NATIVE
ETHNOGRAPHY

H. Russell Bernard and Jesús Salinas Pedraza

Frontispiece

NATIVE ETHNOGRAPHY

A Mexican Indian Describes His Culture

H. RUSSELL BERNARD
JESÚS SALINAS PEDRAZA

Illustrated by
Winfield Coleman

SAGE PUBLICATIONS
The Publishers of Professional Social Science
Newbury Park   London   New Delhi

Gracias a mi padre, Sebastián, y a mi hermano mayor, Heriberto,
por todo su apoyo.

—Jesús Salinas Pedraza

With thanks to my parents, Herman and Lillian, and to Aunt
Sylvia for all their support.

—H. Russell Bernard

For information address:

SAGE Publications, Inc.
2111 West Hillcrest Drive
Newbury Park, California 91320

SAGE Publications Ltd.
28 Banner Street
London EC1Y 8QE
England

SAGE Publications India Pvt. Ltd.
M-32 Market
Greater Kailash I
New Delhi 110 048 India

Printed in the United States of America

Library of Congress Cataloging-in-Publication Data

Bernard, H. Russell (Harvey Russell), 1940-
    Native ethnography.

    Bibliography: p.
    Includes index.
    1. Otomi Indians.   I. Salinas Pedraza, Jesús.
II. Title.
F1221.086B47   1989   972′.00497   88-18628
ISBN 0-8039-3017-8

FIRST PRINTING 1989

CONTENTS

PREFACE

This book is an annotated translation of work written by Jesús Salinas Pedraza in his native language, Ñähñu (generally called Otomí. See Introduction). All the Ñähñu text is available on diskette. Write to H. Russell Bernard, Dept. of Anthropology, University of Florida, Gainesville, FL 32611. In the introductory chapter that follows, I explain how the orthography used in this book developed. Ñähñu is a tone language, but it is not necessary for native speakers to mark tone, and Jesús opted early on in the project to drop tone markers. In fact, as I have shown elsewhere (Bernard 1966, 1974), *most* (but not all) tones can be generated by the application of three ordered rules. For most linguistic work, it is unnecessary to mark tone, except at the discourse level. The phonology of Ñähñu is shown below.

Consonants

p	t t'	ts ts'	ch	k k'	
f	th	s	x	j	h
b	d	z	ẕ	g	
n					
l					
r					
y					

Vowels

i	ṵ	u
e	o̱	o
e̱	a	ä

The apostrophe is used as a glottal stop. The sounds t, th, and k are phonemically glottalized and nonglottalized. Glottal before m has the effect of making it a bilabial, glottalized stop, like a hard b, as opposed to the phonemically distinct b, which is a bilabial fricative. The "z̲" represents the sound of the consonant z in the English word "azure." The sound of f in Ñähñu is bilabial. The aspirated t sound is represented by th. This sound varies a great deal among speakers; it is sometimes an interdental fricative rather than a stop.

The high-mid vowel u̲ is between the vowel sounds in English "sit" and "put." The mid-vowel o̲ is similar to the vowel sound in English "but." The e̲ represents the vowel sound in English "cat"; the low-back vowel ä is nasalized. It is close to the vowel sound in English "mod," but is more rounded, as the vowel sound in "saw."

The numbers in the English text are keyed to the numbered chunks of the original Ñähñu text, so that the interested reader may compare the translation against the original. Once in a while, the reader will note that one of the numbers is missing in the English text. That occurs when my translation covers more than one numbered chunk in the Ñähñu. I felt that it was messy to insert numbers into the middle of translated text, so I skipped over those numbers when necessary.

The annotations fill in where I think the reader might find some extra information useful. For example, I have provided biological taxonomic labels for the plants and animals named by Jesús in the original Ñähñu. To do this, I took flora and fauna field guides with me to the Mezquital desert and worked with Jesús to develop some personal knowledge of the plant and animal life of the valley. Where I was unable to identify the scientific labels for flora or fauna myself, I have had access to the advice of excellent scholars. These include Dr. Earl Smith (ethnobotanist), University of Alabama, Dr. Louis Guillette (herpetologist), Dr. Thomas Weber, Dr. John Hardy, and Mr. Carlos Martínez del Río (ornithologists), and Dr. Craig Shaak (geologist), all of the University of Florida. Dr. Guillette consulted with Dr. Hobart Smith (retired), dean of scholars on North American reptiles and amphibians, in order to resolve some particularly difficult problems. I am very grateful to all these scholars for their help.

I was able to identify on my own *most* of the true bugs, other insects, and arachnids mentioned by Jesús (the solpugids were not easy!). However, the variety of insect life in the Mezquital (as elsewhere) is so great that some creatures simply could not be identified with surety.

Indeed, the illustrator for these texts, Winfield Coleman, collected several dozen species of insects in 1966 when he was studying in the Ixmiquilpan Field School in Ethnography and Linguistics (see Introduction). He brought the actual specimens to the University of Washington in Seattle and was unable to get several of them identified. I suspect that entomologists at the University of

Arizona might have had an easier time of it. In any event, the Ñähñu are intensive utilizers of their environment, exploiting everything possible to wrest sufficient protein from the desert for human survival. Traditionally, they consumed several kinds of insects regularly, especially larvae (because they are easier to catch and easier to eat and to digest). I have identified all the edible insects. I did the footnotes to each volume independently of the notes to the other volumes. There is some repetition of information in footnotes.

I have used many Spanish words in the English translation, sometimes because it just felt right to do so, but usually because it made more sense. So, for example, I usually call small agricultural plots "milpas"; ceramic plates for baking tortillas are "comales"; "prickly pear cacti" are often "nopales"; "open upland desert country" is often "monte"; and "agaves" or "century plants" are *always* "magueyes." In every case where I have used a Spanish gloss for a Ñähñu word rather than an English gloss, I have noted the use in one of the footnotes, except where the meaning is given by Jesús in the text or in cases of words like "tortilla" that are in common usage in English. Furthermore, the index provides a comprehensive guide to all usages of Spanish words. There are many places in the text where I had to use Ñähñu words. All instances of Ñähñu words are listed in a separate part of the index.

There have been many people and organizations who have helped over the years to make this project work. I am grateful to the American Philosophical Society (Phillips Fund) for their support of the early phases of this work (grants in 1972 and 1974), during which Salinas and I worked out the logistics for this project. The National Science Foundation (1978, 1981), and the National Endowment for the Humanities (1976, 1981) provided essential support for the writing of the ethnography presented here. West Virginia University and the University of Florida provided me with time to pursue this work. West Virginia University Foundation also provided some financial support, as did the vice president of the University of Florida, Dr. Robert Bryan.

Jesús Salinas has had the support of his superiors at the General Directorate for Indian Education (DGEI) in Mexico. Without that support, he could not have spent a total of ten months in the United States between 1976 and 1984. In particular, we are both grateful to Professor Salamón Nahmad Sittón (Director, DGEI, 1977-1982) and to Professor Cándido Coheto (Director, DGEI, 1983-1988).

Ms. Liliana Montano and Ms. Carole Bernard did all the word processing on the mainframe computers at West Virginia University and the University of Florida, respectively, during the years that I was experimenting with ways to make mainframes adjust to the needs of printing native-language texts. The tedium involved in feeding text that you do not understand to a computer cannot be described. The possibilities for massive input error are clear. And yet, somehow, they just wouldn't let that happen. I cannot express sufficiently my admiration and gratitude for their work.

Dr. Ole Renick, formerly professor of surgery at West Virginia University and now in private practice in Roanoke, Virginia, played a pivotal role in making it possible for the work to continue. No one can thank another person for selfless acts; but one can acknowledge.

Readers of this book should know that the idea for a native ethnography emerged from discussions in 1963 with Kenneth Hale, Duane Metzger, and Oswald Werner. I have benefited from the example of their fully collaborative, collegial work with Native Americans. I wish to acknowledge my personal debt to these three scholars, for their instruction and criticism, and for giving me courage early on, when I really needed it, to take on a project of this kind. I have benefited also from discussions of this work with Eric Hamp, Del Hymes, John Roberts, Marvin Harris, Alan Lomax, and the late Carl Voegelin. Each gave me encouragement and advice; I hope that they can tell that I've followed some of it.

H.R.B.
Gainesville, Florida
December, 1987

INTRODUCTION

This book is a native ethnography of the Ñähñu (pronounced Nyaw-hnyu) people. It was written between 1976-84 by Jesús Salinas Pedraza, a Ñähñu Indian from the state of Hidalgo, Mexico. The Ñähñu are generally known in the literature as the "Otomí," but Ñähñu is what the people call themselves, and Salinas has asked that his language and people be called Ñähñu in this book.

And with good reason. The word "Otomí" has ugly connotations in Mexican Spanish. Santamaría, in the authoritative *Diccionario de Mejicanismos* (1974), describes the Otomí people as "undoubtedly one of the inferior races today" in Mexico. "They are distinguished," he says "by their distrust, laziness, guile, hypocrisy and treachery." By extension, the noun "otomía" in Mexican Spanish, he says, refers to "barbaric acts, savagery, villainy, vulgarity, or merciless atrocity." No other Indian group in Mexico has had its name become such a pejorative adjective. Honoring the request of the Ñähñu people to use their own name for themselves is thus more than just an innocuous courtesy.

In the rest of this chapter, I will place Jesús Salinas's work in the larger context of the history of native ethnographies in general, and I will lay out the history of my work with Salinas. I will conclude with comments on the importance of native ethnography both to anthropology and to native peoples throughout the world.

To anticipate the conclusion: Native peoples of the Americas and elsewhere have not learned to read and write their own languages in any significant numbers. One reason is that there is nothing for them to read. Of the 3,000 or so languages of the world, most have no major literary tradition. An orthography may exist, and there may be a few examples of written texts, but literacy is not a feature of everyday life. Most of these nonwritten languages are spoken by fewer than 100,000 people. Hardly anyone could afford to publish works that were written in those languages. With so few potential readers, it just wouldn't pay. And with nothing in print, it just isn't worth the effort to learn to read.

A vicious cycle . . . until now. After reading this chapter, it will be plain that this particular problem no longer needs to stand in the way of native literacy in the Americas, or anywhere else in the world for that matter. Much of Jesús

Salinas's monumental ethnography of the Ñähñu people was produced *in* Ñähñu, on a Ñähñu word processor, *by* a Ñähñu. Microcomputer technology—including both the hardware and the software—is available *now*, at sufficiently low cost, so that virtually every nonliterate people of the world can develop their own machine-readable data banks about their own culture, and can have their own independent publishing capability in support of native ethnography. And native ethnography can help to preserve the cultural heterogeneity of the planet.

Native Ethnographies

The term "native ethnography" can cover a lot of ground. At one end of the spectrum are the works of professional anthropologists who write about their own culture in English or in one of the other major literary languages of the world (Japanese, Hindi, Korean, French, Spanish, etc.). Included here are the works of scholars like Jomo Kenyatta (1938) and Victor Uchendu (1965), the former a Gikuyu from Kenya, the latter an Igbo from Nigeria. Both wrote ethnographies of their respective peoples, and though they were native speakers of either Gikuyu or Igbo, both wrote in English and were trained as anthropologists. Kenyatta was a student of Bronislaw Malinowski's at the London School of Economics in the 1930s. Uchendu's ethnography of the Igbo was written as his MA thesis in anthropology when he was a student at Northwestern University (Uchendu, 1965).[1]

At the other end of the spectrum is this work by Jesús Salinas. It was written by a native of a culture that had no previous literary tradition. Salinas had to learn to read and write Ñähñu at a level that no other Ñähñu had ever reached. In their encyclopedic treatment of ethnography, Werner and Schoeple (1987) classify Salinas's work as an example of *monolingual ethnography*. The works that come closest to Jesús's are those of Crashing Thunder, a Winnebago Indian who worked with the anthropologist Paul Radin early in this century; of Abel Hernández Jiménez, a Zapotec Indian from the state of Oaxaca, Mexico who works with the anthropologist Fadwa El Guindi of the University of Southern California; of Ignacio Bizarro Ujpán (a pseudonym), a Tzutuhil Maya Indian from Lake Atitlán in Guatemala who works with James Sexton, an anthropologist at Northern Arizona University; and of Refugio Savala, a Yaqui poet from Arizona who worked with Muriel Thayer Painter, an anthropologist, and Kathleen Sands, a professor of English literature at the University of Arizona. A special case is that of George Hunt, Franz Boas's chief Kwakiutl informant.

George Hunt was born in 1854, the son of a Scot father and a Tlingit mother. He was raised at Fort Rupert, British Columbia, where he learned Kwakiutl as his native language. Boas met Hunt in Victoria, British Columbia, in the summer of 1888. They corresponded for five years, and Hunt became Boas's informant—that is, he received payment for the data he collected (Rohner, 1966). In 1893, Boas brought Hunt and several other Kwakiutl to the Chicago Exposition; it was in Chicago that Boas trained Hunt to write Kwakiutl phonetically.

Before he died in 1933, Hunt provided Boas with at least 5,650 pages of text, which formed the data for over two-thirds of Boas's reports on Kwakiutl life (ibid.; also Rohner, 1969; Cannizo, 1983). The impact of Hunt's work on Boas, and on anthropology in general, has never been adequately assessed. All their correspondence is archived in the American Philosophical Society library, however, and that body of data will doubtless be the subject of a full historical investigation someday.

Boas recognized the importance of training native informants to record their culture in their own language, and one of Boas's students, Paul Radin, obviously took the lesson quite seriously. He did fieldwork among the Winnebago for five years, and in 1913 published, in the *Journal of American Folklore*, the autobiography of Jasper Blowsnake. Boas was editor of *JAF* at the time, and Radin was able to publish the original Winnebago along with the translation (Krupat, 1983). In that article, Radin noted that ethnologists had been indicted for portraying only the "skeleton and bones" of the cultures they describe. What was needed, Radin said, was an insider's view, where informants could express their own feelings and emotions, as they saw fit. Radin's monumental ethnography of the Winnebago, published as the 37th Annual Report of the Bureau of American Ethnology, is filled with direct translations of Winnebagos talking about their culture and their lives in their own words.

One of Radin's informants was Sam Blowsnake (Jasper's brother), who is the speaker in *Crashing Thunder, Autobiography of a Winnebago Indian* (Radin, 1983: orig. 1926).[2] Apparently, Sam Blowsnake was something of a rake, and Radin pursued him for three years until, as Radin put it, "temporary poverty induced him" to write his autobiography. Sam Blowsnake wrote his autobiography in a syllabary that was in common use among the Winnebago at the time. After one day, he came to Radin and was worried about what White people might think when they read it (he confesses to murdering a Potowatami in the narrative), but Radin reassured him, and he finished the manuscript in just two days. Radin's insistence that he "in no way influenced [Crashing Thunder], either directly or indirectly in any way" seems ingenuous today, and from today's vantage point he may have failed to exercise good professional judgment in publishing the part of the narrative where Crashing Thunder confesses to murder. But the book is a milestone in the history of anthropology.

Abel Hernández is the colleague and compadre of anthropologist Fadwa El Guindi. El Guindi actively trained Hernández to write ethnographic descriptions of four Zapotec rituals (a baptism, a child's funeral, a wedding, and an adult's funeral), and to treat a specific set of topics in each one. She used open-ended interviewing to get Hernández to discuss each ritual "in general terms of its ordering of event, categories of participation, meaning of ritual objects, ritual speech impressions, and so on" (El Guindi, 1986: 25). After each discussion, Hernández wrote up his description of one of the rituals and El Guindi collected parallel data on her own to compare with those of her colleague. Hernández apparently wrote some of his descriptions and analyses in Spanish and some in Zapotec, although this is not clear from El Guindi's introduction.

Ignacio Bizarro is the long-term informant and friend of anthropologist James Sexton. Between 1972 and 1974, at Sexton's urging, Bizarro wrote an autobiography in Spanish. He also began a diary in 1972, which he kept for five years. Sexton edited the diary, removing repetitious events and what he felt was trivial material detailing "the kinds of meals he [Bizarro] ate each day, the saying of his nightly prayers, his daily work routine, how well he slept, and common illnesses like colds and headaches" (Sexton, 1981: 4). Sexton supplemented the diary with taped interviews. He inserts his questions in italics into Bizarro's narrative, to show "what kind of information Ignacio volunteered and how much of it is material I solicited from my own perspective" (ibid.; see also Sexton, 1985 for the continuation of the Bizarro diaries).

Refugio Savala, the Yaqui poet, worked originally with Muriel Thayer Painter and later with Kathleen Sands on his long and richly detailed autobiography. According to Spicer (1980), Painter had been inspired by Bronislaw Malinowski in 1939 when Malinowski came to Arizona to study Yaqui ceremonies. Painter, Spicer and Savala worked together to translate a long Yaqui Easter sermon by Maestro Ignacio Alvarez, which the latter had allowed to be recorded on discs in 1941. After that, Painter worked with Savala on various aspects of Yaqui ceremonial life. Between 1964-68, at the urging and with the guidance of Painter, Savala wrote his autobiography. In his narrative, Savala tries to describe Yaqui culture in general by showing his family's participation in it (Sands 1980). The work somehow found its way to the archives of the Arizona State Museum, and was rescued in 1974 by Kathleen Sands who brought it out, along with her own interpretive chapters, six years later (Savala, 1980).

Other North American Indians have written and published autobiographical narratives in English. These include *The Middle Five: Indian Schoolboys of the Omaha Tribe* by Francis La Flesche (1963, orig. 1900), about life at a boarding school; *Wah'Kon-Tah: The Osage and the White Man's Road*, by John Joseph Mathews (1968, orig. 1932), about life under a particular Indian agent on the Osage reservation in the late 1800s; and *The Way to Rainy Mountain* by N. Scott Momaday (1969), in which Momaday, who holds a Ph.D. in English from Stanford, tells of his attempt to seek his identity as a Kiowa from his grandmother and from other elders with whom he consulted.

Another genre of native ethnographies includes the several "as told to" autobiographies, primarily of North American Indians. Some of these were told in English, while others were narrated in the Indian language and translated. Perhaps the most famous example of this technique is *Black Elk Speaks*. John Neihardt, an epic poet from Nebraska, met Black Elk, an Oglala Sioux, in 1930. A year later, Neihardt and his daughters went to Black Elk's home on the Pine Ridge Reservation. Black Elk spoke in Sioux and his words were translated by his son Ben, who had been to Carlisle University, a fact that Neihardt makes clear in his introduction. Neihardt says that it was his own function "to translate the old man's story, not only in the factual sense—for it was not the facts that mattered most—but rather to recreate in English the mood and manner of the old man's narrative" (Neihardt, 1972: xii).

Other examples of this genre include the autobiographies of Don Talayesva, a Hopi (Simmons, 1942); John Lame Deer, a Miniconjou Sioux (Lame Deer and Erdoes, 1972); Left Handed, a Navaho (Dyk, 1938; Dyk and Dyk, 1980); Two Leggings, a Crow (Nabokov, 1967); and Mountain Wolf Woman, a Winnebago (Lurie, 1961). There are few enough examples of autobiographies or ethnographies written by Native American men. Such texts by Native American women are thus particularly important.

Mountain Wolf Woman's autobiography was recorded in Ann Arbor, Michigan in 1958, at the home of anthropologist Nancy Lurie. Over a period of five weeks, during which Mountain Wolf Woman lived with the Luries, she told her story in Winnebago, and Lurie recorded it on tape. Then, using the Winnebago tapes as a guide, and a second tape recorder, Mountain Wolf Woman told her story again, in English (Lurie, 1961).

Lurie and Mountain Wolf Woman translated the Winnebago tape together, and Mountain Wolf Woman's grandniece, Frances Thundercloud Wentz, helped Lurie to produce the final detailed translation. Lurie, however, is critically aware of her influence on the final product: "The final preparation of an acceptable English narrative from a literary and scholarly point of view required decisions for which I must take full responsibility: choice of tenses, equivalents of idiomatic expressions, insertion of words necessary for clarification, and the like" (Lurie, 1961: 95).

Lurie also recorded comments that Mountain Wolf Woman made during the five-week stay, and inserted some of these comments into the final published narrative. She had them set in italics to show where she had added text from materials other than the original tapes.

And here is how Left Handed's story was recorded: "Since Left Handed did not know English, he told his story in Navajo, and it was translated bit by bit by Philip Davis, a Navajo. Left Handed would speak a minute or two, Philip would translate, and my husband would write down the translation" (Ruth Dyk, in Dyk and Dyk, 1980: xvii).

Background

Jesús and I met in June 1962 when I went to the Mezquital Valley, Mexico, to study his language and to collect data for my MA thesis in linguistics. I had spent the previous academic year studying linguistics in a class taught by Kenneth Hale, who advocated that Indian informants be instructed to become full colleagues in the analysis of native languages. Hale practiced what he preached, and his work with Albert Alvarez on the Papago language has become a model for collaborative linguistic fieldwork (see Hale, 1965).

In the early summer of 1962, Hale took a group of his students to Tepoztlán to study Nahuatl, and suggested that I go to Ixmiquilpan to study Ñähñu. The idea was for us to use in the field what we had studied in the classroom. On the drive down to Tepoztlán, Hale stopped in Ixmiquilpan to locate a native language informant for my work. He met Raúl Guerrero Guerrero, a resident of the area and one of Mexico's great folklorists. Guerrero happened at that time to be running a feed and building supplies store in Ixmiquilpan. He suggested that Hale contact Jesús Salinas, younger brother of Heriberto Salinas, of Orizabita, a Ñähñu community of (then) around 800 people, located 12 kilometers east of Ixmiquilpan by dirt road. Heriberto was already a well-known bilingual school-teacher, and had been one of the people whom Guerrero consulted in his studies of Ñähñu folklore (see Guerrero, 1983, 1985).

I was slow in getting to Ixmiquilpan, and Hale had to leave to attend to the rest of his students in Tepoztlán. He left Ixmiquilpan and headed for Tepoztlán, but only after leaving instructions for me to contact Guerrero. All southbound cars on the Pan American Highway in those days had to stop at a customs check point just north of Ixmiquilpan. Hale left the message with the customs officer and described my 1959 green Rambler station wagon to him. Several days later, I was in Guerrero's store, being introduced to Jesús Salinas.

Jesús did not attend school regularly, or speak much Spanish, until he was 11. In 1962, he was 19 years old (I was 22) and in his third year of high school in Ixmiquilpan. He walked back and forth from Orizabita each day, and the job as my informant brought in some much needed money. We worked together very closely that summer, as I studied Ñähñu phonology and verb morphology, and learned about the desert environment of the Mezquital Valley. As Hale had suggested, I taught Jesús the elements of phonological analysis so that he could help me to understand how tone worked in Ñähñu. (It's complicated and not particularly relevant to this story, but for the interested reader, see Sinclair 1948; Bernard, 1966, 1974.)

The Mezquital and the Ñähñu

The Mezquital Valley varies in altitude from about 5,000 feet to about 10,000 feet above sea level, with correspondingly great variations in moisture and vegetation. The bottom of the valley is mostly desert, with mean annual rainfall between 12 and 15 inches. Those Ñähñu who live at the bottom of the valley can scarcely eke out a living from the harsh desert environment, while communities along the upper slopes are often shrouded in mist and are blessed with the flora of the Mexican highland junipers and pine. One community at the upper reaches (Gundho) has even developed apple orchards.

The Mezquital takes up about 40% of the state of Hidalgo. It is bounded by the Valley of Mexico on the south, the Sierra Madre Oriental on the east and north, and by the state of Querétaro on the west. It covers nearly two million acres, or over three thousand square miles, and most of the land is too high and too dry for consistent agriculture. Only about 5% of the Mezquital, known as the "zona de riego" (the "irrigated zone") around the city of Tula and along the Tula River, has adequate natural water. By far, the largest majority of Mezquital Ñähñu live in the "zona árida" ("desert zone").

During the last 20 years, irrigation canals have been built extensively throughout the low-lying areas of the desert zone, bringing effluent from Mexico City for use on crops. These "aguas negras," or "black waters," carry the sewage of the largest city in the world to the countryside, and they do, indeed, produce healthy crops. But because children bathe in those canals, and because women wash clothes in them as well, the canals are a source of as yet unmeasured amounts of disease. Many of the Mezquital Ñähñu continue to live along the valley slopes—too high up for the irrigation pumps to push the precious water.

Of the approximately 350,000 people in the entire Mezquital in 1970, 37% lived on the 5% of the land that constituted the irrigated zone. The population density of the arid zone at that time was around .10 persons per acre, or 64 people per square mile, while the corresponding density in the irrigated zone around the city of Tula was about ten times that. Despite the new irrigation canals, which had brought water to about 75,000 acres of land (4% of the Mezquital) by 1982 (Ergood, 1983), the relative population distribution has not changed much in the last 15 years. Some Ñähñu have come down to the lower elevations to find wage labor on the newly fertile lands, and a few (only a few) have even managed to acquire irrigated land themselves. Many others have moved to Mexico City. But the very high birth rate among the Ñähñu (I estimate that it is still over 3.5% per year, while the national rate for Mexico is just over half that) has kept the population of Ñähñu in the Mezquital stable.

The Ñähñu make up the fifth-largest group of native language speakers in Mexico, after Nahuatl (1.4 million speakers), Maya (about 800,000), and Zapotecs and Mixtecs (around 400,000 each). I estimate that there are today around 350,000 Ñähñu speakers, distributed across eight dialects: Tixmadeje, in the state of México; Amealco and Tolimán in the state of Querétaro; Mezquital and Tenango de Doria in the state of Hidalgo[3]; Huayacocotla in the state of Veracruz; Huauchinango in the state of Puebla; and a small group of isolated speakers in Tlaxcala.

In 1972, Benítez noted that there were 97,700 Mezquital Ñähñu, and that they constituted 44% of all 220,000 Ñähñu speakers at that time (p. 292). His figures were based on the national census of 1970, however, in which just 7.1% of the then 50 million Mexicans claimed to speak an Indian language. In 1980, 9.1% of the then 71 million Mexicans—or nearly 6.5 million people—claimed to be Indians (Roth, Seneff, and Morzón, 1987).

And that figure must *still* be an underestimate. In the Mexican census, persons are counted as being Indian if they claim to speak an Indian language when asked by the enumerator—usually a mestizo enumerator who asks the question in Spanish. An unknown number of bilingual Indians state that they do not speak a native language, fearing that to state otherwise might place them in some kind of jeopardy. Many Indians who live in hard-to-reach areas are simply never counted at all.

In 1970, the (reported) 220,000 Ñähñu constituted about 7% of Mexico's (reported) Indian population of just over three million. If that ratio held true for the 1980 census, there would be at least 450,000 speakers of Ñähñu today, not counting those who avoided divulging their Indianness to the census enumerator and those who were never enumerated. If there had indeed been 220,000 Ñähñu in 1970, and if their birth rate had been 3.5% over the past 18 years, then there would be some 400,000 Ñähñu today. My estimate of at least 350,000 Ñähñu is therefore conservative. Supposing that the 1970 *ratio* of Mezquital Ñähñu speakers to all Ñähñu speakers has remained stable, there are at least 150,000 Mezquital Ñähñu speakers today, about evenly split between the Mezquital Valley and Mexico City, with a few speakers in other parts of Mexico and in Texas.

Traditionally, the Ñähñu lived in nonnucleated, highly dispersed settlements, extracting all their needs from the desert. Even today, many Ñähñu live in sparsely settled areas throughout the Mezquital. They still rely heavily on the maguey, or century plant, for some of their food, clothing, and shelter. They extract the sucrose-rich nectar from the maguey and ferment it into pulque; the fermenting yeasts raise the protein level from .30 to .44 grams per 100 grams, and provide a potent source of vitamins C and B-1 (Cravioto et al., 1951). The Ñähñu extract fiber from the maguey and weave it into carrying cloths and wraps. This is now rare. Some still use maguey leaves for making waterproof roof thatching.

Development and Change in the Mezquital

During the past 35 years there have been profound changes in the Mezquital, brought about by upheavals in the Mexican economy, by Protestant evangelism, and by government-sponsored programs aimed at reducing poverty and increasing the level of health care and education. The principal government agency responsible for development in the Mezquital is the Patrimonio Indígena del Valle del Mezquital (PIVM). From its headquarters in Ixmiquilpan, on the Mexico City-Laredo highway, one hundred miles due north from the capital, the PIVM has transformed the valley—building roads, clinics, and schools; digging irrigation canals; and running electricity and phone service to remote parts of the area. The Ñähñu remain one of the poorest Indian groups in Mexico today. The PIVM has cut back on its activities and, in 1985, even began to close its massive headquarters in Ixmiquilpan. Nevertheless, the agency continues to be the most important single source of development funds and programs in the Mezquital Valley.

It will become clear in Salinas's narrative that the PIVM is held in contempt by many Ñähñu, principally because the mestizos who run the organization hold the Indian people in contempt and treat them with disdain (see also Ergood, 1983). Between 1952 and 1985, only one director of the PIVM actually spoke Ñähñu. Despite the PIVM's weaknesses, it has changed the life of the Ñähñu people, and in many ways for the better. The Ñähñu have not generally been able to gain access to the newly irrigated lands (Nolasco Armas, 1966), and the PIVM could do a lot more with the money it has had. But the fact remains that the agency has built those schools, roads, and clinics, and these infrastructural efforts have resulted in lower disease rates, higher general education, less isolation, and improved access to markets.

The material changes in Ñähñu life have been accompanied by some important behavioral and attitudinal changes, as well. The most obvious is the exchange of Spanish for Ñähñu as the everyday language of children and young adults. When I first went to work in the Mezquital in 1962, I estimated that more than half the women over 40 years of age were monolingual Ñähñu speakers. More recently, Hamel and Muñoz Cruz (1986) estimated that 30% of the Mezquital Ñähñu remain are monolingual. Since Indian women are twice as likely as Indian men to be monolingual in Mexico, 40% of the adult women Ñähñu are still monolingual, if Hamel and Muñoz Cruz are correct. The big change, though, is among the children. One hears less and less Ñähñu among children in the school playgrounds as the years go by, and many Ñähñu parents of my acquaintance seem unconcerned that their children are, at best, only minimally fluent in Ñähñu.

Let me not be misunderstood here. The increased command and use of Spanish among the Ñähñu is all to the good. I see nothing useful or charming about remaining monolingual in any Indian language if that results in being shut out of the national economy. On the other hand, there is definitely something wrong with increasing the use of Spanish (or English, for that matter) at the *expense* of one's native language. There is no linguistic or pedagogical reason to do so. Children learn two or three languages easily if given the opportunity to do so, and without one interfering with the other, after about five or six years of age. There are, of course, political reasons to obliterate native languages (Heath, 1972), and that is what is happening in Mexico.[4] The erosion of native languages further disempowers the poor by making them culturally indistinguishable from one another—by removing whatever unique claim they might otherwise have on public resources.

Why Indians Don't Read and Write
Their Own Languages in Mexico

Jesús Salinas and I conceived the idea for him to write this ethnography in the context of this problem. When Jesús was 23, after graduation from high school and teacher's college, he became a public school teacher—a member of the federal teacher corps of Mexico. He wanted to promote Ñähñu literacy in the classroom, but found himself frustrated by the lack of effective bilingual educational materials and by the absence of a curriculum for integrating native and Spanish literacy. This problem was addressed by an interesting joining of interests between the Mexican government and the Summer Institute of Linguistics.

The SIL is an evangelical missionary organization. One of their principal goals is the conversion of the indigenous peoples of the world to Protestantism by providing each group with its own native-language version of the Bible. Members of the SIL take the original premise of the Reformation quite seriously: if every man and woman could read the Bible in his or her own language, then truth would work its own way and people would convert from their previous religion (whether Catholicism or a native religion) to Protestantism.

The SIL signed an open-ended agreement with the Mexican government in 1952—an agreement that gave the SIL tacit government approval for the institute's evangelical activities. In 1960, a presidential decree gave the SIL a grant of land for 30 years in a suburb of Mexico City. The SIL was to build its headquarters on the land and return the land and the buildings to the government in 1990. In fact, the SIL began to turn over parts of the complex in 1988.

In return for the loan of the land, the SIL undertook to produce and distribute pedagogical materials that supported the government's goal of universal literacy in Mexico. The agreement was peculiar in that the Mexican Constitution expressly forbids the support of any religion by the state. But the government tacitly agreed to turn a blind eye to the evangelical activities of the SIL if the institute fulfilled its part of the bargain.

The Mexican Constitution also guarantees freedom of religion, and there is thus no legal reason to prohibit evangelical work. In heavily Catholic rural Mexico, however, as elsewhere in the world, the proseletyzing activities of the SIL have been the focus of bitter, even violent disputes. In 1962, many homes in Ixmiquilpan and in surrounding Ñähñu communities displayed a sign that read, in Spanish: "THIS IS A CATHOLIC HOME. WE DO NOT ACCEPT ANY PROPAGANDA FROM OTHER RELIGIONS." There are still faded copies of that sign on some homes in the area today. (Jesús describes the animosity and distrust between Catholic and Protestant Ñähñu in Volume IV of this book.)

The SIL counts many fine scholars among its ranks—scholars who use linguistic science to produce better translations of scripture. In fact, a lot of what is known about problems of cross-cultural communication and translation has come from publications by members of the SIL (see particularly Bartholomew and Schoenhals, 1983; also Nida, 1958, and Grimes, 1980). Many of these same scholars have produced superior descriptive linguistic works, and masterpiece dictionaries of native languages. Were it not for the complicating issue of religion, the SIL would be uniformly seen as the world's most effective organization in getting native people to read their own languages. But religion *does* complicate things, and in 1990, when their 30-year land grant ends, the SIL is scheduled to vacate their borrowed property and turn over their multimillion-dollar headquarters facility to the government.

The coming of the SIL to Ixmiquilpan coincided with the establishment of the PIVM in Ixmiquilpan. By 1960, the SIL had built their most important New World Bible-translating research complex—the Centro Lingüístico del Manuel Gamio—right in Ixmiquilpan. Under the PIVM's auspices and logo, the SIL produced instructional material for reading and writing Ñähñu. But the SIL materials piled up in warehouses around the Mezquital and went unused.

I have written elsewhere (Bernard, 1980) about the failure of the SIL's efforts to produce a single truly literate Ñähñu—that is, someone who can sit down, take pen to paper, and compose long texts, freely and comfortably, in Ñähñu. The teachers in the Mezquital were not trained in bilingual education and did not know how to use the materials produced by the SIL. Furthermore, even if people took the trouble to become literate, there was nothing to read in Ñähñu except the Bible (which the SIL was translating and publishing in pieces). Many Ñähñu educators (and others) rejected the orthography that had been developed by the SIL because of the opposition to the institute's Protestant missionary work. And, most importantly, it seemed pretty clear to most Ñähñu that it was being Ñähñu (which means *speaking* Ñähñu) that made them poor and kept them poor.

To this day, this is the single most important impediment to the development of native literacy in Mexico. I have seen irate parents at rural school meetings demanding that teachers stop teaching the children to read and write Ñähñu, and concentrate instead on making the children less identifiable as Indians. These parents do not want their children even to *speak* Ñähñu because they fear it will make their children speak Spanish with an identifiable accent and mark those children for discrimination. There is good reason for this fear, and the parents' behavior conforms closely to national policy. Most observers would agree that, despite all the rhetoric about "the great Indian heritage," tacit government policy in Mexico has been to promote Spanish at the expense of native languages. Jesús and I discussed all this during the summer of 1971. Perhaps if there were an orthography that Ñähñu people could call their own? Perhaps if it were simple enough and could be typed on any standard keyboard without the need for special characters? Perhaps if there were something else besides the Bible to read? Would the Ñähñu people then want to become literate in their own language? Would they see its preservation in written documents as desirable, or would they continue to eschew their language and culture in pursuit of a place in mainstream Mexican culture? Is there an essential conflict between maintenance of one's native, Indian culture in Mexico and participation in the national economy?

How Jesús Salinas Came to Write This Book

I completed my fieldwork for the MA in September 1962, and did not return to the Mezquital for five years. Jesús and I corresponded, but went our separate ways. I finished my studies, and Jesús became a licensed school teacher and took up his first post in the community of Dextho, about five miles north of Ixmiquilpan. I went back to the Mezquital in June of 1967 with the first group of graduate students in the Ixmiquilpan Field School in Ethnography and Linguistics. The field school ran for five years (through 1971) under support from the National Science Foundation, and ultimately became the first field training experience for more than 50 anthropologists. Each student was assigned to a different village in the Ixmiquilpan area; but before they went out to the villages, students learned to hear and transcribe Ñähñu so that they might record data on all aspects of Ñähñu culture. Jesús had already studied the phonology of Ñähñu, and he was hired as a native informant for the school.

As summer after summer went by, Jesús and I began to develop some ideas. By 1971, I was moving away from formal linguistic analysis, and was becoming more interested in writing an ethnography of the Ñähñu. Jesús was becoming more interested in writing about Ñähñu culture himself—to preserve it, to correct what he though were superficial or incorrect descriptions by non-Ñähñu of his culture, and to provide something besides the Bible for Ñähñu people to read someday.

These many years later, there are still very, very few Ñähñu (or members of any other Indian group, for that matter) who are truly, spontaneously literate.

But in those days, we were more idealistic about getting people to read and write Ñähñu than we are today. I envisioned myself teaching Jesús how to take field notes and how to observe his culture. As I had taught him to intellectualize about the phonology of Ñähñu, I would instruct him in the subtleties of ethnographic reportage. I would teach him to conduct unstructured interviews with old people, to make detailed observations of ceremonies, to record the mundane aspects of life (what people eat, what time they go to work, etc.) that outsider anthropologists might miss, to enlist the cooperation of other "informants" (particularly women) so that he could cover more ethnographic ground, and to integrate his observations into a coherent whole.

I saw him writing up a bunch of raw facts and me guiding him in the analysis of those facts, as we teased out the "underlying meaning" of the texts produced by his unschooled efforts. I saw myself guiding Jesús, monitoring and supervising his work, and seeing to it that the ethnography he would produce would meet the high standards of modern anthropology. I wanted to be able to say that, as the professional anthropologist of this team, I had laid academic hands on Jesús's work and that the result was much better for it.

But that's not how it worked out. The fact is, this ethnography was written by Jesús Salinas, with very little active coaching from me on how to do it. As all readers will surely note, this ethnography looks nothing like the ethnography that I, or any other university-trained anthropologist, would have written. I am convinced that had I taken a more active role in teaching Jesús how to write this ethnography, the product would have been the poorer for my effort.

This does not mean that I had *no* influence on the content of the final product. Jesús and I have known each other for 26 years, and we've had a lot of influence on one another. I never told him what to write, or asked him to include a particular cultural episode that I knew about, but I'm sure that through our long conversations during his writing stints I indirectly influenced his selection of topics for this book. I asked him countless questions about Ñähñu culture, and forced him to think out loud about things that he might otherwise never have contemplated consciously. At another level, my instruction on the use of punctuation must have played some role in the evolution of Jesús's writing style.

If my influence on the content and style of Jesús's original Ñähñu text was indirect, my *translation* of Jesús work is another matter. Not only have my decisions made a difference in the content and "feel" of the English narrative, but those decisions have changed over the years. In an earlier version of Volumes I and II of this book (Salinas and Bernard, 1978), I translated the sentence "Rä fooho t'eents'uä ha rä nthuki t'o'tuä yä bätsi" as "Dogs' excrement is used in cleansing of children from the evil eye." In this book (Volume II, #476), I render it as "Dogs' excrement is used in purifying children of evil eye." In both cases, I render "Rä fooho" as "Dogs' excrement" even though, strictly translated, the phrase means "Its excrement," because the prior referent in the paragraph is to dogs and I try to make the text flow properly. But in the present rendering, I've decided that "purifying" better captures the meaning of the verb than "cleansing" does. There are hundreds of such examples, and I am conscious of the risks that I've taken trying to convey what I *think* Jesús meant at so many turns.

I was aware of the risks early on in this project. My decision to back away from the coaching role that I had originally conceived for myself was at once conscious and also not taken with ease. I wondered whether native ethnography was just laziness on the part of the anthropologist. Would my failure to train Salinas in the ways of modern anthropology make his efforts trivial compared to what they could otherwise become? And was it science? Peer reviewers of one of my applications to the National Science Foundation produced the legitimate critique that the work might *not* be science. After all, this book comprises the subjective ethnographic observations of just one member of Ñähñu culture. How can we know that Salinas's descriptions are an accurate reflection of Ñähñu life? What if other Ñähñu don't agree with Salinas on some issues?

But I reasoned as follows:

(1) *All* ethnographies are subjective and selective. Why should anyone find *my* subjective ethnography more interesting than Jesús Salinas's?

(2) Suppose that other Ñähñu *do* disagree with Salinas, even about *key* issues of Ñähñu life? That's what intracultural variation is about. Disagreement by natives couldn't be less valuable than anthropologists disagreeing over what they both thought they saw in the same culture, could it? In fact, Jesús has suggested that one day a seminar might be held by a group of Ñähñu to read the original Ñähñu version of this book, to write responses and additions, and to offer new interpretations.

(3) Not only would this project produce interesting data about Ñähñu culture that could not be produced in any other way, it would also produce a running record of an experiment that has been conducted millions of times in history and has never been recorded—the experiment in which someone becomes literate in his or her native language *after* learning to be literate in their second language. If we could get the support for Jesús to write the ethnography, we might be able to get the whole experiment, from start to finish, into print. And, if I were to enter his work into a computer, the Ñähñu text would be retrievable on magnetic

tape and could be printed out at will. (In 1971, of course, we were dealing with mainframe computers and magnetic tape. It would be a decade before microcomputers would become practical for this work.)

How Did the Ethnography Actually Get Written?

My doubts were resolved, but in 1971 Jesús was a long way from actually writing an ethnography. It is one thing to be able to sound out a few words, or to write one's name; it is quite another to sit down, take pen to paper, and produce a free flow of ideas in writing. I suggested to Jesús that we take it in stages. First, he would learn to *transcribe* long oral texts of Ñähñu. Then he would write a description of his culture. The Phillips Fund of the American Philosophical Society gave us a small grant so that Jesús could come to the U.S. and begin work with me on a volume of folktales and jokes (Bernard and Salinas, 1976). At the time, I was doing research at Scripps Institution of Oceanography, a branch of the University of California at San Diego. San Diego was a convenient and comfortable place to work; it was a nonstop plane ride from Mexico City, and it was a city with a lot of Hispanic influence.

Jesús left his village of Orizabita at around four in the morning; by around seven he was in Mexico City, and by ten he was airborne for San Diego. He was supposed to call me and tell me his flight number, but somehow things didn't work out and I sat around waiting for the inevitable call to come fetch him at the airport. When the call came, it was from the Immigration and Naturalization Service. The man with whom I spoke told me that they had a Mexican national in custody who was telling an unlikely story about how he had come to the United States to work with a professor at the University of California at San Diego on a book about the Ñähñu. He only had 400 pesos ($32. at the time) and immigration officials were astonished, I was informed, that a "wetback" would waste so much money trying to sneak into the country on an airplane. Still, the voice on the phone said, nothing surprised him anymore in this business, and he thought he should check things out. I think he was more astonished to learn that Jesús had been telling the truth.

My family and I were living in an apartment complex; there were several single-bedroom apartments empty and the manager allowed me to rent one of them for the six-week period of Jesús's visit. We got down to the business of reducing a body of oral literature to writing. Jesús's father is a superb storyteller, and Jesús has followed in his father's footsteps. Jesús recited several hours worth of parables, folk stories, and jokes into a tape recorder, and we began listening to the sounds of Ñähñu together.[5] It did not take long before all the phonetic symbols that I was using made sense and we were able to transcribe the tape together. Within three weeks, Jesús was transcribing the tapes on his own, and I was correcting them. Within four weeks, Jesús was on his own, and for the last two weeks of that summer session we did nothing but work through the transcriptions so that I could translate them into English.

We developed a system where Jesús would translate the Ñähñu, phrase by phrase, into literal Spanish. I asked Jesús not to translate into idiomatic Spanish. I wanted to know what Jesús saw as units of thought in his Ñähñu text. An idiomatic rendering into Spanish would have obscured that. After Jesús did the phrase-by-phrase translation, we worked together, elbow-to-elbow, until, using both the Ñähñu and the Spanish, I felt I could translate the Ñähñu into idiomatic English.

We modified our working style only slightly when we began the ethnography. Jesús would write a small chunk of Ñähñu, and then I would translate it into English. Since Jesús doesn't know much English, and since my Ñähñu is not good enough for direct, independent translation, we used Spanish as an intermediary language. Jesús would read a phrase from his Ñähñu text and then he would render it into literal Spanish. I would produce a free, idiomatic translation into English and discuss what I'd done (in Spanish) with Jesús to make sure I'd captured the sense of the Ñähñu.

This was a grueling procedure, but it was necessary for my training as a translator of Jesús's work. I needed to get a feel for the nuances that he felt were in his Ñähñu words, and this long, often frustrating procedure seemed like the only way for me to achieve that. After several weeks, however, the work became easier. Jesús would write several pages of Ñähñu text, and then interlineate with a literal, phrase-by-phrase Spanish translation. I worked from the Ñähñu and the literal Spanish, translating into free English, while Jesús wrote more Ñähñu. Each day we spent some time going over my translation, to make sure I'd gotten it right. Quite often, the literal Spanish translation made no English sense at all. I was able to handle many of these cases by following the Ñähñu, but there were also many cases where I had to check with Jesús to clarify his meaning. In particular, jokes and double entendres were impossible to translate into English without a lot of discussion.

By the time we got to the third volume of the ethnography, Jesús was so comfortable writing in Ñähñu that he didn't want to interrupt his train of thinking and would wait until he had entire yellow pads full of Ñähñu text before going

back to do the interlinear translation. Despite all these modifications in our style
of work, they were minor compared to the change that occurred in 1983 when
we began Volume IV on religion.

At that time, Jesús stopped writing by hand and started using a
Ñähñu/Spanish word processor that I built (with one of my students) from off-
the-shelf software (see Bernard and Evans, 1983). After writing for a few days
in Ñähñu, Jesús would translate the text into *idiomatic* Spanish, using the same
word processor and a split screen to scroll through the Ñähñu. By then, I felt
confident enough in my understanding of his texts to skip the literal Spanish
step, and the possibility had come up that we might be able to publish the Ñähñu
and Spanish texts in Mexico, as well as the English version in the United States.
But this is getting ahead of the story.

The Next Step: Printing the Ethnography

By the time Jesús left San Diego in the fall of 1972, we had all the folktales
and jokes transcribed and translated into Spanish, and we were planning the ethnography. Given the work we had accomplished in the six weeks in San Diego,
I calculated that it would take about four months for Jesús to write an ethnography of about eight chapters, and to do the phrase-by-phrase literal translation
into Spanish. I thought that it would take me about a year to do a polished translation. I should have known better. It took me a year to translate the jokes and
folk stories, and almost another year to enter all the material into a word processor on a mainframe computer.

It took another two years to publish that first effort. At the time, Eric Hamp
was editing the Native American Texts Series (NATS) of the International Journal of American Linguistics. The purpose of NATS was to publish large
amounts of primary text material for linguistic analysis. The idea was quite
visionary, and the volumes that were produced (University of Chicago Press)
are a trove of information for linguists, folklorists, and members of Native
American groups. But, alas, economics prevailed and NATS ceased production
after a few years.[6]

NATS required that authors submit camera-ready copy. The University of
Chicago Press was taking a financial risk to begin with, and the added labor cost
of setting type (a lot of very strange looking type, at that, for American typeset-
ters) would have been prohibitive. I talked with colleagues who were preparing
camera-ready copy for NATS; it was tough going on a typewriter, even when
special IBM typewriter elements were available for the particular language in-

volved. But Jesús and I had formed an orthography that could be typed on any standard keyboard and this made it relatively simple to use mainframe computer-based word processing. The output that I produced in 1974 on an IBM-360 mainframe was crude compared to what we can do today on a desktop computer—but it was effective and our first book was published by NATS in 1976.

When NATS accepted the manuscript for the folktale volume, I applied to the National Endowment for the Humanities and asked for support for the Ñähñu Bilingual Ethnography Project. NEH funded the proposal and in the fall of 1976 Jesús came to Morgantown, West Virginia for the first of two, two-month writing stints. We discussed how he might start.

Recall that I was still harboring notions of training Jesús as an ethnographer, more or less like the students I had trained in the Ixmiquilpan field schools. In teaching students to take and code field notes, I use the table of contents of the *Outline of Culture Materials* (Murdock, 1971). The OCM contains the coding scheme developed by the Human Relations Area Files for handling all ethnographic text, and I've always found the scheme to be easy to teach, and sensible to use.

I presented Jesús with a Spanish version of the coding scheme and told him that I wanted to go over it with him so he could learn about the various components of an ethnography. After a short time Jesús became impatient and said that he preferred to get started writing. So, I suggested naively that he start with something "relatively simple" like the "setting." After all, this was the first time that Jesús was writing directly from head to paper, and I thought that the "setting" (rather than, say, politics, economics, or family life) would be less complex and easier to do for a start. I found out pretty quickly how wrong I was.

Jesús asked me to explain what I meant by the "setting." I told him that it consisted of a discussion of the physical characteristics of the region in which he lived—the geography, the fauna, and the flora, for example, and referred him again to the OCM guide.[7] He asked if it were legitimate to discuss the various kinds of winds and frosts—where they came from and what they meant for crops, animals and people in the Mezquital. I was nonplussed. The fact is, *I could not have formed the appropriate questions in Ñähñu that would have retrieved that kind of information* from a Ñähñu person. I was totally unprepared for the richness of detail that his ethnography would provide, and for the questions it would answer that I would never have thought to ask.

Jesús began writing a chapter on the geography of the Mezquital. He moved around the valley, naming communities and discussing their characteristics; which community produces charcoal, and which produces lime for making tortillas; which communities get rain and which do not. He described the soil types, and named the prominent mountain peaks. He discussed the color of ice when it forms on plants during cold weather, and noted that dark ice is colder than white ice. Three weeks into the first two-month session, Jesús finished the "chapter" on the geography (which had grown to 9,000 words), and began working on the fauna of the valley.

He divided the fauna into categories (insects, domestic fowl, predators, etc.) and made a list of creatures that he felt had to be discussed. Then he began moving through the list, systematically treating each creature, discussing its habits and characteristics, and noting any folklore associated with it. By the end of our first two-month session on the ethnography, Jesús had written (by hand) what I calculated to be about 120 double-spaced typewritten pages (about 30,000 words). He was, by his estimate, about half way through the fauna. When he returned to Morgantown in September 1977 for another two months, he completed the "chapter"—now a book of over 50,000 words—on the fauna of the Mezquital.

As I had done with the folktales and jokes, both the Ñähñu and the English texts were entered into a word processor on a mainframe computer. The University of New Mexico Press looked at the book and (to their everlasting credit) decided to take a chance. Given that I would provide them with camera-ready copy (thereby eliminating the costs of setting the book in type), they would print the volume in facing pages, English and Ñähñu. The book was illustrated by Winfield Coleman, who also illustrated this book. Coleman is an anthropologist-artist who was a student in the first Ixmiquilpan field school; he spent the summer in 1966 in Dextho with Jesús.

All together, it seemed like a pretty good package: there was a large corpus of rare Ñähñu text for linguists; there was an English translation for anthropologists, folklorists, and the interested public; and there were those beautiful drawings by Coleman. Perhaps with all this, and the low cost of production, the book might be economical to publish. But it wasn't, and when we came back to the University of New Mexico Press with the next volume (on the flora of the Mezquital), they were forced to turn us down. They were sorry, but there were just not enough sales.

When the University of New Mexico Press turned us down, it became apparent to me that I was on the wrong track. After all, even a very low-budget operation like NATS couldn't make it. How could anyone expect university presses, which have to pay their own way, to operate at a profit by printing books in American Indian languages—or any other indigenous languages, for that matter? Camera-ready copy does reduce the costs of book production, but that just isn't enough. If native peoples (especially those who use nonstandard scripts) were to have books, I concluded, they would have to publish those books themselves, using some very inexpensive technology.

Microcomputers had made their appearance in 1975; the ham radio club that I belonged to in those days built one as a project. By 1978, it was apparent to all the early tinkerers that microcomputers could be made to do a lot more than anyone had imagined. I started thinking about the possibility of using microcomputers for the storage, retrieval, management and printing of native texts.

In 1978 I proposed to both the National Science Foundation and to the National Endowment for the Humanities that they fund another volume of the Bilingual Ñähñu Ethnography. Joint funding was provided and Jesús came to the University of Florida in September 1979 to begin writing. This time I was more realistic; I did not say in my proposal that we would produce "an ethnography," only that we would produce a volume on the "flora of the Mezquital Valley." By the end of the second two-month session in early December 1980, Jesús had written a volume on the major cactuses and succulents of the region. It is Volume III of this book.

A Native Orthography Forces the Use of Microcomputers

During these years some important events were taking place. Under the government of López Portillo in the 1970s, Mexico had launched an ambitious new program of bilingual education. The goal was to develop bilingual educational materials and curricula for all of Mexico's 56 native languages. The materials would be developed by educators who were themselves members of Mexico's native cultures and speakers of those languages. The program began with half a dozen of the most common languages and now encompasses 26 of them. As a member of the federal teacher corps, and as a published Ñähñu author, Jesús's skills were appropriate for this new initiative.

The agency in charge of the initiative was the Dirección General de Educación Indígena (DGEI) or General Directorate for Indian Education (a part of the Ministry of Education in Mexico), and the director of that agency was Salamón Nahmad Sittón, an old colleague and friend. Nahmad, in fact, had written a letter of support for my application to NEH, so he knew all about the project and followed it closely. In January 1979, Jesús went to work in Mexico City for the Technical Division of the DGEI.

One of the critical issues in native literacy programs involves standardization of orthographies. We take this for granted in English. Listen to a New Yorker and someone from Illinois pronouncing the word "dawn." The New Yorker draws out the "aw" sound with rounded lips; the Illinoisan pronounces the sound more like the broad a in father, and very close to the way the New Yorker pronounces the o in the name Don. Similarly, the word "greasy" is pronounced either "gree'see" or "gree'zee" in the United States, depending on the region. The fact that there are quite radical differences in pronunciation of words in English only rarely leads to disputes over proper spelling.

But it *was* once a major problem in English, and after hundreds of years of developing standard spellings we still are concerned about the proper spelling of "archeology" ("archaelogy" or even "archæology"). It is only quite recently that most English language publishers abandoned the circumflex accent over the o in the word "role" (rôle) or the cedilla under the c in "facade" (façade). For native languages, these problems like the following are massive and current. Since there are seven dialects of Ñähñu, and they are all represented in the program of the DGEI, whose pronunciation shall be used as the benchmark for reducing words to written form? Should it be the Mezquital pronunciation simply because there are more Mezquital speakers than there are of the other six dialects? That would be politically unacceptable to those representing the smaller dialects. It would be prohibitively expensive to publish a Tenango Ñähñu version and a Mezquital Ñähñu version of the same curriculum materials, but what compromises can be reached?

Standardization of orthographies gives native groups greater power because it eliminates one source of internal dissension and fosters literacy as a source of political power. The effectiveness of standardization has been recognized by native groups in Canada, some of which are actively working on the problem (see Burnaby, 1983). The Ñähñu bilingual educators at the DGEI also defined standardization as their first task, and early in 1980 they held an open conference, attended by several hundred bilingual teachers. The object was to hammer out an orthography that they could all agree on. There were some disputes,[8] and some debates are still going on, but in the end, the teachers reached a compromise and agreed on a common orthography for all Ñähñu bilingual educational materials.[9]

My carefully laid plans to foster a simple alphabet that could be typed easily and directly on any computer keyboard were overturned, and when Jesús came to Florida in the Fall of 1980 (right in the middle of Volume III on the flora) I learned of the decision to go with an alphabet that contained many special characters. I balked and asked that we finish the book using the orthography that we had used for so long. Jesús agreed to finish writing the book with the now-obsolete orthography, since we were right in the middle of it anyway. All future books, we agreed, would use the new orthography (by then Jesús had planned seven volumes in the project).

There is a low, back, nasalized vowel in Ñähñu that is represented in phonetics by the character "ɔ". In our IBM mainframe-compatible orthography we used a "c." The mid-vowel sound of the "u" in the English word "but" is represented in phonetics by the character "ʌ". We used a "v." The *new* Ñähñu orthography, agreed upon by the Ñähñu themselves, used the symbol "ä" for "ɔ" and "o̲" for "ʌ." There were several other, equally inconvenient (to me) changes. I convinced myself that the simple alphabet, with diacritics, was better for the Ñähñu, and I tried without success to convince Jesús.

I was reacting to the problems that the new orthography would cause *me* in the computer printing of the special characters. I had only recently written a polemic entitled "Orthography for Whom?" (Bernard, 1980). It was written in response to SIL critics who had expressed concern over the fact that, in our 1978 New Mexico Press volume, Salinas had not marked tone in his writing. As I noted earlier, tone is, indeed, phonemic in Ñähñu, but it is unnecessary to mark it in writing—if you are a native speaker of the language, that is (see Bernard, 1966, 1974). In that polemic I asked: Who is the orthography for, anyway? The Ñähñu are never going to write *anything*, I pointed out, if they have to mark tone. Salinas found it utterly redundant; "una lata" ("a pain in the neck") he called it, in Spanish. Here I was, defender of the rights of native speakers of Indian languages to define their own orthography, actually asking Jesús to adjust to the needs of the computer and its inflexible keyboard, while Jesús was demanding that the machine adjust to his, and to those of his bilingual educator colleagues. There can be little doubt about who was correct.

We finished the third volume using the old, comfortable orthography, but events forced me almost immediately to figure out a way to put the entire text into the new orthography. Then the Instituto Nacional Indigenista (INI) (which by then was headed by Salamón Nahmad, the same anthropologist who had headed up the DGEI's initiative to produce bilingual educational materials in Mexico's 56 indigenous languages) offered to publish all the volumes that were ready (geography, fauna, and flora) in both Spanish and Ñähñu. They would work from my English translation and produce a Spanish version, and Jesús would go over the Spanish and check it directly with the Ñähñu.[10] But if INI was going to publish the work, then the entire corpus of the ethnography, including the first volume, would have to be reprinted, in camera-ready copy, using the new orthography.

Actually, making the changes was quite easy, but the result was very . . . well, "user hostile" would be a good description. In order to print the character "ä" (an "a" with an umlaut), for example, all I had to do was to replace, globally, every instance of the letter "c" with a set of three instructions in the word processor that went like this: first print the letter "a," then backspace, and then address the spoke on the daisy wheel that has the umlaut and print it. Now, the way you instruct a computer to print the letter "a" is simple: you type the letter "a." The other two instructions are a bit less straightforward. First you tell the computer, somewhere in the word processing program, that, for example, the character "&" means "go back one space." Second, you tell it somewhere else in the program that, for example, the character "$" means "strike an umlaut." So, if you type "ha&$a&$" ("yes" in Ñähñu), when the material is printed, it comes out "hää" on paper. The result, on a low-speed, letter quality, daisy wheel printer is perfect—but the screen text looks very, very messy since the sound "ä" is the most common one in the language and there are thousands of "a&$" sequences on the screen!

I was able to produce camera-ready copy for INI but there was no way for a Ñähñu typist to see, *on the screen*, what would eventually come out on paper. This is called a WYSIWYG (pronounced "wi'seewig") system in the computer business, for "what you see is what you get." A WYSIWYG system for Ñähñu, or any other Indian language, required two things; a way to produce the special characters on a screen, using computer graphics, and a way to "dump" those graphics to a printer, the output of which was good enough for publication.

The problem was solved in 1981 by advances in microcomputer software that made possible inexpensive, easily available word processors that will handle any symbols in any language, no matter how "exotic," and will allow the typist to see on the screen exactly what will appear in print. Techniques for doing this are described in detail elsewhere (Bernard and Evans, 1983). Suffice to say here that it is now possible, in 1989, for less than $3,000, to provide any native group with a WYSIWYG print shop that lets people use any orthography they choose. The cost includes the word processing software, as well as the machinery for printing, photocopying, and binding the output for distribution.

The low cost and easy availability of these systems make them immediately accessible to many ethnic and tribal groups in the United States and Canada. And they are certainly within easy reach for governments of Third World nations that want to provide native peoples with the means to record their own history and folklore. All it takes is for native speakers of indigenous languages—people like Jesús Salinas—to become fully literate in those languages so that they can write the books, and for them to have access to the technology.

Anthropologists can make that technology available, but time is short. There are about 3,000 languages in the world today. About 20% of the world speaks Chinese; English, Spanish, Russian, and Hindi account for another 25%. The 100 languages of the world with the most speakers account for about 95% of the planet's population. In other words, of the five billion people in the world in 1988, a mere 5%, or a quarter of a billion people, speak about 97% of the languages (Katzner, 1986; Voegelin and Voegelin, 1977). These "small cultures" are in trouble. Everywhere in the world, the number of speakers of languages that have no previous literary tradition is dwindling.

Nothing less than cultural heterogeneity is at stake. In July 1987, a group of Indians from all over Latin America gathered in Pátzcuaro, Mexico, for a three-day symposium, titled "The Politics of Linguistic Revitalization." The symposium was held under the auspices of the Instituto Indigenista Interamericano and resulted in a unanimous declaration from the 23 delegates. "The loss of a language in the world," they said, "means the disappearance of the cultural heritage transmitted by it, and the truncation of an alternate route of cultural development for humankind." They call for all nations to support work that will "guarantee at least the constant use of indigenous languages in written form and thus guarantee their use in larger contexts." In the context of an emergent literary tradition, some—not all, but surely some—speakers of native languages (in the Americas and elsewhere) would be emboldened to speak their language openly, and to teach it to their children.

Of course, some may disagree with the idea that cultural heterogeneity is all that good an idea. Perhaps all I'm doing is asking for the preservation of quaint, small cultures for us to gawk at. Maybe those Ñähñu parents are right, after all. Maybe the best thing for them is to shuck all that cultural baggage that they believe keeps them poor, hungry, and sick.

I don't think so. If the past is any indication of the future, native peoples everywhere will abandon their languages and will *still* not be integrated into their national economies and cultures. In other words, they will participate in the loss of whatever special identity they now have, but will remain, as groups, just as poor and just as hungry and just as sick as they are now. They will find themselves with neither economic power nor ethnic identity. They will lose whatever economic and political clout they now have (in democratic societies, at least) to negotiate with national governments as separate entities, entitled to some portion of the national resources.

Suppose that, *in addition to* (not in replacement of) doing traditional ethnographic fieldwork, every anthropologist were to teach just one native informant to use a microcomputer-based word processor. Suppose further that every anthropologist helped just one native person or group to acquire the technology and the skill to produce a truly native ethnography. Within a matter of a few years, the data base describing the world's extant cultures would double or triple, and a qualitative dimension would be added to the ethnographic record as well. It is clear, from the work of George Hunt, Crashing Thunder, Refugio Savala, and the others mentioned at the beginning of this essay, how much we have learned whenever we have given our informants the opportunity to tell us, in their own words, and in their own narrative style, what their cultures are all about. Their works are monuments both to our ignorance and to the possibilities for understanding the cultural worlds of other peoples.

Notes to the Introduction

1. Kenyatta's ethnography of the Gikuyu people, *Facing Mount Kenya* (1938), was written partly as a defense of Gikuyu culture in the face of great pressure from Europeans to give up the practice of clitoridectomy (Ronald Cohen, personal communication). Kenyatta, of course, later served as president of Kenya after that nation's independence from Great Britain in the 1950s.

When a member of a native culture writes a description of his or her people's beliefs and practices, no one expects him or her to be anything but subjective. But when a professional anthropologist tries the same thing, the enterprise is fraught with difficulties because the assumption is that the anthropologist is at least trying to maintain some semblance of objectivity. This is a very complex issue that I will not resolve here (see Kim, 1988; Ohnuki-Tierny, 1984; Messerschmidt, 1981).

2. Actually, it was Jasper Blowsnake, whose name meant "Terrible Thunder Crash" in Winnebago. The narrator of the book *Crashing Thunder, Autobiography of a Winnebago Indian* is definitely Sam Blowsnake, but for reasons that are not clear to me, Radin chose to assign the name Crashing Thunder to Sam, not Jasper Blowsnake.

3. The Ñähñu people who live in the Tenango de Doria zone of the state are mountain people who speak a very different dialect from the Mezquital Ñähñu. They also differ in dress, food habits, religious life and kinship. The Tenango Ñähñu, known as the Sierra Otomí in the literature, live at much lower altitudes

and have access to fertile lands on which surplus agriculture is possible. Dow (1975, 1986) has written thorough descriptions of the Sierra Ñähñu.

4. The history and politics of bilingual education and language planning in Mexico has been treated extensively elsewhere: Aguirre Beltrán, 1973; Arana de Swadesh, 1979; Caso, 1954; de la Fuente, 1964; Heath, 1972; Horcasitas and Pozas, 1981; Nahmad, 1982; Scanlon and Morfín, 1982; Villa Rojas, 1971.

5. Many of the jokes that Jesús recited were obscene. Jesús insisted that we try to publish them. There is a tradition of insult exchange among Ñähñu men (much like the dozens among American Blacks), and Jesús wanted to bring out a representative sample of the stories that people actually tell one another. We agreed that the popular portrait of the stoic Indian was distorted. Ñähñu people don't laugh with mestizos, Jesús said, because Ñähñu have nothing to laugh about with those people.

In fact, there is virtually no literature on American Indians that portrays them telling dirty jokes. There are obscene texts available for native African languages and for native Asian languages—but not for native American languages. Historically, even linguists and anthropologists (not just missionaries) balked at collecting the material. When they did collect it, they archived it and used Latin translations for the obscene words. I have discussed the reasons for this prudish behavior elsewhere (Bernard, 1975).

6. The early volumes of NATS are still available from the University of Chicago Press, and the series has recently been revived, on a trial basis, by Mouton Press.

7. I still use the OCM to teach students to take and code field notes. In fact, an entire chapter of my research methods text (Bernard, 1988) is devoted to this particular method. I was so attached to the scheme in 1976, however, that I continued to hold on to the idea that Jesús was following the OCM, and even said as much in the introduction to the first two volumes, which we published in 1978.

8. I was not at that conference, but from what informants tell me there were some serious disagreements that continue being debated to this day. For example, there is an apicodental, unaspirated stop in Ñähñu that is represented by the letter "t." There is also a highly aspirated "t" that is phonemically distinct. It is so aspirated, in fact, that in some persons it is an interdental fricative. The sound is represented by "th." The particular debate in this case among the bilingual educators is whether the "th" sound should be considered a *separate* entity, with its own place in the alphabet (right after "t"), or as a compound sound since it is represented by two letters. Strong positions have been taken on the matter.

This and similar discussions are made more more complex because of the presence of the "etnolingüístas"—a corps of university-trained linguists, all of whom are members of the various major Indian groups in Mexico. During the 1970s, the Mexican government selected and trained several hundred Indian linguists at a special university-level school in Pátzcuaro. The idea was for them to form a national corps of leaders in the revitalization of Indian languages. Many of the graduates of the school now work in conjuction with the DGEI, but it is too early to tell what, if any, has been their impact.

9. Another conference took place in Ixmiquilpan, the heart of Ñähñu country, in May 1984. It was held with flourish and fanfare, complete with wall posters and visits from government dignitaries to ratify the agreement on the orthography and to set an agenda for revitalization of Ñähñu culture. At the big annual Ixmiquilpan fiesta (described in Volume IV) in August 1985, I watched a two-hour performance of native songs and dances by the newly formed "Grupo Ñähñu," a troupe of school teachers who hope to revitalize Ñähñu culture through the performing arts. It is led by a highly respected teacher, in his late sixties, and it has attracted over a hundred members, according to persons in the group. All the members are bilingual school teachers. There were over 300 people in the audience at the outdoor theater set up on the enclosed fiesta grounds, but only a handful were mestizos, as far as I could tell. The troupe's leader announced over the microphone that the group was prepared to send performers to private fiestas held in Ñähñu homes in the valley for baptisms, weddings, saint's days, and so on. The three Ñähñu whom I asked to comment on this were very cynical. One of them said "The mestizos will let them do a few of these shows at big fiestas, and then the group will get bored with it all, and that will be the end of it." Another said "Only teachers, with good jobs, can afford this kind of thing. They'll make some noise, but that's all." The third said "I just don't know."

10. As it turned out, the book was printed but never released, because of political problems. At the time, however, I was working under the assumption that I would have to produce camera-ready copy of the Ñähñu using the new alphabet.

VOLUME I

Geography

Location

01. The Mezquital Valley, as we know, is located in the state of Hidalgo. 02. Hidalgo is bordered on the east entirely by the state of Veracruz. 03. On the west it is bordered by Querétaro. 04. On the north by Tamazunchale in the State of San Luis Potosí. 05. On the south it is bounded by Tlaxcala and by part of the states of México and Puebla.

06. Now we will consider the location and the boundaries of the Mezquital Valley. As before, we begin on the east, 07. where it is bounded by the State of Veracruz. 08. On the west it is bounded by San Juan del Río. 09. On the north it is bounded by Tamazunchale. 10. On the south is Tizayuca. The Mezquital Valley is very extensive. 11. Each part of the valley has its own characteristics. 12. In area, it is about 100,000 cuartillos of planting.[1]

Climate

13. The valley is not uniform in climate. Each part has its own characteristics. There are some parts which are quite wet; others are dry, and desertlike.

14. We begin in the north. It rains a lot there and there is much moisture in the earth. Harvests are possible from Jacala to Tamazunchale. 15. The entire area of Chapulhuacán is humid and mountainous.

The south is not like the north. 16. The north has a very wet natural climate but the south is partly wet because there is irrigation. The irrigated lands have been developed by the mestizos, with the help of engineers, throughout the area of Jilotepec, Chilcuautla, Yolotepec, and El Alberto. 17. The same goes for Tizayuca. All these places border on Tizayuca.

18. On the east the mountains are also quite wet. They begin in La Vega de Meztitlán and Tulancingo. The western region is totally different. The arid section begins in Huichapan and runs through Alfajayucan, Zimapán, and a part of Tasquillo. This aridness is the major characteristic of the Mezquital Valley.

19. The central part of the valley is varied. There are some parts which are very wet and others where the irrigation waters don't reach. In the latter, there is moisture only when it rains; and when it doesn't rain the dust of the earth takes over everything because it is a desert. 20. During those times of the year when there are strong winds the flying dust of the earth looks like mist, and when it gets very hot the dust burns the feet of those folks who go around barefoot. The soil moves all around because of the winds. Sometimes the earth piles up and pushes down people's houses because this is open country. The most desertlike areas are places like San Miguel Tlazintla, San Cristóbal Pozuelos, La Florida, San Andrés Daboxtha, and El Saúz. This is in the eastern part, or the east-central part of the valley.

21. The other part on the west comprises places like Alfajayucan, a part of Tasquillo, and all of Zimapán. This is the western part of the valley. Portezuelo, López Rayón, and a part of Ixmiquilpan are also desert. A part of Ixmiquilpan is irrigated. 22. The following are the most desertlike areas in the valley: Orizabita, Megui, Nasthey, Dexthí, Boxhuada, Defay, El Olivo, El Espíritu, Los Remedios, a part of Capula, Nith, Taxadó, Maguey Blanco, Mejay, Panales, and a part of San Juanico. These are the lands in the heart of the Mezquital Valley. 23. El Arenal, Pachuca, and Tepenene to the southwest of Actopan are also part of the heart of the valley.

The north begins in Jacala, Chapulhuacán. In the north, the entire area is hot all year long. These are very hot lands.

24. In the south the lands are wet because they are irrigated. It is hot during the hot time and cold during the cold time. 25. The winds in the Mezquital Valley blow from the east to the west and from the west to the east. These are the dominant winds; they begin in January and last all through February and March. 26. These winds are not cold like those of September. Those winds are very cold and carry cold rains which last the entire month and sometimes continue into October. Sometimes they last until November. In December the dew begins to freeze on the ground. 27. Sometimes there is white ice and sometimes dark ice. The dark ice is the coldest and it makes the people put on their blankets—those who have blankets. 28. And those who don't have blankets wear their little ayates, generally the heavy, thick kind.[2] These are the really poor people. These frosts last all through the months of December, January, February, March, and sometimes into April.

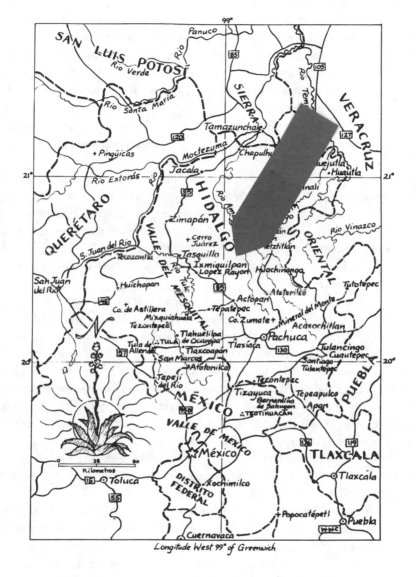

Longitude West 99° of Greenwich

The Mesquital Valley is located in Hidalgo

Geography 01

29. These frosts begin with the warm winds which go eastward. Two or three days after such a wind, it returns to the west as a cold cloud cover with freezing drizzles. Sometimes when it stops raining at daybreak there will be ice, either the white or the dark kind. 30. As I said before, the people wrap themselves in their blankets, and those who don't have blankets sit at the fire where they burn old stumps and dried maguey leaves. 31. This is how it is in the valley, but in the mountains they burn oak, pitchpine, junipers, and other woods. They sit around the fire until their knees are covered with ashes. There are days when people never leave the fire. They only go out to go to the bathroom. Some people, especially children, are bothered by the smoke.

32. Thus begin the frosts and cold periods in the valley. The frost is not easy to see because there aren't many trees in the valley. On rare occasions, though, when the ground is covered with frost, people can tell whether it is white or dark ice. 33. Of course, in the mountains it gets all white because there are trees. There are even times when it snows there. It isn't like that in the hot areas, however, as I said before. In those areas it is warm all year. Once in a while it frosts there, but not every year.

34. I've seen the warm winds make sprouts occur on the trees, on the nopales,[3] and on all the green things in the valley. Then the cold wind blows from east to west. 35. This is the prevailing wind for most of the year, sometimes cold and sometimes normal. 36. When the cold clouds come up it gets very cold, and this wind is not good for plants. It is the opposite of the warm winds. 37. Sometimes the cold wind burns the trees and the new shoots brought by the warm wind. Sometimes it kills the flowers on the peach trees. 38. What the cold doesn't kill the wind does. This wind is of use only when it is hot; then, it brings coolness to the land. 39. Sometimes it brings a good rain.

The area most affected by the frosts, either the white or dark kind, is the irrigated land. If the cold comes when the corn is at the tender stage, then it destroys it. 40. Green plants are weak against the cold.

41. This cold is equally harmful in the valley and in the mountains. The people are sad when it frosts over, because they lose their harvests. In the areas without irrigation the cold desiccates the leaves and flowers of the peach trees, and burns the fig trees. There have even been years when the cold burned magueys, garambullos, viznagas,[4] and mesquites.

43. When the warm wind blows it comes from the west. One can not even see the sky for the dust it raises. 44. The wind only rarely blows from the north or the south.

The Rains

45. The rains come in their own time wherever there are forests, such as in the northern region of Chapulhuacán, Jacala, and Nicolás Flores. 46. This whole area has forests and this is why it rains there. It also rains in the south, but with less intensity than in the north. It also rains in the east in places like La Vega de Meztitlán, Tulancingo, and Real del Monte. 47. All these parts of the valley are green.

48. The west is lower on this scale. That is, with respect to rain, it doesn't equal the other areas of the valley. There aren't as many large trees in this area, and for this reason it doesn't rain much.

49. The poorest part of the valley, with respect to rain, is the central area. 50. All that comes is thunder and lightning, along with strong winds that make dust devils. 51. And when there isn't any rain, there just isn't any, and that's why there are no harvests. The rain that does get to the center of the valley comes from the south. 52. This is what generally happens. Once in a while it rains from the north. It seems to rain from the east or the west when there are hurricanes.[5] 53. When there are hurricanes, then it rains hard in the valley. That is, when there are cyclonic winds on the coastal areas, either the east or the west, then these rains come to the valley as drizzles which last one or two days, and sometimes a week. 54. Then there are harvests in the Mezquital. Even though it's just drizzle it's enough to maintain the lechuguilla, the maguey, and the pasture for the animals.

Topography of the Mezquital Valley

55. As we said in the beginning, the valley has many parts with different characteristics. This is what we will look at now, part by part. 56. There are parts that are very high. Some of those are forests, some are tall mountains, some are just slopes, and still others are hillocks and small valleys.

The North

57. This is all forest. It begins over in a part of the municipio of Zimapán. From Jacala it continues toward Chapulhuacán, adjoining Tamazunchale. All

these areas are mountainous. 58. Another section consists of Nicolás Flores, Dos Pilas, Itatlaxco, La Misión, Cobresito, Chapulhuacán, and San Andrés Pisaflores. 59. All these areas I have mentioned are mountainous. Some of the mountains may be considered just hills, but others are great peaks. In these places I have mentioned, one rarely finds small valleys, as I said earlier. 60. Because the land is mountainous the people have cleared away the trees and brush for planting. The slopes are so steep that the people working them look like they might fall over. 61. Yet, every year they reap a harvest and never lose what they have planted. They plant wherever they can, but where it is too steep or too rocky they don't challenge the forest.

The South

62. The south is dominated by the valley. There are only a few mountains and hills. Mostly, there are cultivable lands. One part starts in the municipio of Actopan. It continues to Poxindejé, San Salvador, Mixquiahuala, Tepatepec, and Progreso. 63. If we return towards the north, then we come to the municipio of Chilcuautla, but only a part of this is cultivable. All the arable lands are irrigated by the sewage waters that come from Mexico City. They come up a great canal which was built some time ago. This is what is used to irrigate the lands in these parts. 64. The mountains I am speaking of are very dry. Even the plants that are there don't develop well. There are no large trees except some big mesquites, and where these are gone, there are just bald, eroded mountains; just boulders, strewn about at the foot of the mountains. The hills have the same characteristics as the mountains. 66. The altitude of the tallest of these mountains does not exceed about 1000 hand spans, and the rest are about 500 spans. 67. The mountains are tall in the south and in the north. They reach about 500 or 600 brazadas.[6]

The East

68. The eastern part of the valley begins in Meztitlán, and runs through San Pablo, Jonacapa, and Vega de Meztitlán. All these parts have the same characteristics as the mountains in the north, which are the tallest. Here, too, it is rare to find a level piece of ground. Those that do exist are the many large and small barrancas.[7] 69. There are places where rivers run. They carry great amounts of water. When it rains a lot the water carries away trees and rocks. In places, the

water can drag away animals, and even houses if they are in the path. When there is a lot of water the rivers jump their banks.

70. The other part of the eastern portion of the valley is a plain, just as in the south. It begins in Tulancingo and goes south to Real del Monte, Pachuquilla, and Pachuca. 71. Tulancingo and part of Real del Monte are the most level areas in the valley. To the north of Pachuca there are many mountains. 72. The rock which forms these mountains I have mentioned is grey in color, but very hard. In places it contains a kind of soapstone which is white in color and in other places the soapstone is also grey. 73. These mountains are in the northern and easterns areas. Towards the south there are some rose colored and some blue rocks. Some are hills of white tepetate.

The West

74. The western part of the valley is toward Chapantongo, Alfajayucan, Huichapan, and Tecozautla. There are great mountains there also. Many of them are of blue rock and arc high. 75. Over towards Chapantongo, Alfajayucan, and Huichapan there aren't so many mountains. In fact, they are rare. Mostly, there arc low hills and these are mostly rose colored rock. Around Donguino and Golondrinas they quarry a lot of this rock for repairing churches and for building houses. People really like this rock because it's a very pretty color. 77. There is also dark flagstone for house patios and churches, and for house walls, too. The stone is cemented to walls because it is so beautiful.

78. In Zimapán there are also many tall mountains and many hills, too. Some of them are very eroded but others have trees and plants—though they are small varieties, like ocotillos, capulín, and thorny cacti, including cardón blanco, etc.[8]

The Heart of the Mezquital

80. Now we return to the heart of the Mezquital to look at each part mentioned here. In the eastern part of the center are the communities of Orizabita, El Espíritu, Cardonal, San Miguel, El Saúz, San Andrés Daboxtha, Pozuelo, Capula, and Nequetejé. 81. North from Orizabita are the following places: El Banxu, La Lagunita, La Pechuga, La Bonanza, Gundó, La Nuez, Cuesta Colorada, La Palma, Cantamayé, Dachí, and Megui.

82. To the south of the very center are Ixmiquilpan, Maguey Blanco, López Rayón, Panales, El Maye, San Nicolás, El Nith, and Los Remedios.

83. To the west are San Juanico, Tasquillo, Dexthí, and El Dextho. 84. There are some mountains in the Orizabita region called Banxu, La Muñeca, Punti-agudo, and Juárez. 85. All are quite high, and reach an altitude of about 2,000 to 3,000 brazadas.[9] They are eroded mountains, and only have small shrubs on them. All are of bluish rock. 86. There is another mountain called Nando at the foot of which is a spring. The people of Orizabita all drink this water. 87. La Muñeca also produces water, but it disappears through the barrancas. It smells of iron and is very cold. 88. Those who have tried it say that nothing boiled in this water ever cooks well. 89. Also Palma Mountain has a spring used only by the people in La Palma.

90. There are other small mountains called Colorado, Puerto, Azulado, El Boye, and Abultado. All these are eroded and have very little vegetation. 91. La Lagunita, La Pechuga, and Bonanza are all forested. In that area there are large junipers, pines and oaks.[10] 92. In El Espíritu there are only hills, not big mountains. These are hills covered with stones. There are mesquites and other shrubs.

93. Cardonal has a mountain called Juxmayé which has an abundance of lime. There are other mountains to the north where there are trees. 94. Over where Cardonal is, it is covered with tepetate.[11] The hills are made of hard tepetate, and white tepetate. There are hard areas and there are soft ones which turn into whirlwinds of dust.[12]

95. San Miguel is all valley land, with cultivable soil. However, it doesn't have water beyond what the rains bring, so they can't produce anything. But the hills are large and the earth is very fertile for planting.

96. El Saúz is about the same as San Miguel which borders it on the east. A part of that area is composed of eroded mountains. 97. Its vegetation does not support the keeping of animals, and is only good for firewood.

98. San Andrés Daboxthá has the same characteristics as the valley and the lands around there are like those in the preceding two communities. There are no hills to mention.

99. Pozuelos is located near the mountains. On the east and on the west they are like those we have mentioned. There are also some small hills in the central area of the valley. 100. In the mountains the vegetation is all sampedro, thistles such as the darning needle cactus, the tuna de coyote, and other thorn bushes.[13]

101. Capula is like Pozuelo, but with other kinds of spiny vegetation like cat's claw, junquillos, and flowering shrubs.[14]

102. Nequetejé is where one really sees the valley with all its characteristics. The people there make charcoal from whatever wood there is on the slopes, including nopales and órganos.[15]

103. El Banxu, La Lagunita, La Pechuga, La Bonanza, El Gundó, La Nuez, and Cuesta Colorada are heavily forested. There are high mountains in that area, and it's rare to find even small flat spaces where the people can plant crops. 105. Many people there plant right on the steep slopes. 106. La Lagunita, La Pechuga, and La Bonanza, all have black earth; in Cuesta Colorada and El Gundó there is red earth; Defay also has black earth. 107. At least there is earth where the water hasn't washed it away. Otherwise only rock remains. There are no trees there any more. The people cut them all down, and so now they are gone. 109. When they cut them down, the roots went also, and nothing was left to hold down the soil. When it rained, the water took all the soil on the mountain. So now, because of this, one sees only rocks. 110. Thus we note the importance of knowing how to protect everything, whether it is a mountain or a valley. Everything is important. Each in its own way is indispensable.

111. La Palma, Cantamayé, Dachí, and Megui also have their own characteristics. Only maguesys, sampedro, and miel de jicote[16] grow there. There are also a few clusters of lechuguilla. 112. Here, too, the earth is slowly being washed away by the rains. 113. It doesn't rain all the time, but when it does it sweeps away everything it touches. There just isn't enough arable land here, either. It is mostly rocky hills. 114. In the small spaces between the barrancas, the people have terraced the earth with dirt and stones in order to conserve the water for the magueys. But if it rains a lot, then they plant seed crops. 115. They plant corn, dark beans, and broad beans. The surface of these small plots is never more than six brazadas square.

116. When they plant they guard it with everything they have, because there are no other milpas. They take turns protecting the milpa, sometimes the man, sometimes the woman, and sometimes the children, if they have children. Once in a while they plant peas. Whatever they plant must be rapid growing so that when the rains end the seeds won't have much more to go before they mature. 118. They really have to protect the milpas if they are going to bring in a harvest; if they don't, the crops will be ruined by animals such as squirrels, foxes, badgers, and bobcats. 119. These are the visitors in the milpas.

120. Los Remedios has hills near the church. The hills are rocky and have thorny plants all over them, including tunas de coyote, mesquites, cardón blanco, and other woody plants which we will see when we take up the flora. These hills are up to 100 meters in altitude.

121. In San Nicolás there are a few hills of tepetate. There is one called
Calavera which is all tepetate. Some parts are hard and some are soft. They used
to quarry rock there for house construction, but this was abandoned after the
irrigation system arrived. Since then the people there have worked irrigated milpas. Only fragrant herbs grow on the hills I'm talking about. 123. But in the area
where the irrigation canals have reached there are now pepper trees, peach trees,
walnut, and ash. 124. Ixmiquilpan is like San Nicolás. There are walnut, peach,
ash, and cypress trees.[17]

125. In Maye there are mesquites and rocks. There is a mountain called
Sauzal which is about 500 meters high. There are mesquites there and garambullos, cat's claw, and a type of giant viznaga.[18] 126. Panales is located on a
mesa of tepetate. It extends a long way towards the east and the people quarry
construction slabs. They export these to whoever needs them for building
houses. 127. Heading west there are just mountains that reach up to about 1,000
meters. There is a lot of cardón blanco, tuna de coyote and capulines. 128. There
are irrigated lands in Panales today on its eastern side. The western part is very
arid. On the north it borders on López Rayón.

129. El Dextho has a barranca running across its eastern side. Before reaching the barranca are the milpas cultivated by the people. Then there is the barranca. 130. There are mountains on the west which border Portezuelo. These
mountains are about 500 meters high. 131. On the north there are two large
mountains. One is called Mt. Mayor and is 1200 meters high. There are
lechuguillas and palmas.

132. El Nith is located on a tepetate hill. There are mesquites, and some
clusters of maguey and prickly pear. 133. In San Juanico, the eastern lands are
cultivable. On the west is Mt. Mayor where there is lechuguilla, mesquite,
palmas, huapilla, and pitahayas.[19] 134. The entire western part is mountainous
and borders on Tasquillo. The northern part of the community is all cultivated
land and borders on Dexthí. 135. Dexthí doesn't have cultivable, irrigated
lands. It is very arid. In the northern part, though, there are yellow-flowered
aloes, mesquite trees, lechuguilla, capulín, Spanish moss in the mesquites[20] and
sisal.

The Lands

136. There are many kinds of land in the Mezquital Valley, each with its own
characteristics. We will look at each of these, one by one, so we may know them
all. 137. We begin in the middle and work our way slowly towards the edges.

Many of them there plant on the steep slopes
Geography 105

138. The part of this area in which the village of Orizabita is located is all tepetate. Some parts are yellow tepetate, and other parts are white. Parts are soft, and parts are solid. For example, a part of the area where the cemetery is located is soft. Towards the west it is hard; but the entire hill is tepetate, nonetheless. 139. It is mixed in some places with a kind of soapstone. Towards the west all the hills are tepetate mixed with solid, dense rock. Blue and pink rock is most abundant. Sometimes the hard rocks are large, but others are small pieces, the size of gravel.

140. Sand from this region is mixed with lime in house construction. 141. There are barrancas at the foot of the hills. It is these barrancas which carry sand and gravel during rainy periods, and this is mixed with cement in the construction of roofs and columns in houses. On top of the tepetate the soil is mixed with compost from rotting plants. Aloe and huapilla are the plants which fertilize the ground most when they rot, and other plants also decompose into the ground. On the east there is a section which is cultivable. 142. It is about 500 meters wide and about 400 meters long. It runs from north to south. The land is very fertile because it contains a lot of nutrients brought by the runoff from the mountains when it rains.

143. Two barrancas cut through Orizabita. One is called Nando. It has this name because it begins in the high area of Nando. The other is called "La Barranca de Agua Olorosa" or "Barranca Hediondilla." It starts up in Mt. Puntiagudo in the north, and comes down to Orizabita where it irrigates the milpas whenever it rains. 144. Then it continues on towards Remedios. Finally, it goes into the great barranca in what is called the "nitrous zone." The great barranca joins the river in San Juanico. This river goes to the sea, east of Mexico City. 145. Other tepetate hills are on the east of the barranca. They begin in the north and descend towards the south. They end at the Orizabita hill. 146. Immediately after this hill are milpas; then the hills continue. One of these is called "Cazadora de Liebres," and that is where the boundary of Orizabita is.

147. Many of the hills I have mentioned are composed of tepetate. On top there is a shallow cover of earth. This is what gives life to the plants. One of the hills which stands out is called Däxt'ooho in Ñähñu, so the pueblo near it carries its name. This is its name in Ñähñu; all the people in the valley know it by this name. Its name in Spanish, Orizabita, was given to it when a saint arrived there who came from the town of Orizabita, Veracruz. It is said that the people brought him to the valley, and he went around and visited various pueblos. When he got to Däxt'ooho the people wouldn't let him return to his homeland. 149. That's how the name of Orizabita came to be used, in honor of the place from which the saint came. People say this is the same saint they have in Defay.

They still carry around his image there from house to house. Many people like to invite the saint to spend time in their homes, sometimes for three days, sometimes for a week. Perhaps this is a continuation of a religious practice from prior times. 150. During the annual festival in Orizabita the image of the saint from Defay comes to the church and is presented in the mass. The people follow him in the procession just as they do other images which come from various parts of the area of Orizabita.[21]

151. In the communities toward the northwest, there are rocky hills. Some parts have a little soil. It is black from the aloe and huapilla, with some clumps of lechuguilla. 152. Not too far from these hills there is a mountain called El Candó. It is not known why it has this name. All the rock from which it is formed is reddish. Part of this mountain is the border of the territory of El Espíritu. 153. South of El Candó there is a large area which is a flat plain that has cultivable lands. But it is very dry, even though the land is quite rich and naturally fertilized. 154. It is hoped that when the irrigation arrives it will extend into this area. It's really a shame about these beautiful lands; but that's how it is in these parts.

155. Heading north from Orizabita we come first to Boxhuada, then to El Nando, La Lagunita, La Pechuga, La Bonanza, and so on until we reach Nicolás Flores and Chapulhuacán. 156. The land is rich. Unfortunately, it is also mountainous and the people can not work these lands easily. Some parts of these lands, from Nicolás Flores to Chapulhuacán, are orange-colored. Some areas are orange-colored, and some are red, but one can get a harvest from all of these lands because they are rich in nutrients from the trees. 157. There are these rich lands in La Vega de Meztitlán also. However, the arable lands are located on the mountainsides.

158. Tulancingo is flat and the earth is fertile. Real del Monte and Pachuca are dark, rich lands. The wetlands begin in Real del Monte. 159. In Pachuca the fields are very dry. All these places plant wheat and barley, and only these grains, every year. 160. San José Tepenene is located near the foot of some high, eroded mountains which are about 2,000 meters. The lands around Tepenene are open fields, but the land is arid. The only thing that grows is mesquites, pepper trees, prickly pears, and other scrub bush.

162. Actopan has a lot of arid land in the eastern sector. There the same vegetation is found as was mentioned above. Tepenene borders on Actopan and this is why it has the same characteristics. 163. The tall mountains to the east of Actopan also reach a height of 2000 meters. At the top of these mountains there are some boulders that look like people. Their name in Ñähñu means Friar Mountains. 164. Going west, all the land is under irrigation. The land is fertile

because it is irrigated with the sewage water that comes in from Mexico City. 165. These waters contain a lot of natural fertilizer.

In Santiago de Anaya the land is completely dry. 166. There are many earthen hills where garambullos grow, along with nopales pintaderas,[22] and mesquite trees. 167. Parts of this section are made up of good, fertile earth, but it needs water. We know that without water there is no life. In Mixquiahuala, the entire region is under irrigation.[23]

168. Progreso is the same, except the lands are rocky. The earth cover is superficial and the tepetate layer is near the surface. The tepetate in this area is of the hardest variety. The lands are irrigated by sewage water. These are the waters which help plants grow best, because the tepetate layer is everywhere. Chilcuautla is only irrigated in one sector. Only the eastern half is irrigated; the western half is dry. 169. Mostly it is hilly, and most of the hills are just tepetate. Other hills are full of rocks; but the soil cover is good quality, especially where there are flat areas.

170. In the southern part of Ixmiquilpan there is a mountain called Zuja which is about 1500 meters high. To the east, directly adjoining it, there is another one with tableland at the top. There is another to the west which is more or less rounded. It doesn't have a proper name. The irrigation system extends to all of Ixmiquilpan. The water comes from Tula, and this is why the river is called Río Tula. A dam has been constructed on the river at Maye, and through this dam all the arable lands are irrigated, including Ixmiquilpan, Panales, Progreso, El Nando, El Dextho, and San Juanico. In Panales, the eastern lands are rocky with a lot of tepetate. This class of land is no good for planting. In San Juanico the soil is rather nitrous. In Dextho, the ground near the irrigation canal is nitrous, and the land going eastward is fertile. 175. In Tasquillo, starting from the corner which borders on Dextho, the cultivable land is mixed with tepetate. However, these areas are only recently cultivated, so they still give good harvests. Similarly, the lands in Arbolado are rocky. Juchitlán has no cultivation at all because the land is arid and hilly. The greenery one sees in Tasquillo is walnut trees. They grow well there because they have plenty of water. 176. This is why they grow to be such big trees in Tasquillo, like the great ashes which also grow where there is enough water. The great walnut trees, however, predominate in Tasquillo. Towards the north there are only hills of tepetate. Wherever there is soil cover there are ocotillos, lechuguillas, cat's claw, and mesquites.

177. Alfajayucan has very little dirt land, but what it has is really good. A small part of Alfajayucan is irrigated by the dam located near the road to

The people follow him in the procession
Geography 150

Huichapan. 178. Mostly, though, one can see that the hills of Alfajayucan are made of rocks, with patches of arable land in between.

The hills are like this all the way to Huichapan. 179. Wherever there is workable land the people labor constantly to keep up the rock dams they build to conserve water. There is water all year when these dams are built large enough. The people use the water to irrigate their milpas and water their animals. All the way to Querétaro, the lands are black and contain a lot of natural fertilizer. Pasture grass grows on the hills, which have a soil cover there, so people raise cattle, horses, goats, sheep, and burros.

180. These are the different characteristics of the lands of the Mezquital Valley. As I said before, all the parts of the valley are not the same. 181. In some places the earth is black, containing many nutrients. In others it is light because it is mixed with tepetate. Other places still are nitrous because the tepetate layer is so close to the surface. Some of the terrain is mixed with sand. 182. Some soils are smooth, and others are mixed with clay. Where the land is still good, it is soft; where it is run down, it is hard. 183. Sometimes water erodes the soil and other times planting itself ruins the land if crops are not rotated every year.

184. Nothing grows well in the sandy and nitrous lands, and there are no harvests. It's useless when the people spend their money without getting a harvest back. Where the land isn't nitrous, it is all slopes, and under such conditions it is impossible to plant anything. 185. This is why the people are poor. It is true that they get a harvest once in a while, but this is only when it rains a lot, as for example when there are hurricanes on the coastal areas. This is when there are strong rains in the Mezquital Valley.

186. Nowadays, the people are slowly starting to take care of the little land which they have. They are guarding against wind and water erosion. 187. For the latter they build barrier mounds, or they plant magueys in the milpas. They plant lechuguilla on the slopes of the hills, or maguey if the land is good. These are the plants which resist drought best. In the land serviced by the irrigation system, the people practice crop rotation. In this way the plants themselves maintain the earth in good condition. If the natural resources which feed the plants become exhausted, then people apply manure. Goat manure is the best kind. 188. It lasts for five years and is not expensive. There is now a kind of manufactured fertilizer, but it doesn't have the same potency as manure. It's also more expensive than manure. For these reasons, most people prefer to fertilize their fields with manure. They also notice that their harvests are better when fertilized with manure.

189. There are not many cultivated fields in Zimapán, so I won't say much about that area. Agriculturally, it is poor. One sees only mountains and hills covered with scrub brush there.

Mineral Resources

190. There are not enough mineral resources in the Mezquital. The region is simply poor in them. I will mention only those places where there are mines where gold and silver are exploited.

I have seen several places where they extract something called "caolín." We will see what is made with this tepetate. 191. The tepetate I'm speaking about is very fragile. There are places where there are small lime quarries, as well as sand and rock quarries. There are many people engaged in transporting the rock to sell to those who use it in building construction. 192. I also include charcoal made from wood as a mineral resource. Even though it was a tree once, the moment it is burned to turn it into charcoal it ceases to be a living thing. 193. We can thus consider that it has been turned into a kind of rock, just like the mineral coal taken from the big mines. The charcoal I'm referring to looks like coal. When it comes out of the furnace in which it is made it looks like rock. It is not as hard as coal, but it is the same color. 194. I will begin by mentioning each area and will cover the various parts of the Mezquital Valley where there are mines and quarries. As before, we begin with the north.

195. Zimapán is the area with mines. 196. To a small extent, the miners there exploit gold; but to a greater extent, they extract silver. Trucks carry the ore from the mines to Huichapan. The train from Mexico City stops there, picks up the crude ore and takes it to Monterrey for refining into pure metal. 198. A great many folks in Zimapán work at this trade, digging underground for the metals I have mentioned. Others work at loading the trucks which transport the ore. This is also done in the western part of the municipio of Nicolás Flores. The workers come from Pila.

199. Generally, the Zimapán people work in minerals. The folk from Pila harvest crops every year. 200. Even though they don't harvest much, still they do get a crop. The money they get from their crops is used to buy clothes and shoes and other necessities of the household. 201. Those who can't find work in the mines go to Mexico City in search of jobs. The mines are still not exhausted, even though people have been working them for hundreds of years since the

Spaniards first came and dominated the Indians. When the people first saw what was happening to them, they should have confronted the Spaniards and sent them back to their country. The Spaniards were like squirrels, digging everywhere. 203. They lived in Mexico more than 300 years and exhausted the wealth of the mountains, especially those mountains rich in metals.

204. Now we go back towards Cardonal to see what there is in that area. This is the area that is second to Zimapán in minerals. There used to be a lot of gold in Cardonal, but the Spaniards exhausted it. 205. A few years ago, a local person from Cardonal tried to reopen the mine. But the effort was abandoned because they found nothing. 206. When the Spaniards lived there many years ago, they worked the mine and it is said that there was a lot of precious metal. They built a foundry right there to refine the ore, and shipped the metal out in pure form. This way they avoided the transportation of ore. 207. Eight years ago in San Miguel Xiguí there were other excavations by mestizos. 208. They worked the area for four years and exhausted it. They, too, shipped the ore to Huichapan, so it could be picked up by the train on its way to Monterrey where the blast furnaces are for purifying metal.

209. There are some rocks in San Antonio from which people make lime, and they have been doing this for many years there. In fact, this area has supplied sufficient lime for the people of the entire valley. 210. Because it is such an old operation, I mention it here as a sort of mine. Everyone uses lime. It is what one puts in the nixtamal[24] to give consistency to the masa and the tortillas. 211. If a mixture of nixtamal does not have lime in it, the tortillas will break into pieces and won't have any flavor, either. This is why it is essential to put in lime.

The people of the valley only use lime produced in San Antonio when they make nixtamal. This lime is not ground up, but is sold in lumps which are white in color. Before these rocks are fired in an oven they are blue. They change color on baking. The lime traders sell the lime chunks in the Ixmiquilpan market on Mondays. Sometimes they take it to Cardonal, Actopan, Zimapán, and Alfajayucan.[25]

213. There is another kind of lime made in Tula, but it is not used in making nixtamal because it doesn't have the nutritional strength of the lime from San Antonio. The lime from Tula is used instead in building houses. It comes ground and packed in paper bags. Each bag weighs 25 kilograms. This kind of lime has only recently become known to the people. Previously, only unground lime was used; that was what was used in constructing house walls before cement was known. 214. We can see this in the old big walls and chapels which still stand in the valley, and in the dams built in the barrancas a long time ago. These dams were what made it possible to reap harvests. In this way, this class of lime is part

We can see this in the old big walls and chapels

Geography 214

of the nourishment of the Mezquital, because it is a complement to the food of the people. 215. Rich or poor, everyone needs lime. In the whole valley it is manufactured only in San Antonio Sabanillas, and nowhere else.

216. Charcoal is made wherever there are many mesquites, and also where there is rubble collected from clearing out the milpas. Tree stumps and other plants are fired into charcoal. Charcoal is mostly made in El Espíritu, Nequetejé, and a part of Remedios which lies east of Orizabita. 217. Those who make charcoal sell it in Ixmiquilpan. During the cold part of the year there is much demand for charcoal. During the hot periods, not many people work at charcoal making, because they know it won't sell well. Charcoal is most desired in the city because there are more people there who don't want plain wood smoking up their houses. 218. Burning charcoal doesn't produce smoke when it is well made. There is only one kind of wood in the valley which can be made into charcoal, and that is mesquite. Either the trunks or the branches; both are good.

219. Lime is indispensable for the entire population of the Mezquital Valley. It is made as follows: Those who want to make lime first look for a place where there is sufficient raw material. They must ensure that the results of their labors will be worthwhile. 220. Next, they find a spot where there is tepetate near the lime rocks. This is to avoid problems of transport. The rocks are carried to the furnace in an ayate or in a rope bag. 221. In this part of the operation the entire family cooperates; the children as well as the mother and father all work. Of course, only the big children, who can lift the rocks, work at this. The small children are left at home to stir the bean pot left on the fire by the mother so that, on returning home, she only has to make tortillas for everyone to eat.

222. Before making the pit for the furnace a spot is selected where there is a ridge of tepetate. It must not be too solid, so that it can be dug into. 223. It is important that it be a ridge or clifflike formation so that a hole can be made at the bottom of the pit. In this way, fire can be put into the pit, and wood can be introduced as needed. The hole should be about two and a half meters deep and close to the edge of the ridge. At the same time the edge of the ridge must not be too narrow, so that it doesn't get broken by the lime ore when the fire is introduced. 224. The fire itself can break through the side of the pit which is where the lime maker stands and where the fire hole is. 225. The diameter of the pit is about a meter—if the lime maker decides this is big enough. If he wants, he can make it bigger. This depends on how much he wants to make. Of course, it musn't be either too wide or too narrow. It has to be the right size for the amount of lime being made so that one does not have to use more wood than necessary in the fire. 226. After scratching out the outline of the pit, one must check and be careful that everything necessary is on hand. One uses a pickaxe, shovel, and some-

times a chisel or a club to dig with, so that if large rock is encountered it can be chiseled out even if it can't be dug out in one piece.

227. After doing all this, next comes the selection of rock for making the lime. The rocks must be chosen specifically so they won't explode when they are in the fire. The lime makers test the rocks by breathing on them to make sure that they are good lime rocks. If the rocks become moistened when breathed upon, they can be used to make lime. When they don't become moistened, then it is believed that they can not be thrown into the fire because they will explode. 228. And this is why the pit must be of tepetate, so that even if there are rock explosions, nothing will be at risk, neither the furnace pit, nor the lime maker. 229. There is no way that the pit will split because it is thick tepetate all around, except for the side where the person who stirs it stands. This is the thinnest part, where the hole is bored out on the bottom so the fire can be put in.

230. The lime maker has to use a pole, about three meters long, to put the wood in the fire. He mustn't get near the fire because it is dangerous. If one of the rocks explodes, it could hit him in the eyes or some other part of the body. The heat from the rocks alone is dangerous, and the burns are painful. For this reason he has to use a long pole to push the wood into the pit as it is needed. 231. Garambullo wood is used by lime makers because it is thought that the fire it produces is the hottest. When this is not available, then another wood is used, called sampedro. It is a species of bush which grows in the mountains, and it is said that its fire is very hot, too. 232. But when none of these are to be found, then mesquite is used, or other kinds of wood found in the mountains. Naturally, when wood is scarce near the fire pit, one must go far to find fuel to make lime.

233. It is not difficult to fit the rocks into the pit. One just puts some metal rods across the middle of the pit, and these rods hold up the rocks. 234. From halfway down the pit, then, it is filled with rocks, and from the middle to the bottom is the wood. Once this is arranged, the fire is set and kept going for three days, day and night. The person who fires the lime sleeps next to the pit and watches so that the fire doesn't go out. This goes on for three days, or more, until the rock has turned completely white. 235. Before being fired, the rock is blue; when it changes into lime it turns white. This means that the lime is done, and when the lime maker sees this, he lets the flame go out slowly, so that it all cools down a little at a time.

236. When it is well cooled, the rock is removed and put into sacks made of hemp rope. These sacks are the strongest kind and the rocks are very heavy. Less sturdy bags won't stand the strain if the rocks are put in them. Less sturdy bags can be hoisted, but they won't last many days, and in transporting them by truck to market they break and the lime falls out. This is the only means of

making a living for some people—that is, they get money for feeding their family by selling lime. 237. They take the lime to the market and sell it to individuals a little at a time. From what they say this is how they make the most money. Sometimes they sell it in bulk to the people in the valley who build houses, because they say that whole lime rock is very strong. The ground up, packaged lime doesn't have the same strength. This is the opinion of stonemasons.

238. When the fire pit is used for the first time, the sign of the cross is made over it as the first rock is put in. They say that this is to ask God's permission, and in this way one ensures that the work being started will be fruitful. The lime maker takes off his hat, crosses himself, and says the names of those saints whom he has heard are miraculous.

239. When the lime is sold at retail, the wife of the lime maker goes about in the market offering it to customers. She sells it to other women so they can make nixtamal. Men don't ever prepare nixtamal, and this is why the man, who has made the lime, does not sell it. It is sold in quantities of 50 centavos or one peso.[26] 240. Sometimes all is sold, and sometimes not. If a woman can't sell all the lime, she seeks a house of someone she trusts in order to leave it there. If she had to haul it back to her house, she would have to pay freight costs, and then the whole enterprise wouldn't be financially worthwhile.

241. This kind of lime is whole rock, not like the kind that comes packed in paper bags and is sold in the hardware stores. When someone buys lime and returns home, they look for a container to do what is known as "quenching." 242. Lime is powerful stuff, and when it comes into contact with water it crackles as if it were in a fire. It may even toss little pieces of lime about when it is dunked in water. When lime rocks are put into water to dissolve, all the lime boils. It is left to cool down slowly.

243. Until recently, people would buy lime for house construction. They bought ten sacks, and sometimes more, depending on how much they calculated they would need. 244. To quench it they would seek out assistants, because it is hard for one person to quench a large quantity of lime. First you have to dig a hole in the ground and throw the lime in it. The hole has to be very wide so the helpers can move about freely. Each helper carries a shovel with a long handle, so that when the rocks fly around none of the pieces will hit anybody in the eyes. 245. When water comes in contact with lime the lime explodes and the rocks fly about, hitting anything in their path. When lime is mixed with water, it gets very hot and comes to a boil. Once it has been quenched the lime is left to cool down slowly. Lime is very potent when it is hot, and if you get it on your hands it raises small blisters. It turns clothing and even soil yellow wherever it comes in

contact. 246. If the peons who help in quenching the lime don't have any other work to do, then they are paid half a day's wages for their help. They are given their pulque first, and then they are paid. The amount of pay depends on what peons are getting at the time; whatever the daily pay rate is, they are given half.

247. Everyone in the valley knows about lime because it is a part of the diet. It is used in making nixtamal and to give tortillas strength and consistency. If tortillas don't have lime, then they break into pieces, and also don't have a good flavor. This is why lime is so indispensable to the inhabitants of the valley. 248. The place where lime is made is San Antonio Sabanillas in the municipio of Cardonal, at the foot of a mountain called Juxmaye. Only a few people work at this, and they have been doing it for a long time. Lime makers are easily distinguished by the lime powder all over their clothes.

249. Lime is used in medicine also. If a person has been bitten by an ant, and if the bite becomes infected (or if the bite swells even though it is not infected) then recently quenched lime is put on the area. This cauterizes the area around the bite and prevents it from becoming infected. 250. The red fire ant has a poison that really hurts when one is bitten by it. At first it hurts, and then it itches a lot. Sometimes it becomes infected and this is why the bite must be taken care of quickly. Sometimes new lime is put on warts and they burn away. 251. Slowly, the warts dry up and are removed. Lime water is used for boiling nopal pads so that they will cook well. Also they maintain their green color when lime water is used.

The pot of lime water is left to settle before cooking is done, so that only fairly clean water is used with the nopal pads. 252. Usually tequesquite[27] is put in with the pads but if there isn't any, then lime is used. Those who have no money to buy tequesquite use lime because they always have some of that. 253. Lime is also added when cooking quelites so the leaves will cook up green. However, lime isn't added to all quelites, only hediondilla, quintoníl, nopal viejo, and endibia.[28] Putting lime in with vegetables is not just to keep them green. It is also done so that people can eat certain vegetables without harm to their stomachs. This is because certain vegetables are believed to be hot and others cold for the stomach. Lime and tequesquite are used to control the power of the vegetables, so that they won't cause harm to the stomach.

254. A woman who grinds corn for tortillas uses lime a lot in the kitchen. She puts it on the comal, which can be either of clay or metal. She does this when she puts the comal on the fire as she starts making tortillas. She uses a little brush made from palma or from ixtle. 255. She mixes the lime thoroughly in the water, then dabs it on the comal with the brush. This is helpful because the tortillas won't stick to the comal when they are turned. When tortillas get hot, they

stick; but if the comal has lime on it, then they don't. Thick tortillas don't stick so much; but the thin tortillas break apart if the comal does not have lime. 256. The lime water is dabbed on and the comal is left on the fire to dry out. Then the little pieces of lime left on the comal are brushed off. In this way only very fine lime dust is left on the surface. 257. This is how the tortilla maker flips her tortillas quickly and easily. She treats the comal frequently prior to preparing the tortillas.

258. Lime is also used to cure new water pitchers. When a new pitcher is purchased in the market it is filled with water. The water filters through the clay and drips out of the pitcher. On the first use of the pitcher the people put on fresh lime and this closes the pores. Then, when water is put in the pitcher, it doesn't drip, but simply filters and evaporates out over the surface of the whole pitcher.[29]

260. Now we will see how charcoal is made. First the mesquite tree is cut. Then it is cut into sections very carefully so that the pieces are more or less the same size. This way they will fit together well. 261. The pieces are about a forearm's length. All the little branches are removed so that there are no obstructions in fitting the wood together. The pieces are cut with an ax rather than with a knife. Then they are fit together and a small opening is left in the pile of wood. 262. First, a layer of wood is built in a semicircle, with an opening left where fire will be introduced. This is the hole left open from the beginning. Nothing is used to hold up the pile except the wood itself. In this way, as layers are added the pile doesn't fall in. 263. After the pile is built in the proper form the fire is introduced. Sometimes these all-wood ovens are small; other times they reach a height of one and a half meters.

After the piling and fitting of the wood comes the covering. 264. The pile is covered over with branches of mesquites, órganos, and various thorn bushes. 265. Then earth is put on so all the holes that remain are covered and no fire will escape from anywhere on the pile. 266. When the pile has been completely covered, the fire is put in and allowed to burn for three to seven days, depending on the size of the oven. 267. Some ovens produce up to 20 sacks of charcoal. When the demand is high, it is sold for 30 pesos a sack. The charcoal maker must stay by the oven day and night to make sure no flame escapes. 268. If air gets to the burning wood, then the whole pile might collapse, and all the work would be lost because some of the wood would burn and some would not.

In hot weather and cold, the charcoal maker must guard the pile. One person is not enough for this. Two or three are needed to help out. 269. And among the charcoal makers it is believed that if the oven is seen by a "bad person," then the charcoal will come out uneven. In other words, some of the wood will be

The woman who grinds corn for tortillas uses lime

Geography 254

properly fired and some won't be. The term "bad person" is used for women who are pregnant. If they happen to see the wood oven, then all might be lost. 270. Cardones are hung over the entrance to the fire, or when cardones aren't available, then aloe is used. These things keep away the "bad air" or "bad luck." This is the belief in the valley. 271. If the charcoal is lost, then there is no money. If there is no money, then there is no corn. If there is no corn, there is no life.

272. There are other mines in Pachuca, but they yield the same metals: gold and silver. Sand is another resource which nature has provided. Many people in El Xothi and El Mejay excavate it to sell to others who use it in house construction. When it runs out, they go back and dig more.

273. In Orizabita there are mountains with a lot of rock, and these mountains can be considered a kind of mine. Trucks come and cart it off to where it is needed. Rock is purchased like sand. There are other rock quarries in Golondrinas. The red rock is very pretty and it is used to cover walls in houses. 274. Rock has been quarried for a long time and it doesn't run out. People polish it for house patios. Many houses in the Mezquital have been built out of this rock.

275. These are some of the mineral resources. The people excavate them and the minerals are their source of work. They sell what they find and the money they earn sustains their families. 276. We have already noted that there aren't many mines in the desert. 277. Only recently they dug up a kind of tepetate at the foot of a mountain in the south of Orizabita. It is said that the rock is for making pitchers. This also happened in El Espíritu around seven years ago, but the effort has been abandoned. The community expropriated the business from the mestizos who ran it. The mestizos cheated the people and didn't pay them well and this made the residents of the community angry.

278. What happened was that a local man sold his land to a mestizo from Ixmiquilpan. The man from El Espíritu was cheated because they didn't pay him well for his land. Even though the land was not good for planting, still it has a lot of subsurface resources. 279. The mestizo found some workers to excavate the land. It was a kind of tepetate that they worked there, and the mestizo said it was called "caolín." 280. The material was transported to Mexico City by truck. No one knows exactly what is made from this. Some say that they make cups; others say plates. 281. But actually, no one knows. The land was a large parcel, but the mestizo only paid 400 pesos; by contrast, he took out thousands from the land and became a millionaire when he was once a poor man himself. This was in El Espíritu; that is, the same place from which the man came who sold the land. 282. The original owner of the land was paid 10 pesos for each truckload

taken out, in addition to the money he had already received. He was taken advantage of, and the people of the village became angry over what was done to this man. They got together and expropriated the operation because mestizos always like to cheat poor people. These people believe that Indians don't think. But in fact, even though many Indians don't speak Spanish, they are very intelligent. 283. In reality, even though they are very poor, the ordinary people have a lot of courage to defend their own rights.

Notes to Volume I—Geography

All derivations from Nahuatl are taken from Santamaría's *Diccionario de Mejicanismos* (1974).

1. The "cuartillo" is a measure of grain used in the marketplace. It is approximately one liter. Ten cuartillos are enough to plant one hectare of land in corn. Cuartillo is "huada" in Ñähñu. Twelve cuartillos are one "uatra." During periods of economic stress it is common for people to lend each other maize, and the loans are measured in uatra. Land holdings are also measured in uatra.

2. Salinas refers here to a "suthi," or a heavy, thick ayate. It is made from the dregs of the ixtle fiber, after the ixtle has been carded and combed. This heavy ayate is used with a tumpline for carrying heavy loads, and as a cloak by poor people in cold weather.

3. There are a great many of these cacti that belong to the genus *Opuntia*. They are called "prickly pears" in English and "nopales" in Spanish. They produce fruit known in English also as "prickly pears," and in Spanish as "tunas," a word apparently brought to Mexico by the Spaniards from Haiti in the sixteenth century. The most desirable variety is the "tuna blanca," which are very popular in the cities and were fetching 800 pesos (about $2.50) for a 20-kilogram case in August 1985. Throughout the text the words "prickly pear" and "tuna" are used interchangeably, as are "prickly pear cactus" and "nopal." These cacti are treated extensively in Volume III.

4. Viznaga is the Spanish name for a number of cacti collectively called "barrel cactus" in English. The smallest variety in the Mezquital is the *Stenocactus phyllacanthus*, which reaches only 15 centimeters in height by about 10 across. *Echinocactus grusonii, Ferocactus latispinus*, and *E. ingens* are larger; their meat can be used as fodder, or squeezed for water in an emergency. They generally reach about one or one and a half meters in height, by half to one and a half meters across. *E. grandis* grows to a spectacular two

meters in height, and is found only at the higher elevations, above Dexthí. The other plants mentioned here are annotated in Volume III.

5. This refers to hurricanes in the Gulf of Mexico or on the Pacific Coast. When there are destructive hurricanes in those regions, the Mezquital often gets the soft rain fallout, producing harvests. There is no harvest during most years. People plant corn and beans in their milpas during April, but the harvest is usually just the corn plants, without any ears, because of lack of rain. The plants, called "zacate" in Spanish, are used for forage.

6. "Ueni" is the Ñähñu word for "brazada," which is a measure of the length between the fingertips of the outstretched arms. Clearly, this measure varies with the size of the person, but among the Ñähñu it is generally around one and a half meters. "Nagi" is the measure of a hand's span, or about 20 centimeters. "Nagi" is also used as a measure of a forefinger's length, or half a hand span. When Salinas says that a hill is 1000 hand spans high he is measuring from the valley floor, not from sea level. The Tula River, which runs through Ixmiquilpan, is at 1,825 meters above sea level. The highest peaks in the Mezquital are around 3,100 meters above sea level.

7. The barrancas in the Mezquital range from small gulleys to great washes that have clifflike sides and look like canyons. The large barrancas are called "hñe," and the small ones are "sa'mhye" or "barranquillas," in Spanish. "Sa'mhye" connect to "hñe" and the latter connect to rivers. The barrancas are dry most of the year.

8. The capulín is a member of the genus *Prunus*, which includes the cherry, plum and peach trees. The capulín tree is a wild cherry, the *P. capuli*. In Ñähñu the word "pe'mni" refers to a white-thorned cactus, glossed as "cardón blanco" in Spanish, and "silver cholla" in English. It is part of a large class of thorny cacti known as "'mini" or "long thorns" in Ñähñu. These are glossed as "cardones" in Spanish, a term I have adopted in this text. Cardón blanco is the *Opuntia tunicata*.

9. In fact, these peaks rise to an altitude of up to 3,100 meters above sea level.

10. The junipers are *Juniperus flaccida*, the Mexican drooping juniper; the oaks are netleafs, *Quercus rugosa*. The pines referred to here are the Mexican pinyon (*Pinus cembroides*), which form part of an oak-juniper forest complex above 2,400 meters.

11. Tepetate (from Nahuatl "tetl," meaning "rock" and "petatl," meaning "mat") is pyroclastic, friable, volcanic tuff, composed mainly of silicates and some feldspars. Much of the the Mexican altiplano is tepetate, variably covered thin layers of soil. Tepetate is quarried in blocks for use in house construction.

12. During February, March, and April, the winds sometimes erode the tepetate so badly that huge dust clouds are formed in the valley, along with localized dust devils.

13. Sampedro is a bignoniaceous bush, possibly *Tecoma stans*. It is also called "tronador," according to the *Diccionario*. The "kahmiñ'o" (literally "tuna de coyote") is also called "velas de coyote" in Spanish. It appears to be the *Opuntia kleiniae*. Another similar variety, "xim'axt'ä," is *O. imbricata*. It looks like tuna de coyote but has more fleshy branches. The third member of this group is the "n'o'mä'mini," *O. pallida*, which grows to about one and a half meters and has straight needles.

14. Cat's claw is translated from "uñas de gato" in Spanish. Uñas de gato in Mexico generally refers to thorny shrubs of the acacia and mimosa families. In the Mezquital it is probably *Acacia greggi*. It is often mentioned along with compite, one of the most dangerous of the large branching cacti, with long, needlelike spines. Compite may be *Opuntia imbricata*. The Ñähñu word "tha'mni" refers to a short, round agave with many sharp-pointed, thin leaves. The Spanish gloss is "junquillo" in the Mezquital region, and I have maintained that name. This plant is discussed in detail in Volume III. What Salinas calls "pext'o" in the original Ñähñu has no common name that I have been able to find in Spanish. It is a common, wild Mexican flowering plant, with white flowers; I have glossed it here simply as "flowering shrubs."

15. Along with the nopal, and the fiber producing agaves, the órgano is one of the most widely used plants. The órgano grows as a series of straight columns, and was used in the past to make house walls and corrals. The use of órganos for house construction is now limited to rather isolated, very poor people, though corrals are still widely constructed from this plant. Corrals can be constructed of órganos that are of varying heights. House walls, however, are a different matter; they must be composed of órgano columns that are pretty much the same size. The órganos are cut to length and placed closely together, forming a wall. They are watered and nurtured, and take root. Every ten years or so, the thatch roof of an órgano house must be changed (see Volume III). At that time, it is common to trim the órganos again so that they are the same size. The walls of the traditional Ñähñu houses, made of either órgano or ocotillo, are alive. Consequently, they can not be attacked by termites or several other pests. Living houses also flower in the spring.

It is tempting to call the órgano an "organ-pipe cactus" in English; indeed, it has some resemblance to the organ pipe cacti of the American Southwest. The plant referred to by Salinas, however, is *Pachycereus marginata* and is sometimes mistaken for *Lophocereus*. There is a very large variety of Pachycereus in the Tolontongo area of the Mezquital, that grows to a height of 15 meters. It is called "viejecito" in Spanish, or "old man," because of the white fuzz, or "beard," that grows at the top of the plant. The particular niche is influenced by the presence of a hot springs waterfall; the vegetation at the border between the desert and the hot springs is unlike any other part of the Mezquital.

16. Miel de jicote is a direct translation of the Ñähñu "t'afigäni." I have not been able to determine its Spanish or English common name. It is a member of the *Compositae* family and resembles in form and smell a very large oregano bush, but is not used in cooking. It has small blue flowers. Lechuguilla is one of the most important agaves, and is dealt with at length in Volume III.

17. The American pepper tree is the *Schinus molle*. It is an evergreen, and does not produce pepper; its seeds, however, have been used in some countries as an adulterant for black pepper (Elias, 1980: 811). The cypresses referred to here are the Montezuma bald cypresses, *Taxodium mucrunatum*, found everywhere on the Mexican altiplano. They are also known by their Nahuatl name "ahuehuete" in Spanish.

18. This is the *E. grandis* in Note 4 above.

19. All these trees and plants are dealt with at some length in Volume III. "Palma" is a generic term in Mexico for a variety of plants that look somewhat like palm trees, but which are not true palms. The variety referred to here is a liliaceous plant sometimes called "palma china" or "palma ixtle." One variety is called "'mahi" in Ñähñu; its leaves are used for roofing thatch. Another is called "denthi" and is used for weaving hats and petates. Fiber is extracted from the heart of the 'mahi to produce crushed-fiber saddle blankets for burros. Huapilla (or guapilla) is the *Agave stricta*, or is perhaps in the genus *Hechtia*. It is a palmalike plant from which fiber is taken in other regions. The variety found in the Mezquital is not used for fiber. Pitahayas ("koua" in Ñähñu) are *Hylocereus undulatus*. These are enormous cacti that run over trees and walls like vines. They produce abundant fruit and are raised commercially in the state of Jalisco (Bravo H., 1937: 191)

20. The long, hanging variety of Spanish moss that grows in the mesquites is *Tillandsia usneoides*. The more ball-like variety is *T. recurvata*. Along the river banks, in the barrancas, and nowadays along the main irrigation canals there are pockets of more lush vegetation, including what appears to be yet another variety of Spanish moss. Goats eat *T. usneoides* and it is used as a decoration in fiestas, particularly at Christmas.

21. Salinas mentions both the *village* of Orizabita and the *area* of Orizabita. This is because Orizabita is a geographic administrative unit, comprising many villages, including Orizabita itself.

22. "Njo̱xikäähä" in Ñähñu are spotted tunas, or "pintaderas" in Mezquital jargon. They appear to be *O. robusta*, but may be *O. cantabrigiensis* with mottled fruit.

23. Twenty-five years ago Mixquiahuala was an isolated area and very poor. Today, as a result of the "aguas negras" project (the project to irrigate part of the Mezquital with the sewage from Mexico City), it is green, and the cabecera, or county seat, has grown towards Progreso, a major town that has developed on an industrial base, principally the manufacture of cement.

24. Nixtamal is from Nahuatl "nextli," meaning "ash," and "tamalli," meaning "tamal." It is the corn from which tortillas are made. The corn is boiled first in water mixed with lime (or in water mixed with ash in some parts of Mexico) in order to make the kernel covering come loose. The lime also provides vitamin C, of course and, as Salinas notes, it adds consistency to the "masa." The nixtamal is ground to form "masa," or dough, from which tortillas are patted out. Most villages today have a shop where one can bring nixtamal and have it ground into masa and, if one wants, made directly into tortillas by machine.

25. This refers to the towns rather than to the municipios. When he says that people from the "western part of Nicolás Flores" work in the mines, however, Salinas refers to the municipios. The weekly markets are on different days in the municipal seats throughout the valley, so people who sell various products go from market to market with their wares.

26. This volume was written in October and November 1976 and during the same months in 1977. When Salinas was writing these words in October 1976, the peso had just fallen to 19 to the dollar. It had been the most stable currency in Latin America and had traded at 12.50 to the dollar for nearly two decades. The prices he quotes, then, are in predevaluation pesos, and I have left them as he wrote them. One peso's worth of lime was about eight cents in U.S. currency at that time, and was sufficient for making nixtamal for several days for a family of six. The same amount of lime was selling for 100 pesos in August 1985, or about 30 cents USC, when the peso was trading at around 350 to the dollar. As a result of borrowing heavily against anticipated oil revenues that did not materialize, Mexico (and other Third World nations that export oil) has experienced massive inflation and deterioration of its economy in the last decade.

27. Tequesquite is a grey mineral, abundant throughout the Mesa Central of Mexico. It is found on the surface of dried lake beds, and is formed from sesquicarbonate of soda and salt.

28. The word "k'ani" in Ñähñu is glossed "quelite" in Spanish. "Quelite" is from the Nahuatl "quilitl," meaning "edible greens" and may be glossed in English simply as "greens," a word (and a food) familiar to all rural people in

the United States, particularly in the South. In Mexico, "quelites" refers generally to "green vegetables that poor people gather." Specifically, many of the
greens in the central plateau of Mexico belong to the genera *Amaranthus* and
Chenopodium. Common quelites on the Mesa Central are *A. chlorostachys* and
C. mexicanum. "Quintoníl" is *A. hypochondriacus*; it is known variously as
"quelite de espiga" and "quelite manchado" in Mexico. "Hediondilla" is *C.
foetidum* and *C. Album* (see also note 31, Volume IV); "endibia" is *Sonchus
oleraceus*. "Quelite verde" is a fast-growing weed that grows in cultivated
fields. It is not found in the wild. It comes up quickly after a rain, and is plucked
to feed to chickens and turkeys. "Nopal viejo" are prickly pear pads that are past
their prime and are no longer tender. Though they are cacti, they are classed as
"quelites" because they are part of the class of green things that poor people
gather to eat.

   29. This technique for keeping water cool by evaporation in very hot
climates is known to peasant peoples throughout the world, and probably dates
to the Neolithic.

VOLUME II

The Fauna

01. There aren't many animals in these lands. In the first place, there isn't much for them to feed on. In the second, the ones that exist are hunted down by the people and killed. 02. Under these conditions, animals don't thrive. The ones that manage to survive are feeble because there isn't much to eat, as I said before. I will mention here the animals I know about and have seen, along with their habitats.

03. We can see that there are cattle in Jacala, Chapulhuacán, and Nicolás Flores. This is because there is pasturage in the mountains on which the cattle feed. There are also burros; the people breed them because they are very helpful in the things people have to do. For example, burros are helpful in the planting of corn because it is difficult for people to walk in the mountains, and so animals do the work. 04. Burros do not provide meat for eating. They only help in the portage of goods when there is a need for it. Cattle provide meat. The hides are sold, and everyone knows that cowhide is used to make shoes, belts, jackets, bags, and so forth. 05. Some people make combs, knife handles, and pulque ladles from the horns.

Horn is the simplest form of pulque ladle. The handle and bowl is of one piece of horn, and the bottom is made of wood. 06. The handle is made of horn that is bent double. First, one selects a good horn, more or less straight, which can be cut. In order to make a good ladle, one selects heavy horns that are not too curved. 07. The part which will be the bottom of the ladle is cut so that it is even and straight. Then a thin piece of wood is chosen to make the bottom. The wood is worked all around its edges so that it is the same size and shape as the horn. 08. After it has been properly worked, the wood is fitted into the opening in the horn. It will become tight by itself from the pulque. Now the horn is cut all around except for the part which will be the handle. 09. The part which will be the handle is left to soak overnight in water. This makes it a little softer. When it is taken from the water, it is placed in a fire to make it more flexible. Then it can be bent without breaking it. 10. After it is bent, it is tied with a piece of rope to keep it fixed and prevent it from returning to its original shape. After about two days it is untied, the base is inserted if it has not already been put in, and it is ready to draw pulque. The handle must be long so that it can hang on the barrel.

11. The people in olden times spent a lot of effort making these things. They used to be different sizes. Rabbit hunters carried a horn for their gunpowder, and they decorated the horns very beautifully. 12. I remember that once a man came from the north to stay in these parts; he went off for a walk in the mountains. He came upon a horn which contained gunpowder. Some hunter had lost it and the man liked it a lot. 13. It was afternoon when he found it and the next day he went immediately to the municipal slaughter house, and returned carrying around four horns, and wishing that someone would make a powderhorn for him.

The people where I worked really had a good laugh over this man. One of the people did it for him. 14. First he got an iron rod red hot in order to pierce the horn through its thinnest part. The man was there observing everything. But when the hot iron hit the horn, it made a lot of smoke and it stank so much that it drove off the man who wanted the horn in the first place. 15. All night his head hurt from the odor of that horn, and when the people found out about this, they couldn't contain their laughter. They talked about it all the time at work. It made the man even more nauseous when they told him that horn is used as a kind of medicine. First it's burnt well until it becomes charcoal, and then this is ground up. It is drunk together with pulque before breakfast. 16. People say it cures anger and fright. Even though it made him nauseous, the man took the horn home with him to his land, along with a muzzle loading gun.[1]

17. Cattle bones are given to dogs to gnaw on. 18. Cattle manure is very useful in the milpas. It is put on the irrigated milpas to fertilize the lands, even though it doesn't have the same power as goat manure. Cattle manure is also used for fire as if it were kindling wood. It is mostly used where wood is in short supply. People say that its fire is hotter than wood fire. It doesn't flame up, it just burns like it was a cigarette. 19. The people who live in the irrigated zones mostly burn cattle dung. Only the whole pieces are burned, not the powder. The powder is thrown on the milpas. Cattle dung doesn't smell bad when it burns.

20. They breed horses in the places I'm speaking of, principally in areas where cars can't enter and only animals can go. Horses help a lot in transporting people from one pueblo to another. 21. There are also goats, but in less quantity because of the difficulty in moving about on the mountains to herd them. Goats are valuable for their meat, and for their skins which are used to make pulque containers. 22. In order to make a pulque carrier the skin is turned inside out. What was outside goes inside so that the pulque won't take on a bad odor. But first the skin must be washed very well, and then it is turned. Also, the hair must

be thoroughly pulled out. 23. The outside part is daubbed with whitewash made from tepetate to give the skin color and strength, and thus, when the pulque is put in, it doesn't smell at all.

24. There are sheep in the areas I've mentioned. Their meat is most exquisite in barbacóa. Later we will see how to make barbacóa. Sheep's skin can't be used for making bulk pulque carriers, because wool shreds on contact with pulque. So we don't see these used anywhere in the valley. 25. Everyone knows that wool is useful for making clothes such as blankets. Warm blanket robes are also made from wool.

26. The meat of the pig is eaten and it has a very good taste. The skin provides cracklings which are delicious, as are the deep-fried chunks of meat made from pork. The pig also yields lard which many people use to fry all kinds of foods, including nopal pads, quelites, and maguey flowers, and the lard imparts a good flavor. Lard is used as a medicine as well. If someone has pain in the stomach, or inflammation, then a mixture is made of lard, ashes and tomatoes. This is warmed over a fire and put on the patient's stomach. With this, little by little the swelling will go down. 28. Cattle are almost never killed by individuals for consumption at home. Instead, they are sold live to the butchers. If someone killed a whole beef, they wouldn't eat it all themselves; they might not sell it all, either, and then it would spoil. 29. Calves are sometimes killed, because they can be fully consumed.

There are chickens in all the places I mention here, again in small numbers. 30. Cats, dogs, and pigeons live in houses. These are the domestic animals.

Now I will list the wild animals. 31. In the same places where we began earlier, there are the following wild animals: foxes, coyotes, ringtails, possums, armadillos, bobcats, badgers, rabbits, hares, skunks, squirrels, and mountain lions.[2] 32. Sometimes deer come around. Foxes sometimes cause harm around houses because they eat chickens. Sometimes they eat baby goats. People eat fox meat, and its skin can be sold for making carrying sacks. 33. Some people believe that when you hear a fox calling out it is a harbinger of bad luck. Some people believe that this announces hard freezes. If it is known where a fox is calling from, hunters get together and go look for it. 34. If they kill it, they make barbacóa. Its meat isn't very tasty. But those who know how to prepare fox leave an opening in the pit so all the bad odor will leave. In this way fox meat is made to taste good.

35. The coyote. No one eats coyote meat. The skin is the only thing taken. When one is killed, whoever helped in running it down carries it around, passing from house to house so that people will give him pulque or food. The people are glad that a destructive animal has died. After it has been carried around, it is

skinned. 36. No one eats the meat because it smells rotten. Only dogs and vultures eat it.

37. The coyote is very scary to people when they meet one. It even makes people's hair stand on end from fright. Sometimes it makes people dumb, and it is said that coyotes bewitch people who see them. 38. In order to prevent any harm, as soon as one sees a coyote the person must scream very loudly, and wave his sombrero around. They say that the sombrero scares a coyote a lot. It gives the coyote diarrhea and it runs off. 39. If one is carrying a slingshot, then one should hurl rocks at it with so much force that the sling makes a lot of noise as it is spun in the air, and this scares the coyote more. This advice is from shepherds who always carry either slingshots or a noise-making whip which they crack in order to frighten off coyotes when they come upon them. 40. Coyotes are also afraid of firecrackers and gunshots. When they come to a house, people who don't have a rifle throw firecrackers at them to scare them off. 41. It is said that its witching power is in its forehead. When it is killed, the forehead skin is cut off. Those who skin a coyote forehead will carry this around, or they will sell it; they say that whoever carries this is always a winner in everything he does. He wins in work and in play, and beats anyone who fights him.

43. The tail is another part of the coyote which contains witchcraft. The people say that when a coyote attacks goats he only has to wave his tail and the animal stands still. Coyote tails are also carried around by people. The witchcraft is found in the tip.

The coyote is the most hated animal because it causes a lot of damage. 44. If one of them happens on three or four goats or sheep, he doesn't eat them all, but just kills them. He bites them on the neck. Even if they are large sheep or goats, the coyote brings them down.

45. The coyote's skin is sold. People buy it a lot for making hand bags, such as those carried by mestizo women. 46. Coyote dung is very useful in medicine. Whenever they find coyote dung, shepherds collect it so they'll have it on hand when it is needed. 47. Some people buy it because they know it is a necessary item. It is useful for evil eye sickness. This sickness occurs when an adult smiles or laughs at a child or a baby, either a girl or a boy. 48. As we know, children smile a lot. When they begin to crawl and to walk, they smile a lot. Adults laugh at this activity, and so it is said that they "make eyes" at them. 49. If a child is not cured of this sickness, it may die. Only the Ñähñu know how to cure it; nobody else, not even medical doctors, know the proper medicine. The sickness begins with vomiting and temperature in children. These are the most powerful symptoms. Then they get diarrhea and when all three symptoms occur together,

The coyote is the most hated animal

Fauna 43

then the child is gravely ill. This illness strikes children from one to three years of age; older ones aren't affected. 51. If a child is gravely ill, medicine is sought that goes with the coyote dung. When there is no coyote dung in the house, then someone has to be sent to the mountains to look for it, because it is urgent to cure the child. 52. The child won't last many days. Those who go through three or four days of this illness die.[3] Therefore, at the onset of the illness people perform a cleansing ritual. All the following medicines must be brought together: heart of palma,[4] the hem of a woman's skirt, the tips of a woman's braid, and alum. All these things are used in purifying the patient.

53. First, the head is cleaned, starting at the eyes and proceeding back towards the neck. In front, the cleaning reaches only to the chest. After cleaning comes the smoking or fuming. 54. The things required for fuming are a blessed offering,[5] hair, a piece of a petticoat hem, coyote dung, hummingbird nest, and lark nest. All this is put in a fire to make smoke, and with the smoke, the entire body of the child is fumed. Afterwards, the child is wrapped up so it will sweat, and with this treatment the illness is alleviated.

55. If the mother knows who put the evil eye on the child, then she asks that person to cleanse it, because in this way the child will get better more quickly. The person asked to cleanse the child does not refuse because he or she knows it's important to save the child. 56. If it is a woman, she cleanses the child with the hem of her skirts and the ends of her hair. If it is a man, then he is given all the medicine so he can cleanse the child. If it is the person who put the evil eye on the child, then the illness is cured more quickly.

57. There is another cleansing agent that is purchased in the pharmacies in town. It is called "ixaai" in Ñähñu[6] and is purchased with money. It's a kind of white rock; it looks like rock salt, but when it's heated in a fire it appears to boil. It doesn't burn up, it just gets white. 58. When it stops burning, it is ground up, and the powder is put on the infant's eyes. 59. If the child has already been cleansed, and on drying the surface of the powder is pitted and uneven, then it was, indeed, evil eye. If the telltale pitted surface doesn't appear, then it isn't evil eye, and the child has to be taken to a doctor. 60. If it is evil eye, and if it is cleansed, then that day or the next the child can eat again. When a child is being cured of evil eye, it is given no food; it is only cleansed and fumed. This is the benefit offered by the coyote.

61. These are the animals that go about at night: coyotes, foxes, cacomixtles, rabbits, hares, opossums, bobcats, rats, screech owls, barn owls, bats, lesser nighthawks, armadillos, frogs, spiders, scorpions, centipedes, carrier ants, spiny lizards, solpugids, daddy longlegs; also some snakes. Some of these animals are

dangerous. Badgers and crickets are also night creatures that are native to these lands.[7]

62. The following are the animals that go about during the day: cattle, donkeys, birds (buntings, skylarks, thrushes, turtledoves, cactus wrens, hummingbirds, mockingbirds, white winged pigeons, woodpeckers, crested woodpeckers, silkies, orioles, nightingales, shrikes, swallows, red cardinals), dogs, fowl (turkeys and chickens), eagles, hawks, quail, roadrunners, reptiles (coachwhips, house snakes, rattlers, afternoon snakes, spiny lizards, whiptails, víboras de aire, black snakes, horned toads), and squirrels. 63. The insects include flies, mosquitos, butterflies, large red bees, and various ants (black ants, red ants, yellow ants, black and yellow ants, escamol ants, large black ants). There are also beetles, capulín spiders, fire moths, pinacate beetles, tumblebugs, red wasps, yellow bees, black wasps, biting flies, green flies, azotadoras, gallina ciega, corn earworms, fly larvae, mesquite bugs, garambolas, carrier ants, large and small grasshoppers, locusts, rain bugs, lice, fleas, chicken lice, squirrel fleas, ticks, ground lice, hog lice, pig lice, maguey grubs, rock wrens, earthworms, tortilla weevils, burrowing field mice, and glowworms.[8]

64. The cacomixtle or ringtail. Now we will look at some characteristics of the cacomixtle in the Mezquital. The cacomixtle looks something like a cat. Its ears, eyes, whiskers, and body are like those of a cat, except a little larger. It lives in the mountains and feeds on rabbits, hares, and other smaller animals it finds. 65. Sometimes it comes to the people's houses and eats chickens. It eats the corn in the fields, and it drinks the aguamiel from the magueys in the monte. When tlachiqueros see that a cacomixtle has been drinking aguamiel, they set a trap, and if a cacomixtle falls in it, they beat it to death with a long stick because it is very wild and it bites.

66. Once it has been killed the cacomixtle is brought home to be skinned and made into barbacóa. Its meat is very tasty. It is fat because it feeds well and eats chickens. In order to roast it, one dabs on ground chile, and this is how the best flavor is obtained. 67. The skin is taken to market, and there is a great demand for it. People pay 20 pesos or more, depending on the size. Small carrying bags and change purses for ladies are made from these skins. Sometimes they make Daniel Boone style caps out of cacomixtle skins. The meat is as tasty as mutton. 68. When cacomixtles are in a group, they cry like cats. They only go about at night. Their fur is generally white and yellow. Some are grey and black. Their paws are identical to those of cats, as are their tails. They live on slopes and in cliffs where they dig their dens. Sometimes they like to sleep on the branches of trees.

69. The possum. The possum is also very mischievous. Wherever it leaves its tracks it looks like a baby has been there. It, too, likes to drink aguamiel. 70. At night, it uncovers the aguamiel and drinks. It pushes the stone cover off with its snout, as if it were a pig. Its snout is long and it's not difficult for it to suck up the aguamiel. If it is a female possum, and it's carrying its babies, then the mother drinks and the babies on her back drink, too. 71. They have a tail which they use to hold on with, so they won't fall off. That is, the little possums steady themselves with their little tails. The mother's tail has long since lost its hair. 72. The male possums also lose their tail hair, because they climb on trees and hang by their tails. They like to go up into trees to sleep. They generally feed on corn, and they are very harmful to young, tender ears.

When people find out that possums are about they set traps to catch them. 73. Possum meat is as sweet as pork. Possum meat, too, is roasted; no one eats it boiled or fried. 74. It is eaten as barbacóa. It is carefully prepared for roasting, and ground chile is put on it. The chile has been mixed with other spices, including mint, cumin, cloves, and pepper. These are what give it flavor. 75. The possum is not skinned. Its fur is first burned off in a fire, and then the animal is ready to put in the oven. It is grey in color and its hair is soft, not like that of the pig which is tougher.

76. The armadillo. The armadillo is more adapted to humid places where no one hunts it. It is very smart about hiding from its enemies. If it sees that an enemy is getting close, it retreats into its shell. Then it rolls along the ground, and it's impossible to catch it because it rolls into the gullies. 77. If one manages to catch an armadillo, its meat is very tasty—even tastier than that of the possum. First, it is killed, and then the shell is removed.

The shell is very hard, as it is made of bone. 78. Some folks I have seen make hand bags out of it. They paint it black and it is pretty. This animal doesn't drink aguamiel, nor does it eat corn. It isn't harmful. It seeks its food away from people. 79. It can't eat hard things because its teeth aren't very strong. 80. By contrast, the possum has strong teeth like a pig's. It also has fang-like teeth. The armadillo has nothing like this. They say that armadillos beat other animals to death with their tails, which are also very hard, in order to feed.

81. The bobcat. The bobcat also looks like a cat and is also very dangerous because it eats chickens when it can. It also drinks aguamiel. In fact, this must be its everyday drink. It causes damage wherever there are milpas. It is very smart and not easily caught. You have to go out at night with a light and a rifle. It can only be shot by shining a light on it. 82. It is eaten roasted, like the cacomixtle. In the same way, too, it is skinned and the pelts are sold. Handbags are made

Then it rolls along the ground, and it's impossible to catch

Fauna 76

from the skin. Its shape is the same as a cat's, but the bobcat is a little taller. It is spotted, sometimes yellow, sometimes yellow and white.

83. The badger. The badger, as its name in Ñähñu implies, eats corn wherever it finds it. It's very harmful, and wherever it has eaten it looks like a pig had gotten in there. One knows right away what kind of animal was eating there. 84. One sees where it has trod; its footprints are like those of a chicken, but crossed. It also drinks aguamiel. At the beginning of and during the summer they come out to cause damage. When they are caught they're made into barbacóa. 85. Its meat is tasty like that of the possum. Its skin is not thick. To cook it, you pull out the hair, wash it very well, add spices, and put it in the oven.

86. The cottontail rabbit. Rabbits sometimes cause damage in the milpas. They always eat the young, recently germinated bean shoots. They saw away at them and hurt the crops. 87. Also, when bean plants are young, rabbits strip the outer leaves and eat them. Usually, they leave corn alone, but once in a while they eat some leaves. They come out in the mornings and afternoons. People look out for them and hunt them, and in this way the plants are left to grow up well.

88. Rabbit meat is exquisite. It is very nutritious. Rabbits like to be in the shade, underneath the plants. 89. They seek out places where there is a lot of pasturage. For liquid they eat purple tunas. This is the cactus which supports rabbits.[9] Rabbits are grey on top and white underneath. They have one distinguishing part: their tail is whiter than all the rest. It is believed that this is where good luck resides. Some people keep the tail. Some put it on their sombrero. 90. If a person is going along a road and a rabbit crosses the road, then the person will have good luck. This is the belief people in the Mezquital have about rabbits.

Rabbit hair is very soft, like cotton. Some people have handbags made from it. Of course, it takes about four pelts to complete a bag, but if it is just a coin purse, for women, then one skin will do. Rabbit meat is tasty in barbacóa, but it is usually eaten fried. 92. Rabbits are born in threes and fours. When they are in the fields and have plenty to eat, they are born twice a year, first during February and March and then again in August and September.

93. Coyotes are born three or four at a time. Foxes, too, are sometimes born four at a time. Foxes feed on the fruit of the pepper tree, especially the ripe, red fruit. They also like capulín cherries a lot. 94. If a fox finds a rabbit, it chases it down, kills it, and eats it, skin, bones and all. It drinks aguamiel from magueys when it can.

95. The rabbit digs its hole in the earth; sometimes it makes its burrow in tepetate. It builds its hollow in the ground when it is going to bear young. When

it is not bearing young, it lives in open country. It sleeps under shrubs where no one can see it. 96. The rabbit doesn't bother any other animal. It likes to play with others of the same species. Of all the animals, this is the one which most likes to live in peace. When baby rabbits are born they don't have open eyes. After three weeks they open their eyes. During all this time they nurse. When they open their eyes they begin to walk. Slowly, they begin to eat small grasses. 97. Sweet pasture grass is their favorite, the large as well as the small kind. At three months they reach the limits of their development. When they are small they are very quick.

98. When rabbits lose their young, they call to them. Their call is like the sound made when someone sucks on the palm of their hand. There are a lot of rabbits, and during the months when they are born they are especially abundant. During the course of the year their numbers diminish. Hunters finish off some, and coyotes and foxes take another part. There is a story about the coyote and the rabbit. It goes like this:

One day the rabbit was going along out in the mountains. 99. Unfortunately, he came on the coyote and the coyote said to the rabbit: "How are you, Mr. Rabbit?"

"I'm just going along here out in the monte," answered the rabbit.[10]

The coyote said "Look here Mr. Rabbit, I'm very hungry. It's been two days since I've found anything to eat, and I'm really hungry. I guess I'm going to eat you now; I just can't take any more hunger."

The rabbit was very scared that the coyote was going to kill him. 100. So the rabbit thought "What will I do? He's going to eat me." So he thought about how he could trick the coyote. He noticed that the coyote was already licking his chops from the desire to eat him. So the rabbit says: "What do you say Mr. Coyote, don't eat me. I'll show you a white sheep I've seen, and I know where it is."

"Good," says the coyote, "but if you're fooling me I will surely eat you. Let's go then, and you show me where it is." The rabbit, trembling, went running ahead to show the coyote where he'd said he'd seen the white sheep.

101. Before getting to where he was thinking of showing him the sheep, the rabbit said to the coyote: "We are getting there; it's close now; just over here. It's very big. You'll see, I'm not fooling you! I'm going to point it out to you from a distance so it won't be frightened off. 102. Get ready to run, and the moment we arrive you jump on it and catch it."

The two stood on a hill and the rabbit showed the coyote a white object across on the other side of the vista. The coyote licked his chops with delight at the fact that he was going to eat. Then the rabbit said to the coyote: "Run, run! If you don't, you won't catch it!" 103. And since the coyote saw that the object on the other side was very large, he took off on the run. He ran fast, and when he got close he leapt up, trying to catch the sheep. 104. What was his surprise when it turned out to be a cardón blanco covered with flowers. He got filled with thorns, and in the meantime the little rabbit, who brought him there, took off running for the hills. 105. He was happy because he had escaped dying.

106. Meanwhile, the coyote was busy removing the thorns from his paws and his snout. 107. His whole chest was covered with cactus spines, and he was very angry because he had been fooled. He was very hungry and at the same time he hurt from all the spines. He said to himself: "That son-of-a-bitch rabbit made a fool of me! But I'm going to look for him, and wherever I catch up with him I'm going to eat him." 108. This is what the coyote thought he'd do when he was finished taking out all the spines. He went looking for something to eat, and at the same time he searched for the rabbit who had fooled him. The rabbit was hiding; he didn't want to meet up with the coyote because he was very afraid of him.

The next day, the rabbit was out looking for something to eat. He was going along in the monte and was shocked to see the coyote who had come out in the open country himself. 109. The coyote said "Now, Mr. Rabbit, I'm going to eat you. I won't let you go this time because you tricked me yesterday. You made me grab cactus spines."

The rabbit shook, not knowing what to respond to the coyote. But he quickly thought to ask forgiveness from the coyote. He said, 110. "Pardon me, Mr. Coyote, it's just that I thought it was a sheep. But now I won't fool you again. Just today I saw an enormous full-grown sheep. It was huge! If you want to catch it, I'll show you where it is. I saw where it was lying down. In fact, it is practically immobilized from being so fat! If you think you can get it, I'll show you where it is."

111. But now the coyote didn't believe him. "You're fooling with me! You want to trick me again. But now I'm going to eat you just to get rid of you for fooling me," says the coyote circling the rabbit.

112. The little rabbit tried to convince him and make the coyote believe the story. At last he was able to convince him and he went off with the coyote to show him what he was thinking of. The coyote said "Well, let's go. But remember, if you're fooling me I'll eat you for sure."

Well, the little rabbit was scared. He went on ahead to show the coyote where the sheep was that he'd talked about. They drew near, and the rabbit said to the coyote "Look at that! That's it." 113.

The coyote saw something black in a gully. It was very large. "Yes, I see it," said the coyote.

"Well, this is it," said the rabbit. "You must stand on the edge of the gully; approach it slowly, so that before it notices what's going on, you catch it." 114. The coyote was cautious, afraid that the rabbit would trick him again.

The rabbit was interested in saving himself. "Run!" said the rabbit. "Run! If you don't, it'll get away, and then you won't eat anything." Finally, the coyote listened to the rabbit and he took off at the run. He got to the edge of the ravine and stood there. He saw the black thing which was in the ravine. 115. He leapt to grab it and his forehead went "crack!" The coyote was knocked senseless by the blow because it wasn't a sheep; it was a large tree trunk that the rabbit had showed him.

116. The rabbit wanted the coyote to die. The rabbit escaped. But now he was more afraid than ever. He thought to himself "If this doesn't kill him, then he'll kill me." This is what he thought to himself. He had to get even further away. 117. He sure didn't want to meet the coyote again if the coyote hadn't died.

118. Little by little, the coyote came to. At first he couldn't remember why he had passed out. Slowly, he opened his eyes. 119. He saw the trunk on one side of him and remembered that it had been the rabbit who had fooled him. He was very angry, sitting there in the ravine. 120. He said to himself "I think Mr. Rabbit is smarter than me to have done this to me." 121. Then he said "I'm going to look for him. I'll do everything possible to find him so I can ask him why he always gets the better of me. I'm going to look for him. He must be about somewhere in the mountains."

So the coyote began looking for the rabbit in the mountains. The first day he didn't appear; nor the second day, either. 122. "Where could he be that he doesn't show up anywhere?" said the coyote. "Hopefully, he died and won't be able to fool me again." This is what the coyote was thinking as he walked and walked. Just when he wasn't thinking about it, he saw something moving in the grass. Sure enough, it was the rabbit, which the coyote hadn't seen. The rabbit immediately hid himself so the coyote wouldn't find him. 123. But because the coyote kept looking, after a while he found the rabbit.

"Mr. Rabbit!" he said. "Mr. Rabbit, either you come here or I'll come over there and get you." The little rabbit, still not wanting to, nevertheless came out of the grass to obey the coyote who had called him. 124. The coyote, said, "I've been looking for you a lot, Mr. Rabbit," and he caressed the back of the rabbit with his big paw. "Now I'm going to eat you. There's nothing else to do. You're always tricking me."

125. The rabbit felt like he was being swallowed by the coyote because the coyote already had his paw on his back. The rabbit just trembled. He couldn't think of what to say to the coyote. He said to himself 126. "I'll ask him to forgive me. We'll see if he accepts my plea; but if not, then God help me."

Then the rabbit said "Mr. Coyote, hopefully you'll forgive me and accept my apology for all that has befallen you on my account."

127. Well, the coyote was licking his whiskers with desire to start eating the rabbit when he heard the rabbit asking forgiveness. So the coyote said "Yes, I'll forgive you, but only if you show me where there is something for me to eat. I can't always find food. Wherever you see something to eat, you report it to me. 128. But if you don't inform me then hunger will hurt me and I will eat you."

129. "Yes, all right," said the rabbit; "as soon as I see something I'll advise you."

The coyote let the rabbit go and as the rabbit ran off; he was so happy he was wagging his tail. He was happy, but scared that he wouldn't find something for the coyote in time. He said to himself "If he starts to hurt from hunger, then he will eat me." This is what the rabbit was thinking. 130. He went on and on in the open country, always thinking about what he would do about the coyote. He knew that sooner or later the coyote would eat him.

131. Around midnight he came to a wide, deep lake. There was light from the moon. The rabbit looked into the water and saw that the moon was reflected there. Once again he saw how he could trick the coyote.

At dawn the next day he went to look for the coyote. He didn't appear, but late in the day the rabbit found him. The rabbit made a false show of laughter to the coyote. "How are you doing, Mr. Coyote?" he asked.

"And how did you sleep, Mr. Rabbit?" responded the coyote.

132. "Look here" says the rabbit.

"Yes?" answers the coyote.

"Last night," says the rabbit, "I saw where someone had left a cheese. I wonder if you'd like to eat it?"

"Of course, I want it. I'm very hungry," said the coyote and he looked like he could just fairly see the cheese.

The rabbit saw that he had tricked him again and he said 133. "I saw a person throw a big cheese into a lake."

"Where?" asked the coyote with joy.

"Over that way, far from here" said the rabbit. "Let's go, then" says the coyote. "Let's go!"

The coyote was knocked senseless by the blow

Fauna 115

The coyote was really glad. 134. He was dancing there where he stood. "Not yet" says the rabbit. "Right now it's too early. We have to go at night, so the owner won't see us; because if he sees us, he'll kill us both."

"OK, then" says the coyote. "You tell me when we go. On another matter, I don't know how to swim. How am I going to get it out?"

135. "I'll help you" says the rabbit. "I'll help you, don't worry."

"Fine" says the coyote. He was quite happy knowing he was going to eat cheese.

The rabbit waited until it was night and the moon was out. "Let's go!" he said. 136. "Let's go, and I'll show you where it is. Just follow me."

The coyote went bounding along after the rabbit. The rabbit thought about what he would do. They arrived at the lake, and now the rabbit says "Mr. Coyote! You who have strong teeth, cut off a piece of root. We'll need it so you can fish around in the water. 137. Without it, you'll just push water around."

Then the rabbit looked for a big rock. He tied it around the middle for the coyote to carry on his neck. It was around midnight when they got to the lake. It was deep, about nine meters. So the rabbit says "Hang this on yourself, Mr. Coyote, so you can descend." 138. The rabbit was just able, with a lot of effort, to lift the rock he had tied up with the root. He said "The cheese isn't going to run away from you, because it's way down there. So it's alright, even if you descend slowly."

139. The rabbit showed him where it was. "Did you see it, Mr. Coyote?"

"Yes, I did" answered the coyote.

"Well, go straight ahead" and the rabbit hung the rock on him.

As soon as they got to the edge of the lake, the rock went in with a big noise and pulled the coyote right to the bottom. 140. Of course, it wasn't a cheese, but the moon which shown in the lake. The coyote drowned and died. The rabbit was saved, and he lived happily ever after because the coyote died.

141. This has been a story of two animals that live in the Mezquital. Both wanted to survive, and the one that was smarter prevailed. Such were the stories that the old people used to tell. There are other beautiful stories published in our earlier volume (Bernard and Salinas, 1976).

142. The hare. The hare is bigger than the rabbit. One can tell right away if it's a hare or a rabbit because the hare's ears are very big. It is the same color as the rabbit, grey and white, but has a bigger tail. 143. It has lively, bright eyes, like a rabbit's. Its skin is the same size as a rabbit's. Its food is pasture grass, miel de jicote, and purple prickly pear pads. Hares rut in February. By June and July they give birth. 144. They are born two, or sometimes three at a time. They bear young only once a year. They are sometimes eaten for their meat, especial-

ly by those who don't have money to buy meat. Those poor people do whatever they can to catch hares. 145. Sometimes they get them with a rifle. Other times they put out traps. Hares always travel the same path. They never vary unless scared suddenly by someone. 146. Thus, people who know this put out traps in the evening and the next day there is meat for the whole family. Generally, hare is eaten in barbacóa. If it is a large hare, it may reach two kilograms in weight.

147. The hare is notorious in the milpas.[11] When it comes upon a planted area, it parks itself for the night and strips the leaves off the corn and the beans. It strips the plants clean, even though it doesn't eat all it takes. When people find out that a hare is about, they hunt it down with a rifle, or set traps. If the animal catches on that it is being hunted, then it doesn't return. They are very clever. 148. There aren't many because people hunt them and kill them continually.

Hares nurse like she-goats. They mature slowly in their nests. They make a burrow in which to put in their offspring, and they line it with grass so it will be soft and warm. 149. In this way the little ones don't feel the cold. Hares only use their nests for bearing and raising babies. Then they abandon the nests to go about in the monte. They sleep under shrubs and bushes. If they are caught, they cry out. Their cry is like a goat's. They move around by bouncing. If someone frightens them, they take two or three bounces and they're away. 150. When they go about they are careful to hide themselves so no one will see them. To do this they flatten their ears against their neck. Some people believe that if a hare crosses their path it means bad luck. It is not known precisely if this is true or not.

151. The skunk. Another nocturnal animal is the skunk. There are two classes of skunks in the Mezquital. One is called the "table skunk" and the other is called the "jumping skunk" in Ñähñu.[12] The table skunk gets its name from the long spot on its back. It looks flat, as if it were carrying a table. 152. The spot is white; it starts at the head and runs all the way to the tail. The black part begins below the jaw and passes along the belly to the tail. Its snout is very long. It is believed that it is used to catch the little creatures it feeds on. It likes to eat beetles, and it likes to drink aguamiel from the maguey plants. 153. It also digs at the maguey roots to find grubs. It is really hated by the people because it uproots the magueys and interrupts the plants' growth. It digs all night until it finishes off the entire row of magueys. 154. This begins in October and lasts all winter. This is when these animals are most abundant. There is no way to set traps for them because they don't follow stable routes. They come from every which way.

155. Some people like to hunt skunks in the moonlight. They make long sticks to hit them with. Some times they kill them by stoning. If the killing is not

done carefully, skunks will "bomb" you in the eyes and it's really painful. Everyone I've known who has been bombed by a skunk has been left with red eyes. 156. People hunt skunks in the middle of the night. The odor of a skunk's discharge travels a long way and is very strong. Besides being pungent, it lasts a month, or a month and a half. Some folks believe that anyone hit by skunk odor shouldn't spit. 157. Otherwise, he will get prematurely grey. Some people believe this and don't spit. Instead, they swallow the odor. The skunk's fart smells bad, but its meat is delicious. Skunk in barbacóa is tasty, and may be compared to pork when well prepared. 158. In skinning a skunk, one must be careful not to burst the odor sac, because this will ruin the meat.

The skunk is notorious for drinking aguamiel. It drinks up people's aguamiel from the magueys. Traps are put out to catch them. 159. But it's difficult to un-snare them because of their farts which smell so bad. Skunks feed on beetle larvae and chiniquiles. When baby skunks are born, no one goes near them to see them because it is dangerous.

160. The jumping skunk is all black. It is given the name "jumping skunk" because it goes bouncing along. The jumping skunk is smaller than the other kind, but both are eaten. It nurses its young the way rabbits do. 161. If a dog and a skunk fight the skunk wins. The skunk farts in the dog's eyes, and leaves it blind, and so, the dog can not attack.

Sometimes skunks come around to houses and do bad things. 162. They suck eggs, and wipe them all out, spoiling all the eggs in the henhouse. 163. Since a skunk's snout is pointed, it just makes a hole in the egg and sucks it out. In a short time it can finish off a dozen. If there are chicks, it eats them, too. The skunk is a very harmful animal. Small bags are made from its skin. The bags look nicer if they are from the multicolored variety, because one part is white and the other is black. 164. The skunk doesn't have a cry. Only its fart makes a noise.

The squirrel. The squirrel is a really obstinate animal, notorious in the milpas. 165. It is really abundant. It prefers to make its burrow at the edge of the milpas. It is about the same size as a rabbit. It is completely grey, and has a long tail. It cleans off the spines on prickly pears with its tail. 166. It feeds on various cactus fruits, such as compite and pintaderas.[13] It cleans all these with its tail. It simply turns its back, puts its tail on the prickly pear, and in just a moment it starts to eat. These are what it uses for water.

Its way of eating is like a pig's. 167. It tests the corn stalks to see if they are strong enough to climb. If not, then it cuts down the stem to eat the tassles and the young corn ears which are its favorite. If no one pays any attention they will finish off an entire milpa. They eat some and take away the rest for their dens. It's like they were human; they choose what is good and ignore whatever doesn't suit them. 168. During planting time squirrels are most abundant. They are born four at a time, once a year. People say that when a lot of them are born it will be a bad year.

When squirrels sense that someone is going by they just stick their heads out of their burrows. 169. When the person goes away, then they come out to eat. Some squirrels will just look right at someone going by and mock them, waving their tails at them. 170. Sometimes they go up a garambullo and whistle. When they are near their den, they clasp their hands together, whistle, and look at the sky. They have a lot of thoughts, as if they were people. When they see a person coming to the milpa they jump down from the cactus in one jump, even if it hurts them. 171. On the ground they go running along, moving away from people, through the furrows of the milpa. They know they aren't going to be caught, and they run.

If you set a trap for them, it must be buried very well, because if it isn't, even though the trap is there for three or four days, the animal won't come out. 172. It just sticks its head out from its den. It doesn't die of hunger because it always has something put away to eat, enough for the whole winter. It stores up garambullo fruit, mesquite fruit, and corn, so that when all the food is gone from the monte, it has enough to maintain itself. 173. When the plants are in season, the squirrel devotes itself to carrying and storing food. We say "carrying" because the squirrel has little bags in its jaws where it deposits what it is gathering. When the bags are full, it heads for its den and then goes back for more. The prickly pear of the nopalillo and the other prickly pears I mentioned earlier are its source of liquid. The nopalillo is covered with spines, but the squirrel cleans them with its tail.[14]

174. There is an old belief which says that the squirrel was once a human being who committed a sin, and because of that it now carries the curse of being a squirrel. Others say that the squirrel was a priest who deceived God, and so God turned him into a squirrel. 175. This is what the people believe because the squirrel sits with his hands clasped and looks at the sky. It is believed that he is asking God to forgive him so he won't be condemned to be a squirrel any more. When the sun comes out, around 7 or 8 in the morning, the squirrel comes out of his den, faces east, clasps his hands, and whistles, looking at the sky. His hands are clasped as if he were a priest, celebrating mass in the church.

People also believe that if a squirrel crosses their path then something bad will happen. 177. Everyone who crosses paths with a squirrel is afraid. It is a time when one thinks about God, so that the Devil, who is the squirrel's companion, will go away. There are still many people today who believe that the squirrel is a symbol of bad luck.

Squirrel meat is eaten in barbacóa, but it is also eaten fried because it is fatty, like pork. 178. The animal is passed through flames to burn off the hair. The skin is not removed. The skin is removed later, and then it is fried separately. It produces chicharrón, like the cracklings from a pig. The meat is delicious. The hair is hard and dry. 179. It is almost like hog hair. Everyone says that the squirrel doesn't cry out, but rather that it whistles. But it is impossible to write here the sound of its whistle. This is how squirrels live.

180. Some people dig for squirrels during Holy Week. But if the squirrel hears the noise, it digs further into its burrow to escape. If the person hunting isn't observant, before he knows it the animal has escaped from the other end of the burrow. As I said earlier, they are really smart. To avoid danger, they make two or three holes to escape from. So, in case someone tries to dig them out, they have exits to get away. 181. The big ones and the little ones alike escape. Few people will risk catching them by hand because they bite and their teeth are very pointy; the uppers as well as the lowers can pierce the flesh. Rattlesnakes don't try to eat squirrels because the squirrels would win. The squirrel has big claws and, together with its teeth, it digs its hole where it is accustomed to live. Sometimes, it sleeps on garambullo branches. It is also an avid drinker of aguamiel.

182. The weasel. The weasel is the fastest animal in the valley. In the twinkling of an eye it disappears, and one doesn't know where it has gone. It is dark red, more slender than the squirrel, and shorter of body. It is not often seen, and not much is known about what it feeds on. 183. I reckon that it eats other, smaller animals, because I know it to be another of the notorious eaters of hen eggs. If it comes on a nest with chicks in it, then it eats them, too. Because of this I can state that it is a carnivore. As I said, it is rarely seen, and it is not known how many babies it has at a time. Neither is it known how many times a year it gives birth. 184. Very little is known about this animal.

I believe it is eaten, but I don't know how it is prepared. On market days, people carry the pelts for sale. I saw a weasel once out in the open country. 185. I tried to catch it, but I didn't know where it went. I guess it must have gone in some hole. It is not troublesome in the milpas, nor for magueys that are giving aguamiel. If it happens to drink, one couldn't tell because it doesn't drink much. 186. That is to say, it doesn't have a large stomach. It is not known if it cries out. Its size is that of a recently born cat. I think it nurses its babies. The pelts I have seen have little teats on them, and they are on the stomach. The footprints from

His hands are clasped as if he were a priest
Fauna 176

its tiny feet are like a cat's. This is one animal whose way of life is not yet well known because it doesn't allow itself to be seen much.

187. The mouse.[15] The mouse lives in the fields and in houses. Those that live in the open country are the most harmful to the milpas. At the start of the planting season they dig out the seeds. They carry corn as well as bean seeds home to their dens. 188. Once they get some seed they go back for more. The field mouse can not be trapped because it doesn't weigh anything and thus doesn't break the seal and fall into the traps. Of course, it can't carry much, either, but it is still harmful. The color of these mice is grey. 189. They dig holes to live in. They take grass and viznaga fuzz[16] to their holes so they won't be cold. This is how they sleep warmly.

No one eats this class of mouse. Only cats eat them when they find them. They are born three or four at a time. When they are born, their eyes are not open. After about a month, the little animals open their eyes. 190. Since they can't see right after they are born, the mother feeds them on her milk. One knows right away where they are because they squeak. The mice that live in houses are fatter. 191. This is because they eat the food of the people. You can't leave anything out to eat because they are very mischievous and will be the first to try it out. They shred paper and clothing and they make their nests out of these things. They make their holes at the base of walls, and sometimes in the ceiling.

192. The owl. The owl is a nocturnal animal. It is said that the reason it is nocturnal is because it doesn't see well during the day. One can hear its cry only at night. Its cry is "Tukuru,u,u,u," and this is why it has this name in Ñähñu. It's about the size of a hen, but the owl's head is larger. 193. Also, its ears are bigger. Its eyes are like a cat's, round and yellowish.[17] It can see perfectly at night. This must be why it is nocturnal. Its beak is curved down toward its lower jaw. This is probably for hunting mice, which are a part of its diet. It also eats bats when it finds them. For this reason we consider the owl a carnivore. It is spotted, with black, grey, and yellow patches. These are called brown owls. People say that the owl was once a cat, but it got old, sprouted wings, and flew. Its face is like a cat's. It has two feet, like those of a hen. 194. Its talons are more curved. It generally lives in cliffs, where it makes its nest. The babies are born in the nest.

I remember once, I found some of them. There were two baby owls and that's how I know that when they come out of their shell they look a lot like chicks. The ones I found were on the ground between two junquillos. The nest was between the plants. 195. The little owls were yellow. The mother got furious with me for disturbing her young, and she chased me around, trying to attack me. I visited them every day. Some people lied to me and told me that the mother would take my eyes out. Because of this I never went back to see them.

The mother owl feeds her chicks with insects and pieces of meat. 196. Surely this must be mouse meat. This is the benefit to humans offered by owls. They kill mice. If they didn't, there would be too many mice and all the things planted in the milpas would be lost. Owls cause no harm, neither to the home nor to the milpa. 197. It has young once a year, during June and July. There aren't many of them. They mostly emerge from their nests around the beginning of the cold season.

198. If an owl calls out during the late afternoon or early evening, people say it announces cold the next day. People are afraid when they hear an owl calling close to a house, because it announces bad tidings. Whenever it comes around it goes up into the tallest trees, such as the mesquites or pepper trees. Sometimes it screeches and sometimes it hiccoughs. Other times it calls out the names of people. Whoever is mentioned is the one on whom ill tidings will fall the next day, or soon thereafter. 200. Everyone is scared, especially those who heard the owl the night before. People tell each other about it, and everyone prays to God so that nothing will happen. The ills heralded by owls are such things as fights, murders, illnesses, and other bad tidings. The owl foretells people's deaths. 201. If someone is sick and the owl calls out, then the person will not recover. We have seen many bad things happen when an owl talks or hiccoughs. 202. When someone hears this animal, they burn plants that have been blessed in the church to make the evil go away. It is believed that the owl is the messenger of the Devil, that is, the Devil's hen here on earth. When an owl is heard calling, people shoot at it.

203. I remember a man named Eulogio who lived in Orizabita. He said he had heard an owl speak the night before, and on the third day he was killed. Just like this thing, other bad things have happened. Whenever a nesting owl is found it is not spared; the person who finds it, kills it.

Owls fly. 204. None of their parts are useful for medicine. Their eggs are like a hen's, and mottled like a turkey's.

The wood owl. One doesn't see these creatures very often because they live in the barrancas and on the cliffs. 205. They are nocturnal and are seldom seen during the day. I've seen one once, and it looked like a small screech owl. It is believed that the barn owl also has evil power. The truth about this is not precisely known. In reproducing it hatches about two birds at a time. It lays two or three eggs, which take a month to hatch. Its eggs are like a pigeon's in size, or like those of a quail.[18] 206. They are spotted, black and white, like the eggs of curve billed thrashers.[19]

The wood owl feeds on mice. At night it can see where mice are. It is not harmful to milpas. On the contrary, it is beneficial because it drives away mice.

It uses its hook-like beak to tear apart flesh. Its beak is hooked like a sickle. 207. It builds its nest up in the cliffs. It collects little twigs, dog hair, and hair from mausoleums. It goes into coffins and pulls out the hair of the dead. It is said that this bird eats the flesh of the dead.

208. Tazegu, or lesser nighthawk.[20] This creature looks like a bat. It is black and about the same size as a bird. It starts flying around at about seven in the evening, and sings "tazegu, tazegu"—the same sound as its name in Ñähñu. 209. It ascends and descends as it goes along the road. No one knows what it is looking for. Perhaps it is searching for food; perhaps it is just following the road. When it encounters a person, it follows him, passing very close.

210. Its diet is based on nocturnal insects, like centipedes, maguey grubs, and crickets. It likes most to live in open country because no one bothers it there. If one comes on a nighthawk on the road, and shines light in its eyes, they glow like two pieces of gold. It is not known where they nest, nor how many offspring they have, nor how many times a year they reproduce. 211. No witchcraft is known to be attached to this animal. It sings when it's cold. Maybe it doesn't like the cold. There are many of them, and in the evening they criss-cross the sky in all directions. I think they must reproduce by eggs, only it's not known how long they incubate. They all live in the high cliffs. They like to live there in the dark, because they shun the light of day. Their plumage is black, and this is why they're confused with the night. Their name is not known in Spanish, and the name given here is the onomatopoeia in Ñähñu of their song.

213. The frog.[21] The frogs are not large, and there is no way for them to develop because there is not sufficient water. They come out only when there is water, after three or four days of hard rain. 214. All winter they bury themselves in places where there is some moisture. The frog has the characteristic of inflating its abdomen whenever it sees a person coming close by. It is said that at this moment it is sucking the person's blood. 215. Also, if it farts on a person's hand or foot, this is dangerous. According to what is said, the part which was farted on will swell up.

When there are lasting pools of water, I've seen that they lay their eggs. These look like quintonil seeds. After a while they become tadpoles, and this is how other frogs grow. 216. Frogs are not harmful to planted fields. They feed on small gnats, worms, and flies which they catch by sticking out their tongue. As soon as the insect sticks to it, they draw back their tongue. During the rains, they all croak, possibly from joy. Their back is spotted, and easily mistaken for the color of the earth; this must be their defense mechanism. They can't be seen by other animals, and if they don't move, then people can't see them either. Frogs don't have tails.

It is said that this bird eats the flesh of the dead

Fauna 207

217. I have not seen what their excrement is like, possibly because it dissolves in the water. Their hind legs are long. Between each toe they have a thin membrane with which they paddle water. They have goggle eyes. During the winter, since they have no way to come out to feed, I've found their stomach filled with earth. 218. Thus, I know that during this period frogs feed on dirt. When it rains, they return to the surface in search of insects on which to feed.

219. The bat.[22] This creature is the size of a mouse. It is grey and its fur is exactly like that of a mouse. The difference between bats and mice is that bats have wings, but the wings are not feathered. They are membranes of skin and with these the bat can lift off into flight. 220. The wings are one piece. They begin on the right and proceed back to the tail. The tail is attached to the membrane, which serves as the wing, and which ends on the left side of the animal. Its feet as well as its hands are attached to the wing. 221. Its face has more hair than a mouse's. It has a pair of fangs that it uses to bite with. Its ears are larger than a mouse's, and it has whiskers like a mouse.

The bat's name, "tsaxmagu," is composed of four Ñähñu words. 222. The first word is "tsa," which means "to bite"; the second is "xui," meaning "night"; the third is "ma," meaning "to go"; and the fourth is "gu," or "ear." Put together it means "it goes about at night biting ears." This is, in fact, what it does. It goes around at night biting the ears of animals. The blood it takes from the ears of the sleeping animals is its food. It spies on animals at night when they are asleep and then bites their ears. 223. It likes to bite the ears of burros, horses, and sometimes goats and sheep, especially the ones that live in the monte.

Bats live in large caves because they like to live in darkness. They hang by their feet when they sleep, with their head pointed down. Their excrement is pure blood. The caves in which they live are really foul smelling. Wherever there is an abundance of guano, though, it is removed and used as fertilizer. 224. It is said that it is better than animal manure. The people of the valley don't know how to use it, because they fertilize their fields with animal manure.

Bats give birth like mice, and bear their young in small holes. When the little ones learn to fly, they hang upside down, too. There is a little story which tells how the bat was once a mouse. But, with the passage of time, it got very old, and because of this it grew wings. 225. This is what is said because of its resemblance to the mouse. The bat doesn't do any witching.

Occasionally, bats go into houses in search of darkness, but only when the dawn takes them by surprise. Their excrement is used in the smoking procedure done on children against evil eye. 226. This is only used when there is some. When there isn't any, of course it is not burned because it is very difficult to find. The people who live in the mountains know where bats live.

227. Bats nurse their young as if they were mice. I've never seen another animal which is a mammal and also flies. 228. All the mammals I know go about on the surface of the earth. No one could fail to say that the bat is an animal of the Devil.

Spiders. There are different types of spiders all over the entire valley. Some are large, others are tiny. There are black spiders, red spiders, and small spiders. There is a little jumping spider that bites.[23] 229. It only does this when provoked, however; when it is left alone it doesn't bite, but is really afraid. It has the name "jumping spider" in Ñähñu because it runs and jumps. It lives in maguey trunks, under rocks, and everywhere.

When someone is bitten by this spider they put on human excrement to cut the venom and ease the pain. 230. It must be recent excrement. This custom is from the time when there were no trucks to take people to the doctor when they were bitten by spiders. This is no longer the case; there are now roads and trucks, and so a sick person can be brought in to the city to be attended by a doctor. Of course, this is for those who have money. Those who don't have any follow traditional medicine. This type of spider dies a few minutes after it bites. We will look at the spiders one by one.

231. The scorpion.[24] These creatures are not large; they are small. The largest is the female, while the male is smaller in size. Their color is a greyish yellow. 232. It appears that they feed on dirt. Those that I have seen have earth in their stomachs. They don't have intestines, just a part of their body where they deposit food. They hide under rocks and garbage. They live everywhere, including houses. They are abundant during the hot season, and this is when they multiply. 233. They bear six or seven offspring. I've seen them carrying their babies on their back, as if they were possums. Before being born, the children are in the womb. They are not little eggs, but fully formed little animals. This is why the female gets bigger when she's carrying babies. The only thing I haven't seen is how many times a year they give birth.

If one isn't careful about these creatures, they go up in one's clothes and when one least expects it, they bite. 234. They bite when one presses a bit on their body; otherwise they don't do anything. Their stinger is in their tail. When they bite they deposit a kind of fluid and this is what causes pain. The sting is sharp, and sometimes is accompanied by pain. The bite swells up for about eight days, and when the swelling goes down there is a lot of itching. If one scratches it the bite fills with pus. People don't die from the bite, because the venom is not dangerous. People who are bitten by scorpions don't consult doctors. They cure it themselves by putting on garlic and onion.

When a scorpion fights with an ant, it cuts it in two. It cuts it in half with its pincers. The scorpion is not used in medicine. Nor does it do any harm, except when it bites. 236. There are many, all through the desert. It has two pincers which it uses to guide its way. The ends of the pincers are open, like tweezers. I think it also feeds on insects, and it catches them with its pincers. When it walks it supports itself on eight legs, four on each side of its body. Its belly is soft, but its tail is stiff, as are its pincers. 237. If you crush one you can hear it crack. In Ñähñu it is given the name "sticky tail" because when it bites, it is sticky.

The centipede.[25] The length of a centipede reaches a hand's breadth among the most fully grown. 238. There are two kinds, a white one and a grey one. The white one is the one which grows big. The grey one doesn't develop much. They have been given the name "hundred feet" because they have many feet, but there aren't a hundred. This is the name in Spanish, but its name in Ñähñu means "gropes through tortillas." This is probably because there are many feet, and they move fast when they go about, as if they were looking for something. The same thing happens when a person is hungry and they scratch around in the petaca,[26] looking for a tortilla, or something else to eat. The same goes for this animal I'm speaking about.

239. Once, I wanted to know if it was true that it had 100 legs. I counted the legs of an adult, and of an immature one. The adult centipede had 70 legs. The immature one had only 30 legs.[27] 240. Of course, in counting these, one doesn't include the antennae on the head. This is how I know that those which live in the desert don't have 100 legs. Sometimes one sees centipedes with grey backs. This is its food which is seen through its transparent skin.

241. When it bites it pushes down with all its feet, putting pressure with its whole body to sink in where it wants to bite. Afterwards, the person's skin swells up, showing the outline of the entire body of the animal, and there is a lot of itching. This bite, too, is cured by putting on garlic, and with this treatment it slowly calms down. When garlic is not used, then onion is put on. 242. The centipede uses its antennae to find its way, as it searches for food. If it perceives that something is good to eat it brings its mouth up to it. Otherwise, it leaves it alone. It usually comes out in the hot season. They are always about, but they are generally more abundant during hot periods, and then they go into houses as well. 243. Centipedes are much faster than scorpions. When chickens see centipedes they eat them. They also eat scorpions. They take off the stinger first so they won't be bitten. Then, they eat them whole.

244. In the mountains centipedes are used as a medicine. The smaller, grey one is the one used. In the mountains there are very dangerous poisonous snakes

It cuts it in half with its pincers

Fauna 235

that bite. 245. There is a snake called the "rattler." It is very dangerous. Once, a friend of mine and I went to the mountains to visit some acquaintances. The house where we wound up was also that of a friend, and he told us about this. Previously, I had seen a bottle which contained water. I picked it up to look at it, and the man noticed me doing this. 246. I asked him what he wanted with those little creatures he had put in the water. He told me "Don't open it, because it's not water. It's medicine, made of alcohol and centipedes. We keep them because sometimes we really need them."

I asked him what illness is cured by this, and he told me that it is used when a person is bitten by a rattler at work or on the road. 247. The bottle is opened, and placed near the nose of the victim so he can smell it, with all its pent-up odor, and with this he won't die and he can hold on until the doctor arrives. This kind of medicine is only to be smelled, and not given to drink. 248. Also, some of it is dabbed on the part which was bitten. This medicine can be kept a long time, for as long as one wants. This is what the man told us. When one of them travels they carry their bottle with them because it's very dangerous to walk about up there where it's all mountains. 250. Also, the paths are very narrow and there is no way to escape.

The rattler is most active in hot lands. All the land I'm talking about is hot land. Most people say snakes are boldest and most dangerous in hot lands. 250. What I have not been able to understand is what power centipede blood has that allows it to control rattler poison. The physicians can investigate this. What the man told me, though, was that the small centipede is the one with more medicinal power. 251. "This is because the large one doesn't have much potency," he said. Centipedes do live in the desert, but no one there knows they are medicinal. But then, there aren't that many very poisonous animals in the desert in the first place.

252. The harvester ant.[28] There are different size ants in an anthill. There are big ones, and others which can scarcely be seen. The harvester ant's head is larger than the rest of its body. The part which forms its stomach is thin. 253. I think its head grows big because it is always cutting leaves and branches off plants, and it spends a lot of energy doing this. Maybe because of this its head develops. 254. This class of cargo ant is red, a dark red. They have a distinctive characteristic in that they form a line and none of them deviate from it. They come and go, cutting leaves off plants. They don't get separated, but just go along in file, some of them crossing over others in the branches of the line. Great and small, they go along, cutting off the leaves and shoots of the plants. 255. They branch off in the trees, and go to their separate branches. Their principal food is leaves from trees and plants. Only rarely do they come out during

the day. But at night it is a veritable parade. Even though it's very dark, one can see where they go. You can hear them, because the leaves make a sound as they pull on them. 256. If no one bothers them, they will strip a tree in one night, leaving only the branches. They are completely herbivorous.

They, too, breed during the hot season. At first they are small larvae, and then, little by little, they take on the form of an ant. Inside the anthill there are a great many little holes where they lay their young. Cargo ants dig their holes very deep. From what I've seen, they can dig down about five meters. 257. To get rid of them you have to dig down all the way. Otherwise, they get away because they are down very deep. Someone who dug them out once told me that he found a snake at the bottom of the hole. He said this was the queen of all of them. He told me it was about half a meter long, with some parts red, others white, black, and yellow. This is how the man who found it described it to me. Also, one can tell where these ants live because their excrement is yellow.

Their anthill lasts a long time and there are some around from long ago. Some are still standing from when my father saw them as a boy. He is sixty-nine years old. One anthill is still there, and the ants are still living in it.

It is not good to plant fruit trees near anthills, because the ants won't let the trees grow. They kill them by cutting the young shoots. 258. Peach trees are their favorite fruit trees. Their other foods are capulín, mesquite (when they are young), and miel de jicote; these are the green things it harvests to store in the anthill. When winter comes, the plants are eaten. If they threaten fruit trees, one must give them something else to eat to get them to leave the trees alone. If someone tries to get them out in anger, then he will get sick.

259. Ants are all over the desert. They eat young frijol shoots when they want to. They also eat corn plants if someone gets them angry. They have very powerful pincers on their heads. They cut through leaves and shoots quickly. The people hate them but, knowing that ants have witchcraft, they don't dare do anything to get rid of them. 260. Harvester ants use the same fresh leaves for water as they do for food. Their legs are longer and thinner than those of the little black ant. When harvester ants are pestered they move more slowly than other ants. The little red ant is very fast. The harvester ant doesn't run. This is possibly because its legs are accustomed to holding the weight of what it carries. 261. One cargo ant can carry half a peach leaf. The little red ant only carries a little something once in a while. This is why I think the harvester ant has slug-gish feet, because it is always loaded down.

The alligator lizard.[29] The alligator lizards around here aren't very big. They reach a length of only 25 centimeters. 262. Their body is thicker than a whiptail's and a bit less wide than a spiny lizard's. The back is grey and it has four feet. Its front legs are fatter than its hind legs. It has fingers and palms on rear and forelegs. It is very sluggish. Sometimes it is confused with the larger whiptails. To tell whether it is an alligator lizard you have to look at its head; this is what distinguishes it. It looks like the big toe of a person. 263. Also, the tail is fatter, and not pointed at the end. It is blue along the sides, and there is a stripe down each side. It is believed that when it bites, it opens one of its sides to take hold of the flesh. Also, they say that it does not let go when it bites; it has to be cut off. I've never seen this occur. 264. It has sharp teeth like a mouse's; it has fangs. These lizards which inhabit the monte are not easily scared. They jump up and bite you. Their flesh is brittle. When you throw stones at them, they split open easily.

They live under junquillos, huapillas, and granjenos.[30] They like to live in thick grass. It is hard to see them for the green. 265. They blend into the grass because their backs are greenish blue. Their belly is white. They eat small insects, larvae, spiders and dung beetles which are under the junquillos. They bear only once a year during July and August. This is when they are below ground. In September and October they start to come out and they stay above ground all winter. When it starts to get hot again, they bury themselves once more. They don't offer a single benefit to people. There aren't many because as soon as people see them, they kill them because it is believed that they are very dangerous.

266. The solpugid.[31] Some are big and some are small, but all are very quick. They are yellow and white in color. They have soft, downy hair on their body, and a pair of antennae on their head which they use to feel with as they find their way about. Their bite is like a spider's; it hurts a lot. They bite with their mouth where they have two small stingers which they sink into the flesh. 267. There are many of them during the hot season. They go into people's houses. They live everywhere, in the rocks, in garbage, and in maguey trunks. Their sting doesn't kill people. Occasionally it causes fever. This creature does not weave a web; it lives beneath the rocks. No one knows how many times a year it bears young. Apparently it, too, feeds on earth; when it is killed, it has dirt in its stomach.

268. Daddy-long-legs. The daddy-long-legs is the spider with the longest legs. Its body is round and totally black. 269. It makes a web, and the mosquitoes and flies which stick to it are its food. The spiders suck out whatever is in the insects' bodies. Some of them have very long legs. Their body is about the size of a pea. In spite of having long legs, they don't run. They don't lay their eggs in their webs but put them in small holes between stones. 270. They make a kind of ball in which they deposit their eggs. The little ball contains many tiny

eggs and if a bird finds it, it eats it. The bird that feeds on daddy-long-legs is the cactus wren.

There is a story about the daddy-long-legs which I will tell here.

271. A person is speaking with the spider and other animals. P = person, D = daddy-long-legs.

P: "Where are you going, daddy-long-legs?"

D: "I'm going over there."

P: "What are you going to do over there?"

D: "I'm going to fetch a white flower."

272. P: "What will you do with the white flower?"

D: "It is for putting on the feet of a girl."

P: "What happened to the girl?"

D: "She was bitten by a white snake."

P: "Where is the white snake?"

D: "We killed it."

P: "Where is it thrown away?"

273. D: "We tossed it in the fire; it burned up."

P: "Where are the ashes?"

D: "The old church was patched up with them."

P: "Where is the old church?"

D: "It collapsed."

P: "Where is it, and who knocked it down?"

D: "The crippled sheep came by, gave it a kick, and it collapsed."

274. P: "Where is the crippled sheep?"

D: "The coyote ate it."

P: "Where is the coyote?"

D: "The vulture ate it."

P: "Where is the vulture?"

D: "He flew away."

275. The cricket.[32] The cricket is small and has two antennae on its head. Its back is black, and its belly is black and yellow. It has two wings and this is what helps it jump. It also has two hind legs with strong muscles which give it pushing strength for jumping. 276. Just before and during the hot season it comes out and sings in the open country. As soon as it's dark it begins to sing. People think that when crickets sing the insects "see the rain." There are none during the winter. They take refuge under rocks and trunks where the temperature is favorable and they are protected from the cold. I think that they multiply during the hot season.

277. They don't cause any harm. Children like to play with them when they find them because they like to see them jump. Children get whooping cough during the hot season. In preparing the tea which they are given, one looks for the legs of the cricket. The two hind legs are removed, and these are boiled along with other medicines, because it is thought that these are very good for reducing the force of the cough. I wouldn't know what medicine is in its blood; but this is its contribution in medicine.

279. The wood owl, or "barks-like-a-dog." This animal has the same characteristics as the screech owl, except that the wood owl is smaller. It has an oval face; its back is black, mixed with grey. Its stomach is yellow, with a little black. It is a carnivore, and it feeds on mice which it catches at night. Some people have seen these animals go to cemeteries and eat the flesh of the dead if they are not securely sealed. 280. Some people are afraid of them, because they think this animal is from the Devil. Others have seen them pull out the hair of the dead to make their nests. This is attested to by those who have seen their nests in the burial vaults. When they don't make their nests in the mausoleums, they make them in dark caves in cliffs.

281. It is rare to hear them call, but if they fly over a pueblo and call out, then this announces bad luck. In a short time there will be a fight of some sort, a murder, or a sickness. Its call causes terror. When people hear it, they give praise to God and ask for help. Its call is like the yip of a puppy. This animal calls out at the approach of winter.

282. Since wood owls can not be seen at night no one knows how many of them are born at a time. Some folks who are afraid of their call light a candle to God to scare them off. No one knows how many times a year they bear young. In my opinion they are born twice a year, the same as the huitlacoche.

283. The cat. The cats in these parts are not like those that live in cities. The difference is that the ones in the country are smaller with shorter hair. There are various colors: greys, blacks, and yellows as well as tricolored ones that are yellow, black and white. 284. People keep them because they help frighten away the mice; and when cats catch mice, they eat them. In houses where there are cats, there aren't so many mice. Mice are dangerous, because they carry disease. For this reason, it is important to exterminate them. Mice multiply the most whenever there is a harvest in the milpas. When there is no more to eat in the milpas, they go into houses. 285. This is why they multiply so much.

There are big mice and there are others no bigger than a walnut.[33] Both small and large are harmful. They gnaw at everything they find in the house. When they come to a closet they gnaw until they can get in. Then they shred clothes, and papers, like documents. Sometimes they make their nests of these. If some

Where there are cats, there aren't so many mice
Fauna 284

food is left out in the kitchen, they either eat it or urinate on it. Then someone comes along and, not knowing better, eats the food. This is how disease starts. 286. Even if people do notice, they don't throw out the food because they don't think it is contaminated very much.

Sometimes the only way to kill mice is to put out traps called "barricades." These are similar to ordinary traps, but they are called "barricades" because they are made of three little pieces of wood of different sizes. A kind of hook is cut into each one so they will latch onto one another. On one of these, on the edge which leads inside, a piece of bread or tortilla is tied, or whatever the mouse eats. 287. The other piece of wood stands holding back a rock. When the mouse comes to eat, he has to pull on the food because it is tied on, and since he is already inside, he can't get out because he is trapped. The rock must be flat. This is the knowledge that the ancient people have left us. Until recently, squirrels were caught this way, too.

288. People like to have cats as pets and also they are needed to hunt and kill mice. During May, when cats are born, there are three or four at a time. When the babies are born their eyes aren't open. They open about 15 days later. The mother cat nurses the babies for about three or four months. Cats have a very notable characteristic. When they need to defecate, they dig a small hole and squat. When they are through, they scratch the earth and cover it up. It is like a small lesson in cleanliness for the people.

289. The birds. Among the inhabitants of the desert are birds of various classes, sizes, and colors. They feed in different ways and also have different songs. During the hot season they come back to the Mezquital Valley to sing to the desert. Every year it's as if they came to teach the people to sing, and to teach people to live a better life. They even show us this by putting all they have into the building of their nests. We will look at them, by name, one by one.

290. The varied bunting.[34] sparrow. Among the birds most esteemed in the valley is this one, which has a beautiful song. When winter is over the hot season starts, beginning with spring and the song of the bunting. It bears its young in April and May. In May the trees fill out, and the buntings build their nests there. It's a small bird but its color and its song are beautiful. The male has a red chest with a small beak. 291. Its back is grey. The female is grey and a bit smaller. They mostly go about together, and rarely separate. They feed on garambullos, figs, and insects, along with corn seeds wherever they find them. They drink water like a chicken.

They help each other build nests. One brings in the material while the other weaves. 292. The male carries, and the female fits the pieces together. First she puts in the heavy sticks, and then a layer of grass where she will lay her eggs.

They use viznaga fuzz, or very fine grass. 293. After building the nest, the female lays her eggs over a period of a week. For 24 days they tend the nest and then the little sparrows are born. The male brings the female food and puts it in her beak so that she won't get up during the incubation period. Once the chicks are born, they both help feed them. 294. They give them water, garambullo, and little insects.

At about 15 days the little birds begin to fly.[35] Their parents go with them to make sure they don't stray too far, and to keep an eye on them. When the young can fly well, the parents abandon the little birds. Usually 3 or 4 are born at a time, no more. Buntings help laborers in the field, because the birds' song gladdens the heart. 295. They relieve the tiredness of the traveler because their song is wonderful. They follow the shepherd, as he tends his flock in the fields, even though on occasion he takes their babies and later sells them. Some people like to have buntings in their houses, keeping them in bird cages. They feed them on garambullo, prickly pear, and ground nixtamal. 296. People mimic their song, saying: "If we don't see one another today, we'll see each other in eight days."[36] Field laborers made up this saying.

The lark.[37] This bird has a ring of black on its chest. It is spotted with black, grey, and sometimes red. 297. It looks like it has its eyes painted on. It feeds on insects like spiders, gallinas ciegas, and tree grubs. It builds its nest on the branches of trees and on darning needle cacti, granjeno, and tunas de coyote. 298. This bird makes the largest nests. It makes a big pile of garbage. Then it brings together small, dried mesquite twigs, maguey roots, rags, grasses, and fuzz from barrel cacti. Even if it rains hard, the bird doesn't get wet. Neither do the little birds during breeding time. 299. It is easy to spot their nest because it is big. They sit on two or three spotted eggs which are black and white, like turkey eggs.

When the young are born they also feed them on small grubs. The sound of their song is like someone grinding a piece of iron. The male sings as much as the female does. The female is the most grey. Sometimes they cause harm in the milpas, scratching out the corn seeds, because they feed on them, too. 300. They live all over the valley. When winter comes, they don't migrate like other birds which seek warm lands and which return at the end of winter. The lark doesn't go anywhere else, possibly because it makes its nest the best of all the birds. A piece of its nest is used in the purifying ritual against evil eye. People believe that evil eye is warded off by animal things, so they pour the smoke from burnt nests and burnt animal excrement over children who are afflicted.

When a lark sees a snake, it seems to warn people. 301. This is how one knows that a snake is about. Sometimes casera snakes eat lark's eggs or even the

little birds. They go into the nest, force the adult bird out, and then they just sit
there. Field laborers like to touch larks' nests; they go to put their hands on it and
realize there's a snake in it, sometimes the chirrionera. These snakes really like
to eat small birds. The lark has a long beak.

302. The huitlacoche. This bird is totally grey. It is the largest bird in the
valley, and the one with the largest beak. It feeds on insects and prickly pears in
season. The insects it eats are spiders, scorpions, and mesquite grubs. It eats
white and yellow prickly pears. It prefers white tunas because they are sweeter.
303. When these are finished off, then it eats whatever is left over. It makes its
nest on the nopal cactus pads, on palmas and mesquites. But it likes the nopal
best because of the food it has close by. The huitlacoche builds a large nest, too,
but the lark's is larger. It makes its nest from mesquite thorns and grass. The
female lays three eggs. Some lay four. They are blue with dots of black.

304. They breed twice a year, first in February and March, and then again in
July and August. People catch the ones born at the beginning of the year to keep
in their homes, or to take to market to sell to the traders. The traders pay six
pesos each for them. No one takes birds from the second laying, because they'll
wind up with lots of bugs. 305. These bugs are fly larva. They are white and are
layed by the green fly. So these birds nauseate people and they don't want them
either in the house or to sell.

The huitlacoche's song is very pretty. It goes up into the highest part of the
garambullos and mesquites and sings there. If, while singing, it is facing east,
then it is said to be calling the cold east wind. If it is facing west, then it is calling
the west wind. 306. It is very rare to see it facing either north or south. What they
say about it must be true, because when it sings to the east there are winds on the
same day coming from the east. The same thing happens when it faces west—
that is, there are winds from that direction. The people who have noticed this
speak the truth.

During the prickly pear season people listen for the huitlacoche. 307. They
rush to cut off the tunas quickly before the wind gets to them, because it scatters
the fruit's thorns all over the place. If these thorns get in one's eyes, they are
dangerous. The huitlacoche announces what we may call the state of the
weather. If wind is coming it announces the direction, east or west. Its song has
a lot of joy, too. When there are no cenzontles,[38] then huitlacoches appear.
Their song brings joy to the Mezquital. 308. They adorn the sky that covers their
area. Even though it is a desert, it still has its joy. When shepherds find a
centzontle nest they take it to market to sell after the baby birds have gotten big.
If they don't go themselves to sell it, then they send someone with it. These nests
sell well; that is, they fetch about five or six pesos for each bird. 309. If there are

three or four birds then the money is enough to buy five cuartillos of corn, though selling off the little birds seems like cruelty. When they are killed, they are eaten, roasted in a fire.

310. The dove.[39] It is grey and has a little red on the chest. It is medium sized. Its beak is black and its feet are white. It is distinguished by its plumage which is smoother than that of other birds. It feeds on insects, ant stones, large ants, maize when available. It lays twice a year with two babies each time. It generally nests in the nopal groves, and among the mesquites. It makes its nest from dried mesquite twigs, and grass to keep itself warm. 311. It feeds its offspring on grubs, chicalote seeds,[40] herb seeds, amaranth seeds, garden sunflower seeds, wild sunflower seeds, and seeds of smooth pasture grass. It also feeds them large ants, and it brings them water that it puts in their beaks. It multiplies for the first time in March, and then again in May and June.

These birds are eaten, sometimes roasted, sometimes fried. The meat is sweet, and not smelly because they only feed on seeds. 312. This is a benefit that they give to someone who doesn't have money to buy meat. Doves don't cause any harm, either in the home or in the milpas. Neither do they eat the tunas. They are harmless birds. They only build nests when they are breeding, and when they are not mating they sleep in trees. 313. They seek out leafy vegetation so no one will see them. They flock together in small groups of two to six and they all sleep together. They sing beautifully, especially when the sun is hot.

When a dove walks it moves its head back and forth in rhythm with its steps. It doesn't hop when it goes about on the ground; it just moves along in a uniform manner, moving its feet one after the other. It is not used in medicine, nor is it known if it has witchcraft associated with it. It generally goes about in groups. Its eggs are spotted with white and black. 314. They don't sell when they are brought to market. This is probably because people don't appreciate their song. Its excrement is black and white and round. It is immediately recognizable as that of the dove, since the excrement of other birds is marble-like in form. Its footprints are well marked, and look like those of a chicken, one behind the other.

315. The cactus wren.[41] This is a bird of small size. Its entire back part is grey, and its belly is white, or, better said, it is ash-grey. It is very small and goes everywhere in search of spiders and flies. It feeds exclusively on insects, and doesn't eat plants. It hunts scorpions and centipedes. 316. It even goes into the roofs of thatched houses to eat insects it finds there. It likes to go into roofs made of palma, maguey, grass and herbage, because it knows there are insects there. It enters the roof in the hole left by the crossbeam made of maguey stalk.

Some people hang jars, pots, and bags on the roof eaves, either empty or with things in them. Others keep medicinal herbs. If the wren finds these things it steals some to make its nest. It uses garbage, rags, hair, chicken feathers, wool and snake skin in making its nest. By the time the person in the house notices anything, the eggs are laid, or the babies have even taken flight. 318. The only thing people don't like is that the birds bring in snake skin. This is not enjoyed at all. The birds lay two eggs which are blue with black spots. They are in the nest for three weeks, and at the end of that time the babies are born. They lay twice a year. I believe that they bring benefit to people by eating spiders, such as solpugids which go up into the roofs.

319. They are not harmful to people, nor are they mentioned in connection with any beliefs. They don't provide any benefits for medicine, either. A lot of people say their song is beautiful. There is a Ñähñu phrase regarding their song that goes: "Turn around little girl, turn around little girl." This can be interpreted in two ways, depending on how people think. 320. The first interpretation goes like this: "Turn around little girl" is said when a girl is passing by where a man is standing and, out of shame, doesn't turn to look at him. Then one says "turn around little girl." The second interpretation has been thought up by day laborers. They say that when you are in bed and a woman has turned her back, then you say "turn around little girl" so you will be front to front. 321. These are the stories invented by the people from the songs of birds. This is what they do when they work in the milpas; this is what they say to pass the time laughing. In this way they don't feel tired, and before they know it it's gotten late and everyone goes home. The next day they return to make up new jokes. Wherever they go they try to make light of their work. Sometimes, they make up jokes about birds, sometimes about their companions at work, and sometimes even about tree trunks. They say whatever is in their heads. When this bird sings, it raises its tail.

322. The hummingbird.[42] The hummingbird is the smallest bird in all the Mezquital. Its body is small but it has a rather long beak. The long beak must be part of nature's design because the bird feeds itself principally on the honey from flowers. It sucks on the flowers of órganos and gigantes,[43] on marigold flowers, squash flowers when there are any, and on other flowers that it finds. 323. There are three classes, according to color: dark green over the entire body, brown, and grey. Hummingbirds are very quick in flight. They draw from "their magueys" three times a day: at dawn, at midday, and in the late afternoon. People, too, scrape their magueys three times a day. There is a story which tells that the hummingbird is the tlachiquero[44] of the Devil.

324. The hummingbird works here on earth; it sucks the honey, and brings it to its master's house. The master has seven bulls' skins where he deposits his pulque. This is known because once a mortal person did the bad deed of stoning a hummingbird while it was sucking aguamiel. He killed it and pulled off its feathers. 325. But then the Devil saw that this man had mistreated his peon, and this made him very angry. So the Devil sent someone to fetch the man from the earth so he could ask him why he had struck his worker. When he arrived, the Christian saw the hummingbird he had killed on earth. 326. As the story goes, he stripped the bird of its feathers and left it naked. And this is just how he found the bird in the sky in the house of its master. As soon as the man got to heaven, they took him over to show him the hummingbird he had stoned. It was lying there in bed, complaining of the pain from injuries to its head. They had fixed it up, and bandaged its head and covered it well so it would get better. 327. But it was complaining a lot because of pains in its body. 328. So then the Devil said to the Christian: "Look what you've done to my tlachiquero. Tell me, what did it do to you that you beat it so?"

The Christian was so scared he didn't know what to say. So the Devil said: "Now we are going to do the same to you so you'll know the hurt you have caused my worker." And saying that, they stripped him and whipped him. All the Devil's helpers beat him, and the man fell, near death. 329. Then, the patrón ordered his helpers to leave the man alone. The man was left there; they had stripped him, as he had done to the hummingbird.

Afterwards, he came to and tried to remember how he had come to this place. He was thirsty, and so he asked for pulque because he thought he was in his own house. The Devil heard him ask for pulque and he ordered his servants to give it to him. 330. He said to them: "Give him pulque to drink, a measure from each of the skins." The servants helped him stand up, and brought him to drink pulque where the skins were hanging. The man drank the first jícara, and the second, and the third. But on the fourth he didn't want to drink any more, because he was full.

"You must drink," they told him. "You must drink, because if not we will beat you again." So he began to drink and get drunk, and he hadn't even finished half of it. They punched him and he turned to fall.

Then the Devil said to the man: "For now you will return to your house. I am going to pardon you for what you did to my servant. But the day you do it again, I'll kill you."

331. "Yes, yes," responded the Christian, already quite drunk. He was so drunk he couldn't get up. The Devil ordered his helpers to throw the man out on

the road. They did, and when the man woke up he was lying by the side of the road. Still drunk, he got up and went home. When he arrived, his wife asked him where he'd gone. The man told his wife he'd encountered some acquaintances; they had invited him to drink pulque, and he got drunk. 332. That was why his eyes were black and blue, he said, because he had fallen on the road. Later, slowly, he told his wife what had happened, and this is how it is known that the hummingbird is the tlachiquero of the Devil.

The hummingbird makes its nest on mesquite branches, and on the branches of other trees. Its nest is small, but perfectly woven. 333. It lays two or three eggs, and no more. When a person tries to look at it, it comes out mad, trying to peck at the eyes. It lays twice a year. The first time is in March, and the second is in July. Its nest is also used in medicine, in the cleansing procedure for evil eye. A piece is taken off and put together with the rest of the things used for fuming a child. 334. This is why, whenever a hummingbird nest is found, it is taken and kept. This way, it will be available when required.

There is a belief regarding its brain. It is said that when someone kills a hummingbird, they should cut open the head. Then they should remove the brain, dry it, and grind it up so it can be carried around. Then, if a man wants to talk to a young woman, all he has to do is throw a little of the brain on her. 335. Want to or not, before she knows it the girl has said "yes" to the man. Some say you have to actually throw the brain powder on the girl; others say you only have to carry it around with you. The truth is not precisely known.

The hummingbird doesn't sing well. It just makes a sound like the grinding of teeth. It doesn't do people any harm in their gardens. It doesn't drink aguamiel.

336. The cenzontle. This is a long, thin bird, grey on the back with white in its wings. It has a long tail which it fans out beautifully when it sings. Its song is pretty because it mixes up its own song with that of other birds. In other words, it mimics other birds. It imitates buntings, huitlacoches, calandrias,[45] larks, cardinals, and even people if it hears them whistle. It goes to the top of the tallest mesquites to sing, and its voice is very strong. Because of its pretty voice, people hunt it to catch it. 337. During April and May, there are bird hunters about. They carry around cages, in which they place a tame bird. The bird is locked up in half of the cage, while the other half is left open. In the open part, they put some food, such as pirul seeds, or masa with garambullo. 338. When a bird enters the cage, the man pulls a string from a place where he has hidden himself. The string is fastened to the cage. The hunter catches other birds, like buntings and calandrias in the same way.

339. The cenzontle feeds on pirul seeds, especially the red ones which are well ripened. It also eats garambullos and insects. It lays twice a year, and each

And saying that, they stripped him and whipped him

Fauna 328

time it lays two or three eggs. They are mottled, with white and black spots. 340. Its nest has the same characteristics as that of the huitlacoche. If one does not look carefully cenzontle and huitlacoche nests are not distinguishable. The centzontle generally builds its nest in garambullos and mesquites.

341. As I said before, this bird is in great demand in the market for its song. People pay 20 pesos for one of these birds. The merchants shout in the market to attract attention. Some people pay 15 pesos. But, generally, whoever pays more gets the bird. I've heard that they are sold in big cities for up to 40 and 50 pesos each. 342. If shepherds come upon a nest they keep it from harm, so that when the baby birds get all their feathers they can take them to market. If there are two or three birds, the shepherds bring enough corn for a week. This may be thought of as a kind of benefit which the cenzontle provides for shepherds. Also, it offers the most beautiful song to be heard in the desert. When the heat gets up to a certain point, one sits in the refreshing shade, listening to the cenzontle playing its beautiful music. The ravines echo and repeat the sound. In the spring, there are mesquite, garambullo, pitahaya, and tuna de coyote flowers. 343. The cenzontle sings at the marvelous color and fragrance of these flowers. It sings at the darkness when the moon is full.

344. The white winged dove. The dove[46] has a really large body, not like the huitlacoche which just has a lot of plumage. The dove has a lot of meat and is plump. It has a lot of fat run off when roasted or fried. Hunters catch doves when they see them, because they enjoy their meat. Their feet are black and their bodies are grey. Their wings have some white, as does their tail. 345. When they are flying, one can recognize what kind of birds they are by looking at the wings. They feed on seeds. They eat chicalote seeds, piedritas,[47] grass seeds, amaranth seeds, and sunflower seeds. At the end of summer and the beginning of autumn, when the plants dry up and scatter their seeds, there are lots of doves. They generally go about in squads of around 10 or a dozen. 346. When they take flight, their wings whistle in the air.

They normally build their nest on mesquite branches. They look for thick stands of mesquites, especially those with a lot of moss hanging from them so that no one will see them. Though it is a large bird, it doesn't build a large nest. 347. It builds a small nest, big enough to lay its eggs. They use dried mesquite twigs, dried maguey roots, and sometimes huapilla root. The only thing one sees in the nest is their eggs. If someone frightens them and makes them take flight, they step on the eggs, which fall and break. They lay two eggs a year. They are large eggs, about the size of a quail's. Because they, too, sing prettily, people hunt them. 348. They are taken to merchants who pay 10 pesos each. Some people prefer to raise doves than to sell them. They like to raise them because they are strong, unlike cenzontles which are more delicate. People give doves nixtamal made from cracked corn. The corn has to be washed really well so the birds don't get constipated. 349. It causes constipation because it is difficult for the seed to go through their intestines. The outer husk of corn kernels is sticky. Every day, the first thing the mistress of the house does when she gets up is begin washing her nixtamal.

Wild doves are afraid of people and like to live far away. Their song is "domitsu, domitsu, domitsu," which means "what are you doing? what are you doing?" in Ñähñu. They have been given their name for their song. It is said that after taking part in mass in heaven, the white-winged dove sang with joy as the glory began.

350. The cocolera.[48] The cocolera is the same size as the dove. Its color is greyish red over all its body. It feeds on the same things as the dove. Whatever the dove eats, so does the cocolera. Both the dove and the cocolera drink water. When it doesn't rain, they go to springs where there is water. But when it rains, they drink the water that collects in the little holes dug out by the rain. They also drink water that collects in the maguey leaves. The meat of the cocolera is also eaten, just like that of the dove. All its plumage is smooth. It lays once a year, and has two white eggs like those of the dove. 351. Its nest is small. It is made of small twigs, which the bird weaves together with mesquite thorns and grass. Cocoleras take turns sitting on the eggs (first the female, then the male) because they go far in search of water and don't want to leave the nest alone. They have white feet.

There is a story which tells how this bird washed its feet in the river. When the Jews killed Christ, they put him in a sepulcher. 352. On the third day he rose to give advice to the apostles and then he went to heaven. In heaven, out of joy for the arrival of God's son, they prepared a beautiful welcome. They called in all the animals of the earth to consult with them. God was not dead in heaven; he only appeared dead on earth. 353. In heaven, they called in all the animals of the earth and had a grand reunion. They told all of them to get there right away. Some of the animals got the announcement the evening before the reunion; some went right away, and others got up early the next day and went. 354. The cocolera thought: "Who will I go with? I haven't got anyone to accompany me." It thought about this and soon ran into the dove. They agreed that as soon as dawn broke they would go.

And so it was that early the next day the dove, who was escorting the cocolera, arrived at the cocolera's house.

355. "Let's go" said the dove "because it will be evening and we'll miss the mass."

"Well, let's go then" said the cocolera. "And don't worry; we'll get there on time."

So the two began the journey. It was just dawn when they set out to go to the mass. 356. They saw that they were getting close and that it was still early. The cocolera said to the dove: "It appears to be early. How about waiting for me? I'm just going to wash my feet a little. I forgot to wash them at home."

The dove saw that the river was close by, so he waited. The dove didn't want to wash his feet because he saw it was getting late. The cocolera went in the water quickly. He washed his feet because they were dirty. The dove saw it was getting late and that the cocolera wasn't returning. So he called to him: "Have you finished? Let's go, it's late."

"Coming, right now!" said the cocolera. "If you want, just go on ahead, and I'll catch up with you there."

"All right," responded the dove. "All right, but don't get there late or you'll miss everything. It's important that we all be there." 358. That's what the dove told the cocolera.

"I'm finishing right now! I won't be long. Go on ahead, and I'll catch up with you there."

So the dove went ahead. When he arrived, all the animals were already in the church. If he hadn't hurried he wouldn't have made it at all. 359. God was giving advice, telling the animals all they had to do on earth. Pretty soon, the gathering was over. All the animals left the church after hearing mass. Some were singing with joy because they had seen God. The dove was in the sun, singing. 360. After a while, the cocolera arrived. Seeing that everyone was standing outside, he asked the dove if the mass had not started. 361. "It finished only a moment ago. What were you doing that you didn't get here on time? I told you that if you bathed you wouldn't get here on time. Now you've come in vain," said the dove.

The cocolera was standing there with very clean feet. Then the dove began to sing and the cocolera began to cry sadly. The rest of the animals returned to earth singing. 362. Meantime, the cocolera remained there crying. Later, he came back alone. That is why now he always sings sadly. Only rarely do people raise these birds because they sing with sorrow. Its song is "huui hu, huui hu." Only *they* sing like this. All the other birds always sing with joy.

363. The woodpecker.[49] This is a bird of several colors, that is, mottled with black and white mixed together. The female is all mottled grey. The male has a red head. The red continues to its chest and part of its tail. It doesn't have a long tail. It is bobtailed. 364. The female is like the male.

The cocolera went in the water quickly

Fauna 357

The woodpecker's beak is very strong. It uses it to make holes in tree trunks where it builds its nest. It works on green as well as dried trees. It makes noise wherever it pecks, making holes in the wood as it builds its nest. It drills the wood out, and then brings trash to put inside so it won't be cold. 365. It builds its nest in órganos and mesquites. Even though mesquite is the hardest tree of all, the woodpecker still drills holes in it. It is always on the sides of trees. It isn't like other birds that sit perched on trees. The woodpecker is always stuck to the side of a tree, with its head pointed toward the sky, and its tail to the ground. 366. It is never seen on a branch, but is always trying to drill holes in trunks. It feeds on insects, like those it finds in tree trunks. 367. I've never seen it on the ground looking for food. It is always on tree trunks. It eats tunas in season, and sucks on the flowers of the nopales. This is probably how it gets liquid, because it is never seen in water. 368. It breeds its young in the holes it makes. It has two or three offspring. It lays only once a year. The young are born during April and May, and the little birds are totally bald when they come out of the egg.

369. Some people catch woodpeckers to sell them. Others don't do this because there is a belief that woodpeckers, too, are the Devil's creatures. This must be why many people are afraid to catch them. They do sell well in the market, though.

370. Old people believe and tell how a woodpecker announces bad luck when it sings on the road. Sometimes it comes and pecks at trees near a house and sings. When it does this, it announces that something bad will happen to the people of that house. Truly, this is so. This bird follows people when it flies around. Sometimes it flies in front of a person, sometimes in back, and it "laughs" at them. 371. They say that in order to frighten a woodpecker away, one must make the sign of the cross with spit on a rock and throw the rock at the bird. This will make it take off because, people believe, the spit of someone baptized in the church is blessed.

When woodpeckers fly they go up and down. They don't fly in a straight line like other birds.

372. There is another belief that woodpecker brain is good for witching; anyone who has some can do this. One dries it and grinds it so it can be carried around. The Devil helps anyone who has this to defend himself when someone wants to do him injury. Woodpeckers are not used in medicine, however. 373. Nor do they cause harm in the gardens, except that when they find fig and peach trees they peck holes in them.

There is another class of this bird called the teco. It is larger than the usual woodpecker, but has similar coloring. It has a long tail. Its call is different and it also likes to live where there aren't many people. When it calls out it seems to hiccough. 374. By comparison, the ladder-backed woodpecker seems to laugh. It is believed that both announce bad tidings. The teco has a crest; the male has a red head, and the female has a mottled black head, but also with a comb. These woodpeckers are most in demand in the market. Both the ladder-backed woodpecker and the teco peck at maguey stalks, where they also nest. Sometimes they make holes in palmas. If someone hits them with a rock, these birds don't die easily. They are very hardy.

375. The cardinal.[50] There are two kinds of cardinals, both equal in size and shape. The only difference is in the color. The black one is much hardier. It is a very strong, brilliant black over its entire body. The male has white in its wings and sometimes in its tail. Both the female as well as the male have a kind of comb on their head. 376. They feed on pirul seeds and insects which they catch in flight.

Cardinals build their nests on mesquite branches. They make the nests from dried mesquite twigs and Spanish moss, and they lay two eggs a year. People hunt the birds to sell them, even though their song is not so harmonious. The song is made of short whistles. The cardinal lives in the valley all year; even in winter it doesn't migrate to other regions. This bird doesn't harm the fields. 377. It doesn't have any use in medicine. Neither does it announce bad tidings. It is a good bird.

The red cardinal is not very hardy. It dies easily if it is kept in captivity as an adult. It inhabits areas where people rarely go; it is very untrusting. The male is beautifully colored. Its entire body is red. Only its eyelids are black. It has a head comb and a long red tail with patches of black. 378. At the time of year when the countryside turns green, the red cardinal comes and sits in the trees; it looks like a flower. The female is red on part of her head and chest. Her body is a pale yellow, as are her wings and tail. Whenever one sees these birds it is easy to tell which is the male and which the female. They build their nests on mesquite branches, and lay just two eggs, once a year. 379. There aren't many of them in the valley because they are hunted by people to sell. They are in demand, not only for their pleasant song, but also for their lovely color. They don't harm anything. They live in peace.

380. The calandria. The calandria is about the same size as the lark, but its coloring is totally different. The male is characterized by its beautiful color. Its entire belly and chest is yellow. It is a brilliant, beautiful yellow. The head is black, and this color extends to cover its back. The black, too, is brilliant. The whole body of this bird is very beautiful. 381. Its tail is long. Its whistle is pretty

to hear. It seems to dress up the mesquites with its song. The trees don't look very nice when they are alone. But when the calandrias sit on them, they present another appearance.

The female is not the same color as the male. It is a greyish yellow on the sides. Its neck, chest, and belly are pale yellow. Of course, it doesn't compare with the male in color. It is pale. 382. Both sing beautifully at the beginning of spring. When the mesquites and miel de jicote are in bud, and the garambullos are in flower, that is when these birds arrive. They stay through the spring and summer. In the autumn and winter they migrate to other places, hotter lands. They build their nests by hanging them from the leaves of the palma. They weave the fiber from the palma leaves. They hang the nest and don't put it on top of the leaves like other birds. 383. They hang their nest like a small bag. They only use ixtle from the leaves of the palma in building the nest. They don't mix in any other material. They weave it very well; it looks like it was woven by a person. They always build their nests on the palmas. This is probably because of the fiber they need, the fiber which they loosen from the edge of the leaves.

Their food is insects which they get on the branches of the trees. 384. They nest twice a year, producing two offspring each time. They are hunted because folks like to have them in the house. Sometimes they are taken to market, where people pay 25 pesos for one that's more or less grown. Small birds fetch less. They are of no use in medicine, and don't do any witchcraft. 385. Everyone in the valley likes to see them and hear them sing. No one's eyes are ever tired by seeing this animal which offers its affection to the desert. When a wood collector[51] hears a calandria in the country something makes him stop and listen to the song first, before breaking and gathering his wood. The pulque vendor goes along with his heavy skin of pulque, and is tired. But when he hears the song of this bird he forgets his tiredness, even if only for a moment. A shepherd is always working under the hot sun out in the monte; the song of this bird refreshes his or her heart and thoughts. The houses of families between the mesquites have no other music more beautiful than the song of these little birds which sing to the campesino's house.

The nightingale.[52] The nightingale is about the same size as the calandria. Its color is entirely ash grey. 387. It feeds on insects like spiders, grubs, and moths.[53] It scratches in the fields because it also likes to eat corn in recently planted areas. It prefers to eat the germinating kernels. It eats mostly corn. Though it doesn't eat bean seeds, it nevertheless stops the beans from growing when it digs around in the milpas. It, too, builds its nest on mesquite branches, and in maguey trunks. It puts in trash for a nest, and lays its eggs there. 388. Just like other birds I've mentioned, this one lays twice a year. It lays two or three eggs each time. It sits on them for three weeks so they will hatch. Practically no one hunts nightingales, possibly because they don't like the bird's song. In my opinion it sings well but just doesn't have a strong voice. 389. Though the people say it has "five guitars" I don't think it plays them well.

It does not bring bad tidings, as it is believed other birds do. Some people believe that when they hear it sing, it is announcing the rain. This is the belief that some people have. It is not used in medicine, neither any part of its body, nor its nest. 390. Some people kill it, pluck it, roast it, and eat it. They just put salt on it. When a family eats it then each person has to take a piece. Even if there are four or six in the family, each person must get a piece.

391. The four-eyed cenzontle.[54] The entire head and dorsal area of this bird is black. The wings are also black. The chest and belly are mostly white, with some grey. It is called the four-eyed cenzontle because it has white eye rings, and black eyes. It looks like each eye is double and so it is called "double eyes" or "four-eyed." It whistles in a chirping manner. It doesn't have a true cenzontle call. 392. For this reason it is not hunted. Its eggs are white. It lays them in its nests, which it makes from maguey roots, grass, and old rags. It is very clever in hiding itself. One sees it one moment perched on a plant, and the next moment it is somewhere else. You can't tell how it got to the other place because it flies practically at ground level. 393. It only does this when people are watching. When no one is looking it flies normally.

It feeds on insects which it catches in flight, such as red flies, hornets, and butterflies. It also eats the ones it finds on the ground. In one quick jump, it comes down from where it is perched and grabs things like grubs, scorpions, centipedes, and spiders. 394. Generally, it doesn't stay on the ground to find its food. Rather, it sights the insects from above where it perches. It doesn't harm the fields, nor is it used in medicine. There are no beliefs about it. It is very similar to the cenzontle, and this is why it has been given this name.

395. The swallow.[55] The swallow's head and sides are black, and it has thin wings. The belly of some of them is white, while the belly of others is dark orange. It is about the same size as the bunting. It has been seen that this bird is a powerful flyer, reaching great heights in flight. 396. Sometimes it flies fast, and sometimes so slowly that is seems to just hang in the air. It doesn't perch on plants or trees; it usually just sits on electric wires, taking in the sun. When they notice that it is going to rain, they all take off in flight. 397. At the end of the rain they fly around as well. It seems that they like to fly when the weather is cool.

They feed on insects which they catch in flight, such as moths and ants which fly about when the rain stops. Red ants and black ants come out and fly around when they sense the rain.[56]

398. Swallows build their nests near the entrance to houses. They stick them on the outside walls where the roof sticks out, and in this way the nests don't get washed out. The nests are built entirely of earth. The bird carries mud, a little at a time, and sticks it to the wall. Once it is stuck on, it continues to put on layers of mud. Then the swallow uses its body to make a hole in the mud where it will lay its eggs. 399. It always makes its nest in the roofs of houses or churches. But it has to find a place where the rain won't hit the nest and wash it away. It carries the mud in its beak. It uses its wings and feet to form the mud.

This bird, too, lays two eggs. 400. It lays them in the earthen nest and sits on them. This is where its name, "kahai," comes from in Ñähñu. "Kai" means "to sit on, as eggs" and "haai" means "earth." "Kaai" and "hwiits'i" both mean "to incubate eggs by sitting" in Ñähñu. The swallow doesn't do any harm to people, nor does it hurt the milpas or the fruit trees. Neither is it a bringer of bad tidings, like some other birds. During the winter there are practically none of these birds around, and it is rare to see one. 401. When the hot season comes people are happy to see these birds because it is believed that they attract the rain. This is another bird which is not used in medicine. No one catches them to sell, because no one buys them. They don't sing well. Nor are they killed for food; no one eats them. This is the only bird in the valley which makes its nest of earth. It always lays during the hot season.

402. The rock wren, or "tepetate worker."[57] The rock wren is a little bigger than the cactus wren; it is pale grey in color. Its head and dorsal areas are slightly red. Its name in Ñähñu means "worker of tepetate." To build its nest it first scrapes away some of the tepetate. Then, it slowly fits its nest into the hole. It always nests in tepetate. 403. It never nests in trees like other birds. People have always seen it living like this, and have thus called it "the tepetate worker." It feeds on the spiders in the tepetate. It eats centipedes also. It is always found in the tepetate; no one catches them to sell because they don't sing well. No merchants ask for them in the market. Its song is like laughter. It doesn't cause any harm to the planted fields. 404. This is because it doesn't eat corn. It only looks for holes in tepetate, because that's where it finds spiders and other insects. No one needs it for medicine. No one kills it to eat because its body is very small and doesn't have much meat on it. The female and the male are the same size.

El dominico.[58] This bird is about the same size as the cactus wren, but different in color. 405. The entire belly area is yellow. Its back and head are black. It is like a miniature calandria, and it is the male which has these color characteristics. The female is grey in front and brown on the back and sides. It comes to the desert at the beginning of spring, and stays to nest. 407. When winter comes, it migrates to warmer areas, like Meztitlán. If it didn't migrate, it would die of

When it is going to rain, they all take off in flight
Fauna 396

cold. During the summer its song predominates in the mesquites and bushes where it makes its nest. One can tell where it has nested because the chicks whistle. Also, when another type of bird perches near its nest, it whistles. When snakes hear it whistling, they go up in the trees to eat the eggs or to eat the chicks. The chirrionera is the fastest snake in going up trees,[59] and if it finds the mother in the nest, it eats her, too. 408. Then the other birds make a hubbub flying and screeching around the snake as if to defend the bird that the snake is eating. When people hear this they find out where it is happening and this is how we know which animal attacks these birds. When the snake sees that people are gathering it jumps to another tree and is gone. One can tell if the snake has eaten the bird, because its belly is all inflated.

409. The dominico feeds on insects it finds in trees, as well as on spiders and insects found in flowers. I've seen it drink water. It also brings water to its young when they are born. It doesn't eat corn, so it doesn't hurt the fields. Nor is it used in medicine. Its nest is made from tree leaves, such as mesquite and pepper tree leaves, and from hanging moss which it puts inside the nest. 410. They build their nests on mesquites, and on pepper trees. It isn't known whether it announces bad luck, as is thought to be the case with other birds. No one takes the babies to sell because they aren't commercially valuable. Their song is not very nice. 411. As I said earlier, it lives in the valley during the summer. When winter comes, it migrates to escape from the cold. It only has two young each year.

412. The grey-breasted jay.[60] It's about the size of the huitlacoche. It is blue on its head and also on its back. Its chest and belly are grey. This is the male; the female is entirely grey. Those who don't know this bird well think it is a huitlacoche. Its cry is strong; it isn't really a song, but rather a call. It comes to the valley at the beginning of spring. Then it leaves when spring is over. It doesn't stay around. 413. I've seen it in the mountains, north of Orizabita, in Banxu, and throughout the region beyond there. They move in flocks and make a lot of noise. They don't build their nests in the valley because they are only there for a short time each year. They arrive as soon as the trees bud and when the budding is over they leave. 414. They don't stay for the summer.

They feed on the insects on the shoots of the trees. They make their nest in pine trees in the mountains. They gather up the needles which they weave together with other twigs. They nest only once a year and lay only two eggs which are about the size of huitlacoche eggs. They are blue, a kind of pale blue. No one captures these birds to sell. 415. No one will buy them. They say that their meat is not good tasting.

When these birds encounter some animal they gather together to shriek at it. Since their call is strong they make a real ruckus. They don't do anything bad to the fields; nor are they used in medicine; nor do they announce bad luck like other birds we have seen. 416. From what I've seen, they don't like the desert, so they return to the mountains where they always live. They are a kind of bird that isn't afraid of people. Wherever they live, no one bothers them.

417. The filomena.[61] This bird is like the jay. It comes every year. There are a lot of them at the beginning of February. During the windy season is when they come. They don't fly alone. They fly in groups, sometimes 20, sometimes many more. One can tell where they are passing by from the noise those squadrons make with their wings. When they perch on the trees, the branches bend from the weight of so many birds. When they perch, they stay where they are for a long time and don't leave. 418. They aren't afraid of people. They are about the size of a bunting, except that the filomena has a crest. The male has plumage of mostly grey mixed with some red. Its beak is similar to that of a bunting. The filomena looks better, though, because its plumage is smoother. The female is totally grey and is also characterized by her crest. 419. This migrating bird also doesn't build a nest because it is in the area too short a time. As soon as the trees begin to bud, this bird disappears from the valley and goes to other places. Some people, knowing a lot about these birds and when they will arrive, make a slingshot to hunt them with because these birds are fat. They can be roasted and eaten. Possibly because of this they don't stay long. Where I've seen them make a nest they use grass and twigs which they set on large trees such as oaks, pines, and junipers. Their eggs are white and they lay two, once a year.

420. The vermilion flycatcher.[62] This bird's face, chest and belly are red. Its head is also red, with a crest. Its wings and its tail are a clear coffee color. The red part is very pretty. Wherever it perches it looks like a red flower. It may be compared to the color of the red cardinal. 421. However, the flycatcher has a round body, while the cardinal is thin. The flycatcher lives in the valley all year long. The male is red, while the female is completely different. The female is grey on the belly and brown on the back. Its head is topped by a crest which is also brown. Wherever they go, it is easy to distinguish the male from the female. Both the male and the female have round bodies. When the male flies it's like someone had shot a red flower into the air. 422. It generally perches on magueys, órganos, or wherever it finds a single, solitary tree. It sings nicely and says "tu tu bi xi" and this is why it has this name. It is like the cenzontle.

It sings whenever it sees the light of the moon, even though it may be midnight. 423. This is the way the cenzontle is, too. This may be just out of its own joy at seeing the moon, but people say the moonlight fools it into believing that it is dawn, and so it sings. It, too, feeds on insects which it catches in flight. It doesn't sit on the ground, but on a maguey, and when it sees an insect go by it makes a quick jump and grabs it. If the insect escapes, then the bird follows it until it catches it and eats it. It does this with moths and butterflies, wasps, red flies, and other insects which it hunts in flight. 424. Insects that live on the ground, such as crickets, some spiders, and maguey grubs are what it mostly hunts, but without staying on the ground. It catches them in a single bound, and then goes back and eats them where it was perched before.

425. There is a belief that if someone hits a vermilion flycatcher with a stone, the bird will tear his hand off; this will happen whether the stone is hurled by hand or by slingshot. 426. Because of this belief, it is not often killed. It nests once a year. It lays its eggs in its nest which it makes on granjeno bushes, or on maguey leaves. Other times it makes its nest in maguey trunks. It doesn't do damage to planted fields.

427. Some people gather the red plumage of this bird so they'll have it on hand when children have measles. The feathers are tied to the child's neck, hands, and feet. It is said that this is so all the lesions will turn red. 428. Sometimes they turn mottled and this isn't good. The child might even die. Of course, it isn't just these bird feathers that are used against measles. There are other medicines as well. But we will see more about this when we discuss medicine. Then we will see all that is done, and what kinds of medicines are used for measles.

429. No one hunts this bird to eat because it isn't fat. Also, if someone finds it while it is nesting, they don't take the birds to sell; there is no demand for them. They sing prettily, but perhaps others don't like their song, because they never catch them like they do buntings.

430. The spotted towhee.[63] It is the same size as the bunting that I mentioned earlier, but different in color. It is called the "bird with the dickey shirt" in Ñähñu because a part of its chest is black, like it had a bib hanging from its neck. So, people gave it this name. Male and the female alike have the same chest coloration. The belly is white and grey. The head and back are brown. The beak is not long, but rather short. When they are first born, it is easy to confuse them with buntings because when they are small they have the same coloring. But as they grow the differences in plumage are notable.

431. They always live in houses, under eaves which project from roofs. This is where they build their nests. They need to eat corn, so they don't make their nests in the fields. If they don't make their nest under the eaves they make it on the branches of garambullos, mesquites, and wild capulín trees that are near

houses. These birds always hang around near houses. At dawn, they walk around the patio, gathering corn and little pieces of tortilla thrown to them. From what is known of them they don't go to the open country to search for food, but always eat the corn fed to the chickens. Even when chickens peck at them, these birds just avoid them and eat.

433. The color of the bib is completely black. It begins at the neck and comes to a point on the chest. They live all over the valley in small flocks. They are abundant in towns because there is a lot to eat, such as the corn that grain sellers throw out in the market place. These birds gather up these kernels, along with other crumbs of food. 434. Some make their nests on roofs, others on the branches of trees. They lay twice a year. They bear two or three young each time. The nest is made from rags, and trash that they find in dumping areas. There are many of these birds because they breed twice a year.

In the morning and again in the evening they come together and make a lot of commotion with their calling. 435. They rush about, fighting over what they find to eat. The males fight for the females, too. These birds are not good for anything much. Only rarely do they dig around in the fields in search of corn to eat. They are not used in medicine, neither their body nor their nest. Neither are their feathers taken. They don't announce bad luck like other birds we've seen before. No one hunts them to sell because they don't sing. Neither are they hunted to eat. 436. They do get fat from eating corn, but I've never seen anyone eat them, except cats when they catch them.

437. The black bird.[64] This bird's body is completely black. It is larger than the huitlacoche and has a long beak. It has only recently come to the Mezquital to stay. Possibly, it likes the climate in the valley, or perhaps it found greater food resources and stayed on. I remember it used to come in earlier years, but they were perennial then. 438. They arrived at the beginning of autumn in large flocks which caused shadows where they passed. They arrived around September and they returned to their place of origin during March and April. A few years ago they stayed in the valley to live the whole year. I've seen them living in Querétaro. 439. They are the predominant birds from there to other parts of the lowlands. They soil the area where they perch to eat. They used to emigrate from their home area, eating up the harvests and the green leaves of the fields there. Then they would leave and come to the valley. They don't like to live in arid areas, only in the irrigated zones. They find places like the green milpas in the valley.

440. The people don't like these birds because they are harmful to the planted fields. They eat the young corn and they eat the mature corn when ears are fully formed. They eat a lot, because they do nothing else and they do it every day,

and so the campesinos hate them. They say that these birds not only eat the corn, but also dig up anything else that is planted when there is no corn. 441. They eat alfalfa, too, but the people say that the birds are most harmful to corn fields. Recently, they've come to live more in the heavily populated areas, because this is where they find most corn to eat. They build their nests in tall trees, such as casuarina and ash. These are the tallest, leafiest trees. 442. They build their nests from trash, grass, and rags. They lay two eggs and nest once a year. Far from offering any benefit to humans they cause a lot of harm. Since they have only recently arrived in the valley they have no known medicinal use, if any. Nor does anyone know if they announce bad luck. Their call is like a teco's, but black birds only squawk and don't sing. There are those who say its flesh is tasty when roasted. It will be necessary for others to try it before the truth can be known.

443. The white pigeon.[65] The white pigeon has the same characteristics, in form and in size, as the wild pigeon which we have already seen. The white pigeon is domesticated; they are born and they grow up in houses. There are white ones, grey ones, black ones, and yellow ones mixed with white. They feed on corn thrown to them when chickens are fed. They eat together. They only need to be fed some corn, and then they go off and supplement their diet themselves in the fields. They eat small pebbles. People think that the pebbles help the birds to grind up whatever hard substances they've eaten. When someone kills one, they open up its gizzard and see that it contains pebbles. Sometimes these pigeons go off to the milpas and eat chicalote seeds, and the seeds of other plants.

445, They nest twice a year. People hang old pitchers or petacas from the eaves for pigeons to nest in. When they are nesting, these pigeons bring in twigs and trash to build the nest. But when they aren't nesting, they don't fetch anything. They just stay in the jug with the male pigeon. Each nesting produces two offspring.

They are not kept in bird cages. 446. They all roam free. The little ones don't leave and fly away. When they grow up, they fly out of the nest in search of food, but then they return. People like to raise pigeons because these are edible birds. They are cooked with rice and they are very tasty because they are fat from feeding on corn. They cause no problems, either in the fields or at home. 447. They are not used in medicine, nor do they announce bad luck. People like to raise them because these birds are in many ways like chickens. Sometimes they nest in the church tower. The little birds are born there, but if an owl finds them, it eats them. It either eats the eggs or the little chicks. 448. I've seen people who wanted to raise them, but didn't have any. So they traded other animals for pigeons. For example, if they have a dog, they trade it for a pigeon; or they may trade a cat. These birds are never brought to market because they don't sing like wild pigeons. The latter has a pretty song, while the domestic pigeon just moans but doesn't sing. It doesn't have any use in medicine; it just lives to live.

449. It seems that it doesn't eat insects because none are found in its gizzard. It always lives in houses and is totally domestic. Even though they don't let people handle them, still, they always return to the house. They are found in every kind of house, from maguey houses to solid stone wall houses alike. Sometimes pigeons like to sleep with the chickens, and sometimes they play together, pecking at one another.

450. What we have just seen are the birds that live in the Mezquital Valley. The majority of them are resistant to winter and dryness. Others, a few, migrate to regions where the climate is more favorable for them. But as soon as they see that the good weather has passed they return to live in the desert. Some help people, and others harm the fields. 451. Sometimes people love them, and sometimes they harm them and kill them to eat them. Sometimes people kill things even though the animals don't do any harm. This is the most harmful practice. In this way humans run the risk of exterminating all the animals just by not knowing how to protect them. 452. It is very important to take care of the animals and the forests, for all of them bring well-being to the places where they live.

Conservation is even more important in the desert. Some plants and animals are already extinct because no one knew how to protect them. Some people don't think about this and blame others, saying that God doesn't want to give rain. 453. But how can it rain if there are no forests to attract the rain? If this goes on, there will never be any more rain and all the vegetation will dry up and disappear. If there isn't any vegetation there won't be feed for animals, and they will die. It is the same with human beings: if they don't have resources they just get poorer and poorer.

454. Everyone knows that birds bring joy to the fields, and not just to the Mezquital, but all over the world. There are trees that don't have flowers. But if a bird perches on it and builds its nest, then the nest will have little birds that sing, and it is as if *they* were the flowers in the tree. This is how everything has its function. It is all right to cut down trees that have died from lack of water or rain, because we know it won't grow any more. 455. But we must protect those that are still green—because they give us shade when we rest, and because they will die from lack of water if we don't take care of them. Then who can ask for more? No one.

The same is true for animals; if we kill off the birds I mentioned, they will slowly become extinct. We know they are important. They give us joy with their songs. Even though some of them harm us, we must understand them. 456. If we imagine that we were birds and birds were people, and that they did the same to us as we do to them, we wouldn't like it. We would be sad. Sometimes, without thinking, we take the life of the mother of recently hatched birds. We must consider that so long as the parents live, they take care of their offspring, feed them and keep them warm. But, if we kill off the parents, the babies will die also. 457. It is very important that we learn to respect the life of animals. Whether large or small, they all need to live.

458. Those which truly are not needed must, indeed, be exterminated. Far from helping us, such things as mice, flies, and other animals that cause disease only make us poorer. Mice and flies go about wherever they please. They touch everything dirty and then they touch what we eat. This is how diseases start. Many of us don't know this. 459. For this reason, we don't know what illness we may have and we try to cure things with various medicines. What we think is going to alleviate a sickness may only make it worse. By the time a doctor is seen, the case may be serious and the result is that the medicine is more expensive.

460. The dog. There are different kinds of dogs, of different sizes. Some are fat, others skinny and weak. There are also different colors. They are different in size because there are different breeds of dogs. That is to say, this is their natural state, to be different. 461. But sometimes they are different in size and fatness just from great differences in feeding. A dog that has things to eat grows big and fat, while a dog that doesn't eat well doesn't grow much and is weak and skinny. They may have fleas from being so weak. 462. They don't have any desire to move around, or run, or bark. They are bent from weakness. They are hardly ever lively; they are worn out because this is how their masters treat them. Sometimes their masters train them and sometimes they give them a little something to eat so that they will be animated. 463. Dogs that eat well are lively and have smooth fur. They almost never have fleas. They also go around playing and running. Each has different coloring. There are black, yellow, white, brown, and orange. These are the dominant colors. The ones in the valley don't have long ears like some that live in the city.

464. People in the valley like to have dogs because they need them to guard the house at night. Dogs help protect the animals that people raise, such as chickens, goats, and sheep. Those animals are in danger if left alone because coyotes would eat them. Families that raise a dog take good care of it. They make it its own special tortilla, and give it food just as if the dog were a servant.

465. They make a gordita but don't give it to the dog right away. First it is cooked and then you wait until it has cooled off, because if you give a dog a hot tortilla, people say that it will slobber a lot. This is how it gets sick, so it is always given cold tortillas. Some folks have only one dog, while others keep two or three. The tortilla is made separately for each one.

Many people train their dogs to be aggressive. Some put red ants in their food. 466. There is the belief that the red ant is exceedingly ferocious. It bites anyone who bothers it. This is how dogs are that are given red ants to eat. Ten or more ants are thrown in and ground up with the masa from which the tortilla is made. People have to watch out because these dogs bite people, too. Many of them turn on their owners, without even barking first. When an owner least expects it, the dogs bite his leg. 467. And it hurts a lot where they bite. It is very dangerous, too, because if the dog is carrying rabies then the person whom they bite gets sick, too.

Many dogs are also trained to control flocks. They learn quickly, and then go about their business by themselves, herding the goats. They nip at any goat or sheep that wants to wander off from the rest of the flock. Even if they cry out, the dogs return them to the flock. 468. Other dogs are trained to hunt. Their masters slowly teach them to run down animals, by throwing out stones for them to chase. When they have learned well, they go alone to open country to hunt for rabbits and squirrels. If they are big dogs, then they hunt hares, and sometimes they eat them as soon as they kill them. 469. Other times, they hold them in their jaws and bring them to their master. Squirrels are dangerous for dogs to hunt because squirrels bite. The dog grabs the squirrel by the neck so the squirrel can't get its teeth around and bite the dog. Hares and rabbits don't bite.

There are dogs that are very smart; they dig into squirrels' dens to get them out. When they come to roots of plants they cut them with their teeth. The ones that know how to hunt are beautiful; they never lack for something to eat. 470. Dogs that go to the monte regularly know what green plants they can eat. Some dogs eat wild capulín seeds, and seeds of garambullos, and mesquite beans when they are ripe, and grass. When a dog knows how to control flocks and hunt, it is very much appreciated by its master. 471. Other dogs are lazy or mischievous. No one wants them and they are always chased away with sticks, or aren't given anything to eat. There are others that learn to eat eggs. They spy on chickens, and as soon as the hen lays an egg, the dog eats it. They just poke a hole in it, so it doesn't run out, and then they suck on it. Still others, learn to eat newborn chicks; or even if the chicks are big, they eat them.

There are others that go around drinking aguamiel. They remove the stone cap from the maguey with their forepaws, and shove the stone aside. 472. After they lap up the aguamiel they abandon the plant. When the tlachiquero comes, he has to scrape the plant because there is no aguamiel to take out. If a tlachiquero gets mad he may set a trap and kill the dog. All dogs that do these things are hated.

Dogs that know how to dig for squirrels first smell them out. When they sense that a squirrel is near by, they dig, and if they smell it and know it is too deep in the ground, then they abandon it.

There is also a belief about dogs. It is said that when someone in a family is sick, and a dog howls, this announces the person's death. Or, if it doesn't announce death, then it announces that the person will get sicker. This really happens a lot when dogs howl. It is not known if they are really saying this or if they want something else. But I've seen that wherever dogs howl, something bad happens to people. Either they get sick or someone does something bad.

474. Where there are dogs, coyotes practically never come around. Neither do foxes or skunks. Even though dogs don't kill them, it is said that they bite them. So they don't come around houses or corrals where dogs are. Sometimes, though, the coyote wins, and gets into the corral to eat the goats. Once, I saw a case where there were five fierce dogs in a house. 475. When anyone approached who wasn't a member of the household, the dogs didn't let them enter. They chased them off. But I remember that one night a coyote got into the corral and ate one goat, and killed three more. The dogs did absolutely nothing, and the masters didn't wake up. They said that the coyote bewitched the dogs so that no one would get up. 476. The next day, they tried uselessly to follow the coyote's trail, but he was gone.

Dogs are very smart. If they lose their master (for example, on the road, or out in open country) they just find the trail by smelling it. When a dog senses that the trail is its master's it follows the trail until it finds him.

Dogs' excrement is used in purifying children of evil eye. 477. No one cares for dogs that live in the Mezquital like they care for the ones that live in the city. Dogs go around wherever they like, and sleep anywhere. No one bathes them like they bathe city dogs with soap. There are many dogs and they roam loose. No one cares for them. 478. The female gives birth twice a year, and in each birth has two, five, seven, or up to nine pups, from what I've seen. They are only given bones and tortillas. They aren't given bread because it gives them fits when they eat it. When they have fits, they roll around on the ground from the pain. But it isn't known whether the part that hurts is the stomach or the head.

During May, when the so-called "hot rains," as people call them, begin, dogs get a disease called rabies. 479. It is very dangerous, especially because there are no herbs in the countryside to cure it. It can only be treated by a doctor who

There is also a belief about dogs
Fauna 473

prescribes injections. He injects into the navel of the person who has been bitten by a rabid dog. The way one knows if a dog has rabies is it smells like a skunk, pants a lot, slobbers a lot, and doesn't hear when you call it. 480. It leaves the house and bites other dogs. It does the same when it finds pigs, or goats. It bites them, too. When people know that a dog is rabid they shoot it. When a dog has been bitten by another with rabies, one locates the bite from the drool around it, and the fur around the bite is burned. With this, nothing will happen. 481. Of course, this must be done immediately, or rabies will break out in the bitten dog.

All the dogs here are domesticated, and live with people. They aren't wild. When they are born, their eyes aren't open. Their eyes open a month after they are born. When they open their eyes, they go out in search of food. When they are born the mother nurses the pups. Some people trade a chicken for a dog, when they want a dog. Or they may trade a cat for a dog, or a small turkey. 482. This is the custom which the people practice. Sometimes they trade a domestic pigeon. All the animals we will see from now on are tame and always live with people. Dogs are not allowed to belch around where people eat, because it smells very bad.

483. Turkeys and chickens. These are domesticated, for they live in houses. Turkeys and chickens are both called "oni" collectively in Ñähñu. They are raised because they offer highly nutritional food for people. They lay eggs, which people eat, and which are very nutritious. The same goes for the meat. It is generally eaten in clear broth with salt, onions, and potatoes. 484. Other flavorings are added when the meat is made into barbacóa. It is also eaten in mole, but with more condiments, as well. The eggs are eaten boiled, fried, and roasted. Eggs have to be watched when they are roasted because if they are overcooked they explode. 485. Eggs are mostly eaten boiled; one simply puts them in water, and the water is put on the fire. Afterwards, they are peeled, salt is added and they are eaten together with sausage. This is how the Mezquital people eat eggs. Some people fry them with lard, and others fry them in oil.

There is another way they are eaten: they are put on a comal which has been placed on the fire. 486. First, the eggs are beaten well in a dish. Chopped onion and salt are added, and beaten together. A little ash is put on the comal so the eggs won't stick. In one flip of the griddle, the eggs are done, and this is much faster cooking than boiling them or frying them. This is how women cook eggs when they have to get their men off to work in a hurry.

487. These animals are very beneficial to those who know how to raise them and take care of them. They are self-supporting; the income from their eggs pays for their feed. A lot of families have chickens but don't know how to take advantage of them, and only rarely eat what they produce. Such families only

eat eggs once or twice a month, for example. Their diet consists of tortillas and chile in salsa; this is what adults eat, and this is what they give their children. 488. In spite of the fact that they have fat hens that lay eggs every day, they don't eat the eggs. Instead, they think only of selling the eggs to buy corn, or sometimes only pulque. They do this because they believe pulque is more nutritious.

When these people buy meat in the market they are always given more bones than meat by the merchants. 489. The butchers keep the best part back for mestizos. The merchants always cheat the Indians. They sell them whatever will bring more money. In fact, it's almost as if the people of the Mezquital didn't even own the chickens and goats they raise with such care; for as soon as any animal has grown large enough, they bring it to market and the merchants give them anything they feel like giving them for it. They do this sort of thing even more when they see that the seller doesn't know how to read. 490. This happens to many people who bring in their nice, fat animals to sell. But, because of their lack of sophistication, they wind up bringing in meat and taking away chiles which don't have a lot of food strength. When they want to buy meat, all they are given is cartilage or bones. 491. And, I repeat, they give away practically anything they have of value in the house. They suffer a lot in taking care of the animals. Hopefully, little by little they will reflect on how to take advantage of the resources they have. As it is now, the people get poorer every day, and the merchants get richer. Though they see what's going on the authorities don't do a thing about it, either.

492. The chicken. There are brown ones, spotted ones, red ones, and white ones. Some have crests. These are the kinds of chickens in the valley. Those raised in the country are more resistant to disease. Those raised in the city die easily. The chickens raised by the people of the valley are not penned up; they roam free. They find roosting places by themselves in the house. Sometimes, if no one watches them, they will make their nest and lay their eggs just anywhere. 493. Dogs will find the eggs and eat them. Or, if it isn't a dog, then a cat will eat them, because they, too, like to eat chicken eggs. Chickens only have to be thrown some corn to eat. They supplement their diet themselves with insects they find by scratching in the ground. Corn is thrown on the ground to them, and they are given water in troughs made from specially cut stone. People have thought about it and make the troughs out of stone so they won't rot or break.

494. Chickens lay eggs during two periods of the year, and produce a dozen eggs each time. When the mistress of the house sees that the hens have gone with the rooster she puts the hen in the nest. But if the mistress sees that the hen was not mounted by the rooster, even one time, she doesn't nest the hen but eats

it instead, or brings the eggs to market to be sold. 495. They pay 60 centavos each in the market for eggs which have not been fertilized by a rooster. These eggs are called "eggs of earth"; if they are sat on none will hatch. So the mistress of the house knows not to put them in the nest, because she knows that's a lost cause. The hen, will, indeed, set on the nest, but when she notices that none of her eggs hatch, she will abandon the nest. 496. And, since the eggs have been heated by the hen's sitting, they are ruined and smell awful. This is how the hens I have seen act when there is no rooster around.

Sometimes, eggs which have been nested are boiled. Though they smell foul, they are eaten anyway. Of course, people who do this are few; they probably do it because they hate to throw out eggs. 497. When a hen has been fertilized by a rooster the eggs are gathered and kept in a jug or pitcher. According to what people say, this is so the eggs will not be "sucked by the air." If the air "sucks them," then eggs don't hatch. After hens are finished laying they have generally produced about a dozen eggs or more. This depends on how well they eat. 498. Around here hens usually lay a dozen eggs. The mistress of the house cares for the eggs with great effort. As I said before, she puts them in the nest. Before doing this she prepares the nest so the cold won't get to the eggs. Before putting each egg in the nest she puts it in a deep dish of water that she carries. 499. She watches each egg carefully; if it sinks to the bottom of the dish, this means it is good. But when it floats it is no good and has been sucked by air. When the mistress sees this, she doesn't put the egg in the nest because it would just spoil. She only puts those in which pass the test. Even if there are just six or eight good ones, these are the only eggs she puts in the nest of a brooding hen.

500. Other folks like to trade off eggs that would otherwise be wasted. A woman goes to houses where she knows there are hens and asks people to trade for good eggs. Since this is the custom and people all know it, they give her the eggs in exchange. But, in order to know that the eggs are good, the woman puts them in water, too. 501. When she finds someone who will trade eggs for her, the woman who lends the eggs will make it an even dozen.[66] These are the eggs that the borrower puts in the nest back at home. If the hen is very big, it can cover more eggs, so the woman may put in a dozen and a half. The woman nests the hen in a corner of the house where the wind doesn't blow and where out-siders won't see the hen. This is because it is believed that if the hen sees a "bad person" all the eggs will be lost. 502. A "bad person" is what a pregant woman is called. Also "bad person" is used to refer to a man who has just had sexual relations with his wife. The mistress must attend to all these details. When the hen is put in the nest, she is not given water for three days. It is said that if she is given water right away her eggs will become water and will spoil.

Hens appear to enjoy nesting. After starting to nest hens don't get up; they don't even want to eat corn. The nest is made of xite and bounded by stones. Old rags are used when there is no xite, so neither the hen, nor the chicks when they are born, feel the cold. Hens nest for three weeks to a month so the eggs will hatch. 504. When they are born the chicks are given preground corn to eat. White corn is ground and they can eat this; if it were not ground, it would get stuck in their throats. For about two and a half months after birth, they are fed this food. Afterwards, when they are larger, they are given whole grain. At first they don't want to eat corn, because it looks big to them. But if they are left alone, hunger eventually gets to them and they slowly begin to eat it. 505. When they are chicks, they are fed four times a day. When they are full grown, they are only fed once a day.

Many women know how to raise chickens and have a lot of them. It is said of these women that animals "follow" them. And so it is; when a woman knows how to care for an animal well, regardless of what animal it is, it is healthy and fat and doesn't get sick. 506. Other women, though they might want to have chickens, don't have any luck; the chickens don't grow well and have feathers that stick out, or they get sick and die, despite having enough to eat well. When other women see this, they say that animals don't follow the woman, and that she doesn't have good hands. 507. Women whose chickens do well take a lot of pleasure from this. They take a lot of trouble caring for the chickens, and the birds develop well. Some women have two or three dozen. They raise chickens rather than turkeys because chickens are more resistant to disease.

Every year in May there is a sickness which attacks chickens. Just when the hot weather begins to build up they get sick. They can be cured, but more of them die than not. This is especially true among those whose chickens don't follow them. Among them, when the sickness comes, all the birds die and there isn't a one left. Some people put medicine in the water before the sickness comes. 508. They use lemon; it is said that this cools the chicken's body because it is heated from the hot weather. It is said that lemons are cool, so they are squeezed and put in the water. Also, there is a woody plant called the "chicalote de arbol."[67] It is found in the monte and is cut and brought in. The ones with the thickest branches are cut. When whoever went to cut it comes back, he hacks it up so it can be put in the chickens' water trough. 509. The sticks are left in the water for about a week and in this way the medicine slowly comes out of it. The center core of the stick is yellow. When it is put in the chickens' trough, the yellow comes out. The water is colored yellow by it.

510. The name of this plant in Ñähñu means "yellow chicalote." As soon as one sees that chickens have white diarrhea one looks immediately for this plant

so it can be chopped up and put in water. The color goes out of it into the water. 511. Sometimes, it gets rid of the sickness, and sometimes not and the chicken dies. In cases where there are one or two or three dozen chickens, they all die because of the contagion. Sometimes they are bathed in tequesquite water, and sometimes in lemon water. 512. Sometimes three things are mixed together, including nejayo,[68] tequesquite, and lemon, and these are put under the wings and all over the body. 513. I've seen cases where this has saved many animals.

514. Chickens are indispensable in Ñähñu life. They are mostly consumed at fiestas such as baptisms, masses in honor of godchildren, weddings, flower offerings in church, various festivals for saints' days, fiestas in honor of the various virgins (Guadalupe, Mary and others venerated in the valley), and the blessing of new houses. 515. They are also on the tables set on All Saints' Day. These are tables set in honor of one's relatives or any other dead person who, it is believed, is punishing the family because no one remembers them. For this, one prepares a special meal which is brought to and left at the place where the person died who is punishing the family.

516. A sorcerer tells what must be done to offer the dead person food, and then this must be brought to the person being remembered. The meal is put into small ceramic pots and jars, along with spoons and plates which go into a new basket with a new napkin. 517. The first thing that happens is that the pots are filled with the meal which is removed from the big table. Then the people who helped prepare the meal of chicken and goat are served their portion. A woman who really knows how to fix up meals is invited to prepare the chicken mole. In this way a good, tasty meal comes out.

518. At midnight, the sorcerer and the master of the house go to where the person died and they bury the meal for him. They go to the dead person's house, or to the place where the ruins of the house are. 519. They bury the offering really well so that dogs won't be able to dig it up. After it is buried, candles are lit. 520. The sorcerer speaks to the dead person, and asks his forgiveness, telling him not to send sickness to his relatives. The master of the house also asks to be forgiven for having insulted the dead person at some time by speaking ill of him. 521. Once all this is finished, the sorcerer goes back to his house. Now, only the healing of the sick person remains to be awaited. Sometimes he is cured, and sometimes he gets worse and dies.

522. People are accustomed to lending things for fiestas. The man who will be mayordomo of the fiesta is lent animals. His acquaintances lend him one or two animals, and in this way he doesn't feel overly obligated by the cargo debt he has acquired. 523. When the one who is lent something gets his turn to reciprocate, he returns the loan in kind. The person who will be mayordomo

At midnight... they go to the dead person's house

Fauna 518

asks around to find someone who will lend him chickens. As I said, one may be lent, or two or three. A person who has a lot of chickens may lend a dozen, or six chickens. 524. When he needs them again, they are given back to him, if that's what he wishes; but if not, he may ask for one or two cartons of beer.

525. The mayordomo doesn't get the animals immediately after the lender agrees to give them. Instead, the owner delivers the chickens to the mayordomo's house two or three days prior to the fiesta. 526. Sometimes only the woman goes, sometimes the man. If the mayordomo has already killed some goats or other chickens besides the ones being lent, then there is blood stew, and he invites the person, who has come to leave chickens, to have a taco. He also invites him to participate in the meal on the appointed fiesta day, so that all the food will be shared.

527. Now, when the day of the fiesta comes, all those who have lent animals arrive at the mayordomo's house and must be are served. They are fed very well. A plate of food is prepared for them to eat, and another for them to take away to their families. 528. The custom is to pile extra pieces of meat on their plates when they are given the meal to eat. Then they are given some tortillas to take home as an "itacate."[69] They are given beer and pulque, and they are invited to take a drink of wine when there is some. 529. Then they won't feel badly about lending something when the occasion arises again, whether it be a goat, or a chicken, or corn or pulque or tortillas. These are the things that are normally lent when religious festivals are celebrated.

530. Loans are not only made between neighbors, but also between persons in different pueblos. For example, those from Nequetejé go to Remedios, and those from Remedios go to San Nicolás. Those from Orizabita go to San Juanico when they have a fiesta, and they exchange visits and loans.

531. I will mention the parts of the chicken that are eaten: head, neck, breast, wings, back, ribs, heart, liver, intestines, gizzard, kidney, tail, thigh, feet, and blood. The following parts are not eaten: lungs, crown, craw.

532. Chicken blood is prepared in the following manner, according to what I've seen. When chickens are killed women help each other. When women have cargos[70] for fiestas, they invite their neighbors over to help them kill the chickens and other animals, and to help prepare the meal. 533. Some wash the tripe, others grind the chile, and others boil the blood. Someone selects the spices that will be put into the meal. Someone else grinds up these spices, such as mint, pepper, clove, garlic, onion, cumin, marjoram, and thyme. 534. These are the condiments put in the blood to give it flavor when it is cooked. This is the food that is eaten first, and the meat is not eaten until the fiesta itself, so that it can be served to all who were invited.

535. When they arrive some visitors bring pulque with them; others bring beer. Others bring raw corn and still others bring already made tortillas. 536. People used to lend money. Sometimes a peso, sometimes five pesos. Though it might be only six centavos,[71] whoever wished to show goodwill would come and leave some money. As I said a moment ago, when the lender's time came to do a fiesta, it would all come back to him. 537. That's the way it was: if a man was mayordomo this year and received loans, then next year the people who came to visit this year would redeem the debt; it would then be the person who first received the loans bringing the needed material to the new mayordomo. 538. This is how a person with a cargo one year pays back the debts, a little at a time, to those who brought gifts. Though it might take one or two years, or more, he has to reciprocate to all who came with gifts. If a debtor gets sick or dies, then the debt may be ended. Generally, if a father dies, then the children pay the debt. 539. However, if the children are grown up and gone, or if they are minors, then they don't pay. In these cases, the lender of the gifts loses, but this only happens once in a while.

540. This is the nature of friendship among the people of the valley. Slowly, this is dying out. Nowadays, there are few people who visit one another with cargos. This is because the cargos are disappearing along with the fiestas, and this is because it is very expensive to buy the things. 541. People get poor buying things for fiestas. I must say, however, that people still visit each other, but not to exchange these gifts. People are rare nowadays who have achieved a level of friendship where they exchange gifts. Between such people, when the cargo draws near, each person carries a chicken or a tom or a hen turkey under his arm to go visiting.

542. All the parts of the chicken which I mentioned a moment ago are eaten. I should say that the people prefer to raise chickens because they are more resistant to disease. Turkeys are more delicate and die, and are more difficult to raise. 543. You only have to grind corn for chickens, and this is what they eat, along with water. Greens are very important for turkeys if they are to grow. Sometimes, when there are no greens, the entire nest of birds will die.

544. Turkeys have a characteristic that if they are born during the time of the warm winds the whole nest comes out with crooked feet and all of them die. Their little feet get all twisted and perhaps they are in pain. They stop eating and they die slowly because of this. Those who know about this don't nest them on just any day. 545. They choose a month when it isn't cold so the birds will grow up well. The woman always checks their wings, plucking out the sick feathers. If she doesn't do this, the animal won't grow. This is a disease that affects feathers. 546. The disease starts with the root of the feather filling up with a kind

of greyish liquid. Usually it is the recently developed feathers on the bird's wings and its tail to which this happens. When the woman sees that the animal is down with the disease she plucks out the sick feathers; when this is done the bird returns to health. 547. Care is taken to throw the feathers far away so other birds don't eat them. Otherwise they'll catch the disease, too. People don't know if there are injections for this disease; and so they don't give them any.

548. We return now to the chicken, and some things associated with this animal. When a person comes down with "mal aire" their head hurts, and they get fever and become nauseous.[72] 549. Some people cleanse a patient who has mal aire by using pirul leaves and an herb known as "nidi"[73] in Ñähñu, along with some flower offerings and candles that have been blessed. First, the patient is ritually cleansed with these, then the things are burned. The patient is fumed with the smoke. Then he or she is covered up well so they will sleep and sweat. When they get up, the pain goes away slowly. 550. Boiled water is prepared with a kind of leafy tree moss, and this is given to the patient to drink. This tree moss is mixed in the smoking with the relic; it, too, in fact, is also considered a relic. But it is boiled separately because it does not have a bitter taste. Others use the chicken to do the cleansing. The chicken must be black in order to frighten off this illness. 551. Others do the purifying with one or two chicken eggs. Afterwards the eggs are thrown out far away in the thorns so that even dogs can't come upon them and eat them. It is believed that the eggs contain the disease after they are used in a cleansing of this kind. 552. The chicken used in the cleansing is also killed and thrown far away, or buried. Neither turkeys nor their eggs are used for this operation. It is said that they aren't good for this purpose.

These are the uses made of the chicken and the turkey.

554. The falcon.[74] There is a small eagle-like bird that isn't very big and lives in the open, wild country. The biggest are about the size of a pigeon. Its stomach is off-white, and its wings are black, with a little yellow. 555. Its beak is curved and pointy. It eats meat, especially little rabbits wherever it finds them. It flies around looking for them, and when it sees an animal, it dives and it always catches its prey. Whether it's a mouse or a rabbit, it hunts it down and catches it. The falcon subdues its prey by pecking out its eyes. This is the first thing it does. 556. Then, at its leisure, it eats the body.

When it flies it calls out and brings out the rabbits and the mice it is hunting to eat. If it finds baby birds, it catches and eats them. If it finds whiptails and lizards, it eats them, too. 557. It likes to fly around between four and five in the afternoon. It makes its nest in the tepetate cliffs. Falcons are born two at a time during the hot season, such as the months of May and June. No one eats them. On the contrary, they are hated because they eat baby birds wherever they find them. 558. They are called "t'itxaka" in Ñähñu because they move their claws rapidly when they fly and their feet are suspended in the air. They don't do anything else bad. They aren't used in medicine and neither are they sold in the market. They aren't commercial things.

559. The quail. The name of this animal is taken from its cry. It goes "tsa-tsa, tsa-tsa, tsa-tsa." It has a crown. It is totally grey in color and is bob-tailed. Hunters like to hunt and kill these birds. 560. Its meat is very good. This bird is very clever in hiding itself. When it sees that someone is approaching, it flattens out on the ground so it can't be seen. They go around in groups of one or two or three, or up to a dozen, both mature and immature birds together. Sometimes, they hide by getting in between the junquillos, and sometimes they go up into the mesquites. They really know how to hide themselves well. One could almost step on them and not see them.

561. Their eggs are like a dove's, also white and of the same size. The female lays a dozen eggs at a time. They are delicious to eat. Once I was out shepherding and I came across a nest. So, I gathered up the eggs, put them in my hat, and brought them home. 562. We boiled them and ate them with salsa. Though there was only one for each person, we ate them. They don't cause any harm to people. They feed on the seeds of wild plants such as chicalote, and quelite verde. They also eat garambullos, and they sing the most during the spring. They nest twice a year.

563. No one catches them for sale. They are always caught to be cooked and eaten fried. It is plump and has a lot of fat which runs off when it is fried. There are a lot of them because many are born every year. They are everywhere in the Mezquital. This bird hides and protects itself by running, but when it sees it is going to be caught, it flies away. It runs along the ground more than it flies. It doesn't provide any kind of medicine.

564. I can say that its song makes many people happy. It sings with a strong voice, making an echo in the barrancas, and bringing joy to the open country. Sometimes it goes up into the mesquites and sometimes onto the garambullos to sing.

565. The roadrunner.[75] This animal also gets its name in Ñähñu from its song. When the sun is hot, it goes "pu, pu, pu." There are spotted ones, and greys, and oranges. Some are as big as 50 centimeters in length. Its eggs are like a turkey's, but smaller and spotted. It lays two or three eggs at a time, and they take a month to hatch. They look like chicks when they are born. 566. The roadrunner is like the quail; sometimes it moves on the ground, and sometimes it flies. Some hunters told me once that its meat is delicious. These birds are pretty to watch as they go along, because of their crests. Both sexes have the

crest. No one raises them at home because these birds aren't accustomed to living with people. If one brings them to market, they don't get sold.

567. The vulture.[76] Everyone in the world knows about this animal. The vulture lives in the area I'm describing, the Mezquital, and they are thin because they don't have enough to eat. This is the animal that cleans up the valley, because it eats the animals that die, such as dogs, cats, chickens, burros, horses; the vulture eats all of these. It does good, and if it weren't for this bird, the community would stink wherever dead animals were thrown out, and this would bring continuous sickness to the people.

568. Vultures live in the open country, and they band together to eat dead dogs. These vultures I'm talking about are always black, and their heads are bald, stripped of feathers. Of course, we all know that they stay aloft a long time. They go long distances without touching down. They don't do any harm in the monte; that is to say, they don't eat live animals. 569. They never catch live chickens or rabbits. They only eat whatever they find already dead. One can say that they are the "sweepers of the country." We can say that this is true all over the world.

570. Vultures make their nests on the faces of cliffs. They find holes in the cliffs, and this is where they make their nests. They use high cliffs so no one can take away their young. No one hates this animal, because it doesn't do anything bad. It brings life and joy to the place where it lives. 571. There are places where I've seen neither plants nor birds, and the place looks sad. Animals are always useful. Whether it's a forest or a desert, it's the animals that give it life.

No one eats vulture flesh because it is said that it stinks. 572. I know this because a man told me about it who tried it once during the Revolution when the merchants hid all the corn, beans, and other food stuffs. The poor people ate whatever they could find in the monte and on the mountainsides. Sometimes they ate moss off the trees, and barrel cactus meat mixed with a handful of nixtamal. 573. At that time, this man had gone without food for two days, and he was going about the mountains. He saw a vulture perched on some órgano. 574. So he thought about killing it, because he was carrying a slingshot. He was looking for a rabbit and instead he came upon the vulture. He saw the vulture sitting there on the órganos and he said to himself: "Since there's no rabbit, I'll settle for a vulture. I'll give it a try."

575. Saying this, he let go a rock and the vulture fell to earth with a thud and died. He tied it up and took it home to be prepared. He thought it would be delicious. But on trying it, it stank. It made his whole family nauseous. And this is how he knew that the vulture flesh is not good to eat. 576. The thing that made him try it was hunger. That is how it was with many who went through the

They are pretty to watch as they go along

Fauna 566

Revolution; they talk of what they ate at that time. People today don't eat vulture meat; they just see the bird eating dead dogs, and this is enough to keep them away.

577. The vulture always has white excrement. One can always tell where its perches are, because they become white with the excrement. It has a habit of always perching on órganos. 578. It doesn't like other trees; it always likes to perch on órganos. From morning to night they perch on the órganos, taking in the sun. We can't really know why they prefer this plant. I think it is because these plants are the tallest around, and they allow vultures to see long distances. 579. Even though it doesn't attack other animals, it still chooses this plant because it can survey everything. They only perch on órganos to rest during the day, because, as I said a moment ago, at night they sleep in the cliffs. They stay in the small holes in the cliffs where they make their nests from twigs they find among the thorns in the monte. 580. They weave their nests, first putting in the bigger pieces, then lining them with soft plant material to sleep. They don't foul their nests. The tepetate on the cliffs is stained; when they defecate they leave their nests and go outside.

581. How many vultures are there? Two or three are born at a time; this is what we have seen sticking out of the nest. One day, when I was out shepherding with other boys, we had brought our goats together and we were going about in the monte. We felt, from the noise it made with its wings, that a vulture was taking off. 582. It must have kicked its nest hard in taking off, and the babies fell to earth. We were surprised by the noise it made; but after a while we slowly returned from where we had run, and that's how we saw those little vultures sitting on the ground where they'd fallen. We left them there and didn't pick them up because there was no way to put them back; the cliff was high. 583. And this is how I know the number of babies it has.

There is a story about the vulture in Ñähñu. Once a vulture was basking in the sun behind a house and it spoke to a little boy there. The entire story may be seen in the first book of stories, published in 1976 (Bernard and Salinas 1976). 584. There is also a story which tells how the vulture is the skunk's compadre. Once upon a time the skunk wanted to fly. So he said to himself "I want to learn to fly, so I can feel what it's like to be flying. I'll try it, just to see if it's possible." He tried, jumping along, but couldn't.

585. Then he thought of his compadre, the vulture: "He knows how to fly." So he said "I'll go look for my compadre to tell him to instruct me. He knows." So, he went off to look for his compadre, and the skunk asked him to teach him how to fly. 586. He found the vulture and said: "Compadrito vulture!"

"Compadrito skunk! How are you?" answered the vulture.

"I want to ask you a little favor, compadrito. Are you willing?"

"Yes, compadrito. What is it?"

"It's nothing, really, compadrito. It's said that you know how to fly. What I want is to learn to fly, because I notice that one moves more quickly this way."

587. "Yes, OK, compadrito." And for a moment, the vulture thought about how he could do it. Then he said he would teach the skunk how to fly. He took the skunk up for a trial run. Well, the skunk, having never flown before, liked it very much. He asked the vulture to help him the next day. But the vulture was already planning what to do with him. On the first day, he took him around, close by.

588. The next day, the skunk was out, looking for his compadre, the vulture, to fly again. He was thinking about asking to be taken out for a longer spin, further away. The skunk said: "What do you say, compadrito? Let's go to Rome. I want to go to Rome. Carry me and let's go. Go straight, so we get there quickly!" said the skunk.

589. The vulture was happy. He was happy because they would go far. "Let's go compadrito! Of course, I'll carry you. But you have to hold on tight to my back."

590. The vulture sat down so that the skunk could get on him. "Grab onto my wings, compadre! Hold on tight compadrito. I'm going to go fast so that we get there quickly. Let's go, straight away!" said the vulture, as he carried his compadre.

591. The skunk was on top, and he said to his compadre: "Don't go sideways, or I'll fall off."

"You won't fall, compadrito. We'll go straight, crossing one barranca after another," said the vulture.

But the paws of the skunk were getting tired, and the vulture was going higher and higher. 592. The paws of the skunk were falling asleep. "I'm going to fall, compadrito. My paws are falling asleep" said the skunk.

"Hold on, compadrito. I'll hurry. Hang on!"

"Ai! I'm falling off! My paws have gone to sleep," said the skunk.

593. The vulture knew that the skunk wouldn't be able to hold on. He made a sharp turn, and the skunk fell off, spinning to earth. Spinning, he fell to the ground. Now the vulture saw that the skunk was dying, so he flew down after the skunk. 594. As soon as he got to where his compadre was lying, the vulture began to eat. He began to peck out the eyes of his compadre. And the skunk, sensing that his compadre was pecking out his eyes, said: "Ai, compadrito, why are you doing this to me?"

And the vulture just said: "While you're still warm, compadrito, I'll eat you. Next time don't ask for help from someone until you know the conditions of the aid."

595. The eagle.[77] There aren't many eagles in the valley area. It's rare to see one. But when they come, they do a lot of damage. They eat the chicks of the hens and turkeys. If it's a large eagle, it will eat the big chickens as well. 596. We've seen them carry off chicks on occasion. Eagles don't just eat chickens, but also hunt rabbits to eat. They also eat mice when they find them. These eagles are the same color as falcons. Sometimes, black eagles come. But these come from outside, only; they don't live in the valley.

597. Eagles are eaten. I haven't tasted eagle, but I've been told about it by persons with whom I've gone rabbit hunting. They said that its meat is very good in barbacóa. 598. One day, we were out hunting and we saw an eagle flying around close by. My friends said to me: "Shoot it! It's meat is very tasty in barbacóa."

I asked them: "But, isn't it foul smelling, like the meat of the vulture?"

599. "No," they said, "you just have to prepare it well. First it must be washed thoroughly. Then you grind up chiles with all the other spices. These are mixed together, and wrapped in maguey leaves. Then it is all put in the ground to roast. When it's cooked, it's like eating chicken," they said. This is how I know that eagles can be eaten.

600. The eagle makes its nest in the great steep cliffs. Sometimes it nests in trees, too, but far away, so that people can't get to them. I think it's good that they catch mice, because those mice eat the seed and seedling in the fields that people plant. When this happens, the farmer's work is useless. 601. The eagle eats small snakes, too, although snakes also help farmers by catching mice in the fields. But people don't like snakes very much, because snakes frighten them. 602. Sometimes, snakes such as the rattler bite people, or, in the case of the chirrionera, they whip people. Eagles can't multiply because whenever people see them they hunt and kill them for the harm they cause. It isn't good for people to hurt animals.

603. The metorito.[78] Very old people used to say that this was the rat which first showed them how to scrape magueys for aguamiel. People didn't know how to make pulque, or to drink it. It is said that some people were going around the country, and they saw a maguey with a hole in it. 604. It had a hole in its center and contained some liquid. Possibly they were thirsty. Anyway, one of them, it is said, tried the liquid they had found. 605. He noticed that it was sweet and he finished it off. In those days there were a lot of really big magueys with a lot of aguamiel. Those people wanted to know who had made the hole, that is,

He began to peck out the eyes of his compadre

Fauna 594

who had bored it out. They looked around and saw that a field rat came to drink aguamiel, too. This is how they knew it was probably the field rat that had dug out the hole in the maguey. 606. This was when they learned that magueys produce aguamiel. Afterwards, the people scraped the maguey. They knew how to break the heart out of the maguey and make pulque; but the people always thank the field rat because it was the first to scrape the maguey. People in olden times used to tell about this.

607. Nowadays people really don't believe this, because now pulque is made in a different way. I have personally seen a field rat scraping away at the base of the maguey heart. I have found small magueys which the field rat has operated on in this manner. But the small magueys don't give aguamiel. Once there was a time when I was out herding animals. 608. I saw, among a row of magueys, a plant which had been bored out by a field rat. It had aguamiel and I was thirsty. Seeing that it was giving aguamiel, I knew it had been bored out by a field rat. 609. I looked for a piece of wooden reed which we call "nts'ii." This is hollow, and can be used like a straw to suck up water or any other liquid.

610. Well, with this straw I drank it all. It contained about half a liter. And now, knowing where there was aguamiel, every day, when I was thirsty, I would go to that maguey to drink. The rat scraped it out, and I drank the aguamiel. 611. This may have disturbed him, but anyway he abandoned the maguey and I couldn't drink any more because my "assistant" got mad at my finishing his work.

612. I got to thinking about how he could scrape like people do, morning and afternoon. He bored and threw the scrapings away from the heart of the plant. He didn't use a metal scraper or an acocote, just his teeth and claws.[79] This creature still scrapes the magueys he finds in the open country. He doesn't do the magueys in the milpas, because the people scare him off.

613. This is the type of rat which is eaten. It is said that its flesh is tasty, but I've never tried it. It can easily be eaten because it is a big kind of rat. It weighs about a quarter kilogram. It has big whiskers, and has a very long, bald tail. It generally lives where there are piles of rock, where it makes its nest and gives birth to its young. 614. It moves about day and night, carrying thorns to put in its den. The thorns are from darning needle cactus, and tunas de coyote; it cuts and gathers other thorns, too, wherever it finds them. It makes a big pile of these, possibly so that no other animal will enter its nest. 615. Sometimes, it makes its nest on the garambullos; but it mostly likes to live among rocks.

616. It feeds on garambullos and on hearts of magueys. During times of heavy drought it eats plants, branches, and the tunas of the purple prickly pear cactus, along with tunas de coyote, compite, and nopal pads. 617. During the

planting season the field rat digs up peoples' corn, but doesn't do much damage. This animal is grey in color and has longer hair than the ordinary rat. They don't generally live in houses, but they do come in once in a while.

618. People kill them by hitting them with sticks. Then they are skinned. Sometimes they are roasted, sometimes fried and they are eaten with salsa, even though each person only gets a little piece. 619. Some time back, I recall that during Holy Week, beginning on Thursday and ending on Saturday, men would get together and hunt field rats. There would be about six men, or however many wanted to go out hunting. Each person prepared his own long stick, about two brazadas in length, and made a point on one end to stab the animals. 620. They took their pulque along, and went out for the whole day in the countryside, yelling and carrying on as they went. They made even more noise when they saw a rat, running it down until they killed it. They had a fine time, passing the day by telling jokes.

621. "Look there goes a rat, you son of a bitch," one would say to another who didn't see it.

"Where did it go? I'll stab you."

"Your sister will prick me, you idiot."

"I'm an idiot for not fucking you."

"I'm not a wall for you to screw."

"You'll be my dog."

"You show me how."

"I'll teach you to hunt."

"Well, here we are."

"I'm not a rope that you can take with you."

"I'm not your burro."

"Did you say cunt?"

"I said prick."

"Bite it!"

"Aren't you ashamed to ask for prick?"

"I'll give it to you slowly."

"You'll give me your ass."

"I'll give you my balls."

"I want you to give me twins, as you said."

"Make me tortillas, you idiot!"

622. They would practically drown in laughter,[80] and then they would start again. "Clean up your mouth for me, like you said."

"Why did they mess yours up?"

"Your sister got me dirty when I had her."

"You fucked the rocks in the road."

"You're the one who gets fucked in the road."

"You're the one who follows the road like a dog."

"Have I, by any chance, gotten your face dirty?"

"I'll get on you whether you like it or not."

"Get on the pole."

"I'll put it in you."

"Put your chin on the fence."

"You're talking about your burro, cabrón."

623. And so they go all day. They may not kill anything on the hunt but they are happy just from going out together, and the others in the group who aren't involved directly in exchanging these foolishnesses are also happy from the laughter. When the sun gets strong, or they are thirsty, they look for a shady place to rest and drink their pulque. And then they begin again the exchange of insults and jokes.

624. They go along talking of many things, sometimes animals, and sometimes sisters. If, by chance, they kill a rat or a rabbit, they return home. They tell their wives to roast the animal they found. Sometimes the men do it themselves. 625. On the last day of Holy Week they say "We have met and gone out together. Let's hope that next year God will give us health and life to go out again."

"Let's hope!" say the others. 626. They say this because they really do get together each year for a day or two to pass a moment of happiness together. Then, when the fiesta is over, each goes back to his own work. 627. Certainly, they meet one another on other days, but not to go out together all day like they do in Holy Week. This is how some animals that live in the countryside help the people to pass their lives.

628. Field rats live all over the valley. They don't eat other animals. Snakes eat this rat wherever they find them. The casera snake eats rats whole. Some time ago, I saw one that had eaten a rat whole. It had a bulge in its stomach. My father and I helped each other to kill it. This snake also eats birds, not just rats. When we killed it, we removed the animals it had eaten, and that's how we know.

629. Snakes. Different snakes live all over the valley; some are big and some are small. Also, there are different colors. There are black ones, yellow ones, blue ones, and brown ones. There are some that go up into the trees; others like to go into houses. Those that go into houses frighten people. Still others bite. Some race along and others are slow.

630. Here I will just mention all of them, but afterwards I'll describe them one by one, because they don't all live at all times of the year. Some come out during the hot season; others after the cold season begins. This is why I will mention them one by one.

631. Chirrionera.[81] This is one of the fastest snakes, especially when it sees someone coming. It is very intelligent. When it really gets going fast it goes along making a hissing sound, the same as swinging a pole through the air. Its body is blue and its tail is red. From this comes its name in Ñähñu, "red tail." 632. They are abundant from March to August. One can see its tracks where it's been; the tracks are smooth. Everyone in the valley knows that snakes have cold blood. This is thought to be true because they only appear when the sun is hot.

633. They go into house roofs when they are hunting mice. They go right into where people sleep. They stay there and sleep, too. They run out when people shake out clothes, and this is how they frighten whoever finds them. There are times when people who are frightened by a chirrionera have gotten very sick. 634. There have been people who have died of the fright—not right away, but they slowly stop taking food, and get sicker and sicker. If they aren't cured quickly, they die. But those who know get cured. Some eat sugar.

635. There is a medicine sold in the city called "'ret'amä'rato," or "sixteen." Many people know about it and say that it's very good for susto. This is taken in a fast, at four or five in the morning. There is no set dose. Some take half a topo, others a whole topo.[82] 636. There are two kinds of this medicine. One is for adults, and the other is for children. Since it is made from aguardiente it makes those who take it dizzy. The one taken by children isn't very strong. But the one taken by adults is really strong. If the children don't want to take this medicine, then it is daubbed all over their body. 637. Then they are wrapped up well so they'll sleep. This medicine is called "'ret'amä'rato," or "sixteen" in Ñähñu, but in Spanish it is called "espíritu."

638. It is called "sixteen" because it is said that to make it they mix 16 medicinal herbs. Then the herbs are put in the aguardiente so that, slowly, the force in the herbs will come out. What I don't know exactly is how many days the herbs must be in the aguardiente to mix up right. 639. It is sold in drugstores for a peso or two. Those who buy it ask for a sample first in order to see if it's all right. If it's good, then they buy it; but if not, then they'll go and look for it elsewhere. It is pinkish in color, and sometimes reddish brown. 640. On Mondays one can see many people carrying empty bottles around, and this is what they are looking for. The susto caused by a snake is very bad.

Sometimes this snake goes into houses because it is following mice. It goes in their holes to catch them. After it eats something it doesn't move very fast.

641. Sometimes it is in the ceramic urns in the house, coiled up there. Sometimes it is up in the thatched roof, and you can tell this because the mice shriek. 642. If you see a snake, you blow cigarette smoke on it. One lights a cigarette and blows smoke on the snake. This makes it groggy and it doesn't run, and then it can be killed.

643. It lives in holes when it bears its young. Otherwise, it goes about on the surface of the ground. They are found at the foot of trees, and at the base of magueys which are no longer being scraped. This snake flies between trees. When it is among birds, it goes from one tree to another by flying. 644. It is very bad for women who are pregnant. It hates them a lot. When this snake meets a pregnant woman on the road, it doesn't let her pass, but makes circles around her. There have been cases where the snake has whipped such women. It stands upright like a pole. 645. Then it throws itself and whips the person. This really doesn't hurt, but it frightens people. Sometimes, the babies of the poor women who have been whipped are miscarried because of the susto. 646. So, whenever people see this snake, they look for a big stick right away to beat it so that it won't do anything. But if it meets a man on the road it runs away. It doesn't confront him. And when a woman isn't pregnant, the snake doesn't stop her as it would if she were pregnant. 647. People say that the snake probably hates the child that's inside. No one knows the exact motive. These snakes are killed wherever they are found, because they frighten people a lot.

648. One can touch snakes after they've been killed and feel their bodies are cold. This is why it can be said that they have cold blood. Some people say that touching a snake makes one's skin peel off. I can attest that this is not true, because once I and some other children killed one and I wrapped it around my hand. Nothing happened and my hand didn't peel. 649. Those who saw me said that I would wind up with skin like a snake's on my hand.

This snake changes its skin at the beginning of the hot season. The old skin is called "kwisi." It does this every year. Sometimes it leaves its skin in the trees, and sometimes on the ground where it has passed. Other times, it leaves the skin in the hole where it lives. 650. This snake skin is used in medicine for whooping cough and evil eye, also called, simply, "eye." This evil eye in which snake skin is used is different from the evil eye in which the person gets bloodshot, bleary eyes. In the former, evil eye children are afflicted after someone has laughed at them. This is the evil eye in which one mixes snake skin with medicinal herbs for the smoking procedure discussed earlier when speaking about the coyote. 651. For whooping cough, however, some people hang a piece of snake skin, along with other medicines like red ants, around the neck.

There is a kind of large red ant which comes out after really hard rain. Those who know about this gather them and dry them, so that when they are needed they will be available. 652. Some people hang these ants in their doorway, along with zábila and cardón blanco, in order to divert mal aire from children who are sick with measles. This is the use made of snake skin.

653. As I said a moment ago, when they are found these snakes are thrown far away so their bones won't do anything bad. When someone gets pricked in the foot by these bones, their foot will swell up with pus, and the bones don't disintegrate in the flesh. This animal is important in the milpas, because it gets rid of mice. The ones that grow big get to be a full brazada in length. 654. Some people, when they find a full, unbroken chirrionera snake skin, give it to a tanner to make them a belt. It looks nice because the stomach part is white, and the back is brown. These are the characteristics of the chirrionera. Sometimes it helps, and sometimes it frightens. It doesn't bite, but only whips.

655. The casera, or "housekeeper snake."[83] This is different from the chirrionera which I mentioned a moment ago. The casera doesn't go fast. It crawls along slowly. Its particular characteristic is that it also likes to go into houses. It goes up into the roofs and hunts mice to eat. It catches them by wrapping its body around them. Then, it eats the mice slowly.

656. Its back is spotted with yellow, pink and brown. Its skin is more beautiful than the chirrionera's. It also grows bigger and thicker. It can coil around a rabbit. I saw it once while I was walking along. 657. It was in the middle of the road. If it hadn't moved, I'd have stepped on it the very next step I took. It was taking the sun, and when it moved off I threw rocks at it. The rocks just bounced off its back because it was big. It was too quick for me; it went off into the thorny brush and I didn't see it again.

658. This snake also sheds its skin every year. When people who aren't afraid to kill it do so, they strip its skin as a belt cover. A belt looks nicer with this cover. It is said that this snake likes milk.

Some day laborers told me that a woman was once nursing her child in her house, and she suddenly got tired and fell asleep. 659. Since the monte was close by, there were animals about. A casera snake was out there. Or perhaps it was in the house and the woman just didn't see it. 660. This isn't known exactly. She lay down for a while, nursing her child, and she soon got tired and fell asleep. She was snoring when her husband arrived. It was about two in the afternoon. The sun was probably hot, and this is why the snake was about. The man arrived and saw his wife asleep. 661. "Something's amiss; something's just not right," the man said to himself. "What could've happened that this woman is sleeping? Something's wrong here." Saying this, he came close to have a look.

662. He looked and he saw the child waving its arms about. He was thinking that it was sucking milk, when he saw something moving that was starting to run. 663. He saw that it was a big snake that was sucking his wife's milk while the child was sucking on the snake's tail. This is why it wasn't crying; the snake had put its tail in the child's mouth to pacify it, and the snake was sucking the milk.

664. The man looked for a stick to scare the snake and separate it from his wife's nipple. The snake was going to run, but the man killed it and woke up his wife to tell her about it. She didn't want to believe it. 665. This is why no one likes the casera snake. It is said that it bites, but it doesn't have venom and doesn't do anything. It is said that it enchants women and makes them fall asleep; then it sucks the milk. Its power of enchantment is to make people fall asleep. It eats mice and birds that it finds in their nests. This snake is also made groggy by cigarette smoke. Even if one doesn't smoke this snake, it isn't hard to kill it because it isn't fast.

666. The rattlesnake.[84] This is one of the many snakes which live in the Mezquital Valley, and is the most dangerous of all, because when it bites someone the person dies. This is because its venom is very strong. When it's going to bite, it coils up. One can hear where it is because it rattles the end of its tail.

667. One day—it was about six in the afternoon—I was out with my father. We were returning from cutting maguey leaves in Naxthey. It was around May because I remember that the afternoon was hot. We were hungry and thirsty. 668. My father said to me "Run, man, and we'll get home to eat." I followed him, running. We used to cross open country and barrancas to go to work and to return to our home. 669. My father had long footsteps, and I followed him, practically running. We came close to a barranca called Barranca de Panteón. It connects with another bigger barranca called Barranca de Agua Potable. 670. We were just going to enter the Barranca de Panteón, just where it dips into the bigger one. That was where the rattler was. As we appeared, it sprang and went to bite my father. God just wanted a pintadera nopal to be there, because that's what took the rattler's strike. It was so strong that the nopal rang out. 671. If it hadn't been there, the rattler's bite would have struck my father.

672. He was carrying an ayate full of ixtle which he had cut that day. He threw it off immediately and picked up rocks to kill the animal. It frightened us a lot. It was already getting dark. Then, after that, he carried a stick to hit the snake if he met it. 673. We lost our hunger with the susto we got from that snake. I was carrying a small load of wood that I had cut. This is how we know that this snake is dangerous. At that time, during the canícula,[85] is when animals become

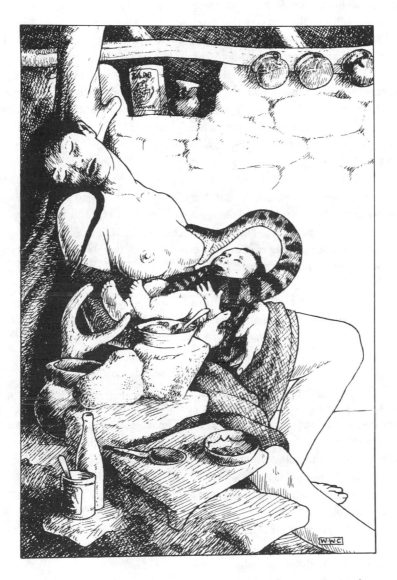

Saying this, he came close to have a look

Fauna 661

active and bold, including snakes and other creatures. 674. Sometimes, even a mosquito bite swells with pus. Ant bites also swell with pus.

675. Out in the valley, that is, in open country, it is rare to find large snakes. Small ones are the most abundant. It is said that the number of rings on the rattler's tail shows the number of years since it was born. In a pueblo called Dextho there lived an old man who had a large rattlesnake skin. 676. He showed me the rattle he had and said, "You know how to count, tell me how many rings there are on the rattle of this rattlesnake." I counted up 32 rings. 677. He was joking with me, because he knew how to count. I asked him "Why do you want me to count it?" "I want you to count it so you'll know how old it is," he said to me. Then I asked him if each ring represented a year. "Yes," he said. "Each ring is one year that it lives. So, the number of rings you counted is its number of years when it died," said the old man, whose name was Tío Bito. 678. He had no children. He and his wife lived alone. He returned the skin to an old disintegrating bag that was hanging on the main crossbeam of the house. He put it away and then told me how he'd found the skin.

679. That old man was a seller of firewood. He bought his corn and other necessities with the money he got from selling the wood. He said to me "Pay attention well." Saying this, he went to fetch about a half cup of pulque and began to drink it a sip at a time. Then he put his cup in a stone molcajete that was there.[86]

680. "Don't you drink pulque?" he asked me.

"Yes, I drink a little" I answered.

"Ah, excuse me, I thought you didn't drink" he said. "Listen!" he said to his wife "bring a clean cup over here, man."[87] The woman went to take down a cup that was hanging on the wall, and she gave it to her husband. 681. Then the man went to fill it with pulque, and offered it to me. "Drink it" he said to me; and saying this, he raised his cup.

682. "With your permission," I said to him. I drank only a little; it was very bitter pulque.

He must have seen me wince and he said "The pulque isn't very good now because the sun is very hot, and the pulque just gets sour. What do you say? I'm going to tell you the story of this rattlesnake."

"All right. Good," I said, and he began.

683. "Once, I'm not ashamed to say, my wife and I had nothing to eat. I would go and cut wood on the mountain; that mountain there," he pointed with his hand. "I saw a big mountain called Dä'tho. That's where I went to cut wood. I had to go to the bathroom, and I squatted," he said. 684. "I was squatting there and I heard something make a sound. I started to look to see what it was, but

didn't see anything. And there was a maguey trunk nearby, which was already scraped out. 685. I heard the same sound again. All of a sudden I saw a pile of something next to the trunk, and it kept making noise. Now I noticed that it was all coiled up and was a snake. I quickly picked up my pants and started to run."

686. He laughed when he said he picked up his pants. He went back to drink a little more pulque and then told me the whole story. "Well, that's how it was. It really scared me. Finished or not with my bathroom needs, I ran. The maguey wasn't far from where I was squatting. It was about a brazada and a half away. 687. I saw that big animal. It was getting ready to bite me. I'm not lying; it had scales on its back and on its head, too. 688. I picked up some rocks to hit it. It got mad and started to bite the rocks, and I threw more at it. Even when it was near death, it still struck at the plants there. Anyway, I subdued it and killed it, and since I was scared I didn't go on cutting wood. The next day I went back to work, but I took that snake home. 689. I skinned it and on cutting it open I saw it was fat like pig meat. I only cut off the skin and the rattle, and threw away the meat. This is the skin you see there." He showed me a skin that was hanging up by a rope and rolled up.

690. Saying this, he got up and went to get it down and unrolled it and we looked at it. It was more than a hand span in width, and it really had scales on it.

691. "What do you say? If you'll sell it to me, I'll buy it from you," I said.

"Well, what do you think?" he said to me. "I'll sell it to you. What do I want it for?" he said. And he actually sold it to me.

"How much do you want for it?" I asked.

"Give me 15 pesos" he said.

692. This is what I gave him. I took that skin to the teacher's house.[88] I wanted to send it to the tanner's to prepare it for me. But I don't understand what happened next. I had the skin; I don't remember exactly what day it was, but it may have been Tuesday. 693. About the third day snakes began to come. There were different snakes, some large, others small, and in different colors. They didn't come all together, but they kept coming. I killed one in the morning and in the afternoon another came. 694. One time, a little snake startled me. I had gone out on a visit to a house. I returned just about when the sun was going down. I opened the house where I used to sleep. There was a little snake there. Its head was all black, and its body was yellow. 695. When it saw me it stood up and jumped; it wanted to bite me. It jumped about a hand span off the ground. I left to go look for a stick to beat it with. I killed it; and so they came, one at a time.

696. I told some people about it and asked why so many snakes were coming around. One of them said "Maybe there are a lot of mice, and the snakes are at-

tracted to them." "No, there aren't any" I told him. "What could it be then" they said to each other. 697. The days passed and different snakes kept on coming.

698. So now I started to think and asked myself "why?" I went on for about three weeks like this. When it wasn't snakes, it was spiders, like black widows and tarantulas, which came on some days, too. 699. Saturday came. I worked from Tuesday to Saturday in those days. Saturday came and I went home. I took the skin. I had a bicycle and I tied the skin to the handle bars. Since I had to pass through Ixmiquilpan, people who knew me saw me and asked me about the skin. 700. One of them wanted me to sell it to him. "No, I won't sell it" I said. "I need it. I just bought it myself" I said. I took it home to my house. I arrived home and hung it up in my room. 701. I said to myself "Now that I have money, I'll bring it to the tanner to fix it up for me." This is what I thought. I hung it up and left it there.

702. The next day was Sunday and at about midday there was a chirrionera on top of the house. I knew it because some birds were squawking. So I went up to see what it was, and it was a snake. 703. The house is not made from thatch. The walls are made of rough stone and the roof is laminated metal, and the door is iron. I killed that snake and threw it out without thinking anything about it.

704. Tuesday came and I went to work again. I returned the next Saturday. On Sunday I went to the city and my wife stayed home in the house. 705. When I came back she told me that a chirrionera had come into the house again. My older brother had killed the snake. It had frightened my children and my wife. It had tried to whip her. 706. Now I got to thinking and I said to myself "Why? Why are snakes following me?" I was sitting there and suddenly lifted my head up and saw the skin that I had bought. 707. I said "I think that's what's doing it all, because when I didn't have it, no animals came around. I'll get it down and go ask my father about it; maybe he knows."

708. He happened to be in his house. He saw I was carrying that skin. "What's this you're carrying?" he asked me.

"It's a snake skin I bought," I said.

"What do you want that for? It will only attract other animals," he said.

709. "What attracts other animals?" I asked him.

"God only knows why it attracts them. This is what happened some time ago when I killed one and took its rattle to keep it. Afterwards, a lot of snakes came here to the house. I knew that was what it was, and I threw it away, and those animals didn't come back any more. This is how I knew it was those things; I had kept its rattle and its shed skin. 710. The snakes came practically every day. Throw out that old skin. What do you want it for?" he asked me.

711. So now I knew what had happened to me, and I told him that I had killed many snakes and of different kinds. "Yes, that's how it is" he said. So I listened to what he told me, and I gave the skin to the dog. 712. It was difficult for the dog to eat it. Afterwards, no snakes came to my house. I knew well that it was the skin of the rattler that had attracted all the animals. 713. Later, I told others about it. I told some peons who had helped me one time. They said "Yes, it's true, that's how it is. When someone keeps the skin or the rattle of a rattlesnake it attracts other animals. But no one knows why."

714. What I think is that since it is the most violent in its class of animals, the others come to defend it when it is killed. Why is it that the snakes that come to one's house are very angry? 715. Perhaps this is what happens to those who go after snakes. I don't know. Field laborers say that the others of its class smell the odor of the skin, and so they go where it is.

The rattle is hung on the neck of children who have whooping cough and measles, so the disease will progress normally.[89] 716. Musicians use it, too, and put it in their instruments. It is said that the music sounds better. When they go to play at a dance and encounter another group that doesn't have a rattle with them, then whoever is carrying a rattle causes the strings in the other group's instruments to break. 717. Some acquaintances who are musicians for many years told about this. They have experience concerning this matter. They told me that one time they didn't have a rattler's tail with them. 718. It turned out that they were playing with another group hired for the same occasion. The other group probably was carrying a rattle. The strings on the instruments of my friend's group all broke. "Now that we know, we always carry one," they said.

719. There are people who eat rattlesnake. An old man named Ruti once went to a place called La Palma. He was the representative of Orizabita.[90] 720. In this pueblo there is the custom to celebrate the Fiesta del Sexto Viernes each year, and the mayordomos must be named. These mayordomos are named at the "change of the pueblo."[91] 721. This man I'm talking about went to La Palma to remind the mayordomos about when they had to get together and do their shopping for their fiesta. 722. There were several who were responsible for the masses, and others for the music. 723. He got up early one morning. He woke up one of his peons and went off with him. 724. They didn't eat anything, but just went out after they got up. And La Palma was far; about three hours on foot. They got where they were going and the man told the mayordomo what he was supposed to. They finished, paid their respects and were about to return. 725. But since this man was highly respected, they didn't let him leave just like that. They detained him and gave him something to eat. He didn't refuse, but

stayed. 726. They gave them coffee to drink. "Drink your coffee; they are preparing a nice taco for you to eat. How can you return like this without eating? It's a long way back," said the mayordomo. 727. Saying this, the owner of the house took his kit bag and went out.

728. Those visitors thought he was going to bring something back from the store. There was a mountain close by there, and the man carried a forked stick. 729. He came back shortly, wearing his kit bag on his shoulder, and it was full. They saw that it was bulging. 730. And the man of the house said "Relax, relax a while. They'll fix up a nice taco right away and we'll eat it." Saying this, he went to the kitchen to deliver that kit bag he was carrying. 731. They heard the noise of something being thrown into hot lard, and it smelled good. The men thought it was pork that they were cooking. It was cooked, the table was set, plates were put out, and hot tortillas were brought out.[92]

732. Now they began to eat because they were hungry. The man said to his helper "Eat up quickly, man; let's go because it's late and we'll not get back soon." And, since they called him "tío," the helper said 733. "Yes, tío; yes, tío." They were eating hot tortillas, salsa, and the meat that was put there. It was fatty, like pork.

They finished eating and were sitting there with the man of the house. 734. And the man of the house saw that they were done and he asked "Did you like the meat, tío?"

735. "Yes, I liked it and I ate it up. Thank you. What kind of meat is it; it was good and fatty. Did someone kill a pig?" asked the old man, because in Ñähñu the word "zajwa" is used for pig.[93]

736. "No, it's just a 'smooth animal' I brought from the mountain," said the man.

And the visitor didn't know it was a rattlesnake. He thought it must have been a hare or an armadillo, because those animals are smooth on their surface.

737. "Perhaps you don't know what a 'smooth animal' is. The rattlesnake is what we call the 'smooth animal,'" said the man.

When the old man heard that he had been given snake he got nauseous, and was afraid because it was in his stomach. 738. He asked "Do you people eat snake?"

"Yes" said the man of the house. "Yes, hereabouts we eat it. It's very good, like it was the meat of a pig."

"But doesn't it do harm with its venom?"

739. "No, it doesn't do anything. We take off a hand span from the head, and another from the tail, and with this it doesn't do anything" he said.

The old man listened to this, got up, said goodbye, got on the road, and went home. 740. He was nauseous, but he'd already eaten it. He told us this story once, and that's how we know this. Prior to that, we didn't know that this snake, the rattler, is eaten. But it's only in this place that I've heard of this, that is, La Palma. 741. There are no others. They say that to catch it, one uses a forked stick. In this way, pressing hard on the head, it can't bite. That stick is like a small pitchfork.

742. The afternoon snake.[94] There is a small snake that lives in the open country. It is like other snakes. It comes out when the sun is hot. During cold times, it is nowhere to be seen. 743. Its color is like the casera snake's. The afternoon snake has a slightly greyer body. Its back is multicolored with black and grey. The largest are about one and a half hand spans in length. 744. It feeds on small mice. It goes into their dens to catch them. Its belly is swollen when it comes out. It also feeds on insects such as the gallina ciega. They come out when the hot season arrives, and they are everywhere. They go into houses, especially those that are close to the monte.

745. When it encounters a chicken the chicken pecks at it to kill it, but the snake defends itself by biting. 746. When the snake gets angry it jumps or springs. Each spring is to bite; it makes a noise which goes "joä, joä, joä," and opens its mouth to bite. 747. Some say its bite is dangerous. I can't confirm whether this is true or not, because I haven't seen its bite. It is generally found among dried maguey leaves. Once, one of my brothers was sent out to cut fire wood. He went to the milpas to collect the dried maguey leaves. 748. He brought back a large load. When he got back, he unloaded and threw the leaves down. Later, when fuel was needed in the fire, and when the snake felt the heat it came out. Fortunately there were no children seated there, because if there had been, it would have frightened them. This is not the only instance of this; it has happened to others as well. And so, those who collect dried maguey leaves bang them against the ground before bundling them up.

749. I said that it had the characteristic of going out in the late afternoon. During the day one cannot see them anywhere. When the sun goes down they come out to go about. And they *do* go about. 750. You might be going along, and just as you get a pace away from it, it moves and goes away. It doesn't move fast. It can be killed easily. It always goes out during the season when the sun starts to get hot. 751. From September to January there aren't any. It stays in the earth until the cold passes. As we know, during this time many farmers prepare their land, so that when the next year comes, the milpa is ready for planting. 752. Some folks clean up the plant rubble to put in nopales or magueys, and in digging up the old trunks they find this particular snake, the afternoon snake.

753. It doesn't provide any medicine. On the contrary, one must have money to buy medicine. Though it is small, it frightens people. Once, a woman left her small children alone at home and went out. She went out shepherding. She left just one small girl child who was about three years old. 754. It was about four in the afternoon. She went to take one more turn with those goats, and then she returned and penned them up in their corral. The sun still hadn't gone down completely. The corral was in back of her house.

755. As soon as she got home, she penned up her goats, and went to her house. She found her little girl seated there in a nice sunny spot, taking in the sun. The mother thought the child had a toy she was playing with. But then she saw it was a snake that was coiled around the child's leg, and she was very afraid. 756. She didn't cry out in order not to scare her daughter. The mother didn't know how to get it off her daughter. The snake had wrapped itself tightly around the left leg. The little girl saw that her mother had come home. 757. She called to her mother to come and see the "grub." The little girl had never seen a snake, but only knew about grubs. She said to her mother "Look at this grub. It's caught hold of my leg." Saying this, she pointed it out. 758. The mother was afraid it would bite her child's leg. She told her to stand. The little girl stood, and as she stood, the snake fell off. 759. The woman was carrying a stick to kill the snake and the little girl told her mother not to kill it, that it was just a grub and didn't do anything bad. 760. The little girl wasn't afraid though the woman told us that the snake was coiled around the ankle and its head reached the child's calf. It had coiled around twice. This is how animals are; *they* don't know whether they frighten people or not; it is the people that have to be careful of them, not the other way around.

761. The spiny lizard.[95] This animal is distinguished easily and is different from both whiptails and snakes. It is called "tsa'thi" because it goes up into the tree called "t'ähi," or mesquite, and eats its fruit when it is ripe. The word "tsa'thi" is made up of two words. The first comes from "tsa," to bite, and the second from the end of the word for mesquite, "t'ähi." 762. This animal has a multicolored back. There are two or three kinds. One is brown, and one is grey. Sometimes they go up into the garambullos. But they don't eat their fruit; they just go up on them. Their back is colored with black and orange and grey splotches. 763. When they are on the ground and not moving one cannot see them because they blend in with rocks and earth. They like to perch on large rocks to take in the sun. 764. When basking in the sun they close their eyes and sleep. When they hear a noise they move quickly and go into their holes. Their food is the mesquite fruit and insects, such as those they catch in the mesquites

and on other plants. 765. At night they stay in their holes. They dig it out and it is about the same size as a squirrel hole.

766. Their body is bigger than a whiptail's. Some people say that these animals may be eaten. This may be possible because they are fat. They have four feet and each foot has fingers like those of a person. 767. I said that it is different from the whiptail, because the lizard's back is rough. Its roughness is like a rasping tool used in filing down wood. 768. The little "teeth" this tool has are like the roughness of the lizard's skin. The rough skin goes from its head to its tail. Its tail is not very long. Its stomach is kind of white, or between lemon yellow and white. 769. People who have rough hands are told "your hands are like a lizard." Whoever is seen to have rough hands is told that their hands are like a lizard's back.

770. Sometimes it does a bad thing—it digs up the freshly planted things in the milpas. It doesn't eat corn, but looks for the beetle larvae under the germinating corn. Sometimes it digs its holes on the bordos.[96] When the rushes of water come after the rains, they go through the holes and undermine the mounds, and leave a lot of work for the poor people to do. 771. They don't even get their milpas watered because the bordos are made for this purpose, that is, to channel and irrigate the land with the water that comes when it rains.

772. What we have not observed is how long the spiny lizard lives. From what I have seen of them, they last a long time. Casera snakes eat lizards when they finds them. Once my father and I were going along together, spinning ixtle. 773. The house fence was near there, and so was the open country. There was probably a lizard in among the thorns of the fence. My father heard a noise coming from the thorns. I was spinning the malacate and didn't hear. 774. He went back to the edge of the fence. He heard a noise and thought it was a mouse, at first, but since the noise continued he went closer and he saw that something was moving among the thorn bushes. 775. He called to me and told me "Come here!"

"What is it?" I asked.

"Look what's here," he said. I came closer and it was a big snake that was trying to swallow a lizard. It had already swallowed the head and the front paws. It had done half of it. 776. The lizard was struggling; we looked for a stick to kill the snake. We don't know how it did it, but the snake let the lizard out of its mouth and ran off. Meanwhile, that lizard was dying. We left it there. My father said to me "Let's leave it there. You'll see that it will return. It knows where its meat is and will return to take it away." 777. Sure enough, we soon heard a noise, and even though we were there, it came back. It came back twice and didn't let us to beat it to death. 778. As soon as it saw us getting near, it ran off. And since it kept coming back, it eventually killed the lizard. 779. Now my father ordered me to remove the lizard.

"Why? What for?" I asked him.

"Take it out, and we will tie it. You'll see that the snake will be back." That's what we did. He tied a wire to the lizard's leg. 780. Then he tied it to a branch of a mesquite, and we went back to work. My father went back and forth with his ixtle, giving them twists and making rope. A short time later, he heard the noise again. 781. He knew it was the snake. He said to me "Let's leave it alone there so it will eat the whole lizard. In the end it won't be able to do anything with it." Later we saw it and it had swallowed the whole thing. 782. It was trying to get the lizard out again but it couldn't, and we killed it.

When someone throws a rock at a lizard and doesn't hit it, it seems to mock or sneer at the thrower. When it sees that the rock has gone by, it sticks its head up again. 783. It doesn't bite people. On the contrary, it is afraid of people and runs to its hole. It just lives its life and there are no beliefs associated with it by the people. It offers nothing for medicine.

784. The whiptail.[97] It has some lines on its back. Sometimes they are white, sometimes brown. They start at the head and go to its back. Most of its back is brown; it is blue on its sides, and white on its stomach. 785. Its tail is longer than the lizard's, and it also makes its holes. These are narrower because its body is thin, but longer than the spiny lizard's. And it is faster. 786. Both go along without making any noise. When the sun is hot, the whiptail pants. It is worse than the lizard. 787. It digs at the roots of the planted corn, and if no one watches, it digs out a lot of corn. It likes to eat small roots. It sneers at you if you throw a stone at it. It runs to catch the stone and bites it.

788. During the canícula they run all over the place. If one throws a rock at a whiptail it chases the rock and bites it. Since whiptails don't bite, people play with them. They throw little stones at them, and the animals catch them in their mouth. 789. Whiptails don't go up into trees like lizards do. Once in a while they go into houses, but then they leave after a bit. They are accustomed to living in their holes. At school students like to get together and hunt whiptails. 790. They go after them during the recess hour. They shout and run through the thorn bushes after the whiptails. They laugh as they close in on the whiptail. If they get out of the thorns, the whiptails go through the children's legs, and run off. 791. The children go back and forth, pursuing the animals, and sometimes they do kill one. They kill it and bring it to school and start throwing it to their friends. There is a lot of laughter because some are afraid of it. There are many whiptails during the hot season. During the cold season they are underground.

792. They don't slither along like snakes, but rather walk on feet. They have parts of bugs in their excrement. They eat ladybugs, and small gallinas ciegas, scorpions, sopulgids, spiders, and weevils. 793. They scratch the ground with their mouths and not with their paws to look for things to eat. The whiptail also offers no use in medicine.

794. The borer snake.[98] It's been named the borer snake because it doesn't run to hide itself. Instead, it starts poking its head into the ground; it pokes and bores until its whole body goes into the ground. It is completely purple. 795. It is about a hand span in length and no more. We can say that its life develops completely in the ground. When we dig in the earth, that's where it is. It doesn't like to have the sun hit it much; it shuns the sun and runs from it. 796. It is practically not seen during the day; when the sun is hot, around midday, it is gone. One sees it in the morning and when the sun goes down. This is when they come out. It goes along a little bit and then goes back to sticking itself in the ground and goes under rocks. 797. From what can be seen, it likes to live in the shade and this must be because it is transluscent. It is pointed at both ends, head and tail. One cannot see where the smallest ones have their eyes. Chickens eat them when they find them; they eat them in one peck.

798. When anyone bothers these snakes they get angry and try to bite. They throw their heads forward, but one can't even see their mouth. When they don't hit anything they get mad and roll themselves up and tighten their bodies. It isn't known what they eat. 799. If one crushes them, there is a little mud in their stomach. It isn't known if it is mud or an insect called cochinilla.[99] These insects are under rocks and are grey in color.

800. The brown racer.[100] The name it has been given means, in Spanish, that it runs fast when it moves. Its speed is like the wind. Its whole body is brown, with streaks of white which run from head to tail. 801. Its stomach is white, combined with yellow. It lives in the open country, where one cannot see it. It is necessary to really open one's eyes, so that when this snake is running one can spot it, because with two moves of its body it's gone. 802. When it is in an open space one can kill it but if there are thorn bushes one can't even see where it's gone.

803. One time my father and I went out to cut lechuguilla. It was about ten in the morning. We went down a barranca. On the edge of the road something moved and I noticed it. Then I really saw that it was a snake. 804. I told my father right away "there goes a snake!" Saying this, I picked up a rock and threw it at it. That snake was going to cross our path. The rock I threw lifted the snake and tossed it into a clump of cardon blanco. 805. My father threw another rock and pushed it further into the cardones, and we finished it off there. Then he told

me it was the snake of the wind. 806. "This one doesn't bite; it only runs fast,"
he said to me. "It's lucky you saw it, because otherwise it would've gone
through our legs," he said. "Since the barranca isn't wide, it would've beaten us
and gone off."

807. It was approximately a meter in length. From what my father told me,
this is as long as it grows. I haven't seen what this snake eats. It lives where there
are a lot of junquillos, huapillas, and lechuguillas.

808. I saw it another time when I was out hunting with friends at a place
called Iglesia Vieja after the fact that there is a church there built by people long
ago. 809. I was on a perch waiting for the rabbit while the others were doing the
driving. The others were on their perches also. The drivers arrived and there
were no rabbits there. We got together to go somewhere else. 810. One of us
there saw something. He thought it was a rabbit, but it was a snake. It went into
some lechuguillas, and we lost it.

811. It lives over towards Cardonal, Tasquillo, Zimapán, Huichapan, and
Actopan. The people there mention this snake. Like the chirrionera, the rattler,
the casera, the lizard, and the whiptail, it lives in Chilcuautla. It is also dry land
there and this is where these animals like to live.

812. The black snake.[101] Its name is the same as its color. It's as black as coal
on its back, and a little white-ish on its belly. It lives mostly in the sierra.

813. One time we went to Meztitlán. We went along, following the bank of
the river, because this was the road there. We walked along, and we were doing
fine. One man named Tilde knew the place. 814. He knew the way, and we followed him. We were just coming to a pueblo called Ixtacapa. There were some
milpas near there and the hot lands begin there. 815. There is sugar cane, orange
trees, black zapote, and yellow zapote.[102] The river we were following was very
beautiful. The water is white, like someone had thrown lime in it. The water
comes from a place called Tolantongo. 816. This water is very hot. We wanted
to see this place because we hadn't seen it before, and it wasn't anything like our
pueblo. We were coming to a field and, since they are irrigated these lands can
be really well planted. 817. There are fruit trees, and there was a lot of fruit at
the time. So we were going to eat fruit. We were about 20 meters from that
field. So now the man said to us "Look well, because there is a snake that lives
near the retaining wall, and it is a black snake."

818. The retaining wall he told us about was nearby. It was about two meters
high, and about 40 meters long. We knew the black snake is dangerous and we
looked for it. 819. Tilde knew where the snake's lair was because he had been
shown it. We watched the path where we were going, and he looked for the
snake's hole along the wall. 820. Soon he saw it, and he said "Get ready,

They eat ladybugs, scorpions... and weevils

Fauna 792

cabrones! There it is!" We all looked towards the wall. And sure enough, there was the snake on the wall. Tilde said that it was baking in the sun. 821. The path passed close to there, just alongside the wall, and there was no other way for us to get by. Now this man said to us "Let's wait a bit and see if it doesn't go in its hole soon." So we waited. 822. He told us again, "If we pass, it'll chase us." Of course, we were afraid and we didn't pass. We stayed there a long time, and the snake stayed put. It did not go. We were hungry because we had left about five in the morning from Orizabita.

823. It was around one in the afternoon when we encountered that snake. We stayed there about two and a half hours. That snake just wouldn't get away from there. 824. It started to go into its lair, but came back to where it was laying. And it started to get late. We said among ourselves "There's no other way; let's go into the river." We all got undressed and put our clothes on top of our heads, and went in. 825. We didn't want to go into the river because it was deep and there was a lot of water. But, like it or not, we had to cross it slowly. We weren't really enthusiastic about killing the snake. 826. We had heard that its venom is dangerous, and that it squeezes and crushes whatever it grabs. Tilde told us that the man who owned the land didn't want to kill the snake, because he didn't want people getting to the fruit trees and eating the fruit, even though it is said that the snake had chased the owner himself once. Everyone from around there, big and small, carries a machete in a sheath when they go to the mountains. 828. They always carry a rope and a machete, because there are many snakes there and their venom is dangerous. Wherever they go, they carry a machete in their hand, and they cut the vegetation as they go along. They sharpen the machetes really well. Wherever they cut its like the vegetation was wiped away.

829. These snakes live in the area comprising Orizabita, Boxuada, Naxthey, La Palma, El Cerro de la Muñeca, El Cedral, La Lagunita, El Banxu, Tasquillo, Portezuelo, El Alberto, and over towards Alfajayucan, and Patria Nueva, but they are small snakes. They barely reach three hand spans in length. When people see them, they kill them right away. They kill them because they know the venom is dangerous.

831. One time, I was walking along a barranca. I had returned from hunting rabbits and it was getting dark, and since it was getting dark, I could scarcely see. I was going along and when I looked down I saw something moving. 832. Since gravel is black, it looked like it was gravel moving. I went a little closer to get a better look. It was rolled up and it tried to spring and bite me. I immediately jumped backwards. I saw it was a black snake. 833. I put down the rifle I was carrying and picked up rocks to throw at it. With the first stone I threw the snake struck again. It got so mad it twisted and coiled up again; it tried to do

something. 834. About the third stone I threw, I managed to hit it in the head, but it got even madder, and started to bite the rocks. I looked for a much larger rock which I dropped on it and it died.

835. Now it was night and I could barely see where I was going. I went home, and very early the next day I got up to go see it. When I got there, I saw that it was, indeed, a black snake. Its color is like dried, rotten branches, that is, black. 836. They live where there are lots of thorns. It appears that they like to go about mostly at night because they come out of their lairs only when it is late. 837. They don't grow very big in the valley, possibly because they don't have a lot to eat and because people kill them. Or it may be because the ground is cold. It's not like it is in Meztitlán. The ones there really grow big, reaching a length of two brazadas and they are much thicker.

838. There once were some traveling salesmen. Some time ago the inhabitants of the Mezquital went out carrying trade goods to sell in the mountains. Sometimes they carried jugs, casseroles, jars, and ropes. These were things that sold most where they went. 839. They sometimes drove one or two burros. Sometimes they loaded themselves with a tumpline. They carried their food with them also. They carried their own plates and pitchers to make their meals on the road. 840. Well, those men I'm talking of went around carrying their wares on their backs. They were caught late one night in the middle of the forest. They couldn't see their way and they couldn't go on.

841. One of them said to his fellow worker: "What are we going to do, man? It's gotten to be night and we can't see the way. It's dangerous and we could fall here in the mountains."

"Yes, man!" said the other. "What do you say? Let's find a place to stay. In the morning, with God's help, we'll continue our trek again." That's what they said to each other. 842. "I know where there's a cave and we can stay there and sleep," continued the second man. "And it's not far from here."

"Let's go, then," said the other. So they went, the first man following the second one who knew where the cave was.

843. They arrived and each one let down his pack. They left the packs at the entrance of the cave. They each took off their ayate and spread it out as a bed. They used their sombreros as pillows. A long time ago there were many people who wore sombreros woven from palma. 844. They were sewn together with special ixtle thread from the small lechuguilla. Those sombreros are called "xamti," or alfajayucans, because the people who make them to sell are all from Alfajayucan. It must have been about nine at night when those men lay down to sleep. Since they were tired, they fell asleep immediately.

845. Around one in the morning, one of them got up, and felt that something was pushing against him. He didn't say anything because he thought his friend was dreaming and thrashing. He said to himself, "Poor man, he must be tired out." He turned to cover himself to go to sleep. 846. But he felt, again, that something was pushing at him continually. So he said to himself, "He probably aches somewhere and it makes him move around." He said, "What's the matter, man? Where does it hurt?" And he felt that the man was moving. 847. He didn't answer so he asked him again. He asked him three times, and the man didn't answer.

848. Now he began to be afraid. Something kept pushing and pushing on him. He couldn't see because the cave was dark. He was very afraid and he said "It looks to me like this isn't my friend. He doesn't answer me." He began to touch the man's body and he felt something rough. He got even more afraid, because he knew that whatever was moving around wasn't his friend.

849. He had touched the chest and head, and he felt something strange. He searched for some matches so he could see. He saw a great bulk, with shining eyes. "Holy Mother of God! You're a creature of God or the Devil" he cried. Taking nothing with him, not even his blanket, he got up and ran out, because he saw his friend being eaten by a snake. 850. It had swallowed his friend's head. It was a big snake, so big it had scales on its head. He wasn't carrying anything to defend his companion, and he was afraid because the snake was so big. He had felt its head. 851. He left the cave, and went up into a tree where he tied himself up with his belt, and waited there until dawn to continue on his way.

852. At dawn, he waited for other travelers so he could return with them. Slowly, he told them of what had happened. The others told him they were going to look in the cave. But that man didn't want to go in because he was very afraid. 853. When he got back to his own land, he told the man's wife that her husband had been eaten by the snake. He lost his wares and also lost his friend.

In this way, it is known that there are large black snakes in the mountains. 854. Just as in this story, there are other people who have been bitten by black snakes. Others have been whipped; others chased. I have seen other people, in other lands, who keep snakes. They are big snakes which people allow to curl over their hands and their backs.

855. The horned lizard. [103] This animal looks a bit like the spiny lizard. It is like the spiny lizard in form; its back is rough like a spiny lizard's and it has little horns on its head. The horned lizard isn't very fast, and can be caught when it is running. It can be caught because it does not bite. 856. I've seen that some people keep them in their house. The horned lizard has a broader, flatter back than the spiny lizard's. It lives in the desert. It doesn't move when it is poked,

He saw a great bulk with shining eyes

Fauna 849

but just keeps its eyes open. If someone is drunk, it is said that they have eyes like a horned lizard, because they can't move them easily.

857. The horned lizard has an unusual trait. It changes its color. It takes the color of the place it is in. When the earth is light colored, this is the color it takes on. If it is brown, then likewise; it takes on this color. In this way, it is difficult to find them. 858. Once, I was out in open country, collecting firewood. I was piling up the wood that I had cut. There were some plants there that we call "hierba fria." 859. I went over to pick up a piece of wood that was near the plants. As I came closer to pick up the wood, it went running off to get away. I had been standing there for some time. The horned lizard has four feet like the spiny lizard.

860. On another occasion, I went with a truck to bring a load of red stone from a place called Golondrinas. I went with two helpers. We loaded up quickly because the rock was already piled up. We only had to load, and we finished quickly. 861. My helpers had brought along their pulque. They sat down to drink it, and I went for a walk out of the barranca. I walked along looking at the vista. There I was, looking at those beautifully colored rocks. Some were red, others a pretty pink color. 862. I wanted to sit down for a moment, and I noticed that something ran off, away from me. When I took a good look, I saw that it was a horned lizard. It was the same color as those rocks. Its back was reddish with a little brown, just like the rocks.

863. I called to those who were going with me, and showed them this thing. They helped catch it, and we took it along with us. One of them took it to the market to sell, but I don't know how much they paid him for it. 864. I know that they don't do anything bad. They have rough scaly backs. Those men started to play with the lizard, throwing the animal back and forth to one another. They played and told jokes.

865. The horned lizard feeds on insects. It eats mosquitos, flies and small spiders. It sits and sticks its tongue out to catch these insects. It doesn't move. It just waits until these little creatures come to its mouth. 866. When it feels an insect is near, then it catches it with its tongue. As soon as it feels it has caught one, it puts its tongue back, and the insect goes with it, and it eats it. 867. The horned lizard is lazy. It doesn't chase around looking for its food, it just waits for its food. Perhaps this is why it appears to be lazy. 868. This animal is not hated, because it doesn't bother anyone. It always goes around in the open country, searching for its own food. If someone bothers it, then it gets angry. 869. When it gets angry, the little horns on its back stick up. The roughness on its back is what it uses as a defense. They say that these creatures are most abundant around Alfajayucan. 870. We haven't seen if it makes a burrow. It must be

protected now in order to preserve it, because it is slowly becoming extinct. There aren't many anymore; just a few years ago one could go out in the country and find them. But now that is no longer so; one can walk two or three days, and find just one.

871. The raven.[104] This is possibly the blackest creature in the valley. Its body is totally black. It is a brilliant black. Its beak is black, as are its feet. It is totally black and has no other color combined with it. 872. It lives in open country, searching for its food. It feeds on corn when it finds it. It will take a whole new ear in its beak and take off. It goes off to find a place to sit and eat it. It pecks at it a little at a time, as if it were a chicken eating corn.

873. It moves its wings to fly. It isn't like the vulture that just stretches its wings out. One distinguishes whether it's a raven or a vulture from the manner of flight.

874. The raven is not bald. The vulture looks like it has a red head, because it is bald, and people call it "baldy." 875. The vulture has transparent wings when it extends them to fly. The raven is not like this, but has dark, opaque wings. It, too, makes its nest in the cliffs. 876. Everywhere it flies it squawks, saying "kaa, kaa, kaa." This is why it has been given the name "kaa" in Ñähñu. It doesn't do bad things to people, nor do people like to hunt it because its song is not pretty. 877. Most people don't like its color, because it is too black. But, like other animals, it is necessary. Even when there are no beautiful birds in the desert, or in the great areas of denuded rock, at least one hears the cry of this creature and is happy, because one does not feel alone.

878. The snail.[105] The desert has its own, special kind of these animals. They are different from the ones that live in irrigated lands. The dry zone has a snail which is different from the irrigated zone. 879. None of these grow well if they are in environments other then their own. The irrigation land snail dies when there isn't much moisture, and the desert snail dies from too much moisture. 880. The ones in the irrigated zone multiply more quickly because they have a lot to eat. There are many there, and they say that they help in the fields by eating insects that would be bad for the useful plants like beans, corn and tomatoes. 881. The snail eats up the insects which threaten the plants.

The irrigation land snails are out when it's cool. They all come out to go around in the early morning, and in the late afternoon, and all night. The snail puts out its saliva and then slides along to move. When someone touches it, it rolls up and gets into its shell. This is how it hides itself; it sits there like it was dead.

882. This snail has two little horns on its head. It is thought that this is what it uses to find its food. And, indeed, this is how it is. When it moves, its horns

move as if it were feeling its way along. 883. When it senses that it cannot pass, or that it's too rough for it to slide over, it turns off and goes in another direction. Its saliva looks sticky. Dead snails are stuck on maguey leaves, or on some other plant, and if you pull them off the skin of the plant comes off, too. 884. One can tell where an irrigated land snail has passed because it leaves a trail of its saliva.

If we compare this with the desert snail we see that the desert snail is bigger. Also, the snails come in different colors. The one from the irrigated lands is slightly yellow, combined with black on what we can call its back. 885. We see it stuck to maguey leaves all the time, and on plants, and on the stems of grasses. Men have made up verses about it, because it isn't bad. 886. We know that there is a type of snail eaten by mestizos. We can't say whether they are the ones that live in the irrigated lands, or the ones that live in the ocean because these are also called "tsimxi" in Ñähñu. 887. They are also larger than the ones I'm talking about here. They come in different colors, including white, pink, and brown. Their shells are much larger, too. But there are also those which are much smaller and live in the sea. 888. The snail that lives in the desert has a different colored shell. It is somewhere between grey and white. Others are brown. There are other little creatures that are a bit more blackish, combined with yellow. 889. They live amongst the junquillos, lechuguillas, and sangre de grado.[106] They come out only when it rains. When moisture really penetrates the earth, that is, when there are two or three strong rains, they come out to go around on the ground. 890. But when there isn't any rain they remain hidden in the shadows where there is some moisture. These snails seem to be very hardy, because there have been whole years without any rain and when the rains finally arrive the snails appear once more.

Their shell reaches about four fingers in length, and is about two fingers wide. 891. The widest part is where the head of the animal comes out. On the end, at the part we can say is its tail, it comes to a point. Since it doesn't run fast, it eats black ants as it comes on them. 892. There aren't many of these animals; it is rare to find one. It moves in the same way as the other snail; that is, it slides along, little by little, on its saliva. Sometimes, when it comes out of where it is hiding, farmers see them. They say that seeing a snail means that rains are near.

893. They start to come out in May. But what they are really doing is going somewhere else, searching for a place where there is moisture. 894. Old women and men also say that snails mean rain is coming. The people who are old are very observant about the weather. Usually, what they say is true; when they say it's going to rain, it rains. And if they say it will freeze, it freezes. Since they have lived many years, they have observed what goes on in nature. 895. To make their predictions, they observe the vegetation, animals, sun and moon.

It feeds on corn when it finds it
Fauna 881

Sometimes, when their body aches, they say it will rain. There are so many beliefs which we will see when we look at religion. 896. There are no bad beliefs about snails.

Some people who find them on the road put them off to the side so that nobody will step on them and kill them because, as I said a moment ago, it is believed that they help bring moisture and rain. No part of its body is used for medicine. 897. The hardness of its shell is the same as that of the irrigated land snail. But the ocean snail has a much stronger shell. When a campesino finds a snail he looks for a place to put it, such as a mesquite. He doesn't want to break it because campesinos believe that snails call up the rain. 898. Campesinos really need rain for the growth of maguey, lechuguilla and nopal plants. These are the plants which give him subsistence.

Some sheep have twisted or coiled horns and are called "snails" because this is the shape of the snail shell. Many people like to have these sheep because they have snail-shaped horns.

899. Insects.[107] We have finished looking at some of the large animals that live in the desert. We looked at and learned the way each of them lives, the beliefs of the people about them, and the uses each one has. 900. We have also seen that some of them are slowly becoming extinct because of lack of knowledge about how to preserve them. We have wiped out the animals that are eaten, without giving any thought to whether or not they will reproduce. It is important to heed the advice of the scientists who say that we must protect the animals as much as the trees so that they won't become extinct. 901. If we don't listen to this advice, the day will come when we will finish off all those animals. By the time we get around to thinking about it, they will be gone. Of course, we must get rid of creatures that don't do us good, but rather do us harm. 902. In this way we can improve our lives, little by little. Many of the insects we will look at here do bad things to us. We will look at them, one at a time, in the same way we did with the larger creatures. Thus we will see how they are named, what they do to us, and if they help us or not in medicine, farming or in growing trees. 903. We will look at the way of life of each one. I'd like to clarify the fact that this book only describes the exterior of the animals. For the internal systems we really need a Ñähñu scientist who knows the life of these insects to really understand them. 904. We therefore explain now to those who read this, that the insects are described superficially.

905. The fly.[108] This is the creature, the insect, most hated by people in the Mezquital. Surely this is true in other places, too, and not just here, for they live all over the earth. They generally live where there is filth, which is their principal food. They sit and rub their front legs together, and then they stick out a

kind of tongue, and with this they lick filth. 906. Thus they flit around all over the place, coming to rest on the nostrils of some persons. When it isn't pestering people, the fly bothers animals, any animal it can. Sometimes they pester dogs by lighting on their noses. Dogs snap at them and sometimes they catch them and eat them. When they don't catch them, the teeth of the dog can be heard snapping.

907. There are people who observe dogs and if they hear someone make a noise with their teeth, they joke about it in this way: 908. "Your teeth are making noise. I think you're eating flies." In this way he is calling the other person a dog.

The one who was called a dog responds: "I'm going to bite you."

"You'll bite me but I'm not a bone."

"I'll hurt your bones."

"I'm not a burro for you to hurt my bones."

"You're the one who takes my strength away."

"I'm not a plow to take away your strength."

"I'm not your ox."

"I'm your ox and I'll chase you to screw you."

"You can screw me but I'm not a zacate."[109]

"I'll take it out of you."[110]

"Take your tongue out for me."

"We'll put it back in."

"Put back your food."

"Make it for me."

"I'll make a child for you."

"You're the hijo de la chingada."

"I say it to you."

"You're saying it to me, but I don't want to now."

909. And thus they go along talking and laughing. But they are careful that children and women don't hear this. The people who tell these jokes are all men, and it is rare to hear women saying these things. This is the kind of fun that men have.

910. The fly is very dirty. It comes and goes wherever there is filth, and then goes to rest on foods. It touches the food people eat; people eat the food, and this is where sickness starts. Sometimes this insect lives in the stomachs of dead dogs. When it comes out, it goes to the houses. 911. Dead dogs are very dirty. They stink more than anything else. Sometimes dogs die by themselves. Sometimes they are killed because they are rabid. They have a disease called rabies. This is the most dangerous thing for people. This is where flies are often found.

When they leave this place, they go to houses. They land on people's hands and faces. Many people don't know about this, yet. That is to say, they don't know that this is the creature that carries disease to people.

912. Sometimes a fly will fall right into the food one is eating, like bean soup, sopa de pasta, and salsa. The person dips his tortilla, and just scoops out the fly and throws it away. Then he eats the food. We can say that he is eating the disease. 913. He sees it in there, but doesn't know about it. Others just don't believe that an insect can kill them. 914. These people are correct, in their own way, because they haven't had any education. They have not gone to school and don't know how to read a book, and so they don't know about these things, such as where the diseases come from that infect the society.

915. The house fly[111] is the most abundant. These flies light on anything sold in the market which is not covered, like fruit that has been cut up to sell by the piece. 916. The same holds for meat put out on tables and sideboards for sale. During their mating season, they light in pairs on served food. They are born during the hot season. They lay their eggs wherever there is moist garbage and are born there. But when they breed in houses, they "hang" their eggs on flat surfaces. 917. There are people who believe that when flies light on their plates this means bad luck is destined to come from this food. It can not be known for sure whether this is true or not. The fly I'm speaking of now is the first kind of fly. We will see how many other kinds there are right away. They are also born where there are piles of cattle dung; when it is humid, they like to go there and live.

918. The green bottle fly.[112] This is one of the largest flies. Its entire body is a brilliant green. One can always tell when it's around because it buzzes very loudly. When it goes into a house, you can find it and kill it because it goes buzzing around all over the house. They must be killed in order to stop them from depositing their larvae in babies' ears. They will do this to adults, too, if they find them sleeping. 919. These flies are the least abundant. They only go into houses when something smells rotten. There are days when a chicken is killed for the family to eat; then, like someone had called the greenbottle fly, it comes and lights on the meat.

920. The green bottle fly doesn't live just anywhere; it goes where there is meat, and lays its eggs there. After a day or two, these larvae grow up and are called "donxi" in Ñähñu. They are a kind of white grub-like insect. If they are allowed to develop normally, they will eat up the meat and they look really ugly. They make one nauseous and disgusted just to see them boring through the meat. 921. The flies keep moving around, and each time they light they lay 40-50 eggs. There is a custom that when one kills a goat, one cooks the head

separately. The head has a special flavor and so it is cooked separately. Anyway, one looks for a place on the patio where there is sun so the head can dry out. 922. By the time it is taken down, the green bottle fly has already deposited its larvae in the mouth, eyes, and in the cavity where the neck is separated from the body. When this happens the head is thrown into the fire so these grubs will be burned up. Then salt is put on the head so the fly won't come and deposit eggs again.

923. Sometimes the tripe, lungs and liver are put aside, too. They are cooked separately and spiced in a special way. The tripe is dried well, and salted a lot so the greenbottle fly won't deposit larvae on it. The tripe is kept for a month. When it is desired, it is cut up into pieces, washed well, and boiled. A good mole is also prepared and this dish also has a special flavor. 924. Salt is put on meat to preserve it, and in this way, even though the green bottle fly may fly around it, it doesn't deposit its eggs on the meat.

925. When someone dies, people seek a piece of cotton to plug up the nose and mouth so that flies won't enter. There have been times when flies gathered around the body trying to get in as soon as a person died. This is why the fly is dangerous.

And it is everywhere. 926. The people of the valley have an expression for people who show up at fiestas without an invitation. When people notice this, they say "There goes that person who is like a green bottle fly. He's everywhere. He likes to go get a drink of pulque." 927. Of course, this is not really an insult, just an expression. Some people believe that if a person is very sick and green bottle flies swarm around his bed, the person will die. 928. The color of the larvae is white. The body and head of the fly are brown. Wherever the green bottle fly goes, it is dangerous.

929. People customarily neuter their male goats so they will get fat. If the goats are not castrated they run around trying to mate and don't get fat. The eggs of both male and female pigs are removed so the pigs will fatten up. To remove the testicles, one must cut the skin and take them out one at a time. 930. When the testicles are removed, the cavity is filled with ashes, and sewn up. I guess everyone knows in what part of the body they have their testes. The same is done for the female, except that with her one opens a part of the belly, for that is where the eggs are. She is neutered so that she won't have more offspring, and she'll get fat. I repeat: the female as well as the male are opened up, and there is a lot of blood for this reason.

If the green bottle fly shows up, it deposits its larvae in the wound of the animal if the wound has not been properly taken care of. 932. This is where the larvae begin to grow. If the pig's owner doesn't notice it early, then the animal begins to fail, and the larvae grow, eating the animal's flesh. I don't know if it itches or hurts them, but I've seen animals infected with those grubs, and they run around and thrash. 933. So, it is very bad when the flies come to deposit their larvae. To cure the animal you have to take out the larvae one by one and then put on a medicine called "nthots'we" or "criolina," in Spanish. And with this, it gets better, little by little.[113]

934. The biting fly.[114] This one looks like the house fly in color. The wings of the biting fly are more open. It lives mostly where animals such as horses, cattle, and goats are penned. These flies mostly bite the ribs of cattle and horses. During the hot months, parts of these animals appear black from having so many flies on them. They have a stinger which they insert in the animals' skin to drink the blood. 935. When we look at this fly, we see it has blood in its stomach. It always lives on animals. When it gets hot they mass together to drink the blood of cattle. They probably tickle the animals, because the animals stamp around. 936. Very rarely they go into houses and bite people. It itches where they bite and blood comes out. They generally bite hands and feet.

937. It is very quick. It stings and takes off. Its sting is not dangerous; it just itches afterwards. One can tell where it is because it buzzes with its wings. But the buzzing of the blow fly is stronger. The biting fly does not deposit its larvae on meat, or in the cuts made in animals.

938. The vinegar fly.[115] Its name in Ñähñu means "it smells maguey." It probably got this name because it is always going into the magueys to scrape them. This is the first little creature to come and visit the maguey when it is opened. When the maguey begins to produce aguamiel a lot of gnats come around. Each maguey being scraped has about a hundred of these creatures. 939. They come to magueys that are being scraped; they live there and drink the aguamiel because it is sweet. When the tlachiquero uncovers the maguey, the insects get stirred up and come out. They don't bite people; they are small. It's hard to even see them. The ones that live in the fields are clean; but the ones in the city are dirtier. They go and light on dead dogs, and then go sit on food. They surely carry diseases with them.

940. When they fall into the aguamiel they are absorbed. When the tlachiquero puts the aguamiel into the jug or in a barrel he first has to strain it with a strainer made of lechuguilla ixtle, and clean it so that when the pulque is drunk it won't contain gnats.

941. The red fly.[116] This is a big, red fly that goes around everywhere. During the hot season it buzzes around all over the place. It seems to be the fastest of all the flies. Its name is composed of two words. The first means "to follow" and the second means "ant stones." Together they mean that it seeks out rocks. We

call the little stones around anthills "godo" in Ñähñu, and these are gathered by the red fly. 942. Sometimes this fly is sitting there among the stones. One cannot say what they are doing, but I have seen them there, sticking out what we can call their tongue, as if they were trying to lick those little rocks. Then, suddenly they jump and go away. 943. When they aren't on an anthill, they are in the barrancas where there are little stones. When they see people sitting close by, they come near and fly around. They get scared off, but then come right back again. It is said that they are "taunters." If you throw a rock at them, they take off after it. As often as you throw one, they follow it. 944. They like it when people play with them. One can get tired playing with them, but they don't get tired. Children like to play with them a lot.

945. This animal is different from the ones we have already seen which are less clean. They like to lick the sap of the mesquite; or they are found among the flowers of other plants like the ocotillo, or the capulín. But they are never seen on the flesh of another animal. They sleep by going into the holes made by insects which eat the wood of trees.

946. The ant. Many, many classes of ants live in the desert. Many of them bite, while others do not. Some are large, some are small. Some of them go about day and night; others only during the day. Many build anthills on the ground, while others live in the stalks and branches of trees and other plants which they bore into. Some are believed to be the carriers of bad luck. We will examine them one by one so we can see them all and know what they do.

947. The little black ant.[117] Its name is made up of two words. The first comes from "mbooi," black. The second comes from "xäju," ant; and together they mean "black ant." The black ant is very small. It lives at the base of plants. They go up and down on the branches, where they probably find their food. 948. They also live at the base of garambullos. During the months when garambullos flower, ants go up the plant to eat the honey. When the fruit is ripe the honey comes out, and that's where the ants gather to eat. This is their food; they always go on plants. These are the smallest ones. 949. Sometimes people go to eat the fruit of the garambullos, since this is the custom when they are ripe. People really like to eat them because they are very sweet. One goes out into the country to find them and eat them. But if you are not observant, and the fruits have black ants on them, then the insects get in your mouth. And then, when you least expect it, the ant bites your tongue. Their bite isn't dangerous, but they are bothersome.

950. There is another ant,[118] but it practically never goes up into the trees. They're the ones that go along the ground. They dig out their anthole and nest in the ground. They feed on the seeds of the grasses they gather. They carry grass

seeds, and quelite seeds. They eat larvae that have died; they also slowly eat other dead animals they find. 951. They also bite when people bother them. But otherwise they do nothing.

952. The other ant we know about is slightly larger than the two previous ones.[119] It is completely black in color. Their mouth is notably stronger. They make holes in the trees where they live. They make holes in the hardest wood in the Mezquital, the mesquite. 953. They make holes in the trunk and bear their young there. Their tail is more pointed. They are out more at night than during the day. When one looks for firewood for the kitchen one goes and cuts the dry branches of the mesquite with a hatchet. If the ants are in the tree they come out and look for whoever is bothering them and try to bite him. 954. If one is not careful one can just tie up a bundle of wood and then, while carrying it along, the ants come out slowly and go on one's neck and back to bite. Their bite hurts more than that of the two ants I mentioned previously. They only live inside tree trunks. These are the three black ants which are about. But it's important that people notice their different characteristics in order not to confuse them on sight.

955. The large black ant.[120] I have seen this large black ant living all over the desert. It is around all year. They go out of their ant holes in search of pieces of leaves to put around their hole. When it rains very hard, water may go into their hole. The old ones leave; they are the ones that have wings. When the sun comes out and heats up the hole, they come out in a glut. 956. Some go off, and others just die; others look for a place to dig out a new hole. These are the ones we call old ants. When a bird comes upon these ants, it eats them. Centzontles, cactus wrens, and nightingales, for example, are birds that eat them.

957. They begin by eating the wings if they find the ants on the ground. But if they come upon them in flight, then they just grab them. 958. These ants, too, feed on seeds of quelite verde, grasses, and seeds of quelites such as quintoníl and hediondilla. This class of ant doesn't eat meat, even when it encounters it. 959. They just smell it and leave it alone, and go to their anthill.

960. There is another ant which is the same color as the one we just saw, but which has a more elongated body.[121] Like the one we saw before, the one we'll see now doesn't bite. It goes up one's legs and body but doesn't do anything. It is esteemed because it gives honey. It digs its anthill deeper than the other ants—up to a meter and a half deep. Sometime around November its belly begins to swell up with a yellow, very sweet honey, like someone had put sugar in it. 961. The little sac which forms on it is about the size of a little pea, and this is where it deposits its honey. It doesn't have honey all year, only during the end of the season when garambullos are in fruit. This is because this ant eats the

honey of the garambullo fruit when they are ripe. It drinks aguamiel also, and this also forms part of its honey.

962. Once I was walking along with two workers who were helping me to dig up a patch of rocky earth so I could level it out between the bordos. We were digging and we saw that these little ants were coming out of the ground. 963. Right away these workers thought that these were the ants made of honey. We continued digging them out, and in a little while we came upon those ants with their bellies formed into little honey sacs. I saw that the workers began to eat them and so I ate them, too. They were very sweet. According to what they told me, the honey is good medicine for those who have a cough; with this, it is eased.

965. We finished eating the ants we found, but those ants that turn into honey ended their life there because they were eaten. What I want to make clear is that the ants that turn into honey never come out of the nest; instead, the other ants, the workers, bring them their food to the nest and this food is the honey they eat. We have found them like this twice, and they live deep in the earth. This ant is seen all over the valley. I've heard some people say "there goes a honey ant." This one, and the one I mentioned first run the fastest when they are on the move.

966. The red harvester ant.[122] This is the most savage of the ants, more so than any we've seen previously. It is very abundant. It is everywhere, even in the barrancas. It is easy to spot this ant because of its red color. There are many in the anthills, and they build little caves inside where they have their offspring and where they store the seeds that they gather to feed on. The anthill is easily recognized because this is the only ant that brings in little stones to put all around it. These are the things we call "godoxääju" or "ant stones." 967. The red ant is always carrying pebbles and seeds. It only puts the stones outside, never inside the anthill, but it brings in all the seeds it finds. It carries chía seeds;[123] it carries them off as they mature from the fields where they are growing. If one doesn't reap them quickly, this ant will finish them off. 968. They also feed on grass seeds, and seeds of quelite verde, xoot'o, verdolaga, and e'yo.[124] They gather them up and store them, and then, when the dry season comes, they eat them.

969. When these ants build their anthill in a milpa they don't let the corn grow and people try to get rid of them. Also, they don't let the draft animals work; they bite them, injecting venom, which isn't deadly, and going from one animal to the next, and so people try to get rid of these ants for this reason, too. 970. Theirs is the most painful of ant bites. It hurts a lot when they bite people's

legs. After two days the bite starts to itch and swells up with pus. 971. When it doesn't itch, it hurts even more, and leaves a kind of lump on the person's groin. Since it hurts a lot it sometimes causes fever. If it bites one on the foot or on the heel, it leaves the lumps we've been talking about. They are like little sacs on each side of the groin, and one can only walk with difficulty because it hurts so much. 972. To cure it, one must heat a rock in ashes until it gets warm. Then, one slowly massages the area with the stone, and with this it goes away, little by little.

973. When little boys are sitting around nude, these ants bite their little testicles, and this makes the children jump around in pain. Once red ants bite, they die. When they are found living near a house, they are dug out to get rid of them. 974. It is believed that it isn't good to burn them, so no one burns them, but just digs them out. If they are burned, they leave a sickness in the family. 975. When they won't leave, some folks give them food. They tear up tortillas for them, and then they don't do anything, even if children are there.

There is also the belief that rainbows originate from the red ant's anthill. This is the thing we see that has many beautiful colors. 976. Many people in the Mezquital believe that rainbows come from there when it rains. We have seen that when a rainbow is near these ants they go crazy like they don't know where to go. But when there's no rainbow, then these ants don't get all agitated.

977. It is also said that anyone who points out a rainbow will get warts on his hands. So, hearing about this, one doesn't want to point out rainbows. But when people who already have these warts see a rainbow, they take a piece of lechuguilla stalk and go to the anthill to "brush" those warts on their hands and feet, as they say. These are the parts of the body where those warts come up. There are people who say that only by brushing those warts right at the entrance to the anthill can one be cured of them. 978. I don't know what there is about these ants, but I've seen times when people were cured of warts by cleaning them with a lechuguilla leaf brush at an anthill. I'm referring here to the lechuguilla leaf used to clean metates. It is cut from the heart of the lechuguilla, because there is another brush made from lechuguilla ixtle and sometimes these are used to clean metates also.[125] 979. As I said before, there is a belief that it is not good to burn red ants because they will bring sickness to the family. The children get pus-filled pimples on their head.

980. This ant has a characteristic which is different from the others. It comes out of its anthill at around seven in the morning. It goes around and carries its food and the little rocks. At twelve o'clock they go into the anthill and none of them come out. After about an hour they come out again and work. 981. Those who have observed this say that at this hour they all go to eat. They have their

"kings," but they don't come out much. They only come out when there is a strong rain. Then they come out to fly around. Some of them fly off, and others go back into their anthill. The ones that fly off make another hole, and start another anthill. 982. Those that have wings are big ants and they are redder. Huitlacoches, with their large beaks, like to eat them. The other, smaller birds don't like to eat these ants, probably because the ants sting their throats and so they are afraid of them.

This is the way of life of the red ant. It doesn't go up into trees but generally moves around on the ground. When dangerous animals (such as scorpions, snakes, centipedes, and sometimes lizards and whiptails) are caught, people throw them into anthills and the ants kill them. 983. Snakes are thrown in dead, but the others are thrown in alive. The scorpion defends itself with its pincers, cutting in half the ants that come near it. It cuts them in half at the stomach. But then the other ants come out to help, and they always win. 984. This ant doesn't bite with its mouth, but with a little stinger it has on its hind end. When whiptails feel the ants all over them, they twist in pain, but then the ants cover them and they slowly die.

985. There is also the belief that if one gives a dog these ants to eat, the dog will become very aggressive. One puts these ants in tortillas given to any dogs one wants to make fierce. The dogs that we have seen that are given fire ants to eat really do become fierce. If they see someone who isn't their master they chase him around to bite him. 986. The same goes for other animals, like pigs. Dogs are made fierce, not to bite people or animals that live in their home, but rather for shepherding. They help shepherds keep coyotes from getting the upper hand and eating the goats. This is what these fierce dogs are used for. 987. Coyotes and foxes make idiots of tame dogs. Dogs are made fierce by putting five or six ants in their tortilla to eat. But it must be done when they are small, because they don't turn fierce when they are already grown up.

988. The red ant lives in the same spot for many years. It's been about 18 years since I first saw ants living in this one anthill and they still haven't changed residence; they still live there. These are the years which I remember seeing the anthill; and, of course, it's still there.

989. The yellow ant.[126] This is a small ant and its body is totally yellow. It lives under rocks, where it lays its eggs. Sometimes they can be found on the dried up branches of garambullos and mesquites. They, too, go up to eat garambullo fruit. 990. They don't come out in the sun much, because they are nocturnal. Their bite burns a lot, and a small pimple comes up when they have stung. They are also called "silk ants" because they shine in a golden hue. After the hurt of their bite is gone, only itching is left; it isn't dangerous. 991. There are

no beliefs associated with them, neither in religion nor in medicine. It is often hard to find where they are living; they don't eat seeds, just the juice of fruits. Young mesquite shoots give off a kind of sap, and this is what they eat.

992. The yellow and black ant.[127] It is multicolored; it is yellow around the mouth, and has a black head. Its belly is yellow again and black, and its tail ends in yellow. Its feet are multicolored, too, and long; it runs very quickly. 993. It lives in decayed wood. It doesn't make an anthill in the ground, but always lives in the dead branches of organ pipe cacti, garambullos, and capulines, and in the buried part of the trunk and roots. 994. This ant also doesn't like to go around in the sun, and it is rare to see them. When one goes out collecting firewood, then they are seen on the woods that I've mentioned. When the wood is split with an axe they go running all around, looking for the person who has disturbed them, and they bite their legs. But it doesn't hurt. 995. When chickens get them they eat these ants. They kill them first by pecking them, and then they eat them. Even more, when they find immature ants, they eat them up. These ants live in dried out branches of garambullo. There are no beliefs associated with these ants. No medicine has been discovered in them, neither for animals nor for people. They penetrate the insides of woody plants. They go along, penetrating and eating.

996. Ant larvae.[128] Of all the ants we've mentioned this is the one most hunted by the people. They don't live in larva stage all year long. They live out in the open country, where many people don't go. 997. They are black, like other ants we have seen. They look like the big black ant in size. They lay their larvae during March or April, around the time when Holy Week is near. 998. There is the belief that it is not good to eat beef or pork, or goat or sheep when Holy Week comes. That is, it isn't good to eat mammals. 999. So, fish, shrimp, ant larvae and chicken are eaten—all animals which aren't mammals. There aren't many fish in the Mezquital, nor shrimp, and these have to brought from the sea.

1000. There are some fish in the Tula River, but not everyone can fish, and the ones sold in the market are very expensive. Campesinos don't have enough money to buy fish. 1001. It costs around 40 pesos per kilo, so only those with money can eat it, and those without money can't, so they look for other animals to eat. The animals they eat are the ant larvae which are around only at Holy Week when mammals aren't eaten. Two or three men get together and go out to look for ant larvae. They take their pick-axe and pole and go out to the open country where they look for larvae at the base of junquillos. One can tell where they are because those plants turn black. 1003. The black color they leave on the plants is from the ants' feet which stain as they go up the plant or the maguey.

Rainbows originate from the red ant's anthill

Fauna 984

One must look really well to see if they are really there and then begin digging. One of the men loosens the earth and the other pries out the trunk with the stick. 1004. They dig down about a meter or a meter and a half. The work is hard because you have to watch out for the ants which bite your legs; so first they must be picked off and tossed away. Slowly, they dig. When they find the larvae, they put them in an ayate brought along for this purpose. 1005. They keep digging until they get to the very bottom of the ant hole. When they get to the bottom the work ends. They collect a cuartillo or a cuartillo and a half if there's a lot. It looks like they are carrying rice, because the larvae is white. Those little animals barely move when they come out of their hole, and when they hit the air they die.

1006. When the larvae diggers get back they divide the catch equally and each one takes a little to his house. When they get home they give it to whoever will prepare it and the woman then begins to put them up to boil. 1007. Since they are very delicate these little animals are just given a quick boil and they're done. Then they find a nopal (this is the time when nopales begin to ripen) and a pad is cut and cooked separately. 1008. When the larvae are cooked, spices are added so it can all be put in a casserole and fried up together. The chile has been ground up separately, either red or green. When it's all cooked, there is a delicious meal. 1009. Pork lard is used for frying, but if there's no money for lard then the larvae are just boiled and mixed with salsa. Otherwise, the larvae aren't boiled. Mint is cut, and onion, garlic, marjoram, thyme and ground chile are mixed together in another casserole to marinate. 1010. It is all wrapped together in corn leaves which have been previously washed. The mixture is put in the leaves, one by one, and when this is finished, they are put on the comal. Sometimes they are buried in a fire to cook.

1011. They take on a special flavor this way and this is called "roasted." This is how ant larvae are prepared and it is one of the exquisite foods eaten in the valley. Mestizos like to eat it, too. There are people who dig up the larvae and sell it. 1012. Other larvae diggers go out and look, but don't find anything; then it is said that they don't have any luck, that "they don't follow them." And then they don't go out another time to look for larvae. These larvae can only be eaten once a year, though their offspring, the ants, live all year long. People sell them either by the puño[129] or by the half cuartillo. 1013. They sell them for 10 pesos a puño, which works out to 40 pesos a cuartillo. The money gained is used to buy corn. A plate of the stew made from this food is served to each person, and they dip their tortillas to eat.

1014. The escarabajo.[130] Two words make up its name in Ñähñu. The first comes from "tsits'i" and the second is "mada." Together they mean the place where one puts the molcajete. The head of this creature looks like the feet of a molcajete when someone puts it upside down so it won't fall. 1015. The molcajete has its own special place in the kitchen where it can't be knocked over by carelessness. It is very useful for grinding salsa which is eaten every day. 1016. There are no houses of poor people where they don't make salsa, either in the morning or in the evening. So the molcajete is taken very good care of so it won't break. If it does, there won't be anything to grind chile with. 1017. This is how the head of this insect looks, like someone turned a molcajete upside down in its place with its feet up in the air. 1018. The head of this animal has horns, like it had a molcajete on its head.

1019. It is dark red in color and bright colored on its back. They fly around at night when the lights are on. They don't do anything to people; they just follow the light, coming and going around and around. 1020. They only come out at night and aren't around during the day; at night they go into the garbage from the house. Sometimes they are under rocks. They go buzzing around at night and one knows that the beetle has entered the house. If someone catches it, it plays dead and doesn't move; but when it is let go, it moves around again.

1021. The gallina ciega.[131] These are of different colors and different sizes and they are born and grow in the same place; so we'll treat them all together here. The white gallina ciega is always born in garbage and dung. Many large gallinas ciegas live in goat manure. 1022. They have white bodies and their heads are black. They have some down-like, reddish hairs, and chickens like to eat them a lot. They get them in the goat pens, because they know they're in there. 1023. Pigs also like to eat them; when pigs chew them it makes a crunching noise you can hear.

1024. They are born when it rains and the manure gets wet. The gallina ciega is the thing that turns into the black beetle. When someone touches them, they stop moving and play dead. This is to fool whoever is touching them. They are always under rocks and manure piles because that's how they keep warm. 1025. There are others that are brown but with the same characteristics as the white one. From what we can see, only the color and size are different; they are smaller and they turn into green June beetles.[132] We will treat these insects separately, later on. 1026. There are other, smaller gallinas ciegas that are black, and some of these turn into tumble bugs and others into Mexican bean beetles. They are of different colors, including green, red, black, and spotted backs. Some are large, some are small.

1027. Many insects come from animal pens, so it is necessary to put the pens far from the house so the insects won't come into the house. Sometimes insects come in and go on food just like flies do. By the time one notices, an illness has come and if there is no money, then there is no way to cure it.

1028. When gallinas ciegas are under the roots of flowering plants, they stunt them and the plants grow up yellowish. This happens to flowers by throwing manure on them; since the manure is warm, the insects follow. 1029. The gallina ciega feeds on earth; that is to say, on the manure where it lives, and on the roots of plants. When they kill plants, one can tell this is the cause. One can say that they feed on earth combined with manure. 1030. It does not offer any benefit to medicine, nor does it announce bad luck, as is believed for some other animals already noted. I repeat: it can only live in manure and in wet earth.

1031. The black widow spider.[133] In the description of snakes earlier we saw that the most dangerous is the rattler. Its venom is dangerous when it bites. Among the ants, the most violent is the red fire ant. The insect we will look at now is called the black widow, and it is the most dangerous of all the spiders in the valley. 1032. Its body is completely black, a strong, deep black, and this is probably why people call it the black spider. There is no other that compares in color. It has a small patch of red on its underbelly. 1033. Some of them are about the size of a pea, while others in the valley reach the size of a grape. Its feet are very long and there are four of them on each side. It is believed that it uses them to bite with, along with its stinger. 1034. Its venom is white. We always smash it whenever we see it, and it bites the stick we hit it with; this is how we observe its venom. We throw it into an anthill; it kills a few, but then many ants come and, though the spider is strong, the ants win and kill it.

1035. Black widows are all over the valley, and all over Mexico, but they are especially abundant in the valley. They are everywhere; they can be found between rocks, sometimes in dried out lechuguilla trunks, and sometimes in little holes on the edges of barrancas.

1036. They are born from eggs. We have seen that there are no more than two egg balls hanging in the webs; this is the strongest of all the webs. 1037. The two balls, that is to say, the eggs it has hung in its web, are guarded by the spider. They take turns guarding them; the female guards for a while, and then the male. The egg balls are white, but inside there are smaller, white eggs, and these are the spiders. 1038. They are incubated by the heat of the spider; inside the two balls there are about a hundred spiders. What has not been observed is how many days they take to hatch.

1039. When this insect bites a person, the person dies if they aren't taken to a doctor right away. Once, I saw a person who was bitten by a black widow. There was a moment when he doubled up. This is said to be the moment when the spider is dying. When the spider draws its legs together, the person does the same thing.[134] 1040. They had to give injections to that man in the hospital to dilute the venom of the black widow.

It is the most dangerous of all the spiders
Fauna 1040

1041. The food of this spider consists of flies, mosquitoes, daddy long legs and other small spiders. It catches them all in its web. As soon as a fly sticks to the web, the spider grabs it and begins sucking on it. Perhaps it absorbs the blood of the fly. 1042. It grabs the fly, sucks on it for a bit, and lets it go. It gets it out of the web, grabs another one and eats by mixing many insects together. It sort of hugs the insects to eat them. This is the way of life of this spider.

1043. When people go to collect dried maguey leaves for firewood they must shake them well, because sometimes they have black widows in them. When the leaf is thrown into the fire, the spider comes out, and there is the danger that it will bite whoever is in the house at that moment. 1044. If an adult sees one, then they know about these spiders and kill it. But if a child sees it, they may not know any better and pay no attention.

What I said a moment ago about its eggs hatching from the warmth of the spider's body is true. When someone kills the spider, its eggs don't hatch; they just dry up where they are. 1045. It doesn't deposit its eggs in the earth, but hangs them in its web. Its web is very strong, in comparison with the webs of other spiders. When the web is pulled off of where it is stuck, one can hear the noise.

1046. It doesn't come out during the day, but comes out later on. If a light shines on it at night, its eyes show brightly. When one goes hunting at night one can tell what animals' eyes are really like, that is to say, how they shine. One can tell which animal is which from the way their eyes shine at night. 1047. It is very important to know which animal is which so one doesn't kill something one doesn't need. It is also important to know how snakes' eyes shine at night. If one knows what animals look like at night when light is shone on them, then one won't make the error of killing a domestic animal. 1048. This is what happens sometimes when a cat goes out in search of mice. If one doesn't know what it looks like at night, one may think it is a rabbit and kill it. This happens because it's hard to see the bodies of animals at night; one can only see their eyes which show up by the light carried by the hunter.

1049. The tarantula.[135] This is the largest of all the spiders in the Mezquital. It has hair all over its body and legs, and is brown or dark red. Sometimes it makes its hole in the ground; other times it lives in dried, rotten maguey trunks, or dried, rotten thorn bushes. It seems to like these places because it is the same color and can hide from its enemies. 1050. This spider has brilliant eyes when light is shown on it at night. It is said that it also has venom and is dangerous, but we haven't seen anyone who has been bitten by it. 1051. The tarantula has another special characteristic: it is the only spider that carries its young around, as if it were imitating one of the mammals we saw earlier, called the possum.

The possum carries its young around wherever it goes. The tarantula's back is filled with its young, the little spiders. 1052. We have seen them going about loaded down in this manner, many times. People always joke about someone who is loaded down with things, and they call him "tarantula." Sometimes people are loaded with firewood when they return from collecting, and they put something else on top of the load, that is, another sack of something, like xite for washing dishes, or greens for feeding the animals. 1053. And when people see them carrying a very large load they say they're like a tarantula carrying her young.

Wherever the tarantula goes, it leaves its mark, so one knows it's a tarantula. It is like the black widow in that it doesn't come out during the day. It only comes out in the day when it's cool, or at night. It comes out when the sun goes down, probably to look for its food. 1054. When chickens find tarantulas carrying their young, they eat the young and then kill the mother to eat her, too.

When tarantulas get angry they bite whoever is bothering them. 1055. They eat little insects they find in the earth. They also eat little grubs that live at the base of maguey trunks. If one crushes their stomach, a kind of mud-like substance comes out. Its saliva is not strong, and it doesn't weave webs like other spiders do, in a circle. 1056. The tarantula makes a kind of misshapen ball and sleeps in it. Sometimes it lives deep in the ground where it digs. Other times, it finds a hole in dead tree roots and lives there. The roots are those of plants like the garambullo, which are not very hard; the spiders live in there, generally one at a time.

1057. There are no beliefs associated with this spider. No part of its body is used in medicine. We have never seen its eggs anywhere. When they reach their full size they are about as big as a newborn chick. They come out and move about on the ground in the hot season. During the cold season they stay in their holes in the ground. They move very slowly.

1058. The fire moth.[136] There is a great variety of small moths of this class. Some are big, some are very small, and they come in many colors. Some are very beautiful, others not so beautiful. Some are grey, yellow, red, orange, violet or black. 1059. Some have their bodies covered with a kind of fuzz. They are all nocturnal. There are hardly any firemoths that fly during the day. The name is formed of two words: the first is "zoo" and the second is "faspi." Together they mean that they fly and go into flames. 1060. Thus, this moth goes into flames, and, indeed, this is true; this is its way of life. If a fire is burning, it goes right into the flame and dies. The same goes for lamps, which are often made from a can. A hole is punched in one end of the can and then a cork is inserted. A hole is also punched in the center and a cotton wick is inserted all the way to the bottom of the can. Or a piece of old rag is put into the can which contains lamp oil and this is how a light is lit. This is the original lamp we know of.

1061. When this lamp is lit, the fire moth tries to go into the flame. When it is a big moth it puts out the flame because it makes so much wind. This is how it is so well known that this insect goes into flames. They are born from the larvae in trees where they mature and turn into moths little by little. 1062. After transforming, some go about during the day. We'll look at them presently.

1063. A fire moth that goes into flames generally dies. This is its principal characteristic: it goes about at night and goes into the flames and burns up. Sometimes, when a person has just been served his food and begins to eat, a moth goes into it. It is said that it isn't good to eat it, because there is a kind of earth-like powder on its wings. This is what isn't good to eat, because it can make a person sick.

1064. The larvae in the zapote tree turn into big fire moths. Those larvae are really ugly. They have the same color as the tree they are in. During the day they stick to the tree, without moving, like nothing was there. About 50 or more are bunched together in one spot. 1065. When it gets dark they begin to move, and they eat the leaves of the tree, not the fruit, just the leaves. If someone touches them, they remain immobile, as if they were dead. In a single night they will eat a lot of leaves. Their excrement is green. When they turn into firemoths, they grow big, are red in color, and are very pretty.

1066. Many small grubs turn into firemoths. There is another firemoth that is much bigger, but no one knows what larva it comes from. Its wings are about the size of a hummingbird's. If it gets caught out in the daytime, it stays plastered to the ceiling of the house. It doesn't offer any medicine.

1067. The pinacate.[137] There is a little animal called the pinacate that lives all over the Mezquital. It has long legs, an elevated rear end, and is totally black. I say that it's "elevated" because when it walks it squats down in front. This is its way of life; its back legs are tall and its front legs are a little shorter. This is why it looks higher in the back. 1068. It is found underneath maguey trunks and in piles of rocks where it makes its hole. It doesn't come out when the sun is very hot; when the day is cool they come out and one can see them. They are out mostly at night. They don't bite. People don't like them because when these insects go into a house they let out farts and it smells awful. 1069. When they are provoked, they raise up their rear end and shoot out a fart; this is their defense. When they are seen in houses they are thrown out right away, so that when they let their farts they'll be outside. Even when they aren't provoked, they sometimes give off these really stinky farts which have a kind of bite to them. The smell lasts one or two days and even causes headaches.

It goes right into the flame and dies

Fauna 1069

1070. When they are provoked, they point their rear ends in the air to release their farts. They shoot out a yellowish liquid that smells bad. Adult turkeys kill them and eat them when they find them. But if they sense that it is going to shoot a fart into their eyes, they leave it alone. Chickens are afraid of them and don't bother them. 1071. Since pinacates go about at night, skunks eat them. Some people say that it's because they eat pinacates that the farts of skunks are so awful smelling. There are parts of pinacates, such as the legs, in the excrement of skunks. 1072. The pinacate has a sort of shell on its back, divided down the middle, lengthwise, like wings. But pinacates don't fly. They don't have any benefit for medicine, and neither is there any belief associated with them in religion.

It is not known what the pinacate feeds on. It isn't known if it eats grubs or earth. It doesn't cause any harm in the fields though there are a lot of them among the rows of maguey. But it doesn't do anything to the crops. The only thing that people don't like is its awful smell.

1073. The maguey weevil.[138] Its color is much like that of the pinacate; that is, it's also black. The "mone," as it is called in Ñähñu, is smaller than the regular pinacate. Its legs are all on the same level. Its head is about the same size as its body. A part of its mouth juts forward, and it uses this to feel its way along. This is one of the insects that belong to the maguey. 1074. It lives in no other plant, only in the trunk of the maguey. When a maguey starts to be scraped these beetles appear, and if the scraping is left and not done, they multiply and eat up the soft part of the trunk. They make holes everywhere in it. 1075. This is the most harmful of the insects for the maguey. If they get into the trunks of the young, recently planted magueys, they don't let the plants grow. The plants grow slowly or dry up altogether.

1076. If these insects live in a maguey trunk, then that maguey will be different from the others in that its heart will become twisted and grow down instead of up. It can't mature like this because there is no way to sprout its leaves. 1077. People who know take a knife and cut out the twisted little sprouts at the base of the heart. Then they make two crossed cuts at the point where they cut the twisted heart. This is done so that the leaves will open up quickly and in this way the plant can grow properly. 1078. Plants that have a lot of beetles in their trunks have droopy leaves; even if there is moisture at the roots they won't grow. When they are like this, they are pulled out and pruned back. A part of the trunk below ground is cut off; then the plant is left in the sun for a few days so the insects will leave. Then it is replanted and it grows well. 1079. This is why these insects are harmful to the maguey.

1080. These insects don't run. They arc lethargic. We can say that this insect is the death of the maguey, because whatever they invade, even a big maguey, they leave rotting. Sometimes there are magueys that don't have far to go before they can be scraped; and from one day to the next, their trunk and leaves rot. 1081. When they're like this, they don't get broken open to be scraped. The owner of the plant loses because he can't scrape it. He loses at least 50 pesos if it is a large plant.

1082. The dung beetle.[139] This bug has an ovular body, almost circular. Of all those we have described this has the shortest body. It is black, like the pinacate and the maguey beetle. Tumblebugs, too, are born in wet dung. They dig in manure and make little balls which they then carry off. They push the dung balls along with their hind legs. They go backwards, that is, with their head in back and their rear in front. 1083. They push the dung ball they have made. The more they roll it, the rounder and more ball-like it becomes, like someone had made it with their hands. They lie motionless when bothered, with their legs all bunched up like they were dead. But when left alone, they start again to push the load they were carrying.

1084. They push and push their load around without anyone knowing where they go, because they have no home. Sometimes they go along two or three at a time, each one with its own ball. When they come to a drop, the bug and the ball roll down together. It digs in wet dung of cattle, pigs and dogs. There are a lot of them when it rains. If there is a pile of human excrement, about 10 get together and each one starts his own trip. They each make their own ball of excrement, and then each one goes off on its own. 1086. When the terrain is flat, they carry their burden about 20 meters. But when it is rocky, then naturally they don't go far because they can't push the balls. It is considered a dirty creature because it is always carrying excrement.

1087. When it comes upon human excrement, it digs in and makes a ball which it carts off. Sometimes it seems like it's mocking people; it carries the dung to the patio of a house and leaves it there. This smells very bad and no one likes it. The ball it makes is like a marble. 1088. It only makes what it knows it can roll, because when the bug is big, the ball is big; and when the bug is small, the ball is small. We can't know why it does all this since it doesn't have a hole in which to deposit the balls. It just goes around all over the place, carrying excrement. When it gets tired, it abandons it. I have heard some people say that the ball is its house and is where it lays its eggs. We can't confirm if this is true or not. God only knows!

1089. The wasp.[140] This is a little creature with long legs and two wings, one on each side; with these wings it can fly far. Its body is completely red. It hangs its hive in mesquites and garambullos, in pepper trees and in palmas, and sometimes on maguey leaves. Sometimes it builds its hive on fruit trees because in this way it is close to the juice of the fruit when they mature. 1090. They also go into rock walls to make their hives where they hatch their young, and where the young grow up. They don't let anyone get near. They chase them, defending their young and their nest. 1091. The nest is made from a kind of paper that doesn't come off when it sticks. Two wasps hang the hive. After 15 days the young hatch and thus they really multiply. When the young grow up, they help to build the hive bigger. If no one interrupts them, the hive will grow as big as a ceramic plate.

1092. When people go out into the open country they have to be really alert, because wasps will sting their ears when they least expect it. They sting hands or other parts of the body, also. To sting, they alight and insert their stinger. It hurts a lot, more than if a person had a needle inserted in their hand. 1093. The sting burns, and it swells up, and when the swelling goes down it itches a lot on the third or fourth day. Its sting is much worse than the red ant's. 1094. As it passes over the place where it will sting, it sticks out a small needle-like stinger, and injects a liquid. This is what hurts. If it stings a child, it makes him dance around from the pain. It practically makes an adult cry because it is a very deep pain.

1095. When we were kids there used to be a bunch of peach trees that had beautiful fruit during peach season. We used to go out shepherding, but the peach trees were near the house. About three of us, I think, got together and said "Let's go pick some peaches, but let's do it so that no one sees us." 1096. We all wanted to pick them. We slowly crept closer along the bordo. The peaches were above that bordo. There were three yellow peach trees. The bordo I'm talking about is what holds back the water when it rains, and keeps it from washing away the plants. 1097. Those trees were really loaded with big, juicy peaches. People generally plant magueys all along the bordos. Well, the magueys and peach trees were planted there along that bordo. 1098. There were some really big magueys, almost ready for scraping. Among the magueys were some peaches that had fallen; the wind had knocked them down.

One by one, we stuck our necks out. I poked up first, but I didn't see anything. Then the next one poked up and looked around for the owners of the peach trees to check that they didn't notice us. If no one was around we could quickly go and gather up what we could. 1099. The third compañero was the first to start gathering up his share. The other two of us were walking along all crouched down at the base of the bordo. The other was not up very long when we heard

They push the dung balls along with their hind legs

Fauna 1091

him scream. We didn't even wait; we just took off running and our compañero run after us, yelling. At first we thought that the owner of the peach trees had hit him with a rock. We ran to a nearby barranca. 1100. When we got there we asked him what had happened to him, but he was crying and didn't answer us. Then we saw him rubbing his ears and he began to laugh. We asked him again what happened. He told us he'd been stung by a wasp. He wanted to laugh and cry at the same time. One of his ears was bitten by two wasps, and the other was bitten by only one. 1101. Soon his outer ear began to swell up. We laughed because we were scared off and didn't eat any fruit. Much later we returned and saw that wasps were living in the magueys near the peach trees, and they had built their hive there. It was large and there were many wasps inside it.

1102. When it is cold, they are not so fierce as when it's hot. Some people in the valley eat wasps. Once I was working with three laborers who were making bordos. 1103. A wasp came to where one of them was working. He hit it with the stick he was carrying and the wasp died. He picked it up, and I thought he was just looking at it; I was surprised when I saw him pluck out the stinger and the wings and eat the insect. His head rang with the sound of his eating it. 1104. Then the others said that it was delicious. "It's as good as if one were eating squash seeds," they said. And they said that there are many who eat them. I have seen three people eat them.

1105. Wasps like to drink aguamiel. If a tlachiquero isn't careful when he uncovers magueys the wasps sting his hand.

1106. The caterpillar.[141] Caterpillars are among the insects that specialize in being on one certain plant in the Mezquital. Various plants have them, and the various caterpillars only feed on the leaves of certain plants. They don't eat all plants. Sometimes one kind will go on another plant than its own, but it doesn't eat the leaves. 1107. The mesquite caterpillar is mostly black. It has little feet under its belly that allow it to crawl, and it goes pretty fast. When the mesquite is sprouting it has a green caterpillar; but during the months of September and October it has a black one. 1108. There are more of these than the green ones. When the black ones are on the mesquite its branches look black. If you squash it, the stuff it has in its stomach is green, because it feeds on the mesquite leaves.

1109. The green caterpillar lives in capulín trees and eats the leaves during March and April when the tree is sprouting and the leaves are fresh and tender. Its whole body is green and it is fatter than the black one. Its whole body bites, causing a lot of pain. Any part of a person's body that it touches swells up, and it leaves its track there. It doesn't use any "thorns," as we call them, to sting. It just exudes a liquid that is hard to see and this is what causes so much pain. 1110. If it bites a person on his palm, it doesn't hurt. But if it stings on another part of the body then the pain penetrates and swells up. The black caterpillar stings in the same way. What we call its "thorns" leave a mark on the skin.

1111. Some years they are abundant and when old people see this they say that during the winter it will be very cold. Sure enough, it freezes, and when it is bad, it freezes the leaves and branches of trees.

1112. There is another kind of caterpillar, but not of the mesquite. It is the caterpillar of a plant called "romero silvestre" which lives in the bottom of barrancas. But when it rains, this caterpillar grows in the open country. It is red. It has long hair and doesn't sting, and moves faster than the two we saw earlier. 1113. This creature eats the sprouts of the romero. There aren't many of them; only two or three are found on a plant. This one goes around to different plants, and eats them. The three caterpillars don't harm peach trees or fig trees.

1114. The grasshopper.[142] The grasshopper that lives in the dry open country of the valley isn't the same color as the one that lives in the irrigated zone. The dry country grasshopper blends in with the color of the earth. Its back is grey and its body is reddish, and it doesn't grow very big. 1115. It has two hind legs. They are longer and thicker and help to make the grasshopper jump. The front legs are thinner and not as long. There are many during the hot season, like other animals. They cause no harm to corn or bean plants; they just eat the weeds in the milpas. 1116. They have bulging eyes and don't blink, but have them open all the time. They also have two little horns on their head. They are not eaten, but just go about free in the countryside.

1117. There are other grasshoppers that are green. They multiply only when it rains and when there is a lot of greenery because that is what they feed on. This one is really harmful because it eats corn plants, and also the ears when they are mature. They eat the leaves of the plants when the young ears are sprouting. They eat bean plants, too, because people generally plant corn and beans together. 1118. They plant vine beans, which climb on the stalks of the corn. When grasshoppers multiply a lot, they eat up the bean plant leaves and the young bean sprouts. They can finish off a whole row in a night. They make a noise when they eat, like there was a strong wind. They are big and all green.

1119. During the day they avoid people and fly around in swarms that create shadows when they go by in the sun. The people are afraid of these insects because they cause a lot of damage, and eat up the plants. They eat the hay and the beans, and thus one may harvest nothing. All the owner of a field can do is put his animals out to eat the stubble that remains.

1120. The green grasshopper eats mostly at night, and apparently rests during the day. It reaches four fingers in length. It has sharp nails on its jumping legs, and these nails keep it from slipping when it jumps. 1121. When one grabs it one notices how much power it has in its jumping legs. Its excrement is green because it feeds on plants. Some farmers say that when there are a lot of green grasshoppers it means that a period of hunger is approaching. It won't rain and thus there will be no crops; then the price of food goes up. 1122. This is what happens sometimes; there will be no rain for a year or two, and no one in the dry zone plants crops. Then, the sellers of corn, knowing that the people have not harvested, raise the price of corn and beans and all foodstuffs. 1123. The same thing happens when there are lots of caterpillars; in that year there is no harvest, and everything is lost.

1124. Sometimes one doesn't want to believe that these animals announce the coming of things. But when one sees it oneself, then one knows it is true. Sometimes there is no rain for two or three years; we have seen up to eight years without rain. Animals begin to die, magueys start to dry up and only the quiotes remain standing. The maguey leaves shrivel up and droop. 1125. Great hunger starts and people begin going far away to look for work to get money to buy food. This usually happens when there are many animals or when the vegetation bears a lot of fruit; then, the next year the people don't reap anything. Those animals announce what will occur the next year.

1126. The green June beetle. This animal is very pretty. Its stomach is all green, and the color shines like glass. Its back is green and yellow. They are born in manure, just like the gallina ciega. 1127. When they come out to fly about, they are in the treetops. When they tire of flying, they land on one of the branches, in a large group. They go after the pepper tree flower, and feed on its honey. When there are figs, they go together into the fruit and suck on the sweet insides. 1128. They have two strong wings which cover the wings they fly with. When provoked, they lie still. When they see no one is watching, they fly around again. Children catch them when these bugs are on plants and they tie a string around one of the legs. Then they let it fly around, but they don't let go of the string, so they play with it. 1129. The insect goes round and round, up and down; children like to watch it because many children don't get toys bought for them. So at least they play with creatures.

1130. This animal doesn't do anything to the plantings. Its most common enemies are chickens which eat them. If a chicken sees them flying close to the ground, it jumps and catches them. First it kills them and then it swallows them; if the beetles are very large, then the chicken's neck twists around as it tries to swallow them. 1131. If one turkey catches a June beetle and others see it, they pursue the turkey and try to snatch the bug away. This is called "hñändui" in Ñähñu; that it to say, the turkeys "snatch" it, or "dundui." Now, these are the same words, but we use the verb form "dundui" for animals. People snatch

They just go about free in the countryside
Fauna 1125

things with one verb, "hääni," while animals snatch things, "tuuni," with another.

1132. Moth larvae.[143] This is the largest and fattest of all the larvae. They come in two colors. One is all green with stripes on its back and a pair of small horns on its head. The other is brown, and this is the only difference between them. They aren't always around in the valley; when it rains there is a lot of quelite verde and then these insects are around. They eat the leaves of the quelites and the leaves of e'yo and xoot'o. 1133. Sometimes, when one goes out weeding corn, one comes suddenly upon this larvae. At first, one can't distinguish it very well, and one may think it is a snake. But when one looks carefully, then it is seen that it is the "kueta." 1134. It eats the leaves of bean plants, so it is really necessary to weed around the plants thoroughly so the larvae won't get to the beans. They have very soft bodies; when one touches them they curl up in one's hand, and make one afraid. They don't bite but just move around and they are very strong. We throw them into anthills, and with one sudden movement this bug can throw off the ants. But when other ants come out they overcome it. 1135. When it grows up it turns into a large, beautiful yellow moth. Some people catch this moth and dry it to keep, and it looks really pretty.

1136. The millipede.[144] Some people call it the "water carrier." It comes out only when it rains. Otherwise, it is found at the base of junquillos or magueys, or anywhere else where it finds moisture. During this time it is waiting for the rain to come so it can come out and move around. There are white, black, brown, and reddish ones. 1137. Farmers are happy when these insects come out because they say that this means rain is near. Sometimes what they say is true, and it rains right away. When it rains hard, many rain creatures come out to go around in the valley. But once the birds see them, they eat them. When people see them, they don't do them any harm; that is, they don't kill them. On the contrary, they like them because they believe these creatures bring rain. 1138. It looks something like a centipede but the centipede has its legs on its sides. By contrast, the millipede has its legs under the part we call its stomach.

1139. The centipede's legs are more spaced out, while the millipede's are more close together. Also, the centipede is much faster than the millipede, which is slow by comparison. The millipede's body is fragile while that of the centipede is stronger. But if one sees them at a distance, it is easy to confuse them.

1140. Millipedes are found when holes are dug to remove old maguey trunks, and to plant prickly pears and magueys. When a person finds a millipede, he picks it up and puts it off to one side, and doesn't kill it. They begin to come out in April, and, as with all insects, they are eaten by chickens that find them.

1141. The louse.[145] This is a very small creature which is very bad, not only for people in the valley, but probably in many parts of the world. We will see what problems this insect causes for people. First we will talk about the ones that live on people's bodies, and that grow in their clothes. If one doesn't watch out, or change clothes, or bathe regularly, lice begin to multiply. 1142. They start by laying their eggs in clothing, either in shirts or pants. The mother stays there waiting for the eggs to hatch. This takes about a week. If they aren't killed, the baby lice multiply much more. Those little lice are the ones that cause the most itching. They cause chills when they bite. They feed on people from the shoulders down.

1143. The white lice are the ones that live in this part of the body. This is a very bad insect. They are always making children scratch from so much itching. Children mostly have them; adults rarely do. 1144. Of course, this was the case a long time ago when there was no water to bathe children, only for adults. Thus, there were many of these parasites which are like flies that go wherever there is filth. But now, all the people have worked to bring potable water to the community; it isn't in everyone's house, but there is water in the pueblo for everyone. 1145. There is enough for all the necessities: for drinking, for washing clothes, and for bathing. In this way the people have slowly fought to extinguish these parasites which do so much harm to people's bodies. Wherever there were many of them they caused diseases like typhus. 1146. People who have a lot of lice get very lethargic because the lice suck their blood and make them weak. Blood is very important if one is to have strength at work.

1147. The lice that live in head hair are a different color than the previous ones. They are totally black, and are camouflaged in hair. When one of these goes into a person's hair, they multiply. First they lay their eggs, and when they are born the lice stay in the hair. People who have them are always scratching their head because lice cause a lot of itching. 1148. If someone who has them stands in the sun, then the lice cause even more itching because they get hot. They are very harmful; one loses strength because those animals suck out people's strength. Continual bathing is important so that these creatures won't follow you. It's also important to keep clothing and bedding clean to get rid of lice.

1149. The harm they cause has been known for a long time. They are slowly being wiped out by cleanliness. So it is important for each person to care for his or her body and to keep their house clean. It is well known that there used to be no potable water in the valley. 1150. People used to dig out big catchment ponds for water. That is, they dug out the earth so it would fill up when it rained. This is how people got water for cooking and for washing clothes. These things were done while the water was still clean, because if it was dirty nothing could be washed. 1151. For the same reason, there was no water for bathing; for this, people went to the hot springs. It took people a half a day to go and come back from the spring just to bring a jug of water. Years ago people really suffered. Many diseases exist because there wasn't enough water in many villages to keep things clean. 1152. Everyone must exert every possible effort to bring this about. If there is no money, then one must work hard. Only in this way can the things people need be gotten. What's important is that there not be diseases that make everyone suffer.

1153. When lice defecate on clothes the stain doesn't come out. Even if they are washed well, the clothes don't lose the color of excrement; they just remain stained.

1154. The flea.[146] These "jumper" creatures are all black, different in size and live everywhere. There is one that lives amongst people, in beds and bedding; sometimes it goes onto people's bodies and when they lay down to sleep the fleas start to bite. 1155. They are also very bad; they tickle as they move about on one's body, and don't let one sleep. They are very difficult to kill because they jump. What must be done is to put all the clothing out in the sun so all the fleas will go away. 1156. Everyone knows that fleas are bad things. It is known that they cause people many diseases. This is probably so because they go all around like flies and suck people's blood and the blood of animals such as dogs, too. 1157. Then they go and bite someone else, and this is how they transmit diseases. The skin gets red where they bite, causing a lot of itching. This flea only bites people's bodies. If there are a lot of them they jump on people's legs in one or two leaps from the ground.

1158. There is another one called the "nail flea" in Ñähñu because it sinks its head into the skin when it bites in order to suck blood. When it is sucking its bite causes a lot of itching. One goes to scratch it, but it jumps and goes away. This flea likes to live on cats and on squirrels because they have fur and this is where they stay "nailed in." 1159. On cats these insects are found around their eyes and in their ears. They aren't easily noticed because they are covered by the fur. Squirrels and mice also have fleas. Wherever these animals are, there are fleas.

1160. If one goes and looks in squirrel holes there are fleas jumping around everywhere. If one isn't careful, they go up onto your clothes, and before you know it they are biting your legs and they go onto your hands. The fleas of mice, squirrels and rabbits are the same size. Dogs have larger fleas. 1161. The skin turns red wherever these larger fleas bite. If you squash one, the blood they have sucked squirts out. When dogs scratch it is because they have fleas, and the fleas have to be killed by putting on a medicine which keeps fleas from multiplying.

1162. One *cures* dogs and cats of fleas; but the thing to do with mice is to *kill* them so they won't transmit their fleas. They just transmit diseases to people, and so a solution must be found.

1163. The nigua. These are the same size and have the same characteristics as squirrel and cat fleas. The nigua also jumps and goes everywhere. One can see them in the feet of pigs. The feet are cut open by the fleas which deposit their eggs between the toes. The eggs are in a large, white ball in the pig's flesh. 1164. This is cured by putting on criolina so that the foot of the animal supurates and the flea egg-balls run out. This flea also affects people's feet; they go between their toes. At first they just itch; though one knows it itches, one may think it's just any old flea. 1165. But after three days the itching gets worse, and it begins to supurate and it grows worse and worse; sometimes it causes itching, and other times it both itches and hurts. When it gets like this, it is opened up with a needle, and a ball comes out, filled with eggs. 1166. A hole is left where the ball is taken out, as if a piece of flesh were removed. One must burn the ball so that the fleas won't be born. It is said that if it is thrown on the ground, the heat from the earth will hatch the eggs. 1167. So that they won't hatch, the balls are removed from people's feet and thrown into the fire to burn up. If one allows the swelling on the feet to burst by itself, it hurts more. 1168. Fleas lay their eggs in the webbing between the toes. Of course, this happens to people who don't wear huaraches; fleas afflict those who go barefoot.

1169. The chicken louse.[147] This is one of the insects which is most harmful to other animals. It lives on the body of chickens. This louse gets all over the chicken, on its back, stomach, and head, and it gets thick around its eyes. 1170. Chickens that have lice are addled and don't want to eat. Those parasites make them stupid. One buys DDT; it is sprayed on, and with this the lice die. Then the chicken begins to eat again, and slowly gets fat.

1171. This louse is orange in color and it is smaller than the lice that infest people. The chicken louse is much faster. Its feet cause a lot of tickling when they go onto people. If a lot of them go on a person, they don't let him sleep as they run around all over him. 1172. This louse also bites people; wherever it bites, it causes a lot of tickling, and little pimples come up. Their feet cause more tickling than a flea's. If they go up onto a person's head, one knows what it is right away. 1173. Some people are more afraid of chicken lice than of fleas, because the lice bother people more. When chickens have a lot of lice, they get sick; so they have to be checked once in a while to see that they don't have lice. 1174. If they do have lice, they must be cured so that they will give the benefits one expects of chickens. Turkeys also have lice. This can be seen because they scratch themselves all the time when they have lice.

1175. The hog louse. Pigs also have their own lice, like chickens and other animals we have seen. These particular lice are larger and are stuck to the skin. They are mostly found in the pigs' groin area, perhaps because this is the warmest part of the body. Pigs with lice get stupid also. 1176. They begin to get thin and become xirgos.[148] One must buy DDT to kill the lice. If the lice don't die with this medicine, then the pig is shaved, and when it is bald then more medicine is put on and the lice die. It must be shaved because it has many lice eggs in its hair, and that's why the lice don't go away. (The medicine doesn't kill the eggs.) 1177. People in the valley don't have many pigs. They usually have no more than one or two; rarely, a person may have five or six, including piglets.

1178. When pigs sit in the sun the lice begin to get active as they feel the heat. The pig feels the itching, gets up and goes to scratch itself on a mesquite trunk or a boulder or whatever it finds. One can hear it when it rubs its rump; this is the part where it has the most lice eggs. Sometimes its hair is white from so many eggs. 1179. When a pig lies in the sun, chickens come around and eat the lice. Turkeys also like to eat them. Pig lice are black and ugly. Piglets that get lice can't resist and die. The bite of the lice is probably too much for them.

1180. Earth lice.[149] This is a small insect whose color is the same as the ground it is on. It is very smart; if it senses that someone is coming to touch it, it lies still and doesn't move. It stays like that for a while, and then goes running along. It, too, bites. 1181. It bites people's legs. Its bite is not painful, but causes a lot of itching. One scratches and scratches until blood flows, and still the itching doesn't stop. 1182. When they really bite someone, they raise hives on the body. These lice are buried in powdery earth. One can see them when they make their nest. To make their nest they tumble over and over and make a small, circular depression. The little creature is not even seen, just the earth that is moving. 1183. If one digs then the insect is found, but they lie still so that they won't be seen. They aren't everywhere, just around where pigs are tied up. They probably feed on pigs' blood, and that is why they are found there.

1184. The tick.[150] It looks like the earth louse. They hold onto things very hard with their feet. They hold and hold, and though one pulls at their feet they don't let go of what they are holding. 1185. They are found stuck on the ears of hares; during the dry season ticks multiply most on hares. They suck on the hare's blood and leave them addled and thin. And during this time the grasses die off in the open country. 1186. Hares and rabbits mostly feed on grass. Those that are full of ticks are no good for people to eat because they are so thin. 1187. Squirrels don't let ticks stick to them. Nor do cattle have ticks, as they do in other regions where, from what I've heard, cattle are full of ticks all over their body.

1188. Sometimes they go into people's ears, but it isn't known for sure whether this is the tick or the earth louse. Some say it is the tick, while others say it is the earth louse. Once I saw a child that had a swollen ear. He said that it itched and that it felt like something was moving inside it. His mother thought it was probably a tick. This woman is my godmother. 1189. She took a little stick and moved it around in her son's ear. Then she saw that something was moving inside and she knew it was a tick. She tried to get it out several times with the stick, but it just wouldn't come out; it wouldn't let go of the flesh. 1190. Then she thought it would go out if she put on salt and water. She ground the salt, mixed it with water and put it in the child's ear. About an hour later, the animal came out slowly. When it goes in it is small; but once it's inside it grows, and it's hard to get it to leave. 1191. This is not the only case; there have been others. It is said that it makes a person lose his hearing. Years ago, people used to sleep on petates[151] and on the ground because they didn't have beds. That's probably how those bugs went into people's ears, that is, while they were sleeping. In those days there weren't many doctors to consult about what to do. And anyway, they charged a lot of money.

1192. The corn grub.[152] They go where there is corn. Whether there is a lot or a little, they go and eat it. At first, one sees a very small insect, and that's what eats the corn. Then it grows and turns into the palomilla moth. 1193. It starts to fly around at night. It seeks out shade; sunlight kills it. It is grey and yellow in color. This is the most harmful insect for corn that's been stored. 1194. If this grub finds any corn at all, even a quarter cuartillo, or a cuartillo, it turns it into dust and ruins it. If one does not stop this from happening, it leaves only dust instead of corn. If it gets into a lot of corn, and ruins part of it, people will sometimes prepare nixtamal anyway. But the tortillas smell of rotten corn, and are dark in color. 1195. Hot storage places, like large ollas and crates, attract palomilla moths.

1196. There are years when there is a good harvest and people make "hangings" of corn; that is, they hang ears of corn to keep them. First the harvested corn is put on the patio; then the largest ears are chosen; a few husks are taken off, and the husks that remain are tied together to hang up the corn. 1197. The first husks are removed with the purpose of tying together the husks that remain. The leaves taken off are kept apart; they are stacked together, one inside the other so they form a tight unit, and these will be used to make tamales. 1198. The hangings are first put out in the sun so the corn will dry well, and then they are put in the house. Others are left in the sun so that palomilla moths won't do anything to them. But others are dried and hung in the cooking area where there is a lot of smoke. 1199. In this way, though it is very smoky and the corn turns black, it can be kept for one or two years and palomilla moths won't do anything to it. When the rains come again, the seed corn is taken down and stripped for planting. 1200. If this is not done, the palomilla moths will eat it all; that is, when you take down the seed corn to remove the kernels, they are all full of holes and can't be used for planting. Thus, we know that smoke is like poison for the palomilla moth. 1201. Other people put on lime dust to keep their seeds. It keeps the palomilla moth from doing anything, but smoke is considered to be the most effective thing against it.

1202. The bean borer.[153] This insect is much like the palomilla moth, in that it does a lot of damage. It can't be seen when it enters a bean. Beans are stored in baskets. But when the beans are selected for cooking, the beans that have borers in them are found. 1203. At first it is like a little grub, or larva, and then it grows, with feet and wings. When it is found at this stage it is white. When it gets bigger it changes color and becomes brown. 1204. When one sees it, it looks like a beetle, but the borer is very small and doesn't have horns like the beetle. It develops inside beans and eats as it grows, until it destroys the bean. Once it is grown it leaves and flies away.

1205. The beans that are still good can still be selected for cooking, but the soup is very salty and the beans themselves don't taste good. Beans are different from corn. Even though the grub has bored it, if a bean is planted it grows and bears fruit, as if nothing had happened. 1206. By contrast, corn doesn't sprout, and even if it does, the plant is sickly yellow and doesn't grow up; it dies. People put a little powdered lime on beans, too, so beans won't be eaten by grubs. It doesn't do any good, though, and the borers eat them anyway. 1207. Each bean seed has one or two or three grubs and they ruin the seed. These creatures are bad. Some of them eat beans before the beans are mature; other insects eat them when the beans are fully developed.

1208. The cockroach.[154] It lives in houses. It is yellow, combined with brown, in color. They go in houses and they are everywhere. They are very bad because they defecate on plates and in the cupboard, and they dirty foods that are stored. When this happens, the food is inedible, and people don't eat it. 1209. Then they multiply and there are little ones and big ones in the kitchen. They are fast; sometimes one cannot catch them to kill them. They have wings but don't fly, only run. 1210. During the day they stay in nooks and crannies and don't come out. When it starts to get dark they come out all crazy and run around. Sometimes they get into the petaca and eat the tortillas. This is why they are called "tsihme" in Ñähñu. 1211. They spoil the food. When they don't eat it, they defecate on it. When they see that people are coming to kill them, they run. They stay in the roofs of houses if the roof is made of maguey leaves. They go under plates that are turned upside down. 1212. They can go hungry for many days. You can abandon the use of a kitchen or a house for a few days, but when you go to use it again, there they are, like new. The cockroaches come out and run around. 1213. Sometimes they go into ovens to make their nest because there is a kind of fiber on the insides of ovens that they use. This is where they live and multiply a lot. One must put in a fire to kill them. 1214. After a while there are more. Cockroaches, palomillas, and borers are all very harmful.

1215. The shrimp. The shrimp is not of the desert. I mention it because it is eaten when Holy Week approaches, and during Holy Week. People bring it from the market and prepare it to eat. The one they buy is not fresh, but dried, because the dried variety is not ruined by the heat. 1216. During the dry season the sun is really hot; so if one buys the fresh kind of shrimp it will be ruined and no one will eat it. Dried shrimp can be kept a long time and they don't spoil, so this is the kind brought from the sea. 1217. Those who have money can eat shrimp several times during Holy Week. Those who have less money eat it at least once. They buy it, grind it up well, and then make some oval shaped tortas. 1218. But in order to shape the ground shrimp meal it is mixed with eggs. The two are mixed together and the tortas are fried in lard, one at a time. 1219. They are left to cook, and then they are removed from the fat. The chile is ground separately; and if nopal is to be added, then it is boiled separately, too. The ground chile has spices in it, such as pepper, oregano, marjoram, and cumin.

1220. The chile is fried. Then the nopal is added. Finally, the shrimp, which has already been cooked, is added, and the whole meal is very tasty. The word for shrimp in Ñähñu "maai," should not be confused with the other word "maai," which means "sprout" and refers to the sprouts of beans and squash.

1221. The earthworm.[155] It generally lives where there is moisture. It doesn't live in dry earth, but always seeks wet earth. There are a lot of them in the irrigated zone because there is plenty of moisture. In the dry zone it is rare to find a piece of ground where there is water and mud, but sometimes there is some. 1222. Whenever it drizzles for three days there are small earthworms about. Their body is all red. They feed on the earth they dig through, and the holes they make serve as their nest. That is, they eat what they dig, and then defecate it. 1223. The earthworm is very slow and doesn't run. All domestic fowl, including chickens as well as turkeys, like to eat worms. They scratch the ground wherever they see it is moist, and if there is a group of chickens and one of them gets a worm, then the others chase it to take the worm away.

1224. The black butterfly.[156] It comes from the same caterpillar that turns into a moth. The black caterpillar is the one that turns into the black moth. It is very black, but even though it is black it looks pretty. It has some orange spots on its wings. It has four wings. The two next to the head are slightly wider, while the ones nearer the hind end are narrower. 1225. Caterpillars start to change into moths in December. They're the ones I already mentioned that live on mesquite branches. That's where the moths hatch. The caterpillars that are totally black turn into black moths. 1226. The ones that are black and yellow on the sides turn into orange moths, and they are also beautiful. 1227. They leave their skin in the mesquites and go flying off to flowers where they drink the nectar with their antennae. These antennae that they have aren't for stinging, but for sucking the nectar of flowers. There are no butterflies that bite; they all just look for flowers to suck on.

1228. One can say that the caterpillar lives twice. The first time is in the form of a caterpillar in the mesquites, eating the leaves. The second is when they turn into butterflies. But this time they don't bite as before. Now they are beautiful, and though one might put it on one's hand, it does no harm. 1229. We don't know how many days butterflies live, because no one can observe them since they don't live in one place. They go all over, and when they die the caterpillar's life is over. Butterflies suck the flowers of the gigante and the órgano.

1230. Mexican bean beetle.[157] They are of different colors and sizes. There are white ones, black ones, red ones, yellow ones and brown ones. They all live in plants. Plants grow when it rains. And when it doesn't rain, then there are none of these insects, either. They live in the plantings all over the irrigated zone. 1231. These beetles do a lot of harm because they eat the leaves of bean plants which are just blossoming. They are found stuck to the leaves, and they feed by sucking on the leaf. Furthermore, they only eat the tender plants and leave tough plants alone. When they finish one leaf, they go to another. 1232. Where there are a lot of these beetles they really hurt the plants; there is no way to avoid them because they fly. When they finish eating the leaves, they start on the flowers, and that's when they finish off the plant.

1233. When the plants start to form beans, they eat them, too. They do the same thing they do to leaves, that is they suck them dry. If a strong rain comes it knocks them off and they die. But the bean plant doesn't come back; it remains withered. They get two or three sprouts and the vines get twisted. 1234. The leaves that are left sometimes shrivel up before the beans are fully developed. Those beetles are "teasers," that is, they make fools of people. They are like dung beetles; if someone touches one it goes completely still, like it was dead. 1235. This beetle draws in its legs and puts them in its shell. It is called "ximozu'ue" because its back is a little ball when it walks, and it looks like a half gourd for drinking pulque that someone has turned upside down. 1236. It

Even though it is black, it looks pretty

Fauna 1233

doesn't only live on bean plants, but also on weeds in the milpas, and it eats their leaves.

1237. Mantis.[158] This is also called "fani rä zithu" in Ñähñu. Its head is like a horse's. Its legs are very large, that is, they are very developed. The back part of its stomach towards its rear end is thicker than the front end. Its neck is very long and thin. It has bulging eyes like a grasshopper's. 1238. Mantises are different colors; there are green ones, red ones, orange ones, and grey ones. Each one goes with a plant that is its own color so it can hide. In this way, birds can't find them easily. Birds hunt and eat them. Even people can't find them when they blend into the color of the plant they are on. 1239. There are different sizes, both large ones and small ones. They are found on leaves and they drink the juice of the leaves. The one on bean plants is green, and it eats its leaves. The ones on capulines are brown, even though the leaves of the capulín are green. The capulín mantis goes onto the stems, rather than the leaves, which are brown. The ones on dried plant stalks are the same color as the dried plant.

1240. When mantises see someone, they raise up their head to look at him. Its mode of walking is different from other insects. Many call it the Devil's horse; it is said that wherever the Devil goes he is mounted on this insect. We don't know how we know that the Devil has his own horse. 1241. Everyone says it is bad to kill this insect, because if its master finds out, he'll punish human beings that mistreated his creature. Of course, this is not certain because, if it were, people whom we've seen kill these animals would be dead. 1242. Those people have no problem and are healthy. What we don't know is what animal turns into this one. Possibly they are right where these animals are, but are hard to see because they change color and blend into the plants where they are perched.

1243. The inchworm.[159] Like the bean beetle and the mantis, these are of different colors and sizes. There are green ones that live on mesquite leaves, and there are a lot of them when the mesquites sprout. They have legs on their head and near their hind end, but in the middle, that is, their stomach, they have no legs. 1244. They inch along. First, they draw up their hind end to their head, then they thrust their head forward, and that's how they move along, like they were measuring the plant or the earth they are walking on. This is why it is called "the measurer" in Ñähñu. 1245. They also take on the color of the plants they live on, and birds eat them. They aren't harmful to bean plants or plantings in general. They feed on leaves, but not in large quantities, and it is not known exactly where they are born.

1246. The bedbug.[160] This bug is worse than the flea. Even though fleas multiply, they don't go up on walls like bedbugs. The bedbug goes up on walls, gets into little holes it finds there, lays its eggs, and multiplies a lot. It lives everywhere in the house, even in the roof, and lays its eggs everywhere. One can see where it lives because the wall looks spotted. 1247. The spots are dried blood, because the only thing this insect tries to do is find blood to drink.

1248. During the day it doesn't move. But at night they come out and run around like they were crazy. These parasites act like they can think. If they see that people are moving about, they remain still. When they see that people aren't moving, they start to run again. 1249. When lights are turned on they remain still again, stopped where they are. If the lights are turned out, they start running around again, and if they see that someone is going to get them, they fall to the floor.

1250. They have oval, red bodies, and have feet like a louse's. Their bite causes itching. They suck blood, about a drop at a time. When it's a large one, it may drink more than that. If they are larger, it is easier to find them and catch them. But when they are small, they can't be seen, and their bite is even more disturbing. 1251. The large ones and small ones alike run around. When a lot get together and bite a person, welts come up and they produce chills. One can get rid of fleas by putting the bedding out in the sun. But bedbugs don't go away. 1252. They find a place to stay and don't leave. People who use petates to sleep on get bedbugs. The bugs go between the weave of the palma and then come out at night. There is no other solution except to throw out the petate or burn it and buy another one. But the bugs that remain on the wall multiply again. 1253. People who have two or three rooms abandon a room for two months in order to let the bedbugs die. When they return, they think that all the bugs are dead. On the first night they are surprised that the bugs return and bite them even more crazily than before because they are hungrier. 1254. Thus we know that these insects are very hardy.

The blood they suck lasts them many days. When they have been starved, their stomachs are transparent, like they were close to death, and they move with difficulty because all that's left of them is skin. But when they find food again, they get fat. They are very bad. 1255. Even if one sprays DDT on them, they escape by going elsewhere in the room. They are a little bit like the earth louse in form. It is very important to find a way to exterminate bedbugs wherever they are, because they are very bad. 1256. They drink people's blood, and possibly transmit diseases, too. As I said earlier, they don't drink the blood of any other animal, just people. They, too, hatch from eggs like fleas and lice. Bedbugs lay their eggs in holes in the wall. They cover the eggs with their own body so they'll hatch.

1257. The large black wasp.[161] Most of its body is black, combined with a little orange on its stomach. It is generally larger than the ordinary wasp. Its stomach is fatter than the other wasps'. 1258. Its head is larger, and its feet are longer and black. Its wings are yellow and transparent. There aren't many of these insects. It is rare to see them, and one can't even see them well when they are around because they fly faster than red wasps. One can see them well when they are sitting on trees or rocks looking for spiders to eat. 1259. They don't eat the whole spider; they just suck its blood, it dies, and they leave it. This wasp sometimes stings cattle. It probably hurts a lot, because the cattle run around, like they were going crazy. They kick up and run around. 1260. The poison must hurt a lot, because cattle have thick skin and the pain gets to them.

1261. Once, a day laborer told me that a big black wasp had bitten his hand. We were working on a bordo for magueys, and the insect was sitting on a rock. That man took off his hat and hit it to kill it. 1262. By luck, he hit it and we saw very well how it was built; the man looked for the stinger in the tail. He found it and said "This is what stings." And saying this, he yanked it out. The point looked like the pointed end of a maguey leaf. 1263. "Once, one bit me," he said.

I asked him if it hurt. "Aa! yes, that son-of-a-bitch hurts a lot," he responded.

"Which hurts more, the red or the black wasp?" I asked.

"There's no comparison! The black one hurts more," he told me. 1264. "One day I was out working as a laborer," he said, "digging out maguey trunks. I had just gotten the leaves free; there was a wasp there, and I didn't see it. It bit me near my elbow. It felt like someone had stabbed me with a knife. I felt like I wanted to cry," he said. "This is how I know its sting hurts more than a hornet's or a red wasp's," he said. "I went for a week, and my arm it still hurt," he said. "When it hit me I wanted to faint and I got chills. But this soon went away," he said.

1265. Fish. They live in the waters in back of dams. They are brought by the Tula River that runs through Ixmiquilpan and San Juanico and then goes off towards Tasquillo, passing through other, smaller villages. 1266. In all these communities where the river passes they eat fish. They catch them by going into small pools where the fish are. They get one or two. 1267. Others go where the river is straight and build rock channels which guide the fish to a narrow opening. The fishermen stand there with their ayate nets extended. 1268. When they see a fish go into the net as it is trying to pass, they quickly lift the net and catch the fish. Sometimes they catch big fish, sometimes small ones. To catch them, they spread their legs out and let the water pass through. They have their ayate tied around their neck; they wait for the fish to go into the net, and they pick it up quickly. 1269. A fisherman might catch just one or two, but he puts them in an olla or whatever he's carrying to store the fish, and then he puts his ayate

Many call it the Devil's Horse

Fauna 1249

down again. He fishes about half a day, and then goes home with what he's caught.

When he gets home, he gives it to his wife who prepares it. 1270. If they are big fish, then they are made in soup, but when they're small this can't be done. If they are small they are washed well and spices are added to the whole fish, including onion, garlic, chile, salt, and mint. They are all cut up very well and then mixed together with the fish. 1271. Then they are wrapped in corn husks to make a kind of tamal. When this is done, the tamal is put in the fire to roast. Sometimes it is put on a comal. Since fish aren't very meaty they cook easily. They cook in ten minutes in the fire. When they're cooked, they are very tasty. 1272. Large fish can be roasted, too, but first they have to be scaled and cut into pieces. Then they are prepared in the same way as little fishes. They are thrown on the comal and they cook quickly. 1273. Small fish don't have hard bones yet, so they are cooked whole. They only have to be washed well.

1274. In another dam lake at a place called Debode in the jurisdiction of the town of Capula there are many more fish. Many people go there early to fish; they are there before dawn. They begin to fish as dawn comes up because the fish come to the surface at night and go back down into the deep water at dawn. 1275. This big area of water is called a dam by the mestizos. These dams have been built to store water for irrigation, and they've stocked them with fish for whoever wants to catch them. But it is only for individual consumption; it is not permitted to catch fish for sale. 1275. Some people take a net and tie lead balls on the edges so that when the net is cast it will sink and catch fish. Fish come to the surface in the pre-dawn hours. One can see them with their mouths open, making bubbles in the water. 1277. But if they see that people are coming they go back down. Fishermen need to have clothes that blend with the plants where they are standing so they won't be seen by the fish. Then, when the fish aren't paying attention, the fisherman throw the net.

1278. The bee. The yellow and black varieties. We begin with the black bee[162] which lives all over the valley. It is known simply as "gäni" in Ñähñu, or "jicote" in Spanish, in order to differentiate it from the other one, called "k'aaxt'ägäni" or "jicote amarillo." The only thing different is the color; they are the same size. The black bee always stays out in the open country. 1279. This bee has hair on its back. Its wings are orange and transparent. Its legs are also black, and have hair on them. This bee has non-closing, bulging eyes, and some of them have yellow stomachs.They feed on the honey of flowers on plants like órgano, quelite verde and all the other flowers it finds with its antennae.

1280. It digs out its nest in maguey quiotes and in plants called "uambo" in Ñähñu,which are between a maguey and a lechuguilla. It bores into any soft wood it finds and lives there and deposits its little larvae. It stings, too, if anyone provokes it. 1281. Its sting is as painful as the red wasp's. They multiply in the spring when there are flowers. One knows where they are because they buzz their wings. They like plants called "t'afigäni" in Ñähñu and they drink the honey of its flowers. Perhaps, observing this, people have given the plant the name "miel de jicote." 1282. The black variety hangs around plants more. It brings pollen, stuck to its feet, back to its hole. But it doesn't make its nest like the honey bee does. The black bee, we can say, is wilder, because it just sticks the pollen it carries any old place and doesn't make a honeycomb hive.

1283. Now we will see the way of life of the yellow bee. This yellow bumblebee hangs around more where there are flowers and green trees. When the garambullos, mesquites, and other trees are in bloom these bees are about in the open country. When the trees I mentioned finish flowering, the bees go where there are other plants in flower. 1284. This kind of bee is yellow all over its body, and its wings are yellow, too. It has hair, like the black bee we saw a moment ago. It is a little dangerous for animals, especially for cattle. When it stings a cow, it makes it jump around with pain from its venom. 1285. According to what is said, it has caused cattle to die. Some people say that when a yellow bee stings cattle the animals die from the pain of the venom. The mountain people say this. 1286. This bee also buzzes its wings when it flies. These are the two bees that are alike in size.

1287. The honey bee. Now we see this other one called the honey bee. In Ñähñu it is more commonly called "kolmenä" to avoid confusing it with the ones we just saw. This bee is small in comparison with the other two. It can live in the cliffs, and it can live in houses. They come in two colors; one is yellow, and the other is a little black. 1288. The ones that live in the cliffs look for holes in the rocks. They construct their hive there, like those that live in houses. They work, gathering up the honey in the flowers of the monte. They make "ñ'eext'ä," or "nopal leaves" as we call them in Ñähñu; but these are of wax and honey.

1289. Sometimes one can find hives in holes in large boulders, or in holes in tree trunks which have rotted out. One knows right away where they are because they buzz wherever they go. Shepherds are always the first to find them because they are always out in open country with their flocks. 1290. When they find a hive they try to knock it down to get the honey. They cover their eyes with their ayates so the bees won't sting them, because the honey bee goes after people's eyes. 1291. If they can't get at the eyes, then they sting wherever they can. Their sting is very painful. If one's eyes get stung they swell up and close. 1292. When these bees sting, you must remove the stinger right away and suck on the wound. Whoever is with a person must suck on the wound to get out the venom; then it doesn't swell as much. But if it is allowed to swell, it gets big. 1293. At night it itches a lot and one just has to scratch it. When the honey bee stings it leaves its stinger in the wound; and once it stings, it dies.

The honey bee uses pollen to make wax and carries the pollen on its feet, or on its legs. 1294. When it gets to the hive, it deposits the pollen, going around in circles and making the holes in the honeycomb. It also deposits honey which it carries in its stomach. 1295. It sucks on different flowers. When the hives of the ones that live in the open country are knocked down they get angry; they swarm out and fly far away from the hive. The ones that live in the open country are fiercer and sting more because they are not used to seeing people.

1296. The ones that live in houses are somewhat tame and don't sting their masters all the time. But if a stranger comes, then they sting one of his eyes when he least expects it. Though he may jump with pain, the bee returns and stings his neck or one of his ears. The Ñähñu word for the sting of this animal means "stoning," because it flies in like a stone being thrown. It is so fast that you can actually hear it coming, and in an instant it drives in its stinger.

1297. Some people are interested in raising these bees, others aren't. These insects know who likes them and who doesn't. If they know they are held in esteem by the people in the house they are in, then they stay there. Otherwise, they leave. One night they just go away, and the next day they are gone. 1298. Also, if they see that the family members don't get along, but are always fighting with each other, they leave. They like to live with people who respect them, including both the woman and the man, as well as the children. 1299. When this is the case the animals work and produce honey and wax as is their custom. They go flying around the patio of the house, and they don't sting; they are happy. 1300. It is said that they are very jealous. If their master doesn't come home one day but stays to sleep at another house, then the next day they sting him. This is what those who raise them say. What they like best about these animals is their cleanliness.

1301. A person who sweeps out the patio every day finds their hive where they live. The bees, too, clean out their house. If one of them dies, they take it out and throw it far away. Those that die outside the hive are also picked up and thrown away by the others. They don't like to strew things around close to the hive where they live.

1302. One must give them a plate of water and some twigs to light on. Otherwise, the bees fall into the water and drown. 1303. Sometimes a mesquite lizard gets into a beehive. This is bad for the bees, because the lizard eats them. When things go wrong, the bees leave and go away. If they don't want to leave the house they go to a tree nearby. There are a lot of them in a hive, up to one or two cuartillos. 1304. They follow the queen. If she leaves, they all go. Some also leave the hive when they multiply. But division of a hive is a slow process.

1305. First, they come out and hang on the entrance of the hive. When the owner sees this, he looks for another hive to put them in so the hanging bees can make their own comb. 1306. The ones that separate off are the offspring and the ones that remain are the adults. If they aren't given a new hive right away, then they leave and go off on their own. Sometimes one sees them separating from the hive. They make a lot of noise and then one knows that they are getting ready to leave. To keep them from leaving, you quickly look for a big iron bar or another piece of metal that makes a lot of noise 1307. and you run after them banging the metal with the other hand to keep them from going. The bees, hearing the metal, stay and look for somewhere to go. It might be a plant or a wall, but they stay, just from the noise of the metal. We've seen many, many bees that have been kept around in this way.

1308. In order to put them into the hive one burns palma wood and makes a lot of smoke. This makes the bees groggy and keeps them from biting the person who puts them into the hive. Once they're in the hive it is brought to the house so the bees will make their honeycomb and stay there. 1309. They like to live in hives made of palma trunks rather than of board wood. The palma hive is warmer. Though it may be cold outside, the hive remains warm since it is narrower. Also, the boards that are usually used to make wooden hives are thinner than palma, and thus colder. Moreover, it's harder for the bees to stick their wax to boards. The palma hive is narrower.

1310. Beehives are made from palma trunks. The straightest trunk one can find is cut down and the ends are cut even. Then the trunk is hollowed out with an adze that is good and sharp. After a hole has been cut, it is left in the sun to dry out. 1311. When it is to be used for a hive it is fumed with smoke from beeswax so the bees won't feel out of place when they enter.

The black bee is raised by people who live in the country. Mestizos raise yellow bees, and they keep them in hives made of board wood. 1312. Both kinds offer the same benefit. Honey gives one strength, too. Many people like to eat natural honey, not the kind cut with water. Bees collect honey all during the time when garambullos, mesquites and other plants are in bloom. 1313. But there are years when it doesn't rain, and there are no flowers, and the bees start to die from hunger.

1314. When honey is removed from a hive, a part of the comb is left so it will continue to be produced. Honey is removed in April when the hive is full. People eat it with bread during Holy Week when they go to town. But they prefer to eat it with lettuce. 1315. People who have these creatures have a valuable economic resource. They sell the wax and honey. The honey is sold for 40 pesos a liter, and the wax for 30 pesos a kilo. Wax is purchased for making candles that are burned for the images of saints and virgins in church; candles are also used for everything that has to do with religion. This is the aid offered by the bee.

1316. Bees only have one leader, called the queen. She lays her eggs in the holes which the worker bees make in the wax. The workers just collect honey. They don't have offspring. The queen is larger, longer and thinner than the other bees. 1317. The male bees are fatter, and don't go out to work; they just live inside and mate with the queen. There are many male bees in the hive; they abuse the workers, and the workers leave. 1318. This is the life of these creatures. Lizards and birds called huitlacoches eat them. They eat bees.

1319. The black and yellow wasp.[163] There are two classes of wasps, as there are of bees. We begin with the black one to see what it does, and then we will look at the yellow wasp. We won't look at them separately because there isn't much to say about them, and they have practically the same way of life. 1320. The black wasp is named like this because it is black with yellow lines that run all around its body. It has two wings that are brownish and transparent. It also stings and hurts, although not with the same intensity as bees. It stings with its hind end when it is provoked. If it is left alone it doesn't sting. 1321. Yellow jackets go around alone, one at a time, and suck on flowers and drink the aguamiel of the maguey. They live in groups to help build the hive. This wasp has a different kind of wax. When one sees the wax, it looks like paper that has disintegrated.

1322. It builds a big ball that it hangs on mesquites where no one will see it. It seems to be able to hide very well in the open country. Sometimes it sets the hive very low, and other times very high. Shepherds and rabbit hunters see them first. They lay their eggs and deposit their honey in their hive. The young are in one part of the hive, and the honey is in the other. 1323. It is necessary to get the wasps away to get to eat the honey. Palma wood is burned; it has the strongest smoke, and this gets them away from the hive. Once they are away, one can take the honey. Sometimes they build the hive very big; up to two hand spans in length. 1324. This is when there are a lot of wasps and they all help to build the hive quickly. Its honey is very sweet, and has a special flavor. One eats it together with the honeycomb in order to get out the honey. Once the sweet part is out, the rest is thrown away. Then, the hive is useless. 1325. No one catches this wasp to raise it. It lives by itself in the open country, and sometimes comes into houses. It hangs its hive from the ceilings of two story houses in the city.

1326. The yellow one is like the honeybee in form. The size of this wasp is smaller; its body is smaller in comparison to the bee. Its color and its wings are much like those of the bee. 1327. It is wilder and lives far out in the country where a lot of people don't come. It only rarely comes into pueblos. It, too, has a hive like the one we saw a moment ago. It has a lot of honey and it's as sweet as if it were the honey of the honeybee. 1328. It eats the honey of flowers wherever it goes and it makes its hive with the honey it collects. Wherever they are, there are lots of them. There are up to a half cuartillo of these animals, making noise as they pass by. They are also called "large wasps." The black wasp builds hives all year, and the yellow wasp builds them only during the season when flowers bloom. When the flowers stop blooming they stop working on the hive and just live inside, eating the honey they have collected. 1329. Of course, they come out. But they don't work like they do when there is a lot of sun and the plants are in bloom.

1330. This is the way of life of the animals that live in the open country. Some cause harm to people, but there are others that offer a bit of joy to people, like the ones we just saw that offer their honey. They all give life to the desert.

1331. The corn earworm.[164] There are many grubs of different sizes and different colors, like the ones we have already seen. We will look at this grub separately because it is eaten, and it eats corn. It eats the corn when it is in the tassel stage; when the ears are young and fresh this bug is there eating. The harvesters find these grubs when they harvest. They each carry a rolled up maguey leaf; they gather the grubs and put them on the leaf. 1332. Some people like to gather them, while others like to eat them raw. When people eat these grubs their heads make a loud noise from the crunching. People laugh and go along making jokes. Those who collect them squash the grubs' heads so the insects won't abandon the leaf; otherwise, by the time you know it the grubs are gone.

1333. When people are through harvesting they go to their homes carrying the grubs they've collected. If there are only a few, then they are roasted on the comal when the tortillas are made. They are "toasted," as it is called. Once they are cooked well, they are eaten plain, or with a tortilla with salt and chile salsa on it. 1334. When at least a handful are collected, then condiments are prepared. The condiments are things like mint, hot chile and marjoram if there is any. They are mixed together well, and wrapped in corn husks to put them in the fire to cook. When they are cooked they have a lot of flavor. 1335. These insects are not selected by color or size; all are eaten because they only live in corn. Only the grubs that live in corn ears are eaten; those that go about on the ground are not eaten.

1336. The mesquite bug.[165] Its name means "stinky animal." Its odor comes from a yellow liquid that comes from its sides. When someone grabs it, it shoots this liquid at the person who provokes it. 1337. It shoots whenever it is provoked. This liquid stains any hand or clothes it is sprayed on. It doesn't go away, even if one puts soap or xite on it. It lasts about two weeks on one's hands. If it goes in one's eyes, they get red because it burns a lot. 1338. Many folks gather these bugs to roast and eat when there are a lot of them around. They let them toast up well, and then eat them. Others gather them up, bring them home, toast them on the comal, and mix them together with chile to make salsa. 1339. It's as delicious as ground squash seed, and gives a special flavor to salsa. If shepherds see mesquite bugs out in the open country, they take them from the mesquites and bring them back to roast. Others like to eat these insects, too.

1340. The insect is spotted, but most of its body is black. It is patched with white and red on its back. They must be brought in to eat when they are still in the larva stage. Once they start to get wings they are called "old grubs," and they aren't any good because they are tough and rubbery. The same is true for when they are in the flying stage. 1341. They always live in mesquites. That is where they grow when the mesquites sprout in the spring. This is when these animals begin to be born. They feed on mesquite leaves, and if one squashes them one sees that what they have in their stomachs is green. 1342. They only eat mesquite leaves. They do go around to other plants, but they don't eat them.

1343. The firefly and the glow worm.[166] These are nocturnal; they appear in the hot season and fly at night. They are dark green and are easily confused with the plants they are on. One of them has wings, and flies; the other only goes about on the ground. Their characteristics are about the same, including their color. 1344. Both the flying one and the walking one give light and they are very beautiful. The nights in May are very hot and these insects go all over the place. Each time they strain to fly, their light goes on. When it is seen that they begin to fly it is said that it will soon rain. 1345. This happens sometimes; the rains come and the people begin to plant. This insect is the same size as a fly. It is the one that gives light to the desert, and it isn't sad, as some people believe.

1346. The chinicuil.[167] Its name means that it is a "red grub." Of all the larvae we've seen, this is the only one that has a beautiful color, the color of the rose. It is the size of a maguey grub. Its whole body is red and its head is brown. The chinicuil is faster than the corn earworm. 1347. The chinicuil lives only in the heart of the maguey, and especially in the young plants that are only one or two years old. If there are a lot of them in the heart the maguey withers and doesn't grow. Even if there is moisture at the roots, the leaves wither. 1348. If not attended to, the plants die. When they look withered they are pulled out, pruned back, and left in the sun so the grubs will leave the heart of the plant. Once it's dried out well where it's been pruned, it is replanted and gets better again.

1349. The chinicuil is not always seen on the ground. At the beginning of September skunks start to dig at the base of the magueys. When skunks find a maguey that has chincuiles, they dig it up and uproot the maguey. People don't like the fact that skunks interrupt the growth of magueys. 1350. In October, on Saint Francis's Day, it sometimes rains very hard. After the rain these grubs come out and there are so many that they color the whole row of magueys. People who like to eat these grubs go out to collect them and toast them on a comal; or sometimes they fry them in lard. These grubs are delicious and their grease comes out when you fry them because they are fat. 1351. Some folks also eat them raw. They are only out during these two months, and in other months there are none. Birds like to eat them, too. This is when skunks feed most on grubs. People who eat a lot of them get a cough. It is said that these grubs are hot animals.[168]

1352. The grubs of the maguey, the junquillo, and the prickly pear. To finish the animals which live in the Mezquital Valley, we look at one that lives on maguey leaves, and at two others that live on the junquillo and the nopal, or prickly pear. We will treat the three together because they are all called "thet'ue" in Ñähñu and they are about the same in their characteristics. 1353. With all this we will finish looking at all the animals, including the big ones and the insects. Possibly, one has escaped us and we have not treated it, but this is because it doesn't always live in the valley, but only passes through.

1354. Let's look now at the nopal grub. When the nopal begins to get old it starts getting grubs. They are small insects, which are white and are called "thet'ue," possibly because they look like maguey grubs which are white. They are different in size and in body form. The nopal grub is a little thinner and its body is rough. 1355. It lives in the nopal trunk and it can be seen because it leaves its excrement on the outside of the trunk. When it bores into the nopal a lot, the plant dies. When a nopal falls over by itself the grubs are collected. When the nopal does not fall by itself, no one wants to chop it down. Nopals are needed since they give tunas and nopal pads. 1356. But when they fall over by themselves they are hacked up to get out all the grubs they have. These grubs aren't toasted, nor are they eaten raw, but are always fried to eat.

1357. The "thet'ue" of the junquillo looks more or less like the nopal grub. It, too, is white, and has some fuzz on its body. Nopal grubs always live in the trunks. The junquillo grub is around in April or May. 1358. During Holy Week, people go out to look for these grubs in the open country where there are many junquillos. They carry iron bars to root up the junquillos to see if they have grubs or not. Some junquillos have them, and others don't. These, too, are eaten fried.

1359. The maguey has the tastiest chinicuil. The maguey grub is white, and its head is brown. It, too, has little hairs on its body. There aren't many in the valley. It isn't like the red chinicuil that can be gathered up in quantities when they come out. 1360. These grubs are also around in the hot months. During March, April, and May they are on the maguey leaves. The day laborers who are hired to take out old maguey trunks find these insects when they prune the magueys near the ones they are taking out. 1361. The chinicuil is near the heart of the maguey, about where the leaves come out. When the maguey is pruned these grubs are found. Some who remove maguey hearts eat the grubs raw; others take them home to toast. Not a lot of them are to be found, only four or five. 1362. Since there aren't many, they aren't fried and they aren't wrapped in corn husks, but are only toasted on a comal. Some people go out to look for these grubs, too, during Holy Week. They go along, looking at the base of the magueys along the row. Leaves that have grubs are distinguished by the fact that they have a kind of growth near the ground that eats at the plant. This is the leaf that is cut to see if it has a chinicuil. 1363. Sometimes it has one, and sometimes it doesn't. There might have been one there, but if it turned into a moth, then it would have gone. Leaves that don't have this mark are not cut because they won't have any grubs. A person who collects up to around sixteen grubs is said to have good luck.

1364. The chinicuil makes its home in the leaf it is on. It bores a hole by eating the pulp of the leaf. Mestizos like to eat them, too. In the State of Tlaxcala, since there are a lot of magueys, people collect them and sell them. It is said that they are delicious when combined with other condiments. 1365. These are some of the little insects eaten here in the valley. As we have seen, not all are edible. Some are beneficial; others aren't, but instead give diseases to people.

1366. With all this, the first volume, that treats the environment and the animals in the Mezquital Valley, comes to an end.[169] Many Ñähñu know what the land is like, and what the animals mentioned in this book are like. What is written here is what is known because it has been observed. What has not been observed can not be written. 1367. What is needed now is that this book be studied in order to know the way of life of the Ñähñu people. The Ñähñu is a person like the inhabitants of other parts of the world. 1368. Like others, the Ñähñu knows how to give respect, how to work, how to laugh. And he knows a lot about happiness, too. There are some people who believe the Ñähñu are sad people. Fortunately, this is not true. 1369. The Ñähñu knows how to make jokes, and sing songs, and knows how to play musical instruments, too. What he is concerned about a lot is maintaining friendship with everyone and with all peoples. Thus, for him, the most important thing is the well-being of all, in work as well as in the rest of life.

Notes to Volume II—Fauna

1. The visitor was an anthropology student whom I placed in the village where Salinas was teaching school in the late 1960s. At that time, muzzle loaders were still used by some Ñähñu rabbit hunters. Thus, this docs not refer to an antique gun taken home by the visitor from the "North." Salinas (1975) mentions this same student, and others, in his article describing "The Clan of Anthropologists."

2. I have not actually seen all of these animals in the Mezquital. All of them are fairly rare, except for the cottontails (*Sylvilagus auduboni* and possibly also *S. floridanus*), jackrabbits (*Lepus alleni*, judging from its enormous ears), skunks (both striped skunks, *Mephitis mephitis*, and spotted skunks, *Spilogale putorius*) and squirrels (*Spermophilus variegatus*, the burrowing rock squirrel). There have been several reports of blue foxes (*Urocyon cinereoargenteus*), and possibly kit foxes (*Vulpes macrotis*) recently. The coyote *Canis latrans* is very rare in the Mezquital nowadays. The ringtail, known as "cacomixtle" in Spanish (and in English in some parts of the American Southwest), is the *Bassariscus astutus*. There are two varieties of oppossum reported in Mexico, the *Didelphis virginiana* and the *D. marsupialius*, and there is some debate as to whether these may in fact be the same species. In any event, neither has been reported recently in the desert region of the Mezquital, but I have heard several reports of oppossum in the mountain section. The armadillo (*Dasypus novemcinctus*) is found throughout North and South America, and there are dozens of subspecies; I have not been able to determine the local variety. The bobcat is the *Lynx rufus* which occurs throughout North America. The badger of central Mexico is the *Taxidea taxus*. The weasel is *Mustela frenata*.

3. Infant mortality during the first month of life was 53 per 1,000 live births in Mexico in 1984. It was 12 per 1,000 in the United States. As in all Third World areas, children up to three years of age are at very high risk from dehydration due to diarrhea.

4. The "heart of the palma" is the point where the leaves of the palma grow away from the trunk.

5. "Xäpi" in Ñähñu refers to any offering to the saints which has been blessed by the priest in church. These are referred to as "reliquias" in Spanish, and I have glossed them as "blessed offerings" or "relics" or "religious mementos" in English. Reliquias are treated at length in Volume IV. The relics used against evil eye sickness are generally rosemary, camomile, and epiphytic bromelias, or air plants ("xikri" in Ñähñu), that grow as leafy vegetation on large trees such as oak in the more humid mountain regions and in the Tolantongo area of the Mezquital. Embellished candles, known collectively as "escamadas" in Mexico, are also used in smoking out evil-eye sickness from children. Escamadas are also "reliquias" because they are used to decorate altars to saints, and are blessed by priests. Escamadas are also discussed in Volume IV.

6. This is alum.

7. I do not know the species of nocturnal rat referred to here, though certainly some of them are pack rats or wood rats. These junk collectors are mammals of the genus *Neotoma*. There are also several kinds of true mice, including *Heteromyidae* such as Kangaroo rats (genus *Dipodymus*) and deer mice (genus *Peromyscus*). The barn owl and screech owl are the familiar *Tyto alba* and *Otus asio*. There are also great horned owls (*Bubo virginianus*) in the Mezquital. I do not know the species of bats in the Mezquital. Salinas's descriptions indicate either *Tadarida mexicana* or *T. brasiliensis*, the Mexican and Brazilian freetailed bats. There are undoubtedly others, possibly including *Myotis* spp., *Glossophaga* sp., *Leptonycteris* sp. and *Eumops* sp. (Carlos Martínez del Río, personal communication). The lesser nighthawk (*Chordeiles acutipennis*) is often mistaken for a bat; it is nocturnal and has quick, darting movements. The black harvester ants are either *Veromesser* (possibly species *pergandei*) or *Pogonomyrmex*.

8. Most of these birds, mammals, and insects are dealt with separately below. "Escamol" is Mexican Spanish for ants whose larvae is eaten. This is described below in the section dealing with insects. The burrowing mice (*Microtus mexicanus*) seem out of place here. They are voles that bore into the maguey plants to drink the aguamiel, and are classified as pests.

9. This may be what Salinas describes as a purple variety of *Opuntia ficus-indica* in Volume IV. However, this might also be *O. cantabrigiensis*, or purple prickly pear. It has relatively few spines, and is eaten by rabbits and other animals.

10. "Mbonthi" is best translated as the Spanish word "monte." In non-nucleated Ñähñu territory, it suggests all the open country between habitation sites. I often use the Spanish gloss in the English text because no English word is quite appropriate. The "Mezquital" as a region is variously called "Mbonthi" or "Bot'ähi" in Ñähñu. The capital letter "M" is used to distinguish "Mbonthi" (Mezquital) from "mbonthi" (monte).

11. The word "milpa" is used everywhere in Mexico to refer to the small plots of land that are farmed by rural peoples.

12. The "table skunk" is commonly called "striped skunk" in English, while the "jumping skunk" is the smaller "spotted skunk." The striped skunk favors moister areas, such as the barrancas, while the spotted skunk is found more in the arid lands.

13. Tunas are covered with very fine, hairlike thorns that must be cleaned off before the fruit can be handled or eaten. People roll the fruit in the loose desert earth; squirrels use their bushy tails to clean tunas before eating them.

14. The nopalillo is of course, a small nopal. It is the *O. microdasys*. It appears yellow from a distance because it is completely covered with very fine, yellow needles.

15. The field mice in the Mezquital are mostly members of the genus *Peromyscus*, of which there are many species throughout North America, including the brush mouse (*P. boylii*), the piñon mouse (*P. truei*), and the deer mouse (*P. maniculatus*), among others (Miller and Stebbins, 1964: 315-320). From my observations, one of the most common field mice in the Mezquital is actually a vole, known in Spanish as the "métoro" (*Microtus mexicanus*). The term "métoro" is an old Spanish word, and is now antiquated in Mexico, possibly because most Mexicans do not distinguish among various kinds of field mice (Carlos Martínez del Río, personal communication). Salinas and other Ñähñu, however, use the word "ratón" in referring to most field mice, and to the introduced house mouse (*Mus musculus*); they use "métoro" in referring to the *Microtus*. See Note 78 below.

16. There is a yellow, woollike fuzz that grows around the top of the barrel cactus, or viznaga. Salinas counts these field mice and the ones that live in houses as the same animal.

17. Salinas deals with two owls here. This first one is the common screech owl, *Otus asio*. The second is the wood owl, the *Ciccaba virgata* which usually inhabits the lowland forests of Mexico, but also extends into the mountain desert regions (Dr. Thomas Weber, personal communication).

18. I have called this bird a "quail" because that is what Salinas calls it in Spanish (codorniz). However, this bird is the common bobwhite, *Colinus virginianus*, which is one of the wood partridges in standard U.S. terminology.

19. The "däskäähä is glossed "huitlacoche" in Spanish. It is the curve billed thrasher, *Toxostoma curviostre*. Huitlacoche is an alternative pronunciation of "cuicacochi," from Nahuatl "cuicatl," meaning "to sing" and "cochi," meaning "night."

20. Salinas has not been able to identify this creature in Spanish. From the description of its behavior, it would appear to be a lesser nighthawk, also known as the trilling nighthawk (Dr. Thomas Weber, personal communication).

21. These are toads of the genus *Bufo*, possibly *B. punctatus* or a close relative of the *B. compactilis*, known as Couch's spadefoot (*Scaphiopus couchii*) for its ability to dig burrows. The toads in the Mezquital have an amazing capacity to hibernate and withstand drought, for many months, if required. They evaporate quickly through their water-permeable skins, but they absorb water just as quickly and their habit of burrowing underground prevents evaporation. According to Costello (1972: 205) Couch's spadefoot toad can lose up to 48% of its body weight in fluids before it dies.

22. This is probably the western pipistrelle (*Pipistrellus hesperus*), a small bat found throughout western and central Mexico (Miller and Stebbins, 1964: 278). It conforms to the description given here by Salinas. It may also be the Mexican free-tailed bat, *Tadarida mexicana*, judging by Salinas's indication that it lives in caves (see Costello, 1972: 133).

23. These are jumping spiders in the family *Salticidae*. The little jumper described here appears to be either in the genus *Phidippus* or *Metaphidippus*.

24. Scorpions (*Centruroides* spp.) are an evolutionary success story. They saw the dinosaurs come and go, and have survived for over 400 million years. Perhaps no other creature is so synonymous with the notion of "desert danger" as is the scorpion. Yet there are only two North American species, of the more than 600 worldwide, whose venom is deadly to humans. (Until antivenom was developed, human deaths from scorpion bites was fairly common: Arizona recorded 54 deaths between 1935 and 1949. See Larson, 1970: 194.) Neither is found in the Mezquital.

25. These appear to be *Scolopendra heros*, true centipedes made up of a series of somites, each of which (except for the the first one and the last two) has a pair of legs. The first segment has a pair of fangs, used to inject venom, which is not lethal to humans, but is very painful.

26. A petaca is a woven basket, specifically made for keeping tortillas warm at the table, or for carrying tortillas to the fields.

27. Depending on species, there are between 15 and 173 somites on a centipede (Larson, 1970: 196).

28. Compared to other insects, species diversity in ants is rather low, and varies directly with rainfall. Consequently, desert speciation of ants is particularly narrow (Crawford, 1981: 160). The large red harvester ant discussed here is genus *Pogonomyrmex*, probably *barbatus*. There are also small black army ants in the Mezquital, probably genus *Neivamyrex*. The small red ants mentioned by Salinas are *Atta* spp.

29. These lizards are called "escorpiones" in the Mezquital, which can be a bit confusing since these reptiles are clearly not related to scorpions. They are members of the genus *Gerrhonotus*, and are related to the Texas alligator lizard which gets as far south as San Luis Potosí (Smith, 1946: 463). Salinas says that these lizards are not very big, but the 25 centimeter measurement that he gives is about 40% larger than the largest Texas alligator lizard, and the latter are huge compared to most desert lizards in general. From their color, they might be the subgenus *S. tourquatus*.

30. Granjenos may be "Christ's crowns" in English, but I am not certain. They are rambling xerophytic bushes, possibly *Koeberlinia spinosa*. They are green, without leaves and grow up to two and three meters in height.

31. These solpugids are a variety of windscorpion, and appear to be members of the *Eremobatidae* family. They are sometimes called "vinegaroons" (family *Thelyphonidae*), despite the fact that they do not give off the characteristic vinegarlike odor of true vinegaroons, or grampuses (family *Thelyphonidae*). These hair-covered creatures are nocturnal, and hide under rocks like scorpions.

32. These are gryllid crickets (*Gryllus* sp.).

33. Adult western harvest mice (*Reithrodontomys megalotis*, for example), found throughout the Mexican plateau, weigh only eight to thirteen grams (Miller and Stebbins, 1964: 314).

34. This is the *Passerina versicolor*, called "gorrion" in Spanish. "Gorrion" is usually translated as "sparrow," but the nomenclature for birds has not been standardized in Spanish, as it has in English. In addition to the varied bunting, there are probably other sparrowlike birds in the Mezquital, like the lark bunting (*Calamospiza melanocorys*), and possibly the black-throated sparrow (*Amphyspiza bilineata*).

35. The Ñähñu reference to 15 days is borrowed from the Spanish expression, "quince días," meaning "two weeks." The term for "one week" is "eight days," and is also borrowed from Spanish.

36. In Ñähñu the rhythm of the saying ("nu'mu hingä nuhubye, gä nuhu nubye rä hñäto mäpa) conforms to the rhythm of the complex call of this bird.

37. There is only one species of lark, out of 75 species of that bird, in the New World. It is the horned lark, *Eremophila alpestris*.

38. Cenzontles are northern mockingbirds (*Mimus polyglottos*). Centzontle is from Nahuatl "centzontlatolli," meaning "bird that sings a lot," according to Santamaría.

39. This is the common ground dove, *Columbina passerina*.

40. Chicalote is the *Argemone mexicana*, an annual herbaceous plant, with spiny and denticulate leaves. It is used for medicinal purposes in many areas of Mexico. In the Mezquital it is used for curing sick chickens, as seen below.

41. Salinas may be referring here to either (or both) the spotted wren (*Campylorhynchus gularis*) or the cactus wren (*C. brunneicapillus*). Both birds inhabit the Mezquital and he may be referring to both with a single gloss.

42. There are several species of hummingbirds in the Mezquital. The green bird described by Salinas is the magnificent (Rivoli's) hummingbird (*Eugenes fulgens*). It is twice the size of the brown bird he describes, which is either the Lucifer hummingbird (*Calothorax lucifer*) or the sparkling-tailed (Dupont's) hummingbird (*Tilmatura dupontii*). Both are found in the Mezquital. The grey bird described is the dusky hummingbird (*Cynanthus sordidus*). (I am grateful to Carlos Martinez del Río for help in identifying these hummingbirds.)

43. Gigantes are huge, delicate, plants, with leaves like those of *Myrtinia*. They grow up to six meters tall, and are used for roof thatch in the Mezquital. They have large, flimsy, soft-petalled white flowers. They are also called "marijuana" in the Mezquital, although they are unrelated to *Cannabis*.

44. A "tlachiquero" is a person who extracts aguamiel from a maguey plant in the making of pulque. When the maguey plant is mature it sends up a flower stalk ("quiote" in Mexican Spanish). The stalk may grow to ten meters in a matter of weeks, fed by the sucrose-rich nectar, aguamiel. The plant is broken open, a bowl is left in the center (where the stalk would have been) and the aguamiel flows into the bowl. It must be extracted several times a day or it overflows the cavity. The aguamiel is fermented into pulque, the staple drink of the Ñähñu. Aguamiel is also called "tlachique" in some areas of Mexico, especially in the Nahuatl speaking areas of Mexico. The process of breaking open magueys and making pulque is described in detail in Volume III.

45. "Calandria" is a generic name for the *Icteridae*, or orioles. There are two species in the Mezquital, Scott's oriole (*Icterus parisorum*) and Wagler's oriole (*I. wagleri*) (Mr. Carlos Martínez del Río, personal communication). Scott's oriole is more common in the desert zone.

46. This is the *Zenaida asiatica*. It lives in open country throughout Mexico, except in rain forests and higher mountains. Although it also lives in towns, the Ñähñu distinguish subspecies of town and house doves (see below).

47. "Piedritas" or "ant stones" are the tiny gravel used by harvester ants to build the familiar crater around their nests. Some birds apparently eat this gravel as grit.

48. The cocolera is the mourning dove (*Zenaida macroura*).

49. There are two kinds of woodpeckers described here. The first is the ladder-backed woodpecker (*Dendrocopus scalaris*). The second is the lineated woodpecker (*Dryocopus lineatus*).

50. Salinas calls these birds "cardenales" in Spanish, but they are actually silkies. The glossy black bird described here is the phainopepla (*Phainopepla nitens*). Both the phainopepla and the red cardinal (*Cardinalis cardinalis*) are placed in the same category in Ñähñu.

51. Throughout the text there are references to "wood collectors." Traditionally, all cooking was done with wood fires. The desert does not produce a lot of wood, and a great deal of time is spent in collecting it for home use.

52. Several different thrushes are called nightingales in Mexico. This is the slate-colored solitaire (*Myadestes unicolor*). Salinas notes that, in his opinion, the song of this bird is not all that good, and he knows that his is a minority opinion. The slate-colored solitaire "makes all other finches sound like amateurs" according to James Fisher (quoted in Peterson and Chalif, 1973: 186). It is this legendary singing ability that is referred to by the "five guitars" in the next paragraph in the text.

53. No distinction is made in Ñähñu between moths and butterflies. Generically, they are both "tuumu." But see Note 136.

54. This is the loggerhead shrike (*Lanius ludovicianus*).

55. This is the cliff swallow (*Petrochelidon pyrrhonota*).

56. Harvester ant males and females fly from the nest to mate. The males then die and the females lose their wings.

57. This is the rock wren (*Salpictes obsoletus*).

58. This is the black-headed siskin (*Carduelis notata*).

59. The chirrionera, or coachwhip, is described below. It is, in fact, one of the fastest snakes in North America (the closely related brown racer is faster yet), and is known to climb trees when pursued (MacMahon, 1985: 444).

60. The grey-breasted jay is the *Aphelocoma ultramarina*.

61. The filomena is the cedar waxwing (*Bombycillax cedrorum*). It looks somewhat like the pyrrhuloxia (*Pyrrhuloxia sinuata*), also seen in the Mezquital on occasion. In Spanish it is known as another form of nightingale.

62. This is the *Pyrocephalus rubinus*.

63. This is the *Pipilo erythrophthalmus*, also known as the rufous-sided towhee. Salinas calls it "pájaro con pechera" in Spanish, or "bird with a dickey shirt."

64. The Ñähñu word for this bird literally means "black bird." It is the great-tailed grackle (*Cassidix mexicanus*). It looks like the melodius blackbird, the Mexican crow, and the giant cowbird. This bird has come into the Mezquital in the last 30 years as irrigation has spread through the lower reaches of the valley.

65. This bird is called "white dove" in Ñähñu. It is the rock dove (*Columba livia*), also known as the domestic pigeon.

66. Women lend each other fertilized eggs. If a woman brings four or five unfertilized eggs for trade, then the lender will give her friend a full dozen or a dozen and a half fertilized eggs, depending on the size of the borrower's hen. The idea is to provide enough eggs for the capacity of the hen to sit on them. The extra eggs are then a debt which the lender will collect at a later time.

67. This is not the same plant as "chicalote," mentioned earlier. This is a papaveraceous bush (*Bocconia arborea*) that produces a yellow tint much like the herbaceous chicalote plant. According to Santamaria, this plant was used by the Aztecs for making yellow dye for feathers, and it also contains an alkeloid that has an anesthetic effect.

68. Nejayo is the Spanish gloss for "gini" in Ñähñu. It is the water left over after cooking nixtamal. There is no gloss in English.

69. An itacate is a meal prepared for a trip. By extension, it refers to the custom of sending guests home from a fiesta meal with an extra plate of food.

70. Although women do not receive formal cargos for fiestas, they have joint responsibility with their husbands for the meal that must be prepared as part of the cargo.

71. This refers to a unit of currency from earlier times.

72. The sickness is called "ndähi" in Ñähñu, and has no simple gloss in English. It is often called "evil eye" but this is the English gloss for "uda" in Ñähñu, or "mal de ojo" in Spanish. "Mal aire" has no convenient gloss in English. One of the terms for "Devil" in Ñähñu is "ts'ondähi" which also means "bad air" ("mal aire" in Spanish). It is used in order to avoid saying "zithu," which also refers to the Devil, but is considered very strong language. See Note 158.

73. I have not been able to identify either the common English name or the scientific name of this plant, nor could Salinas provide a Spanish gloss. It is a short, bushy green that spreads along the ground. It has lanceolate leaves, and very small yellow flowers.

74. This is a small falcon, the American kestrel (*Falco sparverius*), also known as the sparrow hawk.

75. This is the familiar greater roadrunner of the Southwest U.S., the *Geococcyx californianus.*

76. The carrion bird in the Mezquital is the turkey vulture (*Cathartes aura*), also knows as the buzzard. This bird ranges from southern Canada to Tierra del Fuego, and from sea level to high mountains. While "vulture" has a sinister sound in English, this is not the case with the Ñähñu word "pada."

77. Eagles are fairly rare in the Mezquital, but are seen on occasion. There are two varieties. The more common is the golden eagle (*Aquila chrysaetos*), and the other, casual visitor is the great black hawk (*Buteogallus urubitinga*), which Salinas calls a black eagle in the text. The great black hawk is, in fact, larger than many eagles, commonly reaching 50 centimeters in body length and up to one and a half meters in wingspan. It is a formidable predator.

78. In fact, the Mexican vole, known in Spanish as the "metorito" (*Microtus mexicanus*), does feed on the juice of the maguey, according to Santamaria. The metorito, which grows to around 16-20 centimeters, is larger than field mice, which are treated separately (see Note 15 above).

79. The acocote is a long gourd, often reaching a meter and a half in length. It is pierced on both ends and is used as a kind of straw by tlachiqueros to draw up the aguamiel from the heart of the maguey.

80. These lines of repartee are very subtle. They do not translate well because the humor lies in the pattern of rhymes which the men create in Ñähñu. There is much reference to fornication with another man's sister or, homosexually, with one another. These rhyming duels are reminiscent of duels in Turkish described by Dundes, Leach, and Ozkok (1972). For example, in this exchange, one man says to the other "Look, there goes a rat." The one who didn't see the rat asks "Habu xä maa'ä gä suut'ä'i," "Where did it go? I'll stab you." The appropriate response is "gä suut'ä," "I'll stab *it*," referring to what one does to the mouse with the long stick. By putting the ending "i" on "suut'ä'i," the verb becomes "I'll stab *you*" and now "stab" becomes "penetrate" because it is used with the objective case, second person singular particle. Hence, the phrase now means "I'll screw you in the ass."

81. This is the *Masticophis flagellum*, or blue and red racer. It is commonly known as the "coachwhip" because its tail looks like a braided leather whip.

82. "Topo" is the local Spanish (and Ñähñu) word for a small-sized Coca-Cola bottle. Hence, any small bottle of about a quarter liter is a topo.

83. Two species of snake fit the description given here, the speckled snake (*Rhinocheilus lecontei*) and the banded king snake (*Lampropeltus triangulum*) (Dr. Louis Guillette, personal communication).

84. There are three species of rattler in the Mezquital. The diamondback (*Crotalus atrox*) is found scattered throughout the area. More common, however, are two varieties of the Mohave rattler, the *C. scutulatus* in the lower deserts and the *C. triseriatus* in the mountains (Dr. Louis Guillette, personal communication).

85. The "canícula" is the middle of the summer, the "dog days."

86. The cup referred to here is called a "ximo" in Ñähñu. These are half gourds which may be from one-half to three liters in volume. These gourds are the traditional cups used for drinking pulque. They have round bottoms, so they are placed in molcajetes to keep them from spilling.

87. In the Ñähñu text the man calls his wife "ñ'o." This use of the word "man" is addressive, and is a sign of familiarity. It may be used for either a man or a woman.

88. At the time of this story, 1966, Salinas was the teacher in the community of Dextho. His home was in Orizabita, where he went on weekends. Small villages, such as Dextho, reserve a room, attached to the school, for the teacher to live in during the week.

89. It is believed that measles must run a certain course; all the blotches and pimples must be given a chance to appear, and they must be a certain color red. If a person from outside the family gives a child evil eye, then the disease may not come out completely, or the pimples may turn black. The use of the rattle is to avoid the evil eye.

90. Each pueblo has a representative to the municipal authorities in Ixmiquilpan. The election of local authorities is described in Volume IV.

91. The Fiesta del Sexto Viernes is on the sixth Friday of Pentecost. The mayordomos who are in charge of this springtime festival are charged with their obligations each year, after the festival of the twelfth of December. All the mayordomos, judges, and other village functionaries are named at this event. This is described in Volume IV also.

92. In the original, Salinas uses the Ñähñu word "manza" for "plate," referring to porcelain-quality dinner plates, rather than "'mohi" which refers to rustic ceramic plates. The use of "manza" implies respect for guests.

93. The word "zajwa" is used only by some persons; the old man is said here to have used it instead of "tsu'di," the usual word for pig or pork.

94. According to Drs. Louis Guillette and Hobart Smith, this is probably the spotted, juvenile phase of what Salinas calls the "borer snake" (see Note 98), the *Ficimia olivacea*.

95. These are the spiny lizards of the genus *Sceloporus*. The one described here is the mesquite lizard (*S. grammicus*).

96. Earth is mounded up in long rows called "bordos" in Spanish, and "t'a'tsi" in Ñähñu. The mounds are formed in order to keep the rushing rainwater channeled. When lizards make holes in the bordos, they open channels for rainwater and this undermines the plants. Making bordos is described in Volume III.

97. The whiptails, or race-runners, are members of the genus *Cnemidophorus*. This is probably *C. sackii*.

98. This is the *Ficimia olivacea*.

99. These are isopods, the familiar, grey, armadillo-shaped grubs that live under rocks.

100. The brown racer is called "víbora de aire," or "wind snake" in Spanish because it runs like the wind. Indeed, it is one of the fastest snakes known. This is the *Masticophis taeniatus* and is closely related to the *M. flagellum* or coachwhip.

101. I have been unable to positively identify this snake. According to Drs. Hobart Smith and Louis Guillette (personal communication) it may be the indigo snake (*Drymarchon*). The indigo is black and is a huge animal (up to 260 centimeters) that lives in the habitat described. However, there are no all-black snakes that are poisonous. The indigo catches its prey by biting and holding on with its powerful jaws. Its bite causes great tissue damage, with extensive bruising and infection, and it may be that this is seen as venomous. This is a very intimidating snake.

102. There are apparently several different fruit trees in Mexico called "zapote" or "mamey." The common zapote referred to here is the *Mammea americana*; other related species are *Lucuma mammosa*, according to the *Diccionario de Mejicanismos*, and the *Colocarpum mammosum*, according to Cravioto (1951: 140).

103. This reptile is called "camaleón" in Spanish in the Mezquital. It is sometimes called a "horned toad" in English. In fact, it is neither a chameleon nor a toad, but is a horned lizard, the *Phrynosoma boucardi*, that changes its color like a chameleon.

104. This is the common raven, the *Corvus corax*.

105. I have not been able to identify this invertebrate. The desert snails are surprisingly large. One nearly round, coiled, white specimen I observed, among a group of lechuguilla plants, measured almost seven centimeters across.

106. The sangre de grado is a member of the genus *Jatropha* sp. Its juice is used to reduce pain on cuts and burns, and to reduce inflammation from insect bites and cactus spine punctures. I have had numerous opportunities to test its properties. It grows abundantly in the desert part of the Mezquital.

107. Wherever possible I have given the common English name for these insects and have noted the genus and species in these notes. However, the invertebrate life is so varied that I have been unable to identify taxonomically a few of the forms described by Salinas.

108. Salinas is talking about flies in general here. Particular flies are treated separately below.

109. "Zacate" refers to the dried corn plants. The inference here is that the other man usually fornicates with zacate.

110. Here one man refers to the fact that by screwing the other from behind he'll make the other defecate. Since the ox feeds on dry zacate, or "zafri" in Ñähñu, this creates a subtle play on words producing the humor. In the previous riposte, the other man used the word "zafri." In the next jab, "tongue" refers to a vagina. The verb "mbuu" is used here next; it is onomatopoetic and refers to the sound made by a bull when it chases a cow to copulate. "We'll put it back" refers to the one man poking it into the other with his penis, and "put back your food" is a subtle reference back to the zacate again, which is possible because cattle chew their cud.

111. This is the common housefly *(Musca domestica)*; 98% of all flies caught in houses are of this cosmopolitan species. They are a serious disease threat in the Mezquital.

112. This is the *Phaenicia sericata.*

113. Criolina is a brand name product of an insect killer in Mexico. It is DDT.

114. This is the biting stable fly *(Stomoxys calcitrans).* If feeds on the blood of large animals.

115. The vinegar fly *(Drosophila spp.)* is a pomace fly, family *Drosophilidae*. It is sometimes erroneously called the fruit fly, family *Tephritidae.* The vinegar fly gets its name in English from the fact that the larva feeds on yeasts in fermenting juices. The adult flies, however, drink sugary nectars, such as aguamiel.

There may be two different flies discussed here, what Jesús calls the "country" and the "city" gnat. I can not identify the "city gnat."

116. The "red fly" is *Bombyliopsis abrupta,* family *Tachnidae.* It is also known as the beelike tachnid fly.

117. This is the familiar *Monomorium minimus.*

118. This is a harvester ant, probably genus *Pogonomyrmex,* and possibly *Veromessor.*

119. This is the Texas carpenter ant *(Camponatus festinatus).*

120. This is another form of harvester ant, probably also in the genus *Pogonomyrmex.*

121. This is the honey pot ant *(Myrmecocystus* spp.), also known as the arid lands honey ant. The adult workers collect honey from plant exudates and from aphid secretions, and transfer it to young ants by regurgitation. The gaster swells until the ant reaches up to five milimeters in diameter. These "repletes," as they are known, cannot move, and cling to the ceilings of chambers in the nest. The stored honey is used by the colony during times of food stress, and is a favorite sweet delicacy among many Native American groups, including the Ñähñu.

122. This ant's name in Ñähñu means "red ant." True red ants (genus *Formica* spp.), do not build the pebble nests that Jesús talks about and their bite is not painful. Harvester ants *(Pogonomyrmex* spp.), however, are another matter.

123. "Chía" are seed of the *Salvia chian.* The genus *Salvia* includes the sages.

124. I have not been able to identify these plants, nor has Jesús been able to find common names for them in Spanish. E'yo may be fennel.

125. These are the escobetillas discussed at length in Volume III in the chapter on lechuguilla.

126. These "yellow ants" may be termites, family *Rhinotermitidae.*

127. I have not identified this yellow and black ant.

128. These ant larvae are either *Novomessor* or *Pogonomyrmex.*

129. A "fo'ye" in Ñähñu is glossed "puño" in Spanish, and is equal to one-fourth a cuartillo.

130. This beetle is simply called "escarabajo" in the Mezquital. There are many beetles and their larvae are considered as separate animals in Ñähñu (see below). The problem with identification of the various beetles is that the Coleoptera are the largest order in the animal kingdom, with perhaps 30,000 species in North America alone. The family *Scarabidae,* which is well represented in the Mezquital, has 1,300 species on this continent. With this caveat, the beetle described by Jesús here is probably in the genus *Phyllophaga,* known variously as May beetles and June beetles.

131. "Gallina ciega" is a generic term for the larvae, called grubs, of various beetles, particularly *Scarabidae*. Some of these larvae are a rich protein source.

132. The green June beetle (*Cotinus nitida*) looks like the beetle referred to by Jesús here. In fact, when he was writing this volume, he picked a picture of the green June beetle from a book as looking like the creature he wanted to describe.

133. This is *Latrodectus mactans*. Unlike some other venomous creatures whose reputation is worse than their bite, the black widow spider's reputation as potentially lethal to humans is deserved.

134. The black widow is said to die after releasing its venom. Just as she is dying and doubling up, the person she bit is said to have the same reaction.

135. The desert tarantula is the *Aphonopelma chalcodes*. Its bite is painful, but very rarely more harmful than that of bees. The genus *Tarantula* is not found in the Mezquital; it comprises whip scorpions rather than spiders.

136. This is the principal distinction made in Ñähñu between butterflies and moths. That is, moths are night creatures that seek flames. The following appear to be some of the more common butterflies and moths in the Mezquital: Boisduval's yellow (*Eurema boisduvaliana*), the desert grey skipper (*Yvretta carus*), the swallowtail (*Papilio* spp.), the coyote skipper (*Achalarus toxeus*), the Texas crescentspot (*Anthanassa texana*), the painted lady (*Vanessa cardui*), the grey metalmark (*Apodemia palmerii*), the bordered patch (*Chlosyne lacinia*), and the monarch (*Danaus plexippus*). Of course, this is a layperson's guess; there appear to be some dozens of species of moths and butterflies in the Mezquital, from the rather nondescript, small patches and crescentspots to the spectacular Sphyngidae with their four-inch wingspan. These latter are the moths mentioned by Jesús as putting out flame with their wings.

137. This is the circus bug (*Eleodes armata*).

138. This is the agave billbug (*Scyphophorus acupunctatus*), one of the snout weevils, family *Curculionidae*. It may develop from the maguey grub or from one of the chinicuiles described by Jesús below. Cravioto (1951: 153) identifies "gusano de maguey" ("maguey grub") as *Aegiale (Acentrocneme) hesperiaris.*" These are the most widely eaten insects in central Mexico, and are served as a delicacy (usually fried) in fine restaurants in Mexico City. Cravioto (ibid.) notes that they provide 13.65 grams of protein per 100 grams.

139. The scarab beetle is a member of the genus *Canthon*. It is called "cangrejo," or "crab" in Spanish in the Mezquital.

140. This is the paper wasp *Polistes canadensis.*

141. The mesquite caterpillar probably becomes the grey metalmark (*Apodemia palmerii*) or the Antillean blue (*Hemiargus ceraunus*). The green

caterpillar mentioned here is likely the Io moth (*Automeris io*), which appears in the moister barrancas where the capulín trees are found. According to Jesús, the caterpillar of the "romero silvestre" plant may become a species of monarch butterfly.

142. The arid zone variety described here is the pallid winged grasshopper (*Trimerotropis pallidipennis*). The green, crop-eating insect appears related to the Carolina locust (*Dissoteira carolina*).

143. "Kueta" in Ñähñu is the caterpillar stage of a large moth, probably one of the sphynx months (also known as hawk moths), judging from the size and the presence of horns. I have not identified "romero silvestre," but it looks like a menthaceous shrub, something like rosemary (which is, of course, what "romero" means in Spanish).

144. The millipede referred to here is known in the Mezquital as "gusano de lluvia" and is *Orthoporus ornatus*.

145. Jesús discusses two varieties of human body lice, both members of the genus *Pendiculus*. Body and head lice (*P. humanus*) are commonly called "cooties" in English; pubic lice (*P. h. capitis*) are commonly called "crabs." Head lice especially prefer to attach their tiny eggs, called "nits," to hair on the back of the neck, hence the English expression "nitpicking."

146. The "jumper" is either the human flea (*Pulex irritans*) or the common flea (*Xenopsylla cheopis*). The "nail flea" is almost certainly the cat flea (*Ctenocephalides felis*), and dog fleas are *C. canis*. Squirrels and mice have fleas in the families *Dolichopsyllidae* and *Hystrichopsyllidae*. The "nigua" in Spanish is sometimes glossed "chigger" or "jigger" or "chigoe" in English. They are mites of the family *Trombiculidae*, probably *Tunga penetrans* or *Sarcopsylla penetrans*.

147. Chicken lice are members of the family of bird lice, *Philopteridae*. Hog lice are *Haematopinus suis*.

148. "Xirgo" is the Mexican Spanish for "xii'tsi" which is a condition when an animal (cats, dogs, rabbits, pigs, sheep, goats, etc.) has ruffled fur, with hair standing on end. This only happens to scrawny, sickly animals.

149. This may be the larvae of antlions, sometimes called doodlebugs, of the family *Myrmeleontidae*. They build small pits in loose sand and wait for their prey to fall in.

150. The tick referred to here is the *Ornithodorus* spp. Ticks are arachnids rather than insects.

151. Petates are woven mats, made from fronds of the various palma plants (see the section on palma in Volume III).

152. This is the caterpillar stage of what is generically known as "palomilla" in Spanish. This moth is probably in the family *Noctuidae,* but it may be the sod webworm moth (*Crambus* spp.) of the *Pyralidae.*

153. This is a "gorgojo," the Spanish name in Mexico for any weevil that eats beans.

154. These are the American cockroaches (*Periplaneta americana*).

155. These are members of the family *Lumricidae.*

156. This black butterfly is probably the grey metalmark (*Apodemia palmerii*).

157. The various insects described here are probably members of the *Curculionidae* family of beetles and weevils.

158. There are several mantids in the Mezquital; this one is probably the obscure ground mantid (*Litaneutria obscura*). The name given in Ñähñu is "rä fani rä nts'o" or "rä fani rä ts'ondähi." The latter means "Devil's Horse," where "ts'ondähi," or "evil" is used to refer to the Devil. The Devil's real name in Ñähñu is "zithu" but this is considered very strong language and is avoided. It translates into Spanish as "pinche" or "chingado," as in "Rä zithu ñ'ääi xä xe̱'tä yä 'uada," "The fucking skunk has dug up the maguey plants."

159. Inchworms are members of the family *Geometridae,* also known as measuringworm moths. In fact, this insect is called "el gusano medidor" in Spanish, literally "the measuring bug."

160. This is the cosmopolitan *Cimex lectularius.* They are very annoying, but do not transmit disease. These flat, very small true bugs (order *Hemiptera*) are noted for their amazing speed, and for the fact that they can go for up to 15 months without food (human blood), both traits remarked on here. These bedbugs do not transmit disease and should not be confused with the so-called Mexican bedbug (*Triatoma sanguisuga*), which does transmit disease, but which feeds primarily on mammals other than humans (Milne and Milne, 1980: 475).

161. This is the blue-black spider wasp (*Anoplius* spp.)

162. This black variety is the female of the Mexican carpenter bee (*Xylocopa mexicanorum*). The male is the abejorro, mentioned earlier. The yellow bee and the honey bee are both members of the family *Apidae.* The former is a bumble bee (genus *Bombus*), while the latter is (*Apis mellifera*).

163. The black and yellow insect here is the yellow jacket (*Polybia occidentalis*) of the family *Vespidae.* The bee cited here is the stingless bee (*Melipona* sp.).

164. This is the familiar worm that shows up in the ears of corn. I have not been able to establish its taxonomic classification.

165. These are truc bugs, members of the family *Pentatomidae*, and known for obvious reasons as "stink bugs." The local variety in the Mezquital feeds exclusively on the mesquites.

166. In Ñähñu the glowworm and the firefly are classed together because of their luminescence. In fact, rather than being two separate animals, as classed in English common terminology, the glowworms are the larvae of fireflies. The fireflies are member of the family *Lampyridae*.

167. Chinicuiles are edible grubs, that is, larvae. One variety burrows *into,* rather than under magueys. This is the agave billbug (*Scyphophorus acupunctatus*). Other chinicuiles are associated with the junquillo and the nopal. The cochineal bug (*Dactylopius confusus*) infests the nopal, covering the trunk like chunks of thick, white carpet as they die and pile up. This may be considered the excrement of the beetle larvae that lies inside the trunk of the nopal, but I have not had an opportunity to discuss this with Jesús in the field.

168. Animals and plants are divided into hot and cold varieties. All larvae that are eaten are hot; flowers and the fruit of órganos and garambullos are also hot. They are called "hot" because they cause coughing if eaten in excess. When people eat a lot of squash bugs (which are "hot"), they get welts. Fish, for example, are cold and cause stomach pain. There is, of course, a large literature on the concept of hot and cold foods in Mexican culture.

169. The volume on the geography and the first half of the volume on the fauna were written in 1976. The second half of the volume on the fauna was completed in 1977. We thought of these at the time as a single volume. They were published together, in Ñähñu and in an earlier English translation (with less annotation), in 1978 by the University of New Mexico Press (see Introduction).

VOLUME III

The Flora

1. This book describes the plants that live in the Mezquital Valley, and are of benefit to the people of the valley. Many of these plants are of economic use; that is, they are worked and made into many different things which are useful in the home and in work. 2. Others are also used by the people as medicine. Long ago there were no doctors. In those days, many people of the valley were cured with the plants we will look at here. 3. We know that the natural world provides many things—often all we need—and that is how we are able to live. We will move along in this book, examining each plant in order to see the benefits it offers. 4. In this way we will see which plants are used as medicine, and which ones provide economic benefits to the people. 5. We will see that many men and women have become accomplished scholars; some are teachers, some are lawyers, and some are doctors, and this is due to the plants we will be looking at, and to the benefits these plants offer.[1] Of course, these benefits have been for those who knew how to use the plants well; those who have abandoned these plants have received nothing from them. 6. In order to succeed one needs to have money, but what is important is that each person must work to be able to get the necessary things in life.

7. Years ago people knew how to make medicines, and many of these were made from the plants we will mention here. There are still many people who are not cured with the manufactured medicines sold in drug stores. Why? 8. Because these medicines are very expensive and sometimes do not cure. This is why many mestizos prefer to be cured with plants; they have more confidence in the plants, and they know that the plants cure some diseases which manufactured medicines do not alleviate. 9. Many Indians, and especially the people who live in the mountains, cure themselves by using plants.[2] In the Mezquital Valley, poverty is severe, and the people don't have money to buy commercially-made medicines. Also, people live far from the city. Because of this, when people are sick, the first thing they do is look for the plants that will be used to cure them. 10. The physicians do, indeed, cure people. But their services

are expensive; doctors never ask for less than several hundred pesos. For ordinary laborers, this is an impossible cost to cover.

11. Many parts of the body are cured by the plants we are discussing here. As a guide, here is a drawing of the human body and its parts.

12. Now we present the plants used by the people of the Mezquital Valley in medicine and other things necessary for life.

The mesquite.[3] 13. This is the most abundant tree in the valley, and it is why the region is called the Mezquital Valley. In this region, everywhere one looks there are mesquite trees—in the barrancas, in the mountains, and even in the badlands, though they grow there with difficulty. 14. Some of these trees are huge and have great trunks. Others are small, but they all have a particular characteristic which is interesting to know about. These trees simply do not die from lack of water. Even if there is no rain, these trees resist drought and don't wither. 15. Sometimes there is no water for a year, or even for two, three, or four years, and sometimes even longer.

16. Other plants start to shrivel up or just die from lack of water. We all know that green plants bud and put out shoots in the spring; but if there is no rain, then the other plants we will mention in this book don't send out spring sprouts. But with the mesquite, rain or no rain, when spring comes, deep green buds come out all over it as if it had plenty of moisture at its roots. 17. Many people who have observed it say that this is the most drought-resistant tree, and this is due to the depth of its root system in the earth. One can see how long the roots are by observing the steep drops in the great barrancas.[4] Consider that some of these gulches are 10 meters high, or more; this is where one can see that the mesquite roots indeed go deep. And they go even deeper, continuing into the ground, and no one knows where they end. 18. The mesquite is the only tree that pierces the earth so profoundly with its roots. It gives a lot to the people, and is a resource which the earth has provided for the people to use as food.

19. Many inhabitants of this region rely on this tree for their subsistence. Some people search the open desert for dead mesquites, known as "'yot'ä ñ'ee'thi," or "dried branches" in Ñähñu. They hack these up and make small bundles which they carry into town and offer for sale from house to house. There is no firewood in town for use in kitchens, and people there need wood to burn. So, all the wood collectors who live outside the city sell the firewood they collect in the open country. 20. Sometimes the woodsellers have the misfortune not to sell their wood quickly and have to go around from place to place, carrying their load and offering it for sale to the houses. They might ask five pesos for a load, or sometimes twenty,[5] depending on the size of the bundle, and when they come to a house they say: 21. "Buy your wood, madame," and sometimes

hmi (face)
xiñu (nose)
né (mouth)
xiine (lip)
ts'ii (teeth)
juni (chin)
gone (jaw)
si'nsi (shoulder)
tiñä (chest)
'mots'e (rib)
ts'ai (navel)
nts'u (penis)
uantsu (shaft)
ñänts'u (glans)

ñäñ'e (finger)
muñ'e (palm)
mädo (testicle)
dut'i (pubis)
ndemfó-huxäxoni (rump)
xingu (body hair)
ñämo (toe)
saha (nail)

gu (ear)
xiigu (auricle)
hyuja (nape)
ñuxtha (back)
'roonzu (vert. column)
xiiñ'e (scapula)
yuni (elbow)

stää (head hair
ndehe (crown)
dé (forehead)
ngaxtá (eyebrow)
da (eye)
xiida (eyelash)
'yuga (throat)
kaxkjo (axilla)
juxkjo (axillary hair)
'ma (breast)
ñäx'ma (nipple)
mui (stomach)
ximui (abdomen)
juxi (genital hair)
turu (vagina)
jäne turu (labia)
pooho-xiji (anus)
damfo-nemfo (rectum)
xiinthe (thigh)
ñähmu (knee)
zats'u (tendon)
mantiyo (shin)
'mada ua (calf)
qut'egi (Achilles' tendon)
duqua (heel)
mhengua (sole)

Many parts of the human body are cured by plants
Flora 11

they say "Buy your wood, my lady."[6] Whether it's a man or a woman who is doing the selling, either might say these things; but a man might say "Buy your wood, old lady."

22. As I said a moment ago, if the woodseller does not make a sale quickly, then he or she has to walk through town the whole day, sometimes accompanied by a small girl or boy. The woodsellers suffer a lot as they go about, offering their wares for sale. Sometimes they find a buyer who is a good person, and who pays them well. Such a buyer brings the seller into the house, offers coffee and food, and then the poor woodseller is well satisfied. 23. Only a few years ago there were no automobiles for people to travel around in. In those days, people went on foot into town[7] to sell their wood, mostly mesquite. They carried the load the entire distance, and even though they stopped at resting places[8] along the way, they were always exhausted. 24. Even today, when they get to the plaza,[9] they keep carrying the load around until they find someone to buy it from them. These woodsellers always suffer; even though they may be hungry and thirsty, first they have to sell their wood to be able to buy something to eat.

25. Only a short time ago tortillas sold for 20 centavos each,[10] as did a plate of beans. Now these things cost a peso or more. This is what the people buy to eat if they are woodsellers. When they finish eating and drinking their pulque, they buy chiles and corn which they take home to their families. The next day they go out collecting wood again, and the day after that, very early in the morning, they start out again for town to sell their load. 27. Often the father of the family goes alone; other times he is accompanied by his wife, who goes to the plaza carrying her own load of wood. Other times, those children who are old enough to withstand the walk are taken along, and they carry their own small load of wood, too.

28. If a mother is carrying a child whom she is nursing, then she carries the load of wood on her back, and the baby is placed in an ayate, rocked to sleep, and carried in a sling across her chest. Whenever she gets tired, the mother will stop and rest in the shade of the mesquite trees along the sides of the road. She nurses her child while she rests. 29. Many of these people used to go barefoot, but no longer. People now wear shoes, even if only huaraches, so they don't hurt their feet on the rocks. Also, few of these woodsellers walk to town anymore. There are trucks now in which to transport their wood—and not just a single load, either, but two or three loads, and the people don't suffer like they used to when they went on foot.

30. Mechanized transport is changing the way of life of the people of the valley; and not just how they live, but also their way of thinking and other aspects of their life have changed. 31. There are now people who aspire to make

Woodsellers suffer a lot as they go about

Flora 22

a lot of money. These people don't sell the wood they collect, or rather they don't sell it green. Instead, they burn it and make charcoal, which is more valuable. Many people clear wild land to plant things that will be useful in making a living. They clear away brush and thorns, and in clearing everything they amass a lot of mesquite wood.

32. A man who collects wood like this goes into town and offers it to those who make bread, because the breadmakers heat their ovens with mesquite wood. Of course, there are some who fire their ovens with other materials. The man who goes around offering the wood considers whether he will make a good profit from all his work. If so, he sells the wood; otherwise he doesn't. Instead, he makes charcoal and thus makes a bit more money. 33. In the city of Ixmiquilpan, a few years ago, they used to heat bread ovens with green mesquite wood. The bakers used to say that the ovens heated better when they were fired with green mesquite wood, and that the bread baked better. But nowadays they don't use mesquite wood because it's hard to work with. 34. Instead, bakers fire their ovens with fuel oil now, or with diesel oil. Unlike mesquite wood, these products make a lot of smoke.

35. If a man doesn't sell his wood, then he burns it to make charcoal, assuming, of course, that he knows how to do this. If he doesn't know how, then he finds someone who can help him prepare the oven. All the wood gathered in clearing a piece of ground is burned into charcoal. Branches and trunks alike are gathered up and made into a neat pile at the spot where they will be covered and fired. 36. All the wood that will be burned must be mesquite, because it is the only wood that makes good charcoal. Other woods, like capulín, don't work well, and turn into ash. So, it is never fired into charcoal, but only used as kindling.

37. How charcoal is made is described in the previous volume, in the section describing the geographic characteristics of the Mezquital Valley. For this reason, we will not treat this here, but will look instead at the various uses of mesquite.

38. When the mesquites are cut down, some branches are chopped off for making charcoal. Then the woodcutter decides what he will do with all the rest of the wood. 39. Some forked pieces are good for pushing aside thorny bushes, and others can be used to support the wheel used for twisting ixtle fiber into rope. These forked sticks are used to support the entire length of the rope as it is being formed by a wheel and bobbin. Pieces of mesquite are used for making mallets for pounding and crushing lechuguilla[11] and maguey. Some mallets have club-like heads and others, called "thrashers," have no head at all. The part of a club that shreds the fleshy maguey leaf is wide and thick, and the part held

by the person pounding the leaf is thin. 40. The mallet I'm speaking of here has a globular end, and is usually nicely worked so that it looks like a cat's head. This is the part used to crush the fiber in the maguey.[12] 41. A woodcutter also culls out pieces which are straight and thick, and which have a forked end. These pieces can be used as main support posts for houses. 42. Only the valley people use mesquite for house supports. The people who live up in the mountains also use forked posts, but they use oak or juniper.[13]

43. A lot of waste wood is created in the monte when people clear-cut to plant nopal cactus. Mesquite trees are cut down, along with garambullos,[14] wherever they are found. This removes this plant life from the environment. They are needed to attract rain and to hold the earth together so that, when the wind blows hard, or when the little rain there is does come, the soil won't be eroded away. But for those people who have no other resources, all they can do is strip away everything, and plant prickly pears, lechuguilla, and maguey. Then, when these plants become productive, they provide money for the people. 44. The people know the significance of trees, and the good things they bring to the land. So, whenever they can, they plant trees around their living areas, or in the villages. They plant casuarinas and jacarandas, and others which withstand drought.[15]

45. Poverty forces people to find some way to plant something so they can help themselves in time of need. For example, if a person gets sick and has a piece of land which has been cleared and worked, then he has some means to cure himself. He can sell some maguey plants, or lechuguillas; but if he had none he couldn't do anything. 46. So, anyone who has a couple of pieces of property in the monte thinks about what he can plant out there. Nopal and maguey require that all shade be eliminated so that they can grow well. If they grow in shade, they don't develop; and even if they get large they don't produce fruit (in the case of the nopal) or aguamiel (in the case of the maguey). This comes from not having enough sun, so the people have to cut down all the trees wherever they want to plant these things. 47. Also, people who have no regular job, and no prospects for one, go around cutting down trees. Though they may love the trees, they have to do this to make money by selling wood or by making charcoal. Even if they aren't going to plant anything, they have to cut things down to buy food. Probably there is no one who doesn't love trees, because all of us know that they are needed and that they give shade and fruit. But I repeat that the droughts force people to cut down trees in order to buy something to eat so that they can live.

48. This has been going on for a very long time, and now, little by little, the countryside is becoming bare. And now it doesn't rain any more, so the land deteriorates even more. People who have cut down all the trees on their small

pieces of land leave for the city in search of work, or they go to irrigated regions to work as laborers in planting, irrigating, harvesting, or baling of alfalfa. They do whatever they have to in order to make money. 49. The ones who suffer most in this way are those who have had no schooling, or who have studied very little. It is particularly difficult for them to find a well-paying job. But those who made the effort to finish their studies have changed their entire way of life. They have steady work all their lives, and even though the pay may be low, they don't suffer as much as the others. 50. Teachers always have work, and so now they are the ones who think about and protect the trees. They only cut trees when they see that the ground is really good for planting. If it isn't, then they don't remove the trees. But the teachers can really do very little; every day the people are out there making charcoal, because the price of everything keeps going up, and there are few sources of work and money. 51. In San Antonio, Nequetejé, Dexthi, Orizabita, and El Espíritu, where there is no irrigation at all, and in those parts of Capula, Los Remedios, San Juanico, and Panales without irrigation, and in the newly irrigated part of Portezuelo where they are tearing out everything to farm the land, everyone makes charcoal.

52. All the woody plants I mention here benefit the people who still build their houses with tree posts. Those who more or less have some money build their houses out of rubble and masonry, their roofs of cement, and their doors and windows of metal.

Stools are sometimes made from mesquite trunks and roots because around here not everyone has chairs. 53. When a person of humble background gets to have a chair, he really feels rich. Some people have two stools made of mesquite trunks, and also have chairs. The mesquite trunk is the original chair for the inhabitants of the valley, and there are still many who appreciate this type of seat. 54. Possibly they are aware that wherever they go in the valley, they are never without the cool shade of the mesquite. And many of the trunks pulled from the ground are really very beautiful. Some look like cats, and they even have little paws. Others look like dogs with paws and a tail, and a part towards the top that looks like the neck. Others, from their shape, look like different animals.

55. People who clear the cut debris from fields like to find these different shaped trunks and work them slowly into stools and benches. Sometimes they make benches for their own families. They select the smallest trunks and shape them beautifully. They give these to their children. Those trunks have to have at least three or four feet in order to stand. 56. Sometimes very large logs are fashioned into tables. Oh! They really look nice; and even more so when they are covered with an embroidered cloth. Then you can't even tell that it's a mesquite log.

57. Anyone who comes to visit a family is offered a meal. This is the kind of customary goodwill that people show to others in all parts of the world. Though the benches and tables may be humble, friendship is always offered sincerely. In fact, it is often given with greater sincerity by humble folk than by those who have everything. 58. There are some Ñähñu here who pretty much have everything—like a house with masonary walls, and tables and chairs—but they remember their origins. Though they themselves no longer work logs into benches, still, when they send their peons out to work in the open country they say to them:

59. "Don Julio!"

"Yes, what is it don Antonio?"

"Well, now that you are going out to work on my land, as you pull out the trunks, if by chance you find one that can be made into a stool or bench, don't chop it up, but put it aside. Then we'll work on it and make it into a bench, either for me or for the children."

60. "Of course! Don't worry; if I see one, I'll put it aside."

"Fine. And hurry, man, as much as you can, so that you'll be finished with my work before the rains come, and we can plant our nopales. Otherwise, what good is that old land if it gives us nothing?"

"Yes, don Antonio; don't worry, I'll hurry. But don't forget my pulque! Meanwhile, I'll see what I can do. With God's help I'll finish my work quickly."

61. And saying this, he slings his tools over his shoulder and heads off towards don Antonio's lands where he will clear out all the thorns and brush. He puts aside the large logs for benches and stools, as he was asked to do. Of course, before starting to work, he takes off his sombrero and makes the sign of the cross. After crossing himself, the next thing he does is sharpen his tools. He sharpens the axe, the machete, and the pointed metal pole used for levering things out of the ground. Only a few people sharpen these digging poles. People sharpen their tools with a metal file, or a heavy black stone if they don't have a file. Of course, everyone sharpens axes and machetes.

62. When he's finished sharpening his tools, don Julio spits on his hands so they won't slip as he uses the tools, and he begins swinging his axe.[16] If a man is a real worker, he gives it all he's got for two or three hours and then he goes to where he has his pulque, takes two or three big swigs and stands there wiping off his moustache. Then he goes back to work. When he returns to his patrón's house, the patrón asks whether don Julio has done what he was requested to do.

63. "How are you, don Julio? Are you tired?"

"I'm fine, don Antonio; no weariness at all. I had a fine time."

"Good. Very good. And did you put aside the pieces of wood, like I asked you?"

"Yes, I set them apart."

"Very good. Very good, don Julio. Now that there is time left, you can help me for a while to work on shaping the log. We'll do it together."

64. "Why not. If there's a good drink of pulque in it for me, I'll work."

"Now that you mention pulque, did they give you a drink?"[17]

"Yes, thank you. I already served myself, thanks."

"Fine, fine. And thanks to you for helping us out."

"How could I not help you? After all, it's your money that you're paying me, and I'm grateful to you for giving me work. If not for this, who knows how God would help me out and where I'd work. Of course you wouldn't know it, and you didn't ask me, but I need money for my cargo which comes up at the Christmas fiesta."[18]

65. "Oh, what a surprise! Are you the mayordomo?"

"Yes, the mayordomo of the church selected me and gave me the cargo to sponsor the mass on the 24th of December. This is nothing bad; after all, I'll be serving God's son. That is why I am here at your house, seeking work so I can put some money together towards fulfilling my cargo."[19]

66. "It's good that you've told me about this. If you need a loan, I'm at your disposal, and I'll be happy to visit you and bring you maize or some animal. Or if you need pulque, I think I can get it for you. After all, how could I refuse to do this for God?"

"Well, yes, you can do this favor for me, brother. You can visit me with two cartons of beer, and I will be very pleased to have you join me for a meal. I'll hurry up with the work now, but you remember what we've said here today."

67. "Of course I'll remember, since neither of us is drunk."[20]

"Well, that's all for now; I'll be going across the hills now, and we'll see each other tomorrow."[21]

"Good, good. May God be with you."

"Thank you for the rest. May you have a good night. Until tomorrow, then. I'm going now, doña Marcelina. May you have a good night. Until tomorrow."

68. Doña Marcelina, Antonio's wife, says:

"Go, brother, and have a good night. Until tomorrow. Tell doña Hilaria that I send her greetings, and tell her that when she has time she should visit me and have a drink of pulque."[22]

And Julio responds, "I'll tell her. Have a good night."

69. It is customary that when a man returns after a day's work, he and his employer ask after one another. They take these opportunities to find out about

the cargos they have acquired, and this is how the system of loans between people is perpetuated. People ask each other for help in fulfilling the cargos, and when the day for which a person is responsible comes along, he isn't scurrying around trying to get things done.

70. Anyway, the next day, the worker is there again at the house of his patrón, ready to go to work at an early hour. Laborers generally work for those people who have money. When laborers go out to clear land, they are accustomed to working and shaping the wood they find. They make some kind of object. When they come across a large log that can be turned into a bench, they take trouble to make it turn out really nice. Then they try to find someplace to sell their work, and in the evening, when they return to their employer's house, they ask if the patrón wouldn't like to buy a log bench. Don Felipe asks:

71. "Look, here, don Vincente, we found some logs and don Crescenciano helped, and we worked up a really nice little stool."

Crescenciano adds: "Really, it turned out really nice, and looks like a little lamb."

But don Vincente, the patrón, says: "Yes, I agree that it came out well, but to tell you the truth, we don't like those things any more. Why would we want some old logs? There's no reason to bring them here. They don't belong in modern houses. Why would the children want such things? They should just throw them in the fire."

72. So Felipe answers: "Fine. If you folks don't need those things, just give them to me, and I'll take them away. I've got some children who can surely use them."

73. And Vincente says: "If you want them, take them. Why would I want some old sticks? We have *real* chairs and tables. The time is gone when we in this house used log stools and benches. Our grandmothers and grandfathers used those things. For us, the time of log furniture is over. People who extract maguey fiber for a living, and shepherds and day laborers use such things. They suit pulque makers, but not us."

Filipe and Crescenciano answer: "Well, now you've gone too far and insulted us."

"I'm not trying to kid you," replies don Vincente. "I'm telling you the truth."

75. This is how some Ñähñu turn out. What happens is that they want to boast in front of the laborers who work for them. But the workers are insulted by this attitude, and they abandon their work. Though they need the money, they decide to look for work elsewhere, and they talk amongst themselves.

76. "Why are we forced to listen to this? We have been insulted by this man! Look, let's go elsewhere. This isn't the only place there is work. Let's go find work somewhere else."

77. This is how the workers talk about such a situation, and they abandon the presumptuous boss who is trying to pass himself off as a mestizo without being one, and who is ignorant. Even if he has some education, he has no call to act in this manner. What always happens is that laborers work for him for one or two days, but then they abandon him because they don't like the way he acts.

78. We know how some people have spent their lives, and the work they do, and how they have fed themselves. The poor parents have suffered as day laborers, maguey fiber workers, lechuguilla workers, rope makers and charcoal makers. Sometimes they don't even know where they will find work, but they keep working at whatever they can find because they want to help their children go to school to learn to read and write. This is the main concern of those parents. 79. They say, "I'm going to send my children to school so that tomorrow they won't be like me, going around as if I were blind because I don't know how to read and write." Some children try hard to heed their parents' advice, and they quickly learn the lessons offered by their teachers. 80. They grow up and get good jobs and make some money. They provide their parents with food, and help ease their parents' suffering a little. Then the parents can start to take it a little easier, and not work so hard at their usual jobs. The whole family eats better. 81. The child who has a steady job then helps out his brothers and sisters so that they, too, can study. Once they are all grown up, the household betters itself. Then, little by little, they forget their customs and often they don't know who they are, Indian or mestizo. Often they start out to follow mestizo ways, and then, suddenly, they just don't know which way to go.

82. It's fine for people to know the ways of mestizos, and to acquire a knowledge of all wisdom, both Indian and mestizo. But they must not abandon their people. On the contrary, they should pass on the knowledge of their own culture which they have acquired, because "when they die they can't take it with them." These words are what we Ñähñu say when we see someone who has become presumptuous and boastful.

83. While some parents are cared for by their children, others just go on suffering all their lives. Their children spend all the money—money which represents their parents' toil. These children simply don't know how to manage; they think that the money will never run out. This happens to some children because they are stupid, and to others because they are lazy. Parents whose children have finished school and now have good jobs, tell other parents in the community about it. They encourage each other to see to it that their children go to school, saying:

84. "Don Alejandrino, it's really nice that you are helping your son go to school. Tomorrow it will be he who will have to help you."

"That's right, don Alfonso; thanks for counseling me about this. It is my duty to sacrifice, and to do whatever work is necessary, so my José can go to school. I see how your son has acquired a trade; I'm doing all I can so that, tomorrow, as you say, my son will help me. Next year I'm going to send my lazy son Encarnación back to school. We'll see if he can learn his letters this time around. Last year he quit school, and I see that he didn't learn a thing."

85. "He'll learn, don Alejandrino. He'll surely learn. Just be sure to give him a good breakfast, and don't keep him home all the time, for one excuse or another. You have to send him to school every day."

"That's just what I'll do. And I'll recommend to the teacher that he give José a good beating if the boy doesn't learn quickly. In the end, it will be good for him. In the future, he'll see what will happen if he doesn't learn now."

"That's a certainty, don Alejandrino. Thanks for the chat; I'll be going along now. We'll be seeing each other."

"Fine, don Alfonso. May God accompany you."

86. This sort of conversation has been going on now for some years, and continues today. Little by little, people help one another. That is, someone who knows how to read a little helps those who don't know at all. They don't exactly teach others to read, but rather they advise those who have no education to find a way to send their children to school. A man's friends and neighbors, and anyone else who should be in on this, do him the favor of advising him. 87. But, as I said a moment ago, the people who do this are the ones who respect those who are still poor. Those who have become arrogant, on the other hand, don't even want to see their own people. They don't advise those who are uneducated. These vain, prideful Ñähñu are hated by many of their own people.

88. Sometimes the old people are correct when they say: "Ah, knowledge and study are good! How I would have liked to have been able to study in my own day. I wouldn't be so blind now if there had been schools when I was a child. But sometimes all this is good, and sometimes not so good. I look at don Ricardo's children, who have finished school and are living a better life. Then I see don Jerónimo's children; it was useless to send them to school. Look at them. They go around being lazy, and don't work at all. 89. They don't help out their poor father at all. What purpose did that poor man's suffering serve? And he still suffers to feed his children, even though they are grown up."

90. Some children feel superior to their fathers who are unlettered. These children have no respect for their fathers or their mothers. And this is even more the case when the father is a charcoal maker or a maguey fiber worker. Then children are ashamed to tell their friends what their fathers do for a living. It ends up that a child comes to hate its own parents just because they are poor

fiber workers—even though it is from this very job that the child's sustenance comes. That is why I said a moment ago that old people, talking amongst themselves, say: 91. "May God keep the old times. Though there weren't any schools, there was more respect. And now, though there is learning, children don't even greet people any more." They say this because the old people are accustomed to being greeted respectfully, whenever they meet someone along the way. Nowadays some children don't respond, and the old people find this very bad.

92. There are still some old people around who have what is called "deep respect." Whenever they meet another person, these old people extend greetings, and remove their hats. This is what is considered respect around here. Whoever it might be, man or woman, they take off their hat and say: "Good day, son" if they are greeting a man, or "A very good day to you, dear woman" if they are greeting a woman. The very old people may even say "Good day, dear boy" when they meet some youth or boy along the way.[23] 93. Others, when meeting a woman, may say "Good day, elder sister." Even though the word they use for sister means "elder sister of a woman," and should not be used by a man, some men use it by mistake because they've heard it for years. Its incorrect use does not mean any lack of respect on their part, of course.

94. Also, we should note that about 25 years ago, parents didn't want to send their daughters to school. Some fathers and mothers would say that girls should grow up in the home, and that it sufficed if they learned to grind corn, mend clothes and raise chickens and other domestic animals. Older brothers were also against their sisters going to school, because the men were afraid the young women would get involved with a boyfriend. The only thing the brothers wanted was for their sisters to grow up and get married, and that was all they thought their sisters should do. Many, many girls grew up like that, until just recently when parents started waking up and sending their daughters to school. Now, many women are school teachers. 95. Others study nursing, medicine and law. It is rare now that a girl from the heart of the valley does not attend school. This is because all the civil authorities, as well as the teachers, demand that all school-age children attend school.

96. It's really good that everyone is going to school, but the Ñähñu language and customs are rapidly being forgotten. In fact, all the new ideas are good, because they have changed the way people live, and made life better, and new ideas are needed for even more progress now. But learning and knowledge should not make one despise one's parents; knowledge should guide people in seeking the well-being of their whole family. People should respect one another.

97. Now we go back to talking about the benefits of the mesquite. We've gone far afield, but it is important that we look at everything that happens in the valley. What we want more than anything is that the next generation will become aware of the words written here. We have seen what things can come from large logs, and now we'll look at the other parts of the mesquite. As we have seen, some people make stools out of logs, others work large pieces of wood into chopping blocks for meat. The people who make use of this last item are butchers, cattle slaughterers, pig slaughterers and those who roast barbacóa, who are called "maathumgo," or "barbacóa sellers."

98. Why do they cut up their meat on these blocks? Because the heart of the mesquite is very hard, and it can stand all the chopping one can give it. Some people make tall chopping blocks that stand about a meter high. Others send the log to a carpenter to have a wheel cut from the trunk. These might be three hand-spans across. These really take a long time to make; it is especially difficult to cut through the log, because the wood is so hard. This is particularly the case with very old trees. No one knows how long a mesquite tree lives. There are many that are very big. Sometimes the young men ask the old men about this:

99. "You who are older, do you happen to know how old those mesquites are over there?"

"Ah, I'll tell you the truth, I really don't know. They've been there ever since I can remember. Who knows how old they are. The size you see them now is the same as they were when I was just a child."

100. We once asked a ninety-year-old man about the age of some mesquites. "Oh," he said "how would I know how old they are when even my grandfather said he didn't know, and he was a very old man when he died."

101. This is how large trunks are used in the selling of meat. But they are also used for other things, such as in the construction of an instrument known as a "lathe wheel." This is a nearly perfect circle, and anyone who makes one has to take care to see that it is well-formed so it won't create problems for the workers who use it. 102. To make one, a person must select the tree carefully, choosing only those which are well dried out so the wood won't crack in the sun or from the "hot air" of spring. The wheel will last a long time if care is taken, and in fact people try to avoid making them frequently. 103. Some of these wheels have been around for more than 25 years, and they continue to be used every day. They are at work all week, beginning on Wednesday and going through Thursday, Friday, Saturday and Sunday. They are given a rest only on Mondays and Tuesdays[24] and on the saint's day in each community when a festival is held once a year. Then the workers rest, and so do their tools. 104. However, people who use these tools to make rope don't rest much. If they take off too much

time, then after about a week they wouldn't have enough money to feed their family.

105. Lathe wheels are made from mesquite wood, especially. The father of the house who will make a wheel takes a lot of trouble to see that it comes out well. First he finds himself an assistant to help him cut the wood, because it is very tough. They use a double saw, and each one grabs an end. It takes half a day, or even a whole day to cut a wheel, depending on the size of the trunk. 106. The wheels usually run about three hand spans in diameter, but some are two spans wide. Once they are cut, they are planed smooth, though sometimes the wood is so dense that it pulls the blade out of the plane.

107. Once this is done, the wheel is measured carefully so that a hole can be bored exactly in the center. This receives the shaft of the lathe with its handle, and this is placed on the supports, which are also made of mesquite. These supports are called "m'aai," or "forks." The shaft and handle can be made of metal, but are usually made of wood. One tries to find a mesquite root with straight ends and a curved end. The straight end is inserted into the center hole, and the curved part is grabbed like a handle by the person doing the turning. The handle is buried in the ashes of a fire for a short time to cure the wood, so it won't be ravaged by insects. 108. Once this is done, the handle is prepared for insertion in the wheel and it is ready for whoever wants to use it.

109. Recently, some people have been making these wheels out of other things, like bicycle wheels, which are made of metal, and some people find wheels from various machines to use as rope twisting instruments. The one thing that is always made of wood are the malacates, or spindle whorls, because they are never sold in stores or anywhere else. Malacates are made from oak,[25] which is very tough and durable. 110. The malacates turn and spin against other wood, and they take a lot of use. They are greased to make them turn quickly and smoothly. The fat is removed from goats when they are killed, and is kept for this purpose. It is dabbed on the malacates as they spin, right at the point where they touch their supports. If this were not done then the wooden posts and the malacates would grind against each other and cause difficulty for the operator of the wheel. But if the apparatus is greased, then it works smoothly. 111. Grease is also dabbed on the fork of the main support where the wheel shaft rests. But care must be taken so that the grease does not get on the main pulley rope which goes around the whole apparatus, and which make the malacates spin. If grease gets on the pulley rope, then the malacates slip.

112. These tools must be constructed well, because they work continuously, all day long, from dawn until evening. Sometimes it gets dark and they are still working. The spinner goes back and forth, putting on new loads of thread, spin-

Lathe wheels are made from mesquite wood

Flora 105

ning, and so on. Some make ixtle from maguey fiber for weaving ayates; they make lassos, also known as "xidinthäähi" or "crude rope."[26] They spin ixtle for tump-lines, yoke bindings and heavy sack cloth.

113. The spinners of lechuguilla fiber also make rope, and we will discuss them in the section on lechuguilla. For now, we are examining only those things made from or with mesquite. Many people still construct their houses from palmas, and from maguey leaves or some other plant for roofing. But in all this, mesquite trunks are required. If a house is needed quickly, then one or two men go out to look for the proper logs. They select the straightest mesquite trees so the house supports will be really beautiful. 114. Since these trees are very resistant to disease, the house supports last for many years. There are some that are about 30 years old and are still standing. The main supports for a house are put deep into the ground, so even if there are strong winds they can stand up against them.

115. Imagine if trees could talk, the suffering of families they could relate! They would be living testimony to how a child grew up. Indeed, trees are mute witnesses to things. Late at night and early in the morning they see everything. They are witness to whether a father or mother has given love to their children. Though they are made of wood, trees defend the people against the rain and the cold, against stormy winds, and hail. 116. If a person does not want to cut down a particular mesquite, or because he likes its shade, then he puts his house right there where the tree stands. He prunes its branches back almost to the trunk, and they act as V-shaped supports for the house. The tree reacts, and it seems like it enjoys living with the people, and it starts to sprout new growth, and to give shade. It seems to spread its cover over the house that was put there. 117. When winter comes, the tree loses its leaves, and when spring returns it starts to grow again with flowers and then with new shoots. The house becomes almost covered with flowers and foliage and it looks beautiful.

118. And now, those of the house say: "Oh, there's no other mesquite like this one. Why would I build another house?" 119. When the tree has stopped flowering, it becomes filled with fruit. These fruits begin to ripen in May, and by July and August they are at their height. These fruits are eaten by the people of the house if they like them. Otherwise, the fruits are given to the pigs. Sometimes they aren't harvested at all if the people have no use for them, so they fall on the roof of the house and slowly rot.

120. When a mesquite is cut back to make forked house supports, there are branches left over that are left to dry for use as firewood. Mesquite wood is the most prized firewood because it gives good light, with strong flames; and, be-

cause it is dense, its flame lasts a long time. Mesquite wood is used most in making barbacóa, because this wood heats up the stones well.[27]

121. Some time ago, when matches were not common (or because people didn't have money to buy them), the women would select a thick mesquite branch and would set it afire. When they finished cooking and doing what they had to do in the kitchen, they buried the lighted branch and covered it with ashes from the kitchen fire. Then, the next day, when they needed fire again, all they had to do was dig out the branch they had buried. They did this every day, and they could go for two weeks or more without ever being without fire. 122. One woman might get up early and go ask another to lend her some fire. When a woman needed to borrow fire, she would be up and out at first light, standing ouside her neighbor's house.

123. "Hello, doña Pancha," she says. But no one answers because they are still asleep in the house. "Hello doña Pancha." But only the dogs bark and the chickens are startled. Slowly, those in the house awaken, and then the man or the woman answers. If the man answers first, he says "hello" and nothing more, because he doesn't know who is out there.

Doña Gregoria says "Hello, brother!" And the man answers "Hello, sister!"[28]

124. "Is that you, doña Gregoria?" he goes on. "Yes," she answers "and is doña Francisca there? I'd like to give her greetings."

"Yes, she's here, but she's still sleeping. Relax a while, and I'll tell her you're here. Sit, sit." And the man says to his wife, "Someone is out there asking for you. Get up."

"Who is asking for me?" says doña Pancha. "Why don't you tell them to come in and relax for a while?"

So the man tells doña Gregoria, "Come in and sit down, sister. She's coming now. And what do you want to talk to her for? What do you want?"

"I'm sitting and resting, thank you. It's nothing much, really. I just want to ask her for a favor."

125. Women are embarrassed to tell a man why they have come to his house. And even if she were to tell him, he would not give her the fire that she needs. This must be discussed between women.

Doña Pancha says, "Well, so it's you, doña Gregoria! Sit! What can I do for you?"

"Excuse me for coming in like this, sister Pancha, but do you happen to have any fire? Maybe you buried some. I buried mine, but it was made of maguey leaf and didn't last the night. Meanwhile, my worker at home is in a hurry to get to work."

"Ah, why didn't you just come in and take it. You've been out there for some time now," says doña Pancha. "You know where it is."

"Ah, no. I'm embarrassed to come in with your husband there. He's going to say that I'm in the habit of coming on my own into your house."

126. "He won't say anything to you while I'm here."

And so, the woman uncovers the fire that she had buried, and gives it to the other one who returns home. But when she gets home, she's late, and her husband says:

"What have you been doing? You've been gone a long time, and I'm in a hurry to get to work."

And Gregoria answers "I had to wait because our neighbors still weren't up when I got there."

"I always tell you to remember to bury your fire. There are some logs we brought in from the open country a week ago."

127. "Yes, from now on I'm going to do that. Otherwise, all I get is embarrassed with sister Pancha over there. Her husband could say that all I do is come over to get fire. Anyway, don't worry about it. I'm going to light a fire right now and make tortillas and some lunch for you to eat. You're going far and you'll be back late."

"Yes, woman," says the husband, "hurry please."

128. So she gives him some tortillas to eat and some more to take with him. They have salsa de chile on them. Some peons carry pulque with them. Sometimes they pour it into a bottle, or they pour it into a gourd which they carry on a sling. The sling goes across the chest, and the gourd rests on the side of the body. There used to be a kind of pitcher that was flat on both sides and circular in form. They were called "p̲etu"[29] in Ñähñu by some people. Others just called them generically "'mada," or clay pitchers, but they were of this particular shape. They held between four and five liters. 129. Nowadays, they are disappearing because new liquid containers, called "garrafones" in Spanish, have come in. Even if a person carrying one of these drops it, the container doesn't break. But those nice, old clay pitchers lasted only one fall, especially if they fell on a rock, in which case they would just shatter into pieces. Sometimes a person might just be careless in setting a clay pitcher down too hard, without realizing that it contained water or pulque. If a rock banged against the bottom, the pitcher would get a hole in it. 130. The owner then took it home and filled the hole with a chunk of wax. Then he would put pulque in it and the pitcher would be usable once again.

131. Let's see how doña Gregoria sees her husband off to work:

"Here's your meal. Take it with you and heat it up at work when you get hungry. And don't forget your pulque."

"No," he answers, "I won't forget. I'm carrying it right here. Well, I'm going. It's getting late. And don't you forget to check out our milpa. And be sure the shepherds don't let their goats in to feed on our garden plot. As you know, we have to protect the little maguey plants there. Well, I'm going. And remember that you have to scrape out the magueys[30] at midday, so that when I return you can give me a drink of pulque. I hope the new batch ferments well, because the stuff I'm carrying is overly sweet since we used up the base liquid."

This is the style of life in the valley. Each person goes to his or her own work, and in the evening they come together again.

132. We are considering here both skilled workers who have their own peons, as well as day laborers. In both cases, their women give them tortillas to take with them to eat on the job. Morning after morning, the woman of the house rises early to prepare what she will give to her husband (if he is self-employed), or to the one or two helpers he may take with him, depending on how much he can afford to pay. 133. By seven or seven thirty in the morning, the workers are already eating, in order to leave early for work, especially if they have to walk any distance.

134. What do they eat? It is different in each house. Those who have some money eat well, but the poorer people eat only what little they can afford. For this reason it is impossible to think that everyone has the same diet, and eats the same things. Some people say that Indians just eat tortillas made of maize, along with beans and salsa de chile all the time. That is what some mestizos and whites say who have come to the Mezquital Valley to observe the Ñähñu way of life. 135. But a lot of times what they say just isn't true. The truth is not always what one sees. It's one thing to see something, and quite another to live it.[31] Furthermore, not all Indians are poor, nor are all mestizos rich. There are Indians, too— why not say it?—who make this sort of error, just like anybody else in the world. They see a mestizo or white person dressed in nice clothes and they think that person has everything, when the truth is not this at all. Sometimes an Indian may not be dressed well but has more food to eat than a mestizo.

136. There is a saying among the Ñähñu when they see one of their own who is dressed well but who also doesn't have much to eat. This person is called an "o'tsa zaa," or "hollow log." This is because we can look at a log and think it is good and strong, but when we cut through it we find it is hollow, without pulp or substance. 137. This is a person whose fancy clothes don't do him any good when his stomach growls. Sometimes a mestizo might be invited to eat in a

Ñähñu house. Inviting people to eat is a custom among the native people. On these occasions the mestizo will notice that Ñähñu eat more than just tortillas and beans, and he might say "How is it possible for people to live in this arid environment and to eat a variety of things?" 138. But as I said a moment ago, in every family the situation is different, and we can say that even among those who don't have money, each household eats differently.

139. For example, consider a person who extracts fiber from lechuguilla, or consider a peon laborer. They work all week. The fiber maker collects ixtle which he pulls from the leaves of the plant, while the peon awaits the pay which he gets on the last day of the week. Ixtle extractors sell their product themselves to make money to buy things. Day laborers, who are paid in cash, purchase what they need. In either case, they buy as much as they can with the money they have. 140. First they buy corn, and then they see how much they have left over to buy other things. If they see that they have enough money, they buy some meat, but only enough for one meal. The meat might be boiled or fried. They also buy chiles, potatoes, and onions. Potatoes are for once or twice a week. They buy garlic, coriander, salt, tomatoes, and jitomates,[32] as well as different kinds of beans every week, like dried peas and garbanzos. However, mostly people buy the normal type of bean, called "hoogäjuu" in Ñähñu.[33] Of course, all kinds of beans are good, and this is just a phrase used to distinguish the common bean from the rest.

141. Some people buy lard for the whole week. If a man is shopping, he carries his purchases in a large bag; and if it's a woman, she uses a basket. 142. Men generally do not use baskets when they go to the plaza to shop. Things that don't bruise easily go on the bottom of the bag or basket. All the hard things are usually purchased first, but even if they are bought later they go on the bottom, and the soft, fragile things, like green tomatoes and jitomates go on top because they have to be carried a long way.

143. It is not possible to say "this is the every-day diet" because what people eat changes from day-to-day. For example, on Tuesday morning fried meat is eaten,[34] each person getting a piece. Don't think that this is meant to fill a person up with meat; it's just a little meat to go with tortillas. It is fried with ground chiles and green tomatoes or large red ones. This meat is only eaten with tortillas, and there is no other meat or stew. 144. In the afternoon, around four to six o'clock, or even seven o'clock for some folks, beans are eaten. They are cooked during the day with various condiments like coriander, onions, or scallions if there are any. If there are no beans, then the meal might consist of salsa[35] with water or pulque to drink.

Men generally don't use baskets when they shop
Flora 142

145. On the second or third day, the potatoes are cooked. If there is enough corn, then the worker has enough food to take with him on the job, but if there isn't enough, he gets only a little. He takes two or three "gorditas"[36] and four or five regular tortillas, depending on what he is used to eating. Again, if there is plenty, a worker takes enough to satisfy his hunger; otherwise, though he might wish for more, he just doesn't get it. 146. Sometimes they just put the rest of the meal right in with the tortillas, and sometimes a worker may take the rest of his meal in a pitcher which is covered so it won't spill on the way. Usually, salsa is not carried in a pitcher, but is considered a "dry" food.[37]

147. As for fruit, it is rare to see day laborers carry any with their meal, because they don't have enough money for fruit. Furthermore, even though fruit is expensive to begin with, the vendors raise the prices even more when they know that some fruit is not produced in a particular area. Sometimes a worker might take along an orange or a banana because these are the cheapest fruits to buy.

148. Now, about the amount of pulque a worker takes. Until recently, the wages of workers were not high, and magueys were not costly. In fact, until about seven years ago, the patrón used to give all his peons five liters of pulque for the day's work, not counting the pulque given in the morning before work and the pulque given to workers during the course of the day. 149. That was when pulque cost 70 centavos a liter. Then it went up to a peso, and it is now three pesos a liter.[38] 150. Nowadays, workers take about three liters of pulque with them to their work. We have already considered the food they take. They get whatever is available, including simple greens, rice or noodles, and beans. Those who have some money take at least two real, cooked meals every day, such as fried, boiled, or comal-cooked eggs.[39] Those who don't have much money also eat eggs, but more rarely. Those who have money sometimes eat beans and fried egg, or sometimes meat and beans which are carried in separate pots. 151. If one doesn't want to carry pots around, then the cooked food can simply be put directly on the tortilla, but this is a matter of personal taste.

152. When meat is not stewed in broth and condiments, it is fried. Sometimes it is pork, and sometimes beef; these are the kinds of meat which are usually obtained. We will consider the condiments in another book which will deal solely with the preparation of food.

153. We can mention three classes of families,[40] and among the last two (those who more or less have money) there isn't much difference between what they eat at home and what they take to work. Teachers, and others who have been educated, such as lawyers and doctors, work their own land whenever they have time off or vacations. If they have to go really far, they take their food with them. But if their plots are close, say, two or three kilometers, then they eat

breakfast and go off. Then, at midday, their wife brings their meal out to the field and the two of them eat together. And if they have more or less grown up children, then they eat with them, too. 154. Of course, only those who live out in the country pueblos do this. Those who live in the large towns or cities, though they might have workable fields, are somewhat lazy. Generally, they send out laborers. These wealthier folks don't work their own fields and they get easily tuckered out by the heat. Work in the milpas is really very tiring.

155. Everyone knows that in all communities everyone must live well together and develop a means to teach everyone in the community the same thing. In order for a pueblo to be well organized it is necessary for one man to be in charge of the activities, and to represent the community's wishes for a better future. 156. To achieve this, the people in a community exchange ideas, and they select a person whom they believe is appropriate for this sensitive job. Some pueblos, in fact, name a man to function as "juez auxiliar" or village judge or headman.[41] He is the one who imparts justice on the local level; he gives the people direction and purpose; and he sees to it that necessary projects, such as water tanks, schools, and roads are undertaken 157. The men of the village select the judge from amongst those who can read. This is not the only qualification, however. He must also be a hard worker and be respectful of all his neighbors. He must be on good terms with all the people in the community.

158. When the main fiesta in each community is over, the people of the valley gather to name their new judge. There are some communities that have two fiestas each year. If their main fiesta is at the end of the year, then this is when they gather to name their juez auxiliar. But if a community celebrates its main fiesta in the middle of the year, they wait until the end of the year, too, when the judges finish their terms. Sometimes people just wait until the order comes down from the central authorities in Ixmiquilpan, saying that it is time to change judges. 159. But among those people who like to work and who are progressive, they name their new judges before the order comes down. A few days prior to the changing of the personnel, the people are already talking amongst themselves, asking who they will name.

160. Don Antonio says, "Good day, Gumersindo." And Gumersindo answers, "How are you all, and what about this cold weather?"

"We're all fine, thanks. Yes, it's a little chilly in the morning, all right. Come in and rest a while."

"I'm well rested, thanks. I only came by to ask a question."

"Ah, really? What is it?" asks Antonio.

Gumersindo says, "It's nothing very important. I just wanted to ask you folks if you know when we are going to make our change of judges."

"Ah, well, who knows what the judges have been thinking! Personally, I've heard nothing yet, but perhaps two weeks from Tuesday."

161. "Ah, as I thought! I said to myself, I'll go and ask don Antonio when the change will be, so that I can attend the meeting. We all know that the judges change every year. They are like a tired pair of oxen who need to be spelled and allowed to rest. If it were one of us, in fact, I'll bet we'd be anxious to see our replacements by now. That's what I think, but who knows what the rest of the people in the village are thinking?"

"What do you think they will be thinking, don Gumersindo? I was talking with some men the other day, and they were saying that they had already seen who we can name as new judge. We'll see soon, when the time comes. Between us here, I'll tell you that I think they are looking at don Felipe. He'd be fine, as far as I'm concerned. He hasn't had to get out of embarrassing situations, and he is a good man. He knows how to read well. What's your opinion?"

162. This is how they talk amongst themselves. They usually don't say anything to the candidate whom they are considering. He will find out about it on the day the judge is named. But sometimes they do tell him beforehand.

Gumersindo continues: "Well, I think he would be fine. I was thinking of him myself, in fact. Let's just hope, and when the day comes we'll say our piece. Well, that was my only question, don Antonio. Thanks for taking time out, and good-bye!"

"Don't mention it. I don't have anything to offer you. So long for now."

163. The encumbent judges know that the day of change is coming. A week prior to the change, they send out their aides to notify the people that everyone will have to attend a meeting, but they don't say what the meeting is about. And if someone asks "what is the meeting for?" then the aides just say, "Who knows? The judges only told me yesterday to go around notifying the people that next Tuesday they should attend a meeting. But they didn't tell me what it was for. They want the people to get together as early as possible, by eight in the morning, so that they can start early and finish quickly."

"It's good that you are advising us of this. We will be there early," say the people of the house.

164. On Tuesday, the people named by the judges to notify the villagers are up early. The judges name two or three such aides, depending on the size of the community, and they name only the most responsible so that the work will be carried out properly. By five in the morning they are out there in the village square, where the bell is, calling the people together. The bell goes "Ndan. . . ndan-ndan. . . Ndan. . . ndan-ndan," several times. Once most of the people arrive, the judges enter the picture and go to where they will talk to the assembly.

First they take the roll, and then they give an account of what they've done. They talk about their attending the faenas that were called.[42] They also talk about how much money they were able to raise in collections. In short, they talk about all they were able to accomplish.

165. If anyone doesn't hear his name called, he says so, because no one wants to appear badly in front of his neighbors. By the same token, those who haven't lived up to their obligations during the year don't even want to hear their names called.

166. The judges finish their report. Some communities have two judges, and the smaller villages have only one. In the pueblos with two, the main one is called the "juez auxiliar propietario," or "primary judge" and the other is called the "juez auxiliar suplente," or "secondary judge." The primary judge has most of the responsibility for dispensing justice. On days when he is not there the secondary judge takes over. But when both are there, they work together.[43]

167. When the judge finishes giving his report, the people applaud if they are satisfied with his performance of the duties. Otherwise, they don't. The judge speaks to the people of the community:

"Neighbors! We hope that what we have done is acceptable to you. We have tried to do everything in our power. You yourselves have been witness; don't think that we have shirked our work. Thank you for all your help. You all know that every year we change the authorities, and our judges. That is why we have called you together, and you are here now to select those men who can fill the post. Surely, you have already determined who who will be proposed. But we want you to appoint him right here, so that everyone will know what happened."

168. As I said a moment ago, they select a person who is living well with the people, and who is working hard, as he should, in and for the community. So, one of the villagers says, "I propose don Tomás." Hearing his name, the villagers applaud their approval. The old judge says, "Well, you've heard the name of don Tomás proposed. What do you think?" And others say, "Yes, let it be him!" They name two or three candidates, and select one of them as primary judge. Then the second judge is chosen from among the other candidates.

169. A secretary takes down all the proceedings. The election papers are filled out in the pueblo. These documents are provided by the municipal president's office in town. The outgoing judges are responsible for bringing, in writing, the names of those elected at the meeting. Then, the new judges are called to the municipal center from all the villages in the municipality of Ixmiquilpan, so that they might be given proper orientation on the work they have to do in their villages. 170. The municipal president swears each of them in, explaining to them the importance of their posts. He asks them to raise their right

hand as a sign that they are speaking the truth. They put their arms straight out from their chests. Until about six years ago the new judges were called for swearing in on the last day of December at midnight. But since it was noticed that many came from far away, the time was changed. Now it is done on January 15th, and in the middle of the day.

171. We will consider the activities of the judges in cooperation with authorities from other villages in another volume on economics and politics. It is not convenient to do so here. Of course, this depends on our having life and health. I only introduce the naming of the judges here because it is connected with the religious cargos—yet another volume—and those cargos are connected with the use of mesquite in the incense burners.

172. The mayordomos of the church are also elected when the judges are named. First the judges, then the mayordomos. The same procedure for naming judges is followed. First a list of names is drawn up so that one may be selected. He will be the principal mayordomo. Then three more are selected. The people raise their hands in order to see who has the most votes. Whoever has the votes is elected. 173. What the people want in a man who is to be mayordomo is that he be a faithful person in the church, and that he not be a Protestant. If the people know that a man is a Protestant, they get angry and don't nominate him. Not only do they not elect him, but they hate him. No one can stand to see him; everyone shows their disdain, and he is called "'ñä jähñä," or "unbaptized." 174. Another thing that is required is that he be honest, that he not take another's money, and that he not steal the money offered to God in the church. Also, he should not be a drunkard so that he can take proper care of the images of the saints and virgins.[44] Two main mayordomos are named, and it is not necessary that both of them be able to read. But one of them must be able to, so he can keep the accounts. They, too, must be good people in the community, like the judges. They must know respect, and be respectful of the people in church when there are fiestas.

175. Women are not named as head judge for a village. It is very rare to see a woman in this post, but in 1978 there was one in the pueblo of El Maye. This is the only woman I've seen as juez auxiliar; in all the other pueblos the judges are always men. Pueblos have either one or two judges, depending on the number of inhabitants and the size of the village. Some villages have 2000 or 2500 people, like San Nicolás, El Maye, Orizabita, El Espíritu, San Miguel Tlazintla, El Saúz, San Andrés Daboxta, Los Remedios, and Zimapán. These are some of the places that have a lot of people and so they name two judges. 176. In these communities the population is very large and they have subdivided into units called

"barrios." These barrios generally name one judge each; but recently, their populations have gone up and now even some barrios name two judges.

177. The judge who is situated right in the main village oversees the one in the barrio, and gives him advice on how to work with his people. If some kind of emergency meeting is necessary, the main judge sends a notice to the one in the barrio, telling him that he must assemble his people on such-and-such a day. The barrio judge also has his own aides, and they go out to notify the people right away. We will look at these functions of judges in another book, so that what I say here can remain in order, and so that we can understand it better in fuller treatment.

178. Both the judges and the mayordomos must be in agreement for the village church's images to be taken away on a visit to another pueblo. There is the custom that, when a village has a fiesta, they invite the saints from other villages to come over. For example, in Santuario, they invite the Virgin of Cardonal to come over on the "fifth Friday." The "Fridays" I'm talking about are counted after "Ash Wednesday," called this because believers make a cross on their forehead with ashes. After Ash Wednesday, Lent begins. 179. The Friday after this particular Wednesday is counted as the "first Friday." The next Friday as number two, and so on until it ends with the Resurrection of Jesus.

180. We will look more closely at the exchange of visits from community to community in the next volume, which I've mentioned. That is where we will see who visits one another and when. We will also see whether visits are exchanged, or if only some people go visiting. Wherever this custom of visits exists, the judge and the mayordomo, with the consent of the people, get together and agree on a visit. They see if the people agree that the church santitos can go on a visit. If the people say "no" then the icons don't go, because the people have the last word.

181. On the day that the santitos are supposed to go, the judges and mayordomos of the community which invited them come to the pueblo where the images reside. The judges and mayordomos come with a procession of their people. Then they return to their community along with the images and a crew from the images' village. The crew from the images' village are there to see that the images are taken care of, and to help with the transport. 182. This procession takes place a day before the scheduled fiesta. The mayordomos, judges and people of the invited village go to the other village, with the icons. The mayordomos are obliged to stay with their community's images to protect them. They carry the images during the mass celebrated in the other village where the fiesta is. The judges can go home after the mass is over; the mayordomos must stay to

protect the images until they are returned to their home village. When the images are returned, however, the judges have to go back to the other village and accompany them home. The mayordomos stay on, receiving the offerings that the people give to the icons. If they didn't stay and collect, they would get nothing.

183. Women in communities other than El Maye are not named as judges or as mayordomos. In the past, this was because, first, many of them didn't know how to read or write, and second, because it was not the custom to name them to these posts since they could not travel far and go to the municipal presidency to ask for favors for the village. Also, their work at home didn't permit them to go out in the world, and they didn't have transportation, anyway. It would have been necessary for them to have their own cars in order for them to go wherever necessary to get resources for their pueblo. 184. For example, those who had infants couldn't go wherever they had to. They are now overcoming the backwardness they suffered of not knowing how to read or write. Of course, there are still some women who don't read, but more of them are educated nowadays, and they can fulfill the obligations of these jobs efficiently, especially the obligations of judge. In fact, people obey women more than men because women command more respect than men. 185. Women can not be mayordomos, however. Mayordomos must always be men because a lot of physical strength is needed to lift the statues of the saints. Other things are even heavier, so it would be very difficult for a woman to handle.

186. Mesquite fire, as I said before, really lasts a long time, and this is why it is used for so many purposes. For example, when people make a floral offering, they carry a vessel to burn incense and flowers to God. 187. They use mesquite to ensure that the fire lasts a long time. During the fiesta of the sixth Friday in Orizabita, the icons of El Espíritu are invited to visit. The santitos are carried in large showcases, and are accompanied by many people in addition to the carriers. The people who live along the route know that every year the images will be passing by, and that the incense carriers will ask for fire. The people in the houses along the route know this is the custom and set some mesquite to burning. One might say that they make the fire out of faith because they know that the saints and virgins make miracles, and the people think that if they don't adore them then the saints will punish them.

188. Another time when mesquite wood is lit is on the Day of the Little Angels and on the Day of the Faithful Dead. The first day of November is dedicated to the "little angels," or babies and children who have died, and the second of November is the celebration in honor of the "faithful dead," or departed adults. 189. About two weeks before, the wood gatherer begins to collect firewood so he will be prepared on the day dedicated to the dead. He has great

love for the departed and he buys incense for them. Then, on the day dedicated to the dead, he burns incense with mesquite coals.

190. Now that we are talking about mesquite coals, we can see that they have another use in the kitchen, or, more correctly, in nourishment. When someone makes tamales, either for their family, or to sell, or for the spirits of the dead (in which case they are made with great pleasure), the women—that is, the mothers of the family, or the daughters if there are any—all help in the preparation. When tamales are made, there is the belief that if there is a pregnant woman in the house and she looks at them, then the tamales will cook unevenly. So, when the first tamal in a batch is made, people take a mesquite coal and put it in the middle of the tamal, wrap it in corn husks, and tie it around the middle with a maize plant leaf. 191. This first tamal is called "the child." Whether there is a pregnant woman in the house or not, they always make the "child" tamal because it is a custom. Then the rest of the tamales are put in the pot, and the tamal carrying its "child" is cooked in the middle of all of them.

192. Hooks are made of mesquite wood for domestic use, but I emphasize that not all the people use these things any longer. These hooks are used in the home to hang up just about anything, such as sacks, gourds, baskets containing things, and so on. 193. Sometimes they make "garabatos," which are hooks that are different in form from the ones just mentioned. These latter are shaped like horseshoes, with a groove around the front side; a rope fits into the groove, goes around the horseshoe, and goes through a hole on each end of the garbato. 194. These tools are used to twist the binding tight on a rick of firewood being bound up for carrying. Mainly it is wood gatherers who use these tools. If they just used plain rope and no instrument for pulling it, they couldn't get it tight enough and the wood wouldn't bind up properly. When the bundle is carried, the whole thing would come loose and falls apart. But if it's bound really tightly with a garabato then it remains intact.

195. These mesquite hooks are treated by roasting them in a fire to prevent their being attacked by bugs. Another use made of the garabato is in bundling dried maize stalks, or zacate. Whether or not there is any corn to harvest, there are always stalks which are used as animal fodder during the dry period.[45] 196. In order to protect the zacate from rotting, it has to be stored properly, and this requires that it be bound up into special bales; this is done with mesquite roots. Zacate is unruly and sticks out all over the place, and it is because of this that the garabatos and ropes are useful. Two men work on a bundle, pulling one cinch tight, and then moving the garabato up to pull another cinch. The rope doesn't slip well through itself, and so it doesn't tighten up, but it does slip well through a garabato. 197. Thus, the rope is made perfectly taut around the

bundle. Once the bundle is tied up properly, then the roots are tied on. The ropes only serve to bundle the zacate, not to hold it for storage. The roots are pulled out of the ground in preparation for their use in making zacate stacks. First the stack is bound up with a large rope pulling the binding ropes tight, and then the roots are used to keep the stack in shape for proper storage.

198. Really big mesquite trees had a special use for people long ago. In early times, the men used these massive trees, though with great difficulty. They chose the straightest trunks and took great labor to fashion them into proper form. Then they raised them to the top of the churches, laid them across as beams, and mounted the church bells on them. Because these beams were from the heart of the mesquite, they have not been ravaged by bugs. They have remained intact, over these many years, holding up those bells. I would have thought those beams would have warped, considering how huge and heavy the bells are. But not this wood; it just goes on and on. 199. El Espíritu, Nequetejé and Orizabita are places where I've seen these bell tower beams. These beams have never been changed, even though they've been there a long, long time. We can safely say that the heart of the mesquite tree is immune to infestation by borer larvae. Otherwise, the big trunks holding up the bells would have collapsed by now.

200. There are two mesquites by the side of a church in a community called San Andrés. The trees are about two and a half meters apart. Each tree has a major fork, and another beam of mesquite has been laid across the forks between the two trees. Bells are hung from the crossbeam, and when they are rung the two trees sway back and forth, but don't fall over. These trees look beautiful when they bloom in the spring. They flower, and have moss all over them, and the bells chime. When people where they live looking like this, they smile and are happy. They joke among themselves and when they get together for a mass or a fiesta they say: 201. "Look at our nice bells. When there is money we will build a place made of mortar and rubble to hang them, because if those trees ever rot the bells will fall." This is how they talk, seated in the shade of some other mesquites, or drinking pulque. They always enjoy themselves, seated in the shade.

202. Frames for wood planes are made out of the same mesquite wood, because it is very tough. To make a plane such as I'm talking about here, only the most mature trees are selected. The trunk is worked to remove the bark, as well as the entire white part, or soft pulp around the heart of the tree. The heart is a darker, brown color. 203. This is the densest part and no bugs eat it or bore into it. The white, or pulpy part, is easily eaten by insects and is not as resistant as the heart. 204. The heart is then planed down until it is finished nicely, and then an

Garabatos are used to twist the binding tight on a rick

Flora 193

opening is made into which the blade and wedge are placed. In the same way, the handle of the plane is inserted into an opening on the top of the instrument. Once this is all done, the tool can be used to plane pine boards and any other kind of wood needed.

No matter how much use it gets, the main frame of the plane never gets scored underneath because the wood of the mesquite heart is so hard. Some of these tools were made 15 years ago and are still in regular use. 205. Carpenters use them, and they take good care of their tools because it takes a lot of work to make them, and if they aren't careful, then they won't have tools. The mesquite plane doesn't jam up and it slides easily when it shaves wood. Oak gets sticky rather easily and carpenters have to buy petroleum as a lubricant and apply it continuously. In this way they can work smoothly and their shoulders don't get so tired. However, when there is no petroleum, then, like it or not, they just have to work and bear up under the effort.

206. The really huge trunks are also called "mbonza" or "ancient trunks" by some people. These are selected by the people of a pueblo at a meeting where everyone gets together and reaches an agreement. The authorities call the people together. And for what? To tell them that not many days are left until the village fiesta, and that they must "raise the posts" or the "castillo" for the fireworks. The people who are assembled affirm their readiness, because putting up the posts is considered a sort of mandate and they know that they must hurry to find and raise the castillo together. 207. They work it out together and decide on what day they will go to look for the right trunks. For example, suppose they agree to go on Tuesday. A man gets up early to sharpen his axe because he knows full well what kind of wood he is going to cut and that it is thick. He goes off to where they've agreed to meet. Everyone goes to cut down the posts they will need.

There are three or four men who do the cutting, depending on how large the main castillo post will be. 208. They carry it back on their shoulders, taking turns, until they reach the village again where they will set up the posts. They then set to cleaning the support posts so they can plant them in the ground. When all this is done, the people are happy and they say: 209. "We have worked for God and the Virgin; would that they give us life until next year when we will be here again like this." What they are saying is that they will come together again as a group, but not to plant, or to set up the poles. This is because mesquite wood lasts many years. 210. The posts are about two hand spans thick, and about a meter and a half above the ground, not counting the part buried in the earth.

211. When the fiesta draws near the fireworks makers are called in. They might come today, for example, and begin work tomorrow, and by the afternoon

they are ready to set up the "d̲o̲ni," as some people call it in Ñähñu. Others call it by its Spanish name, "castillo." Other men have to be called upon to help raise the castillo. 212. They shout in unison and push against the castillo. Other men, who are not of the village but who are there for the fiesta see this and run to help. Once it has been raised upright those who helped step away and have a drink of pulque, because they really sweated from the exertion. And while they drink they talk:

213. "Those supports for the castillo which we brought were really buried well. They didn't even budge," says one.

And another responds, "We'll see about that when it starts to thunder and shake from the fireworks going off all over it."

"God will help us; nothing will happen to it," responds the other, and when someone mentions God the others quickly take off their sombreros and say, "That's what I say, too."

And they continue. 214. "Nothing will happen to it, nothing will happen to it. God our lord will help us. It isn't possible that we will be embarrassed in front of all the people who have been so kind as to visit us for the fiesta." And so they go to the fiesta, talking about whatever, while they await the procession. After the procession, fireworks castillo is set off, and this happens by no later than one or two in the morning.

215. The tower blasts about three or four times or sometimes more, depending on how much the people have paid the fireworks makers. When it's over, the people say, "Oh, it was really good what we did. Nothing happened to our handiwork!" Then they begin to drift apart and each one returns home, and everyone is happy because the work turned out well. Some men are accompanied by their wives and children, and everyone is glad that they have seen a fiesta. 216. The child goes along recalling the blasting of the fireworks tower; he skips along, kicking stones on the road. Sometimes, if he gives one a really hard kick, it pulls off his toenail. But it's as if he doesn't feel anything, because his joy is so powerful. He limps along after his parents; what's important to him is that they listen to what he says about the fiesta.

217. The branches of the mesquite tree are also very useful. What are called "staked posts" are cut from them. They are put to a great deal of use, so it's important to select them carefully when they are cut. These posts measure about one and two tenths meters and are not of uniform width. Some of them are 20 or 30 centimeters wide, and others only 10 centimeters. They can be cut from single or multiple branches with two, three, four or five parts.

218. They are referred to as "staked wood" because they are cut and then planted in the ground. The word for these is "m'anza" and it comes from "'ma'mi" which means a planted pole. These branches are planted in the ground wherever one wants to make an enclosure. First you plant all the posts necessary to encircle the area you want to enclose. Then you put cross timbers of mesquite or of maguey quiote, or any kind of wood.[46] 219. These cross timbers are used to reinforce the fence. One is lashed towards the top of the fence, and one nearer the ground. They are lashed to the posts with mesquite root if there is nothing to tie them with. They are lashed securely so that even if a bull pushes on it to get in, the fence won't fall. Finally, small branches are woven into the large branches. The points of the small branches are tucked together, and then the whole thing is filled in with thorn bramble. In this way, animals such as goats, pigs and chickens can't get in and do any damage to the house.

220. The branches of thorns that are used are from mesquites, ocotillos, and cardones. These are laid across the branches of the main supports so that goats or cattle can't jump over them. These animals jump their enclosures when they are hungry. Wherever they see any kind of food, they do everything they can to get at it.

221. It's rather difficult to make a fenced enclosure of these staked posts because, first, one has to cut the posts and cart them back if they are far from home. Then second, they have to be planted in the ground, and holes have to be dug for them using a metal rod. These enclosures are usually built around an area where nopal is to be planted. These particular plants are rather delicate and if cattle or goats nibble them—even if they just get saliva on them—the plants weaken and die. 222. Enclosures are also built around clumps of peach and fig trees. These trees require a well-built, durable corral. Staked posts are also used in building corrals for goats and sheep. These animals damage corrals with their horns, so the enclosures have to be built really well, and this is why corrals have very strong stakes.

223. Nopal enclosures and corrals can also be made of órgano. But these have to be lashed together so the wind won't knock them down. When the rains come, the órgano stakes take root. At the point where people enter the nopal patch, a special post is planted. This is the door, so to speak, and is called the "tonts'i" in Ñähñu or the "switcher," because it must be raised in order to go through. Sometimes you have to have something to stand on to open the "switcher." 224. One needs a lot of thorny brush to close off the entrances. This is all tied together and put on the fork of the entrance. But if the switcher is high, then a blockade is not needed.

225. In order to cut posts and stakes for an enclosure, the people who will do the work first see if the day is right for cutting mesquite. If they sense that the day is good, then they go off to work. But if not, then they don't, because they would wind up being sorry that all their effort went into something that won't last. Of course, *all* of one's work would not be lost. But the enclosure will last much longer when the day is right for cutting. 226. It isn't a good day when the moon is new or young. That is, when it's heading towards a full moon. If any kind of wood is cut when the moon is in this delicate stage, the wood gets attacked quickly by bugs, and the thorns are easily broken off by animals when this happens. But if you cut wood when the moon is mature, then the posts last longer.

227. Now we will look at another utensil that many people in the "blessed valley" know how to make.[47] This instrument is used for different needs and is also made from a thick, massive trunk. It is called a "trough"; the word in Ñähñu, "motsa," means "hollowed out wood" and, indeed, that is just what it is. 228. For this, one looks for a log that is thick and straight, and one that is about a meter long. Of course, some troughs are longer and some are shorter. A person who wants to make one starts hollowing out the log, leaving a raised, ungouged edge on each end of about four fingers' width. He digs it out with an adze, and little by little it takes a hollow shape, and he takes care not to go through the bottom. Then, when it's finished, he uses it as a feeder for pigs.

229. Pig troughs are made from wood so that they don't break. If you give a pig a trough that isn't massive, like a log, then it breaks when he dumps it over. Troughs of mesquite last the longest. Pigs have a habit of turning over their troughs when they finish eating. But if the trough is made of a thick log, then even if the pigs dump it over so hard that it makes a loud bang, it still won't break. 230. These troughs are also used to water chickens, and these animals don't try to break their feeders. Anyway, these troughs are very useful because they have many different functions.

231. There are many parts of the mesquite that make people happy, but some people have bad memories from these trees. How can this be? From what I've been told by some people from El Espíritu, about 30 years ago they built a tower on their village church. It was very hard work; it took an enormous effort to haul in the rock required for the church. The person whose idea the project was pushed the people hard to do their part in the communal labor. 232. Anyone who didn't cooperate was punished severely. There was a big mesquite tree there, and the man in charge ordered a rope brought in to tie prisoners to the tree if they didn't cooperate willingly. He forced them to work all day, and in the

evening he had them lashed to the big mesquite for the night. A guard stood by all night, until dawn. And if he didn't guard his prisoner securely, or if someone came to untie the prisoner, then the guard had to spend the next night tied to the tree.

233. In order that the prisoner might eat, his wife would bring him food. The poor man was completely tied up—his feet, his hands, and around his stomach—so he couldn't eat by himself, and he had to be fed. His wife would tear up his tortilla into pieces, and put the pieces into his mouth. Then, after giving him his food, she fed him his pulque. The next day, about ten in the morning, he was untied and put back to work.

234. The sons of men to whom this happened told me about this. The sons of the man who ordered the punishment are also still living there. When the children of those who were punished talked about it, they got angry. I told them that these events were in the past, and that they should forget them. 235. What they need to do is reach an understanding of the situation. And they understood what I told them, and forgot the past. What happened was that the mesquite tree performed its function as a sort of jail. The tree is not to blame, only those who forced those people to stand there all night. The mesquite never chose the people or judged whether they were strong workers or lazy men. No, it liked everyone equally, and covered them all with its shade. For better or for worse, the tree made its own history in this community.

236. Slingshots are made from the thinner branches of the mesquite. The right kind of branch must be chosen for this, and it has to have two prongs. Then it has to be roasted in the fire to make the wood flexible so that the two prongs can be bent back double. When the prongs have been bent back to the handle, they are tied back until they dry, so they will not return to their original shape. The wood is heated in a fire to soften it up so that the prongs won't break when they are bent back, and also so that bugs won't attack the wood. 237. After the wood is dry and has taken form, the bark is stripped off and the wood is polished. One tries to find a piece of wood that has a knot right where the two prongs come out of the handle. Then the knot is carved and fashioned to look like the head of a person, a bird, or some other animal.

238. Other parts of the mesquite are used in the construction of houses. Houses made of maguey leaves have a part on one end which is curved outward. It comes in a sort of circle from the ground to the roof and is connected inside to small posts or sticks which have been shaped to conform to this part of the house, called the "fozu." This part of the house is added on so that the structure won't be completely straight-sided, and also to increase the space in the house.

Troughs of mesquite last the longest

Flora 229

239. This is where the curved branches and roots of the mesquite are used. They are cleaned of spines and thorns so they can be fitted into place. They sit in the crooks of the small forked house supports. They are lashed well so they won't budge when other supports are attached. One has to be careful, for this job, too, that the moon is in the right position; the owner of a house, of course, wants the walls to last as long as the rest of the structure.

240. The children are sent out to the open country to look for wood. They gad about, looking among the thorns, and if they come upon a mesquite branch that has bent over near to the ground they start to hang on it and bounce up and down. When they see that the branch will hold them, they sit on it and make it into a seesaw. They are late getting back with the wood, but they don't want to leave. And their joy is even greater when there are two children, rather than just one. They take turns, and say: 241. "Let's bounce up and down, and then we'll help each other gather wood." And so they take turns, going up and down, one of them moving the branch, the other one on it, both of them laughing joyously.

242. Other children carry a rope with them for tying bundles of wood, and they make a swing out of the tree branch. They do this because they don't have toys bought for them. So whenever they see something they can use as a toy, they set to playing. The other children, who live in towns, have toys bought for them. The toys are made in the big cities. Someone might ask, why aren't toys purchased for all children? And there is one reason: the parents don't have enough money. Whatever money they get they use to buy food to live on.

243. Mestizos may say that Indians are lazy. This is just a big lie. When they say this, the mestizos are talking only because they have a mouth. But they don't go see first whether poor people even have the means to work.

244. Here is an example of the truth of what I'm saying. In the lands where the irrigation canals have reached, one can see that there are regular harvests now. Though the people there don't have much money, they are not as badly off as the rest of the people in the valley. Those people who live in areas without water, though they have land to work, can't plant anything if there is neither rain nor any means to irrigate those lands. The people who live on these lands have no resources and the mestizos, seeing this, believe the Indians are lazy. But it isn't so; it's only the lack of water. 245. If they *had* adequate natural resources and the people still didn't put them to use, then the mestizos could say the Indians were lazy. But some mestizos seem to offer their words and opinions without thinking first. Many mestizos are sent by the government to make studies of the land in order to make it productive. But a lot of times they don't do their work, and just find something else to do. Then the local people, seeing this, don't believe anything the mestizos say. 246. There have been times when the

mestizos were supposed to show the people how to plant maguey, but instead of teaching people, the mestizos were the ones who were taught. It would likely be cheaper if some Indians were to go to the mestizos' offices and teach them there what the mestizos want to teach others—things like the planting of maguey, lechuguilla and other plants of the valley. That way, when they go out to where the Indians live, the mestizos wouldn't run into such major problems.

247. Many of those poor men who are sent out to us suffer a lot. First of all, they've never been out in the provinces, and second, they don't have food they're used to. As they become confronted with these things they become demoralized, fail to accomplish the necessary tasks they were sent to do, and return to the city. This has happened a lot, on various projects that the government wants to effect, and this is why progress doesn't happen. How could progress occur, when its own workers flee?

248. Other mestizos come, also sent by the government to work on various projects. They resent it when they hear the local people talk Ñähñu. Some mestizos think they are being insulted by the native people, but the mestizos never stop to think that the economically poorer people don't know how to express themselves well in Spanish, or don't even know how to speak it at all. When these mestizos hear Ñähñu being spoken, they seem to feel superior to others. 249. They just start giving orders—anything that comes to their heads— to the local people who are accompanying them as aides. Then what happens to these aides is that they are despised by their own people and the aides abandon the mestizos. Then the mestizos inform their superiors that the people don't want to offer any help, that the Indians are lazy. They make up some pretext to get a transfer, and they go somewhere else. Then the same thing happens again. It doesn't matter to them whether they go up or down; any place will do. And no one knows if or when the work will get done. The only thing we know for sure is that money has been spent uselessly for their salaries.

250. When they report to the government they say that they've spent millions and millions of pesos on public works for the Indians. But what works? If we look carefully, we see that nothing has changed. It must be absolutely clear that the Indian is not at all lazy; he is not an ingrate; he is not perverse. But no one wants to hear the Indian's words of respect and gratitude.

251. Some other tools made from small, dry mesquite wood are two pieces which are fashioned by hand, one of them flat and the other rounded and club-shaped. One end of the rounded piece is a blunt wedge, as if someone were making an adze. These pieces are about 25 centimeters long and about four fingers wide so that they can be grasped tightly. Now we will see what they are used for.

252. These two pieces of wood are used together to cut the nerves in the testicles of male goats and sheep. The flat piece of wood is placed on the ground and the other piece that has the blunt edge is held by the man who is going to castrate the animal. He hits the testicle nerves with the blunt edge and severs them so the animal won't be in stud again. With a couple of sharp blows the nerves are severed. Only the nerves are affected, but nothing happens to the skin. It hurts a bit, and a little blood flows, but that is all. 253. When it's over, it's like nothing happened. The testicles still hang down as always, only the nerves have been severed. The animal limps around for about two weeks, and after three weeks is walking as well as ever. From then on it gets fat, and this is precisely why it is castrated. It is allowed to get fat and is then sold or killed and eaten by the family. Sometimes animals are sold uncastrated. This happens when the owner needs money, has to sell the animal in a hurry, and can't wait for it to fatten up. 254. Both goats and sheep, if they are to be eaten by those of the household, must be castrated. Otherwise, the meat causes stomach pain. Whoever eats the meat of uncastrated goat or sheep suffers gurgling stomach and diarrhea. The people who know this don't eat the meat of animals that are still in stud.

255. Whenever it is required, a man who knows how to castrate animals is called in. Both goats and sheep are treated in the same way. The man comes with his two pieces of wood, tied together for easy carrying. The animals have to be hung up by the horns to prepare them for the operation. Of course, only those with horns can be hung in this way; those without horns are strung up with the rope around their chest. Goats and sheep that don't have horns are called "zooñä," or bald, whether they are male or female. 256. A thin string is tied around the animal's testicles so the nerves can be pulled and stretched out. This way, when they are stretched out, the nerves can be broken easily. Male goats make a lot of noise when they are castrated, but sheep just grunt.

257. There is a little story about a sheep and a bull. One day the master thought he would castrate the sheep and the ox. So he went to get his helpers to prepare the animals, and they came. They took the bull out of the corral first, since it is more difficult to castrate because it is very powerful. To castrate a bull one finds a big, strong mesquite to tie it to. 258. You tie up the horns, the front feet, and the rear feet. You have to tie the animal up really well, so that when it starts to kick with the hard blows to its testicles it won't come untied and kick the person castrating it. When it has been tied up, some of the helpers step aside. Only two people do the work of castrating a bull. One pulls the testicles out, and the other, who knows how to castrate, strikes the blows. He is the one who calculates the force of the blows needed. He doesn't want to break the skin.

259. The men who have stepped aside watch the man who is working. The master, of course, has already thought about castrating the sheep. Now both those animals knew about this because they had heard the owner say to his wife that he was going to castrate the sheep and the bull. From that day, the sheep and the bull began to say to each other:

260. "Hey, did you hear, little sheep, what the master said? He said he was going to castrate both of us," began the bull.

Then the sheep answered, "I'm not afraid, I reckon that it's my fate."

The bull, on the other hand, was afraid of being castrated. So he said, "You can't imagine, little sheep, the fear I have."

And the sheep said, "You are afraid even though you are so big, while I'm little and I'm not afraid of them."

The bull didn't believe what the sheep was telling him. "If you're so unafraid," said the bull, "what do you say to a bet, and we'll see who loses."

261. "You name it, and we'll do it," said the sheep.

"Well, they're going to castrate us, so we'll bet on who can take it and who cries out."

262. "That's fine," said the sheep. So when they were castrated, the men started banging so hard on the testicles of the bull and the sheep that it made a loud noise. At first they both tried to hold out and just take it. But when the pain got really bad the bull gave a great groan. Hearing this the sheep asked "What's up?" That's all he said, and then he shut his mouth because he thought he might cry out also. After they had both been castrated, and even though the sheep was limping, he said to the bull, "Well, you lost the bet we made." And that's how sheep are; when they are being castrated they don't cry out; they just kick and groan, but don't cry out. By contrast, goats and the bulls really carry on.

263. The pieces of wood used to castrate goats and sheep are not the same as those used on bulls. The chisel-edged club used on bulls is larger, about the size of the club used to beat maguey leaves. This is because the nerves of bull testicles are bigger.

264. Now we will look at mesquite moss, another resource provided by the mesquite tree. There are two classes of this hay-like moss, one known simply as "hay," and the other called "long hay."[48] The short moss is one of the things goats eat when they roam about the open country and come on medium-sized mesquites. They stand on their hind legs to reach the moss with their mouths, because this plant grows on the branches of the mesquite. 265. As I have said many times, when there is a drought the green plants and grasses don't get new growth, and the animals really suffer. Goats get food off the mesquite trees.

There are some branches that have moss which the goats can reach with their mouths, so little by little they manage to get through the droughts. 266. Shepherds carry long sticks so that when goats can't reach the moss in the tall trees, they can knock it down for the animals to eat. When goats get used to shepherds feeding them, then they don't stray away and they bleat when they are hungry. Sometimes goats act like cats, brushing up against the legs of their shepherd. Sheep eat tree moss, too, but only what is knocked down for them. They don't stand up on their hind legs because they are too stupid to find their own food.

267. When moss gets old, then only the tips of the strands are eaten. Goats won't eat dried up moss; they sniff it and walk away. This class of moss grows in any kind of tree, even on electric wires or the eaves of houses. We have seen hay moss growing in cat's claw, miel de jicote, Christ's crowns, garambullos and pirul trees.[49] But we have also noticed that goats like most to eat the hay moss off of mesquite trees and cat's claw cactus. We don't understand why this is so; perhaps it just tastes better to the animals. 268. Bulls also eat the hay-like moss whenever they find it if they are pasturing in open country. Other plants that get this kind of moss are nopales, fig trees, ocotillos, pines and acacia trees.[50] Some animals like to eat these mosses, while others like to use them in their nests as a soft blanket against their bodies, or, in the case of birds, to protect their eggs. Birds like to have soft nests, and they make them soft by lining them with soft hay moss. Then, when their little birds are born, they feel nice in the soft nest. Turtle doves, sparrows, pigeons, mocking birds and wild canaries have tree moss in their nests. Hummingbirds put a lot of it in their nests. I say "a lot," but many of us know how big a hummingbird nest is. Anyway, it uses the smallest and softest moss.

269. During the Revolution people used to eat tree moss because corn was hidden away and there was a lot of hunger among the common people. Some of them died of starvation, but people survived who ate whatever they could find. There are still some old people around who tell of eating tree moss. They would cut it off the trees and just eat it.

270. In the days when people used to carry water in pitchers it would slop over if it weren't covered with some kind of top. Some folks used maguey leaves, and others used a fistful of washed tree moss[51] so that the liquid wouldn't spill out and their backs wouldn't get wet.[52] 271. We have often seen the pulque vendors going along the road, carrying their pulque on their backs to market. If they meet up with friends on the way they greet them and invite them to have a drink. But the fresh pulque is not strained so they quickly look for a

fistful of tree moss which they put in the mouth of the pitcher to act as a strainer. Of course, it contains desert dust, but it's better than drinking the dregs of the maguey scrapings or the gnats which have gotten into the pulque. 272. One uses the young, tender moss which is pretty clean. The one invited drinks first. The pulquero takes a cup or a maguey leaf and says "help me here." When they are finished, the one who was invited helps the pulquero put his load back on his back, and they both go on their way.[53]

273. The really long tree mosses are not eaten by goats. These mosses also grow on mesquites, but not on every tree. The bald cypresses, along the edges of rivers, have a lot of this moss. The people like to drape the long moss over mesquites in order to create shade. During the time of the posada fiestas, around Christmas and New Year's, the dance halls are decorated with long Spanish moss.

274. Another parasite on the mesquite grows on the young tender branches of large trees. This plant is also eaten by goats, sheep, even kids. There isn't much of it, but they really like to eat it. The form of this plant that grows on branches is like that of siempreviva.[54] Its leaves are the same shape. Some are green and look like they are covered with white powder, while others are yellowish green. This little parasite branch is not hard like the mesquite itself. Its stalk breaks easily. 275. If you cut them off this year then next year other shoots grow in their place. The Ñähñu word "menza" means "a plant which is not well developed," which is to say that it is not hard and tough. This plant is not like hay moss that hangs on trees; rather it actually grows out of the branch as if it were another branch itself. 276. We don't know whether it tastes good or not, but goats and sheep love to eat it. The animals can't get at these plants themselves because the parasites grow high up on the trees. Shepherds pull the plants off them or beat them off with their staffs. These plants surely taste good to the animals, because when they see shepherds go to hit the mesquite branches with a staff, they come running to snatch the plants, and they salivate freely while eating them.

277. Just as many other plants contain some liquid, the mesquite has its own, and it is called "'mi'thi rä t'ähi," or "mesquite urine" in Ñähñu. The color of the liquid as it comes from the tree is yellowish, but when it dries it turns jet black and simply won't come out of clothes. No matter how much soap you use, it won't come out, especially if it stains a white fabric. 278. Until a short time ago, blanket makers dyed their white wool with mesquite sap, and the color lasted until the wool wore out. They boiled the bark first, and then they put in the wool. The wool stayed in the dye all night and the next day it was removed, allowed to

drip off, and then dried in the sun. Then it was washed so it could be carded. 279. Salt was put in the boiling water and, according to those who did it, this made the dye stronger so it wouldn't come out in the wash.

280. There also used to be woodworkers who made guitars out of walnut. One was named Trinidad and he used to stain the wood dark brown with mesquite sap, and then varnish it. When it was finished, the guitar looked beautiful and was sold in the hardware stores.

281. Another liquid that comes from the mesquite is resin, but the word in Ñähñu means "gushes from the mesquite." This is very different from the black liquid which comes out of the trunk and large branches. The resin comes from the thin branches. It comes each year, during February, March, and April, and flows spontaneously in the morning; in the afternoon when the sun shines on it, it shines brightly and it looks as if the mesquite is wearing earrings as the drops accumulate and form hanging clumps.

282. The liquid is transparent and sticky. Only rarely does it drip off the mesquite. Some globs of it are sweet, and others have no flavor at all. Bees don't eat it because it dries hard as it flows out and there is no way for them to suck on it. Until about 20 years ago people used to gather this stuff and sell it. Children who were out herding would gather it all week, and then on Mondays, whoever came to market brought it in a bag. We never knew what it was used for. 283. But people paid 20 or 30 centavos for a kilogram bag, and with this money the seller would purchase five centavos worth of salt and with the rest he or she would buy bread for the person who had actually collected the sap. If it rains, and if the rain is really strong, the hardened sap slides off the branches. Though they may not have any leaves, some mesquite trees have their little balls of resin, and it looks like someone had decorated the tree.

284. Some mesquites flower as early as December, but these trees never develop their fruit. People say that these trees have been fooled by the cold, because the cold is wet rather than dry. Sometimes it gets cold out, and then a few days later some mesquites start to sprout new growth and to flower. Also if the spring winds from the west come early, they make the new growth on the tree really green, and it looks so pretty that one would think there was lots of water around the roots. 285. But the early spring wind also fools the trees, and in January and February, whether it rains or not, the new growth dies.

285. Some trees get their new sprouts first, while others flower, and sometimes they sprout and flower together. They start to sprout, and it's beautiful; the whole vista of the valley changes as it becomes green. If they could be eaten, they would be cut; but though they aren't edible, these green sprouts are a real marvel to see. They produce a really cool shade because the foliage is so thick.

Here, the field worker can get some protection from the heat when he feels the strong rays of the sun and he is tired. He looks up from under the shady tree as if to ask it when the rain will come. 286. He thinks about it and realizes that the tree will not tell him and so he sits in silence for a while. While he rests, the flight of the bees and other insects is like a song for him, and he thinks he sees the first flowers appear. 287. Some birds also chime in with their singing, as they go from one sprout to another, eating the little insects on the delicate, new branches. There are very small green bugs that stick to the new branches of the mesquite, and some birds like to eat them.

288. The birds that eat mesquite bugs come to the valley in great flocks from somewhere else, just as the trees begin to sprout new growth. When the trees finish flowering, the birds migrate again, and then only the birds that are always around remain in the valley. The dominico birds come; they sing in the greenery of the trees and they give more life to the valley. As March begins, the mesquites are at the height of their flowering. Some trees are virtually covered with flowers and they look really beautiful. This is when insects fly around all over the place, going from flower to flower. Some flowers are yellow, others are white. They have a nice aroma, and you can smell it when the air is pure. The birds I mentioned also go from mesquite to mesquite, but only to eat the insects, and not the flowers.

290. At about halfway through the period of new growth, the mesquite becomes covered with little green bugs and inchworms. These are the bugs that the birds look out for. The little insects exist in large clumps, and they are so thick that they can be mistaken for the foliage on the branches. If a person brushes against one of these branches, the insects swarm and go up into the air. 291. They are around for several days, and they ruin the new branches on the mesquites, because they eat the young sap. The young branches get all covered with their own sap, and if a good hard rain comes, the branches break off. 292. When the flowering time is over, the mesquites grow pods that look like dark green, long beans. Some years there aren't many, and others there is an abundance.

293. There are two beliefs associated with the amount of mesquite fruit. When there is not a whole lot, people believe it will be a good year for agriculture. A "good year" means that it will rain a lot, the people will plant and they will reap a harvest. 294. But if there is a lot of mesquite fruit, then people say, "There's going to be a lot of mesquite fruit; it's not going to be a good year." When there's a lot, there's *really* a lot—so much that the branches are weighed down towards the ground. And there are a lot of mesquite grubs, too. The people who say this about not having a good year have watched what happens over the

years, and it is just as they say. There will be one good rain, and the people will plant. The maize will sprout but then the rain won't return quickly, and by the time it rains again, the fields are all dried up.

295. The people just trust in God. One of them says, "God didn't want to give us our rain and our harvest. Maybe next year we can raise some crops, even if only a little." "Let's hope so," answers another. 296. They aren't really remorseful about having lost their crop, because it's a normal occurrence, and the next year they are out on their plots of land building bordos to catch the water if it rains.[55] Thus, most people don't lose hope. It's like a tradition: they plant every year, and reap no harvest. 297. Every year the people take note of how the wild plants and mesquites are doing—how they develop in the flowering stage and the sap running stage, and whether they have a lot of fruit or not, how many caterpillars they have, how cold it was during the cold period. Taking all this into account, they predict how the harvest will be.

298. Many people say that when it's very cold, then there will be a lot of rain, because it is believed that the moisture left by the cold is what becomes part of the rain. 299. It has snowed only rarely, and when it happens it is called "zunza," or "hangs on the trees." This is the sleet that hangs on the trees, and it is the kind of cold that leaves the most moisture behind.

300. In May, the mesquite fruit begins to ripen. These early ripenings are called "me'thi" or "undeveloped"; the word "medi," from which the term "undeveloped" is derived, means "incomplete," and signifies that somethings has not grown properly. For example, a peach which is ripe on one side, and hard on the other, or a squash which ripens on the end connected to the plant, but not on the other end; these are called "medi." 301. So, mesquite fruit which doesn't develop or ripen evenly are called "me'thi" because one part is ripe and the other wrinkled up. June, July and August are when mesquite fruit really ripen up. 302. When this occurs, some people gather up the fruit for feeding to pigs, and they store it for when there isn't any. The animals get fat. Goats eat the fallen fruit which is gathered, as well as the fruit they are given by their shepherds out in the fields. Shepherds carry a long pole to knock down the fruit, and in this way the sheep eat, too.

303. While we're talking about the riches of the desert, why not mention that shepherds, themselves, like to eat mesquite fruit, too. They choose only the juiciest and sweetest fruit; some fruit is fat, but not sweet, while others are thin and sweet. When shepherds are thirsty, they cut a few pieces and this cuts their hunger and thirst as well. Some shepherds rarely take tortillas or water with them to the monte. I say "some" shepherds because they are not all alike in the way they live. Those who work for wealthy employers get a monthly wage.

Their employers also give them a fistful of tortillas to take with them each day. 304. That is, in the morning, the lady of the house grabs a normal handful of tortillas between her thumb and fingers—not too big a handful, and not too small, but normal. This is called a "xo̱'tse" and consists of more or less ten regular, thin tortillas, and five or six of the gorditas. The shepherds get enough to eat right there, and also for the trip to the pasture out in the open country. 305. They put salt, greens and beans on the tortillas first, before going out herding. They can't be given a clay jug in which to carry all this, because it would fall out of the jugs on the twisty trails which shepherds use. A big person is given more, and a child is given less. 306. All this depends on the particular family that a shepherd helps, too. A family that doesn't have a lot can't give a lot. People who have no children, or whose children are away at school, or who have enough money to pay others, look for someone to tend their goats. For example, teachers, who have secure jobs and who keep animals are among those who seek shepherds' help. Ten years ago, in 1969, shepherds were paid 40 or 50 pesos a month.

307. Nowadays, the cost is never less than 100 pesos a month. If there are only a small number of goats, it may be less. But if there are many, say 20, then 100 pesos is the price. And if there are even more, then it costs 150 pesos. Why should it cost so much? Because the more goats, the more work it takes to watch them. It used to cost less because the people did not understand or appreciate their own value. So, whether it was a few goats or many, they charged the same price. Some patrones are really demanding, and they would ask their shepherds to keep the flock out until very late, so the animals would be really well fed. 308. Like it or not, the poor shepherds didn't come in until very late. They would just be getting back at sundown, and sometimes they would be still penning up the goats while it was getting dark, having taken them out at nine in the morning. If shepherds see that their employers get angry a lot, then they abandon their flocks and don't take them out to watch over them anymore. They just finish out their month, and ask for their pay.

309. The next day, the patrones are waiting, but the shepherd doesn't show up. The owners just have to take their own goats out, and they have to look for another shepherd. But if new shepherds see the same behavior, then they leave also. By contrast owners who are good people feed their shepherds well, and treat them as they should treat a servant. These people retain their shepherds for a long time. They may stay for a year, or two years, or they may even live with the patrón permanently. 310. People notice the fact that shepherds are not run-of-the-mill folk, but require respect and must be asked, not ordered to do things. If they are asked politely, then they will take the goats to the open country where

there are greens for the animals to eat. The good patrones who see that their shepherds come in late from the fields give them meals to take with them, and set out all the foods for them that we have seen above. 311. They give them some kind of bag to take their tortillas in; they give them pulque in a gourd[56] that holds two or three liters and no more, because they don't want the shepherds to get drunk and lose the goats. 312. Shepherds eat their tortillas out in the fields. They heat them up if they like them hot, or they eat them cold. Nowadays, shepherds use plastic containers, called "garrafones" in Spanish, which don't break easily.

313. Mostly shepherds are women. When they are in school, very few children herd flocks. But when there are no classes, then children do a lot of herding. It is rare to see adult men herding flocks. They work at other things to make money. Children are not usually given pulque when they go out as shepherds. They are told that they shouldn't get drunk and lose the goats, and also that they must quickly learn to read, but that this will happen only if they don't drink pulque.

314. Mesquite fruit used to be sold. It was thrown into a large, heavy ayate for carrying to market. But we don't know what the fruit was used for. People paid one or two pesos for an ayateful. The fruit was carried in by poor people who had to come on foot. They came from all over, and some people brought it in sacks. 315. Some say they used to boil the sweetest fruit right there in the market, and then people would buy it to eat. Both men and women alike used to eat it. I don't know if it was sold by the plateful, or by the piece. I have tried boiled mesquite fruit, and it is sweet. The sweetest fruits are selected and then boiled. When cooked, they taste as if someone had thrown in sugar, and they are eaten as a kind of sweet, rather than because one is hungry. The whole fruit wasn't eaten; only the sweet part was sucked out, and the skin and seeds were thrown away.

316. The fruit of these trees is particularly good for squirrels. When the fruit is abundant, squirrels come and go through the branches, eating and carrying fruit in the pouches of their jaws. They take what they carry in their pouches home to their young. If they have no young, they store the extra fruit away to eat when there isn't any more on the trees. 317. When there is plenty of mesquite fruit, the squirrels are happy, and they whistle from their perches atop the trees. When they see people coming, they whistle at them and hide in the branches. Squirrels are real jokers. If you throw a rock at them, they stick their tail up, run down the tree, and scurry off to their burrow. This is the time of year when squirrels get fat and when a lot of them are born, because they have a lot to eat.

318. Mesquite fruit is also good for lizards. Lizards are the same color as the branches of the mesquite, so they are camouflaged in the trees and you can only tell that a lizard is there when it moves. Mesquite trees are more or less a brown color, and the trunk is craggy and slit open. As they grow, they continue to split. 319. The trunks are split from the ground up, and the oldest branches are also split. The young branches are light green, and the brand new ones are a brilliant green. The roots are brown, a sort of light brown, compared to the color of the trunk. When the roots are really deep in the ground, they don't split; but where water has eroded the ground, and the roots are exposed to the sun, they get rough and craggy just like the trunks.

320. Mesquites grow to different heights. There are some that are only 20 centimeters high; others are one, two and three meters, and some highly developed trees reach a height of 20 meters. 321. Their trunks get to be approximately three meters around. These are the biggest ones. The size depends, above all, on the kind of ground a tree grows in. If the ground is rocky, the tree grows poorly. But if the earth is good and soft, then the trees grow well, with many branches and much foliage. The shade thrown by a large tree, with all its branches, may reach 10 meters across, measured when the sun is directly overhead.

322. As we saw in the beginning of this section, the mesquite's branches are used as firewood in the kitchen and anywhere else that it is necessary to burn wood. The trunks are not often burned like the branches are. They are put aside and not made into charcoal. Then, when it's really cold—when the cold clouds and cold winds come in November and December, and when it freezes in January and February—then the trunks are put on the fire to give heat to the people. 323. In order to get the trunks lit, one must use a starter fire made of dried maguey fronds and small kindling wood. The trunks don't just catch fire easily because they are so heavy. When they are lit through and through, huge pieces of charcoal emerge.

324. If it's been a good year, that is, if there has been a good harvest and there are large calabasas called "pintas," then one of them can be roasted on the large coals of the mesquite trunks. Or two calabasas may be roasted, so that the whole family can have some.[57] These squashes do not burn as they sit in the coals, but cook up like they were in an oven. The roasted squash is sweet and delicious.

325. As far as medicine is concerned, no one knows how many Ñähñu know how to use the mesquite in curing. But I've heard from many, and seen myself that freshly cut branches and roots are used in medicine. By this I mean the rather thin, young roots and branches that are not dried up. 326. One end is

placed in the fire, and when they are about half consumed, a warm sap flows from the other end. If there is a child, boy or girl, who can not hold its urine, and who wets the bed all the time without feeling it, then this sap is used. 327. Just as the sap comes out of the branch and is warm, the father or mother of the child dips a finger in it and dabs it right in the center of the child's navel. They dab it on two or three times and this stops childhood incontinence. This is how mesquite is used in medicine.

328. The mesquite's seeds are oval, with a thin edge and a thick, bulbous center where the actual seed is located. The sheath of the seed is like leather, and the seed itself looks like a lentil bean, which also comes wrapped in a leathery covering. The wrapping or sheath is orange-brown in color. The seed itself (that is, the part that sprouts a new plant) is white and is split into two parts, down the middle. 329. No one plants these seeds; they just grow by themselves wherever there is moisture, and they prefer fertile soil. They grow wherever there is garbage and moisture. They take about 15 days to germinate. Two thick, roundish leaves appear first, about the size of a fingernail. Between the two leaves, at their base, there is a little ball, and this is the part that becomes a tree.

330. Even though you can just barely see the plant above the ground, its one single root has penetrated deep into the earth, and can be as long as 20 centimeters eight days after it starts to grow. We know this because we are always pulling them up out of the milpas where they are not permitted to grow. 331. At about a month or six weeks the actual tree begins to grow, and those first leaves turn yellow and fall off. The plants start to put out leaves that are different from the ones they start with. The new leaves have a kind of branch or stick down the middle. The little leaves stick out on both sides of the branch in a row. Down at the bottom of the stick is where the thorns grow.

332. This is also where the flowers bloom. When they bloom, three or four stalks appear, and each one has about 50 blossoms. Each node from which the flowers come always has two thorns. Each large twig has about 20 dark green leaves on it, and the new leaves are yellowish green. 333. As they grow, the branches get thicker, lose their spring thorns, and become covered with bark.

334. There are different kinds of mesquites. Some are all leafy, while others have sparse foliage. Some have only a few thorns, while others are covered with them. The ones with a lot of thorns hurt more when they prick you. We say that they "bite." 335. If a child is going along barefoot, and gets pricked by a thorn and cries, he will say that the thorn "bit" him. This is the term used most among the people. Even an adult will say "the thorn bit me." In order to specify exactly what kind of mesquite it was, however, a person has to say "the thorn of the old mesquite bit me."[58] 336. The people who used to suffer the most from these

thorns were the shepherds who went around barefoot. They went running along behind their animals. If they got stuck in the foot by one of these thorns, they would jump in the air from the pain, especially if it was a hard prick. Sometimes the thorn breaks off inside the flesh. In that case you get another thorn from a mesquite and use it to dig the first one out. Otherwise, if a thorn remains in the flesh, it is very painful; you can't put your foot down or walk well. 337. If a thorn has gone deep into the foot, and if it can't be pulled out right away, then the foot swells up and the person limps around.

338. How can the swelling and the pain be gotten rid of? When the sufferer goes home he or she takes a piece of wood from the fire and holds the glowing hot end very near the wound for as long as they can stand it. This is possible to do because the pain of the thorn and that of the hot coal are about equal. With this technique, the pain and the swelling go down. The next day, even though the thorn may still be in the foot, one can walk on it. 339. Then the next evening, the same heat is applied again, so that the problem can be cured. The thorn doesn't come out all at once, however, but little by little. 340. Sometimes a thorn may cause infection on the bottom of the heel, and this is even more painful. If one can, one pinches the sore in order to push out the pus and blood. The thorn may also come out, though it hurts and throbs when this is done.

341. There is one kind of thorn that hurts more than others, called the "hurting thorn." This kind of mesquite doesn't grow very high; rather, its leaves are more toward the ground, and these trees are the ones most used in making fences for nopal patches.[59] If one uses the branches of these trees, the animals don't easily get into the patches. The trees only grow about two or two and a half meters high, and have thin branches, covered with impenetrable, thick foliage and thorns. These trees give very little fruit.

342. When the mesquites are at the height of their spring growth, burros love to eat the branches and foliage. The mesquites taste bitter, but they are eaten by wild burros. This is how wild burros maintain themselves; they eat the new growth, and the green, unripe fruit. Their heads ring with the noise of their crunching the hard buds. 343. Also, green, and black caterpillars eat the new leaves on the trees, just as they come out. They don't eat the little shoots, just the leaves. If a caterpillar is squashed, green stuff comes out; that is what it feeds on. 344. One of the birds that makes its nest in mesquites is the wild canary, or huitlacoche. It builds a mound of dry thorns on a branch, with needles sticking out all over the nest. In order not to hurt the little birds when they are born, the huitlacoche covers the thorns with the fuzz that grows on top of the viznaga, with tree moss and other soft stuff. Hummingbirds build their little nests on the thin branches. As we have seen (in Volume II), they make their nests out of soft,

hanging tree mosses. 345. Another pretty bird that uses the mesquite is the dove or pigeon. It uses only a few twigs of thorns, and lays its eggs. Because it doesn't cover its nest with soft material, the nest remains transparent.

346. Mourning doves and larks also build their nests with mesquite twigs. Pigeons and mourning doves both look for trees with thick hanging mosses in order to hide their nests, and also because the color of these birds is like that of the mosses. 347. These birds sit in the shade of the tree during the heat of the day, singing. Sometimes one, two, or three sing and pick at their feathers with their beaks.

348. To continue, we will look at another small plant that grows on the branches of mesquites. People actually plant these plants in the fresh, wet cracks in the bark where branches come out of the main part of the tree. The little roots can take hold in these cracks. Sometimes these plants just grow there spontaneously, and sometimes people put them into the cracks to multiply because the plants have a beautiful flower. Though the branch of the mesquite is dark, when these little plants flower they give the tree a nice color and decorate the tree they grow on. 350. We call this little plant "doonza," in Ñähñu which means "tree flower". They begin to flower at the end of April, and all during May. They are called "May flowers" in Spanish.[60] They come in two colors. One is white with a yellow center, and the other is violet. Even when the plant has no flowers on it, you can tell which one gives which flowers. The plant which gives white flowers is a pale green, and the one that has violet flowers is dark green. 352. Seeing these flowers, you want to cut them and take them into the house because they are so pretty, both the white and violet ones. Hummingbirds don't seem to want to touch these flowers, perhaps because the birds fear that they will make the flowers lose their beauty.

The maguey.[61] 353. This plant grows in much of the Mezquital Valley, and in other places like Ciudad Sahagún, and Llanos de Apan. These last two places are where there are large maguey farms. These maguey plots cover an area of about two kilometers square. There are many different kinds of magueys, but nowhere are they as plentiful as in the two cities just mentioned.[62] 354. There are magueys on various plots in Actopan. Even some parts of the areas under irrigation have magueys of a different class. Some people use these magueys to make pulque, and others just plant them as a kind of fence.[63] They plant magueys along the edges of the rows in their milpas, in order to protect their other plants. The other plants are more lucrative, so people protect them by fencing off the long mounded rows. Otherwise, animals would get in there and ruin the little plants.

355. Where magueys are really found is right here in the arid lands. In these dry lands you have to be careful in planting magueys to line them up correctly in rows and to space them just right so they will develop properly. If they are planted on top of one another, they just rob each other of the little available moisture and they grow up shriveled. 356. In the irrigated lands magueys are planted close together so that animals, and even people, are fenced out. But these magueys are hardly used to make pulque. This is how it is in the irrigated lands. That is, even the magueys are a good, productive class of plant. The people prefer to grow other things in irrigable land, however. 357. They only scrape enough magueys in order to make pulque for their own consumption or for their laborers who work the milpas. The magueys that we will be concerned with in this section, however, are the ones that grow in the arid lands. These plants are one of the more important economic resources and have to be tended and worked properly.

358. Zimapán is another place where there are magueys, but in smaller numbers than elsewhere. There would surely be lots of magueys in those areas around Zimapán where they are planted, except for the fact that most of the mountains are all eroded, and there isn't enough soil for the plants to grow. North of Zimapán there is a pueblo called Maguey Verde where there is a certain type of maguey that is ashen green. 359. The land in these parts is not flat, but all hilly, even mountainous, one could say. This is where the lands begin where it rains every year, and so the people can plant on the little slopes.[64] The land is very rocky, but whatever is planted grows because of the availability of moisture, and also because the earth is fertile. 360. People plant those magueys I spoke of, all around their milpas. The magueys are bunched together, one after the other in order to serve as a fence and to protect the plants so that cattle, goats, sheep and pigs won't eat them. 361. Magueys don't grow well when they are packed together; we can compare plants that have grown up well-spaced apart with those that are planted as fences. We should note that the magueys planted as fencing are a different variety than the ones that grow wild in the open country.[65] No one plants these latter magueys on purpose.

362. It is rare to see any magueys over towards Chapulhuacán. Jacala lies before Chapulhuacán. The magueys are different in every place. Some are big; some are good for transplanting; and others are only good for use as fences. It is even more arid over around Tamazunchale, and it is really hard to find any magueys there.

363. Heading back towards the east we come to Ixmiquilpan and to Cardonal with its pueblos of San Miguel Tlazintla and El Saúz. East of these places there are magueys.

364. Many people count on the maguey as an economic resource. They scrape the plants to obtain pulque which they sell in the markets of Ixmiquilpan and Cardonal, or deliver to wherever pulque is ordered. This is what is done in the houses of those who make and sell pulque. A lot of pulque is sold where there is lots of work going on, such as road construction or house construction. But even more is sold in the irrigated zone because there are lots of field laborers there all the time. Some of them plant, others irrigate, and others weed the fields. 365. The amount of work that's there is what makes the people work so much. When they work, those who like it need to drink their pulque; and to drink it, they have to buy it. 366. In San Miguel Tlazintla, which is adjacent to Cardonal, and at Vega de Meztitlán, there are magueys, but in smaller numbers. Whatever there are, however, are "good magueys" and, in fact, that is their name. Of course, all magueys are "good" but some of them just aren't scraped for pulque. 367. The really large sized magueys are called "good magueys" in Ñähñu.[66] The size really isn't so important, actually. What is really meant by "good" in this case is that when you break open the maguey and scrape it, it produces a lot of aguamiel. Some magueys, even though they are large, don't give much aguamiel. 368. Later on we will look at all the different classes of magueys, one by one, and what they are called in Ñähñu.

369. To the west of Ixmiquilpan are the communities of Tecozautla and Huichapan where there are magueys, but, again, not in great numbers like the magueys over in the east by Ciudad Sahagún which I mentioned before. That's the part of the state of Hidalgo that has the most magueys. 370. There are also magueys in the adjacent state of Querétaro, but they are sparse. Over in Alfajayucan, to the west, there are magueys of different kinds. In Tasquillo they have very few. Whatever they do have are all planted, rather than wild, and some people continue to cultivate those magueys even though they now have irrigated fields. 371. They plant or, more correctly, they "seed" magueys. That is, first they plant seeds which germinate. When the plants get big enough they are called "t'u'ta," or "maguey shoots," and they are sold off to people in other communities where the people specialize in growing magueys and in making pulque.

372. I will mention a few of these communities in the jurisdiction of Ixmiquilpan. From La Lagunita some people bring their pulque to Tasquillo. Sometimes they sell it a little at a time. Other times they just bring it to someone who has agreed to buy it all. 373. Most people from Naxthey, Cantamayé, and La Palma bring their pulque to Tasquillo. Some carry it on their backs, others drive it in on a laden burro, depending on how much they produce. If a person sees that there is a lot, and that a burro can't carry it all, then the person will

carry a few liters, too. 374. This will be, let's say, 30 liters, which are carried in a goat skin. The skin is specially prepared for transporting pulque and is called a "boota" in Ñähñu, although the word comes from the Spanish "bota."

375. Those from Dexthi also go to Tasquillo, but some of them go to the irrigated zone, close to Dexthi, where they deliver their pulque to their clients. Only a few bring their pulque in to Ixmiquilpan. But some do and they sell one or two liters at a time to people accustomed to drinking it. 376. In Remedios the people who make pulque just sell it to their own neighbors. The pueblo is divided in the middle, with irrigation on one side but not on the other where it is arid and where the landowners cultivate magueys. 377. Orizabita, Nequetejé, San Miguel Juguí, Defay, El Espíritu, San Miguel Tlazintla, El Decá, El Saúz, San Andrés Daboxta, Pozuelos, and part of Capula —the other part is recently irrigated—these are the communities from which people bring small quantities of pulque to sell in Ixmiquilpan.

378. Monday is market day, and this is when people gather to sell their wares. When they finish selling, they purchase what they need. And thus the pulque sellers, too, organize to sell their product. They start selling around seven or eight in the morning and finish around two or three in the afternoon, depending on how their sales go during the day.

379. West of Ixmiquilpan there are magueys in the communities of Panales, López Rayón, Tetzú, Portezuelo, El Dextho, and in the part of La Rinconada that has not been irrigated. Over in El Mandó and in Progreso there are magueys that are different from those around Ixmiquilpan. Turning to the south of Ixmiquilpan, we begin with Maye and La Reforma, which is adjacent to Panales. Heading out beyond Maye there are other communities called Tablón, El Alberto, Mejay, Xothi, Maguey Blanco, Taxadhó, Xuchitlán, Julian Villagrán, El Tephé, Yolotepec, Patria Nueva, Santiago de Anaya and Chilcuautla. 380. And now we go towards Mixquiahuala, Tlahuelilpan, Tula, Pachuca and Tepatepéc.

381. The states adjacent to Hidalgo that have magueys are Tlaxcala, Puebla and México. Magueys are not found throughout these states, but there are some in the parts adjacent to Hidalgo, and the people there make pulque. Tlaxcala is famous as a producer of pulque. 382. Magueys are found in other parts of Mexico, but in less abundance and of different classes and sizes. There are big ones and small ones; the big ones are found planted in fertile soil, while the others don't grow well because they are planted in arid land. Even if the soil is fertile, if there is no moisture the plants can not grow. 383. On the other hand, there are magueys that are just naturally small, even when they grow to their full size.

384. Wherever there are no other exploitable resources, the maguey is a means of getting money, and of subsistence for the people. Like the mesquite, which we looked at earlier, the maguey is a big resource that helps the people a lot. In fact, the maguey is even more important, and enters into all parts of family life among the Ñähñu. 385. Everything that one does either utilizes maguey or some product extracted from it. It enters into commerce, religion, and work. In all these things there are aspects of the exploitation of maguey. I must repeat here what was said about the mesquite; namely, that many students have been able to go to school because of the exploitation of the maguey.

386. As we know, people have always given each plant its own name, in antiquity as in modern times. Not only each plant, but each part of every plant has its own name. 387. In olden times, as people came to need each part of a plant, they gave it its own name. Perhaps this was how naming things began, but today all the plants used by people all over the world, and all the parts of those plants have their own names. And thus, too, have the Ñähñu given names to all the parts of the maguey. When they utilize the maguey they know which part they are talking about, which part is most useful, and which part isn't useful.

388. This is the maguey plant. There are many kinds and sizes, with differences in the width of the leaves, the size of the central heart or trunk, the needles, which are also called spiny points, on the ends of the leaves, and the thorns along the edges of the leaves. All of these are different for each class of maguey. 389. Some needle points are long and thick, others are long but thin. Some are sturdy, others are brittle. Some are not long, and of those some are thick and some are thin. Some are so strong that they can be nailed into things, while others break easily.

390. The size of a maguey depends on what class it is; whatever kind it is, that's how big it can be. There are some that are two and a half meters tall, not counting the quiote, which is separate. The only thing being considered here is the plant itself, measuring from the base where the heart begins. The circumference of this plant is about two meters. And there are other sizes of maguey. 391. Just as there are various sizes, so there are different colors. Each different plant has its name in Ñähñu so that the people can be specific when they speak about magueys. There are plants called "green maguey," "long leaf," "xam'ni," "white maguey," "netu," "i'ta," "gääx'mini," "hmu'ta," "sarabanda," "manso" and "black maguey."[67] 392. The first of these is called "green maguey" because its leaves are truly green. The head of the leaf is not very big. The plant has many leaves that are more or less wide and thick, and is white. The head of the leaf is the part which attaches to the piña, or trunk.

393. This class of maguey has many leaves. Some plants have 20-30 leaves, depending on the size of the plant. From the trunk to the needle point, the length of the leaf of the green maguey can reach a full arm-span. Of course, I'm speaking here of the longest leaves on the largest plants. This class of maguey is found in all the parts of the Ixmiquilpan region which have been mentioned. 394. The places where they are planted in greatest abundance are: El Olivo, El Espíritu, San Antonio Sabanillas, San Miguel Tlazintla, El Saúz, Nequetejé, Los Remedios, Orizabita, San Juanico, Boxhuada, El Nando, Naxthey. 395. In these places the people plant a lot of magueys; the ones that grow by themselves in the open country are sparse, and they don't grow very big, either. They don't have what is called "rä mohi rä nkaho" in Ñähñu or a "plate", that collects and retains moisture for the plant whenever it rains.[68]

396. This class of wild maguey is said to be of a good class, and indeed, it has been seen to be good. It develops better when it is planted by people and cultivated. First a "plate," or water deposit, is prepared, before the plant is set in the ground. This kind of maguey is not planted from seeds. Instead, the little shoots that grow up around the base of the plant are pulled out and transplanted. Usually, most of the shoots are right around the base of the plant, but sometimes the shoots pop up some distance away. 397. When there is plenty of moisture, the shoots will come up relatively far from the plant, up to about two meters away. It sends out what we could call a "root" from the trunk, and this is what gives birth to another plant, which is an extension of the original trunk. 398. Then, little by little, the runner dries up and disintegrates, because the new plant sends out its own roots. Later on, one could not even tell that the new plant was the offspring of the big plant next to it.

399. In order to plant a maguey, it is important to prepare the ground well, and loosen it up. We will describe how this is done now. Magueys are planted in mounded rows in the milpa. Whenever a plant has been scraped clean, and only the trunk remains, with no more aguamiel, then one must replace the plant with another one. In planting one or more magueys, the owner of the land does the work himself, or he contracts it out to a laborer.

400. First, he pulls off the leaves which remain on the plant. If a maguey has not been thoroughly scraped and exploited, then some of the leaves will be thick and juicy. These break off easily. The worker goes along, lifting the leaves off. The leaves have to be pulled out one at a time because they are layered, one atop the next. 401. In order to pull a leaf off, the worker has to give it a really hard yank. It makes a loud, cracking noise, and the worker pulls the leaf away. The juicy ones can be yanked off by hand, but the dried out ones don't come off so

easily. They have to be pried off with a pole, or chopped off with an axe. The dried leaves are very tough because they contain a lot of ixtle fiber, and they take a lot of work to remove. 402. Pulling dried leaves off the maguey causes itching for those who are unaccustomed to this type of work. It's very bothersome, but those who are used to it don't mind. It's not that they like it; it's just that they don't feel it because they do this kind of work all the time. 403. We could compare this to a person who lives in a hot climate going to a cold climate, or vice versa. They wouldn't be used to it.

404. The juicy leaves and the dried leaves are piled up separately as they are pulled off. The dried leaves are brought home to be used as fuel—for making fire in the kitchen, for example.

405. This whole thing is called the piña, or stump. A worker who doesn't want to waste time prying the leaves off the piña will prune the maguey back. That is, he goes around the plant, cutting off the leaves at the base. It is easy to get rid of the leaves this way, but when you go to pull the stump and roots out of their hole, the whole thing weighs a lot more because the thick ends of the leaves are still attached to the stump. 406. To pull out a maguey stump, you have to go round the plant, prying it up a little at a time with a pole. But it's difficult work, in any case. Some are very large and require more than one person, especially the plants that have been pruned. The others are lighter and are less difficult to pry out of the ground. 407. It takes about an hour to an hour and a half to pull a maguey stump out, depending on the size of the stump. 408. Workers who specialize in this chore do it more quickly. For example, if they start at nine in the morning, by four in the afternoon they'll have taken out ten stumps. When they charge by the plant they work more quickly, and when they are paid a daily wage they work more slowly.

409. In order to remove a stump, one begins by digging a hole on one side. The hole should be about 70 centimeters deep, and little by little the ground beneath the plant crumbles away. 410. As the hole is dug deeper and deeper the roots of the plant are cut. The digging proceeds around the plant, and once the stump is pulled out the hole that remains is prepared for the next plant. The roots all have to be pulled out, and the earth has to be loosened and made soft so that the next plant will take hold quickly and will grow. 411. The "plate" or hole that the new plant is placed in is about an arm-span in length by a meter wide, and its depth varies, as I said before. When the hole is prepared, it looks like this drawing:

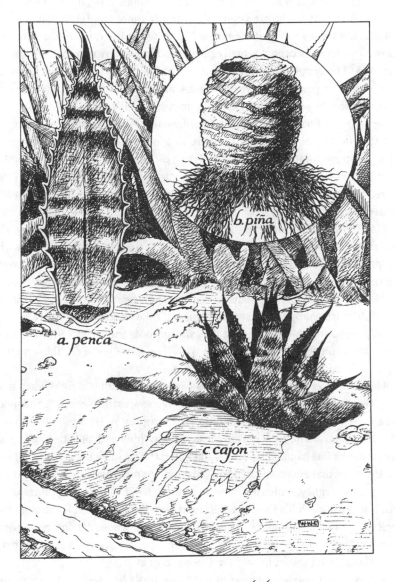

a. penca

b. piña

c. cajón

This whole thing is called the piña

Flora 405

412. This work may be done at any time, but is done more during January and February. However, the prepared holes remain there empty; the magueys are not planted right away, but are planted later when the rains come. One must know that magueys cannot actually be planted in just any month, or on just any day. 413. The people give this work its own time, especially March, April and May, depending on how the weather looks, and whether it seems like it will rain or not. When they see that rain appears imminent, they plant the little magueys in the holes that have been prepared beforehand. Also young magueys are not transplanted right away after they are dug out from around a major plant. 414. The new plants will have been lying out for some time before they are transplanted. The young plants vary in size, from about 40 to 50 centimeters or more, but never more than a meter high so that a single man can transport them from one place to another. If they are too big, then they are too heavy to carry.

415. To transplant a maguey, first it is pulled out from where it shot up. Then the leaves are pruned back, and so are the roots so that new roots will grow when the plant is replanted. Also, the little piña, or central core is pruned, as well as the dried leaves. 416. Then the plant is put out in the sun to dry. It isn't good to replant young magueys right away because their hearts rot and the plants die. But if they are put out in the sun to dessicate, then as soon as they are put back in the ground and contact moisture they sprout roots and the old withered leaves come back to life and begin to grow. 417. The more withered they are when replanted, the more they grow.

418. Whoever owns a maguey takes care that the moon is right when planting. It has to be a good day to plant maguey. We saw earlier what a "good moon" means. And a man who is going to plant maguey must have clean hands. 419. For this work he must not have touched anything bad, or rotten and smelly, because if he has handled something bad then the maguey dies or doesn't grow well. Things that are considered bad or rotten are meat and hens' eggs. Anyone who plants maguey avoids touching these things. 420. When the planter goes to work he must wash his hands with soap, if there is any, and if there is no soap, then he washes it with xite.[69] This is always done whenever someone goes to plant any plant, not just maguey. Of course, the people always wash their hands, even if only with water, in case there is no soap at all.

421. When a person goes out to plant, the tools he uses are a shovel and a pickaxe. The pickaxe is used to loosen up the dirt where it has become hardened. Only the dirt right where the maguey is to be planted is loosened. It isn't necessary to loosen all the dirt around the plant, as was done when the old stump was removed. The shovel is used to pile up the dirt around the base of the little maguey so that it will be firmly placed. 422. Before actually putting in the first

plant, the planter looks around for some aloe. He tears it up and rubs the juice on his hands. People do this if they believe in putting aloe juice on their hands in order to make the new maguey produce a lot of shoots when it is transplanted. 423. This is believed because aloe grows in big clumps and produces a lot of new shoots. I've seen how, when this practice of putting aloe juice on the hands is followed, a new maguey really produces a lot of shoots once it takes hold. And since I've seen this practice followed in many different places, I can be sure that this belief of those who plant maguey must be correct.

424. Now begins the actual setting in of the maguey. The earth is totally dry, without a drop of moisture, and the first rain of the year is anxiously awaited. If it rains and nothing has been planted, then people quickly put in new plants, because the earth contains some moisture and the new plants will take root quickly and won't be exposed to the sun. 425. This is the kind of work that goes on in the replacement of magueys. But if we are talking about new plantings, then a complete bordo, or raised furrow has to be dug. The bordo is made by piling up the earth in a straight line. The size of the bordo, that is its height and width, depends on how much water one reckons will have to be contained. Usually, bordos are about a meter high, a meter and a half wide at the base, and about 60 centimeters wide at the top.

426. Sometimes a man makes bordos by himself, shoveling the earth a little at a time. If he doesn't work all day, he'll work in the morning when it's cool. Then, when the sun gets hot he'll return to his house to do something else. 427. By six in the morning he is already out in the milpa, shoveling earth, raising the bordo. If it's a small plot, then it will be near his house. But if it isn't, then he'll have to go far and stay away all day. The length of the bordos varies because the length of the plots of land vary. The main purpose of these bordos is to contain the water when it rains, so that it doesn't just run off. They help the water seep into the sides of the furrows and in this way the moisture lasts longer. This is what magueys need in order to grow. 428. Magueys are planted on the bordos. Otherwise, when it rains, the runoff would carry dirt and deposit it on the plant, covering its lower part and preventing it from growing. Magueys are planted about 35 centimeters up on the bordo. They aren't planted right on top of the furrow, but on the sides in arid lands so that the moisture will reach them. 429. In irrigated lands the magueys are put right on top of the furrows because there is a lot of moisture.

430. The planter lines up the little magueys along the furrow. He places them one by one so that they are in a straight line. If there is plenty of moisture in the ground, then in two or three months the plants begin to revive and turn green, and their first new leaves open out from the heart. 431. By the end of two or

310   NATIVE ETHNOGRAPHY

three years, they need to be pruned back so that more new leaves will grow. Well-made furrows absorb plenty of moisture. Otherwise it takes four or five years before the young magueys need their first pruning. The leaves that come from pruning a maguey are used as combustible material. First they are dried out, and then they are burned in the kitchen fire or just to create warmth when it gets cold. These leaves catch fire easily because they are relatively thin. They blaze up into big flames and quickly turn to ashes. They don't produce the kind of fire that comes from hot coals. 432. The big, old leaves that are cut off when a stump is pulled out are very hard, and they do produce coals when they are used in fires. Their fire lasts a long time. The only part that lasts, though, is what we call the "neck" of the leaf. The head of the leaf close to the heart is consumed quickly in the fire and goes to ash right away. That is because it is the part that contains the most pulp. 433. The head of the leaf is the softest part; it contains the most ixtle and is thus most easily burned in a fire. Because of this, it is often used as kindling to get a fire going and to set on fire the harder woods that don't catch easily. You put a handful of the dried, pulpy ixtle from the heads of the leaves under the harder woods so that the wood will light quickly.

434. Dried maguey leaves produce a lot of ash, even more than mesquite wood. Maguey leaves are used mostly for heating water when removing the hair from an animal that has been killed for eating. For example, chickens and pigs are the kinds of animals that are not skinned, but you do remove their feathers or their hair. To do this, you boil water. For a pig, much more water is needed; and to heat the water more firewood is needed. And for this we use maguey leaves, because it is the most easily gathered combustible material. 435. The firewood gatherer goes out and brings in a large bundle. However, there is a lot of it, and it doesn't take much effort to gather it up. It is important not to come into physical contact with the heads of maguey leaves when they are being lit on fire, because the pulpy stuff, or "marrow" as we refer to it in Ñähñu, causes itching. It is usually white, and sometimes dark colored. 436. It contains a kind of shiny powder, or crystals that look like sugar, but if they come in contact with skin these crystals cause a lot of itching. 437. The ashes left in the hearth are thrown in a special dumping spot for ashes; sometimes they are taken out and put around the base of nopal plants. This is done to prevent these plants from getting grubs. When we discuss the nopal, we'll see what kind of damage these insects cause. In any event, putting ashes around the nopal keeps it from getting bugs on it.

438. Another part of the maguey often used for kindling is the dried out roots. They are used in the same way that the head pulp is used. They are placed underneath the firewood so that the wood will catch quickly. 439. When it rains, wood gets wet and doesn't light easily. Maguey roots are covered with a brown

skin. Inside, the actual root is purple. 440. The roots are made up of fine filaments that don't break easily and are very tough. This is why you have to use a pickaxe and shovel on them, in order to lop them off. 441. The first layer of the root is soft, but after that comes a much harder layer which is sharp and glasslike. You have to be really careful when pulling out a stump not to break off the roots with your hands, because this layer can cut right through the skin, or the skin can get stuck to the root. There are always sharp, needle-like edges that stick out when these roots are broken. 442. After this layer of sharp material comes the actual root fibers, and this completes the root's structure.

443. In order to plant maguey one should make certain that the day is good for this kind of work. You ask the old people, who continue to believe in these customs, whether the day is good for planting maguey, and if it isn't a good day, then you don't plant. The heavenly body that best indicates whether it is a good day for planting, for pruning, and for taking out the mature hearts of magueys is the moon. The moon, or the "little virgin," as it is also called by many people, must be considered.

444. It has already been mentioned that magueys are pruned back at two or three or four years, depending on how fast they grow, and on how much moisture there is where they are growing. At the first pruning the leaves aren't very long, and are thrown out. But on the second and third pruning the leaves are big enough to be useful. 445. A maguey owner feels badly about just throwing out good leaves that have been pruned off. Some of those leaves are really beautiful, and green, and juicy. These leaves can be used to build house roofs, if one wants to. In order to do this one must put up all the supports first. 446. Anyway, as the leaves are pruned off, they are spread out in the sun to dry. Maguey leaves are not of uniform thickness. The part near the trunk is the thickest, and it doesn't dry out quickly. To make it dry at the same rate as the rest of the leaf, you slit it up the middle to where the leaf thins out.

447. As many leaves as possible are pruned off in order to gather enough to make a roof. Whoever does the pruning takes about six or eight leaves off of each plant, depending on the size of the maguey. Plants are pruned to make them grow well and to stimulate the growth of new plants from shoots. A large maguey that isn't pruned will have leaves drooping on the ground, and these will smother the new shoots coming up. The new shoots rot and die. 448. In putting the leaves out in the sun to dry, one doesn't cut off the thorns. The leaves are left with their thorns because if you take off the thorns the edges of the leaf dry up and crack. When this happens, rain water filters down through these cracks, if you use the leaves to make a roof. 449. The leaves are left out for one or two weeks to dry out well. Then, when they are bent to weave them onto the roof

supports, the leaves will be supple like leather and won't break. After the leaves
are all dried, they are split down the middle. Their thorns are removed from the
edges prior to weaving them into the roof.

450. There are two kinds of roof weaving, called "halves" and "wholes." In
half weaving, the leaves are split right up the center line, the full length of the
frond, and this results in two halves. This is why it is called "halves."

451. In whole weaving, only the thick part is split so that the leaf will dry
evenly, but the rest of the leaf is left intact. When the roof is woven, one simply
removes the thorns from the edges, and the whole leaf is woven into the roof.
452. In both half and whole weaving, some leaves are left with their needle
points intact so that they can be attached to other leaves in the weave. Some
whole leaves just don't dry out properly and they tend to curl up at the tips and
not lie flat; they ruin the weave and other leaves can not be placed on top of
them. To prevent their popping up, their needle tips are simply jammed into the
leaves below them. 453. Half weaving is more work, but more durable. A half-
weave roof can last 20 to 30 years, and both sides of the roof are angled so that
rain will run off easily.

454. In half weaving, the split fronds are woven over and under the roof cross
supports. One must take care to overlap the long edges of the half leaves to keep
rain from seeping down. First one makes a pass to the right, up and over, then to
the left, coming back, and this makes the needle overlap. 455. The weaving
goes back and forth, with no spaces between the leaves. 456. The split leaves are
bent double and woven around the roof supports. They are held in place by the
supports, and don't slip around.

457. Half weaving is very fine, crafted work, and lasts for many years. In
contrast, whole weaving is rather simpler, cruder work. Even though the edges
are overlapped, they don't lay quite as well and the leaves rot fairly quickly. As
is well known, rotten maguey leaves don't hold up well. They don't disintegrate
immediately, but they last only about 10 years at the outside. 458. The shade
produced inside a house with a maguey roof is very cool. When the desert sun
gets really hot, one can take shelter in the cool shade of a roof made of maguey.
Sometimes even the walls of houses are made of maguey, using a simple, whole
weave. 459. This is done if there are sufficient leaves. If not, then the walls are
constructed from other plant material. Some people make walls out of rough
stone rubble and mud; others use a process called "dry wall," where stones are
just fit together without any kind of cement matrix, except for some dry earth to
keep the stones from moving.

460. The disadvantage of walls made from maguey is that small creatures
live in those walls. Various spiders and centipedes, and the chirrionera and

house snake are the animals that live in houses the most. 461. These snakes scare people, even though their bite is not poisonous. The house snake comes in to look for mice, as does the chirrionera. If these snakes are seen in houses, it's because they follow some animal they are hunting, like a lagartija or a lagarto.[70] 462. These creatures try to take refuge in houses as a defense against snakes. By the time a person notices a snake, it is already inside, hanging on one of the roof beams. To kill it, you first knock it out with cigarette smoke. The smoke makes them sluggish, and then they are easily killed. If they are not killed, then they come back frequently and scare the chilren because the houses are built close to open country where all the animals mentioned live.

464. In order to keep a maguey house from being blown away by the wind, the main posts have to be dug really well into the earth. That is, the posts that hold all the weight of the house, and which hold up the main beam on which all the cross beams are tied, have to be really secure. The first rains of the years are generally accompanied by high winds, thunder, and lightning. 465. The winds are very strong, and they cause houses made of maguey to sway. Hail falls; sometimes rain comes first and then hail, while other times hail comes before the rain. This latter is called "dry hail." 466. Houses roofed with maguey just get like leather in the rain. The leaves get wet, but become even stronger than before, because the ixtle inside the leaves gets wet and leather tough. If the maguey leaves are properly placed, one over the other, the roof won't leak even if it drizzles steadily all night long. 467. The roofing sold in the hardware stores is called both "cartón" and "ásbestos," in Spanish and is made specifically for making roofs. It surely does keep out the rain and drizzle, even a drenching downpour. But if there is a heavy hail, the synthetic sheets get pocked with holes, and the wind can lift these roofs right up and tear them apart. Anyone who buys these roofs is just wasting their money.

468. To fasten down the cross beams, sometimes the outer sheath of large maguey leaves is torn off and used as lashing. They are lashed together where the roof supports cross, and the pieces of lashing are twisted together to form a continuous fastener.

469. Now the new plants are in the ground. After three or four years they are pruned back, and some of their leaves are cut off. The best leaves are selected, so they can be used in roofing houses, as we saw. From the time magueys are transplanted until they reach maximum maturity, 8, 10 or 15 years will pass. Then they can be scraped out for aguamiel. 470. Magueys don't all mature at the same rate. Though they may all have been the same size when planted, they grow up differently. Some plants grow quickly, while others mature later.

471. If someone wants to open the heart of a maguey for aguamiel, or "geld" it, as we say, they observe carefully and select only those plants that are ready to be broken open. To know when a maguey is fully mature, one need only look to see if the heart of the plant has begun to shrink and get thin. When this happens, it is a sign that the plant is ready to be broken into. But one must also see that the moon is right; that is, that it is not a full moon, a new moon, or a moon that's just past being full. The moon is observed to ensure that the plant produces enough aguamiel. If you break open a maguey on any of the days noted, it won't produce a lot of aguamiel. 472. To get good production, one needs both of these things; that is, fully mature plants and a good day.

473. When a maguey is mature its center gets thin, and this means that in a short time it will send up its seed stalk, or quiote. If it starts to send up its quiote, then the maguey has been lost, as far as aguamiel is concerned, and it can not be scraped. It won't produce aguamiel because the central core becomes filled with fibrous matter, and this does not permit the aguamiel to filter down into the heart. Therefore, it's best to start scraping a maguey when it is at a medium point of maturity. If it is left to grow too much it won't produce any aguamiel, and if it is broken into when it is still too young, then the pulque will taste of young, or raw maguey. The pulque will not taste good, but will be insipid. 474. When a maguey reaches normal maturity, the pulque is thick and has a good taste. The same is true for the plain aguamiel. When it is removed from the plant it is sweet and not bitter. Sometimes it does get bitter, but only during the really hot period of the year.

475. To break open a mature maguey, one begins by removing the thorns from those leaves on the side of the plant where one will enter to take out the heart. For this work, a person carries a tool called a "gelder." 476. The front end, which digs out the heart of the plant, is a broad semicircle and has a sharp edge. From this part back, the handle is bent like a pipe. This is attached to the wooden part which the worker grabs and uses as a lever for force. The whole thing is about a meter long.

477. This is what a person uses to dig out the heart of the maguey. The entire heart must be cut out and put aside. 478. If the special cutting tool is not used, then a small iron pole is used instead, but it must be well honed down on one end. Using either tool produces just as good results.

479. After this is done, the center, or what we also call the heart, is removed. The leaves that come off the heart are totally white, and are called "nximbo" in Ñähñu. The part where the heart was is all shredded up because it does not slice evenly. 480. It is left as is for one or two months until it is good and rotten, and then the core is cleaned out. The cleaning consists of removing all the shredded

This is used to dig out the heart of the maguey

Flora 477

junk that was left there when the heart was cut, but now it's rotten and there are a lot of bugs in it. 481. The center is cleaned out, and all the stuff called "xi'mfi" is removed. Not all of it is removed at once, but little by little it is removed as the plant produces aguamiel. After one or two weeks the plant will be producing well, and that's when all the waste matter that was left in the center is removed. 482. Some people don't clean the center out right away, but wait five or six months. Some people wait as much as a year before they do it. Some of those magueys will have sent out a stunted quiote even though the plant is producing aguamiel.

483. In the early stages, the plant is scraped out twice a day. People get up early to collect aguamiel at five in the morning, or at six. Then they collect again at five or six in the evening. They remove aguamiel from all the plants that were broken open; whether there are six or a dozen, all of them have to be scraped and the aguamiel has to be absorbed. We say "absorbed" because the person sucks up the aguamiel with an ococote. 484. And we say "scraped" because the collector scrapes the inside of the piña with a special scraper, removing all the waste "xi'mfi," or "honey leaf," so that the inside surface will be new and the aguamiel will flow. 485. After a few days have passed, say, three weeks, the plant is scraped out three times a day in the morning, at midday, and in the evening. The scraping done at midday is called "nho̱'thui" which means literally "to show the honey." This is done so that the pulque will be good; if the midday scraping is done like this, the aguamiel will not go bitter. 486. During the hot period of the year, aguamiel turns bitter very easily, and the pulque doesn't turn out right if this occurs; it turns out watery and insipid. People don't buy pulque from someone if the pulque is cut and not full strength, and so the pulque seller loses his or her money and all their work in making the product.

487. All the magueys that are planted eventually grow, but when the first ones are ready to be scraped, most are still growing. Sometimes there is lots of moisture and the plants grow quickly, while other times they are retarded in their growth. That is to say, some grow while others wither, and while they are in a withered state the plants don't grow. 488. What happens is that the milpas aren't level; the earth is very uneven, with rises and falls. The water doesn't reach evenly to all the plants when it rains. Also, it isn't just one type of maguey that is planted, but several kinds. Many of these different kinds of plants are just naturally faster or slower growing. For these reasons the plants in a milpa grow unevenly.

489. There is a belief that if someone going out to plant eats any part of a chicken, then skunks will come and dig up their magueys. Children are not given chicken feet to eat, even though they want them very much. The mother

says: "We don't give you any chicken feet, Francisco, because if you eat them skunks will dig up your magueys." 490. This is what skunks do. They dig up maguey roots because they are hunting chinicuiles.[71] These insects are red and white. The white chinicuil is born when the hot period begins, and during the hot part of the year; that is, during March, April, and May there are a lot of them. They are down at the thickest part of the maguey leaf, at the head, near the trunk of the plant. 491. During Holy Week people who know how to gather chinicuiles go along the rows of maguey, one by one. To get them out, they have to cut off the maguey leaf wherever there is a chinicuil. 492. But how do they know what kind of bug is in there at the bottom of the leaves? First, they go in close to look at the part of the leaf nearest the ground. Then, if they see a lump with a hole in it, sunken in the middle, they cut the leaf off. If this sign is not there, they don't cut the leaf because there is no reason to abuse the maguey for nothing.

493. There is usually one chinicuil in each plant. By chance, there may be two, but never more than that. And, of course, each one is on a different leaf. The white chinicuil is usually about two and a half centimeters long. It has a little brown ball on its head where its eyes and mouth are. It has two rows of legs. There are about 12 legs, but this depends on the size of the bug. 494. It has very fine hair all over its body. When they mature, these white chinicuiles turn into moths.

495. When there are only a few chinicuiles, one can eat them toasted right off a comal. But when there are lots of them, say half a plate full, they are prepared with other ingredients, such as parsley, mint, marjoram, thyme, onion, garlic, chile and salt. 496. After all these ingredients are mixed together the bugs, which had been collected previously, are put in it. The quantity depends on how much of the other ingredients were prepared. If the whole thing is to be wrapped in corn husk, it is then folded as if it were a tamal. Then the whole thing is thrown on the fire to cook. 497. It only takes 15 minutes to cook well, and it's ready to eat with tortillas.

498. Red chinicuiles are not found inside maguey leaves, but in the trunk of the plant. This insect is very harmful and causes a lot of damage to magueys. It keeps the plant from developing. To fix a plant attacked by these grubs, you have to rip the plant out, prune it back to the trunk, and leave it in the sun for several days until the bugs leave. 499. The meaning of the word "theenk'ue," or red chinicuil, in Ñähñu, is "red worm," and this is really the color of this insect. It, too, has a brown tip on its head, but its body is totally red. 500. This insect has a very powerful mouth, and this is what it uses to gnaw away at things, and so it is tough. There are many more of these than the white chinicuil, and they live in-

side the main trunk of the maguey, in the part below ground. 501. From October 4th onward it rains on occasion, but sometimes it doesn't. In any event, the chinicuiles come out in bunches and go about on the ground. They go all over the place; when it rains there are so many of them that they turn the ground red wherever they go. 502. The little black ants adhere to the bodies of the red chinicuiles and eat them.

503. When people see that the chinicuiles are out, they go after them, and collect them to roast and to eat. These bugs are roasted on a comal; they are also fried in oil, and are even tastier this way. They can be prepared in various ways. If one likes, grubs can be ground up in a molcajete with chile, once they have been toasted on the comal. The chiles used in this recipe are chile de arbol[72] or another kind known as chile rayado or chipotle; the mixture is a delicious dish. 504. However, people who eat a lot of this get a cough, because the bugs are considered "hot" food, and besides, they are very greasy. 505. Some people eat chinicuiles raw; they crunch them in their mouths, and it sounds like they were chewing calabaza seeds.

506. The reason that skunks are always around new plots of maguey is that they want to get at the roots and find red chinicuiles to eat. One day you can look at a maguey and it's fine; the next day a whole row of magueys can be lying on the ground, dug up and tumbled over by skunks. They dig all around the plant, at the base, and keep the magueys from growing. 507. There are no chinicuiles during the first months of the year. Of course, they live inside the trunks, but they don't come out. 508. Perhaps skunks know this, because they don't dig up magueys at this time of year either. But when September comes, skunks start digging up magueys.

509. If someone discovers that a skunk is digging up their nice maguey plants, they will try to catch the animal and kill it. But the skunk defends itself, and unleashes a terrible smelling, asphyxiating odor. This animal doesn't run just to get away, but just runs far enough so it can unleash its gaseous odors. 510. Its gas reaches up a meter and half off the ground, and it can spray three or four times. Just when you think you've got it finished off, the skunk sees what is happening and runs away. It raises its tail, flutters it, and runs into its den. Before it disappears, though, it leaves behind an odor that is so strong that nobody can stand it. If the spray gets in a person's eyes, it leaves the person blind for three days, and with red eyes after that for a while. 511. If the spray gets on clothing, it turns the fabric yellowish, and the color won't wash out, no matter how much you wash it, even if you use lots of soap. 512. For this reason the skunk is considered a fierce animal. If anyone dares provoke it, it unleashes

one of its sprays, and this always wins, no matter how brave a person might be. This is where the great battle is lost. You could call it the fight of the century, because after a spraying no one ever bothers a skunk again.

513. Skunks can be caught and killed by putting out traps in their path. Many people eat skunk, but you have to be careful in removing the viscera not to break its odor sac because if it opens up it ruins the meat. 514. The meat can be fried or roasted. It's very tasty, like pork. Skunk fat is good in medicine for curing soma.[73] 515. The fat is allowed to cool down and coagulate after being rendered; then it is put away. When the scabs appear they cause a lot of itching. It is even worse at night; it hardly allows a person to sleep if they have this sickness. 516. Just when the scabs itch, they are scratched, broken open, and skunk grease is applied. Two or three treatments is enough, and with this the illness clears up.

517. As soon as the little maguey shoots are large enough, they are pulled out of the ground and put aside for later transplanting. When they are taken out of the ground, they are pruned back so they will dry up well. For this procedure, too, one must be careful that the day is good. 518. January, February and March are when little magueys are taken out of the ground around the big magueys. At this time of year the little plants are pretty withered and dry, and this is just right, because juicy plants break off at the base and leave the roots in the ground when you pry them up with a pole. When they break off at the base they make a cracking noise; and even if they are transplanted, broken plants like this won't grow new roots. When the rains come no one pulls up new magueys for transplanting.

519. Pulque is made from the aguamiel taken out of the plant.[74] The aguamiel is put in a wooden barrel, or sometimes in a large earthenware jug. Barrels are more common, though, because they give the pulque a better flavor, and aguamiel doesn't go bitter as easily in wooden barrels. In earthenware, however, the aguamiel curdles into little clumps. It still turns into pulque if it curdles, but it is spoiled and can not be drunk. 520. Pulque spoils easily, so it is important to wash out either the barrel or jug where one will put the aguamiel. In this way, it will keep the aguamiel tasting good; otherwise, the liquid will stink.

521. About 40 years ago, there were no soft drinks in the cities, because no one knew how to make them. In Ixmiquilpan, the mestizos drank fresh water with a little lemon, and many of them drank boiled aguamiel. 522. Boiled aguamiel is just what it sounds like. That is, it is aguamiel from the maguey, but boiled in order to prevent it from making you sick. The good taste is not lost in the cooking, but rather the taste is actually enhanced. Mestizos, who always

went around in suits and were seen as "grand men," bought boiled aguamiel to drink. This is what they used to drink to quench their thirst. They didn't drink pulque, but they sure did like boiled aguamiel. This is attested to by old people who used to go to market a long time ago.

523. Another thing which used to be made of aguamiel, and is still made today, is "atole de aguamiel." To make this, one selects the sweetest aguamiel there is. One uses the best aguamiel for boiled aguamiel and for atole de aguamiel. 524. The magueys that produce the most and the sweetest aguamiel are called "gääx'miini," "xa'mni," penca larga, maguey verde, and maguey oscuro. All these magueys produce aguamiel for a full three months. The ones that don't produce a lot are the "i'ta," "netu," and the maguey blanco. 525. This last plant produces the least of all. Very few people scrape these plants. The best thing to do with them is to plant them as fences to protect other plants from animals. Furthermore, to make it produce at all, one must break it open when it is half grown, rather than when it is fully mature. If it is opened when it is fully mature, then it produces almost nothing. It's as though its bowl had dried up.

526. Once magueys have started to send out their quiotes, it is best to let the stalks grow completely and let them produce flowers. Once they sprout, then, the quiotes are allowed to grow, and whoever wants to can make roast quiote. For this, one must cut the quiote before it grows flowers at the top; that is, at the stage when the stalk is tender and hasn't yet formed tough fibers inside. 527. To make roast quiote one digs a hole in the ground a meter deep by a meter wide. The quiotes are hacked into hunks 50 centimeters long, so they'll fit in the hole. 528. A fire is lit in the hole, just as if one were going to roast meat. One lets the stones absorb the heat and get really hot. Then, when the quiotes are thrown in, all flames are extinguished so that the quiotes cook in pure heat from the rocks. If the quiotes are thrown directly on hot wood coals they get scorched and don't cook up well. 529. The quiotes of the i'ta and gääx'miini are cooked the most. These magueys grow slowly up in the mountains and are not usually broken for aguamiel, so they are a favorite for cooking their quiotes. 530. People who live close by these resources go up into the hills to cut the quiotes and cook them. They cook them up and bring them down, all prepared, to the small villages and rancheras, and they sell the roast quiotes from house to house. Sometimes they even bring them into the city to sell.

531. People snatch up these delicacies quickly, because roast quiote has a good flavor and is good to eat, or, better said, to chew on. Mestizos like to eat roast quiote, and a quiote seller quickly sells all of his or her wares. 532. If the sellers see that there is heavy demand, they go back out to the mountain to cut more quiotes and roast them up. Then they make another trip into the city. They

Once they sprout, the quíotes are allowed to grow

Flora 526

use the little money they get from these sales to buy the most necessary items for their homes: corn, chiles and beans. These are the things most sought after, and the things that have to be worked for to acquire. 533. Quiotes grow during February and March. This is the time when the warm winds of spring come up, and with these winds the quiotes sprout quickly.

When they grow well, quiotes produce yet another resource, their flowers, and they are a choice food. 534. About a week before quiotes actually open their flowers they are cut down and the buds are prepared for eating. They are delicious. The flowers are gathered when they are still in the budding stage. When they are cut down, whoever likes to do this sort of thing minces the buds very finely. Then they boil them and fry them with onion, chile, and salt. 535. You have to squeeze out the water after they are boiled. This food is not eaten with its own broth.

536. They are even more delicious when they are freshly sliced and steam fried with condiments in a covered pan. If the buds are left to flower, then they don't taste as good, but are rather bitter. 537. On certain fiesta days, when it isn't permitted to eat meat, these buds are eaten as a kind of Lenten dish.

538. When the flowers open they are yellow. They are high up on top of the quiote in a great cluster. Bees and wasps come and feed on their honey. They take their pollen and they are there all day, buzzing and making noise on the flowers. 539. The full flowering stage lasts three weeks, and after that the flowers fall. When the seeds are mature they turn black and look like chicalote seeds. Birds such as doves and huitlacoches, and possibly others, eat the seeds. I mention these two birds specifically because the seeds are found in their gizzards and in their craws when they are opened up. 540. The remaining seeds that aren't eaten by birds are scattered by the wind. The wind then covers the seeds with earth, and when it rains, new maguey plants grow.

541. The leaves of the quiote that come loose from around the heart of the plant are very green, and contain a particularly soft fiber. Women see where people have cut out the hearts of magueys to start aguamiel flowing, and where people have just left the leaves they cut from the center in breaking open the plant.[75] Women pick up these leaves and cook them as if they were preparing barbecued meat. After the leaves are cooked, they take them out of the pit, and bury them somewhere else. This is all done so that when the leaves are shredded for their fiber they will be soft, and also to make the ixtle inside the leaf soft. It comes out a bit yellowish, but very soft.

542. The leaves are buried for one or two weeks to soften them up. In this way, the waste parts of the leaf just slip off, leaving the fiber when the leaves are processed.[76] The yellow color can be removed by soaking the ixtle in soap and

water. The ixtle used for spinning is put into soapy water and left out in the open to get rid of the yellow color. Then the fiber is taken out and washed well.

543. A woman who wants to make an ayate finds a barrel cactus and brings her ixtle to the cactus for carding. She arranges the fibers and draws them across the top of the cactus where there are many thorns. This cards the fiber, and prevents it from snagging when it is spun. This process removes any waste and junk from the fiber. 544. The waste from the fiber is not left on the barrel cactus, but is taken back and used when a lot of it has been accumulated. The woman then makes ayates, called "ts'u̱'nänxwa" or "fine ayates," from the ixtle that remains after the carding process. The thickness of the weave in these fine ayates is only two, three, or four threads. 545. Ayates made from two strands of fiber in each cord are the most difficult to weave, and require a special backstrap loom. Fine weaving is needed to make fine ayates.

546. A special tool, called a "malacate," or spindle whorl, is needed for spinning the fiber. It is also called a "dooxthet'i" which means a spinning stone (see p. 325).

547. When the spindle is filled, you remove the ball of thread and keep adding on until there are big skeins of fiber twine. For this process, one uses two posts that spin the threads. 548. You spin enough fiber to make an ayate, and this depends on how wide you want the ayate to be. The amount is kept track of by counting the amount of fiber being spun. This depends on the size of the ayate to be woven, and is counted in "xu̱ni." This means "half an ayate," and so first you count enough for half an ayate, and then you make enough fiber for the rest. 549. Ayates are woven in halves, first one half, then the other. Then the two halves are sewn together.

550. Now we will see the names of the implements needed to weave ayates. These are: two poles, one warp, one "nopal," one opener, one whettle, and one ending tool. 551. In weaving the fiber, it is crossed over and under. This crossing is absolutely necessary, or one can not make an ayate. The warp is used to make the over-and-under crossing, while the whettle goes back and forth. Without this, it would not be possible to make an ayate.

552. The warp goes around each of the threads, with another strand. Then the threads are lifted so the woman can pass the whettle through with the other strand which will make the ayate. 553. The fiber used in the matrix is also called ixtle, and some people roast it, too, to make ayates. But they only do this when the ayate is for family use, not when it is for sale to others. Fiber used for making commercially-sold ayates is not roasted.

554. The waste material from the carding process is also spun, but separately. It is not carded or cleaned again, but is spun as is, just as it comes off the barrel

cactus. This class of fiber is much heavier and requires a bigger, cruder mala-cate. 555. This material is spun into skeins, and then woven into ayates, just like the fine ayates. However, the looms, like the spinning spindles, are also thick and crude so that they can handle the weave. 556. The product is called a "suthi" in Ñähñu, or "crude ayate." Crude ayates are made in the same way as fine ayates; that is, the weaving process is the same. Crude ayates are a meter square, while fine ayates are of various sizes, large and small.

557. There are some fine ayates woven to cover the heads of young, virgin girls. These are the most carefully made of all ayates. Some people embroider flowers on these ayates. There are also ayates that are just regular thickness, neither fine nor crude. 558. These are used by women to cover their heads when they go out in the sun. These ayates are also used to rock babies in. 559. These ayates are also used to carry things from one place to another, to carry home pur-chases from market, and to carry all useful things. They are used for carrying maize when it is purchased. Maize can be carried any distance, no matter how far, in an ayate.

560. Old people tell how they used ayates to carry earth when they used to make bordos in the milpas and had to throw dirt up on the mounds where there wasn't enough dirt. In other words, they had to fill in areas where the earth was not deep enough or thick enough. In those days they didn't have wheelbarrows like they do now, so the laborers were given ayates with which to carry dirt and complete their tasks. For this work, they used the big, crude ayates called "suthi" which were not easily ripped by stones when heaving dirt from them. 561. Also, these ayates were used a lot by traveling salesmen who went great distances and stayed away for a month and a half or two months before returning to their homes. 562. Some of them used to use ayates for carrying their wares. Others, who were poor and didn't have enough money to buy blankets, used to use thick, heavy ayates to cover themselves against the cold. 563. Children who stayed at home were also covered with heavy ayates, especially when the wind blew and when it froze over.

564. Heavy ayates are still used today for carrying skins full of pulque. These skins are very heavy when they are filled with pulque, and so something is needed to carry them in that is tough and won't tear. A tumpline is used with this ayate. The pulque carrier puts the tumpline around his forehead. The tumpline is also woven from ixtle extracted from magueys. 565. The same work is done in making tumplines as in making ayates, and the tools are the same form. The fiber strands are thicker for tumplines than for ayates. Also, the strands used in making tumplines are spun on a wheel, while those used in making ayates are not always spun on wheels. This is because each size and kind of ayate uses a

A special tool is needed for spinning the fiber
Flora 546

different thickness of fiber. 566. Neither fine ayates, nor heavy ayates are sold in the market very often. They are generally made for family use. The ones brought to market are called "selling ayates." 567. These are made from heavy fiber, but not as thick as those used in making the heavy, carrying ayates. Also, fiber for ayates that are sold in the market is spun on wheels. To spin this fiber, one must work at around dawn, when the morning is just beginning, so that the air will be cool and fresh. This is so the thread won't break and get all fouled up when it is being twisted. If you spin fiber later in the day when it's hot, the threads get harder and less pliant, and they break easily.

568. The women ayate makers can weave a dozen ayates a week. The merchants pay the women 25 pesos for each ayate. Tumpline makers turn out a gross a week. A gross is a dozen dozen, and these are sold for 30 pesos a dozen. However, if there are lots of tumplines, then the price goes down. 569. Tumplines are in heavy demand around harvest time. Yoke straps are also made from maguey fiber. They are used to lash together the horns of a pair of oxen. Yoke straps are made the same as ayates and tumplines; that is to say, they are woven on special looms. Yoke straps are four meters long by five centimeters wide. 570. Yoke straps are used to fasten ox horns to the yoke. The yoke has a chain in the middle, between the oxen, which goes back to the plow being pulled to dig up the earth.

571. People used to spin ixtle for making shoulder bags, and men used to wear these bags to carry around whatever little things they needed when they went on a journey. People like the salesmen I mentioned before, who went far from home used to carry their money, a knife and other things in these bags. 572. These bags are woven the same as ayates, except that bags are woven in one piece, then folded over and sewn along the edges. After the edges are sewn, a carrying cord is braided from three heavy strands. This is called "'metä hñuu," or "three weave."

573. Shepherds out in the open country need to do something to keep their flocks together. But they don't have to run all day to do this, because they use slingshots, which shepherds invented, and which they make themselves. To make one, you pull fiber out of the young leaf from the center of a small, immature maguey plant. 574. To do this, you wrap the needle point of the leaf around a stick and pull the fibers out in a bunch. These fibers are called "k'u'nxäähi." This word comes from "k'u'ti," to pull, and "xenxäähi," ixtle. 575. Next, you draw your fingers down the fresh fiber and squeeze out the juice, and then you twist the fibers. The fibers are not twisted on a wheel, but are rolled by hand across the shin until they twist up and become a single rope. This process is

The threads are lifted so the woman can pass
the whettle through　　　　　　　Flora 552

repeated, adding fibers to the end of the rope, until the rope is long enough for the job. 576. After the rope is twisted, the part where the stone is placed is made.

577. Slingshots can be made by twisting or by braiding the ixtle, whatever the person who makes it prefers. It he likes, he can make it thin, and if he likes, he can make it thick and heavy. One end of the sling is left untwisted as a fringe. This part makes a whirring noise when the stone is let go, and the bigger the fringe, the more noise it makes. 578. Slingshots can send stones great distances, up to 100 meters, and by using it shepherds don't have to run after their flocks to keep the animals in line. They round up their herds from a distance. The stones make noise as they are flung out of the slingshot, and the noise scares the goats into line. If a stone from a slingshot hits a small branch or twig, it cuts it right off the tree.

579. Years ago, people didn't have firearms to defend themselves when there were wars, and they confronted their enemies with slingshots, according to what people say. If a stone hit a person in the back, he would fall down from the pain, and if it hit him in the head it would kill him. This is what the old people say. 580. If the stone hit someone in the leg, it would break his leg. That's why shepherds don't sling stones to hit animals, but only to keep them close, and feeding where they should be.

581. Whips are also made from ixtle; they are braided from three or four strands. They have an open fringe on one end. Shepherds carry these whips. They twirl them and snap them towards the ground. The fringed tip snaps loudly from the force of the whip crack. 582. Shepherds that really know how to crack their whips can make them sound like a rifle going off. Shepherds always carry whips, and they crack them when they are out in the hills to keep away any coyotes or foxes that might be in the area looking to eat goats.[77]

583. Another use made of the waste material left over from carding ixtle on the barrel cactus is in making gun barrel tamping. It is called "njäfooxi" in Ñähñu because to discharge a shot you first have to put powder down the barrel and then a wad of the waste ixtle, or "fooxi," from the carding process. Then you put in more powder, then the shot, and finally another wad of waste ixtle as a cover for the whole thing. The waste ixtle acts as a kind of fuse to ignite the powder. 584. When the flint sparks, pieces of burnt ixtle are sprayed about. If the person shooting the ixtle is not strong, he will be kicked back from the force of the blast. This instrument is very dangerous and foxes don't like to risk their lives against it.

585. To shred ixtle from maguey leaves, the following tools are needed: a large, wide, flat stone to crush the leaf; a club for pounding the fiber; a brace or wooden horse; a board on which to work the leaf; a special pole with a piece of

mesquite   ixtle

Slingshots can send stones great distances
Flora 578

sharp metal in the middle with which to scrape the leaf and extract the fiber; a stick about 30 centimeters long with which to roll up the extracted fiber; a clothesline on which to hang the fresh ixtle to dry; and an extra maguey leaf which serves as an apron and which keeps the juice of the leaves from getting on the person doing the job.

586. To extract ixtle, a person first has to cut some leaves. These are taken from magueys that have already finished producing aguamiel and are drying up. The remaining plant is used to make ixtle, and not let to go to waste. 587. Some people scrape magueys and extract ixtle themselves. Others scrape their magueys for aguamiel, but then sell off the plants to others for the ixtle when the plant stops making aguamiel. 588. Or they may give others the old magueys in return for half the ixtle they extract. If someone extracts six bundles for example, then the worker gets three of the bundles and the owner of the plant gets three. This is not very profitable for a worker who has to work all day for just half the product.

589. People who have some working capital buy maguey plants that are no longer producing aguamiel. They extract the ixtle and sell it by the bundle in the market. But if there are women who make ayates for a living in a village where people make ixtle, then these women will buy the ixtle locally. Ixtle workers who know their craft can extract a lot of fiber quickly. They can work through 18 leaves in a day, and ixtle sells at eight pesos a bundle, these days. 591. The word "tu'ti," or "handful," is used to refer to a bundle of ixtle because it is the amount that fits in an open adult fist with the thumb and fingers about two finger widths apart. This is what is called a handful, or bundle of ixtle. 592. If the ixtle buyers see that a bundle is small, they complain, saying to the seller: "Look at that fistful there that you're selling me! I don't think it's a full bundle." 593. And the ixtle seller responds, "Yes, it's a full one, it's a full one. Furthermore, the ixtle is long, and I'll throw in an extra leaf's worth just to make you buy it."

594. In this case, the leaves that the seller shredded were not heated in a pit fire, but were worked raw. When leaves are worked raw like this, the juice causes welts and stinging if it gets on a person who is unaccustomed to touching it. The waste material, the pulp, from the shredding and extracting of ixtle is fed to goats. Goats love to eat this food, as do cattle, and even pigs sometimes. 595. Goats and cattle find the ixtle pulp waste by smelling it, and they eat it. They like it because it's cool and soft, and it gives them something to chew on. Sheep also like to eat it.

The pulp that comes from scraping magueys for aguamiel is white, and this is what pigs like most to eat. People bring it back from their scraping chores, morning, midday and evening, and feed it to pigs. 596. They carry it in an old basket, called "njänxi'mfi," or "pulp carrier." Among men who joke around, if one of them is wearing an old, dirty hat, the others tell him it's a "pulp carrier." 597. If they find themselves in a situation where they have to remove their hats, and if someone with a dirty old hat forgets to take it off, people say to him: "Take off your old pulp carrier for a minute."

598. When maguey stumps are pulled out of the ground, the best of them are selected for use. They are worked and carved, and some of them are turned into benches. Others are hollowed out and used as planters for some seeds, like peaches, or chiles. Then later, the seedlings are transplanted to a permanent place when they are big enough to survive. 599. Some stumps are used to make bee hives. Bees like to live in maguey trunks. They stay in there and make their honey. Only the largest, most voluminous stumps are chosen for bee hives, so there will be room for the honeycomb. 600. The stumps that aren't selected for household use are used to shore up the bordos in the milpas to stop erosion when it rains. Others are split with an axe and used for firewood. These trunks are used especially when it's very cold. They are thrown into the fireplace to keep people warm.

601. The big quiotes, left to grow to maturity and dry out, are also cut down and used. Some are used as fence posts, with bramble and thorns and mesquite branches interwoven among the posts.[78] The largest quiotes are hewn nice and even and are used as cross beams in making house roofs. These are the main roof transits that go right across the center of the roof and hold most of the weight because they hold up all the lesser cross beams. This is especially the case when the house has a double slanted roof, pitching on both sides from a peak. 602. As soon as the main roof beams are put in place and all the cross beams are lashed together, little animals make their home in them. It's like they just want to live around people. These animals are the abejorro or red fly, black jicotes, and a bird called the woodpecker, also called the "quiote pecker" in Ñähñu.[79]

603. The abejorro bores into the quiote, even though the wood is dry and hard. The bee just works away, taking a little piece out at a time in its mouth. When a little hole is made in the shell of the wood, the bee hollows it out and makes it bigger, and stays in there at night. During the daytime it goes about outside. 604. You can tell immediately when abejorros come to the house because they make a loud noise when they fly around. It's like the insect was singing with its wings. When it gets to its hole, it makes a few circles before going in, as if it were looking for traces that something else might have gone in there before going in itself. 605. Wasps also bore out their homes with their pincer mouths.

They have a special kind of pincers that are strong, and that they use to dig out the wood in the quiote. When the hole is big enough, the wasp goes in and raises its offspring. First they are larvae, and then they mature and take on the wasp form. Two or three are in each hole. 606. All these animals seem like they are playing music when they fly around where the owner of the house is sitting. They come and go, back and forth, making their sounds and protecting their offspring in their nests.

607. Woodpeckers like to live in dried out quiotes which they bore into with their beaks. You can hear it when they do this. The size of the hole it makes depends on the particular bird's body size. Whatever that is, that's the size of the hole it makes. Wasps chase anyone who dares bother them, and sting them. 608. By contrast, the woodpecker sings when it sees people. Actually its song sounds like hiccoughs. When it does this, it is believed that it is announcing bad tidings, or that it foresees bad things for the person it sings to. It follows the person, flying back and forth in front of them. If you throw a rock at it, it just makes a circle and goes to the other side of the branch on which it is perched. 609. From what people say, sometimes bad things happen on the day a woodpecker sings. It might be a fight among members of the family, or a child might have an accident and lose consciousness. These are some of the things that happen to people on the day a woodpecker mocks them with its song.

610. Woodpeckers live inside quiotes. In order to fit in its nest, it builds it along the long axis of the quiote. It lays its eggs and bears the young woodpeckers. You can tell when they are born because they are in there squawking away. 611. If you want to chase them out, you just put a cigarette into the nest pole. This weakens the birds and they leave. Maybe they don't like the smell of cigarettes because they never smoke. They like to bore into quiotes because it doesn't take a lot of work. Once they get past the hard outer shell, the inside is fluffy and pulpy. The outside is pretty hard because it contains ixtle. But inside it isn't too tough. 612. Also, woodpeckers have very hard beaks. Otherwise, how could they ever bore into mesquite trees, which are the hardest of all? They bore into them, too, to make their nests. 613. Several kinds of animals live in houses made of maguey leaves, including woodpeckers, wasps, and abejorros. These are the professional singers of the house.

614. Quiotes help out poor people even more, especially those who have neither land nor magueys. These people have only their own physical strength to rely on. A poor laborer has food to eat only when he gets a day's work. Otherwise, he has no food, for lack of money. 615. These people are in really bad shape, especially when they get sick, and they have no economic resources or material goods to sell off so they can get money for doctoring. If the sickness be-

comes grave, then they just die, and then, even when they are dead, there are no resources to bury them, because their families have no money to buy burial clothes. The purchase of burial clothes is a tradition among people who have the money that is needed. 616. Those who have nothing are just buried in the clothes they wore when they were alive and well. Two or three men dig the grave, about one and a half times the height of a man in depth, and they bury the dead person in it. It makes no difference whether the dead person is an adult or a child; when they have no money they are all buried in the same way. 617. There is nothing to put the dead person on to carry the body to the grave.

As we know, it is customary to buy a coffin in which to put a dead person, in which to bring them to the cemetery, and in which to bury them. Poor people have no money for coffins, yet people can not just grab a dead person by the arms and legs and carry them to be buried just like that. People have a lot of respect for the dead. 618. Here is where the quiote comes in. The grave diggers go out and find two or three quiotes. They cut them down and carry them back to the house. When they return, they take a machete and an axe and they split a quiote down the middle. 619. When a quiote is split the long way, this is called "x̱ote." The other quiote, or two quiotes, depending on the number needed, are chopped into four pieces; first they are split lengthwise, and then they are cut into one-meter pieces. 620. After this, all the pieces are lashed together, with all the poles carefully arranged and tied fast on both bends. In other words, all the one-meter pieces are lashed to the long pieces, using the tough skin of maguey leaves. When it is all lashed together it looks like a ladder. But even though it looks like a ladder, this is not what it is called. It is called "m'et'e rä mboo" in Ñähñu or "woven quiote" (see p. 335).

621. When it has been securely tied together, the apparatus is ready to be used to carry the dead person to the cemetery. Only the body is buried, not the apparatus. The corpse is slowly lowered with ropes into the ground and the quiote framework is left on the ground at the cemetery.

622. But the uses of the quiote are still not finished. When wood collectors go out gathering firewood they often find these abandoned burial frameworks. They break them up and bring them home to burn and cook whatever they need. Only some people burn these "woven quiotes"—usually those who do not believe that dead people can punish the living. 623. Those who believe that dead people *can* punish the living don't burn the frameworks. According to them, the dead take vengeance if they see someone burning their burial platform. In their view, the dead continue to feel that the platform belongs to them, and they say that anyone who burns a corpse's platform will get welts, called "'yedu rä ndo'yo," or "rain of the dead," all over their body. If it isn't welts, then

it will be some other illness, and the person will die. That is the belief that still exists.

624. The extra maguey leaves that remain, after the plant finishes producing aguamiel, and after the good leaves are sold off, remain on the plant. They dry up slowly and are not used. The plants that have had their aguamiel extracted really thoroughly wither quickly, and die. Those plants that have not been properly scraped continue to send out new leaves for a time, and don't die right away. 625. These new leaves are used when there is a fiesta, such as for saints' days, baptisms, flower offerings, planting time, and harvest time although this last is not strictly considered a fiesta. 626. At all celebrations people always make a meal to offer a taco to everyone gracious enough to come. The wife of the mayordomo of the celebration kills chickens and goats. Sometimes they cook the meat in mole and with other ingredients, and this goes for chickens as well as for goats. Other times someone is given the special task of roasting the meat, and that person does the cooking.

627. For this job they have to collect maguey leaves. They go out and cut the leaves wherever they are found, usually in milpas. The number of leaves that will be needed depends on the amount of meat being cooked. It also depends on the width of the leaves, because some are wide and others are narrow. 628. They bring in a large bundle of leaves to where the fiesta is being held. When they arrive, someone else is already dressing out the carcasses of the goats that will be roasted. 629. The pit oven has to be lit early in the day, and the rocks have to have been put on top of the wood fire. The fire is made well, with large coals, so that it will heat the stones thoroughly. The man who brings the maguey leaves has to roast them one at a time. This way they will be cooked and won't make the meat bitter when it is wrapped in the leaves. The leaves are cooked on one side only, not on both sides, because if they are scorched they will make the meat bitter, too. 630. The back of the leaf, that is, the curved portion that faces down towards the ground when it is on the plant, is placed on the fire. 631. When the maguey leaves are roasted, and the goats have been fully dressed out and cut into pieces, then you only have to wait until all the wood is consumed in order to bury the meat.

632. When burying the meat, one must remove all the pieces of wood that were not completely burned up so that no smoke will get on the meat. If it does, the meat will smell from smoke, and it doesn't taste good like that. The stones have to be spread out evenly. They have been turned into coals by the fire and they contain all the heat that will cook the meat. The leaves are spread out on the stones, and the meat is placed on the precooked leaves. The meat is spread evenly so it will cook evenly.

When it is all lashed together, it looks like a ladder

Flora 620

633. After all the chunks of meat have been placed in the pit, they are covered with the rest of the leaves, and then the dirt that was removed in digging the oven is put on top of the whole thing. All possible holes are blocked up so that no heat escapes. If heat is allowed to escape, the meat might come out patchy— that is, not cooked in some places, and bloody. 634. Another fire is made on top of the earth that covers the maguey leaves. This is to maintain the heat and to keep the top from getting cold. It takes four hours to cook the meat thoroughly, and when it is done it has an exquisite taste that makes those who eat it lick their fingers. The maguey, cooked slowly with the meat, is what gives the meat its flavor.

635. There is another trick to making barbacóa. Really heavy goats have a lot of fat on them. If the fat is not cut off, then when it renders in the oven it puts out the fire and the meat doesn't cook up well. In order to prevent this, you catch the dripping juice in a drip pan. A large earthenware or metal pot is buried with the meat. It contains water and condiments. This gives flavor to the juice of the meat that falls from above. 636. To do this, all the things I mentioned earlier have to be done. The oven has to be made, the leaves have to be cooked; everything has to be done right. The first thing done in collecting the juice is that the pot is filled with various ingredients including carrots, chiles rayados, thyme, marjoram, cabbage, chickpeas, rice, mint, and cumin. Some people put in xoconostle[80] and corn on the cob, if there is any. If there isn't any, then they don't.

637. The first thing put in the fire, then, is the pot, and it is covered with some metal rods which are criss-crossed over it. Then, on top of those, the maguey leaves are placed, and then the meat, as I said a moment ago. After putting on the meat, it is covered with more leaves, if there is nothing that one wants to cook along with the meat. Some people roast corn on the cob with barbacóa; these, too, give a delicious flavor to the meat. 638. Salt needs to be sprinkled on the meat. It has to be sprinkled on all sides of each piece so that the meat will taste good. No salt is put in the soup because it will be seasoned by the salt coming down from the meat.

639. Some magueys are good for medicine, and one of these is called the maguey pinto.[81] It gets this name because its leaves are variegated. We can picture a leaf: in the middle it is green, but along the edges it is bright yellow. 640. This type of maguey is not broken open to scrape for aguamiel, and it has not been seen to send out a quiote. Nor is it cultivated much because people give more importance to plants that offer larger economic returns. 641. The maguey pinto is good for curing shoulder pain. From what I've seen, day laborers suffer a lot of shoulder pain because they work all day, all week long, with very little rest. 642. You cut a small leaf from the maguey pinto, and you roast it on a fire.

A plate is needed to squeeze out the juice of the leaf. You squeeze out the juice and add tequesquite, which is thought to be cold, as opposed to the ailment being treated, which is hot from the sun in which laborers work all day. 643. Salt is added, along with nejayo de nixtamal. This liquid, too, is considered cool. The preparation is then tested to be sure it is at room temperature. Then the sick person lies face down so the liquid can be rubbed on the shoulders and back. This is done twice. 644. Then the area is covered with a fine cloth so the vapor can penetrate. You can see the vapor rising from the poultice. This medicine is applied late in the evening so the person can sleep with it on. The sick person should not get up once the medication is applied, but the next day the pain will be down.

645. Another medicinal maguey is called the corazón cocido.[82] This maguey is scraped for aguamiel, its leaves are processed for fiber, and the ixtle is woven into ayates. 646. But this maguey is also used in medicine to treat sprains, blows to the body, and painful bruises. Sprains are the most painful. If someone has a sprained leg, they can hardly walk or take a step. And if the sprain is in the arm, it not only hurts but you can't even work. 647. The corazón cocido is used to treat banged up knees and shins and backstrain. Backstrain occurs when someone lifts something heavier than he should, and this causes weakening of the bones and pain. In treating these pains, a leaf of corazón cocido is cut, and thorns along the edges are cut off. Then the leaf is roasted. 648. When it is well cooked, it is removed from the fire and left to cool off just a little. When it is cooled a bit, the leaf is placed on the injured area—that is, the part that was hit or dislocated. The heat of the leaf is placed directly on the pain. 649. The person who has the pain puts the leaf on the sore spot and makes it as hot as they can take it. With this, the pain and the swelling go down.

650. The juice of this maguey is not squeezed out for use in medicine. The plain leaf is used to warm up contusions, and the liquid that comes like sweat out of the leaf is the medicine. The procedure of putting a piece of maguey on some part of the body is called "pa'mi" in Ñähñu, which means "heat turning," perhaps because the leaf is turned on the painful area. [83] 651. For example, suppose the sprain is in the ankle and it is swollen all around. Then, in order to treat the entire area, the piece of leaf has to be rotated around the hurt area. 652. Only the thickest part of the leaf is used; that is, the part closest to the trunk is cut off and roasted.

653. The ashes from all magueys that are burned as firewood are also used in medicine, especially the fresh ashes that are barely extinguished in the fireplaces. The ash is used to treat people who suffer from a kind of inflammation. In Ñähñu it is called nthinmui," or "bloated stomach." This results from

eating something that causes gas and bloating, and is cured with hot ashes from the fireplace—but not too hot, so they won't burn the stomach. 654. The hot ashes are rubbed on the abdomen by the sick person, or someone helping them, and little by little the swelling subsides in the stomach and the person is better. If someone eats an ear of corn that has not been cooked well, or a poorly cooked potato or an unripe peach, these things cause stomach bloating.

655. Continuing now, we will see what uses are made of ayates. Fine ayates are made in different sizes and of different size threads. A woman who makes an ayate does so with enthusiasm so that it will turn out well. 656. If the ayate she is weaving is promised to someone whom she respects, like her older brother, or her father or her sweetheart, then she makes a really fine one. These finely woven ayates are beautiful, and are made with great care. 657. When the woman reflects on one of these promises she sets to work with care, weaving a small section at a time so she can keep track of how it's progressing. It's a shame that the custom of making these fine ayates is disappearing.

658. If someone is obliged to make a floral offering because they promised a saint that they would do so, then a separate ayate is woven. Ayates for floral offerings must be used for the first time in the ritual, and no one should use them before for anything else until after they've been used for their designated purpose. After that the ayates can be used for other things. 659. These ayates are made specifically for carrying the flower bowl, firecrackers and incense, which are the most important ingredients in a floral offering. Once ayates have been used for this, though, they can be used thereafter to carry anything one wishes. 660. There are still men who wear ayates criss-crossed over their chests. Only fine ayates are worn like this. Heavy ayates are hardly worn by anyone because the fiber is so crude.

661. When the judges of the community call a meeting, the men change their clothes before gathering. They used to wear handmade cotton shirts and baggy cotton breeches when these things were still around. In the 1950s there were still some men who dressed in white cotton, in traditional costume, and they wore crossed ayates also. Those ayates were extremely fine, woven of threads that were only two strands thick, and they looked beautiful. 662. They wore those ayates crossed in the front and draped in the back, or crossed in the back, a different position each time. This custom of wearing an ayate crossed over the back or chest was done to make the person look attractive. 663. Other men put things they wanted to carry in their ayate while others wore a bag over their shoulder in which they carried their things. 664. They were like people today who wear suits when they get dressed up. In those days people wore crossed,

fine ayates. If they went to a fiesta, that's what they wore. They dressed in white cotton shirts, with long sleeves, white breeches, a beautiful multicolored sash around the waist, new huaraches and a new palm sombrero.[84] 665. When a man wasn't going out anywhere special, all these clothes were stored in a box so they wouldn't get dirty with grease and dust.

666. People used to know how to make nearly all these clothes, and they only bought a few things ready made. For example, a man made his own huaraches and only bought the leather straps. 667. A woman sewed all the family's clothes and bought only the material. She wove the waist sashes. Only men wore crossed ayates. Women, of course, wore ayates, but only to cover their heads. When they went with their husbands to a fiesta or to an invited dinner they wore those fine ayates over their heads. 668. They wore skirts they made themselves, embroidered around the bottom edge and around the waist. The embroidery was red or black, blue and orange. 669. Women embroidered their own blouses on the chest and shoulder areas.[85] They wove their own sashes. They put metal taps, called "garbancillos" in Spanish, on their huaraches. 670. It was mostly the young women who dressed up; they braided their hair, which they generally wore long, into three or four strands.

671. And so it was that young women used to weave their own fine ayates to cover their heads. From the time they were little girls their mothers would teach them how to weave ayates. In this instruction the mother would not teach with words, but would sit the girl down in front of the loom, and the girl learned by herself quickly. 672. By the time a girl was four or five years old she was already being taught to weave and to grind corn. In fact, girls learned to grind corn even earlier. 673. As they grew up and got stronger they would take on other chores they had to learn. Sometimes they had to process maguey or lechuguilla leaves for fiber, just like men. Girls were taught to weave when they were still very small, so that by the time they grew up they would know how to make different kinds of ayates. 674. They could make crude ayates, medium fine ones, and the very fine ones used for rocking babies to sleep. They made cradles so that when babies cried they could be rocked and quieted, and would go to sleep. 675. This is how many of the men were raised who are today adults in the Mezquital Valley. The maguey is the people's best friend in this great desert.

Lechuguilla.[86] 676. After the maguey this is the most important plant for the people. It, too, is very useful for the Ñähñu. In spite of this, the people don't care for the lechuguilla as they should. It grows wild on the slopes of the mountains, and only a very few plants are cultivated.

677. Some plants are bright green, and others are a yellowish green.[87] If a person grabs a leaf of one of these latter plants, a kind of yellow powder comes off and sticks to their hand. It is easy to tell that the powder is yellow, and more or less brilliant in color. It has a characteristic odor which is pleasant, not foul.

678. Other plants have a green central core, with dotted or dashed lines on the outside portion of the leaf that faces down towards the ground. The leaves are green and the lines are darker green, and they go along the entire length of the leaf, from the needle point all the way to the base of the leaf where it joins the core. 679. The needle points are smaller than those of the maguey. The points are brown at first, when the leaves first come away from the core. The plant looks generally like a maguey, but the leaves of the lechuguilla are very narrow.[88] Some plants are very leafy, due to heavy moisture in the ground below them, and because they are in fertile soil. 680. If someone gets stuck accidently in the hand or foot by their needle points, the sting is quite painful and causes a bad wound. People in this region call the lechuguilla points "xä pa yä ne" or "hot mouth." 681. The thorns along the sides of a leaf begin right below the point and go along both sides all the way to the base. These side thorns hook downward towards the base of the plant, and if they prick a finger they go deep into the flesh, causing intense pain. When the thorns are pulled out, the wound bleeds profusely. To stop the bleeding and calm the pain, you squeeze some juice from the same lechuguilla and rub it on.

682. The size of the lechuguilla varies by terrain and by type of plant. There are some that are very small, and others that are medium sized or large. There are very small plants called "short lechuguilla," or "doots'uada" in Ñähñu.[89] This word is made from three words. "Doo" means "short legged," and in this case reflects the height of the plant. The particle "ts" is from "ts'u'ta" or lechuguilla. And the noun "'uada" means maguey. 684. The small plants are not generally processed for ixtle, because it takes too much work, and it isn't worth the effort. Also, the threads break when they are spun because the strands are so short. 685. The medium-sized and large ones are processed. The people who process ixtle appreciate most the lechuguillas called "penca larga."[90] These are worth the effort; they produce commercially sellable fiber and it practically spins itself. Ropes made from long fibers are smooth, without a lot of rough pieces sticking out. Ropes made from short fibers, by contrast, are bristly and the merchants don't like to buy them. 686. The long leaves are about a meter in length, and they are called "mats'uada."

687. Lechuguilla is not cultivated but grows wild on the slopes and hills in the following places: El Decá, Bingú, San Antonio Sabanillas, El Boto,

Lechugía is not cultivated, but grows wild

Flora 687

Capula, San Juanico, Portezuelos, Panales, El Dexthí, Cantamayé, El Naxthey, Boxhuada, Orizabita, San Miguel Juguí, El Espíritu, Nequetejé, Los Remedios, and in a part of Zimapán adjacent to Tasquillo. These are the places where there is most lechuguilla in the Mezquital Valley. 688. Wherever lechuguilla grows it grows in clumps of 200-300 plants. Some plants are uprooted and replanted by people, so the plants are better spaced apart. When the replanted plants take root they won't be so crowded and there will be enough room between them for a person to go along removing leaves for processing. 689. It is not necessary to dig raised furrows before planting lechuguilla. The earth just needs to be loosened up with a pickaxe, and the plant can be set in the ground. If lechuguilla is planted too deeply, that is, above the root with the "foot" of the plant covered by dirt, then it doesn't grow and just dies. 690. It can go a year out of the ground without being replanted. It dries up completely, as if it were dead. Its little leaves wither and resemble wrinkled chamois cloth. But when the rains come after the plant is placed back in the ground, it soaks up the moisture so quickly one can hardly describe it. It sends out new roots, turns green again, grows new leaves, and sends out new shoots called "bätsi," or "children." A year or two after being replanted, lechuguillas form a completely new cultivated garden of processable plants. 691. Other plants grow only in porous tepetate terrain but they don't thrive well, and remain short and stiff. They only grow to a quarter of their regular length, and these leaves are the most difficult to extract fiber from.

692. When the plants grow leaves, either the newly replanted ones or the ones that were growing by themselves, a person who wants to make ixtle can prune them off. Actually, we don't use the word "m'oki," meaning "to prune" in referring to lechuguilla. That word more correctly describes the work done with maguey. For lechuguilla we talk about "cutting," or "nthet'i" rather than pruning. 693. A lechuguilla cutter carries a well-sharpened tool which he continually hones down because the plant is very fibrous and cutting the leaves dulls the tool. Lechuguilla fiber is not like maguey ixtle, which is soft by comparison. 694. The cutting instrument loses its edge easily because lechuguilla ixtle is so tough. The cutter files the edge of the instrument with the back of a knife, that is, the part opposite the edge. People who do this for a living go out and cut leaves, and then bring them home to extract the ixtle. They sit under some shade to work. But if they don't feel like carrying the leaves a long way, then they might process them right there in the lechugilla field. 695. They find a piece of shade to protect them from the sun and they sit down with the lechuguilla leaves close to hand. When they finish shredding the leaves close to hand, they move so the rest of the leaves are within reach. And thus they move about in the hills, for days, processing fiber from the plants. 696. One must be careful that the moon

is right when cutting lechuguilla, too. Otherwise, if the day is bad, the rest of the leaves on the plants won't grow after some are cut off.

697. Fiber makers prefer the long leaves that have a lot of ixtle in them so their efforts will be productive. They leave aside the plants that don't have much ixtle and whose leaves are all juicy pulp and skin. They let these leaves dry up because the juicier the lechuguilla leaf, the less fiber it contains. Even if the plant is among the best fiber producers, if it has a lot of juicy pulp it won't have much fiber. You'd just get more waste material than ixtle from it, and ixtle is what is important. 698. The leaves that contain lots of ixtle are the ones that are dried up a little, but they present another problem. When they are withered and fibrous the leaves are like leather and the person shredding the leaf gets more tired. However, if he has no choice, he takes what he can get and processes whatever there is. 699. Lechuguilla leaves are dry during April, May and June. They get thin from the intense heat of the sun. By contrast, in July, August and September they are juicy and thick from all the moisture that builds up during the rains. 700. The really top fiber producers extract 10 kilograms a day, starting at eight in the morning and quitting at five in the afternoon. In order to do this, however, they have to go cutting for a full day before processing fiber, collecting leaves and piling them up where they will sit and do the fiber extraction.

701. The lechuguilla is rather like the maguey in that nothing of it goes to waste. Everything is usable. The wastage from the fiber extraction is dried out in the sun so it won't rot and so it will keep its green color. It is hung out to dry on other cactuses. If it is laid out on the ground then little stones stick to it and the merchants won't buy it. 702. The waste material from lechuguilla is not like that of the maguey that stings and causes itching. It is rare that lechuguilla pulp causes itching. Sometimes, if it contains a lot of juice it stings, but otherwise it doesn't. 703. The leftover material, or xite, has various uses in the valley. It is as much in demand in mestizo homes as in poor Ñähñu homes. It is used more in native households for washing dishes used in serving food. On fiesta days, or when someone has a big meal just because they feel like it, dishes get very greasy. Chickens, goats and pigs are killed. They are cooked in large pots and served on plates to those invited. 704. When the meal is over, the dishes are dirty and obviously have to be washed. More than just water is needed so the dishes will be clean and won't smell bad. Xite is what removes any bad odor. 705. All the plates and cooking dishes are washed two or three times with xite, and rinsed between each scrubbing in order to get all the bad smell off. On the first wash, there won't be many suds because there is so much grease on the plates. On the second wash there are lots of suds. On the third and last wash the plates are rinsed with fresh water and laid face down on a rack to drain.

706. People in this region prefer to wash their dishes with xite because it gets rid of bad odors, while powdered soaps are not as effective. Sometimes plates still smell bad when used again after being washed with powdered soaps. 707. Also, powdered soaps are more expensive, while xite is very economical. All it costs is for someone to go out to the country and get it. Women have noticed also that soap wrinkles their hands and cracks their skin, while xite does not. 708. Xite is used even more in washing field laborers' clothes, or those of country people whose clothes get dirty a lot. Their clothes are washed with xite, and the dirt just dissolves. Xite leaves everything it washes nice and clean.

709. Xite can be kept for a long time so long as it isn't stored in a wet place. If it gets wet it loses its soapy quality. But if it is kept properly it lasts for months without losing its effectiveness. 710. When it is well preserved, xite is very dried out. But when it is placed in water, the green substance in it dissolves. It is this bitter substance that makes all the foam and suds. But if it gets wet from the rain before it is put to use, xite loses its power and won't be useful for washing dishes or clothing. 711. Even xite that is washed out is not wasted. It is used in construction of house walls, in houses made of ocotillo poles. These walls are made by setting the poles next to one another, but there are still cracks between the posts that you can see through. Wind comes in through these cracks and makes the house and the people in it cold. Ocotillo is the most common material used for walls. 712. Xite is brought in, mixed with mud and daubed on the walls. The xite helps the mud hold together and stick to the poles in the wall. The mixture is plastered on the surface and the ixtle sticks to the octotillo poles and seals up the cracks. After applying the mud, it can be smoothed into a nice surface so the walls are not rough inside.

713. Xite considered unusable is thrown out like garbage. A hen ready to lay needs a nest to keep her eggs, and the nest needs to be soft and warm so the chicks will incubate and hatch. If the nest gets cold, the eggs will be lost. 714. When hens build their nests in the brooder they gather old, used up xite and place it on the bottom of their nests. After three weeks the chicks are there, chirping away after hatching. 715. After that, you take the old xite and put it around the base of nopal plants. As the xite rots it acts as fertilizer, and it also holds in the little moisture available. This helps the nopal produce nice ear-like leaves and good tunas for eating.

716. Xite is commonly used in personal hygiene. It is used in washing hair. It gets rid of dirt and leaves hair soft. Not only that, but it gets rid of dandruff. People with dandruff wash their hair a few times with xite, and the dandruff is gone. 717. If the dandruff doesn't disappear when washed with dried xite that has been wet again, then you use fresh, green xite, just as it comes from the

processing of ixtle fiber. You wash your hair with the lechuguilla juice, full strength, and this gets rid of dandruff quickly. 718. Other people, especially women, use xite if their hair doesn't grow well. They wash their hair in fresh, green xite, and after a few washings the hair grows well again.

719. Six tools are used in processing lechuguilla fiber: (1) a rock, about a handspan in width, which goes underneath the leaf during the pounding; (2) a club, made of wood, for crushing the leaf; (3) a piece of wood, about a handspan wide, for support during the fiber extraction process; (4) a fiber extractor which can be either of metal or wood;[91] (5) a fixed post, with a hole in it, into which the extractor point is inserted; (6) a stick, used to roll up the ixtle as it is removed from the point of the leaf, back towards the end.

These are all the tools used in pulling fiber out of lechuguilla. 720. The ixtle is hung out in the sun to dry, and then stored or spun if the person knows how to spin. Otherwise, the ixtle is sold as is. Some people just extract the ixtle, dry it, and bring it to market, as is. Others card it and clean it before bringing it in to sell. They make a carded roll, or small bale, and they weigh it right where the merchant is who will buy it. 721. Many merchants try to cheat those whom they see can not read the platform scales. But now people know these merchants' lies and tricks, and they watch the merchants carefully and call them on anything that isn't done properly. 722. When that happens, the merchant is embarrassed, and tries to pretend that he just made an honest mistake. When ixtle is carded its value rises because it is cleaner. When it is uncarded it contains a lot of dirt that adds weight. The merchants know that they are paying for something they can't use, that is, the dirt that adds weight on the scale, so they lower the price for uncarded ixtle.

723. Those who don't sell ixtle make their own rope. This requires that the ixtle be carded in a "carder." The carder is just a piece of wood with about 30 nails sticking in it. The ixtle is thrown across the nails in small handsful, and drawn across, so the dirt is removed. Then, holding the ixtle in one hand, you pull out two or more strands with the other hand and throw them into the air, about head high. The fibers fall to the ground clean, and they form a tangled mass. 724. When the ixtle is all carded it is rolled up into a bale so it can be carried in an ayate, and is taken to the spinning wheel. 725. The whole bale of ixtle is sprinkled with water to keep it soft. This is done by the spinner, who continually blows a fine spray of water on the ixtle with his mouth. This keeps the fiber from becoming brittle, and lets the person spin it. If the ixtle weren't dampened, it would cut the spinner's hands.

726. People who extract lechuguilla fiber and spin ropes begin on Tuesday to cut leaves and extract the ixtle. They cut and extract through Wednesday and

Thursday, and they spin what they've produced on Friday, Saturday, and Sunday. Then on Monday they go to market and sell the ropes they have made. 727. In order to get a good price they have to arrive early. If they get there late, then others will have arrived; and where there are many sellers, the merchants lower the price they will pay. They pay whatever they feel like when there are lots of sellers, saying that they can't get a decent price where *they* will be selling the wares themselves. 728. So, anyone who wants to get a good price has to get up early. By four in the morning they have to be on the road. If they get up this early they will be at the market awaiting the arrival of the commercial buyers. 729. When the buyers get there, they choose what they like and ignore what they don't want. What they like are ropes that are smooth, and not bristly with rough fibers sticking out all over. They buy the smooth ropes first. They only buy the bristly ropes if they feel like it, otherwise they don't. 730. And if they do buy bristly, rough rope, they pay whatever they want to for it. For example, if they bought smooth ropes for 25 pesos a dozen, they would pay only 10 pesos a dozen for rough ropes.

731. Whether they like it or not, the sellers of these ropes have to take the price because they need the money to buy things. People are waiting at home for them, but they don't come because they haven't sold their wares quickly. When this happens, people are pressured to do better work the next time. 732. People who really know how to make rope well produce a gross and a half pieces a week. Others make six or seven dozen, and this is what they have to take to market to sell.

733. Making rope is a laborious, difficult occupation. The ropes are used for tying bundles, and for tying up animals. 734. These ropes are two and a half meters long. When they are selling well, then people make rope, and when the price drops they stop making them, or they make them and store them against a time when the prices are better.

735. When there are a lot of warm winds and rope is made, the ixtle dries out and the fiber continually snaps. 736. Other lechuguilla ixtle extractors gather fiber and weave large sacks, or burlap bags. One type of bag is called "'ro̱zänthäähi," or "rope sack," and is woven of ixtle threads. It is very tough and is used for carrying corn stalks and cobs after the kernels have been removed. 737. These bags are a meter tall, by 80 centimeters wide. When they are filled with corn a man can only carry it with great effort. This kind of rope bag is also called "saaka" in Ñähñu; this word comes from Spanish.

738. Rope sacks are made in El Decá and also in San Antonio Sabanillas. That is where people specialize in making these bags. They are not made in other places, because they require a lot of work. 739. The looms used for weav-

ing sacks are big and heavy, so they won't break when the throw rod is yanked hard to make the weave tight. These bags are woven in a single piece. They aren't like ayates made from two pieces. Sacks are one piece, two meters long. 740. After they are woven, they are folded double and sewn along the edges.

741. Extracting lechuguilla fiber is not very difficult because the leaves are small, compared with maguey. Children and older people can extract fiber; women and men alike can do it, too. Children five or six years of age find a place to sit and extract fiber when it is being done by adults. Girls as well as boys do this. 742. Children who go to school get up early and extract lechuguilla ixtle. The lechuguilla leaves are brought in beforehand. When the time comes to go to school, the children eat and leave. When they get out of school they go back to extracting fiber all afternoon. They buy whatever they need for school with the money they get from making ixtle. They buy pencils and paper. These things cost the least and the children can purchase them.

743. In one way, work on lechuguilla has forestalled the migration of people from the valley to the cities for work. People go out for a week or two but, because they are not accustomed to city life, they return and work lechuguilla. 744. They don't adjust to the city because it costs them more to live there than they earn. They wind up leaving all the money they make in the city because of their expenses.

745. When lechuguilla plants grow to their full size they are like magueys. They shoot out a quiote, but theirs is thinner than the maguey's. Lechuguilla quiotes grow up to three and a half meters high. Their flowers start to appear half way up the quiote and go all the way to the top. Lechuguilla quiotes are not cooked for eating, because they are bitter. Also, they are thin and don't have much pulp. 746. Some people eat the flowers when they are still in bud. They cut the ripe ones, not the ones at the top of the quiote, because those are bitter. 747. They fry the flowers in oil, just as they come from the quiote, and don't boil them first. They first add salt, onions, chiles, and then they fry them. The buds cook up still keeping their green color. 748. Other times, the flowers are cooked quickly on a comal, although they get a little singed like this. This kind of cooking is called "mhät'i," or "light cooking." In this kind of quick cooking salt is sprinkled on the food so it cooks dry on the comal and takes on the salt flavoring. Then the food is mixed with salsa, which has to be already made so that all that is needed is to mix it together for eating. 749. Not many people like to eat these flowers because they are a little bitter.

750. The buds that aren't cut remain on the quiote and come to flower a few at a time. For example, today there may be a few flowers open, and then tomorrow other flowers open further up towards the top of the quiote. They always

flower from the bottom upwards. 751. Small creatures such as wasps, black
wasps, yellow jackets, butterflies and hummingbirds fly all around the flowers,
sucking the honey. These flowers open during the days of the spring equinox.
This is when the maguey quiotes shoot up also. 752. The little creatures that
suck the lechuguilla flowers make buzzing noises with their wings, and it's like
they were a musical band, playing around the quiote. Lechuguilla flowers are
white, combined with a delicate yellow. 753. When the flowers finish blooming, the little bulbs at the bottom of the flowers begin to grow. They grow and
grow, and when they are mature they dry up. Then later the little bulbs open and
the seeds scatter. The seeds are black when they scatter. Birds eat them if they
find them, and the rest germinate in the open country.

754. The quiotes are allowed to finish flowering, and then they are cut down,
piled up and dried out. These quiotes are used as cross beams in the roofs of
houses, because lechuguilla quiotes are not eaten up quickly by bugs. 755. The
parts where the flowers were are cleaned and smoothed before putting the
quiotes up as roof thatch supports. The quiotes would otherwise be too rough. If
they are not used right away, then the quiotes are bundled together and stored
someplace, upright, and not lying on the ground. That way, even if they are
rained on they won't rot. 756. After a plant has sent up its quiote, the leaves are
all cut off. Sometimes the leaves are processed for ixtle, and sometimes they are
just cut off the plant without processing but are used for other things. 757. All
the green leaves are removed. This is called "thots'i" or "removal." In this, the
entire leaf, including the thick part at the bottom, is cut off. In what is called
"nthet'i," or "cutting," the leaf is cut off higher and the leaf's bulbous head is not
removed. 758. The leaves that are removed entirely from the trunk can be used
for making two things. One is called "nt'exke" and the other "sani nt'eke." They
have very similar functions but it would be better to examine what they are.

759. In making a "nt'exke," or pot scrubber, the leaf is removed entirely from
the core of the lechuguilla. Then all the thorns are removed from the edges. The
front, thin part of the leaf is cut off, leaving a piece the size of the hand of the
person who will use the utensil. The part left is the thick, bulbous part attached
to the core. It is white and shiny, and on the end one can see thick, heavy ixtle
fibers. 760. In order to make the fibers stick out more, one cuts up the end with
something rough. This ruffles the xite and makes the big, thick fibers stick out of
the end. If the thorns have been cut off the edges the piece is ready to use.
761. The scraper is used when grease sticks to something and gets hard. The escobetilla, as it is known in Spanish, removes such dirt. 762. Masa dries hard on
the metates used for grinding nixtamal. In order to clean a metate well, one uses
an escobetilla first, to remove the caked on masa, before washing it. The same is

done for molcajetes.[92] First they are scrubbed with an escobetilla. Anything rough and porous is brushed like this, to make it clean.

763. The other instrument is called a "nt'eke" or "comb scraper." To make these, the leaves removed from the lechuguilla have to be processed for ixtle. They are processed thoroughly, until no more xite comes out, and only ixtle remains. One or two kilograms are extracted. If the ixtle is for sale, then more is made. But in this case, the ixtle is not for selling but for something else. 764. The ixtle at the head of the leaf is quite heavy and rough. It is left to dry a bit, and then a handful or so is taken, depending on the size of the scrubber one wishes to make, and folded over. 765. The strands are distributed evenly on both sides, so that one side doesn't become enlarged. The rough, heavy points of the ixtle face downward, and all sides of the scrubber must be even. 766. When folded over, the whole thing is about 15 centimeters long, from the head of the scrubber, which is where the head of the leaf was. After the ixtle is folded over, the bundle is tied with a thin string around the center. The string has to be tied several times around the middle to keep the fibers from coming loose. 767. Sometimes the bundle is not merely tied, but woven together to make the scrubber nicely formed and strong.

768. The instrument is also called a "sani" or "comb" because in olden times, and even until recently, there weren't commercially made combs like there are nowadays. The combs referred to here are the instruments that men and women alike use to fix up their hair. Products made in cities used to reach the Mezquital Valley last of all. 769. Traveling salesmen who went from house to house only rarely came to the valley, offering wares which they had purchased in the big cities. They brought needles for sewing, and thread, and spices such as cumin, and pepper; they brought handkerchiefs, blankets or tablecloths. These were the things they mostly brought. 770. Ñähñu women needed things with which to fix their hair. For this they asked their husbands to make them "sani nt'eñä" or "head combs" as they are called. This is the comb made from lechuguilla ixtle, and which women used daily to comb out their hair. Because their hair was long it got easily tangled and they had to comb it out continually. Also, this kind of comb lasted a long time and didn't get worn out and become soft quickly.

771. Another use of this scraping instrument is for cleaning out pulque barrels. Pulque has a sticky sediment and the barrels have to be washed all the time so the pulque doesn't get spoiled. If you just rinse it out with water the sediment doesn't come off and that is exactly what needs to be removed most. To remove the sediment, people just scrape it with the escobetilla made of lechuguilla. 772. It is also used in washing plates. Anything that has stuff stuck to it can be cleaned off with an escobetilla.

773. As with many things in the Ñähñu world, there are many beliefs associated with the escobetilla. Some people suffer from warts that are callous-covered. These warts never contain pus, and they don't get inflamed. They just grow, and as they get bigger they crack open. 774. These growths are really ugly when they are on someone's hands; that's where they grow, on the hands and feet. They come out below the wrist, towards the fingers. On the feet, they come out below the ankle and down towards the toes. 775. The belief is that when it drizzles and there is a rainbow, a child or grownup who suffers from these warts should bring an escobetilla to an anthill. There, they should brush the warts, whether on the hands or on the feet. They should clean them off in this manner, and slowly the warts will disappear. 776. It must be an anthill of red ants. When the person finishes brushing the warts, they leave the escobetilla there at the anthill.

777. After all the leaves are pulled off to make scrapers and brushes, the lechuguilla trunk that remains is a ball. It is white on the outside, where the leaves were, and is heavy and dense. The inside is pulpy and soft. 778. It is hollowed out and the whole thing is used as a funnel for pouring liquids quickly, without spilling them. Funnels are used a lot in measuring out pulque and for pouring it into the large goat skins, called "botas" in Spanish. 779. When pulque is measured in liters the count must be exact so that the right amount gets where it's going. Otherwise, the buyer will demand money back and won't buy again from the person who gave less than was paid for. 780. Therefore, when pulque is measured out in liters, none must spill back into the barrel or on the ground. 781. The neck or mouth of the bota is soft and loose, and thus it is easy to spill pulque when pouring it. But with a funnel you can fill a bota in a few minutes, with no spillage.

782. Ixtle is also used as a strainer for pulque. When aguamiel is taken from a maguey it is strained because it contains a lot of waste material and insects from the scraping. 783. The ixtle is carded and then washed well so the bitter tasting substances are removed, along with the foam it contains. Some cutters take ixtle from young leaves and make wash rags from it. 784. This is made of only fine, soft ixtle that is carded. These washcloths are collected in a pile and made into packages for sale at public baths. They sell for a peso each. These washcloths are used by people in bathing to scrub their bodies clean.

785. To finish the description of the uses for lechuguilla, I can say that it is a very tough plant that withstands both droughts and freezes. There are some years when it freezes hard and lechuguilla leaves get a little singed around the edges. But this does not affect the plant's growth much.

Sisal.[93] 786. This plant looks neither like maguey nor lechuguilla in size or color. It has its own characteristics and is smaller than the maguey. It reaches a height of one meter and its leaves stretch out to 90 centimeters. 787. Its name in Ñähñu means "maguey quiote" or, in other words, a maguey that has a quiote. This plant needs good soil to grow. It likes heavy, thick soil so it can send out its roots. 788. Its roots resemble those of the maguey and the lechuguilla. It doesn't multiply easily. It sends out shoots, but the shoots do not appear far from the main plant. The new shoots grow practically on top of the main plant and are concentrated right around the base. 787. Sisal grows in clumps of five or ten plants. They are planted near house fences to help keep out animals. Goats can't cross through them because the plants are pretty high. It is important to keep goats out of fruit orchards. 790. As sisal multiplies the new plants are replanted in straight lines as a fence, and they multiply in the lines although they only have two or three shoots each.

791. Sisal leaves are ashen green in color, different from both the maguey and the lechuguilla. All the plants are the same color, and no one could mistake them for lechuguilla or maguey. Sisal is easily distinguished at first sight because its leaves are ashen colored. 792. The leaves have thorns along both edges. The thorns are not like those of the lechuguilla which are spaced closely. Those of the sisal are spaced further apart along the whole edge of the leaf, and they are curved downwards towards the foot of the plant. 793. Sisal leaves have a thorn, or needle, as it is better known, at the top. This needle is not as pointy as the needle on the ends of lechuguilla and maguey leaves. Even so, sisal needle points really hurt when they stick into a person. 794. The leaves, as I said, are long; they are thin at the bottom, wider in the middle, and thin again towards the needle point. The leaves are cut and processed for fiber. Each plant yields about 10 leaves. After the plant is pruned back it is left to grow new leaves. 795. But it takes a long time for sisal plants to grow leaves that can be cut and processed. They take six or seven years, and even more, to generate usable leaves.

796. When these plants are big, some people break them to scrape for aguamiel. If there is a lot of moisture then sisal produces aguamiel. After a month, however, the plants dry up. 797. The aguamiel is sweet, like that of the maguey except that the sisal's aguamiel stings a little. For this reason, pulque is not made for separate serving from sisal juice, but its aguamiel is mixed with that of the maguey to ferment together. 798. After the plant has been scraped, the leaves can be cut for fiber. The leaves are processed using the same tools as those used for maguey because the leaves are long. Children don't usually process sisal because their arms aren't long enough to handle the leaves. 799. Ixtle from sisal is not sold, but is only for household use. It is used to make rope for tying up such animals as horses, pigs, cattle, and goats. For all these animals one needs ropes five or six meters long. The ropes are spun on a wheel, strand by

strand. The ixtle used in making these ropes is not carded. One end of the bundle is held in the huarache of the spinner, and the other in his or her hand. The person doing the spinning then feeds the ixtle from the middle of the bundle, moving backwards as the rope spins on the whorl attached to the wheel. 800. Ropes can be made of four or eight strands. Sisal ixtle is soft, almost like that of the maguey, and not like that of the lechuguilla which is rough and scratchy. As always, goats and sheep eat the waste from the leaf, if it is dried well.

801. It has been found that sisal ixtle is tougher than that of the maguey or that of the lechuguilla. A kind of rope called "dänthi," or "thick rope" is made from sisal. Sometimes it is truly thick, and sometimes not. It gets its name from the fact that the twisting of the rope is different from the process described above. The rope is twisted much more tightly than any other type of rope. 802. This particular type of rope has a special use. It is used exclusively for catching animals that roam loose, including horses and cattle. They are lassoed with this type of rope. The rope is as stiff as a rod. It is carried rolled rather than folded in lengths. It is very good for lassoing; when the loop goes over the animal's head the knot slips easily and the animal can't get out of it. 803. Charros, or roping cowboys, twirl lassos in the air. Sometimes they dance inside the loop, jumping in and out as they spin it near the ground. Lassos are indispensable to horsemen. They always carry their ropes rolled up on the sides of their horse. Sometimes they twist their ropes from pure sisal, and sometimes they twist pieces of horse mane into them because they believe this makes the ropes stronger. 804. When they twist mane and sisal together they card the sisal so it will twist evenly and so that parts won't be white while other parts are dark. 805. Sisal is also combined with other material when making ropes for lashing fireworks towers, or castillos. These ropes are heavier. Ixtle from lechuguilla and sisal are twisted together to make this kind of rope. These ropes have to be 40 meters long, and they weigh about 65 kilograms. These ropes are tied around the base of the castillo and its supports to prevent the tower from falling over when the fireworks are lit.

806. When sisal reaches its full growth it sends out a quiote which grows up to five meters high. The quiote is not as thick as the maguey's, but is thicker than the lechuguilla's. Sisal is like other plants of its class in that it sends out its quiote in February, March, and April. When the quiote is well developed it blooms. First it puts out buds, and then the buds open into beautiful flowers. These flowers are yellow and hummingbirds, bees and other insects gather around to feed on the honey. 807. After the quiotes finish growing and die, they are cut and used as thatch roof supports. Since sisal quiotes are thicker and

longer than those of the lechuguilla, a single one reaches all the way across a roof from edge to edge.

808. Other people pile up sisal quiotes and when they have enough they build a lowered platform ceiling in their house, called a "tapanco." A tapanco is made by laying quiotes side by side from one end of the inside of the house to the other, about one and half meters off the floor, so that an adult can walk upright below it. 809. Platform ceilings are useful for storing things like corn ears. Though sisal quiotes are thinner than those of the maguey, they are called "boo," the same word used for maguey quiotes, and not "ts'ebe," which refers to the lechuguilla quiote. This is probably because it is more nearly like the maguey quiote in thickness. No medicinal uses have been found for sisal. When its trunk is dead and dry it is used as firewood.

Aloe.[94] 810. This is a plant that grows in arid soil. It multiplies where the soil is fine and soft, such as along the edges of barrancas where the earth is rich and mixed with sand. That is where aloe multiplies. The name of this plant in Ñähñu is composed of two words: "ju" means that it is bitter if you taste it, and "ta" means maguey. The whole name means bitter maguey; when you say this quickly it comes out "juu'ta." 811. And, indeed, it is bitter. If you taste it with your tongue it has a pungent, bitter taste. It is sort of pinkish orange in color, just a bit on the dark side, rather than bright, and a little whitish. If you pass your hand across a leaf, the whitish powder comes off and the exposed leaf is shiny. The white powder smells unmistakably of aloe.

812. Aloes remain green even when they dry up. They begin to dry at the tips, and stay green even as they die. Because there is no fiber in the leaf one can break it easly, even though the leaf is hard. They always break off at the juncture where the dry part meets the juicy part of the leaf. 813. Aloe doesn't grow tall, only about 40 centimeters high. But if one counts the height of the quiote, then it reaches one meter, including the flowers. 814. From the bottom up the leaves are thick, and then they become thin and straight about halfway up. They have no needle point on the ends of the leaves. 815. They have very fine, soft thorns along both edges of the leaves. These thorns can be easily crushed with the fingers. When a leaf is cut off, a bright yellow liquid comes out. It smells strong and is slimy.

816. Aloes are found in big clumps. They grow on top of one another and the new shoots can hardly survive around the base, they are so thick. Animals hide in aloe because the clumps are so thick. Spiders, beetles, spiny lizards, whiptail lizards and snakes may be found around the base of a clump of aloe. 817. A single plant can have 20 offshoots, but, as I said, they don't all grow because

they are right on top of one another and many just die off. The baby aloe plants are white and tender and they bruise easily. 818. Because aloes multiply so prolifically, it is thought that this characteristic can be transferred to other plants. When people plant young magueys on bordos they go and get a handful of baby aloe plants and bring them to the maguey field. 819. Before planting the first maguey, they crush the aloe between their hands. One could say they wash their hands with aloe. 820. It is said that with this treatment the young magueys will grow more shoots than they would otherwise. This belief appears to be correct. Wherever the treatment has been applied the magueys have sent out many new plants all over the bordo.

821. Aloes grow to full size in three or four years. When they are grown they send out a quiote. The quiote is like a thin, pink twig, or sometimes white, with straight stripes on it. The stripes begin at the base and go to mid-stalk. Then they change color and become pale green. 822. There are flowers at the top of the quiote. The buds starts about 20 centimeters up the quiote. The first buds bloom first, and they flower all the way to the top. 823. They only bloom for three days, from six in the morning until ten or eleven when the sun gets hot and the flowers wither. 824. Each batch of flowers only blooms for one morning; then they wither and don't bloom again. Their petals fall down and are scattered by the wind. The flowers contain a sweet liquid. People who have the patience for it cut the flowers and suck them out one at a time. 825. Hummingbirds go from flower to flower every morning. They go out earlier than people. When the flowers are still in bud they are yellow, with a covering on the surface that opens into bloom. 826. When the flower opens, the cover falls off. The flowers are yellow in bloom. They bloom in beautiful clusters and have a nice aroma. 827. There is a central staff in the flower, the pistil, which also flowers on the end. At the base of the pistil are many fine thread-like growths which also flower.

828. There are two kinds of aloe, that is, two colors. One kind is what I described above. It is pink, while the other kind is pale green. Some people call the latter "white aloe." They have yellow flowers that are a little paler than those of the pink aloe.

829. Aloe flowers are used as food, and are prepared in two ways, fried or parboiled. Either way they are delicious. The flowers that are cut for cooking are not yet fully open. By the time they bloom the flowers are bitter and have lost their flavor. The flowers are cut while still in bud and are fried in oil. They go right into the pot of oil, just as they come from the plant, with no other preparation. 830. The pot is covered so the flowers don't burn. Otherwise they would get singed and become bitter. 831. Onion, ground or chopped chile, and salt are

added. The dish is served only to people who like aloe flowers, because some folks don't like the taste.

832. The other method of cooking aloe flowers is to boil them. The water in which they are cooked is brought to a boil twice, then left to cool down. Then the water is drained, and the flowers are washed and then fried if one wishes, or left as is, adding only some condiments. 833. Some people also stir-cook the flowers on a comal. They chop in some onion, sprinkle on some salt, add chiles and cover the mixture with a plate so the steam won't escape. They shake the comal continually so the food doesn't burn. 834. Aloe flowers are sold in the market. A bunch consists of six to eight clusters of flowers and costs a peso. They are sold quickly by anyone who offers them. 835. Mestizos like to eat aloe flowers because they say the flowers are medicinal for fighting cancer. That is what is said. It is not known whether this is true or not. The only thing known for certain is that mestizos buy the flowers for cooking.

The people of the valley know that aloe does cure some illnesses that physicians can not cure. Either doctors can't find the right medicine, or they just don't want to cure these illnesses. 836. In these cases, the people go out to look for the plants that they know will cure a particular illness or pain that they suffer. Dried, dead aloe leaves look like they are no longer good for anything, but they are good for use in medicine. 835. They are used when someone has an open, oozing blister or wart growth, and especially when putting modern medicine on it doesn't stop it from festering. This is when you use dried aloe leaf.

Three or four pieces are boiled in water. The substance of the aloe is allowed to come out. 838. When it has boiled awhile, the water is colored like cinnamon. It is left to cool, but not so much as to lose its color. When the liquid is lukewarm it is drunk by the person who has the blister or boil. The dose may be repeated two or three times. If the lesion throbs and stings, the pain is calmed and it stops throbbing. 839. The boiled leaves are removed from the tea so the liquid may be drunk. Sugar may be added if one wishes, but it is better to drink the liquid straight because sugar dilutes the strength of the medicine. 840. The tea does not have a very good taste. Some people like it, others do not. But good flavor is not what is needed; curative power is needed. Having mentioned the tea, I should say that it looks very much like cinnamon tea, with the same color.

841. Green, juicy leaves are used more for medicine when someone has an open, oozing pimple or boil. The raw juice is put on the sore. This requires that the leaf be broken in the middle, at the fattest part, where it is juiciest. 842. Boils often deteriorate and get pus, and turn green. But if you dab aloe leaf on them, they dry out and later the scab comes off. Pimples and boils can also be cleaned with aloe juice, which is taken from the leaf and dabbed on the oozing sore. The

juiciest leaves are used in this case. These leaves are called "fat" or "well formed." The leaves are broken in the middle and the sap is dripped on the sore. Little by little the sore dries up and heals.

843. The so-called white aloe has more sap than the pinkish one, but one is as curative as the other. They are also good for warming up sprains and dislocated bones. For this the aloe must be roasted first so the juice runs out. 844. When the juice is lukewarm it is put on the part that hurts, whether it be a hand or a foot, and this calms the pain. If a child has measles aloe is used to cure that disease, too. 845. Measles usually break out in May and June, and attack children who are one month to two years of age. If these children are not cared for properly, the disease worsens, and they break out in sores. Some sores are bright red, while others are dark. Some of the sores don't rise above the skin, but just form splotches. 846. When this occurs it is said that the sores are inside the body, and if this condition occurs the child's mother gets very worried. She has to find medicine to help the pimples rise and make all the sores turn red. 847. As soon as it is noticed that the child has measles, it is isolated. Measles are easily distinguished because the child develops fever, stops eating, and its eyes get red. The child is put by itself in some part of the house where it remains until it gets better. 848. Only the mother, who cares for the child, goes to its room. Other people should not enter. A piece of aloe is hung on the door to the house. It is believed that this keeps away bad luck. 849. No "ts'ojä'i," or "bad person" should look upon a house that has a child with measles in it. I have already explained what constitutes a "bad person" in the previous volume on the fauna of the Mezquital.[95]

850. When the child is cured, the piece of aloe that was hung on the door to the house is thrown far away, because now the aloe is considered to be ill. Where the plant is thrown, if it senses moisture it sends out roots and begins to grow new leaves again and to multiply. 851. As I said earlier, it grows quickly where the soil is soft. When raised furrows are built, aloe is yanked out wherever it is growing in clumps, and it is replanted on one flank of the earth mound. When it takes root and grows it helps to firm up the soil so it won't be washed away in the rains. 852. "Aloe soil" is used in gardens as a fertilizer to make beautiful flowers grow. Also, seeds planted and fertilized with aloe soil grow well. 853. Mestizos in town order aloe soil by the cartload to fertilize their gardens. Since there are some areas that are just about covered with aloe, people who own a truck set their peons to work removing all the soil in order to bring it in by the cartload for sale to the mestizos. 854. The smell of aloe permeates the soil. And how does one know? When one sprinkles water on the flowers, the dirt gets wet and smells of aloe. 855. Goats eat the dry parts of aloe leaves, and

won't even touch the juicy green parts. When aloe send up its quiote it does not suffer the same fate as the maguey or the lechuguilla. After these latter plants flower, they die. But the aloe just keeps on growing; not right away, and not in the year following the quiote. But neither does it die.

The palma.[96] 856. This is another highly appreciated plant in the desert because it, too, gives much to the people in these arid lands. The form of this plant is different from that of the ones we have already seen. 857. Its roots are like those of the maguey, the lechuguilla, and the aloe, but its roots resemble those of the maguey more. The roots look like maguey roots in their color and in their curved shape, but not in their size and thickness. Palma roots are bigger. They grow to one and a half meters long where the soil is soft; where it isn't the roots are short. 858. From a distance it looks like the palma has a lot of roots, but it doesn't. When you dig up the trunk you can see that the roots are sparse, and even more so in plants that grow in poor, dry soil. 859. The trunk gets bigger and bigger as the years go by. Very old palma plants have great big trunks that spread wide on the ground. I think they do this to keep from being blown over in the wind, because when their bases are wide they can't be pushed over. 860. They can reach two meters in diameter at the base, thinning to one and a half meters just above the base.[97] The main trunk can reach 70 centimeters in diameter. Their branches begin to grow about one and a half meters up from the ground in big plants. The branches grow in different directions. 861. As the branches grow, the leaves fall. They die, rot, and finally fall off. Then the branches are dark, heavy, and naked. The branches become rough as they grow.

862. The leaves of this plant are different from those of other plants. Palma leaves are like knives, straight and inflexible. When there are strong winds the leaves rustle and produce a characteristic buzzing sound. They don't make an ordinary noise like other leaves. 863. They are dark green, and become yellow when they dry up. They contain a few strands of ixtle-like fiber that is more easily seen when the leaves are dry than when they are green. 864. There are no thorns along the edges of the leaves like the lechuguilla has. All it has is something like fibers, loosely laid one over the other. It has a very sharp point on the end of the leaf. As time goes by a transparent sheath drops off the leaf like it was shedding its skin. 865. If one is not careful and is stung by the point, the pain is intense. But not all the points are so sharp.

866. One kind of palma that grows very big gets branches, like a tree. It can grow up to four or five meters high.[98] They generally grow where the soil is soft and fertile. 867. The branches spread out and multiply. These trees can have as many as 15 or 20 large branches, and smaller branches grow on these large ones.

It takes rather a long time for a palma to grow. Many years pass before it is a fully grown plant. I saw some plants some time back (about 20 years ago), and it seemed like they weren't growing. They give the impression that they stay the same size.

868. There is another kind of palma.[99] This one doesn't spread out as much as the other, but just grows straight up, with its trunk slightly at an angle to the ground. Its leaves are all in a bunch at the top, and they are longer than the other plants. 869. Perhaps it is because it gets enough moisture in the leaves while the other kind has to distribute the moisture all through the branches. And since there is not much water in the ground, that would keep the leaves of the first plant from growing well.

870. The so-called "solitary palma," on the other hand, has plenty of moisture for its leaves. The solitary palma reaches five or five and a half meters in height. 871. It has a dark trunk, and its leaves fall as it grows. The leaves dry and fall, dry and fall. 872. They don't fall off immediately after drying up, however. They dry and remain attached to the trunk for days, even years. Eventually, they rot and fall and the trunk becomes naked. 873. The trunk of the solitary palma is straighter than that of the foliated palma and is therefore taller. Various birds spend the night at the top of the solitary palma. These include turtledoves and sparrows that nestle into the thick cap of leaves. Even if it rains, the leaves protect them, and they remain dry.

874. A moment ago I mentioned that palma leaves contain a kind of fiber. Birds use these fibers to construct woven nests. Sparrows and calandrias use palma fibers in their nests. 875. Calandrias make their nests entirely of these fibers. One can not imagine how they weave like that, but they do. They make a pocket of pure palma ixtle, and use nothing else. Though the nest is a bit light and open, the little birds hatch in it. Generally, this bird does not change trees. It always uses the palma, possibly because it likes it. 876. It does not set its nest on the surface of the branches but hangs its little bag-like nest instead. It weaves the nest to the leaves, and there it hangs. It may hang its nest where it is hidden because it is the same color as the dry leaves. The fibers that the bird uses to build its nest are very strong. If one tries to pull the nest off, it doesn't come loose too easily.

877. When palmas are alive their trunks are very dense and heavy. But when they die, the pulp gets soft and spongy. When you cut a trunk down you can see that it contains a lot of juice. As soon as you hit it with an axe the liquid sprays from the trunk. This is how it is when it is green. 878. Palma trunks are cut for different uses among Ñähñu families. Both kinds of palma are much appreciated because they are useful resources. 879. Though the trunk may seem

peculiarly shaped and full of surface cracks, it can be fixed, and cleaned up a bit, and it is fine for what it is used. First, I'll say here that only the big, thick trunks are cut down, whether it's a solitary or foliated branching palma. 880. They are cut in meter lengths, with even ends. Then you hone down a blade instrument called a "tajadera" in Spanish, or an adze scraper, and thin out the trunk, turning it into a beehive. The bees go in there, work, multiply, and produce honey.

881. The trunk is scraped out on one side, beginning in the middle and going towards the end. You leave about three or four centimeters so the hive can be placed on supports and rain will not enter it. Bees do not like it when water gets in their hive. 882. About one whole day is needed to hollow out a trunk from one end to the other. The pulp is adzed out a piece at a time, and the adze is sharpened regularly because the palma juice does not let the adze hold its edge. 883. When the trunk is all hollowed out it is left in the sun to dry. It has to be thoroughly dry or it smells of palma and the bees don't like it. 884. Its odor is not pleasant; it smells rotten, and the juice or sap is also not pleasant. It is pungent and causes itching on the tongue if you taste it. 885. When it is dry the log can be used for bees. But first you take a piece of honeycomb, put it on coals, and smoke the hive so that it smells of the honeycomb. If bees smell that, then they stay, otherwise they abandon the hive. 886. If the bees like their hive, they stay and work. Within a week there are already two pieces of honeycomb in the hive. The bees make their comb as big as the inside of the hive, and they fill it with honey. 887. When the hive is filled with honeycombs it is very heavy. The honey has to be removed so the bees can return to work. By this time, too, they have multiplied, and the new bees have to be separated or they will swarm and fly away. For this, one needs to have another log hive already prepared so the new bees can be just put in when they are ready. 888. Around two hives can be made from a branching palma trunk because those trunks are not very long. By contrast, three or four can be made from the trunks of solitary palmas, which are longer.

889. The large branches that are removed are not thrown away, nor are the thinner branches that have all the leaves. 890. The large branches are split in the middle so they can be scraped out and the pulp removed. The pulp is white and is not dense but rather soft and fibrous. The fibers are all woven together like a net. 891. The fiber of the branches, then, is soft, while that of the trunk is rough. The leaves that come off the center of the plant are also used. They are about four fingers wide, and vary in length. 892. As they are cut off, the leaves are laid out in the sun to dry so that when they are put on roofs they won't warp the cross supports with the weight of their juice. 893. The leaves are only laid out to wither and not to dry out completely, because if they are totally dry then they

leak. Sometimes people just go out and cut leaves for roofs. Other times they use the leaves that result from making beehives. Any way is fine; what is important is not to waste the leaves.

894. When houses are covered with palma fronds they are called "palma houses." When covering a house, you strip about five or six large plants and bring all the leaves to the construction site right away. 895. If you leave the fronds lying about where you strip them, goats will shred them. They don't eat palma leaves, they just tear them up. When the leaves are dry they can be put on the roof, but first all the supports have to be put up, and the roofing goes on these. 896. The leaves are placed one at a time across the supports. Two or three fronds are woven on each support to hold it, so that when the winds blow the roof won't come off. You begin roofing at the bottom of the planted roof and work towards the peak. 897. This is the same for roofs with one side as well as for double roofs. They are slanted to allow water to run off. Palma roofing doesn't last many years. The most it lasts is about ten years. The leaves rot quickly and are scattered by the winds. 898. But the shade produced by palma fronds is very cool when it gets hot out, and when it is cold the chill does not penetrate much. Their only defect is that they don't last long; they are thin in comparison with maguey leaves.

899. The pieces that come out of the core of the trunk in making a beehive are set aside to dry and then piled up. These pieces of pulp are used when removing honey from a filled hive. In order to get out the honey in the comb, a couple of pieces of the dried pulp are burned. 900. They produce a very pungent smoke, and this smoke is directed into the hive where the bees live. The bees huddle to one side and this allows one to remove the honey. When palma wood burns it does not flame but smolders like a cigarette. It is not used in the kitchen for this reason.

901. Palmas that are not cut down bloom in May and June, when they send out a quiote, or flower stalk. Both classes of palma that I mentioned bloom, and they have white flowers. 902. The quiote comes out of the end of the branch. It is white and pretty thick, and comes out with buds already on it. The flower is covered with a shield on the side that faces the sun. It takes about two weeks to blossom, and then the flowers open. 903. The quiotes get about one meter long on the solitary palmas, and only about 80 centimeters on the branching palmas. 904. The quiote on the solitary palma is foliated, because it is not merely a quiote. Small branches grow from it, which also have flowers. Palma flowers are cut and cooked for eating. 905. There is no difficulty in locating the flowers because they are always stark white. The large quiotes are hard to carry for one

person, because they are heavy. A person can carry two if the quiotes are medium sized.

906. After the quiote is brought to the house the flowers are selected and picked off one by one. Those that are three or four days in bloom are already too bitter and are ignored. Only those that bloomed the same day or the day before are selected and the ones that are still in bud are even more preferred because they have no bad taste. 907. A single quiote can produce one and a half quartillos of flowers, enough for a family of six. The flowers are boiled. First water is brought to a boil, and then the flowers are put in. This preserves their color and keeps them from getting yellow. If the flowers are put into water before it is boiling, they turn yellow. 908. When the flowers are cooked, the water is drained into a receptacle, and the pot is washed with fresh water to get out the bitter taste. Then the flowers are combined with other ingredients like salt and onions for eating. 909. Some people fry the flowers in oil or lard. The same ingredients are combined, but tomatoes may be added.

910. The fiber from the branches that were stripped for roofing material is pounded out with a mallet. The fiber is pounded to remove some of the pulp, and to clean it off. The fiber is hung in the sun to dry. 911. When it is dry, one could mistake the fiber for maguey ixtle if one didn't look carefully. The palma fiber is gathered into clumps, and neatly arranged. Then other clumps are piled together, and the bundles are tied with ixtle strands, one band around the middle of the bundle, and another at either end. It depends, too, on the size of the bundle and of the leaves that are pounded. 912. When the fiber is all bundled the ends are cut so they are even. These saddle blankets, used for beasts of burden, are about three fingers thick, about one and a half meters long, and about 60 centimeters wide. 913. These are called "nsi'tsi," or "cushions" for beasts of burden. The cushions are placed on the backs of horses and burros when they are loaded down with things. The cushion blanket is the first thing that goes on the animal's back, to protect it from getting blisters from the saddletree, or "fuste" as it is called in Spanish, on which packs are hung for the animal to carry. 914. The saddletree is made of wood, and is composed of nine parts.

915. People who make saddletrees buy whole palmas to cut the trees up themselves. They cut off the branches and use only the actual branch itself. They throw away the leaves, or they sell them to someone who wants them for roofing a house. 916. Saddletree makers pay 40 pesos per plant for the use of a palma, and they examine it first to see if they can make a profit from it. The price of a saddletree is about 40 pesos, depending on the particular market day. 917. One plant can yield three or four saddletrees if it has lots of branches. The

people who buy the palmas don't cut them down at the trunk base. They just cut off the thin branches and leave the main trunk standing. The next year the trunk sends out new branches again. 918. It is as if the plant likes to be pruned because it grows a lot of new growth wherever it was cut back. At each juncture it will send out two or three new branches. After three years these can be cut again to make more saddletrees, or to roof more houses. 919. It's a good thing palmas are like that, or they would have been wiped out because they are always being cut.

920. In places where there is lots of greenery, such as in the irrigated lands, people plant coriander. Palma leaves are used for tying bundles of coriander when they are brought to market. Coriander is sold in bunches. 921. For this, one looks for the longest palma leaves, which are sort of shredded[100] to make a particular kind of thread. About eight threads or strands of fiber will come from one wide leaf. These strands are used to tie up bundles of coriander, as well as thyme, mint, and marjoram. These are the spices usually sold by the bunch. 922. Lettuce plants are tied up to prevent the leaves from turning green on the inside, and to keep them white.

923. As I said, once a palma has been pruned back it will last for years and continue to put out new growth. From what I've seen, we could compare palmas with mesquites in terms of how long they live. I've seen trees that have lived a long time and they look as if time had not passed. 924. Trees I saw 30 years ago are still alive and they look like they just don't feel the passage of time and who knows how long those trees have been there. No one knows for sure. But it is certain that they live for many years. 925. When land is cleared for planting, all the bramble and thorn bushes are pulled out. But palmas are left for their shade. Sometimes, when a palma is between two furrows it has to be removed, whether one wants to or not. It is cut into pieces and thrown off to one side. The pieces don't dry quickly, and even take root on occasion.

926. Palma fronds that aren't cut continue to bloom and bear fruit.[101] These fruits grow slowly. When palma fruits are not yet ripe they look like bananas, but that is only when the fruits are still green. 927. They look more or less like little green bananas. When they ripen they turn yellow and slightly dark colored. They get like this because their seeds are black inside the fruit, and there are lots of seeds. There are about 30 seeds, in three rows, inside each fruit. 928. The fruits are sweet, and are eaten by birds like huitlacoches and calandrias. Those are the birds I have seen eating palma fruit. People can eat the fruit, too, but not a lot, only one. Eating a lot of palma fruit causes vomiting. They are a little piquant. When eating them one should suck out the sweet juice and not swallow the pulp which is tough and contains fiber.

929. Palma is used in medicine, also. The leaves that grow at the very top of the plant are used when children are sick from someone putting evil eye on them. The white, central heart of the tree at the top is used to cleanse the child, and this is done along with other cures. 930. This central heart of palma is used to cleanse the child's eyes and head so that it will get better. This cleansing is not done in just any manner, or in just any direction. 931. It is done starting from the eyes, going back over the top of the head, towards the neck, and then back to the face and over the neck again. According to the belief, you can't start a cleansing procedure just anywhere.

932. The needle points of the leaves in the center of the tree are also used. Since goats wander around they are herded to help them find food among the bramble. Sometimes a snake is hiding in the bramble, and if the shepherd does not see it, the snake may bite one of the goats. 933. Rattlesnakes are the worst. They usually bite goats on the jaw, and will strike at anything if provoked. One knows that a goat has been bitten by a snake because its mouth gets swollen. It forms a little bag and the goat can't eat. This particular swelling is called "buxhne," and means that the goat is carrying a sac on its jaw. 934. To cure this one looks for a leaf out of the heart of the palma; the inflamed part of the jaw is punctured with the needle point of the leaf. If the cure is done one day, then the next day the goat is better and the swelling is down. The belief is that the mouth sac holds in heat, and it is necessary to puncture the sac so the heat can escape. 935. When the sac is punctured a kind of liquid comes out, and it is said that this is the illness. Four or five punctures are made, and the animal cries out.

936. When palma leaves are burned they produce flames immediately. When one looks at a palma tree out in the desert, it looks like it is not good for anything. But if you know how to use it and to take advantage of each separate part, the plant offers a lot. All that is needed is for people not to hold back and to work as hard as they can.

Huapilla.[102] 937. Huapilla is often found together with lechuguilla in open country. When people see the plants like this they say that the plants get along well together; they are not like other plants that compete for light. When one plant covers another with shade, the one below turns yellow and dies. 938. Huapilla is as tough as lechuguilla. That is, it resists drought and it doesn't dry up easly. Its little leaves just wither back, but they don't die. Of course, when a real drought comes along, it dies. Like all plants it has its limits.

939. Huapilla leaves are smaller than those of lechuguilla, but they look like maguey or lechuguilla in that they stick up. The leaves have thorns along both edges, and the tip has a very sharp point. 940. The thorns on the edges of the

leaves are brown and look like hooks pointing down towards the base of the plant. These thorns go easily into the flesh of people who go about in open country, such as shepherds and lechuguilla cutters. These people get their feet all scratched up from huapilla thorns. 941. These thorns are sharp and they cause a lot of pain. They draw blood wherever they prick anyone. This plant also tears up the pants and skirts of shepherds. 942. The thorns are so sharp it's as if they were honed. If you pull one out of your flesh it cuts like a knife. And if they break off, they remain in the flesh, and they hurt and throb. They have to be removed to stop the pain. When a huapilla thorn gets into flesh it doesn't dissolve or rot, but just stays in there, causing pain.

943. Huapilla plants have ashen green leaves, covered with powder. The powder is like sugar, except this powder does not shine much. There are mature leaves, and leaves that are just opening from the center of the stalk. The center is where there is the most powder. The powder probably does not taste good because no insects eat it.

944. The center or heart of the huapilla is not like that of the maguey or the lechuguilla. The leaves on the huapilla are not attached to the heart, and they do not unfold away from the heart, as they do in the other two plants. Huapilla leaves grow out of the ground with no heart; they are separated from one another right from the beginning. Each new leaf grows by itself. 945. Huapillas are not such a deep green as some other plants. They are pale green. It is a kind of green that tends towards white. If you see it next to a lechuguilla, the huapilla is easily distinguished. But even by itself it is distinguished as pale green. 946. Huapillas grow in clusters, but they don't grow very quickly; they multiply slowly. The older huapillas are the biggest ones. They are like lechuguilla in that they grow well in good soil. There are 5, 10, even 100 in each cluster. Because they grow so heavily clustered they help to keep the soil together, and thus aid other plants by preventing them from being blown away or washed away. 947. They retain the moisture and hold the soil together. Another plant, called miel de jicote, is found inside the huapilla. Huapillas get to be around 30 centimeters in height. The leaves contain thin, strong fibers, but they are not removed because they are so small.

948. The plants live for about four years. The leaves open from the center and when they get big they turn yellow and dry up, and rot. They pile up around the base of the plant and decompose, and in this way they enrich the soil. 949. Goats and sheep break off the leaves to eat them. Though the leaves have thorns, the animals break them off where they won't get cut. They chew the leaves and leave the pulp, because the leaves are very tough. When the rains come in spring, the older, fully grown plants send up a quiote. 950. The quiote has a

brown cover and the inside is green. When the quiotes first come up they are brown and look like they are dead. The quiotes grow to one and a half meters high if they develop well. 951. When the quiote is grown it sends out little branches and little by little its flowers open up. It blooms from the bottom up, a little at a time. Every morning there is a cluster of flowers that bloom. It takes about ten days for all the flowers to bloom, and during this time insects gather, perhaps to eat the honey from the flowers. 952. They come and go, buzzing all around the flowers. The entire area of flowers gets foliage around it, and the weight of the flowers and foliage makes the quiote bend. Hummingbirds go around the flowers to eat the honey, but they can't because the flowers are so tiny. So they go off in search of other flowers to suck on, that is, flowers that are deep enough for them to put their beaks into. 953. Honey-producing bees are attracted to huapilla, and they go around gathering the powder of the flowers on their feet. When they have gathered all they can, they fly back to their hive. They return and once again put their feet on the flowers. They go back and forth, gathering the flower dust on the backs of their upper legs.

954. When the quiote has bloomed it dries up and the plant slowly dies. Shepherds use the quiotes as firewood. As the leaves rot, they fall all around. 955. All that is left is a small, round, black core, and one can see the roots that have gone into the soil. They are black, too. The roots go 40 centimeters into the soil. 956. The little trunk can be used as firewood, and it makes coals because it is very dense. People like to use the roots as kindling for heavier wood that does not catch as easily as huapilla when used in the kitchen fire. 957. The huapilla leaves the ground dark colored wherever it was planted, either because the leaves rot around it, or because the plant contains some substance which discolors the earth. 958. Wherever you see a blackish patch of earth, you know that a huapilla had been growing on that spot. Aloe, on the other hand, leaves a reddish spot. 959. People like to use the soil around a huapilla plant as a kind of fertilizer. They plant peaches, chiles, and flowers in the soil, and use huapilla dirt as a kind of potting soil. Huapilla soil is granular and helps plants germinate and grow roots, because when the soil is loose it doesn't cake and harden. Also, it is possible that huapilla soil contains some kind of substance that helps plants grow. 960. Unfortunately, irreparable damage is being done to huapilla, and other plants, too. They are being burned up, and are disappearing; the mountains are being denuded.

961. In the annual round of fiestas one is Christmas and another is New Year's. Christmas is celebrated on December 24th, and New Year's on the 31st of the month. 962. After 9 PM people start bonfires on the mountainsides to celebrate. They burn plants, and one of these is the huapilla because it burns

easily, even when it is green. 963. The flames are called "t'unza" or "plant fires" because that's what they are. Separate blazes are set for Christmas and for New Year's Eve, and so the plants are disappearing quickly. 964. The belief about Christmas is that blazes have to be set because Jesus Christ was born that night and it was very cold when he was born. People still believe that fires have to be lit for this reason. 965. Blazes are also lit on New Year's Eve, again to help God be well, that is, not to be cold. There is the belief that anyone who does not set fires will be reborn as a weevil when they die. Because people believe this, they set fires all over the mountains. 966. Religion is good for those who truly know what it is all about. But for those who do not, religion loses its meaning and is not good. An example of this is the burning up of plants that I'm talking about, so that the mountains are stripped bare. The plants die and the wind and rain erode the soil. 967. By the time anyone notices, the plants are gone and they won't return.

The junquillo.[103] 968. This is a bushy, bristly plant that grows wild in open country. It is rare to see one of these plants by itself; they usually occur in groups of 5 to 20. They come in two colors. One is dark green, and the other is yellow-ish green. This depends on the kind of soil they grow in. Where the soil is good, one can tell one from the other.

969. They grow about 70 centimeters high, and their foliage measures about a meter across. Junquillos have a round, ball-like appearance because their leaves, or spines grow from a central core on the ground and extend equally in all directions. Also, the leaves are all about the same length. 970. When they are pulled out of the slopes where they grow, their roots leave a circular hole in the ground; the way they grow also makes them round plants. Their leaves are different from those of the lechuguilla. Junquillo leaves are like little twigs, straight and uniform. 971. They grow out of the base of the plant, upward. They are of uniform width and have four sides. They have thorns on two sides. The thorns are very small, and it looks from a distance as if there were none. 972. But if you pick up one of these plants and aren't careful, and if you let the plant slip slightly in your hands, the leaves cut through you like knives. They don't hurt much, but they cause a lot of itching.

973. The thorns are like those of the lechuguilla, hook-shaped, and pointing downwards towards the ground. If you go up close you can see that the plant has many thorns. A single leaf can have 200 thorns. 974. The leaves have a needle point on the ends, smaller than the maguey's. But the roots of junquillos are more complex. When junquillos are in tepetate soil their roots dig in deeply to collect whatever moisture is available. The roots are about 40 centimeters long. Junquillos send out shoots around the base of the plant. 975. The central core is

easily distinguished, and is not like the huapilla which has separate leaves. The junquillo has a core made up of thin leaves that are bunched together. 976. The little leaves contain a fine, soft fiber that is removed and made into washcloths for scrubbing during baths. The leaves are roasted first in order to extract the fibers. 977. The leaves are processed in bunches, rather than one at a time. Until recently, bags were made from the fiber. The fiber was pulled and spun, and then woven like ayates into a mat which was folded and sewn on both sides to form a bag.

978. People who went to market used these bags to carry their purchases. One of these bags used to cost five or six pesos, depending on the size. 979. There were still bags like this in 1964. They were made by people in Capula and others in Pozuelos. But when plastic bags came to the market, these fiber bags disappeared because people didn't buy them from those who made them. 980. This was an economic setback for those who used to make those bags because they lost a source of work. Even though they did not earn much from this work, what they got was indispensable for feeding their families.

981. This plant sends up a quiote, too. It rains in June and July, and when they feel the moisture they send up a quiote. It is black, and not green. Even when the flowers on the little branches bloom, the quiotes remain dark colored. When they start to bloom one can distinguish their flowers. They are white, with a tinge of yellow. 982. The plants get two meters tall, including the quiote. Their growth depends on how much moisture is available. When the quiote finishes blooming it grows little elongated pods. They are green at first, but turn black when they are mature. Then they open and the seeds scatter. 983. The seeds are black. There are four rows of seeds in the pods. The seeds are sort of flat. They scatter all over the place and root by themselves. After the plant flowers, it doesn't die but goes on growing. The central stalk that flowered dies and falls off the plant, and a new center core grows in its place.

984. Small animals like to live among the bushes because these plants grow in clumps. Small snakes and little spiny lizards like to live there. This is known from digging up junquillos with a pole for transplanting as fences or borders. Junquillos are good for making fences because the plants take root quickly when they are transplanted. 985. Even though the leaves are not very thorny, the plants are very thick and goats think that they can't get past junquillos. You put junquillos in a border fence and when the rains come the plants take root and produce new growth, and the fence gets thicker and thicker. 986. Some people set whole clumps ablaze on New Year's Eve, and so junquillos are disappearing. Junquillos also help hold the soil together and prevent erosion. The flowers are not eaten, and neither is this plant used in medicine.

Cucharilla.[104] 987. Cucharillas like to grow in moist areas. They live in the mountains where it is wet. People go there to find this plant when they need it. They pull out whole plants. They are a little difficult to pull up because they grow on slopes and on cliffs.

988. They are about the same color as huapilla, that is, ashen green, but cucharilla does not have powder on its leaves like huapilla. Its leaves are straight and even, from the base to the top of the plant, and it has a needle point end. This plant has thin leaves. 989. They are only about half a centimeter wide. It has hooked thorns on all sides of its leaves, about like those of the huapilla, except that huapilla thorns are not uniformly spaced, while those of the cucharilla are neatly lined up on both sides of the leaf. They look neatly lined up on the leaves, and each leaf has about 80 thorns. Cucharillas grow to about 50 centimeters and look like junquillos in that they are round. They, too, have a lot of leaves which grow from the base and are about the same length and form a kind of ball. 990. Their roots look like those of the huapilla, too, and the ground turns black wherever there are cucharillas. The two plants probably have something in common. The central core of the cucharilla is slightly bigger than that of the huapilla.

991. The leaves of this plant are much sought after, and when they are needed they must be found and brought in, no matter how far the distance. As always, religion stirs up people's heads and they go get whatever they need for their rituals in order to worship the saints. All over the Mezquital Valley people celebrate fiestas every year. 992. Many fiestas require a great deal of work and much expense. Even so, the people have to celebrate the fiestas with delight, whether they have money or not. When a fiesta approaches, the people gather to discuss who will do what in the community in order to make the fiesta successful. 993. Each person is assigned a task. Some will clean the plaza; others will fix up the altar; and others will dig up tree stumps in which posts called "arches" are set. It is customary to set up these posts where the fiesta procession passes. Some men are commissioned to go to the mountains to find cucharilla with which to make the arches. 994. Those men ask their wives to make them some tlacoyos[105] to take with them. As I said, going out to find cucharilla is difficult, because the plants grow on cliffs and on high slopes, so the men have to leave early. Even so, they return quite late. Each man brings back only about six plants, because the plants weigh a lot.

995. A day before a fiesta the people gather to build the arches.

These constructions are made every year and are called "arches." Cucharilla is used when the statue of the saint or virgin of any fiesta goes out in the procession from the church. It is placed around the arch, and all over the posts, and this is how the images are worshipped. 996. The arches are built of split carrizo that is lashed together. Cucharilla, brought from the mountains, is removed from the plants and placed on the carrizo. The leaves are removed one at a time, each one 20 centimeters long.

997. The head of the cucharilla leaf is all white and shiny. It looks very pretty and that is why the people like it. Even if it rains on the day of the fiesta, it doesn't lose its color or go limp. Paper, on the other hand, gets shredded and colorless if it rains. But cucharilla just gets even shinier. 998. When the arches have been all lashed and built, the posts are set in the ground, and the arch remains above ground. When the entire construction is raised, you can see what beautiful work it is. The cucharilla is all white; even when it dries out and dies it remains all white. 999. People like to keep the plant after the procession is over. People have noticed that beautiful things only last a short time. That is how it is with these arches made of cucharilla. They are beautiful and require a lot of work to build.

The construction is used for one procession to honor a saint. After only a few passes of a procession it ceases to be of use. 1000. It takes a lot of work to build it. Some communities make five or six of them for their fiestas.[106] Ixmiquilpan puts up eight, but in that particular case several small communities in the municipio contribute one arch each. The communities that contribute to the fiesta are San Nicolás, El Nith, El Carmen, El Maye, El Mando, Progreso, El Dextho, Lopez Rayón, and Dios Padre.

1001. In what fiesta do they put up arches, and when does this occur? I will describe this in detail in another book in which I will speak only about religion. Floral wreaths are woven from cucharilla leaves. These are placed on the church door and all over the arches. 1002. Very few people know how to weave these floral designs. First they make the petals, and then they make the center of the flower. When they finish, the piece looks like a flower in bloom. Mestizo men and women who attend the fiesta take the flowers home with them as a memento.

1003. There used to be plenty of this plant around and some people would break open the center of the plant and remove the leaves in order to roof their houses. The technique was the same as that used with palma leaves. Cucharilla lasts many years, that is, they don't rot. The head of the leaf goes under the support and faces in towards the house, while the point of the leaf faces outward. 1004. When it is finished, it looks all white and shiny inside the house. These plants are fast disappearing because people pull them up every year to use them in the fiestas and for roofing, and also because it doesn't rain enough for the plants to grow back quickly. The head of the cucharilla is about as wide as a spoon, about three centimeters. 1005. Goats eat this plant. They just eat the tips, and when cucharilla is eaten by goats it sounds like little explosions.

La flor de la chuparrosa.[107] 1006. This is another plant that resists drought well; it looks a lot like aloe and is about the same color. If one does not look closely, one would think that this plant was aloe, because the shape of the leaves and the color of the plant are similar. The leaves are not the same length, however; those of the flor de chuparrosa are shorter. 1007. The plants grow to only 20 centimeters high, and the leaves are only one and a half meters wide. Its thorns are tiny and soft when they are young, like those of the aloe. When the plant matures and the thorns are fully grown, they widen out at the end of the leaf and form a circle, like a flower in bloom. But it is not flowering, because the cluster is green. 1008. On what I would call the back of the leaf there are little sacs that are probably for seeds. The plant sends up a quiote, with little leaves attached to it. 1009. The total height of the plant reaches one meter. The quiote is ash colored. If you wipe off the white powder on the quiote, it becomes very shiny. The quiote also gets little branches on it. It grows all it can and then gets clusters of grey flowers on it. The flowers are hardly noticeable because they are covered with a calyx.

1010. But little by little the flowers appear. The petals are a very beautiful red, and they open slowly. They bloom for three days and then dry up. As always, hummingbirds know best how sweet the nectar is because they go to this flower all the time. 1011. But who knows if the flowers have nectar? They are not horizontal to the ground like other flowers. They bloom hanging upside down, with their petals facing the ground. When they finish blooming the quiote dies, and what I call the mother plant keeps on growing. 1012. The dead quiote is not dense; if it is broken, one can see that it is soft inside. Its pulp is white and does not fill the inside of the quiote. When the quiote is dry it breaks or tears easily. But if one wants to cut the quiote for the flowers when the quiote is green, then it is very tough.

1013. Because the flowers are so beautiful, people have tried to transplant them in their gardens. The flowers last about a week and then they wither and die. They just do not transplant. Children love these flowers and they gather them just to hold them whenever they can. This plant multiplies well when it grows wild. 1014. It has no use in medicine and so no one bothers it. It is very bitter and animals do not go near it to eat its leaves and flowers. The soil in which this plant grows is not used for fertilizer because the plant does not grow much, and without many leaves it doesn't make fertilizer.

The nopal.[108] 1015. This plant has been a major resource for the people for many years. It does not matter whether it is cold or hot, this plant provides food and economic resources for acquiring anything one needs in the house. For many people, this plant is their only hope and support, so they really take good care of it. They protect it from animals, and keep them from eating it, or breaking off its pads. If this were allowed to happen, the plants wouldn't grow well. 1016. Nopales do not last long if they are nibbled on by animals. The part that is eaten gets scarred and new shoots come out from the pads. Nonetheless, the plants get old quickly if they are gnawed by animals.

1017. When one considers making a nopalera, the first thing is to get the ground in good shape. This includes building a really thick fence of thorns and bramble to keep out goats and cattle. Pigs and turkeys also hurt the plants by breaking off the pads and eating them, because they really like to eat green things. 1018. Another animal that likes to eat these plants is the rat. It does not eat enough to kill a prickly pear cactus, just a little piece, and only from the young pads. Rabbits also gnaw constantly on nopales.

1019. The nopal cultivated most produces a fruit called the "white tuna." They are cultivated most because they bring the highest price when they are available. They are mostly sold in the city. In Mexico City tunas sell very well, and it is always the white tuna that mestizo men and women eat. They like them because white tunas have a delicious taste. Of all the tunas, these are the sweetest.

1020. People in the valley help one another to plant nopales. When planting time approaches, people ask their neighbors to help them out, so that when the neighbor's turn comes he will be able to count on having help, too. In this negotiation, people talk to one another in the following manner. Here are don Enrique and don Felipe. They have run into one another someplace, or one of them has gone to the other's house to visit.

1021. "Good day, don Enrique."

"Good day, brother. Come in and sit in the shade don Felipe. There's a stool over there; sit for a while."

"Yes, I'm relaxing, thanks. How are you folks doing? We haven't seen each other in days, and I haven't visited you in ages. It's because I'm herding some goats these days, and I don't get home until late, so I don't have time for visiting. Forgive me for coming over only when I have a favor to ask."

1022. "Let's not even talk of that! That's how things are. Work is never done, and by the time you notice it, the sun's down and it's late."

"That's just how it is, Enrique. Listen, I've come to ask you a favor."

"Ah, well what is it? But relax first!"

1023. "I was wondering whether you had some time to help me out for a few days. If you like, I can pay you in money. But if you prefer, we can exchange work and help each other out. That would also be fine with me."

"What kind of work is involved? If I have the time, I'll help you out, otherwise I won't. Why should I promise you something I might not be able to do?"

1024. "You know the way of life around here. Everyone has to work in order to make a few pesos. With God's help, I want to put in a nopalera; we'll see if God helps make it turn out well. I've been looking at some of our neighbors; they planted nopales last year and this year the plants are big already. That's why I'm considering fixing up a little piece of land that I have, where I haven't planted anything. What do you say?"

1025. "Well, I'm not sure I can do it, don Felipe. We have some animals that need tending, and no one else to leave them with, so I have to keep them myself. But I'll try, in any case, to see if I can help you out for a few days, so that when I need help you'll give me your support. So don't worry; I'll go speak to my comadre Isabel, and I'll tell her that I want to leave my goats with her. She, too, herds by herself, so when I have time I can return the favor to her."

1026. "Great! That's just what I wanted to hear. So if you find someone to leave your goats with, I'll expect you at my house on Tuesday, day after tomorrow."

1027. "Sure, why not. I'll go speak to my comadre. I'm almost certain that she'll agree. She's a really good person and never turns me down when I ask a favor. I'll be there Tuesday nice and early."

1028. The next day don Enrique goes to his comadre Isabel, to ask if she will herd his animals for a few days—"animals" because the same word is used for herding both goats and sheep in Ñähñu.

1029. "Good morning to you, comadrita!"

1030. "Good morning, compadre! How are you?" This is how the comadre responds, and she comes out of her house to kiss her compadre's hand. Some compadres, of either sex, take the other's hand and make the sign of the cross with it, touching their compadres' knuckles to their own foreheads as they bow in greeting. These people have profound respect for one another, and they are compadres from baptisms. There are various kinds of compadres.

1031. "Pardon me, comadrita, but I've come not just to say hello, but to ask a favor."

"Well, who knows what it is that you wish, compadrito?"

"You couldn't know this, of course, comadrita, but don Felipe came to me yesterday and asked if I could help him with some work for a couple of days. He

The rat does not eat enough to kill a prickly pear

Flora 1018

really needs to plant some nopales, and he wants me to help him out. 1032. What I've come to ask you is whether you could take my animals. As you know, I have no one else to watch them, and I was hoping you would be kind enough to take them for me. Just tell me how much you want me to pay you. Or, if you like, I can take your animals and help you out sometime when you need it."

1033. "Why not, compadrito? I'll take them. There aren't many, so just bring them around and put them together with my flock, and I'll herd them for you out in the monte."

1034. "Thank you very much, comadrita. It's settled, then. Tomorrow I'll bring my goats around very early. Thanks for your hospitality. We'll be seeing each other."

1035. "Fine, compadrito. I haven't offered you anything except a rest."

So they take leave of one another and Enrique is happy because he found someone to look after his animals for him. For this reason he will go to work happy and without worry. 1036. The following Tuesday he goes to his comadre's house. He takes his animals there and returns to don Felipe's house to help with the work, as they had arranged. 1037. He goes with don Felipe to the parcel of land where Felipe was thinking of putting in a nopal patch. They start by tearing out the biggest trees, because these obstruct the sun from getting to the plants. If the plants are shaded they don't grow well. These plants like to be in an open space, with nothing blocking them.

1038. The two men clear rubble for two days or more, depending on the size of the plot. When they finish clearing the land they make holes in which to put the plants. The plants are in the middle of larger depressions which fill with water when it rains. 1039. When all the basic work is done, they make sure that the holes and the fencing around the area are all alright before actually planting. Nopales do not require deep planting, but are put close to the surface. If you plant them too deep, they don't produce new growth and rot. You select a day when the moon is right when planting nopales. 1040. The pads that are planted are cut off another plant and left to dry out. If you plant a pad right after it is cut, it will also just rot.[109] The pads are cut and spread in the sun for three months to dry out well. Then, when they are planted, not many are lost. Some will be lost, but this will be from bugs which were not noticed on the plants.

1041. When someone begins planting, they make the sign of the cross and ask God to help make their work turn out well. The plants are set on the day of the full moon. Other people around here plant on the new moon. 1042. Each person has their own belief that they keep. People who plant on the full moon claim that the plant will bear tunas quickly. They say that if you plant on the new moon, then the plant won't bear fruit fast, but will just grow new pads. 1043. From what I have heard, prickly pears that are planted on the full moon bear a lot of fruit three years later. People who plant on the new moon say that the plants grow faster, and that the plants do not get old quickly. They claim that if you plant on the full moon, the plants will become old quickly.

1044. Before planting one must observe which way the rays of the sun fall on the plot of ground. If the rays fall vertically, then the plant is placed straight in its hole. In other words, one edge of the pad faces east while the other faces west; and one of the flat sides faces north, while the other faces south. 1045. They are planted like this so that if it does not rain right away the full force of the sun will not hit the pads. If the sun shines full-force on a new nopal plant before it takes root then it will die. With the intense heat of the sun, and even more because of the heat of the dry earth, the plant shrivels up and dies. 1046. That is why the new pads are planted as I've described. This protects them for a while, and when the rains come they take root. Then the plants can withstand the sun on their own.

1047. Most of the prickly pears are "tuna blanca" or white fruit. Probably 19 out of 20 are tuna blanca. Why is it also called "rock tuna"? Because it is so hard. The word for this fruit in Ñähñu is "dookjä" and is formed from two words, "do," or rock, and "kähä" or "tuna." Together the word means a tuna that is as hard as a rock. 1048. If one tries to squeeze it before it is ripe, one can feel how hard it is. They are harder than the other kinds of tunas. There are two kinds of fruit of the tuna blanca. They are of different shape and color. 1049. Some give white tunas, and others give yellow ones. We will begin by discussing the one that is planted the most.

1050. First one purchases the plants that are to be set in the ground. They are bought in lots of a hundred, and each plant should have two or three pads on it. If there are four pads, then the plant is thought to be too big; when it is transplanted it will break. 1051. Each plant, already cut back, costs three pesos. All you do is bring them to where they will be transplanted. The ones bought and sold have sprouted out of other plants the year before. Those are the best ones to plant. Larger ones are generally not transplanted.

1052. The tuna blanca grows to various heights. A lot depends on the quality of the soil. Where the soil is rich, they grow well and grow a lot of ears. On the other hand, where the soil is poor, they don't grow very tall. 1053. Some grow three and a half meters high. There are not many such plants because the stems break easily. Also, the new, young pads are cut off regularly for transplanting. The tuna blanca is pale green in color. Its pads are covered with a white powder. 1054. The powder is like grease, and when it rains the water just slides off the pads and they don't get wet. The roots of the plants are fairly thick, and grow out about three meters from the plant.

1055. The main root has many little roots coming off it. At the ends of the smaller roots there are yet more roots that form clumps. From a distance they look sticky, but they aren't; they are simply tiny roots that look like little balls of wool. People say that nopal pads are "hot" because if you plant a nopal near another plant the nopal doesn't let the other plant grow but makes it die. 1056. Some people alternate nopales and magueys in the fields. Sometimes deep, mounded furrows are made, and rows of prickly pear are alternated with rows of maguey. Nopal grows faster than maguey. 1057. The nopal overshadows the maguey, and the maguey shrivels up, or it just grows the center trunk without leaves. People who see this learn that their efforts are useless, and they don't plant nopal and maguey together again.

1058. Nopal roots light easily in a fire, but they make a lot of smoke. When the roots are green they break easily, like glass. Roots from the tuna blanca contain white pulp and an oozing fluid. 1059. The roots are tougher when they are dry than when they are green. When they are planted, as I said, they contain two or three pads, and when they get new growth they have five or six little nopal pads. When these grow, they get bigger and change shape. 1060. The next year they grow new buds again, with little pads and fruits, and thus the whole plant gets taller. The first pad planted in the ground doesn't remain flat, nor does the one following it when it grows. They get longer and rounder, and get really thick, like a tree branch. 1061. Who knows how they lose their flat shape, but the pads become completely globular. Though they get thick and round, they don't lose their thorns. Years go by and the other pads get rounder and thicker. This happens so the plant can hold up under the weight of the pads growing above the bottom ones.

1062. When they are dry, these plants do just fine. If a big wind comes along and rocks them, they stand firm. But when it rains, the pads absorb the moisture and get juicy and heavy. When they weigh a lot, a slight wind can break them off. Even the trunk of the plant can sometimes be broken under these circumstances. 1063. It takes another three or four years to grow another plant to bear fruit when this happens. Even though the pulp of the plant is woody, when they absorb a lot of moisture they get soft and brittle, and if the moisture doesn't break them, then the bugs that attack them will.

1064. The bugs are a kind of white larvae, with brown heads. They have little feet. These larvae eat the pulp of the nopal. How can one know that a prickly pear has bugs? It is clear. You can just remove the waste and excrement of the bug from the holes they make to tell that they are in there. 1065. They weaken the plant from within, and the plants break. This kind of bug is found only in the trunks of prickly pear plants, and never in the pads.

1066. The pads of the tuna blanca have thorns all over them. Even the little pads and the tunas that grow from the main pads have thorns. The thorns on the new fruits have a kind of cover over them. It seems that this is to protect the thorns. The sheath only covers part of the thorn, not all of it. The cover is like a very tender thorn in itself, and it is grows together with the real thorn. 1067. The little thorn cover ends in a point which does not prick, but just bends on contact. As the little pads and fruits grow, the little thorn covers fall off. First they get yellow, and then they fall, and the main thorn is left exposed on the tender ear of the plant. 1068. It seems that the first thorn protects the main thorn from the sun and the wind until it grows. When the real thorns first come out they are tender and soft, and if they did not have this protection, perhaps they would die.[110]

1069. All over the pad there are groups of two, three or four white thorns that are very sharp. When they prick, these thorns are painful. At the base of these thorns there are other smaller ones in bunches. Each bunch has about 300 thorns. 1070. When you see them on the pad it is hard to tell that they are thorns, but if you pass your hand across them you know they are. The bases of the thorns are all lined up in rows across the pad. 1071. They are not randomly distributed on the pad although it seems that the younger pads have more thorns. When the pads get big, each clump of thorns is spaced farther apart. 1072. The thorns of the tuna blanca are hard, but they are also brittle. When they stick in someone's hand, they break off and hurt a lot. When other thorns stick in your flesh, they disintegrate and come out little by little. But the nopal thorn doesn't disintegrate.

1073. Nopales bear a lot of fruit one year and then the next year they grow a lot of pads. In the years when they have a lot of green growth there is great demand for the fruit because it is scarce, and the dealers ask a lot for it. 1074. People gather around when they see someone carrying a case of tunas, and the seller gives it to the merchant who offers the most money. In years when the plants produce a lot, the fruit is not worth much because so many people bring it to market. 1075. The first cuttings of fruit are well paid for, but by the time half the fruit is in, during bumper years, the price drops. This phenomenon of years with heavy fruit production and years without is not limited to just one area. It occurs everywhere that prickly pears are planted.[111]

1076. Both the young tender pads and the fruits are eaten. The first pads eaten come out in March and April, and by June there are no more. Nopal pads are cooked in different ways for eating. 1077. In one recipe the pad is cut and cleaned of all its thorns. Then it is sliced finely for cooking. First a pot of water is put on the fire to boil. When the water boils, tequesquite is thrown in. 1078. When that is dissolved the cold nopal is added to boil with the tequesquite. In ten minutes it is all cooked and the pot is taken from the fire and the water drained. 1079. The tequesquite is added to prevent a problem which nopal causes. Anyone who eats nopal gets a stomach ache, and so tequesquite is added to stop this. When the plant is cooked it can be prepared for eating. 1080. Onion, salt, chile, garlic, oregano, avocado, tomato, and rosemary are added and mixed together well. Then it is ready to eat. It is eaten with hot tortillas, straight from the comal.

1081. The other way to prepare nopal is to boil it and add the condiments I mentioned, but then to fry it in lard. First the onions are fried up well, and then the nopal is added. 1082. When the pads are all fried, then the other ingredients can be added. Still another way to prepare nopal is to fry pork and then add nopal pads and the other ingredients mentioned. In this recipe some water may be added to form a broth in which to dunk one's tortilla. 1083. Other times nopal is roasted, together with meat in an oven. In this case the pad is cut into strips and placed on top of the meat. This is delicious because the vegetable takes on the taste of the meat. In fact, all the ways of preparing nopal which I have mentioned are delicious.

1084. Prickly pear cactus pads are eaten by a lot of people in the Federal District, and I have seen them sold in the big markets there. The mestizos who live in the big cities like to eat tunas. Sometimes the vegetable is mixed with crushed chicharrón to give it more flavor.[112] The yellow nopal pads are the ones that are eaten the most, followed by those of the white nopal.[113] 1085. Another one called the "doxhmo xätä," or "nopal without thorns," is also eaten.[114] The reason that other nopal pads are not cut for eating is because they contain a *lot* of thorns, and they prick the hands of people who cut them. 1086. All the varieties of nopal pads are good tasting, but some of them just have too many thorns that stick people.

Nopal pads are also eaten in beans. The pads are sliced and thrown in with the beans when they are being cooked. The beans have already been cooked and are not raw when the nopal is put in. The nopal is just for flavor. 1087. When nopal pads are cooked with beans the preparation is slimy. There is nothing bad about this, but it is definitely slimy. When nopal is cooked separately, however, and *then* added to beans, the meal is not slimy because all the gooey liquid from the nopal pads gets drained off first. 1088. Until just recently people would harvest prickly pear pads, slice them up, and put them aside in the sun to dry. Then, when they did not have any fresh pads they would boil the dried pads and eat them.

1089. In earlier days, during civil wars, people hid wherever they could. They hid all over the place, in the mountains, and in caves. In those days, there was a lot of hunger because there was no corn available. First of all, there was no way to work or to protect one's life and the lives of one's children. 1090. Wherever soldiers went they went into people's houses and stole any nixtamal there was. Many people who suffered through those times are still alive, and they themselves tell of what they went through. 1091. In order to survive they had to eat many different kinds of wild plants. One of those plants is the nopal. Sometimes they ate it boiled, other times roasted. In the latter case they did not add any other ingredients, but just ate it plain. 1092. When it was roasted the nopal pad was simply stripped of its thorns and cooked on coals. Roast nopal is tasty, but you really have to put condiments on it; however, the plain pad tastes fine.

1093. Another way the nopal is prepared is called "mhät'i," or "parboiled." In this recipe the pad is sliced up and the pieces are put in a pot or urn. The vessel is covered and placed on the fire with all the added ingredients. All this is cooked in the nopal juice. That is, it is steamed, and this is called "parboiled." 1094. People who survived the war also cooked it like this, and when there were no more young pads on the plants they cut the bigger, older ones, removed the leathery covering and ate the pulpy inside. The process was called "mboxt'ä" or "stripping," because the entire covering on the pad was removed. 1095. When the covering was off, the network of nerves was removed, and thus the meat of the pad was removed, piece by piece. This method is very time consuming. 1096. But like it or not, the poor people had to bear the suffering brought on by the Revolution in those days. It was started in 1910 by a man named Francisco Madero.

1097. This is how it is described in the books that have been written. I did not see all this personally. But why would I make up things? Also, people who were children in those times remember them and tell about them today. Even though they are very old, the stories are well told, with detail. 1098. These same old people tell how people did not light their hearths, so that they would not make smoke whenever soldiers were around. They didn't want to let the soldiers know their whereabouts, because the soldiers would come and round up the men and impress them into the army. 1099. So people often could not light fires, and in order to eat nopal they had to eat it raw—tender, young pad, or a tough old one, they just had to eat it raw. Even more terrible was that there was no salt to put on it, because there was no place to buy it. There were no shops in the mountains where the people hid. 1100. Today there are still many people

around who survived that war. Those who were the actual revolutionaries went
to war and were carried to the cemeteries.

1101. The most tender pads are eaten, that is, the ones that came out a year
ago. The pads that budded two years ago are already too tough. The heavy
covering is removed from old, heavy pads and the pulp is thrown together with
beans—or they are boiled separately to get the slimy juice out first. 1102. Also,
nopal pads can be cooked, as I've mentioned, along with other ingredients for
flavor. The big old pads have hard thorns. To remove them, one must use something harder, like a rock. The thorns can be cleaned off quickly with a rough or
porous rock. 1103. The baby fruits are also cooked for consumption. They are
cut from the plants and their thorns are cleaned off first. Small tunas have the
most thorns. The fruits are cut while they are still in bud, and those that are
flowering are not. 1104. These are not like other plants that go bitter when they
flower. It's just better to let the fruits that have flowered grow into mature tunas.
The little budding fruits are cut into pieces. Sometimes they are boiled first, or
they are fried directly. 1105. They are boiled to get rid of the slimy juice they
have. They are served as a vegetable with beans, and they give a good flavor to
the beans.

1106. When the pad finishes producing buds the little tunas flower. They
flower every morning. Many insects gather their pollen. The flower of the tuna
blanca is very pretty. At the base of the flower there are many little thorns. From
this will come the fruit later on. 1107. These thorns hurt a little if you touch
them. But the flowers, by contrast, look beautiful and don't hurt to look at. The
flowers are wide and scalloped around the base, that is, the part that will become
a tuna. They have about 20 petals in a scalloped array. 1108. The flowers of the
tuna blanca are light yellow, and they look beautiful. There is a pistil in the
middle of the flower, and there are stamens all around it. The ends of the
stamens look like a little flower, but this is yellow pollen, if one looks carefully.
1109. The pistil is thicker and has a bright green bulb on the end. The green ball
is joined with other pieces, and when the flower opens these all open, too.

1110. When the nopal flowers just begin to open, bees go to them for the
honey and they gather up the pollen on their feet. They take the honey back to
their hive to make the comb where they store honey. 1111. And so, every day
they go back and forth from the prickly pear groves. Hives have honey in them
during the season when nopales and other flowers are in bloom. But after the
flowering season passes, there is no honey. Then the bees begin to suffer and
they consume what they had gathered. 1112. As with bees, other insects that
live from the honey of flowers also suffer when there isn't any.

1113. When the flower withers and falls it leaves a small depression at the top of the still unripe fruit. There are many thorns around the depression. The base of the flower, which was around the top of the tuna, falls off and leaves what looks like a tiny glass. 1114. The base of the flower comes to an oval shaped end. The petals don't come off, but remain stuck to the base. Finally, as the fruit matures, the hollow that was there disappears and the top becomes flat and smooth, with no thorns. 1115. After three months the fruits are mature and ripe. They ripen in June, July and August. That is when there are a lot of them.

1116. When the tuna blanca starts to ripen, the people who have cultivated them cut them off to bring to market. The custom is to pack them in boxes to sell them. They can not be just thrown into a box, either; they must be carefully arranged. 1117. If the fruits are not carefully packed the merchants will not buy them. A box holds about 100 tunas, but it depends on the size of the fruit. Some years it rains when the fruits first appear and flower. Then they grow big from all the moisture. 1118. But in years when there is no rain, they do not grow big and they are said to "grow by the sun." The white tuna sells the most because it is delicious and sweet. It is also the hardiest for transporting over distances. 1119. This class of tuna is more green than white. It has many seeds; they are round and dark colored and have a hard outer cover. The actual seed inside the cover is soft and white.

1120. This is the juiciest of all the tunas and it has a very special flavor. The white tunas that come from arid lands are the best tasting and the sweetest; large or small, they taste alike. 1121. The tunas from irrigated lands are slightly larger and therefore juicier; but they don't have much taste. Before buying them, merchants ask where the tunas comes from. 1122. Or they taste the fruits themselves to find out if they are sweet and have good flavor. If so, they buy them, otherwise they don't. If they do buy tunas from the irrigated lands, they pay less; they pay whatever they decide.[115] The prickly pear plants in the irrigated lands grow bigger and have thicker, juicier pads. 1123. These plants get to be about four meters high. Their little pads are also juicier. More people prefer to eat tunas from arid lands, however.

1124. This class of nopal is used as cattle feed. The big pads are singed in order to get rid of the thorns, and the pads are cut up and fed to cattle. The singeing is not done to cook the pads but just to burn off the thorns so they won't hurt the animals' mouths. After the thorns are burned off, the pads are allowed to cool and then they are cut into pieces so cattle can eat them. 1125. Sometimes goats are also given singed nopal pads to eat. For both goats and cattle, the pads are left to cool off, because if they are served hot the animals get gas. If the animals are not attended they can die of gas, and this is a big loss to the owner.

1126. Lack of water results in the plants not growing, and in the animals not having food to eat. People always like to have animals, which they hope will grow and multiply. Then the people can sell the animals to bring in a little money. 1127. When it doesn't rain there is no hay or other grasses for animals to eat. When they really have nothing else to eat, they can at least be fed singed nopal pads. Once in the morning, and again in the afternoon, they are fed singed pads. 1128. Under these conditions the animals are hungry and barely survive. They get skinny and weak, almost to the point of falling down at times. The bones of their hindquarters and spines show, as well as their ribs. 1129. Their bones are covered by practically nothing but skin. The nopal is the life saver of these animals when there is nothing else to feed them.[116]

1130. White tuna plants can grow from seeds. Birds eat the tunas, fly to other places, and defecate the seeds they have eaten. These seeds get covered with earth and when there is moisture they germinate. They grow slowly, and when the plants are big they produce fruit. 1131. This only happens, however, when cattle do not find the little plants and eat them. Birds eat tunas; they make holes in the fruit so they can poke their beaks in. The birds that do this are sparrows, mocking birds, larks, and huitlacoches. 1132. The sparrows and huitlacoches cause the most damage because they bore into the best and largest tunas, and they do not even eat them all. They just make a hole in one fruit and go on to another. Each large ear on a nopal has about 10 to 15 tunas. 1133. Sometimes birds will make holes in all of them. After birds bore holes in tunas, the fruits cannot be sold and, as a last resort, the tunas are fed to the pigs. In years when there is an overabundance of tunas, they are also fed to pigs in order not to let things go to waste. 1134. Pigs like to eat the fruits; the animals froth at the mouth, perhaps because the tunas are so delicious.

1135. A white tuna plant grows for about 15 to 20 years, and then gets old.[117] At that time the plants have to be removed to make room for new ones. One reason the plants get old is that frosts burn their pads, or animals shove them and disrupt them. Then the pads start to rot and die.

1136. Another kind of tuna blanca is called the "hard, yellow tuna."[118] This nopal has denser, more tightly packed thorns on its pads, relative to the tuna blanca, and also on its fruits. It has many, many very small thorns, and even so, many people grab the fruits with their bare hands to clip them from the plant. These people don't need anything to protect themselves. 1137. They just grab the fruit carefully, with the tips of their fingers, and cut the fruit away with a knife. Some people just cut the tunas; others cut them and peel them right away, without cleaning them, to eat them. The pads of the yellow prickly pear are not eaten much, because they have a lot of thorns. 1138. When the tunas are ripe they are yellow. In shape and taste they are identical to the white tunas, and that is why they are called "hard, yellow tuna." There is yet another one called "hard, red tuna."[119] The pads of this plant are dark green. The fruits are the same size as the white tuna. 1139. The hardness of the fruits and the juice they contain are the same.

1140. The custom is to plant more white tunas than any other, because the merchants like to buy them. When one brings yellow and red tunas to market, they bring a lower price, and so they are not cultivated much. The fruits of the few yellow and red tuna plants cultivated are consumed by the family. 1141. When women bring these tunas to market they sell them little by little to people in the plaza. The women find a place to sit in the market, and they put out their tunas in one-peso groups. A bunch of five or six fruits costs a peso. 1142. Sometimes the women have to sit in the sun, and if there is no shade, then they have to suffer with the heat. They have to sell their tunas before they can go back home. They put the tunas they wish to sell on an ayate. 1143. To sell their fruit, they offer people a sample to taste, and then, when people taste one, they feel obligated to buy. The women offer a tuna so the person trying one will buy at least one of the clusters she has there. 1144. When the buyer gathers up the fruit in the cluster, the seller throws in an extra one, or the "pelón." This is the custom with many things that are sold; people are offered a taste, and then given an extra piece with the purchase. If buyers get this kind of treatment, they feel good about buying another batch.

1145. Sometimes tunas are sold by people who walk around in the plaza. They do this to evade the permit sellers who collect money for the right to sell in the plaza. The collectors charge a lot and harass people who just walk around trying to sell a few things. The tax collectors wind up taking all the money of someone who has only a little to sell to begin with. 1146. This is because the collectors make the small seller pay the same fee as those who sell a lot of merchandise. Sometimes the collectors take half the money someone has made. For example, if someone takes in 20 pesos, the collectors take 10. 1147. Who knows why they do this, whether these are orders they are carrying out from the local government authorities, or if they do it on their own? Like it or not, the small sellers give up their money. 1148. Otherwise, the collectors threaten to take them to jail, or they threaten to go and get the police to put the people in jail.

1149. There are some years when there are really a lot of tunas. When people see this they know what's going to happen. The rains come, with big winds; hail falls and hits the tunas. The tunas get hard and are then no good to eat. 1150. The skin gets all cracked and the merchants won't buy them. When there is no rain while the fruits are flowering, the tunas grow well. But when it rains, then the tunas crack. Sometimes they crack on the sides, sometimes on top. 1151. No one in the market wants to buy them when they get this way. Nor does the family that owns the plants eat the fruit, because when the tunas crack open, the thorns go into the spaces. Anyone who eats them gets their mouth stung. Because of all these bad natural events, the people go on living in poverty and can not escape it.

1152. The next-best-selling prickly pear after the white tuna is the yellow one.[120] This nopal has thicker, wider, and juicier pads. The thorns on the pads are a little longer than those on the white tuna. 1153. But they are spaced further apart; the white tuna has a lot of thorns bristling all over the pad. At the base of the biggest thorns there is a black lump made of very small thorns. If one wants to remove them, a lot of thorns come off. 1154. The flower of the yellow tuna is orange, and beautiful, too. It grows and blooms exactly like the flower of the white tuna. The fruit takes the same time to ripen as that of the white tuna. When the yellow tunas ripen they turn yellow. 1155. The fruits are sweet, and their delicate pulp has a different taste from that of the white tuna. The pulp of the yellow prickly pear is softer and less juicy. Their seeds are also a bit bigger than those of the white prickly pear. If the yellow one grows fully it gets to be bigger than the white tuna. 1156. The yellow tuna is more oval shaped, and larger. The yellow tuna is sometimes preferred for eating because it is less harmful; white tunas sometimes cause cramps for people who eat them. 1157. When there are plenty of yellow tunas they are harvested, cleaned, and packed in wooden fruit boxes for bringing to market. The merchants pay very little for this fruit. They don't want to pay well, and they use the pretext that there is little demand for yellow tunas. Or they say that they don't want to buy the fruit because it bruises easily. 1158. And indeed, these fruits do bruise easily when they are really ripe. When they are still packed in boxes the juice remains in the fruit. But when you peel the fruit the juice runs all over you.

1159. There is another class of tuna called "red yellow." The form of the plant is exactly like that which produces the true yellow tuna. Only the color of the fruit is different. It is red, while the shape and size is the same as that of the yellow tuna. Both kinds of tuna, the red and the yellow alike, are pecked at by birds. The red variety is only rarely brought to market. There are not many of these fruits around. Very few people cultivate them; but wherever they are, they look beautiful, with their completely red tunas.

1160. Another plant found in the prickly pear orchards is the one that produces purple tunas. It is planted in the same way as the other prickly pears which I described earlier. 1161. It has rather greyish pads, more white than green in color. All the pads are covered with an ashen powder, and it is this powder that covers the green and makes it white. The young pads are not very long, but rather oval-shaped and have almost no thorns. 1162. Goats really like to eat these young pads precisely because there are no thorns to stick in their mouths. It is rare to find any large thorns on these pads. 1163. But there are lots of small ones. The pads of the purple prickly pear are eaten because they taste as good as the ones I mentioned earlier. As I said before, and I say again, animals do not avoid these plants; they eat the pads because there are no thorns. 1164. Animals eat these pads as if they were eating sugar, chomping noisily on them because the pads have no thorns.

1165. These plants flower around the same time as the other nopales. The little fruits bud on the pads and they are the same color as the pads, that is, ashen. The flowers are yellow. This plant does not get many tunas. Those that it does bear are large and round; they are not elongated like the others. 1166. When the tuna is ripe it is purple. It starts to turn purple at the top, and slowly turns color all the way to its base. Sometimes it does not turn completely, and remains purple on top. 1167. The rest of the fruit remains green. Even so, if one picks the tuna and peels it, one can see that the pulp is completely ripe, and the color inside is totally purple, a deep purple.

1168. This type of prickly pear has a lot of pulp, but not much juice. One might say that it was dry, but it is delicious nonetheless. It has a lasting, staining color, and you can tell that someone has been eating this fruit because their teeth are all purple, and they have purple all around their mouth. 1169. If there are even four tunas on a pad, and if the pad is rather dry, then the weight of the tunas will break the pad off the plant. The fruits that grow fully are so big that two of them are too large to fit in one's hand. It is rare to see a purple prickly pear plant, because most people do not have them. 1170. Even though the plants look like they are fine, some people just don't like the color. No one cultivates this plant commercially. They are only raised to produce fruit for family consumption. These tunas, too, split open when there is lots of rain. And because they are sweet, insects gather around them. 1171. Although these plants are not useful for making money, still, they provide food for the people.

1172. There is another variety of this same plant, called the "wild purple prickly pear," because it is found growing wild all over the countryside. It has the same characteristics as the domesticated variety, and is delicious to eat, so I will discuss it here. When the fruits are ripe they are the same color as the domestic variety. 1173. However, the difference is that the wild kind are smaller. Another difference is in the thorns. The wild purple tuna has large spines on it, and the pads bristle with many thorns that are very long. The thorns which the domestic variety lacks are all on the wild variety of this plant. It has more than it needs. 1174. When animals go up to eat the wild variety, they decide against the idea and are afraid of this plant. Until only recently, people would pick the wild fruits to eat. No one plants the wild purple tuna in a nopalera. The people who eat these tunas are shepherds who are out in open country, and other people who have no prickly pear plots of their own. 1175. If they want to eat a tuna they pick one of these. The wild purple nopal grows out in the monte, and the fruits which are not picked by people are eaten by birds. Birds have beaks which are not affected by thorns. 1176. Wild nopal plants do not grow very tall, but rather spread out along the ground in all directions, and the new pads take root in the earth.[121] As with all nopal plants, they do not grow from seeds, but from the rooting of their pads. The pads need to be laid out in the sun to dry out before planting them.

1177. Next I will discuss another nopal which is a bit different from the others. It is perhaps the most abundant variety in the open country, and is found among the brambles in the desert. This variety has a beautiful name, "uts'miini," which means "spiny," formed from two words in Ñähñu: "uts'i" which means "has many," and "mini" which means "thorns." 1178. Together, the two parts mean that the plant has many thorns.[122] And this is surely true; this plant has thorns all over its pads. It is probably the most thorny of all the prickly pear plants. The fruits, as well as the pads, have many thorns. The thorns are long on the pads and small on the prickly pears. 1179. Both of them are equally noxious to anyone who is pricked in any part of the body. Each kind of nopal produces a tuna different from the rest. The spiny nopal bears a fruit with a special flavor, but with a lot of thorns on it. This variety of tuna never loses the depression on its top where the flower blooms. 1180. The depression remains hollow, and when it rains, the hollow fills with water if the tuna happens to be pointing straight up to the sky. There are two varieties of spiny tunas that ripen at different times. One variety ripens in July and August. 1181. In other words, it matures at the same time as the white and yellow prickly pears. Because they ripen at this time, almost no one eats these tunas. People prefer the fruits that have fewer thorns. And so the thorny tunas just rot on the plants, and fall.

1182. The other variety ripens in October and November, and there are still some in December and January. They are mostly found in steep mountainous areas, that is, where no one will bother them. The people who live in those areas pick the fruit, pack it in boxes, and sell it from house to house in the city, and village to village. They sell the fruit for a peso or even two pesos, and they do well because there are no other tunas during this time of year. 1183. These plants grow the biggest of all the prickly pears because they are never pruned back, but just grow wild. The pads have a lot of thorns, and are eaten when there are no other nopal pads available from white and yellow nopales. The same people who pick the tunas also collect the pads to sell. They bring in the fruit from far away, walking half a day to reach the places where they sell it.

1184. Because the plants are so big, a long pole is used to pick the ripe fruit and the tender pads from the top. It might be a quiote from a lechuguilla or a sisal plant. A hooked point of some kind is attached to the end of the pole, and this hook is used to cut the fruit. 1185. The fruit is not allowed to drop to the ground, however. Rather the point is stuck into the top of the fruit and brought down. If the tuna falls and hits the rocks on the ground, the fruit breaks apart and is useless for packing. 1186. It is a great sacrifice for the people who collect these tunas and bring them in from so far away. But this is like their "harvest"; like it or not, that is what they have, and so they must do it. Also, the other prickly pears do not adapt well to the mountains, and will not grow there. 1187. So the people of the mountains have only the thorny nopal for eating and for selling. These nopal plants in the mountains bear a small tuna. The pulp is very soft. It is like one were eating a very ripe peach.

1188. There is another variety of spiny nopal which is the same as the one above. It is distinguished by its tuna, which is larger.[123] This tuna is really juicy, and it sprays when you open it up to eat it. It is sweet and red in color, and is eaten with pleasure. 1189. All spiny prickly pears bear tunas in clumps. Each pad bears around 20, in two lines along the edges of the pad. These tunas can easily be distinguished from far away because they are red. 1189. There is another one still, called "dark tuna," and it, too, is one of the spiny nopales. It is called "dark tuna" because the pulp is practically black when the fruit is mature. Its color is also a kind of red, but it has been given its name in order to be able to tell one variety from the other. 1190. Spiny prickly pears are among the nopal plants that live the longest. There are some plants that I have seen for many years, and they are still alive. It is as though time did not pass for them. Maybe they live so long because no one bothers them, while almost all the other prickly pears are pruned back each year. 1191. When spiny nopal plants die and dry up they leave a woody network. This network is what holds up the plant and bears all the weight of the pulpy pads above. The woody nerve system, or network, is found in layers, inside the main branches of the plants. 1192. There are about ten layers in each trunk, and the wood is fairly hard and brittle. It burns easily if it is used as firewood. Even though it is hard, it is porous, and looks like a kind of net, with holes all through it. It is used as kindling to light harder, denser wood. When the pads of this cactus die they exude a thick, foul smelling liquid. 1193. Inside the rotting pad there are many white larvae. And though the pulp may rot away, the woody skeleton remains and dries out little by little.

1194. There is another variety of nopal that is cultivated and cared for so that animals will not eat them. These plants have to be protected against goats, sheep, and cattle, because the plants themselves have no thorns. Sometimes they may have a few, but this is rare. The thorns that they do get are on the edges of the pads. That is where the little thorns are found. 1195. This class of nopal is known in Ñähñu as "bald prickly pear."[124] Many people like to have this variety in their nopal orchards. They like to have at least one because these plants do not have large thorns. They have lots of little tiny thorns, but no large ones. 1196. Whenever someone sees this variety of nopal, they ask the owner to give them a pad, or sell them one. If the plant has many pads, then the owner gives one, but otherwise not. Instead, the owner promises to give one the following year, and asks the person to come by at that time for the gift.

1197. This kind of nopal bears fruit very quickly. When it barely has two or three main pads, it starts budding little pads with tunas. The little pads have small and large thorns on them at first, but as they grow the large thorns drop off, and the little thorns remain. 1198. The pads are long and oval-shaped, and the young pads are picked for eating. They take less work to clean the thorns from them. The pads are eaten roasted. They are also boiled and then fried. The pads reach 40 centimeters in length. The plants grow tall, reaching three meters in height. 1199. Some years they get a lot of tunas and the pads become heavy and break off. The fruits reach up to 10 centimeters in length; they are yellow and have small thorns. The tunas have a lot of juice. They have a distinctive flavor and taste different from the ordinary yellow tunas. These tunas are also not taken to market for sale.

1200. In order to tell one plant from another, like the many nopales, for example, the people give them each a different name, in such a way that the name will not be forgotten quickly. This is what happened in the case of another prickly pear called "Saint John's nopal." It is called this because its fruit ripens at about the time of the fiesta of San Juan. This fiesta is celebrated every year on June 24th. 1201. That is when the long, thin tunas of this plant are ripe. They are among the first tunas of the season to ripen. They are yellow in color, and have a special flavor. 1202. The form of the plant is rather distinct. It looks most like the white prickly pear plant, but the resemblance is slight. Its thorns are long, and so are its pads which reach 40 centimeters in length. The plants grow to two or two and a half meters tall.

1203. The other good thing about the nopal is its use in medicine. The juice of the pad, when boiled in water, is used in curing. In prior times, children would get sick if they ate something that was too hard, and they would get constipated. Then their mothers would boil nopal pads. 1204. When the pads were cooked, the mothers drained the water and let it cool down. Then they gave it to the sick child. The mothers used to say that this cured children quickly. The juice from cooked nopal pads is very thick and slimy, and as it circulates through a child's stomach it surely makes whatever was stuck inside pass through.

1205. With this plant the third book comes to an end. The book has treated some of the plants that grow in the desert valley. Many of these plants flower and die, and disappear. 1206. What does not disappear is our gratitude to, and respect for, all those who have helped us, and who have been kind enough to provide the facilities that made it possible to write this book. Although the plant with which this book ends has little thorns, there are no thorns in our heart. There is only happiness, and respect for all people. 1207. We offer our respect and our sincere hand to everyone, any place we find ourselves in this small world.

Notes to Volume III—Flora

1. This is in reference especially to the lechuguilla plant from which fiber is extracted. The process and the products made from the fiber are explained later in the book. During the last two decades, many Ñähñu have extracted and sold lechuguilla fiber in order to send their children to primary and secondary school. A substantial number have gone on to become grade school and secondary school teachers. It is difficult to get accurate figures. My guess is that, of the 23,000 indigenous teachers in the national teacher corps, about a thousand are Ñähñu (see Introduction). A few dozen Ñähñu have received university degrees in medicine, law, and engineering. Not surprisingly, education is seen by many people as the best way out of poverty. This entails sacrifice by one generation for another, both in supplying children with money to go to school and in postponing the income that children could bring to households were they not in school. The single most important source of income for the Ñähñu in the past has been the sale of lechuguilla (and, to a lesser extent, maguey) fiber, known as "ixtle."

2. Throughout these volumes Salinas distinguishes between the valley people and the mountain people. As is evident from the text, there are abrupt differences in the physical environment between the valley and the mountain areas of the Mezquital, and these differences account for many differences in custom. Here, however, Salinas notes that the mountain people practice traditional medicine more than the valley, or desert people do. This difference in custom is due to the difference in acculturation of the two groups to the national culture. Over the last 30 years, there have been vast infrastructural changes in

the valley, brought about by massive government development programs. The principal agency for this development has been the Patrimonio Indígena del Valle del Mezquital. The agency has been quite justly criticized by Mexican anthropologists and by the native people of the valley for spending a lot of money and for some scandalous behavior toward the Indians over the years. However, there can be little denying that the roads, schools, clinics, electricity lines, irrigation canals, and potable water lines built by the PIVM have had a major, cumulative impact on the lives of the valley people. The mountain people are a more sparse population, and have been largely left out of the development schemes. Consequently, they are today much more traditional than the desert people in such things as the practice of traditional medicine. They are also much poorer than valley people, and are much further from clinics, hospitals and doctors, factors that force them to rely on traditional medicine more than the valley people do.

3. The glandular mesquite predominates in the Mezquital Valley. The mesquites constitute a genus in the family *Leguminosae*, which includes the kidneywoods (*Eysenhardtia*), mescalbeans (*Sophora*), Jerusalem thorns (*Parkinsonia aculeata*, and leadtrees (*Leucaena*), all of which resemble the mesquite, but which are generally found in Mexico at lower elevations than the Mezquital. The mesquites (and several other legumes) are characterized by spiny branches and featherlike leaves. They produce delicate, yellow or cream colored flowers, and podlike fruits that are very sweet. The glandular mesquites (*Prosopis glandulosa*) grow both as shrubs and as trees, up to about 15 meters in height, although most specimens are much shorter, averaging perhaps three to four meters in the lower, more arid parts of the valley. The narrow fruit pods, from 10 to 25 centimeters long, are used principally as fodder.

4. If a mesquite tree is growing on the side of a barranca, some of the roots may come right through the walls, and one may see how deep the roots of this tree penetrate.

5. This volume was written in 1979-1980. At the time, the peso was trading at between 30 and 50 to the dollar. In August 1985 the peso was trading at around 350 to the dollar. In January 1989, it was 2,400 to the dollar. All prices are left as in the original.

6. These are some of the expressions used in greeting. The Ñähñu word "nju" is used for "older sister" and as a general greeting. "Nxumfo̱" is a general term for "lady." "Nänä" is a term of respect, usually reserved for older women. A man would address a woman as "nänä," "nju," or "nxumfo̱," in order of politeness. Women use "nänä" to address other women when they wish to express respect and admiration.

7. Throughout, Salinas speaks about "the town" or "the city." When "town" is not named, it refers to Ixmiquilpan, the "cabecera" or county seat of the municipio of the same name. Ixmiquilpan is 12 kilometers from Orizabita, the village where Salinas grew up. It is understood, then, that people in Orizabita carried wood 12 kilometers to sell in Ixmiquilpan. Wood is carried on the back, supported by a tumpline across the forehead, as are most loads carried by Ñähñu in the Mezquital.

8. There are parts of the road that serve as resting areas. These are usually places where small rock walls, about a meter high, have been built, or where the road cuts deeply into the land, leaving a meter-high natural wall. A person can rest by standing with his or her back to the wall, placing the bottom of the load on top of the wall. This relieves the pressure on the tumpline.

9. The plaza is the center of town (Ixmiquilpan), where the government is located, and where, in the past, markets were held every Monday. In the late 1960s, the plaza in Ixmiquilpan was paved over with native red stone, and an exact copy of the famous Diana statue in Mexico City was installed. A separate market area was built, with protection from rain and sun. The word for plaza in Ñähñu, "ntaai," derives from the verb "tai," "to buy." Nowadays, the word refers either to the central plaza or to the separate market area, depending on context.

10. This was the price of tortillas (60 for a dollar) as recently as 1976, three years before Salinas began this book.

11. Lechuguilla is a general name in the Mezquital for several varieties of agave, from which fiber is extracted, including the *Agave lechuguilla, A. difformis* and *A. lophantha*. It is treated in depth later in this volume.

12. The term "maguey" is a catch-all for a wide variety of agaves from which fiber is extracted, and which provide aguamiel and pulque. The maguey and the lechuguilla are both members of the genus *Agave* and of the subgenus *Littaea* (see Gentry, 1982). Aguamiel and pulque are discussed in the fuller treatment of the maguey plant, below.

13. The Mezquital ranges from about 1,500 meters to 3,000 meters above sea level. At the lower reaches of the central part of the valley (around Ixmiquilpan) around 1,800 meters, there is little rainfall (400 milimeters a year) and predominately desert flora. At the intermediate elevations (around Orizabita), around 1,900 meters, there is still only about 500 milimeters of rainfall a year. But at the higher elevations (in communities such as Gundó), around 2,400 meters, there is much more rain—over 800 milimeters a year, on average. The climate and vegetation change markedly, and so do many of the subsistence habits of the Ñähñu.

14. The nopal, or prickly pear, comprises many varieties of the genus *Opuntia*, which are treated at length at the end of this volume (see Notes 108ff). The garambullo is the common name in Mexico for an entire genus of cacti, the *Myrtillocactus*, which are often called *Cereus*. The *M. geometrizans* is a huge, treelike variety that grows in great abundance in the lower parts of the Mezquital. It bears a small, red fruit which is edible. Cravioto (1951: 150) notes that the garambullo fruit provides 12 grams of protein per 100 grams of fruit, and it is rich in several essential vitamins, as well. Like many large cacti, when it dies it leaves a woody skeleton that is used for fuel, but one that is quite porous and burns up quickly.

15. Neither the jacaranda nor the casuarina are native to Mexico, and are only planted as ornamentals. The casuarina is native to Australia, while the jacaranda is native to Brazil.

16. The verb used in the Ñähñu for "swinging the axe" here is "di n'ontho." This is an onomatopoeia for the sound made by the chopping of an axe against wood. Thus, "he begins to 'thwack.'"

17. Don Antonio asks "did *they* give you a drink," referring to either his wife or to his foreman, if he has a large enough operation. It is customary to supply pulque at regular intervals for field hands. Typically, day laborers were paid in wages plus three to five liters of pulque. Recently, the custom of supplying pulque has come under negotiation as workers ask for higher wages, but pulque is still delivered to field hands and is drunk at regular intervals instead of water. Martín del Campo (1938: 12) in his study of pulque remarked that it was much preferable to contaminated water. In fact, the definitive study of the food value of pulque remains to be done. Pulque is today at the center of a bitter struggle between Protestant evangelists and Catholics in the Mezquital. The Protestants have taken the position that pulque is a scourge that robs people of energy and money and provides no nourishment in return; on the other side, of course, is the argument that it is an essential part of the traditional, balanced diet from time immemorial. A great deal more research is needed on both the dietary and social functions of pulque. (See also Martínez, 1936, for an early study of the value of various Mexican plants, and Cravioto et al., 1951, for the most careful study to date on the nutritional content of various Mexican foodstuffs.)

18. "Cargo" is the Mexican word for obligations to provide food, or fireworks, or other material support for a particular fiesta. The "mayordomo" is the person in charge of an entire fiesta. His cargo is greatest but he may distribute it among several others, according to their means. The cargo system is discussed in detail in Volume IV.

19. Although the person referred to here as Julio is mayordomo for the mass, it is understood that he was selected by the mayordomo of the village church. The church mayordomos are elected for a year's term, while a mayordomo for a single fiesta has only the one cargo to fulfill. He must pay the priest for the mass (60 pesos in 1979 in Orizabita), and he must buy the flowers, candles and firecrackers needed for the celebration. He must also invite his friends in for a first-class meal, with meat and beer. Salinas discusses this in Volume IV.

20. Of course the worker has been drinking, while the patrón has not. Usually, serious business, such as the promise to help a person fulfill a cargo, is not done in the afternoon, but is done from 5-11 A.M. After that, any person might be slightly tipsy on pulque. Hence the need to affirm that neither is drunk and that the promise is binding.

21. The fact that don Julio will be crossing hills is understood in the use of the Ñähñu verb "tonts'gani." If he were going to cross a barranca or a road on the way home, he would have used the verb "'rangani."

22. When men speak to each other, they may use the word "juädä," or "elder brother" as a term of respect. When women speak to men, as in the present conversation, they use the term "idä" (again, "brother") as the equivalent term of respect. Note also here that women and men alike serve each other pulque as the ordinary gesture of hospitality.

23. Here the difference is in the use of the word "tata" or "zo." Both terms are used by men or women to address any male younger than they, but the latter term is used only by old persons. The character z represents the sound of "z" in "azure." It is rare in Ñähñu, but appears also in "nzolo," one of the edible larvae.

24. Mondays are market days in the Ixmiquilpan region of the Mezquital.

25. This appears to be the *Quercus rugosa*. There are not many oaks in the Mezquital; they are generally found in the oak-juniper complex above 2000 meters.

26. "Ayates" (from Nahuatl *ayatl*) are carrying cloths made from ixtle. The word "ixtle" itself is from Nahuatl (*ixtli*), meaning fiber. Ixtle is extracted from a variety of agaves, and comes in several levels of quality. The word "xidinthäähi" means "crude rope," or "hairy rope." When crude ixtle fiber is twisted into rope, it has many rough "hairs" which stick out and do not gather neatly into the rope.

27. "Barbacóa" is not "barbecue" in the sense that Americans usually use the term. Barbacóa is made differently in various parts of Mexico, but in the Mezquital it is made in a pit filled with stones that are heated by building a fire over them. The hot stones are covered with maguey leaves, the meat is laid on

the leaves, and the whole thing is covered with more maguey leaves. Salinas gives a recipe in Volume I.

28. The man uses the word "njuu" in calling the woman "sister" and the woman calls the man idää, or "brother." In Volume IV, Salinas notes that the Protestants in the valley call each other "brother" and "sister" and are therefore called "yä zi ku," or "hermanitos" in Spanish. "Zi" is a diminutive in Ñähñu, so the Protestants are called "little brothers and sisters."

29. "Petu" comes from "pet'i" or "flat." These clay pitchers are rarely sold in the market now, though they were very popular until just a few years ago for keeping small quantities of liquid rather cool. They are made of porous clay, and they "sweat," thus cooling the contents.

30. Both men and women scrape magueys, but women are more often seen at this task since men more often work at day labor or in their milpas. When the heart of the maguey plant is removed, the sweet aguamiel, from which pulque is fermented flows into the bowllike cavity that is left. The aguamiel has to be removed daily, and the bowl must be scraped out in order to induce the continual flow of juice. The "base" referred to in the next sentence is the heavily fermented, sour starter liquid which is used to get fermentation going quickly in the aguamiel.

31. For a discussion of the diversity of the Ñähñu diet, see McCarty (1985).

32. "Tomates" in Mexico are the small green or red fruit of the *Physalis coztomatl*. They are used in making salsa de chile. "Jitomates" are the familiar *Lycopersicum esculentum* (both round and pear-shaped) consumed in the United States.

33. There are many varieties of beans in Mexico, several of which are native. The bean referred to here is the native *Phasoleus vulgaris* ssp., perhaps *P. multiflorus*, which is purple or speckled in color.

34. Since Mondays are market days in Ixmiquilpan, a discussion of a week's activities, such as meals, begins on Tuesday.

35. Salsa is one of the ubiquitous components of meals in Mexico. It consists basically of chiles and tomatoes, ground together in a molcajete. Spices are added, but this varies from region to region.

36. These are thick tortillas, rather than the usual thin ones. The thick ones are called either "lolo" or "pijhme," while the normal tortillas are called "xihme." The word "xini" means "thin" and "pidi" means "thick and flat" and can be used in reference equally to a table top or a fat tortilla. The word "ndää" also means thick, but refers to round things like trees, rope, logs, etc. The word "lolo" refers to thick tortillas that are smaller in diameter than "pijhme." "Lolo" is also used by women when talking to children about food, and refers specifi-

cally to a small, thick tortilla, which children are said to enjoy, that is made with cumin and salt.

37. By contrast, "mole" would be considered a "wet," or liquid food that would have to be carried in a container.

38. Seventy centavos, at the then current value of the peso (8 cents, USC) a liter of pulque was about 5.5 cents USC. The value of the peso when this volume was written in 1979 was approximately 4.8 cents USC, so three pesos per liter was nearly 15 cents in 1979. In July 1985 the peso was trading at .3 cents USC (330 to the dollar), and pulque cost 50 pesos per liter, or 15 cents. By January 1989, the peso was valued at .0004 cents and pulque cost 500 pesos a liter, or 20 cents USC.

39. Eggs cooked on a comal may be sunnyside up or beaten, but are cooked without any grease. A few ashes from the kitchen fire may be sprinkled on the comal to keep the eggs from sticking.

40. This refers to the familiar poor, middle class, and rich socioeconomic levels. The middle class among the Ñähñu are thought to be those who have secure government jobs, such as teachers and other functionaries. Teachers in the national Federal teaching corps were earning around 60,000 pesos a month in July 1985, or $180, after all deductions. Federal employees also are entitled to a variety of benefits, including medical care. The rich comprises people with large agricultural landholdings; professionals such as doctors and lawyers; and successful shopkeepers. The poor comprise all the landless rural folk, along with all those whose land is not irrigated, and all the ordinary day laborers and lechuguilla cutters, etc.

41. Only some of the village communities elect judges. These are official postions in the Mexican jurisprudence and governmental system. The many rural villages are grouped geographically; each village falls under the jurisdiction of a large village. The judge in that village acts on behalf of all the communities in the jurisdiction. More is said about this in Volume IV.

42. "Faenas" are community work projects, in which all able-bodied men (and often women) are expected to participate. Roads are cleared by faena labor; schools are built; water tanks are erected; clinics and basketball courts are built; and electric poles are raised by faena labor. Typically, a delegation from a village will petition local authorities for a grant of materials and will promise to provide the labor for a community development project. Faenas, like corvée labor, were originally exacted by hacienda lords from the peasants. Today, faena labor is common throughout Mexico on a voluntary basis as part of community development.

43. The judges are auxiliary to the central municipal justice system, and are expected to take care of small matters at the village level. They are also expected to bring more serious matters (major violence or large-scale property destruction) to the authorities in Ixmiquilpan.

44. Each church has one or more patron saints or holy virgins. These are either statues or icons (cloth, wood, or paper). They are called "santitos" collectively, in Spanish, and "images" or "icons" in English. This complex is treated extensively in Volume IV.

45. While maize is planted each year, the harvest depends on rain. There are years when virtually no rain falls in certain places, and only the stalks grow, but no ears are produced for lack of moisture. This is no longer a major problem in parts of the Mezquital which have been irrigated over the last 20 years. However, the irrigation canals, which rely on gravity to bring the sewage water from Mexico City, do not reach the higher elevation pueblos, such as Orizabita and those higher up, because they are above the altitude of Mexico City. The cost of pumping irrigation water in sufficient quantity to grow crops at those higher elevations is prohibitive, especially considering that the population is extremely sparse (perhaps ten per square kilometer) and that much of the land is not flat enough to permit mechanized agriculture. These pueblos at the higher elevations continue to wager the success of their agricultural efforts on erratic rainfall. Above the 2,200 meters mark, however, the picture changes, as noted earlier, and there is sufficient rainfall to make irrigation unnecessary. In Orizabita, however, where Salinas lives, there are many years in which only zacate (corn stalks without the corn) is harvested.

46. When the maguey plant matures, it sends up an enormous stalk of rather hard wood. The huge stalk is called the "quiote" (from Nahuatl "quiotl"). If the heart of the maguey is cut out at the time the quiote is formed, then the sucrose-rich aguamiel which would have fed the growing quiote can be collected to make pulque.

47. The phrase "mäkä 'matha," or "blessed valley" is used ironically by some cynics to refer to the generally inhospitable environment, erratic and sparse rainfall, and desert flora and fauna.

48. These are two species of *Tillandsia*. One is *usneoides*, known both as "grey beard" and "Spanish moss"; it grows on the mesquites and on several large cacti; the other is *recurvada*, known as "ball moss," which grows on electric wires, as well as on various trees.

49. I am not certain of this classification. Salinas glosses this plant as "granjeno" in Spanish, which may be Christ's crowns in English. See above, Note 14,

for garambullos. The pirul is the American pepper tree, *Schinus molle*. It is native to South America and grows to about 15 meters.

50. The "ocotillo" is the *Fouquieria splendens*. There are several species of hard and soft pines in the Mezquital, and the Ñähñu word "tuudi" used here is generic. It includes the Chihuahua pine (*Pinus leiophylla*) and the Mexican pinyon (*Pinus cembroides*). The genus *Acacia* is one of the largest of the legume family. Many are bushes. The acacia tree referred to here appears to be a variety of the sweet acacia (*Acacia farnesiana* Willd.), which grows throughout Mexico and reaches a height of 10 meters.

51. The use of the verb "me'te" here, to wash, is for objects which are soft and delicate. Also, it is understood that the object has been soaked first. For hard objects which have the capacity to hold things (i.e., they are hollow or deep) then the verb "ua'ti" is used. For hard, flat objects, like a table, the verb "xuki" is used. Ua'ti is used only when the object has been soaked first and is about to be washed well. Xut'i is used for hollow objects or containers only if they are not soaked first. Ua'ti can also be used without the object being soaked if it isn't really dirty. Rinsing out a cup of coffee in order to put more coffee in it is ua'ti. However, though it refers to a container, the verb ua'ti can not be used to rinse out a cement pond because a pond can not be moved or sloshed around.

52. Here Salinas uses "Xuutha" because he refers to the entire back; the top part, or shoulders is "si'ntsi." The spinal column is "'roonzu."

53. The pulquero says "help me" because he can't pour the pulque out by himself and hold the cup at the same time. The invited person holds the cup or maguey leaf. It is understood that a maguey frond is cut from a convenient plant if the pulquero is not carrying a cup or gourd. The frond has to be dying and limp in order to bend it from the ends into a cup shape. If it is a healthy frond it will snap, and anyway, it isn't considered good to cut healthy leaves just for drinking pulque.

54. There are several plants known as "siempreviva" in Mexico, including the selaginaceous terrestrial mosses, the crassulaceous succulents (such as the *Cotyledon coccinea*), and several parasites, including *Aizoon canariense*, which may be the plant referred to here.

55. These are earthen mounds, called "bordos" in Spanish. They act like short dams that run in rows through, and sometimes around the perimerter of a milpa, or field. Bordos prevent fast run-off, and give the desert rain a chance to break the hard, dry crust on the soil and to soak in, thus preventing erosion.

56. The Ñähñu word used here is "huaxi," meaning "guaje" in Spanish. It is a large, double calabasa gourd, the *Leucanea esculenta*.

57. These squashes are very hard. They are round and green in color, mottled with white, and about 30 centimeters in diameter. They can keep for a year after harvesting, if left in shade. They can be cooked only in extremely hot fires with large coals. They don't cook up in fires of small wood.

58. The "do'thi," or "old mesquite," is one of the varieties of the tree recognized by the Ñähñu. I have not been able to determine the subspecific classification of this tree. From my observations, however, it is possible that distinctions among kinds of mesquites made by Ñähñu are not distinctions made by botanists. This difference in classification is especially evident for the maguey and the prickly pear cacti described later in this volume.

59. This appears to be one of the shrub varieties of the *Prosopis glandulosa*. It may also be *P. juliflora*.

60. These appear to be members of the genus *Plumeria*, orchidlike flowers that come in several varieties. They have four petals in the form of a cross and are called "flor de la cruz" in Spanish.

61. The maguey, or century plant, is the most important plant in the Ñähñu economy. It contributes to food, clothing and shelter, in the form of pulque, ixtle and roof thatching. There are many varieties of this plant, all of the genus *Agave*, which also includes the lechuguillas. I have not been able to determine the taxonomic classification for all the magueys recognized by the Ñähñu, but the main ones (those used for ixtle and pulque) are identified in notes as they are mentioned in the text. A great deal has been written about the role of the maguey in Ñähñu life, and a great deal of work remains to be done on this topic. Important recent work by Parsons and Parsons (1985) approaches the issue from the perspective of ethnoarcheology. The definitive botanical work on the maguey and agaves in general is by Gentry (1982).

62. The maguey cultivated commercially on these farms is the *Agave salmiana*. It is also the maguey most preferred by the Ñähñu for its aguamiel and is known in Spanish as the "maguey de pulque" throughout central Mexico. Gentry (1982: 607-608) guesses that about 75% of the pulque produced in the states of Michoacán, Guanajuato, Querétero, San Luis Potosí, Hidalgo, Tlaxcala, Puebla and Morelos (the 20,000 square kilometer pulque producing area in Mexico) comes from this one species. The other major producer of aguamiel for pulque is the *A. mapisaga*.

63. This appears to be the *A. mapisaga*.

64. The higher elevations get more rain than the lower reaches of the valley, but the land at the top of the valley is very steep. Excellent examples of terracing, reflecting centuries of labor, may be seen around Santuario above Cardonal, and around Defay, just below the pass to La Lagunita.

65. Several varieties of maguey are planted as fencing, or as windbreaks, or for control of erosion. These include the *A. americana*, which is especially good for windbreaks against erosion, and *A. aplanata*.

66. "Good maguey" refers generally to any variety that produces large quantities of aguamiel for pulque. In this instance, Salinas refers to a variety of the *A. salmiana* mentioned above.

67. The "green maguey" ("maguey verde" in Spanish) is a variety of *A. americana*. The "long leaf" maguey ("penca larga") is the *A. mapisaga*. The "white maguey" ("maguey blanco") appears to be the *A. aplanata*, and is not exploited for aguamiel in the making of pulque. It also has characteristics similar to the *A. atrovirens* var. *mirabilis*, and to the *A. americana*. However, since both of the latter (and especially the *A. americana*) are exploited for their aguamiel, and since the *atrovirens* are generally found further south, I think the maguey blanco is more likely a variety of *A. aplanata*. The "i'ta" (for which I have found no common name in either English or Spanish) is the *A. macroculmis*, a short, light grey or green variety that only grows at the highest elevations of the valley, above 2,000 meters. The "manso" is a variety of *A. salmiana*. I am not positive about the taxonomic classification of the other magueys mentioned here. The "sarabanda" appears to be a very large variety of *A. aplanata*, but I am not certain. The "black maguey" ("maguey oscuro") has dark green leaves and red flowers. It does not appear to be the *A. obscura* identified by Gentry (1982: 164). It is an excellent producer of aguamiel. I have also seen what I believe are variants of *A. kerchovei*, with its characteristic widely spaced, shark's tooth thorns along the leaves, and the *A. Weberi* which has no teeth along the leaves.

68. This refers to the area dug out around the base of cultivated magueys, at the bottom of the bordos on which they are planted. This technique of planting the magueys atop bordos and channeling out around each plant gathers and holds moisture and conserves the topsoil as well.

69. Xite is the leftover, rough fiber that remains after ixtle is removed from the maguey or the lechuguilla. Xite contains a foaming agent and is used as a cleanser.

70. These lizards, the "madga" and the "tsa'thi," are glossed as "largatijo" and "lagarto" in Spanish by Salinas. In southern Mexico (Yucatán, Campeche, Chiapas), the lagarto is an alligator. There are at least three genera of *Iguanidae* in the Mezquital, including *Sceloporous* (the spiny lizards), *Phrynosoma* (the horned lizards), *Cnemidophorus* (the racerunners or whiptails), and possibly *Gerrhonotos* (the so-called alligator lizards of the *Anguidae* family). The two animals mentioned here are *S. grammicus* and *C. sackii*. I have not seen skinks or geckos in the Mezquital.

71. Chinicuiles are maguey grubs. They are various moth and beetle larvae that feed on the maguey and at the roots of various agaves. According to Crawford (1981: 174), very little is known about certain subsurface invertebrates of the desert, including the *Scarabaeidae* and the *Monomidae*. These are the beetle larvae known to feed at the roots of the maguey and the lechuguilla agaves. The particular chinicuil described here in the text is a moth larva that bores into the maguey leaf. The beetle larvae that feed on the maguey roots are a delicacy and are served fried to discerning patrons in some of Mexico City's best restaurants. It is clear from this passage and from the treatment in Volume II that the various subsurface larvae and other insects of the Mezquital were an important source of protein in the past for the Ñähñu. The best work on the white grubs of the *Scarabidae* family is by Richter (1966).

72. Chiles de arbol are tall plants, about 40 centimeters high, with many branches. Chiles rayados are large, black, dried chiles. They have long cracks, or stripes from drying, hence their name. They are also smoke dried; hence the variant name "chipotle," from Nahuatl "chilli" and "poctle," meaning "smoke." Virtually all chile peppers in Mexico are *Capsicum annun* spp., but the variety is seemingly infinite. The Spanish names given here are used locally in the Mezquital and elsewhere in central Mexico.

73. These are skin eruptions that break and scab over. They are called "roña," which normally means "mange," in Spanish, although the disease is not the same as that contracted by dogs and sheep, according to local physicians.

74. The best work on the role of pulque in preconquest central Mexico is by Goncalves de Lima (1956). Other evidence (obsidian scrapers) indicates that pulque goes back far longer in the Mezquital than the Ñähñu. Pulque is a vital source of liquid in the desert, and it is an important source of nutrients, containing .44 grams of protein per 100 grams of pulque, along with substantial amounts of vitamin C and B-1, as well as calcium, phosphorous, and iron (Cravioto et al., 1951). Pulque is part of all social activity among adults, men and women alike. It is difficult to emphasize sufficiently the importance of pulque in Ñähñu life.

75. These leaves belong to whoever picks them up. Men and women both cut open magueys, but men do most of the cutting while women collect the leaves that are produced.

76. Maguey leaves are much bigger than lechuguilla leaves and require a physically demanding procedure for extracting the fiber. The leaf is draped over a board that is set between posts or trees, or over a wooden horse, about waist high. The fiber extractor (usually a man, except in the case mentioned here in the text) wears a protective apron (which may consist of another maguey leaf)

and holds the leaf against the board with his body. He leans over the board and scrapes downward, using a tool consisting of a piece of wood with a 10 centimeter-wide piece of iron embedded in it. The leaves are dried and pounded before the extraction begins. A full description of the process is given in Parsons and Parsons (1985), and see below.

77. In fact, as a result of hunting, coyotes and foxes are now extremely rare in the Mezquital, though occasional sightings are reported. I have heard recently from some Ñähñu that foxes may be making a comeback, but I have not been able to substantiate this. Some shepherds, particularly men, still carry whips with them and use them for recreation while herding.

78. This is primarily composed of creosote bushes (*Laria divaricata*), mesquite bushes, ocotillo branches, and cardón blanco (*Opuntia tunicata*).

79. Abejorros are the males, while jicotes are the females of the carpenter bees. The woodpecker referred to here is a local variant of the ladder-backed woodpecker, the *Dendrocopos scalaris*.

80. Xoconostle is a bitter prickly pear, *O. imbricata*.

81. This is a variety of the *A. angustifolia*.

82. This appears to be a local variety of *A. salmiana*.

83. The procedure is known to students of Mexican folk medicine as "caldear" or "heating."

84. The traditional Ñähñu sombrero is made of a single length of yucca thatch material, pieced together and "turned," like a piece of pottery, towards the top. The "palma," or yucca industry is discussed below.

85. The traditional Ñähñu embroidery designs have made local blouses popular tourist items in the Mezquital. These blouses were selling for around 1,400 pesos (about $4.25) during the summer of 1985 in the Ixmiquilpan market. Women in the villages were getting around 800-900 pesos. Despite the low cost, however, external markets have not been established. The Patrimonio Indígena del Valle del Mezquital, the agency responsible since 1950 for economic development of the Mezquital, has built small embroidery factories and has trained young women in the craft.

They have used government program money to purchase the blouses from local women, and have not had to turn a profit from the merchandise acquired. They have taken any merchandise offered in order to subsidize local families, to encourage the development of the industry, and to help develop what several PIVM administrators refer to as a "work ethic" among the Indians.

The problem is exactly the reverse: by buying every stitch of clothing produced, the PIVM has not encouraged the development of stable, high quality goods. They have kept the price artificially low as well, and have not been forced to seek markets beyond the Mezquital. The so-called work ethic—the desire to work, the capacity to put in very long hours, the cultural trait of punctuality—is far more evident among the Indian population than among many of the government functionaries in the Mezquital. One result of the government programs to develop cottage industries of embroidery among the Ñähñu has been mutual dependency between the Indian women in the small factories and the administrators of the government programs. Whether there are long-term economic benefits for the Indian women remains to be seen.

86. There are several varieties of *Agave* that are known collectively as "lechuguilla" in the Mezquital, and which are exploited for fiber by most rural families. Gentry (1982: 156-157) indicates that it is *A. lechuguilla* that is exploited most for its fiber, but I believe that *A. difformis* and *A. funkiana*, both called "lechuguilla" in the Mezquital, are also widely exploited.

The potential for industrial exploitation of *A. lechuguilla* has long been recognized. Martínez (1936: 261) calculated that lechuguilla stands reached a density of 30,000 plants per hectare, and that there was an average of 21,000 plants per hectare. He further calculated that there were about 86,000 hectares of lechuguilla growing close enough to seaports to use for commercial exploitation (reported in Gentry, 1982: 157). Considering the large hennequen and sisal fiber industries of northern Mexico and Yucatan (also based on agaves), commercial exploitation of the lechuguilla (and the *A. difformis*) would seem appropriate for economic development in the Mezquital region. However, the steep, rocky land on which lechuguilla grows well in the Mezquital is not suited to plowing by draft animals, much less by tractor.

Given the abundance of wild lechuguilla, then, it is cheaper to exploit it where it is than to try to domesticate it and grow it on plantations. Furthermore, although the best lechuguilla lands are indeed, close to seaports, the problem is getting the raw fiber to factories for processing into rope and sacks. At a rough guess, a factory in Ixmiquilpan, for example, would have to develop and sustain a network of more than a thousand stable, individual peasant producers to produce sufficient quantities of fiber and fiber products to be commercially competitive with the sisal and hennequen industries in Mexico, and with the other sisal industries of the Third World. Thus, although lechuguilla and maguey plants are a vast resource, it is unlikely that they will be exploited on a commercial level for their fiber in the Mezquital. Given the current demand for high-grade paper, however, it might pay to produce this product from lechuguilla and maguey fiber.

87. This is a characteristic of *A. difformis* in the Mezquital, but there are so many local varieties of lechuguilla in the area that I cannot say for certain which subspecies Salinas refers to here.

88. These are characteristic of the *A. funkiana*, one of the most exploited varieties for its fiber. However, it is possible that this may be simply a local variety of *A. lechuguilla* or even of *A. lophantha*.

89. I am not sure which plant this is. There appear to be stands of *A. xylocantha* in the area, which conform to the description given here by Salinas.

90. These are the *A. funkiana* mentioned earlier.

91. The extractor has an edge over which the leaf is pulled. The point of the extractor is stabilized by jamming it into a tree.

92. Metates and molcajetes are among the indispensable kitchen utensils of rural Mexico. They are quite ancient, and are known in one form or another from the earliest sedentary peoples of the Western Hemisphere. Metates in Mexico today are rectangular stone grinding platforms, usually made from volcanic rock. They are slightly curved on the top surface, and rough (hence the preference for volcanic rock) for grinding maize. They always have three feet, two on one end, one on the other, and angle slightly downwards, away from the woman who kneels before it while grinding corn. She uses a long, thin crushing stone, shaped like a rolling pin, made from the same coarse material. "Metate" comes from the Nahuatl word for this object; the rolling pin is called the "mano" in most of Mexico today, although, according to Santamaría, in some areas it is still called by its Nahuatl name "metlapil" or "child of the metate."

The word "molcajete" also comes from Nahuatl—"molli," meaning "salsa," and "caxitl," meaning "casserole." It is a smaller, bowl-shaped grinding device, also traditionally made from volcanic rock, and supported by three short feet in a tripod arrangement. Grinding is done with another stone, called a "tejolote," from Nahuatl "tetl" meaning "stone" and "xolotl" meaning "doll." Molcajetes are used for grinding up spices and chiles, for making salsa, and for serving salsa at the table. In some parts of rural Mexico I have been served salsa in ceramic molcajetes in restaurants. Molcajetes and metates are very difficult to make because the entire unit, including the working surface and the feet, must be cut from a single block of material. Ceramic molcajetes are therefore very popular because they are inexpensive and can be rather larger than the usual molcajete.

93. This does not appear to be the type plant, *A. sisalana*, but is probably a closely related agave in the *Sisalanae* group. The *A. weberi* has the characteris-

tic grayish appearance and also produces a very fine ixtle, but generally does not have teeth along the edges of the leaves, as does the plant referred to here by Salinas. The *A. sisalana* has unarmed leaves, but is found mostly below the Isthmus of Tehuantepec and in Baja California, where it is raised commercially on plantations for fiber production. A variant of the plant, *A. sisalan* var. *armata*, does have well-developed, triangular teeth like those reported by Salinas for this plant, and this may be the agave called "sisal" in the Mezquital. This variant occurs sporadically in widely scattered locales through the world (Gentry, 1981: 628).

94. The familiar aloe is a lilliaceous plant belonging to the genus *Aloe*. The aloes are part of the same order as the agaves, and look very much like a kind of agave. There are several varieties of aloe in the Mezquital, but I have been unable to identify them at the species level. The juice of the aloe is used as an unguent for skin burns (it is used in patent medicine treatments for sunburn, for example).

95. The word "ts'ojä'i," which translates literally as "bad person," refers to pregnant women and to men who have just had sexual relations.

96. There are several species of plants grouped as "mahi" in Ñähñu. The Spanish gloss for this word is "palma," but the English word "palm" is not adequate as a translation, because the "palmas" in the Mezquital are not members of the palm family. The two plants called "palma" in the Mezquital are both members of the family *Liliaceae*, either genus *Beaucarnea*, or genus *Yucca*. The yuccas include the famous Joshua tree (*Y. brevifolia*). There are some huge examples of heavily branched yuccas in the Tolantongo area of the Mezquital that look much like Joshua trees, but most of the palmas are smaller, single trunk yuccas (*Yucca elata*, e.g.), or branching trees of the genus *Beaucarnea* which grow up to five meters in the lower, more arid reaches of the valley.

97. Here Salinas is referring to the *Beaucarnea*.

98. The description offered here fits the *Beaucarnea* rather than the *Yucca*. Yucca leaves are rather stiff and do not rustle in the wind (Dr. Earl Smith, personal communication).

99. Here Salinas refers to the *Yucca* variety of palma.

100. The leaves for shredding come from the *Beaucarnea*.

101. The fruits are from the *Yucca* variety of palma.

102. The huapilla (also spelled guapilla) appears to be either *A. stricta* or a member of the genus *Hechtia*, which also grows in large clumps in the desert, and has the characteristic four-sided leaves that Salinas describes. It looks a lot like the junquillo, treated below, but the latter are either members of the *Filiferae* group of agaves, or are the *A. striata*.

103. I have glossed this with its Spanish name, "junquillo," because this plant is not a jonquil. The jonquils are members of the genus *Narcissus*, while the "tha'mni," or "junquillo" in Mezquital Spanish are agaves, either *A. filifera* or *A. striata*.

104. The cucharilla is in the genus *Dasylirion*, perhaps the *serratofolium* species.

105. Tlacoyos are a kind of tortilla, only about eight centimeters across, prepared with salt in the nixtamal. The tortillas have washed beans in the center. The beans are prepared with chile, cumin, etc. The tlacoyo is a whole meal in itself, and one need not carry anything else, except something to drink.

106. Once again, Salinas is writing in the "ethnographic present." The construction of these arches is dealt with at length in Volume IV, in the section on "Traditional Religion"—that is, prior to around 1950, by Salinas's definition. Thus, although he says here that Orizabita builds eight arches, he is speaking of a custom that is no longer practiced.

107. The name "flor de chuparrosa" applies to several plants in Mexico, most commonly to the *Loeselia mexicana* of the family *Polemoniaceae*, according to the *Diccionario de Mejicanismos*. However, the plant referred to here is probably a member of the genus *Echeveria*, a widely distributed plant in Mexico known in English as the hen and chicken plant (Dr. Earl Smith, personal communication).

108. "Nopal" is the Spanish gloss for the generic English name "prickly pear cactus." It is part of the huge genus of *Opuntia*. The nopales produce a series of articulated pads, or joints, usually (but not always) covered with thorns. The pads bear fruit, called "prickly pears" in English and "tunas" in Spanish. I have adopted the Spanish term here. One variety of tuna, the so-called white tuna whose skin and fruit are a very pale green, is grown commercially, and produces a good crop every other year. These are the *O. ficus-indica*, which are native to Mexico.

The plant breeder, Luther Burbank, domesticated a spineless variety of this species early in this century and tried to introduce it commercially in California, but without much success (see Benson, 1982: 514). In Mexico, the tuna blanca continues to be a prized fruit in season. Most Ñähñu families have several of these plants in their house gardens, and many families devote a substantial part of their milpas to growing white tunas because they require no water beyond the meager rains in the valley. Nopal patches are called "nopaleras" in Spanish.

There are three varieties of *O. ficus-indica* which produce white, yellow, and red tunas. Several other species are also described by Salinas, but I have not been able to determine their taxonomic classification with certainty. They are possibly related to the *O. phaeacantha*, which produce commercial-grade fruit in the north of Mexico.

Besides the fruit, nopal pads are eaten as a vegetable. It is common to find nopal on the menu in restaurants in the Mezquital, for example, and the pads are sold in the market.

The genus *Opuntia* also contains a variety of other common cacti in the Mezquital, including the various chollas and cardones dealt with in Volumes I and II.

109. As with maguey plants, the pads are left to desiccate. Desert plants have a great capacity to do without water; if they are stressed by water starving first, then they send out roots more quickly (Dr. Earl Smith, personal communication).

110. Salinas is describing the true leaves of the cactus (as opposed to the fleshy pads, which are not leaves). The leaves grow at every spot on the pad where a thorn cluster will erupt. When the leaves fall off, the thorns emerge (Dr. Earl Smith, personal communication).

111. When I first learned of this some years ago, I inquired at the market. I thought that there must be a random distribution of plants that bore fruit or grew pads in any given year, thus evening out the fruit production from year to year. The distribution is anything but random and the years alternate between bumper crops and scarcity.

112. Chicharrón is fried pork rind.

113. These two plants are the same species, but produce light green ("white") and yellow tunas.

114. This appears to be a variety of the *O. rufida*, but it may be a "reverse migrant" of the Burbank hybrid of *O. ficus-indica* (see Note 108 above).

115. At first I thought that this might be a bit of "desert chauvinism" at work, but it is true that tunas from the irrigated part of the valley are less flavorful and consequently of less value than those from the arid lands. As with fruit trees, more than enough water dilutes the taste of the fruit (Dr. Earl Smith, personal communication).

116. Luther Burbank also tried to develop *Opuntia* as commercial cattle fodder, but ran into a serious controversy with scientists at the U.S. Department of Agriculture, and the project never took hold. Prickly pear cactus pads were used in Texas as range fodder before 1920, however, and blowtorches were used to burn off the thorns (see Benson, 1982: 223-229).

117. When these plants are allowed to grow to full maturity they branch out and become huge treelike forms.

118. Despite the fact that this plant is called "hard yellow tuna," its name in Ñähñu means "yellow variety of the white tuna," so Salinas classifies it as "another kind of tuna blanca." I believe it is the *O. amyclaea*, a subspecies of the *O. ficus-indica*.

119. Again, this plant's name, the̲e̲ngä dookjä in Ñähñu means "red variety of the tuna blanca" whose name, recall, means "hard nopal."

120. This is not the same as the yellow variety of the tuna blanca, but is recognized by Ñähñu as a completely different class of nopal. Unlike the white, yellow, and red tunas already mentioned, this plant is not *O. ficus-indica*. It appears to be close to *O. phaeacantha*. I am unable to identify with any certainty this and the other nopales described here. For detailed descriptions of the many *opuntia* of Mexico, see Bravo H. (1937).

121. In the Tehuacán Valley there is a prickly pear called "nopal de víbora," or "snake nopal," that has this prostrate form (Dr. Earl Smith, personal communication).

122. This may be the *O. streptacantha*, which is widely distributed in the altiplano of Mexico. It is cultivated in other states, but not in Hidalgo (Bravo H., 1937: 192), where it grows wild in the monte up to five meters in height, with most mature plants around three meters. There is a wild nopal in the area called *O. cantabrigiensis* that has heavily seeded, dark purple fruits. This may coincide with the wild variety of purple prickly pear described here by Salinas.

123. This may be the *O. robusta*.

124. Again, it is possible that this nopal is a return migrant of the Burbank prickly pear mentioned above (see Note 108).

VOLUME IV

Religion

Traditional Religion

1. This description deals with the years before 1950. First we will discuss the coming of the foreigners to Mexico—that is, to the land of the Ñähñu, the Nahua, the Maya, Purépechas, Pame, Totonac, Mixtec, Mixe, Paipai, Huichol, Mazahua, Ralámulis, and other peoples who live on Mexican soil.[1] 2. Before the white people arrived in Mexico, most of these peoples were free; no one drove them like animals or forced them to do things for others.

3. They went about and lived free wherever they wished. In those times there were no borders on the land. There was no one to prevent them from eating what they wished. They just prepared the foods that they knew were good to eat, and they did not have to explain themselves to anyone. They were like the birds that sing and perch wherever they want to, that fly where they like, with no one to interfere with their desires. 4. That is how those peoples whom I have mentioned used to live. They were as free as the wind that goes everywhere, up and down, east and west. No one holds it back, and no one tries to make it go in another direction.

5. The beloved sun, since time immemorial, gives its light, its splendor, and its heat to keep alive the animals and plants, and even the human beings who have come to the earth. 6. And there is the moon, too, which gives its delicate light at night, and illuminates the surface of the earth. It is as if the moon and the stars help one another to give us light at night. The night is dark, but it is free; it doesn't bother anyone; it doesn't hurt anyone. 7. In the beginning, this is how the people of Mexico lived here; they were happy, living in peace because they were free. The people I am talking about were the first inhabitants of the land.

8. When the foreigners arrived they began to change the way of life of those first inhabitants. From the beginning the strangers were put off by the local people. The people here were a different color; they dressed differently; they ate different foods; they performed their work in a manner different from the

strangers; their speech was different. The foreigners began to punish the natives[2] because they did not understand what the strangers were saying to them. This was the very moment that the troubles began.

9. The people divided into two groups: those who were on the side of the foreigners, and those who fled from them. This happened primarily because the strangers began to displace the native people from the land. 10. They chased the Indians off the land, forcing them to take refuge wherever they could. They dispersed many of them, and left them scattered. But the great majority of the people hid out in the steepest, most inaccessible mountains so that they could not be found. They did this because they were accustomed to going about freely and not living in captivity. 11. At first, some got separated from their own group and so joined up with others. But when they realized that they were not among their own people, they continued to search. When they found their own people, they lived again with them. They tried most of all to ensure that they found a secure place to live, a place where the intruders would not find them.

12. Still, the foreigners kept looking for them. Perhaps it was not their intention at first to cause the people any harm. Maybe it was just that the people didn't understand what the strangers were saying to them. The foreigners sought out Indians in order to send them off to work. Sometimes they needed people to carry things for them; and sometimes they needed people to guard the things they had brought with them. 13. After a while, though, the strangers thought about opening up mines to extract silver and gold; in fact, this was what they wanted most. Once again they rounded up the Indians—but this time they did it by force in order to get the natives to help them excavate the mines.

14. Some old people, who heard it passed on by word of mouth, tell how the poor people in those early days had no rest at all. They worked every day, day and night, some digging and others taking out the dirt from the mines and hauling it away. 15. Without rest, they wasted away quickly, because the Spaniards made them suffer thirst and hunger as well. They didn't even give the Indians any clothes or coats, but made them work naked. Nowadays, some people are asking how much the foreigners paid those people for their labor.[3]

Many natives died during those times. The Nahuas were enslaved and worked the hardest, possibly because they were in the majority. The Ñähñu also suffered through those bad times.

17. As the years went by, the strangers noticed that the natives worshipped some gods that they had never seen and they did not think that this was good, either. So they thought about changing the local religion and they brought over their priests from their own country. Those priests carried with them holy images they believed in, especially those they thought had performed the greatest

miracles. 18. The priests built churches in which to install those images of saints and virgins[4] that they had brought from their homeland. They built towers in the churches and hung bells in them. By contrast, the people did not use bells; they just worshipped their gods. 19. They carved images of their gods out of stone— sometimes black, volcanic stone, and other times red stone. These were the two kinds of stone they mostly used and these are the colors of some of the idols we have found out in the monte where the first Ñähñu lived.

20. As the days and years passed, the religion of those strangers who came across the ocean from the east spread. That religion, which consists of the adoration of saints and images, is what those foreigners left as their legacy, and it is the religion that many people profess today. 21. Many are also moving away from that religion today because they have seen that it isn't practiced the way it should be. We will see in the following pages why this is so and what has caused the thinking of the people to change. 22. We will begin by looking at what happened prior to 1950. This is the period we refer to as "Traditional Religion."

23. Each of the little communities that make up the Mezquital Valley has a different religious icon or statue of a saint or Christ or a holy virgin. We begin by looking at the statue that belongs to the parish of Ixmiquilpan. The people pray to El Sr. de Jalpa, who is the patron here. His festival is celebrated during Holy Week, at Easter time, and it is his image which is taken out and paraded around in the procession on Good Friday. 24. That procession doesn't go far; it just goes from the altar to the main door of the church.[5]

25. Another fiesta celebrated in Ixmiquilpan is the 15th of August. This fiesta has been celebrated since early times, and is known as "The Assumption of the Virgin Mary." A lot of people who live in the jurisdiction of Ixmiquilpan, as well as some from outside the municipio, come together for this occasion. They gather at the church in Ixmiquilpan[6] some days before the actual fiesta in order to sing songs of praise and to say the rosary each afternoon for a week; then, on the day of the fiesta, the people all gather together. 26. On that day, people go to church to leave alms for the poor, or to present a gift to the saint in fulfillment of an oath,[7] or to offer flowers. By these acts they beg God and the Virgin to forgive them the sins they have committed.

27. Musicians come, including string groups and groups with brass; and there are the traditional flutists accompanied by their drummers. The musicians in the bands are paid fees, while the string players, the flutists and the drummers do not charge anything for their playing.[8] Even though they are not paid, on this day they remain outside the door of the cathedral, or just inside, and play for the entire day. Some people come of their own choosing to leave a religious offering. They leave plants, such as fennel, chamomile, air plants,[9] and rosemary.

These are the plants known as "reliquia," or "offerings."[10] 28. Others come to the fiesta with an offering of fireworks. In the 1940s and before, people used to set off pyrotechnic displays called "castillos" and "toritos."[11] A mayordomo[12] was named to take charge of these fireworks, and whoever was named had to pay the entire cost. In those days, it didn't cost a lot of money like it does today; it cost five to ten pesos for one castillo. Even so, the person who had to pay it worried a lot about not being able to pay that sum because that was considered a lot of money then.

29. All the offerings are placed together at the place where the images of Christ and the Virgin and baby Jesus are found. Sometimes the offerings are put at the base of the painting or sculpture, and sometimes they are draped over the top or around the neck. These "necklaces" are made of aromatic herbs strung together on a thread of ixtle fiber and formed into a kind of rope that can be draped over or onto the images. 30. Another kind of offering hung on the images is molded from wax. These are called "escamadas" in Spanish and are produced by candlemakers. First, they melt a pot of wax on a fire, and then they pour the wax into molds. Once the mold has cooled down, the figure they wanted is formed.

31. The traditional figures that they make are of flowers and the leaves of various trees. The designs come in various colors; some are white, and other may be red, green or blue,[13] yellow, orange, and pink. These are the colors that most people like. 32. The candlemakers mold these things, both for the offerings that are draped over the statues and for the ones that are placed near them as adornments. These last are wax candles used as decorations. 33. Other things are offered, too, such as "pastillas," or star shaped figures made out of sugar. The people offer these things because they believe the saint "eats" the taste of the sugar. People say that after three or four days the pastillas and other food offerings lose their flavor, and so they think it is the santito to whom they made the offer who absorbs the taste of the food.

34. With only a few exceptions, the people don't put anything out for an offering unless they fume it with incense first. The incense burner, into which has been placed some hot coals, is held in the hand. The incense is placed on the coals. Then, with the smoke from this, the flowers and wax figures and other things being offered by people, out of the goodness of their hearts, are treated. 35. The flowers are passed directly over the incense so that the fragrant smoke will penetrate them, and then they are put on the altar with the holy images.

36. Those who bring flowers and wax things are inside the church, while outside their assistants[14] are going around setting off firecrackers. This, too, can be done in fulfillment of an oath. Firecrackers make a great "bang" and about three

dozen are set off at a time in fulfilling an oath. Firecrackers are not treated with incense before being lit, but are set off just as they are when purchased. 37. After the priest blesses all the offerings brought by people, someone takes some of the flowers and puts them around the bell in the church tower. The offering is placed at the point where the bell hangs from its shaft. The crosses at the top of the church tower might also be decorated with pieces of the offerings.

38. There are also people called "carolers,"[15] who sing hymns of praise to the holy images. Sometimes, three or four men get together and sing songs of praise on the road as they go to church. Only rarely did one ever hear a woman singing with the men, due to the fact that in those days the women didn't know how to read. 39. This was because their fathers didn't let them go to school. Only recently have parents realized that education is important for everyone, men and women alike.

40. It is the custom in the churches to have many holy images of saints and virgins besides the main ones, and all of them are worshipped by the people. They often have to work very hard so that the flower offerings will suffice for all the images. First they bring the flower offering to the image considered to be the most important in the church, and then they put a piece of it around each of the other images and light a candle for each one also.

41. When the people finish doing all this, they return to their homes. Others await them there, with a meal prepared for all those who participated in the floral offerings. 42. When the supplicants who made the offerings get home, they ask permission to enter the kitchen and to make a floral offering to the fire where the meal has been cooked. They carry ropes of flowers from the cathedral in Ixmiquilpan; the flowers, of course, have already been blessed by the priest. 43. Everyone begins crossing themselves, including those who have returned with the offering as well as those who stayed behind at home. First they put incense on the flowers and on the fire hearth, and then they all kneel, and a man raises a large wooden bowl with the flowers in it up over their heads, and makes the sign of the cross with it. 44. The men, as well as the women who carry the incense burner and the vases of flowers, all kneel at the side of the man who is holding up the bowl and making the offering.

45. The man raises the bowl, asks God in heaven for permission, and says that all the offerings are for him. He raises the bowl and makes the sign of the cross with it in the air; then he lowers himself and makes the sign on the ground, with the bowl practically touching the earth. 46. There are two helpers, a woman with the incense burner and one with a vase of flowers. As the man makes the sign, they do the same. The man ensures that everyone performs the ritual together. When they are finished, he takes a brazada[16] of floral rope from the

bowl and lays it around the fire, and he takes a few pieces from the rope and places them on top of the hearth stones.

47. Once the flowers have been placed on the hearth, the man lights a candle and continues putting strings of flowers on the ceramic pots and jars containing the stew. He puts flowers on the pulque barrel and on the walls of the kitchen and all around the door. 48. All this is done to ask God for his grace and to ask that there be plenty of food for all who were invited and who will be partaking of the meal. God is also asked to banish all evils, such as illnesses that may have struck a member of the family. The fire is also begged its forgiveness for using it and bothering it all the time. 49. Fire is considered to be like a god, since it helps people live and grow, and so, it is said, it is fitting to thank it.

50. The great fiesta of August is not the responsibility of just one person from the city of Ixmiquilpan. People from many small communities around the municipio organize amongst themselves in preparation for their coming to this fiesta and worshipping God. The date of the actual fiesta in Ixmiquilpan is August 15th. The festival has been celebrated for many years.

51. The people who contribute the most money to the festival are the Ñähñu. The mestizos who live right in the city of Ixmiquilpan are kind of stingy and don't spend their money. They don't want to take money from their pocket to give to the church; on the contrary, they want others to give *them* money. 52. They have a different way of thinking, as if they didn't believe in God. When they see the Ñähñu parading through the city on the way to make a floral offering, the mestizos stand in their doorways and just look. A few of them join the supplicants who are going to church. 53. Ah, but these are the ones who set up stalls for selling things so that they can get the little money that the Ñähñu people bring with them from the pueblos. For when the people have finished worshipping the santitos, they go out to the plaza for soft drinks, or pulque or beer, and that's where they spend the little money they brought with them.

54. On the 15th of the month people come into Ixmiquilpan from surrounding communities. For about two weeks, the rosary is said each evening. People from Maye, from the barrio of Progreso, from San Nicolás, and from other communities close to Ixmiquilpan come for this. 55. They pray every evening, until September 7th. Actually, the period lasts for 23 days from the 15th of August, counting from the day after the fiesta, but it is known in Ñähñu as "two weeks" because it is customary for people to speak of it in this way.

56. Prior to September 7th, the people of the various communities have reached an agreement. On the 7th, the people from the communities that have been assigned the duty of constructing a floral-decorated "street arch" gather together. Each community has been assigned a particular spot in Ixmiquilpan

He raises the bowl and makes the sign of the cross with it   *Religion 45*

where they will construct their arch.[17] It could be on a corner or in the middle of a street; wherever they've been assigned is where they put it. 57. All the members of the community have chipped in some money so that the necessary materials for building the arch might be purchased. The people who build arches for the festival come from the following communities: Dios Padre, El Maye, Progreso, Panales, El Dextho, San Nicolás, El Mandó, and the barrios of El Cortijo, El Carmen, and San Antonio. These are, in fact, the communities that continue today to decorate the plaza during the fiesta.

58. The grand procession leaves the church and makes its way into the plaza at about 9:00 PM. Some people carry the statue of El Sr. de Jalpa. Others follow along singing songs of praise. Just about everyone repeats the praises sung by the lead caroler. 59. Women as well as men join in and repeat the prayers. When the procession comes to one of the arches, those carrying the statue stop and wait until all the pilgrims have finished singing the prayers. When they finish at one arch, they continue on towards the next, and they keep doing this until they have completed the circuit of all the arches that have been constructed. 60. The procession leaves the main cathedral and heads towards the barrio of Carmen. From there they go to the barrio of Progreso, and then they return towards San Antonio, and finally end up back where they started. It takes about four hours to complete the procession, and about 1000-1500 people are in it. 61. Many of them carry candles purchased in fulfillment of their promise. As a finale, they sing more praises to the santito but this time inside the church. Then they close everything up. After that, only a regular mass is celebrated daily, led by the priest; or, if there is no priest every day, then on Sunday.

62. When the "great procession," as it is called, is finished, people go to the plaza to buy something to eat. As I said before, the mestizos have already set up their stands and are just waiting for someone to come by and make a purchase. 63. Men buy beer and get drunk; then they start punching and kicking, and taking out knives. In the end, the winners are the rich who covet the money of those who have it least. 64. Pretty soon the police come and take away those who were fighting and throw them in jail. The next day they are brought into court. They deny everything, claiming that they don't remember anything. They just pay their fines and return to their homes. 65. That's how people are; when there is a fiesta they get drunk and fight among themselves. If they come to fighting with knives, then they become entangled on the ground in hand-to-hand wrestling, and the one who is stronger comes out on top.

66. Fiestas are good because people gather and get to know one another. They can establish mutually respectful relations and greet their fellow human

beings with respect. But bitter quarrels are not good. If some poor person is imprisoned, and if he doesn't have money to pay for his wrongdoing, then he can't go free. 67. Every day, the police roust him out and force him to sweep the streets of the plaza.[18] He'll be in jail for a week or two, and finally the mestizos take pity on him and let him free. In any event, the fine has to be paid; it is never forgiven. 68. So, if the man doesn't have any money, he has to sell one of his animals, if he has any. And if he doesn't have any, then he sells whatever he has of any value, such as a steel digging rod or an axe.

69. There is, therefore, nothing good about provoking fights. There is no benefit to going around the plaza, cleaning up nauseating garbage. Ultimately, the only ones who win are the judges of the Ministerio Público.[19] Money flows into their hands by the hundreds of pesos.[20] One of those judges can get rich in a very short time, just sitting and dispensing so-called justice. 70. It has been noticed that when they come to these jobs they are poor, and when they leave they are rich. The people who provide this wealth are the folk who are imprisoned and who give the judges their money. Also responsible are those who set up the stands that sell beer and pulque and aguardiente.[21] Those are the drinks that most people consume; that is why they get drunk and that's when the problems start.

71. We can not continue without taking a look at the church that was mentioned. Once the procession is over, all the people are back in the cathedral. The images are put back in their usual places, and the people bid them goodbye, crossing themselves. 72. Whoever has money, leaves some as charity. There is a bowl there to receive whatever money people wish to contribute, be it fifty centavos, or twenty-five centavos, or five or ten pesos, or whatever anyone can afford. The money is used to buy whatever is needed for the church, such as brooms or, if enough is collected, to repair the walls where the lime has flaked off. 73. Sometimes the money is used to pay the salary of the sexton. During the grand procession, he leads the way, carrying large bundles of a kind of organ pipe cactus. The bundles are used as torches to light the way of the procession.

74. Now we are going to go back to discussing all the things that people sell on the night of the fiesta in Ixmiquilpan. People always hope that they can get some money together some day, and so they set up stalls or just lay things out on the street to sell. There is not much in these stalls, but the hope is that people will buy what there is. 75. Some people sell "tamalitos dulces." They select a spot where they can sit and set up a fruit crate on which they lay out what they are selling. Sometimes they put out a batch of tamalitos worth twenty-five centavos, or sometimes a peso's worth.[22] The Ñähñu like to eat tamalitos as much

as the mestizos do. 76. If there is a lot of demand on the day of the fiesta, then the vendors sell out quickly. This is especially the case if the woman selling the tamalitos has a lot of friends and acquaintances who come to buy from her.

77. Tamalitos dulces are similar to regular tamales. The difference is in the size and the taste, and the fact that they are wrapped in purple colored corn husking. In preparing tamalitos, dark corn is selected. This class of corn has purple leaves. The maize is ground raw, until it is a very fine powdery meal, called "pinole." It must be dry, without any water added. 78. Once the pinole is ground, it is put into a receptacle, preferably a large pot. In another pot, piloncillo, or sugar cane candy has been melted down. This agua de piloncillo is very sweet. It is poured over the pinole and mixed together. It has to be blended together very well. 79. Care has to be taken that the mixture is not watery. It has to be firm, like masa,[23] so that it can be wrapped without running out of the leaves. Tamalitos are small, and not as large as the regular tamales. The lump of masa placed in the husk is about the size of a peanut. 80. Once the tamalitos are wrapped, they are left to dry and brought to wherever one wishes to sell them.

81. These tamalitos are found mostly at festivals. You can spot them immediately wherever they are sold because they are purple in color. They are hardly ever found in the big cities. They are found mostly in the small communities that make up the Mezquital Valley and are mostly made by Ñähñu women. 82. The people who live in the irrigated zone of the Valley grow this kind of corn. This corn is easily distinguished in the milpa.[24] The stalk is violet, and its leaves are dark green. The spikes of corn are white and purple. This type of maize is only rarely used for making nixtamal[25] and tortillas. 83. The people who grow it just sell it to Ñähñu women for making tamalitos. The people who buy the tamalitos at the stands don't just eat them right there. They take them home to those who stayed behind to watch the house during the fiesta. This is a very old custom. Whoever goes to a fiesta buys something to eat—if they have money, of course—to bring back to those who remained at home.

84. Another thing always found at fiestas is a squash seed called "pipián" in Spanish. They are like the seeds of castile squash but the seeds of the pipián are longer. The people who sell these seeds sometimes sell them raw, and other times they sell them lightly toasted on a comal. They toast them on a comal until the skin of the seeds is golden. They don't use a lot of heat because the seeds can get overcooked and then they are bitter. 86. One has to be careful about eating these seeds and not eat too much, because if you eat too many they cause coughs.

87. These seeds are used in restaurants and inns to make a variety of mole. Those who prepare them remove the outside shell and toast the inner seed which

is the part that is needed. First they toast the seeds, and then they grind them into a fine meal, and then this is fried in oil. Some people add a little water and then the mixture becomes a kind of atole.[26] 88. Once this is done, chunks of previously cooked pork are added. Chicken can be used instead of pork.

89. Something else always eaten at fiestas is peanuts. They are sold already toasted or roasted. There are two kinds of peanuts: one is meaty and the other is more shriveled. They taste differently. 90. The meaty variety is not favored much by the people because it smells rotten. People like the less meaty nut because it has a better taste. One hardly ever sees a stall or stand selling raw peanuts. 91. If peanuts are purchased raw, then they are roasted in the shell on a comal. Peanuts, too, if eaten in large quantities, will cause colds and coughs. 92. Both pipián nuts and peanuts are sold by the the puño or by the puño de la mano or by the cuartillo. A person who sells these nuts carries about fifteen cuartillos, or an ayate-full; he or she knows how much they are going to be able to sell.[27]

93. Other people buy up fruit wholesale in the villages and then come to the fiestas to sell it at retail. Some of the fruits sold are: peaches, apples, mangoes, tejocotes,[28] sugar cane, oranges, and other fruits that grow in the hot lands. 94. People who live in the irrigated zone sell walnuts, pomegranates, and sweet potatoes. Each of these products comes according to its season. Also at fiestas, there are whole meals for sale, already cooked and ready to eat. Various kinds of stews are sold. These are some of the traditional dishes of the Ñähñu.

95. For example, there are frijoles quebrados, or "broken beans," where a woman first pounds beans into pieces. She pounds what is needed for the meal she is making; it may be half a cuartillo, or a cuartillo, or whatever she is going to mash up. Next, she puts a pot of water on the fire and then throws in the pounded beans. 96. The skin comes off the beans in the hot water and the pieces float to the surface. She removes all the pieces of skin that float to the top, and then only the pulp remains. This is left to boil, and condiments are added. 97. Ground chile is added, either chile de arbol or chile ancho.[29] A little masa is added to the beans so that it will thicken up. 98. Also, an herb known as "lengua de vaca" is added for flavor. Coriander and cumin are added, and, of course, salt.

99. This class of meal cooks up very quickly; only about an hour is needed before it is all prepared and ready to eat. This is the kind of ready-to-eat meal that some women always make for sale at fiestas. They also make tortillas to sell. Others sell tlacoyos. Tlacoyos are made as if they were regular tortillas, except that a bit of ground frijoles is added to the dough as the tortillas are being formed. The beans are flavored with condiments that have been prepared beforehand. 100. Tlacoyos look thick because they contain frijoles. Some

people call them "tortilla de frijol." Some women make them round, and others make them eliptical and they are called "loló" in Ñähñu.[30] Other women prepare broad beans and bring them to the fiestas to sell at a stand they set up. And of course, they always have tortillas. 101. Still other women sell fried nopal leaves and fried quelites, such as quintoniles, verdolagas, and hediondillas to which has been added some ground chicharrón for flavor.[31] Really poor people buy all these kinds of food that I am talking about here. When people get a little money they buy other kinds of food at fiestas, such as cooked meat or fish.

102. Barbacóa is another food created by the Ñähñu.[32] In recent times, the number of barbacóa makers has grown because there is a lot of demand. Despite the fact that many of these newcomers to this trade don't prepare barbacóa with the same taste that the Ñähñu do, people eat it up.

103. Some men travel to other places in order to trade in products and then return to sell those products to their Ñähñu countrymen. They might sell cántaros, guajes, acocotes, raspadores, or jícaras.[33] Sometimes these last are white and sometimes they are red. 104. The white ones sell most because they are natural in color and are less expensive. In comparison, the red ones are expensive because they are painted with various designs, and this is the value added to the price. 105. Other inhabitants of the Mezquital Valley sell various kinds of rope products made from ixtle.[34] People like this who go around selling various things don't show up at the fiestas just for the sake of going. They do this kind of work as a means of making a little bit of money.

106. There are potters who make stew pots, pitchers, ceramic molcajetes,[35] small pitchers, flat sided water jugs, large standing pitchers, plates and over-sized cooking pots. Many of these products come from far off communities. Some vendors come on foot from their homeland, and others come in trucks. 107. Those who come on foot sometimes carry their merchandise for sale on their backs, or they drive burros loaded down with the wares. How they get there is not so important. What they have to do is get to wherever there is a big fiesta and set up, either in a stall or on the street to sell their wares. 108. They stay at their spot for two or three days, or however long the fiesta lasts, and they are the last to leave. When they finally leave, they go on to another pueblo. If there is no fiesta, then they set up their wares for sale in open markets. And thus they travel, alone, going from one place to another.

109. The people who come down from the mountains bring tree moss with them to sell to the fiesta mayordomos and to those who are responsible for building the street arches. They also bring wooden poles used by merchants as supports for the canopies they set up to keep from baking in the sun all day. 110. The purveyors of wood generally come on foot, carrying their burden on

their shoulders.[36] If they have thick posts, they can carry only two, and if the poles are thin, then they carry four. The thick poles are three and a half to four meters long. The distance that those men come in order to sell their wood is about 20 kilometers. 111. The man who walks fast gets there quickly, and the man who doesn't takes a whole day on the road. Some people spend the night on the road and don't get where they are going until the next day. Older people really hurt on the long walk; but they must walk or they won't have food for themselves, much less for their families. 112. Those who have burros let them do the work and the owner just directs the beast. You can always tell when the wood sellers who own burros are passing by because the poles make a racket as they are dragged along behind the burros.

113. At this time we will leave Ixmiquilpan in order to see how fiestas are practiced in other communities. In order to give some order to what I am going to do, I'll move along a line to the north of Ixmiquilpan. We will see, one by one, what festivals are celebrated every year in each community in this direction. 114. There are some communities that celebrate two or three fiestas a year. In each case we will see which santito they believe in and worship.

115. San Antonio is a small community that borders on Ixmiquilpan. One can even say it is connected to Ixmiquilpan because it is so close by. The church there is large and has two towers. Bells hang in each tower and they call the people to church whenever the priest is going to say mass. 116. This church contains the statue of San Antonio, and this is the name given to the community. San Antonio's fiesta is celebrated on June 10th. More than any other time, this is when the people from around there come together. They celebrate mass there only once in a while when there is no fiesta. This is because the community is so close to the central cathedral of Ixmiquilpan, and whoever wants to attend mass can go there. 117. The festival lasts two whole days. On the third night everything culminates and the festival ends; then people disperse and go home.

118. On the day of the fiesta itself, they decorate the church altar with flowers, and they put vases of flowers near the statue of the saint. They light long, thick candles. The door of the church is decorated with a beautiful archway. 119. Not many people come to this fiesta. Maybe this is because the saint is not powerful or doesn't make many miracles, and so people don't worship him much. People do not come to this church to make floral offerings. The few people who come leave some alms. The saint is taken out on a procession, but the procession does not go far. 120. It goes a short distance, and returns to the church where the saint is returned to the altar. As the procession moves along, people set off firecrackers, and make a lot of noise with them. 121. The bells don't stop ringing up in the bell tower. That is when they get some use;

when there is no fiesta, they don't ring the bells, and so the bells don't wear out. There is no band of musicians at this fiesta. 122. Until around 1940, people used to chip in to put up a castillo, or fireworks tower. That is what the old people say who lived in those times and saw it.

123. From here we walk about a kilometer and come to another little community called "Dähmu" in Ñähñu. This community has taken the name of the saint in the church there, San Nicolás. His day is celebrated each year on September 10th. 124. People contribute to finance the celebration of the fiesta. The amount they each have to contribute depends on the value of the fiesta that they all agree to have, and that way, each one contributes the same amount. The custom is for each person, rich or poor to give an equal share. The poor people have to find a way to come up with the assigned amount. 125. There are still a lot of people who believe that the saints punish those who don't come up with their share of the fiesta. Because of this, they suffer a lot, working and trying to get together their share of the money for the fiesta.

126. This collection of money is for hiring a band, and for paying the fireworks specialists to build a castillo and a torito.[37] These are set off on the actual day of the fiesta. 127. Women who live alone, like widows, are also included in the collection of money if it is seen that they have it. Some of them just put in whatever they feel they can afford, and no one forces them to pay as much as the rest of the people do. 128. Some men refuse to chip in, even though they have enough to give. When the collector sees this, he tells those men about the widows who have already given their share. Then the men are ashamed, and, even though they did not want to, they give the amount that was assigned.

129. Two mayordomos are named for the mass. They help make sure that the fiesta is celebrated. They get together and work things out between themselves for this cargo. It is important to know that in many small communities, there are at least three masses celebrated, over as many days, one for each day of the fiesta. 130. For each mass two mayordomos are named. All the mayordomos are men; only rarely do women want to be mayordomos. The mayordomos consult amongst themselves to determine how much each one will pay. 131. The money that they contribute goes to buy flowers for the altar, for incense, and for firecrackers. Some of them customarily burn candles as an offering, as well as escamadas. 132. These are just wax, but the people who melt and pour the wax use molds and make flower figures. The mayordomos buy wax that has already been melted once and is sold in blocks, so that all their assistants have to do is melt it again for molding into figures.

133. In addition to the money needed to pay for all the things in the church, the mayordomos have to chip in to pay for the priest because he, too, demands

his wages. Also, the mayordomos have to pay for food for their assistants—for the makers of the candles and wax figures. 134. Some people make the candles and escamadas and others offer them in church. The mayordomos also have to pay for the firecrackers set off during the procession.

135. Years ago, the mayordomos had to buy candles to distribute to the throngs of people when the procession started. These candles were used to light the way of the people who carried the images of the saints and virgins. During the procession the band went along playing tunes. 136. In prior days, too, a flutist and drummer were always in attendance, accompanying the procession. If they knew where a mayordomo lived, who was in charge of the mass, they went there to play. This was an obligation they had. People who make flutes and drums are dying out. 137. Sometimes there would be two or three flutists and a drummer. There were generally three to five players in a group, among whom were children who were taught to play the flute.

138. As soon as people started thinking about the fiesta in this community, they began to organize for it. First they named the mayordomos who would be in charge of the masses. The number of mayordomos appointed depended on the number of days the fiesta would last. Once that was done, the mayordomos for the music were named. 139. In earlier times they used to name one mayordomo to feed the musicians for one day. He had to give them breakfast, and then a meal at midday, and then supper at night. There were a lot of musicians—about 25. They didn't have to feed only the musicians, but all those who came to visit, as well. 140. They also fed the assistants who helped them.

There used to be a custom where people lent each other things that were needed for those meals. Things that were lent included corn, tortillas, money, pulque, and animals. In 1940 there wasn't much beer, and so people didn't lend that to one another. 141. Also, they believed that such things were only for consumption by rich people and mestizos. But there also wasn't much of it, and it wasn't sold much. In those times, people had a lot of respect for one another. In making and taking these loans, people visited each other, got to know one another and shared together what God had given them.[38]

142. In order for the meal to feed everyone, they had to kill a lot of animals. They might kill four dozen chickens, a head of cattle, two dozen goats, and some sheep as well. With all of this there was enough to eat for five days. 143. The custom was that the mayordomo put a lot of meat on the plates of those whom he invited to eat. Whoever came by the table to eat got a lot of meat heaped on their plate. They heaped their plates with meat for them to eat.[39] Later, the woman of the house would come by with a basket full of meat and tortillas. She would fill the plates of her guests again so that they could take the

food home with them. 144. This was what was called "making the itacate." This was one of the characteristic customs of the people who lived a long time ago. Whenever they went to visit someone's house, they took along a satchel in which they would take home their itacate, which consisted of the tortillas and meat that they were given.[40]

145. During the fiesta days, people offer their help with preparations, and in payment they are given food to eat. In those times, the custom of making barbacóa was not yet common. If it was made, then it was only for giving to those who were considered the most socially distinguished. 146. Mostly, in those days, the animals that were killed were eaten in stews that were prepared in mole de olla. First the meat was boiled to cook it. Then the chile was ground, along with other condiments including cumin. Then the mixture was poured into the pot in which the meat had been boiled so that the meat would absorb the flavor of the condiments. The whole thing was left to cook a little, and then the meat was removed from the fire and the meal was ready to be served.[41] 147. Goat meat and beef was prepared in this way. Chicken was prepared in a thicker broth. For this, the chile is ground separately. Large, red chiles called "chile ancho" are used. Rarely is chicken made in mole de olla.

148. The people who gather at the fiesta of San Nicolás come from the small, surrounding communities. In San Nicolás it is traditional for the mayordomos to meet a day before the fiesta and prepare atole and tamales together and distribute them in front of the church door. This is considered the beginning of the fiesta. 149. They don't distribute anything else, just atole and tamales. It is given to adults and children alike. The distribution begins at 6:00 AM and by 7:30 AM it is over. 150. The atole given out is sometimes made from pinole with piloncillo added, and that is why it is dark in color. Other times it is made with rice flour with chocolate, sugar, and cinnamon added to give it good flavor. 151. Year after year they do the same thing—give out atole and tamales, and always in the plaza of the pueblo. Though the mayordomos change, the new mayordomos give out the atole and tamales on the day of vespers before the fiesta; this custom has been practiced for many years.

152. A "curado de pulque" is prepared on the third day of the fiesta at the house of the mayordomo. This is a drink made basically from pulque. The mayordomo estimates how many people are invited and that is the amount of pulque prepared. 153. Sometimes they make a hundred and fifty liters so that there will be enough for everyone to have a drink. Such things as chocolate, cinnamon, sugar, and aguardiente are put in the pulque. The pulque is poured into the barrel and then the other things are put in and it is all mixed together really

well. 154. It is mixed with a stirrer and then left to ferment. In the afternoon, around six, the guests come and the pulque is distributed to everyone.

155. This is where the large jarros, or pitchers, that people buy are used. Those whose job it is to give out pulque to the guests carry the jarros. They go to the barrel, fill their jarros, and go around filling up the cups of those who have been invited. People get drunk very easily on this curado de pulque, both because it is a mixture of so many things, and because it is sweet. 156. With a single jug of it, some people wind up staggering home. Sometimes folks drink more than they should, and then there are always some people who start making a racket. Then, if the rest of the people don't hold things down, the drunks wind up slugging at each other. 157. Then people who try to separate the combatants get involved in the fight.

The next day, everyone is calmed down and they go back to being friends again. In earlier times, people actually pulled knives on each other, and someone would get killed. In those days people used to say that it was a good fiesta if one of the celebrants got killed. 158. The murderer had to carry the body on his shoulders to Ixmiquilpan himself so he could stand trial. The murderer used to be locked up for four or five years. If the guards did not pay attention, then the murderer fled, and when they went looking for him, he was gone and no one knew where he was.

159. Continuing to the north, we come on another community known as Los Remedios. A long time ago the Spaniards built a church there and installed the statue of the Virgen de los Remedios, along with other images. However, no one knows exactly what the names are of the other images. 160. They are hanging on various parts of the church walls; some are large icons, and others are small. There are hardly any celebrations in honor of any of these icons, possibly because they aren't so miraculous. Once in a while, someone will light a candle for one of these santitos. Most of the church is dark and poorly lit where these images are hanging.

161. The people believe fervently in the miracles of the Virgen de los Remedios. Her fiesta is celebrated year after year. The organization of her fiesta is more or less like the one we saw in San Nicolás. The fiesta in Remedios is larger, though, and many more people attend. This is because the people believe that the Virgin makes many miracles. 162. It is said that if someone is sick, and they worship the Virgin with all their soul, then in a few days they will feel better and be cured.

Two bands are hired each year in this pueblo. 163. The people get together and organize to do all this. Inhabitants from all the barrios that make up

Remedios are involved. Some of the barrios are Granaditas, Cerro de León, Cerritos, El Banco, Vázquez, El Mirador, and El Centro. 164. Each person contributes a little money; everyone cooperates to pay the costs of the music and the fireworks. Suppose, for example, that the musicians arrive on Tuesday, late in the afternoon. They remain Wednesday and Thursday, and they depart around midday on Friday. 165. The fireworks makers arrive on Wednesday morning around nine o'clock, and they start working right away. That same night they raise the castillo that will be set off around one in the morning. 166. The following morning, they tear down the castillo and begin to build another one from the pieces. On Thursday night, they put up two castillos because that is the main day on which the fiesta is celebrated.

167. In order to get all this done, the barrios organize among themselves, so that while one provides food for the musicians, another provides for the fireworks makers. One thing is the financial support that mayordomos have to provide; and another is the work that goes into feeding the people who have been assigned to them. 168. Both a torito and a castillo are set off on Wednesday. On Thursday, the actual day of the fiesta of the Virgin, two toritos and two castillos are set off. When the toritos are set off, they present a very comic spectacle.

169. The person who carries the torito goes running around, back and forth, up and down. He jumps and runs around, bellowing like a bull. He tries to fool the children and to provoke the adults, pretending that he is going to gore them, and they follow behind taunting him. 170. Before the firecrackers in it are lit, the person carrying the torito runs around, bellowing. Everyone, men and women alike, laugh as the fireworks that were placed on the body of the torito are set off, and the man carrying the piece goes running around, with all the firecrackers going off. 171. There are about three separate episodes of firecrackers that go off, and then the torito goes dead. The torito is the first fireworks display in any fiesta. After that, everyone rests for a bit and then the castillo is set off. The firecrackers go off with a deafening roar.

172. The castillo, set up earlier in the afternoon, erupts, and the firecrackers on the first level explode. Then there is a pause for about three minutes, and it starts again. All the fireworks, including those from the torito as well as those from the castillo, are in beautiful colors. 173. Some are white, and others are violet, red, blue or green, or orange. They all make a lot of smoke; the smoke is suffocating, but not stinging. The colored fire doesn't burn as hot as the normal kind. 174. The fire from the firecrackers is really hot. If that fire touches your hand, it sears the flesh. Children love to follow along in back of the fire that falls from the top of the castillo and try to catch it. 175. When the castillo

He jumps and runs around, bellowing like a bull
Religion 169

finishes burning, the fireworks makers set off some really big firecrackers, called "bombas," as a kind of big finish. These are bigger than the usual ones, and they make a noise that makes it feel like the earth is shaking. The noise can be heard in other pueblos, and then people there know that there was a fiesta and that the castillo has finished burning. About two dozen of these gigantic firecrackers are lit.

176. An even larger number of bombas is lit in Remedios. The people of the community say that when they hear a lot of bombas, this shows that it was a really good castillo. But if there isn't a lot of noise, then they aren't satisfied with the castillo.

177. The musicians play joyous tunes, known as "dianas,"[42] dedicated to the mayordomos who have been placed in charge of making the fiesta happen. Each of the bands takes its turn playing these tunes.

178. We have moved away a little from describing the activities that go on in the church. A long time ago it was the custom that people showed profound respect for one another. People in Orizabita and Los Remedios showed high esteem for each other, and in those days people from these communities visited each other more. This was especially the case when one of the communities celebrated its fiesta. 179. They visited each other for fiestas, and they also visited one another's homes. Back before 1960, the people of Los Remedios came to Orizabita on the Fiesta del Sexto Viernes de Dolores,[43] carrying the statue of the Virgen de los Remedios from their pueblo. Year after year, they always came.

180. Correspondingly, the santitos from Orizabita used to go over to Los Remedios. The Virgen de los Remedios used to be brought to Orizabita alone, and was not accompanied by any other icons. 181. A group of people from Orizabita was sent over to Remedios to bring the statue of the Virgin back. The mayordomos, who were in charge of taking care of everything having to do with the church, and the judges[44] had the biggest obligation to be present in order to receive the Virgin from the hands of the people from Remedios. The authorities from Remedios came, accompanied by their helpers and other invited persons who carried the statue of the Virgin. 182. Starting in the morning, the mayordomos of the church rang the bells to call the people to accompany them in the carrying of the Virgin. First they all gathered in the church, adults as well as children. 183. They set off firecrackers in the church in the morning. We will examine this event more fully when we look at how they celebrate the fiesta in Orizabita.

184. That is how the people of Remedios used to be; each year they requested that the santitos of Orizabita visit them. The authorities in Remedios organized the people to come out for the bringing of the santitos from Orizabita. They started setting off firecrackers at about six in the morning, and the people of Orizabita could hear them. 185. The mayordomos from Remedios hurried to get together with their assistants at the church. The assistants are known as "bell ringers" and, in fact, this is what they do. They ring the church bells at daybreak, and at midday, and at night to call the people to attend mass. 186. Sometimes they play the role of doorkeeper. That is, when the mayordomos are not available, they open the doors to the church. They toll the bells for anyone who has died, or when someone is going to be buried. 187. When someone dies, it is the custom to bring them to the church. It is believed that this is so they might thank God and the Virgin for having let them live on earth in the days prior to their death.

188. The bell ringer helps the mayordomos in church to collect the money from the people who come to mass. He distributes relics to those who want to take them home. That is why he has to be in church on the day of the celebration; it is important that he helps out those who have named him as their helper, that is, the mayordomos.

At about 11:00 AM or noon, the mayordomos from Remedios start to organize a few boys who are strong enough to handle the long walk. 189. He chooses three and lines them up in a row, and gives the one who walks in the middle a metal pole about two meters long. It has a cross bar on top, also made entirely of metal. 190. The two boys who walk alongside carry similar poles. The difference is that theirs do not have crosses, but instead there is a candle holder on the top of the pole. A lit candle is placed on the top of each pole. The candles remain lit when there is no wind; otherwise, they go out. All three boys are dressed up; the color of their uniforms is red and white. 191. The group of three are called "ciriales." They go in front of the procession; behind them come the "ofrecientes" carrying the floral offerings, and behind them come all the people accompanying the procession.

192. The people at the front of the procession carry firecrackers. They set them off as they go along and that is how people know where the procession is passing on its way to bringing back the sacred images. The man carrying the floral offering has to really hold up under pressure. He has to carry a big wooden bowl in his arms, filled with garlands of flowers in his arms, and he can not carry it on his back. It is easy to imagine that his arms get tired, but that is the custom.

193. Many people hurry to catch up with the offerers. All the people who participate in the bringing of the icons go the entire route without resting. On their way back they do stop to rest, and we will see where.

When they get to the church, the mayordomos and the judges from the two communities greet each other. 194. Those from Los Remedios tell the authorities from Orizabita the purpose of their visit— to take the statue back to Remedios to participate in their fiesta with the Virgen de Remedios. The mayordomos and judges agree; this is a show of respect that has been practiced for a long time. The ciriales go in first. They are accompanied by another boy who carries a little bell that he rings all along the way. The ciriales stand aside and make room for the offerers who bring up flowers and offer them to the santitos. 195. The way in which the flowers are offered has been described before, and all offerings are done in the same way. After making the sign of the cross, the person who has been assigned the task uncoils the ropes of flowers and drapes them over the images of the saints and virgins. The statues have been previously arranged so that they can be carried on the shoulders of the men assigned this task.

196. The flower offering at this time is considered a greeting. When the images arrive at their destination, they will receive more. Next, people are sought who want to carry the various images. This is not difficult because many people want to do it, thinking that they will be fulfilling a promise to God. 197. Four men carry the statue of El Sr. del Buen Viaje[45] and four women carry the Virgin. They always do this; that is, each person carries what he or she is supposed to. It is thought that it is offensive for men to carry an image of the Virgin or for women to carry that of Christ. 198. The men and women leave the church and walk about 100 meters to an "ermita," or rest stop. The ermita has its own mayordomo. 199. He has prepared an awning to protect his visitors from the sun. The ermita has two purposes; one is to provide the carriers a place to rest, because sometimes the icons get heavy, and the other is to offer the holy images flowers.

200. The person who has set up the ermita makes the offering. While one person offers flowers, another sets off firecrackers. The ermita is decorated with flowers. It costs the mayordomo in charge of the ermita some money to set things up. He must pay for all the flowers, as well as for the firecrackers and the incense. 201. The canopy cloth that is used to create shade is lent by the church. The mayordomo must work very hard to get all the money necessary. If he can not get all the money together, then he must sell one of his animals to fulfill his cargo. 202. It cost about 300 pesos to fulfill this little cargo. This is the amount it cost a long time ago; nowadays it might cost about 3000 pesos.

203. After finishing at the first ermita, they walk about 300 meters and stop to rest again and to make another floral offering. Another mayordomo has been named for this ermita. He does the same thing here that the mayordomo did who was in charge of the first ermita. 204. Flowers are brought to the statues, and then those who carried them continue on their way, if they can. If they are tired and can not continue, then others take their place. Some people can endure the entire trek of six kilometers with the icons. They make the long walk of their own volition, because, according to them, the pilgrimage pays for the sins they have committed.

205. They pick up the holy images and resume their trek. They go about two kilometers further before reaching the next ermita where they can rest. 206. This ermita is in a small barrio called Granaditas which belongs in the jurisdiction of Remedios. Another offering is made here. If there are carolers who wish to do so, they gather around the images and sing songs of praise. If there are musicians with stringed instruments, then they play tunes to the images. 207. When this is done, then all the people continue on the walk. This is where some people start tiring. They walk another two kilometers and stop at another ermita and make another offering. 208. At this site, some people will have set up some food and drink to sell to the pilgrims who want to buy it. Such things as soft drinks, pulque, and tamales are what are usually sold. Sometimes, rarely, bread is sold. Some women sell the tamalitos dulces mentioned earlier.

209. The entire route up to this point is on dirt roads. Now the procession leaves the road entirely and heads east to the fourth ermita. Next they come to the center of the village and stop to rest again. They then continue on to the last ermita, which is at the entrance to the cemetery. They set down the images here and make another offering; this is the last one. 210. Now the local mayordomos organize the procession with the holy images that have come to visit, and then the images are brought into the church itself. The people call this "la procesión pequeña," or the "small procession," because it does not go very far—just around the church's cemetery, or the "nt'agi," as it is called in Ñähñu.[46]

211. The procession goes once around the cemetery and then enters the church where a place has already been reserved to put the icons. By then, it is getting late and the people come out of church around the time it is getting dark. The next day, the priest celebrates mass in honor of the santitos and the Virgin that have come to visit. 212. A separate mayordomo is appointed for this mass. The mayordomo asks the priest to celebrate the mass on the proper day. I say that he "asks" for the mass to be celebrated, but it is known as "putting" the mass in Ñähñu. That is how people talk about this activity. They might say that

"Don Vincente went to put a mass for Monday." 213. The phrase "put a mass" has been used for a long time. In earlier times, there was no paper money, only metal. The person who went to request a mass brought money with him to the priest in order to pay an advance. When he delivered the money he took the coins out of his "morral"[47] and *put* them in the hands of the priest, and that is why they called this "putting a mass."

214. The mayordomo of the mass also spends money. He spends money to pay for the mass, and for the candles, and for the flowers, and the firecrackers. A lot of firecrackers are set off when this mass is celebrated. Some of the flowers the mayordomo buys are for the altar, and the rest are given to people who make the flower rolls for the offering. 215. He spends about 600 pesos, aside from the expenses of the meal that he provides for his assistants. In earlier times, he had to provide breakfast for the priest. This breakfast had to be prepared apart from everything else. 216. It was not mixed together with the other food that was prepared for the assistants, because they respected the priest a lot. All of the breakfast that they made for him was prepared separately. 217. Sometimes they invited a woman to make the breakfast especially for the occasion. She would make atole with chocolate, fried eggs, and very fine, thin tortillas separate from the rest. This was given to the priest and to the singer who accompanied him.

218. The breakfast was presented in a basket with a handle on it. The basket was lined with a well-ironed napkin, and sometimes there was a hand embroidered cloth. The napkin was for the bottom of the basket and the other cloth was to cover it. They brought it to the priest in the church and when he finished saying mass he sat down to eat. 219. They did not invite him to the house of the mayordomo, because the people were shy and embarrassed to do such things. All this used to happen around 1950. In those days, it was considered an honor for a person to give a meal to a priest, and especially to serve him at his own house.

220. On the day of the fiesta, the mass was celebrated with three priests officiating. It lasted about three hours and was called a "grand mass." When it was over, the people would go back to their homes, but some of them went to the mayordomos' houses to eat. 221. They came back at about 3 o'clock in the evening for the procession. The priest was not present at the procession, only the people of the pueblo. All day long the pilgrims kept coming to the church, going in and out, and leaving alms for the Virgen de Los Remedios.

222. September 1st is the day traditionally dedicated to her fiesta. On rare occasions the date might be postponed. We have already seen, in another volume, the beliefs involved in postponing a fiesta. For example, if the day for

the celebration of the Virgin falls on a Monday,[48] then the celebration is put off until Thursday. 223. But the fiesta actually begins on Wednesday; this is considered the vesper, or pre-fiesta day. Then Thursday is the day of the actual fiesta, and Friday is the finale. 224. Friday is better known among the people as the "dia de la trasnochada," or the "overnighter." If a fiesta falls on a Sunday, then it, too, is postponed until Thursday. By tradition, the fiestas are held only on Thursdays, and on no other day.

225. As it starts to get towards night, the participants keep arriving at the church in order to leave some alms. Mostly, they leave something for the Virgen de Los Remedios because it is believed that she performs many miracles. They only leave a few coins for the other santitos that have come to visit.

226. At this point the statues are taken down from the altar and placed on short pedestals, and everyone gets ready to go out with the procession. As they leave the church, they come out in the following order: in front comes the boy carrying the little bell that he rings as he walks along. 227. Behind him come the ciriales. Next comes the Virgen de Los Remedios, and behind her the Virgen de los Dolores de Orizabita, and then El Señor de Buen Viaje, and finally the band that goes along playing beautiful music. 228. We must remember that there are two bands; when one stops playing the other starts. This is what is know as the "grand procession." It leaves the church and makes a tour of the entire central plaza. The supplicants follow along praying; some of them say a prayer and then others repeat it. 229. It takes about two hours to go completely around the plaza and return again to the church.

230. It has been a long time since they used to put up decorated arches on every street corner. Little by little, those arches have disappeared; people have stopped building them because they were too costly, and also because of the work it took to weave the cucharilla plant used in making them. This plant used to be brought in by people from far away in the wet mountain lands.[49]

231. When the procession is finished, the people once again return the saints and the Virgin to their usual places. People pass by and worship the various images. Everyone goes by and makes the sign of the cross, and kisses the feet of the statue, and says goodbye. Anyone who has money leaves an offering. 232. A mother or father who has one or two children along will ask the mayordomo to "cleanse" the children with a peso that the parent gives him. The money serves as a form of offering. The money for such a cleansing is given only to the mayordomo.[50] 233. There is a kind of hierarchy here. Sometimes the adults ask the mayordomo to do the cleansing on them, and then they leave money as an offering to the santito whom they asked for protection. It is believed that whoever is cleansed in this way is freed from the Devil and from

bad luck because the saint or virgin whom the person worships keeps them away.

234. There is also a belief associated with what are called "lazos para pegar" or "whipping ropes." These are small, tightly wound ropes that are very hard and are also known as "ejotes," or string beans. They are hung at the feet of the statues and are taken everywhere with them. The lazos consist of four such short, hard ropes attached to a handle so that the mayordomo can wield them whenever necessary.

235. Parents who bring their children to the fiesta and to the church, bring them close to the icons and ask the mayordomos to "give the children some ejotes." The mayordomo takes the ejotes from the base of the statue of the Virgin and makes the sign of the cross in front of her face. When he is finished, he brings the ejotes close to the child's face so that the child can kiss them. 236. The child kisses the ejotes. Then the mayordomo makes the sign of the cross and finally he brings the ejotes back to the child's mouth so that the child can kiss them again. Now the "cleansing" begins.[51] The mayordomo passes the tips of the ejotes across the child's back and in front of its face. He goes around the child, touching the shoulders with the ejotes, and then he gives the child a few lashes across the shoulders and on the back. 237. When he strikes hard it makes the child jump because it hurts. It makes small children cry. The mayordomo gives about six lashes. This is what is called "ejotes." There are some adults that ask for the lashes, too. 238. In this case, also, they give an offering. They give whatever they feel like giving. The belief about this is that it will rid people of laziness.

239. When the mayordomo finishes giving lashes, he presents the person with the ejotes and the person kisses them again. Adults, men and women alike, are whipped much harder than children if they ask for ejotes. You can hear the loud crack as the tips of the whip strike a person's back. 240. It makes a piercing pain and people jump as their back is struck by the ejotes. Some people ask for an ejote whipping from those carrying the Virgin of Los Remedios, and others ask for it from those carrying the Sr. del Buen Viaje from Orizabita. They ask for ejotes from whoever is carrying the image in which they have the most faith, and they ask for them only from one image and not from both. 241. When this is over, people ask all the mayordomos of all the images there to give them some kind of relic to take home. Pilgrims to the fiestas burn the relics when there are thunderstorms and strong winds. They believe that this calms the storms. I am referring here to torrential rains accompanied by strong hail. 242. Strong hail and lightning kills animals and people. People put the relics at the base of a big tree, and it is said that this keeps lightning from striking it.

243. The system of loans that people make to one another is very old. Many who are great grandparents recall that people used to lend each other things, particularly when one of them had some kind of reception. The person in charge of the reception went around to the homes of the people with whom he had the greatest trust, respect and friendship. 244. He would leave early in the morning in order to visit those whom he felt could do him the favor of lending him what he needed. He did not go empty handed on these errands, but brought along at least a bottle of aguardiente as a gift for the person whom he was visiting. Sometimes he might bring along a pack of cigarettes, or two pesos worth of bread. Mostly, people brought along aguardiente and cigarettes.

245. Arriving at his destination, he hailed the people in the house and they bid him to enter and rest. Then he offered what he brought as a gift, and began to explain the reason for his visit. The borrower had to make his rounds three weeks or a month in advance, so that the lender might have sufficient time to work and to fulfill the favor asked of him. 246. The lender had to work hard in order to get together the money to pay for what he was lending. If he saw that the date of the loan was very close, then he said no. If he said that he would do it, then the person who asked for the loan was happy; he took his leave and went off to visit someone else.

247. Everywhere he goes, he tells people what it is that he needs for them to lend him. He tells them if he needs corn, or an animal, or pulque. Then it's up to the lender to choose, on his own, what he wants to lend. Whatever he thinks he can come up with is what he chooses. Suppose that a person agrees to lend tortillas. 248. The custom is to lend this commodity in measures known as "uatra" in Ñähñu, or a dozen cuartillos. Loans are also made in half measures, or six cuartillos. A person who is better off says that he will lend twelve cuartillos, and someone who is not so well off says that he can only lend six. In any case, these measures are always used.

249. Once a household has promised to provide tortillas, the woman of the house seeks out other women of her generation to help her make the round, thin type of tortillas. She gets two friends to help her. When they finish making the tortillas, they go to the house of the mayordomo to whom the loan has been promised. 250. There is a special large size basket for carrying these tortillas. It is made of woven carrizo.[52] It is large and wide across the top, and about 70 centimeters deep, and holds exactly twelve cuartillos of maize made into tortillas. There is also a specially made basket that holds six cuartillos.

251. The women have already been advised about what time to go to the mayordomo's house, when the meal starts. Sometimes the man of the house goes along with the women, with one of the women carrying the big basket of

tortillas. 252. Other times, a man might go later, after the women have already gone to the reception. This happens when a man is embarrassed because he has not helped to make the tortillas. Of course, no one forces him to go at all, but he worries that when the time comes for him to be repaid, then the man who asked for the loan won't show up at his meal either.

253. The person who lends whole grain maize brings it about a week before the event. This is so that the woman of the house will have sufficient time to find *her* friends, to bring them the maize, and for them to make the tortillas for her. Maize is always lent in twelve cuartillo lots, or in six. A few people have enough money to lend twenty-four. 254. The amount customarily lent is calculated not to cut too heavily into the finances of the lender, nor does it cost too heavily for those who have to go out and repay the loan later. Everything is designed to be balanced. 255. The woman of the house where the reception is planned receives the maize from her neighbor and she gives it to other women who are her friends and acquaintances. This activity is a kind of labor loan because the women who help take on a repayable cargo when their friend asks for *their* help later. 256. The women never refuse each other and always say yes immediately when they are asked by their friends to help out. When people live in mutual friendship and respect, they help each other with whatever is needed.

257. The lending of animals does not exceed one or two at a time, even when the person being asked has many. In fact, it is difficult to agree to this kind of loan because animals do not multiply very quickly in this region. Animals do not have much to eat because the land is desert, and so they grow slowly and are very thin. 258. They multiply whenever some grass grows for them to eat. Goats and chickens are the animals mostly lent between people. Sheep and cattle are practically never lent because there are not many of them. Of these last two, the one lent the least is cattle. 259. A goat that is lent must be a female or a castrated male. The person asking for the loan would not accept an uncastrated male goat, because it is not customary to eat such goats. Eating a billy goat that has not been castrated causes stomach pain, and so people always eat either billy goats that have been castrated or nanny goats.

260. If the date of the fiesta is near and the mayordomo still doesn't have all the animals he needs, or at least the minimum required, he will accept the animals he is offered, even if they are not appropriate. Then he tries to trade the animals for others that are good to eat. 261. The person looking to trade seeks an animal the same size as the one he has. Everyone in the Valley, or at least almost everyone knows what it means not to want to eat uncastrated goats. Some people say it is because of the power of the semen the goat has in his genitals.

This brings on sickness and causes stomach pain and diarrhea to whoever eats the meat of an uncastrated goat.

262. The mayordomo will ask for four or five animals on loan because he does not want to get into too much debt. People could lend him more, but then it would be difficult for him when he has to repay the debt. If he did not have the necessary animals when he needed them to repay the debt, he would be shamed and he doesn't want this. If he welches on his debt just once with someone who lends to him, from then on that person will not trust him when he goes out asking for a favor. 263. Around here, then, it is pretty bad if someone doesn't know how to keep his word when he commits himself to his neighbors. His co-villagers will spread the word that there is someone around who can't be trusted to pay his debts, and then no one will believe him. 264. When he knows how to keep his word, a man is held in respect because of his honesty. People take their hats off when they meet this kind of man.

265. Hardly anyone lends sheep because there aren't many. For example, if a man has as many as forty animals, only six or seven sheep might be in the herd. Then, too, a person who raises sheep might not lend them because he needs them himself. He knows that sheep provide two different products. The ewe has lambs and the herd multiplies. 266. The other useful thing is that when sheep are big they give wool. The owner can shear it and sell it, or he can send it off to a weaver to make a blanket. If he has about seven, and if all of them give wool, then he has enough to make a blanket for himself. This type of sheep does not grow wool very fast, and that is why they are sheared every year.

267. For one of these animals to be lent there has to be agreement between husband and wife. Sometimes only the husband says whether to make the loan or not. There are families that divide up the animals they have. That is, even though there is one herd, some animals belong to the woman while others belong to the man. 268. This arrangement of owning animals sometimes leads to arguments if there is not a good understanding between the parties. In such cases, whenever someone asks for a loan, the couple bickers over it and can't agree. Sometimes it is the woman who says that the loan will be made and other times it is the man. 269. When it is the woman who agrees to make the loan, then the person who asks for it is embarrassed to accept it. This is even more the case if he stops to consider what will happen if he has to repay and he does not have enough money, and then he worries that he is entering into a debt agreement with a woman. 270. Where there is no division of animals the problem is not so great. But, in any event, the debt remains binding.

271. Asking for the loan of fowl is almost always the job of the wife of the man who has the cargo. She is given the responsibility of getting the loan. Why? Because women raise all fowl, including chickens and turkeys. By contrast, men hardly know anything about them. 272. A woman takes some gift with her when she goes to a friend's house to visit. She may take bread or pulque if the person whom she is going to see does not have pulque. It is not the custom among women to drink aguardiente together or to smoke cigarettes. It is very rare for Ñähñu women to consume these things.

273. The woman speaks to her friend and tells her that she needs a few fowl[53] in order to fulfill the cargo that has been assigned to her husband. If the woman of the house agrees to make the loan, then she asks how many fowl, and what kind—that is, whether the woman who is making the request wants chickens or turkeys. 274. The woman asking for the loan says that she needs six or a dozen. If the woman has a lot, she says that she will lend them, but if she doesn't have many fowl then she lends whatever she can. In this case, as with all such loans, when the woman asking for the loan returns the favor, she gives back the same number that she gets. 275. Chickens are the most easily lent because that is what women raise mostly, and also because they multiply more than turkeys and they resist disease more, as well. Turkeys do not grow fast, and when they get sick they die more easily than chickens.

276. The woman asking for the loan learns whether the loan will be made or not, but she does not take the fowl away with her. She returns two days before she needs them and takes them with her then. Or, more usually, the woman making the loan will take the fowl to the borrower's house and drop them off so that when the loan is repaid the borrower will do the same. 277. Sometimes a woman will not simply ask for a loan, but will also invite her friend to come to the house and help kill and cook the chickens. There is also a set measure, though not a strict one, for the lending of chickens. Either six or a dozen are lent at a time. It is rare that they are lent one or two at a time; only a few people do it that way. 278. Perhaps they are lent in this way so that there won't be any mistakes, and so that no one forgets, neither the lender nor the borrower. Three, four or five years can go by, or even longer, and the chickens are not forgotten.

279. The lending of pulque is also done in its own way, and by particular measures. When pulque is lent, it is given by the barrel or half barrel. The words "cuarto" or "half a cuarto" are usually used in this regard. The capacity of a barrel is 44 liters. These are always the amounts lent by whoever agrees to do the favor. 280. The mayordomo asks that the pulque be delivered on the day of the meal. There are some people whom he won't say anything to; that is, he won't ask them for any loan. But in such a little community everyone knows

who the mayordomo is and it is not difficult for them to attend the meal. 281. So, before he knows it, people are there at the mayordomo's house with some kind of loan. Mostly they bring pulque or tortillas. They don't bring animals because they know that it is the very day of the fiesta and there is no time to cook them.

282. In earlier times, some people lent money to the mayordomo. They came by with the money on the day of the fiesta. The mayordomo would not go out in search of monetary loans. People who had the pleasure of lending money would come by on their own and leave it with the mayordomo. 283. Years ago people used to leave two or three pesos, or even fifty centavos. Someone who was better off would leave five silver pesos, which was the kind of money that circulated in those times. When the mayordomo saw how much was delivered, it made him worry about going into a lot of debt. 284. He was concerned that he would not have enough money to pay back the debt when the time came. Of course, everyone did not ask for repayment at the same time. Some people who made loans would ask for repayment at the end of the year, or after two years, or even three. When a person became mayordomo he would remember all he had lent out to others. 285. If a man is reminded about several of his debts at once, he first thinks about whether he has enough to cover them. If two or three people remind him of his debts, then he will pay one or two of them and will postpone the other until another occasion. A person's neighbors notice it when someone has accumulated a lot of debts, and they refrain from reminding him about it.

286. Just because a man does not have enough money at the time he is asked to repay several loans at once is not considered a loss of honor. If he pays off two debts in one day, then he has acquitted himself for part of his obligation, and he seeks someone else who can help him pay the other part. 287. If a mayordomo really needs to be repaid, and if the man who owes him the money has already made a commitment to another mayordomo, then the person whose debt is being recalled looks for someone who can lend him the money to pay off the obligation. 288. When this happens it is called a "chain loan." If ready-made tortillas are given as a loan, then the same kind must be returned in payment later.

289. Everything we have looked at so far has been in regard to loans contracted by mayordomos. We saw that they have to go out and ask people to lend them what they need. One might be tempted to think, then, that the mayordomos rely only on loans in order to fulfill their cargos. 290. Actually, it is not like that at all; each mayordomo does, in fact, ask for loans, but the amount that he contributes from his own pocket is greater than all the loans put together. He asks for loans only to help him a little with the total amount he has to give. A mayordomo's entire family must work to get together enough to cover what the

mayordomo contributes. Many people who get to be mayordomos have a lot of acquaintances and friends in their own communities and in surrounding communities as well. 291. They are the numerous guests at the fiesta, and that is why he has to make a lot of food. He has to kill a lot of animals for this. Some kill a head of beef and goats and chickens in order to have enough for all the guests to eat.

292. On the day of the fiesta, people from small communities come with loans to all the mayordomos who customarily borrow and lend to others. For example, a person from El Saúz may visit Los Remedios, but he brings one or two barrels of pulque with him. 293. Some loans of pulque come from Defay, and others come from El Naxtey, El Nando, and so on. Some people who lend pulque make an agreement with the borrower to repay the loan in maize and not in pulque. 294. The mayordomo accepts the proposal of the person from whom he is borrowing, because he knows that the person comes from a place where they do not have harvests every year and they need maize. On the other hand, there are not many maguey plants in the irrigated zone for scraping and for making pulque. The man who owes a barrel of pulque pays it back with twelve cuartillos of maize.

295. This is the custom, even though it appears that the monetary value of the pulque is not equal to that of the maize. This does not happen in the lending of tortillas or of animals; they must be repaid in kind. In the case of tortillas it is because of the labor value involved, and animals just cost a lot. 296. There are people who lend maize on the very day of the fiesta. They always bring twelve cuartillos and beg the mayordomo's pardon that their wife did not have time to make the tortillas. The host responds: "this will not terminate our friendship for one another; there will be another occasion."

297. On Friday, the last day of the fiesta, the mayordomo bids farewell to the fireworks masters and to the musicians. He pays them their money and they leave. The fiesta is over, but the debts that remain are many. 298. The people don't let many days go by before organizing to name the mayordomos for the following year. It is important for them to name the mayordomos and to authorize them officially so that they can work to complete their obligations.

299. We are not yet finished with the fiestas of Remedios. We will see that the faith the people there place in the Virgin of Los Remedios puts her in a special place of honor compared to the icons and statues worshipped in other communities. It is believed that the Virgin is very miraculous and the people have developed the custom of requesting that she be allowed to spend a few days in their homes. 300. Those who want to have the Virgin at their homes tell the mayordomo about it. That way, they can come to an agreement about what day the supplicant will bring the statue to his house and the mayordomo can be

ready. The person who asks that the Virgin come to his house must come and fetch her himself. 301. For example, if a person from Espíritu wants to have the Virgin at his house, he starts to get ready early in the morning. This is considered another mayordomía, or cargo obligation, and he has to hire a band and find assistants who will prepare flower garlands for the offering. He has to kill goats and chickens to make mole and feed all the helpers for the occasion.

302. Those who prepare the floral offering begin very early and when they are finished the band has to be ready to go. They go with the people to deliver the flowers and to return with the Virgin. They all go together from the house of the person who will host the Virgin, and they return with her after making a floral offering to her. The musicians play along the way, and other men set off firecrackers, especially when they near the house they are going to. 303. They take turns carrying the Virgin. They put the statue in a glass box about a meter high, and put a rope around the base to carry it. When they get to the house where people are waiting for them, more flowers are offered. Candles are lit, and holy water is sprinkled on the spot where the image will be set and venerated. The people approach one by one and begin censing the Virgin.

304. People ask for holy water from the church. When the priest says mass, people ask him to bless a jug of water. He makes the sign of the cross over the water jug, while looking up towards heaven. From what people say, this is to chase evil from the water. 305. Holy water is sprinkled on the ground wherever a new house is going to be built. It is sprinkled wherever a person has been murdered in order to chase away evil. It is used to make the sign of the cross on the foreheads of gravely sick people who are dying. It is sprinkled in graves and then the corpse is put in. It is used by priests to bless a new house, and is sprinkled on the walls.

306. When people make an offering to the Virgin, they go into the kitchen and offer the flowers to the hearth fire, in the same way described earlier. Then the meal is served and the same evening the people go home and the Virgin remains in the house of those who awaited her. 307. She remains there for three or four days and is returned. Sometimes, another person from the same village might want her, so she passes directly to him and he takes her to his house and she does not return to her own community. She is awaited in the houses of people who have been sick for a while and who haven't gotten better. They ask for the Virgin because they believe she can help rid them of their illness. The Virgin invariably collects offerings that people give her.

308. If she is finished in one place, and if no one takes her home, then she passes to another village where someone else will be waiting to host her in their home. In this way she goes about for a month or two outside her church. She is

called everywhere. Sometimes she is called to villages in the municipios of Zimapán, Tasquillo, Alfajayucan and Cardonal. 309. Towards the end of the year she remains in her church. Around December the Christmas posadas begin.[54] The Virgin is put on an altar, and people come to worship all the other images that are like a family there, all together, and set out on a table in a kind of diorama.

310. The fiesta begins December 16th and ends the 25th. One or two mayordomos are named for each night. Each of the mayordomos spends a certain amount of money in order to fulfill this cargo. 311. He buys some large candles for the altar, and others that are no more than 10 centimeters long. They are various colors and burn for perhaps half an hour or less. These little candles are for giving to the assembled people at the church so they can go out and follow in the procession of the saints. 312. The saints in the diorama are Mary and her husband Joseph. The woman is seated on a burro and the man is on foot, as if he were driving the burro. There is a little child out in front of them who is pulling on the burro's rope.

313. The mayordomos for the first night of the posadas work together to feed the members of the choir and the musicians. The mayordomos of the first night have to hire the string musicians. After the first night, then it is up to the other mayordomos, if they wish, to keep the musicians on. They may hire the same musicians, or they may hire others. The choir members are sometimes men and sometimes women. 314. They sing prayers to the saints at night in the church for about two hours, and then take the images out on the procession. The procession begins at the base of the altar, goes out to the entrance to the cemetery, and heads back. It does not go very far. They make this circuit twice, and the second time they close the church door on the santitos and leave them outside with a few of the prayer singers.

315. The singers beg for permission to come inside for lodging. Those inside the church respond, singing, and deny permission.[55] 316. Those outside ask again, and this goes on about four times, back and forth, until those inside finally relent and open the doors to let those outside come in and spend the night. 317. When the doors are finally opened, people are very happy and they light sparklers that the mayordomos have handed out beforehand. They put the images back where they belong and the choir sings more songs of praise. Then the choir members sing a special carol to say goodbye, and the musicians say goodbye, too, playing a song.

318. When this is all done, the mayordomo calls to the people outside the church so he can distribute peanuts and sweets to them. They have gathered in the meantime, awaiting this event. First the carolers are given the sweets, and

then the musicians, and then the rest of the people. While the distribution of peanuts is going on, the musicians continue playing beautiful tunes. 319. A special, decorated ceramic jug full of peanuts, oranges, sugar cane and sweets is set up for the children. It is suspended on a rope above their heads, and they are blindfolded and given a pole with which to hit the jug. They are amused for a long time with this game, as they swing at the jug. 320. Someone climbs up to where one of the rope ends are tied, and he toys with the children, raising and lowering the jug as they swipe at it from below. When one of the children catch him off guard and strikes a heavy blow, the piñata breaks and makes a big noise and all the peanuts and sherds fall to the ground. 321. The children push and shove each other as they try to gather up the peanuts and all the other things from the jug. Sometimes the mayordomos make piñatas for grownups, too, but only for men and not for women because women don't like to push and shove one another.

322. The piñatas made for men are just a joke because they only contain a few little peanuts, and gravel instead of sweets. Sometimes they find a couple of lizards and seal them in the jug. 323. They decorate the jug beautifully so that one would not know what it contained. At the proper time they hang the jug and set a man to try and knock it down. People stand around shouting, goading him to knock it down as quickly as he can. When he finally swats it, the jug makes a loud noise and falls to ground.

324. People rush in to pick up all the stuff from the jug. They pick up the pebbles and a few peanuts. Their hands work quickly; because it is dark they can't see what they are grabbing. They can feel some kind of little animal on their feet, and it is just the lizard that was put in the jug, of course. 325. They run all around after the creature, laughing a lot, but they don't get anything to eat. This laughing and joking takes place apart from and in a different area from the distribution of peanuts to the people. If someone likes to dance, he starts dancing. He picks out a girl, and asks her to dance, and she accepts. 326. The mayordomos finish distributing peanuts and start giving out coffee and bread. They give out coffee in earthen cups. This fiesta finishes about three or four in the morning and when the people leave they go back to their homes.

327. The next day they return to take part in another posada, and this goes on every day until the nine nights are finished. They give out peanuts, sweets, and coffee every day, and the mayordomos who have money give out alcoholic drinks. Everything the mayordomos give out is of their own volition; no one obliges them to do this. 328. They are, however, asked to purchase the candles and firecrackers needed for the church. The mayordomos provide little baskets of sweets and peanuts that are hung from one of the arms of the small statues

444 NATIVE ETHNOGRAPHY

that are taken around. This is ostensibly for the saints to eat, but in reality the mayordomos of the church eat those things.

329. The last night is the twenty fourth and it is called "rä gäxä xui" in Ñähñu, or Christmas Eve. About six mayordomos are named for this night because a lot of money gets spent. 330. They work together to decorate the entire altar. They purchase moss (the kind that grows on rocks), pine boughs, cotton, and different paper maché animal figurines, such as birds, deer, buzzards, tigers or lions, wolves, eagles, cattle, horses, burros, coyotes, foxes, and others such as elephants that live far away in the wild forests. 331. The fiesta mayordomos buy the figures and bring them to the church mayordomos who know where it is most convenient to put them. A lot more people congregate on Christmas Eve, and the church fills up.

332. The decorations on the altar look like a wild forest where many animals live, and in the midst of it all they put a replica of the baby Jesus who supposedly has just been born.[56] The rosary is said just as it was said on the previous nights of the festival, and then the saints go out in a procession. When this is finished, the images are returned to where they are usually kept. 333. Then the replica of the baby Jesus is put on a table. The choir starts singing carols of praise, and the statue of the child is taken out on a procession. This procession makes the entire circuit of the cemetery.

334. When they are finished, the fiesta mayordomos and the church mayordomos get ready for the "lullaby of the baby Jesus." The baby Jesus has been placed in a little cradle, and two children stand at the ends of the cradle, holding it steady. There are other children, dressed as shepherds, at the door of the church. Each one carries a gourd, and they are holding a little bleating lamb or a kid in their arms. 335. They come up practically to the foot of the altar where the baby Jesus is. One of the little shepherds takes the cradle's cord and begins to rock it back and forth while the others start to dance. The musicians play shepherd tunes.

336. The church is filled with people and not everyone can see what is going on up in front. The mayordomos and their helpers go around handing out whistles and sparklers to light for the little baby. The "lullaby of the baby" is performed at midnight. 337. This is a custom that has been practiced for a long time. It is said that this is how it was when Jesus Christ was born and this is a reminder of that. When this is finished, the baby is put away and the people leave the church, saying goodbye to the santitos, and go to where a dance will be held. The people will be there all night, without sleeping, because the next day, December 25th, is a holiday and there is no work.

338. A week later there is another fiesta in celebration of the New Year. This fiesta also has its mayordomo who must fulfill his cargo. The baby Jesus is adored once again. 339. The mayordomo for the New Year's celebration also spends money. He buys things needed in the church and he kills some animals to provide food for the musicians and the singers. The rosary is said in the church, the baby Jesus is taken out on a procession around the cemetery, and the procession returns and goes into the church. 340. The person carrying the statue this time is the padrino, or godfather, of the baby Jesus. The mayordomo is only for the midnight mass, and after that the padrino brings the baby to the mayordomo's house. The mayordomo does not carry the baby; the padrino does, and he brings the baby to the mayordomo's house. 341. A place is ready to put the baby Jesus when he gets there, so that whoever wants to can adore it. The padrino has been told in advance to do this. They mayordomo invites the padrino to bring the baby to his house. 342. Once he gets to the mayordomo's house, the padrino starts giving out alcoholic drinks, peanuts, and sweets for everyone visiting there. When the padrino finishes giving out peanuts, dinner is served, even though it may be one in the morning by this time. 343. From this day on, the mayordomo and the padrino will show respect and friendship to one another as compadres because the padrino carried the baby during the mass in church and then brought the baby to the house of the mayordomo. This is considered to be the same as if one had baptized the child of the other.

344. We finish here the fiestas of Remedios. At the end we will talk about the big bonfires that are burned everywhere, and not just in Los Remedios, on both Christmas Eve and on New Year's Eve.

345. Now we continue north on the road we have followed. From here we have to go about six kilometers to reach a community called Orizabita. The Catholic religion has been practiced for many years in this community. Five fiestas are celebrated in this pueblo each year. 346. The first, considered the most important, is called El Sexto Viernes de Dolores. It is known by some as "Following the Footsteps." Next in importance comes the Fiesta of the Dead, for both adults and children. Another is the Fiesta of Guadalupe; it is on December 12th. 347. There are the posadas on the nine nights of Christmas, and finally the celebration of the New Year. In addition there are other small fiestas celebrated by individuals as a result of some promise they may have made to one of the other santitos. Such things include the offering of flowers to God or to the saints or holy virgins during a "petition" mass for them or for the dead. There are masses to petition God for rain. 348. Another fiesta that used to be celebrated was called The Blessing of the Candles, in which seeds for the maize

and bean plantings were blessed. This fiesta was celebrated on the 2nd of February.

Regarding the hosting of holy images, people in Orizabita invite the Virgen de Los Remedios; El Sr. del Buen Viaje, who is also the patron of Orizabita;[57] the Baby Jesus of Portezuelos; and the Virgen de Soledad. These are the images that the people believe in most and that are thought to make the most miracles. This is why the people follow them.

349. In order to put on a really good fiesta for the Sixth Friday, it was necessary for the authorities to organize everyone in all the villages that make up Orizabita. The Juez Auxiliar del Centro[58] called on everyone to come to a meeting from all the little communities around Orizabita. He called on those from La Pechuga de Gallina, La Lagunita, El Banxu, El Ojo del Agua, La Palma, El Cantamayé, Boxhuada, San Andrés, Cuesta Colorada, El Gundhó, El Manantial, Agua Florida, and El Defay. 350. All those old enough used to come and participate in the organization of the fiesta. They would set out from their homes as dawn broke and by nine o'clock they would be in Orizabita. In those days there were no cars and everyone came on foot. There were not even roads and people would come straight across the mountains through the passes.

351. When it was seen that most of the people had arrived, the judge would move the crowd to the shade and tell them why they had been summoned. First they named everyone, and as each person heard his name he called out "present!" After reading the list the judge told everyone what was needed for the fiesta. 352. Everyone already knows the date for the celebration. The fiesta is always celebrated on a Friday. The significance of the fiesta that takes place on the Sixth Friday is treated in another volume of this series dealing with the flora. 353. The mayordomos of the church list all the things they want to do for the fiesta. They mention the first mass, and then the street arches, and the firecrackers, toritos, castillos, candles, and relics of one kind or another for people to take home after mass. Sometimes they buy robes for the statues, and they mention the music, too. The mayordomos have to provide food for the fireworks makers and for the musicians as well.

354. Sometimes Sixth Friday comes in March and sometimes in April. The organizational meeting takes place during the first days of February because that is the only way there will be enough time for the mayordomos to fulfill their obligations. 355. They agree among themselves how much each will pay. Suppose they agree to pay five pesos each and they have three weeks to come up with the full amount. 356. Among them there would be many for whom this amount would be a big burden and in the end, some are short a peso or a peso and a half.

357. Another way in which the cargos are distributed is for whole villages to be responsible for particular functions. The people get together and say that, for example, La Lagunita will be in charge of the castillo, or El Defay is responsible for the musicians, and Gundhó is responsible for the masses. 358. In fact, this is what they used to do. The people of those communities would organize and take on those cargos. Of course, this raised the amount of money that each resident had to pay; but then they would be given a rest for two years while other communities took on the obligations, and on the third year they would acquire new cargos.

The residents of La Lagunita organized to fulfill those cargos; no one wants to be shamed for not having pitched in. 359. They chose among themselves who would be responsible, and those who had not had cargos before were selected. They named six people, out loud, one by one, to be in charge of the castillo, and that is how each person appointed knew who his partners were. 360. The mayordomos agreed how much each would pay, and thus they put together the cost of the castillo. The mayordomos also agreed on when they would deposit the money with the fireworks master[59] so that he would know exactly on what day the Sixth Friday was.

361. A castillo used to cost about 15 pesos in those days. A torito cost about five pesos. Two castillos and two toritos were needed, so they paid around 50 pesos for the four pieces along with the big firecrackers that were shot off after the castillo was spent. 362. Once they had made a contract with the fireworks master, those responsible were happy because they had fulfilled their obligation, and on the day of the fiesta they would not look bad in front of their neighbors. They drew up a document that said that the fireworks makers had received the money and had promised to fulfill the agreement with the mayordomos. The name of the fireworks master responsible for the agreement appeared on the paper and he signed it. 363. The mayordomos thus had something to show when they made their report to the people.

364. When they went to drop off the money, the mayordomos did not go alone, but had to be accompanied by the judges and by the mayordomos of the church who went along to where the fireworks makers lived. Sometimes they went as far as La Blanca. This is in the municipio of Santiago de Anaya, and you get there by following the road south from Actopan.[60] 365. They went on foot, crossing directly through the mountain passes because they knew that the fireworks masters who made good castillos lived there. They contracted out everywhere to villages that celebrated fiestas, and that is how people knew of them. Those who went to deliver the money left Orizabita around three in the morning and by eight o'clock they were at the house of the fireworks maker.

366. He knew those mayordomos were coming because he had met them at the market in Ixmiquilpan. He agreed on the time they would come, and was waiting for them when they arrived. 367. If the mayordomos and the fireworks maker knew each other well, then the mayordomos dropped off the money in the market so they would not have to walk such a long way. In that case, though, they had to have witnesses to the transaction. The total cost of the fireworks was not paid out in advance. A portion was left to be paid as dawn broke after the fiesta. The full contract was not paid off until practically the moment when everyone said goodbye to one another.

368. If the work of the fireworks master did not turn out well, then the next year he was not hired again. People are not satisfied if the colored fireworks on the castillo don't burn well and if the wheels of the castillo don't spin around as the powder goes off. Nor are they happy when the big firecrackers just fizzle instead of booming. 369. And they don't like it when the roman candles just shoot up and fall back to earth without exploding and making a lot of noise. Some pieces just shoot up a short distance in the air and fall to the ground before going off. Sometimes a roman candle will shoot up and fall back right on top of someone when it explodes. 370. This is a disgrace for the fireworks makers, as well as for the people on whom the firecracker falls because it is considered a sign that they did not come to the fiesta with full devotion in their hearts. The following year the people contract with fireworks makers from someplace else. If they don't contract with those from Alfajayucan, then they go to those from Chilcuauhtla.

371. After delivering the down payment on the castillo and the toritos, the mayordomos agree on who will be responsible for feeding the pyrotechnists on the first day of the fiesta—who among the six will provide breakfast, who will provide the midday meal, and who will provide supper. 372. They make these arrangements about three months ahead of time so that each one knows just what he has to do. He knows how much he will have to put in himself, and how much he will have to borrow from others, and he starts to work as soon as he can so that he can do everything needed. He goes to people who owe him and reminds them of their debts in plenty of time.

373. There are about ten people in a group of fireworks makers. The master craftsmen are accompanied by their helpers who assist in building the castillo. Some build the frame for the castillo, and others set to making the spinning wheels from split carrizo. Some people fashion the wheels from thin branches of the pirul tree,[61] but they are heavy and the wheels don't spin well, so they are generally made from carrizos[62] that are split lengthwise. 374. Other assistants fasten the colored fireworks, and the ones that make noise, to the correct parts of

the castillo. On occasion, the fireworks master is accompanied by his wife, and sometimes by his children whom he has shown how the carrizo must be split. 375. Splitting carrizo looks easy, but if the person doing it is not careful they can cut their hands or break the carrizo. The chief fireworks master instructs his assistants that they must not drink a lot of pulque and under no circumstances should they get drunk. 376. This kind of work is very dangerous, especially if one is not careful; they are not allowed to smoke either, because that could cause a tragedy.[63]

377. The mayordomo makes them dinner, and even though it is just a single meal, he kills about two dozen chickens and about a dozen goats. This is so that there will be enough to feed everyone who comes to visit him. Some people come just to visit, while others come bearing loans. Some come with loans for the first time, while others come to pay what they owe from previous transactions. The fireworks makers and the visitors all take food home with them. 378. When they are served they get a lot of tortillas and chunks of meat heaped on their plates. The mayordomo prepares, and expects to give, food for everyone. This is the custom of those who follow the Catholic religion in this region.

379. I am saying that everyone comes back for seconds and their plates are filled again; even children are treated in the same manner. The mayordomo is actually throwing bread on the water, because when he goes somewhere to visit friends, they take similarly good care of him. 380. Each of the three mayordomos provide the food on their appointed day. They all do it in the same way; that is, they provide enough food so that everyone can fill their plates twice and take home their itacates. The mayordomos and their wives invite their assistants to the fiesta to help out, and they rush around attending to the guests.

381. The man calls upon his helpers two days before the cargo. He calls on those who butcher goats. The number of helpers a mayordomo needs for this job depends on the number of goats he will slaughter. For example, if he will butcher two dozen goats, he calls on three people to help him. 382. It may take a long time to kill the goats, especially when the man of the house asks the butchers to make pulque bags from the skins of the largest ones. Not everyone knows how to do this; among the three people whom the mayordomo has called to help him, perhaps one of them knows how to make pulque bags from goat skins. 383. Two of them work on turning the skins of the selected goats inside out, while the third kills the other goats. When the other goats are killed their skins are slit open. They are sold in the market to merchants who specialize in this trade, although those merchants only pay what they feel like paying. Even today nobody has complained about them; they just want poor people's money.

384. More skins are slit open than are turned inside out whole; about three or four pulque bags are made at a time.

385. As they kill the animals they see if they like the skin and they also remove the intestines and the liver. The woman of the house has invited her helpers who wash the intestines for cooking. The women who help here are the ones who work the most, actually. The men really work only when they kill the goats and cook the barbacóa. The men don't do anything else. 386. The women, on the other hand, start working the day the goats are killed because they have to wash and cook the intestines. On the third day they kill the chickens. The hardest part of this job is to remove the feathers and gut them; killing them is not very hard. The women just slit the chickens' throats and they die. No one ever pays money for this kind of loan of labor. The payment is just what people eat.

387. So far, the mayordomos for the first day of the fiesta have provided food. For the next day, which is the actual day of the fiesta, the other three mayordomos take over. The ones who have already provided food on the first day now rest. 388. The others have prepared everything and are ready to provide food. They serve everyone who comes with a loan to visit them. Mayordomos invite one another. Those who were mayordomos the day before, for example, now come with their wives to visit those whose turn has come. The mayordomos go out at night together to attend the fiesta and to see the burning of the castillo. 389. When the procession leaves the church, the mayordomos stay together, and thus they show respect for one another for having been mayordomos. Even if they live far away, they find some way to attend the fiesta. 390. If they live really far, then they find some place in Orizabita, where they know people, and ask permission to prepare the food for the fireworks makers right there. The owners of the house who are asked the favor know the custom and give permission gladly.

391. In those days, a lot of people used to come down from the mountains to the fiesta, and in order to eat they would visit the mayordomos. In turn, the mayordomos knew who their neighbors were from the surrounding villages and they prepared enough food and did not let them go hungry. 392. Each mayordomo took care of some people. There were a lot of mayordomos: six for the castillo, nine for the music, and about four more for the masses. None of them would turn away anyone who came to visit or deny them food. They always offered, with friendship and respect, something to eat.

393. The mayordomos for the music take good care of the musicians so that they will play continuously. There used to be fifteen or twenty musicians, and sometimes as many as twenty-five. Those who had more money were selected

to be the mayordomos for the music. 394. They would butcher around three dozen goats or a head of beef so that there would be enough to feed all who came. Some people in those days had wild cattle in the mountains. 395. The owners got six of their assistants[64] together and set aside a day to go out and kill one of the animals. They shot it, butchered it, and quartered it on the spot so that they could haul back the meat on their shoulders, each person carrying a slab.

396. The mayordomos had to pay money in advance in order to contract the music. The nine mayordomos went and talked to the judge. They asked him to accompany them to where the musicians lived in order to drop off the advance money. 397. They used to charge about 100 pesos in total for the music for three days.[65] The musicians arrived on Wednesday around four in the afternoon, and they played all day Thursday. They used to accompany the people to fetch the Virgen de Los Remedios and the images from Espíritu. Sometimes half would go to Remedios and half went to Espíritu. Otherwise they went to only one of those places. When they returned, they gathered again before going into the church. 398. They played all day Friday and most of the night. They rested at four in the morning and began playing again Saturday morning, finishing up by midday. 399. The judge and the mayordomos for the music had to deliver the down payment on the music together; the mayordomos for the church did not go along.

400. One of the mayordomos had to provide food for the musicians when they arrived on Wednesday evening. That was their dinner. The next day, Thursday, another three mayordomos were responsible. One provided breakfast at around eight in the morning, another provided the midday meal around two in the afternoon, and the last gave the dinner. 401. The musicians played some beautiful pieces before eating, and when they finished they played some more. When they left the mayordomo's house they would play a diana which the band leader dedicated to the mayordomo and to all who prepared the meal.

402. The next day, Friday, the musicians get up early to play in front of the church. They greet the Virgen de Dolores with a piece called Las Mañanitas. For this particular piece, some people go along with the musicians and sing, and in this way they "wake up" the Virgin. 403. There are adults, young men and young women, and children, and by five in the morning they are in front of the church to sing. They carry bunches of flowers for the Virgen de Dolores (that is, the Virgin Mary), and some of them set off firecrackers. When they start out singing, the door to the church is closed, and by the time they finish the mayordomo opens the door and lets them all in so that they can bring the Virgin the flowers and worship her. 404. The musicians start playing again, but this time in

the church, and they play songs of their own choosing. This is the first visit of the day to the Virgen de Dolores on this fiesta in her honor. The Orizabita statue of Christ is just there, for the time being, as a companion.

405. At midday the "grand mass," as it is called, is celebrated. It is called this because the mass for the Virgen de Dolores used to be officiated by three priests. In those days the priests didn't say the mass in Spanish, much less in Ñähñu. 406. They officiated in some other language that seemed like it required a lot of tongue twisting. It sounded like when someone eats something very hot and burns his tongue. That's what those priests more or less sounded like when they officiated at mass, and it took a long time to recite. 407. They celebrated mass for two or three hours. Since people didn't understand what the priests were saying, they got bored and some of them fell asleep in church. In those times, the people did not understand Spanish and it was useless for them to go to church because they didn't understand what the priests were saying. 408. The priests officiated at mass for many years in a language they called "Latin." Even the name of the language was not known for many years because the priests never mentioned it. They always sang the mass and spoke in Latin. 409. It is not known whether they spoke it well, since there was no one who could ask them about it; they just used it among themselves.

410. No matter how hard people tried, they could not understand what the priests were saying. Even though the priests spoke Spanish, they never spoke it to their assistants who were Ñähñu. As children we could listen to them talk to one another because we could go anywhere and listen. 411. It has only been a short time since they started saying mass in Spanish. Possibly they noticed that the people did not understand what they were saying and changed languages. In those days when they were still saying mass in Latin the priests used to shave the crowns of their heads, and they went around practically bald. 412. They had hair all around their heads, and shaved it in the middle. 413. It was probably because they thought that it made them look old. But actually, they did not look old. Some of them still looked young. Also, they generally dressed in black robes. 414. They wore a black pullover, dress-like piece of clothing. They tied a braided cotton rope, into which they put a lot of knots, around their waists. Who knows what significance it had?

415. In the middle of the mass one of the three priests climbed up onto a footstool, which was a high place from which to speak. He began to speak, but always in Latin. He held forth for about half an hour but who knows what he said? When he finished, he told the people to cross themselves, and then he turned towards the altar and continued saying mass with the other two priests.

416. A lot of firecrackers are set off when the mass begins. More are lit in the middle. They light about six dozen, and to finish off they light about a dozen dozen. 417. This measure is called a "gruesa" in Spanish, or a "gross." A lot of Ñähñu people used this measure and, of course, the Spanish word for it. (We will discuss the various measures elsewhere in order to keep order to the present text.)

418. This is what the mayordomos of the mass did. They burned a lot of firecrackers during the course of the grand mass. They just made a lot of noise in those masses and learned nothing, because they didn't understand a thing the priests were saying. 419. But they sure had a lot of respect for those priests. Many people who went to mass came up to the priest to greet him, kissing his hand. If there was a little boy there with his mother, the child had to kiss the priest's hand. 420. Some children did not want to come up and kiss the priest's hand because they were ashamed in front of this man. In that case the child's mother or father would give him a knuckle on the head, or slap his face or pull his ear in order to make him kiss the priest's hand. 421. Even though it made the child cry, with tears in his eyes he went kissed the priest's hand so that his parents wouldn't hit him any more.

422. Other holy images are invited to the fiesta of Sixth Friday from communities in the jurisdiction of Orizabita. Some are invited even though they are not from the jurisdiction of Orizabita and they show up. Some images arrive on Wednesday, or vespers, and the others show up on Thursday. 423. Those that arrive on Wednesday are from El Espíritu, the Virgin of Los Remedios, and the statue from San Andrés. The others that arrive on Thursday include the statue of Sr. del Buen Viaje, who resides in Defay; the crosses from Puerto Juárez in the Municipio of Zimapán; the crosses from La Pechuga de Gallina; the crosses from La Lagunita and from Banxu; and the statue of Christ that comes fom El Gundó.

424. These communities are a long way off. Puerto Juárez is about 24 kilometers away. In order to attend the fiesta, the people cross the mountains, carrying the crosses, looking for the shortest route possible. 425. The man in charge of those crosses has been coming for about fifteen years to Orizabita. That old man keeps coming and he says that he likes to come every year even though he is not from the pueblo.[66] 426. The people who live along the route taken by those who carry the crosses to the fiesta have agreed among themselves to receive the pilgrims. They have prepared food for all the walkers. There are two ermitas, or rest stops, where people await the pilgrims and receive them formally. 427. They offer them rest and they prepare a table with a cloth

on it for the crosses people are carrying. The people carrying the crosses are offered a seat and given a drink of pulque and a meal. 428. They don't usually make floral offerings here for the crosses. This is reserved for when they finally get to the church because the crosses have their own mayordomo who has been assigned to attend to them. Those people are given food and when they are finished they resume their march and take the road that goes to Boxhuada.

429. There is another ermita there. They await the arrival of the others coming from the mountains to the north—from La Lagunita, La Pechuga de Gallina, and El Banxu. Those crosses are accompanied by many more people. They all come on foot, adults as well as children. 430. Everyone gathers at the ermita in Boxhuada. People greet each other and ask how they have been. A mayordomo is named for this rest stop. 431. This is the one who is going to offer flowers. He has prepared a long rope of flowers that goes around all the crosses that have arrived. Afterwards, the walkers resume their march and head south to Orizabita where the church is and where all the other statues and icons will be coming together as well.

432. From Boxhuada the walkers still have three kilometers to go before reaching the church. The little community of Boxhuada does not have any holy images of its own. The people go to Orizabita to worship the saints there. 433. The images stop once again at another ermita before entering the church. From the time they leave Boxhuada they are accompanied by a band that plays music along the way. 434. When they get to the final rest stop, they meet up with the people from Gundó and El Defay who have brought their own santitos with them. Those from Gundó have had to walk about 25 kilometers to get this far. Those from Defay have come about seven kilometers. 435. Pilgrims from each of those villages have stopped along the way. They were given food to eat by some houses, and others just gave them a place to rest. All this is done out of respect.

436. When the marchers get to the outskirts of Orizabita they are greeted by the mayordomos who have built another ermita there. They have also prepared a meal, both for those who have come to leave the holy images, and those who have come to see them. The mayordomo of this ermita also makes a floral offering. Then everyone goes to congregate at the ermita built especially for the crosses and santitos that come together every year for the fiesta of Sixth Friday. 437. A floral offering is made to all the images at this final ermita. Meanwhile the musicians continue playing songs. Even more people, coming from different places, congregate here. 438. Some flutists play, accompanied by their

drummers, and there are drummers who go about on their own, unaccompanied by flutists. That is, a solo drummer may go about carrying his instrument. 439. The size of the drum, if you put it on the ground, is about 80 centimeters high, and about 40 centimeters wide. The sides are made of wood, and the striking surface is skin. It appears to be goat skin. It doesn't play any melody, but just amplifies the sound of the hits that it takes. 440. Meanwhile, the bell ringers chime the church bells from the tower. When the floral offering is done, everyone gets together to head for the church.

441. The mayordomos of the church are waiting to receive the images; this is their responsibility. The mayordomos for each of the icons and crosses remain there as auxiliaries to those who are charged with the cargo of the church in Orizabita. This is where all the holy images come together, including those that came the day before. 442. Two images come from Espíritu, one of Christ called El Espíritu Santo, or The Holy Spirit, and the other called La Virgen de Paz y Bién, or The Virgin of Peace and Good.[67] The people of Orizabita always go to fetch them, and these images attend the fiesta every year. They go on foot to fetch the images, a distance of five kilometers. 443. The community of El Espíritu is in the eastern part of the pueblo of Orizabita.

Until about twenty years ago an image of the Virgin called La Purísima Concepción, or The Immaculate Conception, used to attend the fiesta. She was brought from Cardonal. In those days people used to go there to fetch her also. It is about 26 kilometers to Cardonal, and they would go there and return on foot. When they used to carry this Virgin they took an entire day to reach the church in Orizabita. They would return about a week later to bring her back after the fiesta was finished.

445. About 200 people went along to return her. People took turns carrying her along the route. Of course they had ermitas along the way, and they always made floral offerings. 446. In recent times they have stopped bringing the Virgin from Cardonal because it is a long way for anyone to go on foot. But in those days there was a gathering of the images of Espíritu Santo, the Virgen de la Purísima Concepción, the statue from San Andrés, and the Virgen de Paz y Bién. First the people of Espíritu waited at an ermita for those who were bringing the Virgin of Cardonal. 447. Once the two communities had gotten together they would head for San Andrés and then all of them together went to Orizabita, though of course they rested along the way. When they got to the highway that goes to Ixmiquilpan there was another ermita. 448. If those who brought the Virgen de Los Remedios arrived first, they waited there and everyone went

together to the church. If they did not, then the others waited for her. Each of the images were accompanied by people from Orizabita who went out to meet them and escort them to the church.

449. The mayordomos of the church and the judges of the pueblo split up and went to different places. Two church mayordomos and two judges are named each year. That is, one is named each year. So when they went to bring back the images they separated and each went to a different place. That is, one mayordomo and one judge went to El Espíritu. 450. Another judge and a mayordomo went to Remedios. Sometimes these authorities did not go and the people went without official representation. But in those cases the people of those villages did not hand over the images. The mayordomos and judges of El Espíritu would demand the presence of the authorities from Orizabita in order for them to hand over the responsibility for the images. 451. The same thing happens in Remedios. The first thing the mayordomos and judges there ask is if at least one mayordomo and one judge from Orizabita is present. If they are there, then the mayordomos from Remedios are satisfied and don't say anything more about the matter. The authorities of each of the communities are present in order to act as witnesses regarding the condition of the images at their transfer. 452. Those who bring back a holy image have to make sure it does not have any bangs or nicks on it. Then they can receive it. If they find a nick on it, they apprise the owners so that they won't be held responsible when they return the image, and people won't say it was they who damaged it. 453. Thus, when the image is returned, it is examined carefully again to ensure that all is well.

454. The positions, or levels of judge are juez auxiliar propietario and juez auxiliar suplente. The same goes for mayordomos. A primary and a secondary mayordomo is named. Although they are called "auxiliaries" in both cases, they work together as equals. 455. Wherever one goes, the other goes too, and they help each other out. Anyway, whoever arrives first at the ermita at the highway juncture waits for the others. Everyone has to congregate there in order to make the offering to all the images. After that they continue walking together.

456. When they get to the entrance to the plaza in Orizabita, there is another ermita. The mayordomo of the ermita makes another floral offering. Then they go to the entrance of the church where there is another ermita, and this is the last one. 457. They put down all the images and make another floral offering. Then they organize the procession around the cemetery and come back to the church where they install each image in the place reserved for it.

458. Here, in Orizabita, only one band of musicians is hired. This is first of all because the people here do not have enough money for more than that. And

second, the images here don't attract enough money in charity to support paying for music. 459. The musicians also have to go on foot to bring back the images, even though some of them have heavy instruments, like the tuba or drum, that have to be carried and played at the same time. They have to go anywhere people ask them to go, and they have to go on foot. 460. They go along playing and walking without any rest for distances such as those mentioned a moment ago.

461. The Virgin de Dolores is the one whose fiesta is being celebrated, so she is installed on the main altar in the place of honor. She is always dressed in black because they say that she was the mother of Jesus Christ. 462. When the Jews killed him it caused her a lot of pain. Maybe that is why later on someone dressed her in black. She is installed on both sides of the Virgin. 463. People have made beautiful wax flowers for her that look like large pendants. They are hung around the statue and over the altar. She remains there on the main altar for a week. When her fiesta is finished she is put back where she usually stays. 464. The santito of Orizabita is then installed in the spot where the Virgin was during her fiesta. The real name of the santito of Orizabita is El Señor del Buen Viaje. He always occupies the main altar in the church. They put him there because he is considered to be the patron of the pueblo.

465. Three priests used to conduct mass on the Friday, as we said a moment ago, and it was called the "grand mass." Here, too, the priests did not celebrate mass in Spanish but said it in Latin. Even though the people did not understand its significance, still a lot of people attended. 466. They just imitated what the priests did.

Sometimes people buy clothes for the Virgen de los Dolores so that she might wear them for the first time on the day of the fiesta. They also might do some work on the church, like repairing or painting the walls, or repairing the floor. 467. Sometimes they buy a candlestick or two. If they buy all these things, then the mayordomos inform the priest so he can bless them all. They send out invitations to this ceremony to people in the other communities and ask them to be padrinos in the blessing of the items. 468. They would send out the invitations in writing, noting the name of each member of the community whom they were inviting. Then someone would take the invitations to the mayordomo of the village. The mayordomos have to disperse the invitations to those whose names are written down. 469. Those who are invited are notified two weeks in advance so that they can get ready in case they wish to attend the benediction over the newly acquired items. With all the invitations sent out, many people attend. For example, if three hundred are sent out, around two hundred will show up.[68] 470. Everyone who accepts the invitation to be a padrino at the blessing knows what they have to bring. They don't need to be told beforehand, and it does not have to be written down on the invitation. They each know the things needed in the church.

471. The padrinos agree amongst themselves, and with the other members of their village, and decide what time to leave. None of them go empty handed; each has purchased a candle or has put aside a few pesos that will be given as charity for the image they are going to worship. 472. They decorate the candle by putting a flower on it, more or less in the middle, and when they get to the mass they light the candle. All the padrinos bring a candle and this is their contribution. They light it when the mass begins. 473. The blessing given over what they have made or purchased comes at the end of the mass. For example, if there are decorated candlesticks, or dresses as gifts for one of the virgins, then those gifts are placed on a table set up near the priests. When the priests finish the mass, they pray over the gifts and then sprinkle holy water on them.

474. After the priest finishes the blessing, the padrinos come forward to worship the images and to bid them goodbye. As the padrino comes forward to the Virgen de Dolores, he leaves a peso or two as an offering. 475. The poorest person leaves something, even if it is only fifty centavos, and does not return without giving alms. The candles carried by the padrinos are also left and turned over to the mayordomos' assistants. It is the job of the bell ringers to do this and they collect a lot of candles. 476. Besides the candles left by the padrinos, there are those left by the pilgrims who come to the fiesta. Many padrinos request some relic to take home. After the ceremony, everyone goes out and walks around the plaza. Some go home and others go to the houses of the mayordomos to eat.

477. These invitations to padrinos to come and take part in the blessing of things for the church is a custom that has been practiced for a long time. The people from Orizabita invite others from Los Remedios, San Juanico, El Mandó, San Nicolás, El Santuario, El Espíritu, Nequetejé, San Miguel Tlazintla, Capula; and in earlier times they invited people from Tasquillo, El Maye, and Progreso. 478. When any of those people came to celebrate a fiesta, they invited back the people from Orizabita, and there was an exchange of relations. That is how it is done every year. When they celebrate a fiesta the people are there from all around, and right there they invite each other to take part in another fiesta.

479. At around eight o'clock at night the people congregate again in church; men, women and children. Firecrackers are set off and the castillo has been set up and ready for the moment to light it. 480. Inside the church the mayordomos are going around organizing everyone for the procession. All the mayordomos

of the other images that have come are there, too. This is the custom, so that each person takes care of the image from his own community. The local mayordomos are responsible for assigning the santitos to be carried by particular persons in the procession. 481. When they leave the church in the procession they go in the following order. First there is a torito, with someone carrying it; and then a boy carrying a little bell that he rings; then the ciriales; and then come the crosses from Puerto Juárez in the municipio of Zimapán. Then come those from La Pechuga de Gallina, and then come the crosses from La Lagunita. 482. Then comes the Virgin of Los Remedios, and after her El Sr. del Buen Viaje from El Defay, the Christ from Gundó, and the Christ from San Andrés. After that come the crosses from Banxu, the Virgen de Paz y Bién, the Christ from El Espíritu, and then the Señor del Buen Viaje from Orizabita, and lastly the musicians. 483. The drummers and flutists follow along with whichever image they care to. The singers of prayers also follow and pray to whatever holy image they want to.

484. It is a custom to construct arches. Each of the barrios that existed had to build arches adorned with flowers and cucharillas and set up the arches in designated spots. The barrios that used to exist were called El Centro, El Salitre, and Cerritos. These groups were part of the internal organization of Orizabita itself. 485. The group in El Centro had the most people. The barrio in El Salitre had about 80 persons, and the barrio of Cerritos had only 30 persons. The people in each of the groups used to cooperate amongst themselves in building the arches. 486. Those in Boxhuada constituted their own barrio, as did those in San Andrés. Those in El Defay, La Lagunita, El Gundó, and La Pechuga all set up an arch every year, adorned it with cucharillas, and made it look very pretty. There are nine groups here, and each one used to set up its own arch by working together amongst themselves.

487. They begin working on Tuesday by digging the holes for the wood poles that serve as supports. They raise the supports on Wednesday morning and put on the floral decorations they have made. By the time the images arrive, the plaza is all decorated with these arches. 488. Regarding these arches, it appeared as if everyone was a mayordomo because they all cooperated in order to buy the firecrackers. Each group bought four, five, or six dozen. When the procession came out of the church with the images it had to pass through each of the arches. 489. For example, when they passed through the archway built by those from El Centro they set off four or five dozen firecrackers, creating a roar that left one almost deaf. Then they passed through the arch built by those from Gundó and there was another great lighting of firecrackers.

490. Before all the santitos had passed through the arch, there came a roar from the firecrackers being set off at the arch up ahead—the arch built by those from Cerritos. Before the procession got through that arch, the people ahead from San Andrés started lighting off their firecrackers. 491. The procession continued on until it passed through all the arches that were set up. It had to go through the arches of El Salitre, El Defay, Boxhuada, La Pechuga, and La Lagunita, and then turned to go through the arch of Gundó and, for the second time, through the arch, set up by the people of El Centro, at the entrance to the cemetery. The procession passed through these last two arches twice. Firecrackers were set off again so the images would not pass through the arches in silence.

492. Suppose that each group sets off five gross of firecrackers. If we add up all nine groups we get a total of 540 dozen firecrackers. Now we can figure how many firecrackers there are in total, and we see that there are 6480 set off. 493. That's how it is every year. A lot of firecrackers are shot off, but what is burned up in reality is money. Those groups are in a kind of competition with one another. The group that sets off the most wins, and so they each try to be the best. 494. The group from El Centro almost always won. They used to compete most with the group from El Salitre, and occasionally the latter won. The group from El Centro, as we saw, had the most people. 495. El Salitre and El Centro predominated in those activities as well as in the community assemblies. Whatever those groups said was what the people in the minority groups had to accept and do.

496. Once the procession passed through all the arches, all the images that took part returned to the church and the mayordomos arranged to return them to their usual places. This was not done, however, before the people finished praying to the images and left alms if they had money and wanted to do so. 497. Some people don't condescend to help even though they have the money. Even if they are asked directly they pretend they don't understand or they say they don't have the money. This part of the service lasts about an hour and a half because there are a lot of people and everyone wants to pass by and cross themselves before the images. 498. The holy images are then put back in their places and the mayordomos from Orizabita arrange another procession out of the church. This second procession is called "Looking for the Tracks." Many people call this fiesta of Sexto Viernes de Dolores by the Ñähñu name "nheua," which means "following the footsteps."[69] 499. Now we will see what this means and how it is celebrated in order to understand it better.

500. In order for this procession of "Looking for the Tracks" to begin, the mayordomos and their assistants take down the Virgen de Dolores from the main altar. 501. She has been put there because she is the one whose fiesta is

being celebrated. She is at the top of the main altar and she is brought down to the bottom. Some people come forward immediately and begin crossing themselves and kissing her. All who pass by to worship her cross themselves and kiss her feet. 502. The choir begins to pray to the Virgin who has just been set down on the ground. While they are singing, the mayordomos and their helpers, along with other men of the community, think about how they will one day need this kind of help to fulfill their own cargos.

503. Everyone helps the mayordomos position the Virgin on the pedestal, and as soon as the adoration of her is over, the procession leaves the church with the statue. The Virgin is accompanied by a large cross. It is a single cross placed on the pedestal. 504. It is about two and a half meters high and a band of white cloth has been draped over its arms. The band is about 20 centimeters wide and about three and a half meters long. 505. The band is wrapped around the cross and the ends of the band hang from its arms. This cross accompanies the Virgen de Dolores all throughout the procession.

506. When the Virgin and the cross are ready, the procession can leave the church. Two ciriales go in front, and then comes the cross with the cloth strip that we spoke of, and then behind that comes the Virgin. 507. Each of these things is carried by its own bearers. Four men carry the cross. Four women carry the Virgin. The Virgin has been dressed in black. 508. It is said that she is dressed in the color of grief because her son had been murdered. They say that it was the Jews who murdered him and helped nail him to the cross. 509. That's what some priests say, but who knows who saw what they really did to him? He probably owed them something, or he had done something bad to them, and so they participated in his punishment. It is possible that he had made the Jews angry and so they nailed him to the cross. 510. In any case, all this caused the Virgin a lot of grief because they killed her son. Maybe that is why she is always dressed in black; whenever it is her fiesta, that is how she is dressed.

511. The procession is very sad. No firecrackers are set off, and not because they have all been used up. Rather, it is the custom that the procession remains silent, and even the marchers don't talk much to one another. The bell ringer rings a sign of mourning, not of joy. 512. The choir sings songs of sadness. Slowly, very slowly, those who carry the Virgin move, and the same for the rest of the people. They walk like this and make the entire round of the earlier procession. 513. This procession is thus called "looking for the tracks" because it's like when someone goes along slowly, looking for the tracks of someone who is lost. They walk and pause, and we see that one person follows the footsteps of the other. 514. This goes on all night and they get back to the door of the church as dawn breaks. Many people last through the whole march. Some

women bring their eight- or ten-year-old sons along and make them last through the whole thing. 515. Even though those boys are tired, their mothers make them walk because they are following the Virgin.

516. When they get back to the church they take the Virgin from the pedestal and put her back on the main altar. The cross that accompanied her is also taken from the pedestal and put back in its usual place. 517. When all this is over, the mayordomos start collecting everything. The musicians have had to follow both processions, and they played sad pieces during the final procession. By contrast, in the first procession they played songs of joy. 518. When all this having to do with the church is finished, they rest about two hours and return to work again. The castillo and torito are lit once the first procession is finished so that everyone will see it. All these activities are on the main day of the fiesta itself. 519. Of course, now we are already into Saturday because a new day has dawned, but this does not bother anyone. What they are following is their religion and the adoration of the images, because this is the only day of the year that they take part in a fiesta. That is why they don't mind if they are up all night and stay there all day Saturday.

520. There are a lot of people in the plaza and they ask each other how they have been and how they are doing. People who are good friends invite one another to drink pulque, or coffee, or, if there is aguardiente available, they buy a small bottle called a "topo" and drink it together.[70] They comment on whether the burning of the castillo and the torito was good or not. Each one gives his impression of how he thinks the fiesta went. 521. Some of the women buy tamalitos to take home; others buy tamales to eat right there, and others buy squash seeds or oranges, if they are in season. They buy different things to eat there or to take with them if they need something at home. 522. Others, especially the mayordomos, invite people to come over for a visit to eat.

This is the last meal that the mayordomos have to provide to those who have been assigned to them. They may have been assigned to feed the musicians or the fireworks makers. This is the last meal, and now they say goodbye to those whom they have had to feed. 523. The mayordomos invite each other over to eat at the next occasion because they have trusting relations that have been established for a long time. Thus, the next year those who are now invited may be called upon to provide the meals, and then *they* will do the same for *their* friend and neighbor. The person now invited says that he will see his friend the next year on the day that falls to *him*, and he invites his friend to *his* house to eat. 524. Others, who have not been named as mayordomos, but who have nevertheless prepared food, ask their friends over for the following year, too.

525. Some people make an offering of escamadas; they make about six of these pieces. We know that these are called "escamadas" in Spanish. They are made and decorated by assistants to the person who has promised God an offering of these flowers. 526. These escamadas look beautiful; they are decorated with flowers made from different colored wax. The man or woman who has decided to offer escamadas to God holds a small, private fiesta, with a banquet to feed those whom they have called upon to help them. 527. The escamadas are made in the house of the person making the offering. When they go to make the offering to God they are not accompanied only by their assistants. The promise of the offering is made with all their heart. 528. So, they go personally, or send someone, to bring a band of musicians to their house. The escamadas are thus accompanied by music.

529. The musicians are asked to go and play at various houses on the day of the fiesta, and wherever they go, they have to go on foot. When someone wants to make a floral offering, they ask the musicians to play at their house where the offering is prepared. If the musicians do not comply with the requests, then the people who have made the promise of an offering become angry, and they take the matter up with the judge, calling it to his attention when there is a general meeting of the pueblo.

530. The judge suffers more than anyone. He may not eat well or sleep but has to go around everywhere, taking care of everything. It couldn't be said that this work brings great honor or is some kind of high position. To be a judge is to be a servant to the community in which one lives. 531. The judge gets no salary for his work. If he does a good job then he gets the thanks of the community and these are his wages. Many people come to him and ask him to resolve problems that they are having.

532. Sometimes the first judge, the juez auxiliar propietario, is not available, and this is why a second person, the juez auxiliar suplente, is named as his aide. He stands in for the judge when the latter is not available. Practically all of a judge's time is eaten up and he can not even go to work. 533. If he goes away for a day to work, then when he returns there are problems that must be resolved, and he has to use all his experience and good tactics in solving them. He must also really know how to organize things for fiestas. Otherwise, he just creates problems and can even cause people to fight. And if problems arise, then the fiesta won't turn out well. 534. Thus, when the judge is named, people are careful to find someone who does not easily lose control of situations, and someone who is the first to confront problems when they arise. Even if people are shooting at each other, he has to confront the problem right then and there.

535. All during this week people are involved in the fiesta and many don't
work at all during this time. Consequently, many folks do not have enough
money to go to town during the fiesta week, and this is why there are animals.
The animals pay the price of the traditional religious festivals.

Returning to the escamadas, people from the little communities around the
area and those from Orizabita come to leave their wax figures and floral offerings. 536. The people from outside reckon on what time the mass will be and
they show up so that the priest will bless the things they have brought. On Saturday, mass is celebrated at about nine in the morning, and finishes at eleven.
Then the priest leaves.

537. The mass celebrated is in honor of the images that have come to visit
from up in the mountains. The mayordomos of these images get ready to take
their leave from the church. When they leave, all the images from the mountains
leave together. 538. The band and all the people accompany them up to the last
ermita mentioned in previous pages. That is where everyone reconvenes. The
person who has erected this ermita, that is, the mayordomo, brings flowers for
all the images. 539. The musicians play almost without stop, because they, too,
are about to go back home. All that remains is for the floral offering to finish and
for those who are leaving for the mountains to be fed. Then everyone takes to
the roads. The images from Defay and Gundó are bid farewell here at this
ermita. 540. The others go on together and bid goodbye to one another at Boxhuada where they came together in the first place. At this juncture one group
goes off towards the west. Those from Puerto Juárez of Zimapán separate, and
those from La Lagunita, El Banxu and La Pechuga go on together.

541. When they reach La Lagunita they separate again, with those from
Banxu leaving towards their village first and those from La Lagunita going on.
Thus, the crosses arrive back at their church. Sometimes those who remain rest
together at an ermita and then take up the walk again. 542. There is still a two
hour walk for the people from La Pechuga. By the time they get home, it is eight
at night and the others in the village are waiting to feed those who accompanied
the crosses to the fiesta. 543. They do this every year. They name one or two
mayordomos who await the return of the people who accompanied the crosses
to Orizabita. All those who accompanied the crosses are from right there in the
village.

544. Those from Orizabita just say goodbye and go home, and do not accompany the others back up the mountain. But, of course, they thanked their guests
for having participated in the fiesta and they asked God to give their guests life
and health so that they might come back and take part the following year.

545. Meanwhile, at the plaza in Orizabita, the stalls for selling peanuts, tamalitos dulces, sugar cane, coffee, tamales, oranges and pulque are taken down. All the people who have set up the stalls gather up their merchandise and go home. 546. Some of the stalls are set up by people who are not from the local community but by people who come from places like El Mandó, El Maye, San Nicolás, and Ixmiquilpan. These people come every year to the fiesta, and they come on foot. Sometimes they carry their wares on a donkey.

547. The fiesta still is not finished because on Sunday the priest will return and celebrate another mass. This mass is in honor of the images of El Espíritu and Los Remedios. Those who attend the mass are from right there in Orizabita. 548. The mass is celebrated on Sunday, even though it should be celebrated the following Wednesday. However, seeing that there may not be time for it on Wednesday, they say the mass on Sunday. These images remain in Orizabita for seven days and on the eighth day they return to their land.

549. On Sunday another mass is said for the blessing of the palms, and this day is called Domingo de Ramos.[71] Palm branches and young olive branches are blessed, too. 550. Then the people take the palms home as relics. The palms are brought by the mayordomos from far away where the humid mountain zone begins. These plants do not grow in the arid zone. Other herbs, including manzanilla, rosemary, and xikri, or "air plants," are brought. 551. Mostly there are palms. Some people weave three or four branches together and they look really pretty. The palms taken home are the ones that have been blessed. People tie them to the trunks of large trees. The belief is that this will prevent the trees from being felled by lightning.

552. This custom of blessing the palms is practiced in various places. They use a lot of palms in the main church in Ixmiquilpan. People come from all over to set up stalls and sell palm leaves. There are craftsmen who know how to weave different kinds of figures from palm leaves including birds and human images. They copy the figure of the saints and attach these to little crosses that they make. 553. They make all these figures by weaving together palm leaves. No one has taught these artesans how to do this; they just do it out of their own creativity. They already know the craft of weaving palm leaves, because they are the same people who make "petacas"[72] floor mats, and hats all by hand, without using any metal tools to help them.

554. To make finer figures, they just use finer strips of palm leaves. They are so trained that their hands can work without their having to look at what they are doing. A man can just walk along having a conversation with another person while weaving at the same time. Some of these people who come to Ixmiquilpan

are from Alfajayucan, and others are from the west, from Tasquillo. There are some who come up from the Tolantongo River area. 555. Only a few people from there engage in this work. The people from the river don't weave hats or petacas, only "petates," or wide floor mats that they use as beds, either for resting or for sleeping. They weave large mats that can accommodate two adults quite well. 556. They bring their extra palm leaves to Ixmiquilpan to sell at the markets on Mondays. That is where people from other communities come to purchase the palm leaves, which are sold in bundles or by weight. They weigh it in order to know how many kilos there are. The customer pays according to the cost per kilo at the time. 557. There are a lot of hat weavers in Alfajayucan, and so many people come from there to purchase the palm leaves.

558. If the mayordomo for the blessing of the palms has a friend or acquaintance who sells palms, then he doesn't have to waste his time looking for palm leaves. All he has to do is ask his friend to bring some along. On the day that they are needed, the person who was entrusted with the task delivers the palms. Sometimes he comes right to the house of the person who needs the palms. 559. When the mayordomo orders the palm leaves, he does not deliver any money in advance. Even if the mayordomo were to offer it, the seller of the palms does not take it. He responds by saying that among them there is no deceit, and no distrust. He says "we know each other." When the seller comes to deliver the palms that were ordered is when he receives his money. 560. Many agreements are made verbally and no one cheats anybody. It isn't because they don't know how to write that they do this. It is simply the custom that everyone knows how to keep his word.

561. Here is where the fiesta that began two weeks earlier ends. In other words, the fiesta of Sixth Friday ends and then the celebration continues with Holy Week, and that is where it all finishes.

On Wednesday morning the mayordomos and the judges prepare to return the images. People talk among themselves about who is going to drop off the images and about whether they are going to El Espíritu or to Los Remedios. The people in charge of the ermitas start in the morning to get things ready again where the ermitas are usually set up. 562. The people in charge of the images also get ready from early in the morning. Those who are going to return the icons are called "ñ'ente" in Ñähñu, or "people on the way," and those who are coming to get the images, that is, the owners, are called "ndäte," or "people who are going to find something." So the people of Orizabita await the arrival of those who are coming to get the images. 563. The people from El Espíritu and San Andrés arrive first, and they are always together.

564. Whoever arrives first waits for the others who don't take long to get there. Sometimes they get there together. Firecrackers announce the direction that each is coming from. They all come with their ciriales in front. 565. Of course there is also a floral offering. The offerer walks along carrying a large wooden bowl of flowers in his arms, and two more people come with him, carrying the flower vase and incense burner. They leave the church at about two o'clock, and they stop to rest at the first ermita. Then they continue walking. 566. They stop again at the second ermita. Sometimes those from Remedios hire musicians to come along with them when they carry back the Virgin. They hire the musicians from Nith because they are the closest to them. 567. Earlier, there used to be a group called Los Zopilotes, or "the buzzards," from Nequeteje. They used to be hired by El Espíritu. They may have died because the group no longer exists. Or perhaps they didn't raise any little buzzards to play music.

568. There is a fork in the road at the second ermita. One branch goes straight south towards Remedios. The other branch heads east towards San Andrés and then further on is El Espíritu. The floral offering is made at this second ermita. 569. After the offering, they separate and each group goes towards its own pueblo. Two images head one way, and one goes the other. 570. It is more accurate to say that the three head east because there is the Christ of San Andrés, the Virgen de Paz y Bién, and the Espíritu Santo. The only one that heads south is the Virgin of Los Remedios. When the images separate, they fall under the responsibility of each of the separate mayordomos. 571. They each rest along the way. When it gets to San Andrés the image of Christ goes to his chapel. The Virgin and the Christ of El Espíritu continue on for another half hour before arriving home. They all get back around dark. 572. The people do not leave church until the images have all been put back on the altar.

573. At midday on the following day, Thursday, the mayordomos return to the church to cover all the images with cloth. Why? Because Holy Week has arrived, and according to what is believed, this is when Jesus Christ died. 574. The images are covered up for two days, from midday on Thursday, all day Friday, and until midday on Saturday when a mass is said and the images are uncovered. The images are covered with a purple cloth and then the church and the bell tower are closed so that no one will touch the bells. 575. The bells are rung when the mass is celebrated, which is supposed to be when Jesus Christ rose from the dead.

576. We have skipped over a fiesta which used to be celebrated for many years. It stopped being celebrated because people saw that the fiestas were be-

coming almost continuous. The people did not have enough money to celebrate them. The fiesta was known as "The Blessing of the Candles." 577. It was celebrated on February 2nd; the holiday continues to be on the same date, but is no longer celebrated. Other communities used to celebrate it also, but it has been abandoned. The Virgin worshipped on this date is called La Candelaria. Corn and bean seed was brought before her. It was put into a basket and brought to church so that the priest would bless it before planting. 578. Candles were put in the basket. The candles were picked up and lit when the mass began and the candles were also blessed. Not only maize and bean seed were blessed but many other kinds of seeds that people might want to plant.

579. They did this blessing so that when the rains came the seeds would be ready to plant right then. But the weather changes, and despite the blessing, if it doesn't rain then the seed is lost because it is eaten by insects and does not germinate. It is possible that this fiesta was abandoned because people lost faith since it did not rain. The belief in the blessing of the seed is in order to make the seed fertile. This custom of blessing the seed exists in various communities. 581. We will see this when we look at the fiesta celebrated in the community of Candelaria in the Municipio of Tasquillo. That is where the people come every year, bringing baskets of seed to the church.

582. People used to make floral offerings all over Orizabita, and not just in the church, during the festival of The Sixth Friday of Suffering. Long ago, crosses were erected along the paths used by the ancestors to cross the mountains. People in those days may have been more inclined towards religion because they used to erect crosses along the paths. 583. They made the base for the cross of rough stone, and for the cross itself they selected wood that lasted a long time against the sun and rain. Some of those crosses can still be seen where they were put up; they were made of mesquite. The ones left from those times past are about two and a half meters high. 584. One that can still be seen quite well is on the hill between San Andrés and El Espíritu. These crosses are like landmarks. When people talk to each other and one person asks another where such and such a thing happened, the other person may say that it happened "over by the cross."

585. There were other crosses on the roads, but they were not man-made. They were trees whose branches formed a nearly perfect cross by themselves. Over where people used to go on foot towards Ixmiquilpan, if one follows the old road that comes down from San Nicolás and enters the city along the road known as El Cajón, right there is a mesquite that looks like a cross with its branches extended. That mesquite has been there a long time. 586. People have noticed that the tree looks like a cross and so they have worshipped it.

No one knows who started worshipping the tree. In the days when many people still came on foot to the market in Ixmiquilpan, they would stop at the tree and make the sign of the cross before continuing on. 587. Whether they were coming down towards the south, or returning to the north, they did this. Others used to bring a candle back from the plaza and light it there. Some people, like those from El Maye, offered flowers. On their way home they would stop for a moment to drape a rope of flowers over the arms of the cross. 588. Others claimed that the tree made, or makes, miracles, and they would bring oil in a plate and burn it like a candle. Other people brought jars of flowers, or large, beautiful vases. Whenever believers in God passed the spot, they would cross themselves and continue on their way, whether they were just coming south, or returning from the market.

589. The same thing happens in other communities. If the people see a tree that looks like a cross, someone will worship it, light a candle for it, and bring it flowers. It is also a custom to put crosses on top of nearby mountains. 590. When a fiesta is celebrated, the cross is not forgotten. Flowers must be left for the cross or a floral offering must be made to it in some way. The people who actually offer the flowers climb the mountain and make the offering in the manner which we have already seen. 591. They bring firecrackers to shoot off. For this, and for all the fiestas celebrated, they bring the flowers from the irrigated zone of Ixmiquilpan. They buy the flowers in El Maye, and when there are none there, they go to Tasquillo, on foot; it takes a whole day to get there. 592. If they don't find any in Tasquillo, then they have to go to La Pechuga. The mayordomo for the occasion will find out where he has to go, but he must find the flowers that he needs.

593. Many days, even months go by before there is another fiesta that can be considered among the most important ones. While this is coming, the people continue to venerate God. To do this they ask for what is called a "petición de misa," or a "requested mass." These are not just for one of the santitos or the Virgin. Requested masses may be celebrated for fulfilling a vow or for some other event in a person's life. 594. People ask for masses to be said for the saints, or to remember someone who has died, or to ask for rain. These are the masses that are celebrated. As usual, the priest gets the money that people bring when they come to request a mass. Sometimes it is women and other times it is men who request and pay for the mass. 595. Sometimes a request for a mass for a particular image is to thank God because one's whole family is in good health and no one is sick. Before ordering a mass in this case, one agrees to make a floral offering.

596. When a person makes a floral offering, they also generally have to provide a meal and for this they kill a goat or some chickens. Some families request a mass when one of the members is sick. If the sickness is not grave, they ask that the person get well again quickly. If a person is gravely ill, then the family asks God to lessen the severity of the sickness. 597. This is when people take the images into their homes to ask for divine intervention. Sometimes people promise to commission a mass to an image of God or a saint or a miraculous virgin. 598. Then later on they forget to celebrate the mass that they promised to sponsor. It is believed that in this case the holy personage sends an illness to strike the person who cheated him. Because of this, when sick people think about it, they do all they can to fulfill their word. They fulfill it by sponsoring the mass that they thought of making, or by making the floral offering that they promised. Whether the particular image in question is close by or far away, the sick person does all he or she can in order to visit it in its home church.

599. When a person from one community goes to fulfill a vow in another one, he has to notify the mayordomos of the pueblo in question and they give him permission to go to the church to complete his obligation. They always grant permission; that is the custom. 600. Whether they get better or not, they still have to fulfill their vows. If the sick person dies, the burial is just one more large debt left to the family to pay off. That has happened in various cases; a day or two after completing the offering or the mass the sick person dies because they could not fight the illness.

601. Another belief is that the dead reprimand the living when no one in their family remembers them. According to the belief, they make one of the family members sick so that they will remember the dead. 602. Another mass in honor of the dead person is commissioned for this. The people in the family do this to ask the dead person to forgive them for not remembering. No floral offerings are made in the mass for the dead, and neither are firecrackers set off. There is only a special ringing of the church bells. According to belief, the adults who have died do the reprimanding. 603. No special mass is said for dead children.[73] Other people don't petition a mass when they are sick. 604. They do celebrate mass, but in order to mark the anniversary of the death of someone who died whom they want to remember. They kill a goat and invite their acquaintances to eat with them. After finishing the mass the priest goes to the grave site and makes the benediction, sprinkling holy water, as always.

605. The other kind of petitioned mass is in order to ask God for rain. Several families get together and chip in. Sometimes all the members of a community discuss it and decide to chip in together, and they send the mayordomo to request the mass. 606. At these masses there is no floral offering. The people just

When a fiesta is celebrated, the cross is not forgotten
Religion 590

attend, but firecrackers are purchased. The days pass and there has been no other fiesta in the village. Meanwhile, the people go to other villages where fiestas are being celebrated. They either go simply for the visit, or to drop off a loan for someone else to fulfill a cargo.

607. When the festival of All Saints, or The Day of the Dead, comes on November 1st and 2nd, everyone holds a vigil for their relatives who have died. Two mayordomos are named for this fiesta also—one for the mass said for dead children, and one for adults. 608. The mayordomos must ask the priest well in advance for the mass. Otherwise, the mass will not be said on the proper day because there are many mayordomos, from many communities, asking the priests for masses, and in some cases the mass has to be postponed. 609. Even if the mass has to be postponed, the celebration of the Day of the Dead is never postponed. It is always celebrated on November 1st and 2nd. The mass for dead children is said on the first, and firecrackers are set off for it. 610. No firecrackers are lit for the mass celebrated for dead adults. Also, when a child has just died, people light firecrackers until the child is buried. But when an adult is buried there are no firecrackers. And when a child dies the church bells ring in a brighter manner, but when an adult dies they signal sadness.

611. The vigil for the dead children begins on October 31st at midday. Those who hold the vigil start by lighting firecrackers all over the place. It is said that the children return to their homes at midday to receive all that has been prepared for them to eat. 612. Sweets are put on a table, along with flowers and the ever-present candles. Some people have their own bees and so they have wax and they make candles to light for their dead babies. Chrysanthemums are mostly what are used for decorating the table that is set for the vigil. 613. Breads, called "pan de angelitos," are also put out.[74] They are made in the form of a circle and are covered with red-dyed sugar. Everything that children like to eat when they are alive and well is put on the table. 614. All that night the people light firecrackers, ending at midday on the first of November. It all ends with the celebration of the mass, if there is one.

615. Between midday on the first and midday on the second, this fiesta is celebrated. Things the dead ate when they were alive are placed out for them. There are calabasa sweets, tamales, tlacoyos,[75] walnuts, peanuts, oranges and sugar cane. 616. A candle is lit for each person that has died in a family. Cooking oil is also lit for them. There is a plate of oil and one wick for each dead person. That way, it is as if they were partaking from the same plate. 617. Suppose that a person were remembering three or four of his departed family members. In that case, this would be the number of wicks placed in the plate filled with oil. If there is a choir group in a village they go around all night singing hymns

wherever someone has set up an altar of vigil. The bell ringer stays up all night ringing the church bells; he is there until dawn, ringing the bells in a sad manner, and he does not sleep at all. He doesn't come down from the bell tower and go home until about seven in the morning. 618. The bell ringer also finds a helper who accompanies him up there. Meanwhile, the choir passes the night singing hymns, though sometimes they don't get to more than ten houses. 619. People who want them to come and pray at the altars they have set up wait for the singers to finish up at one house and to come along. But the singers sometimes get two or three invitations at once and they don't know whose invitation to accept first.

Wherever they go, the people give them a plate heaped with food; this is how people thank the choir for singing at their house. 620. There may be two groups of singers, but they visit different houses and do not work together. They do not finish what they are offered to eat, but keep it and heat it up later. 621. The bell ringers, coming down from the belfry, also go to people's homes and are treated in the same way. They are given a plate of food heaped with the offering. They are given pulque, and aguardiente, if there is any, and coffee. They are well taken care of because they have stayed up all night ringing the bells. Then they go around all day to various houses being treated.

622. A poor person puts out only candles, incense, flowers, and tlacoyos in order to await departed members of the family. As much as he might want to set up more, there just isn't any money. There are practically no homes where people do not await the dead. 623. Many, many homes remember their loved ones every year. As always, there are beliefs, and so it is with this celebration. The people do all they can to await the dead on their day. 624. The people who come in to the market in Ixmiquilpan from other communities can barely squeeze in. The market goes on for two days with people buying the things they need in order to set up their altars for the dead. Everyone returns on foot carrying their purchases on their backs. If a person has a burro, then the animal does the carrying and the person just drives it.

625. There is a story about a poor man who drank a lot, and he spent all his money drinking with his friends. To be sure, he was also a good worker, but he drank up whatever he earned. As fast as he acquired money, it was used up. He did not have any children, but lived only with his wife. 626. So the Day of the Dead came and he had no money to spend on it. His wife was very sad because they were not going to put out anything for the dead. So she said to her husband: "Well, what are we going to do? What have you thought of that we can put out for the dead?" she asked. 627. The man just shrugged his shoulders, not knowing what to say. The woman told him not to drink any more, with the idea of get-

ting a little money together. The man said that he would not drink, but it was just something he said at the moment. When he got together with his friends, he started to drink again.

628. This made the woman very sad when she saw it. At that moment it occurred to her that she had put aside a little money on her own and had not said anything about it to her husband. She decided to put the money to use. 629. It would be for the dead and for buying their candles, flowers, incense and all the necessary things. So she told her husband that she had a little money. She told him the truth that she had put away this money for the Day of the Dead. 630. The woman said: "What do you say? How about going and buying things so that we can await our departed loved ones? If you don't buy the things, what do you think we'll be able to set out for them? There just isn't anything here," she said. 631. "Go to the plaza, but for the love of God, man, don't go getting drunk. You are going to run into your acquaintances and friends there, and they are going to give you pulque. But don't get drunk until this fiesta is over, and then after that you can do what you want," she said.

632. The man said "yes, of course; yes, I'll return quickly," he said. Then the woman got an ayate and a large, six cuartillo basket, and put it in the ayate. She gave him the money and the basket and he took off towards the road to town. 633. When he left he moved quickly, as if he were truly going to return right away. In the meantime the woman remained at home and sprinkled water on the floor and swept a place where she put a table for her altar. She finished sweeping and put out an old table that she had, but she washed it with clean water first. Then she went out to collect firewood.

634. There is a custom that some people follow where they remain awake all night on vigil at their altar, and watching over the offerings. For this reason the woman went out to gather a big bundle of dried maguey leaves that would last all night. She hurried to gather what she needed and return right away. 635. That way, when her husband returned she would be able to devote her attention to the offerings. She returned from gathering firewood and, arriving home, she thought about when her husband would come back. She considered the distance and how long it would take him to walk to the plaza and to return. 636. The woman waited and the man did not appear. The poor woman began thinking and started to become suspicious and she became sad. 637. It got later and later, and the sun was going down and still her husband did not appear. She watched for him, hoping that he would show up, and there was no one. And it occurred to her that her husband had gotten drunk. 638. She put her head in her hands and began to cry and contemplated God. She begged forgiveness from the dead, and she

said to herself: "Whatever made me send this man, when I could have better gone myself?"

639. Finally it got to be nighttime and the man did not show up. Finally the woman realized that her husband had surely gotten drunk. So she started grinding corn, and making nixtamal; she ground it very fine. 640. Then she boiled quintonil leaves that she went out and collected, and she sliced up onions and ground up some green chiles and mixed it together. With this she made some circular gorditas, or fat tortillas. 641. She put the leaves that she had boiled in these tortillas. When they were all cooked, she took out the tortillas and put them in a little basket in which she had put a napkin. This was all she put on the old table that she had set up. There were no candles, and all night she burned the maguey leaves that she had gone out and collected. She just thought, and she cried.

642. The man who had gone to the market to buy things did, indeed, get drunk. As soon as he got to the plaza he ran into his acquaintances and friends and they began to give him pulque. Since he was friends with them for a long time, he had to accept all that they offered him. 643. And since he did not want to just sit there without returning the favor, he started buying some pulque to offer them. Even though he wanted to leave, they prevailed on him and would not let him go. They kept telling him that they wouldn't be long. Little by little they all got drunk—the man who came to buy things and his friends as well. 644. Once the drunkenness set in, the man spent all the money that his wife had given him for the purchases. He even lost the basket and the ayate that he had been given. He tried to return home, but now he had nothing with him and he was very drunk. So he laid down on the side of the road and slept there.

645. He didn't have his hat or his coat; he just folded his arms around himself and laid down on the side of the road. Around midnight he heard footsteps and the voices of many people who were coming down the road where he was lying. Soon he saw that there were many people; they took up the entire road from edge to edge. 646. They were all dressed in white, every single one of them, and none were dressed differently. Each one carried candles. Some carried one and others carried two and there were some that had a fistful of candles. 647. The man raised his head up in order to see from where he was lying. The people who were walking along were talking among themselves and asking each other if they had been awaited well. Some said that they had, while others said that very little had been set out for them.

648. Many of them passed by the man who was stretched out on the road. The procession stretched for miles. All the marchers were barefoot. Some walked

along eating bread, others walked and ate tamales. 649. The man was still lying there with his arms folded, and he was very cold and still hung over. As those "people" passed by they talked about how they had been received. Some carried beautiful candles and others were eating delicious foods. 650. Not far from them there were others who carried more crudely made candles. The man heard them ask one another how well they had been received. And they responded that they had no one to wait for them and that they did not have relatives any longer. 651. Others responded that their relatives were poor and that that was why they did not set out anything for them. That is, their relatives had not waited for them. That is what the man heard as those people talked among themselves. Those who had no relatives to await them weren't eating anything, nor did they carry any wax candles to illuminate their path. 652. Instead, the tips of their fingers were in flames and they used this to light their way. All five fingers on both hands were lit. Where their fingernails would be was fire, and with these they illuminated the road that they were passing along.

653. Pretty soon more came behind them and they were carrying bunches of dried maguey leaves that were on fire. They lit up the road with these and they were eating thick tortillas with quelites. And they, too, were asked by others how nicely they had been received. 654. And they responded: "We do not have our candles. They just lit some dried maguey leaves for us, and these are what we carry." That is what they said. "In our tortillas they have put only quelites, and there is nothing else," they said. "The man went to the plaza but he just got drunk and did not return home." 655. And that is what those "people" said as they passed near to where the man was lying on the road. Then he started to think about what those people said about how the man who went to the plaza just got drunk. All those people finished passing by. 656. They were saying among themselves "With God's help we'll see each other again next year." Then the man saw that morning was near and that it was only a short time before dawn broke. So he got up. He didn't even have his sombrero or his huaraches. He got up, his hair all disheveled, and started on the road towards his house.

657. He walked along thinking about all that he had seen and heard. He said to himself: "Maybe the dead really do come to visit. Why else did I see them?" He walked with his arms folded around himself because the morning was cold. 658. He felt dizzy because he had not eaten anything the day before. He arrived at his house at around eight o'clock. When his wife saw him coming in she started to cry. 659. She said: "I told you not to get drunk and that was the first thing you did." As she said this she cried, and the man didn't know what to say in response. 660. At last he said: "Well, I really didn't want to drink but my

They were all dressed in white
Religion 646

friends forced me to drink pulque with them, and that is how I wound up spending the little money that you gave me."

Then he started telling his wife about what he saw on the road. As he noticed the burning maguey leaves he recalled what he had seen and how some of those people had burning fingernails with which they lit up the road. 661. The man was hungry and thirsty. He noticed that there were itacates in the basket, the tlacoyos that his wife had made to put on the altar for her dear departed. Then the man said: "I'm very hungry and very thirsty. Heat up those stale tortillas that you've got there in the basket and I'll eat one." 662. The woman obeyed and heated up the tortilla he asked for and gave it to him to eat. She also gave him something to drink. And just as he was finishing eating, a kind of trembling came over him and he died.

663. People believe that the dead come to eat the things that are set out for them, and that if people do not hold vigil for them on the appointed day, then the dead take revenge. People believe what is said and everyone does all they can to get money to be able to await the dead. 664. The people also believe that they must exchange the offerings that they have set out in order to eat them. For example, suppose a family wants to eat the food that it has set out for the dead; they cannot do so until they find an exchange partner. 665. So, someone in the family fills a basket with different offerings such as fruit, chayotes,[76] tamales, and pan de agua.[77] They bring this to the person with whom the exchange is to be made. However, they don't go to just anyone. 666. They go to the house of someone who is known to the family, or to the house of a relative. The person who receives the food empties all the contents of the basket and goes over to where they have set up their own altar and refills the basket.

667. Even though the things they put in the basket may not seem like much to the people who receive them, the important thing is to exchange something that corresponds to the offer that has been made. This is what the people of the village do. They go about exchanging food in a kind of chain. They make a chain of courtesies with each other and they have linked exchanges. What they say is that it is not good to eat the surplus meal of one's own dead relative. 668. Some people go far, to another community where they know someone or where they have a compadre, and they bring the person those offerings. The person receiving the offerings does the same in return, and exchanges the offerings that he or she put on their own altar. Then the person who came over to visit leaves, and when they get home they eat what they received in the exchange.

669. Another circumstance in which the dead are remembered is when someone is sick. Then the family blames the dead relatives. They say that the dead are punishing the sick person for not remembering them by lighting a candle, or

they say a departed relative wants to have a mass celebrated. They say that this is why the dead person has sent the illness so that the afflicted person will remember. They also say that the dead get hungry while they are up in heaven, so they take revenge on their relatives who are still on earth, and that is why a person got sick. 670. Those who believe this are few. In order to beseech the dead to remove the illness that afflicts a person, a relative of the responsible departed buys breads and candles, and piloncillos. They put all this in a little basket that holds about a cuartillo of grain. 671. They cover the basket with cempoalzúchitl[78] and fennel. Then they bring this to the church, sometimes to the main church in Ixmiquilpan, or sometimes to the church where they come from. They ask the priest to pray over the offering that they are making to the dead person who is considered responsible for the illness. Sometimes a list of the names that dead people had when they were alive is read out. 672. The priest repeats the name of the dead person while he prays, and begs the dead to forgive the sick relative if the latter has offended the departed.

673. When this is done, the person who is remembering the dead goes to where the deceased is interred. They light candles that have been prayed over by the priest. There may be two or three dead persons, and they all have candles lit for them. The relative looks for a good spot to leave all the things to eat so that, according to what is believed, the dead can consume them. 674. If they don't go to a priest, then they go to one of their neighbors who knows how to pray. They ask the neighbor to pray over the things that they want to offer. Usually they buy breads and piloncillos. The person who does the praying does the same thing as the priest. He mentions the names of the dead, one by one, and he asks them not to do any evil against their relatives, nor to make them suffer any illness. By coincidence, some people have gotten better and so they believe in this, and then the rest of the people in the community do the same thing.

675. The orphaned dead are also remembered on their day. The orphaned dead are those who have no relatives left on earth. That is, they have all died, and the entire family is gone. Some people believe that these dead also come back. According to the belief, God lets them come back to earth and move around freely when it is their day, the Day of the Dead. 676. So, some people, in consideration of this, light a candle for the dead. If they make tamales in a house, then they set aside a special plate of them, on the usual table that is used as an altar. This is done for the orphaned dead adults as well as for the dead children. 677. If the priest celebrates a mass, he does it at the cemetery, and not in the church. Once the mass is over, he goes to the cemetery and sprinkles holy water on the graves. This is how graves are blessed.

678. When the Fiesta de Todos Santos is finished, another month goes by before the coming of the Fiesta de La Virgen de Guadalupe. This fiesta is celebrated in all of Mexico on the 12th of December. This fiesta has been celebrated in Orizabita for many years, and is second in importance only to the Fiesta del Sexto Viernes. 679. Musicians and fireworks makers are hired for this fiesta also. Mayordomos are named each year for each of these things and they are placed in charge of getting them done. This fiesta, too, lasts three days. It is rarely postponed and is usually celebrated on December 12th. 680. None of the images invited for the fiesta of the Sixth Friday are invited for this one. Neither the Virgen de los Dolores, nor the Sr. del Buen Viaje of Orizabita accompanies the Virgin of Guadalupe when she leaves the church on the procession. She is worshipped all by herself. In order to celebrate the fiesta of the Virgin of Guadalupe every year, the people come together right after the fiesta is finished and carry out what is called "el cambio," or "the change." 681. This is for naming the new judges and mayordomos for the church, as well as the mayordomos who will be in charge of the music and the castillo and the torito for the fiesta of Guadalupe. Thus, by the time the fiesta comes around, everything is organized.

682. Vespers are on December 11th, and by that time the people have arrived from other communities to set up their stalls and sell different things. Some of them get there a day before and by the time of vespers, they are already set up and selling. 683. Many people from up in the mountains come down for this fiesta. The musicians, as well as the fireworks makers, arrive on the day of vespers. The musicians arrive around midday on the 11th and play all afternoon and evening. 684. They rest around one in the morning. Before resting they wait until the castillo has been lit, and before that the torito. The torito goes out on the procession from the church along with the Virgin. 685. The torito goes in front of everyone. It is carried by a man, who is the same one who carries it when it is set off. The man goes along, jumping around, yelling and imitating the bellow of a bull. One torito is lit on the day of the vespers along with one of the castillos.

686. The next day, or the 12th, which is the actual day of the fiesta of the Virgin of Guadalupe, another torito and a castillo are lit. First the Virgin of Guadalupe goes out on the procession. Only she, and no other image, goes out on the procession. 687. She is accompanied only by the ciriales. There are none of those arches that we saw in the celebration of the other fiesta. She goes out of the church and makes a tour of the entire plaza. This procession comes out of the church only once, not twice like in the Fiesta del Sexto Viernes. 688. Of course, there are firecrackers. Only women carry the image of the Virgin, not men. The Virgin of Guadalupe does not go visiting to any other village.

689. A grand mass is celebrated on the 12th. There are three priests and a singer who assist in the mass. This mass is also celebrated at noon. There are the usual floral offerings, and escamadas. 690. The priest takes confession before starting the mass. He confesses anyone who wants to do so. He takes the person aside in order to talk because he asks about all the sins they have committed. 691. After confessing the person, the priest asks God to forgive the person for his or her sins, and then he makes the benediction. This is supposed to drive out the Devil who makes people commit sins. Children as well as adults take confession. After taking the confession of all who have asked for it, the priest begins the mass. 692. Those who take confession do not leave right away, but remain for the mass. Before drinking the wine and eating the little round cracker that he carries, he prays over those things. Then he consumes them and he invites the other two priests to do so as well. 693. After they have eaten it they call up those whom they have confessed and put this little white, round thing in their mouths. Who knows whether they just let it dissolve in their mouths or they chew it? Then the priest gives them a drink of the wine to wash it down.

694. Priests also do baptisms. People bring their littlest children to be baptized. They bring the children before the priests to receive a benediction and to have the priest pour water on their heads. This is supposed to keep God protecting the children. 695. This is also when the priests do another function called "first communion." Children who have already been baptized are given first communion so that they will visit God in his church and keep on believing in him. Padrinos and padrinas are sought for both baptisms and first communions. 696. They carry the baby in their arms at the baptism. The parents simply accompany them. The priests always tell the parents that the padrinos must appear at the mass, and if there are no padrinos then the priests don't want to give the blessing. The same padrinos who took part in the baptism accompany the child in the first communion. Now, though, they don't carry the child but walk with it because it has grown up.

697. The padrinos dress the child all in white. At first communion the child is asked if they know their prayers. The child is given confession, and is given the little round cracker to eat during the mass. Because of all these extra ceremonies, the fiesta of the Virgin of Guadalupe brings in many people. They come from all over, from small pueblos where they don't celebrate the fiesta of this Virgin. The image of the Virgin is taken out for a procession on the day of vespers and on the day of the fiesta, the 12th, as well. The next day, the 13th, another mass is said, but nothing else is done.

698. Meals are prepared in the same way as for the fiesta of the Sixth Friday. The mayordomos, as always, receive loans. When the fiesta of the Virgin of

Guadalupe is finished, then the season of the posadas is near. 699. They begin
on December 16th and finish on the 24th. Each night people come to the church
to take part in the little processions that are made. 700. The images of what is
called the "holy family" are taken out in a procession. Just as we saw with the
celebration of the posadas in Remedios, the same is done in Orizabita, with a
mayordomo named for each of the nights. Some are named, and other volunteer
to host one of the posadas. 701. They provide the things most needed in the
church. If they wish, they also provide the music, and they hand out sweets,
peanuts, and coffee after the praying is finished and the procession has left
the church.

702. The musicians play and a dance is held. They play a style of music
known as "huapangos."[79] In this style of dancing the dancers don't hold onto
each other. Each member of the couple dances alone, moving back and forth
and crossing past each other, back to back. This fiesta goes on every night of the
posadas. 703. Some nights there are piñatas set up for the children. The piñatas
are made from either earthen pitchers or jugs that have been decorated and filled
with sweets, oranges, and peanuts. The piñatas are hung up some place for the
children to break.

704. After the eight nights of the posadas have gone by, then the ninth, or
Christmas Eve, comes, and this is the last night of the fiesta. On this night there
are many people gathered in the church. There are so many that they don't fit
into the church, and many remain standing outside. This is the night that they
sing the lullaby of the baby Jesus. First they do the procession just as on all other
nights. Then they sing the lullaby to the baby Jesus and that is supposed to make
him sleep. 705. Sometimes the priest conducts the mass at midnight in order to
baptize the baby. As we have seen before, here too, there is a mayordomo. The
mayordomo asks someone to act as padrino for the baby Jesus—that is, to carry
the image of the child in his arms and to baptize him. Later, the padrino brings
the child to the mayordomo's house to continue the fiesta and the dance.
706. The padrino contracts for the musicians who accompany the child in the
church and who later go back to the mayordomo's house (that is, the house of
the padrino's compadre) to continue playing. A meal is served and peanuts are
given out. Some people stay all night, and others go to the dance that is organized by the pueblo.

707. Bonfires are lit on the mountains this night. The belief about these fires
is that they light the way for the baby Jesus who has just been born. Others say
that the fires are lit to warm the baby Jesus, because the night he was born it was
very cold. 708. The significance of the bonfires is treated at greater length in the

Bonfires are lit on the mountains this night

Religion 707

third volume in this series on the flora of the valley. Those bonfires are not the work of one individual; they are set by many people.

709. Once the posada of Christmas Eve is over, then a week later is New Year's and another celebration. There is a procession and a mass is said. A mayordomo is named to be in charge. The image adored is the same baby Jesus who was sung the lullaby on Christmas Eve. 710. The same image is taken out on this procession, and the mass is said in his honor. The mayordomo responsible for the fiesta has a meal prepared for his helpers and acquaintances who have done him the favor of making the floral offering. Few mayordomos for this fiesta make floral offerings. They must, however, ask a priest to say a mass.

711. The festival of the New Year passes. Many people are happy for having lived another year. They ask God to give them life and health to live another year. Others hope to realize plans they have for them and their families to live well. 712. Others hope that God, who does everything, will make it rain, so they can plant a garden on their little parcels of land, and so the fields will be green.

713. For most people there is hope and happiness, but there is also sadness. Some old people fear that they will not live another year, and they ask God to take them to his side should they die.

714. The mayordomos of the church change on the 6th of January. They have been named previously in a general meeting of the community. The judges are also named at that meeting, and they take over their responsibilities at the same time. One person is named for each judge post; the outgoing judges have to be there because they and the mayordomos of the church are questioned about matters having to do with the church. Everyone who is old enough to be a citizen is asked to participate in the pueblo meeting. That way, later on, no one can object on the grounds that he was not informed. 715. The citizens most responsible for pueblo life, along with those who are going to receive power, are among the first ones asked to attend the meeting of "delivery and changeover," in which the change of village authorities takes place. These people make sure that none of the mandates received by the previous year's group, who are now turning over the power, has been left unfulfilled.

716. All the mayordomos and judges, who have been named about two weeks before, come together for a meeting. Each of them has also named his own assistants who accompany them to the meeting, and who help check that everything the authorities receive that day is in good condition. They also help ensure that everything is returned the following year in the same condition which it was received. 717. Some of the new authorities are accompanied by their friends and brothers who help check that nothing is missing from the papers and paraphrenalia they receive. Then the following year they won't be

accused of losing something, or of having kept something in their house. When a mayordomo or judge loses something, the people of the community are very displeased and make the man replace it or pay its value, while others at the meeting scold him.

When most of the people have arrived, the changeover begins. 718. For this, a man who knows how to read well calls out the list of things to be found there, spread out on the ground, so the people can see that everything is complete and in good condition. In case something is amiss, he informs the people there and they decide what is to be done. If the object is not of much value, then the people may pardon the mayordomo, particularly if he has worked hard for the betterment of the church. But if he has been lazy, then they reprimand him strongly and make him pay for the object, especially if he is deemed responsible for the object being lost. 720. If everyone agrees that the mayordomos must make reparations, then, like it or not, they have to find the money to restore things. If the mayordomos show hesitation about paying, the people threaten them with suspending the changeover of authority. The most convenient thing is for the mayordomos to accept the fact that they will pay up, and in this way they avoid a lot of problems.

721. Among the things that have to be taken care of are the priest's vestments and the coverings for the images, including some that have been there for around 70 years. All these things are checked and placed on the inventory. 722. Other things are candlesticks, incense burners, and the trunks in which things are stored. These include the vestments of the priest, the dresses of the holy virgins, their rings, earrings, and necklaces. All of these things are put in the inventory because some items are made of gold and people say they are worth a lot of money.

723. Once all the clothing and such have been inspected, the group moves to where the various images are kept and inspects them, too. They check to make sure that they haven't been scratched, banged up or otherwise abused. This is one of the most difficult moments for the mayordomos of the church, because if anything has happened to one of the images the people get really angry, and the changeover meeting can wind up in open conflict. 724. After the images have been inspected, they count up all the money collected in alms, including the money turned over to the mayordomos from the year before and the money that was collected as offerings over the past year. Finally, they weigh all the candles so that everyone will know how many kilograms were collected during the year. 725. Ladders and bells are also checked; even though the former may be made of very old wood, still, everything must appear on the inventory.

Once all this is done, papers are drawn up for signatures, both for the mayor-domos and judges who are now free of their burden, as well as for the new authorities who are taking over the cargo. 726. By signing this document, they show that they accept willingly the receipt of the cargo given to them by all the people, and they affirm that the following year, on the 6th of January, they will return everything to the pueblo.

727. The new mayordomos now receive the keys to the church—huge keys about 20 centimeters long. 728. The changeover has been completed, but by now it is late and starting to get dark. Everyone who attended the meeting stays there, however, because the mayordomos who are finishing their cargos have the pleasure of offering everyone something to eat and drink. The cooks are ready and waiting, and as soon as their assistants arrive at the meeting they serve so the people can eat. They begin by seating the new mayordomos and judges who are the first to be served. 729. They lay out the food on the tables which have been covered with clean, embroidered cloths. This is the moment in which women really shine—that is, those who really know how to make beautiful embroidery.

When they serve the meal, the first thing set out is the salt. If men are being served at the table they have to remove their hats because that is part of the respect that people are accustomed to show. 730. If a man is seen at the table who has not taken off his hat, then someone will comment to someone else that the man is disrespectful. Once the salt is placed on the table, then come baskets filled with tortillas, and then the plates with the main meal. It may be consomé de barbacóa, or chicken in white broth, or goat meat in mole de olla.

731. The two outgoing mayordomos offer the meal. Each one has helpers who serve the tables. They come and go, attending to the people who have come to the changeover meeting, and to the new mayordomos who are taking over. They make several trips, bringing out pulque, beer, and more hot tortillas which they put in the baskets for people to eat. 732. All the assistants to the mayor-domos and the judges are well treated, as are all who have come to the change-over. They are served with kindness.

As I say, the two outgoing mayordomos offer the meal. They have killed chickens and goats, and sometimes even a head of cattle so that there will be enough food for everyone who has come. 733. Once everyone has been served, then each of the new mayordomos and judges are given a cooked, whole chick-en. The first chicken is given to the juez auxiliar propietario, and the second to the juez auxiliar suplente. Then the first mayordomo gets his, and finally the second mayordomo. Each one is applauded as he is given the basket with the chicken, fully cooked and ready to heat up and eat.

734. For the moment, the new mayordomos have been on the receiving end of things; but the following year it will be their turn to provide food for everyone, and each mayordomo will have to present a chicken to the next mayordomo who takes his place. They do this every year, giving and returning invitations. The bell ringers and the assistants to the judges are not given chickens; they are just given food to eat like everyone else. 736. After everyone has eaten, then if music has been brought in everyone starts to dance, and little by little the fiesta comes to a close.

This celebration is always on the 6th of January. Of course, there are times when it has to be postponed if it falls on a Monday because that is market day. The people go to Ixmiquilpan to sell what they have made and to buy provisions to last a week. 737. There are also people who, finishing their cargo as mayordomo, won't hold the changeover on a Friday but will postpone it for a Tuesday, for example. Some people believe that Friday is not a good day to hold a mass because people end up fighting. Supposedly, the Devil roams the earth on Fridays; that is the day he is free to move about as he chooses, and he visits Christian believers.

738. Once the mayordomos are free from the obligation of their cargos, they go back to work as usual. Little by little they earn enough to pay off the loans that people gave them when they threw the meal for everyone. 739. The mayordomos also spent a lot of their own money in fulfilling their cargo obligations; in fact, this class of cargo generally impoverishes the person who fulfills it, because he has to kill his animals. He has to purchase and gather together many things, not for his own consumption but for the meal when he turns over his cargo to the next person who has been named. 740. Some people ask that they be named mayordomos of the church because, according to them, they want to serve God, or they want to serve in the house of God.

Sometimes the system works differently; a group of neighbors from the community get together and name the mayordomos, and then tell them that they have been appointed. 741. The mayordomos are responsible for attending to everything in regard to festivals at the church. For example, they have to open the church doors when mass is said, or when a dead person is brought to church, or when a floral offering is made for a departed adult or child. 742. People are quick to anger if the mayordomo doesn't open the door. They complain immediately about such treatment and bring the problem to the judge so that he will speak to the mayordomo and remind him of his obligations not to mistreat people and make them angry. 743. The mayordomos finish their cargo on the 6th of January, but the judges with whom they have worked have to stay on until the 15th of the month. All of them feel very good about having completed their period of cargo.

744. The judges are obliged to mention, at a general meeting of the community, everything that the mayordomos accomplished during their year. They may have repaired some parts of the church walls, or they may have purchased some things like flower vases or candlesticks for use on the altar. 745. From this moment, the new judges take over. The old ones turn over the community property to the new ones. In this exchange, too, everything has to be done properly or problems arise. If something is missing, then an investigation must be conducted to locate its whereabouts so that the people[80] will be satisfied. 746. It is very important not to make the people angry because then they will not want to cooperate to purchase things that the community needs. It becomes a delicate matter when the people are not well organized, because they become divided against each other.

747. Boxhuada does not have any religious images of its own. The ones that come down from the north pass through there, or they stop and rest at the ermitas that are always set up there. The reason that they have no religious statues of their own is that they only recently separated from Orizabita.[81] Possibly, they will construct a church of their own in the future, as other small communities have done. 748. They do name their own judge although always in coordination and with the agreement of the authorities from Orizabita. Whenever the people from Boxhuada have been called on to pitch in on something, they have never said no and have always been very good neighbors. Many of them are Catholics; those who are not are called "hermanitos" or "little brothers." Most of the people believe in God[82] and they hate those who do not and sometimes they get into fights with them.

749. Why do people fight with the Protestants? In the first place, they hate the Protestants for cheating God by practicing hypocrisy, and because they go around trying to get others to convert and become "hermanitos." This is what their Catholic neighbors detest so much. In the second place, whenever those people are asked to chip in money on any community projects, they refuse to do so. Sometimes they don't even support the school, much less the church; and so the rest of the people pressure them even more to obey and to work like they should.

750. The Protestants simply do not obey; they respond to those requests badly and cause the people who work and cooperate in the village to get angry. Sometimes a few people get together and grab one of the hermanitos and make him drink pulque, and if he refuses in a coarse way, then that's when the fighting starts. 751. The hermanitos have been well schooled by their superiors about

how to avoid bad situations and they generally know how to respond. The children, seeing all this, also come to hate each other, and they fight, too. One can see this most easily in school. A few of the children start picking on one of the others, calling him "hermanito." The hermanitos do not drink pulque, they do not drink beer, they do not drink liquor. 752. But many of them surely scrape maguey plants and make pulque to sell to those who do drink it. Wherever they go they tell people that they cause no one any harm, but this is not always the case. Why do they make pulque to sell to others? Then people drink and get drunk and have words with one another and fight. Isn't this a bad thing that they cause for their fellow man? This is why what they claim is not true. 753. Anyway, it is often worse to confront people because it is possible to get killed that way.

It is true that many people who became hermanitos really used to be drunks, and when they took up the new faith they stopped drinking pulque. Others had good intentions when they converted, but when their thoughts turned to pulque again they came back to the Catholic church—that is, where God and the Virgin are worshipped. 754. A lot of people have not been able to last even a year as Protestants, and then they show up in church again. But those persons who have taken the idea firmly into their thinking never return. Those who have been able to put together some money have built good houses and dress well. 755. Many of them had problems in their natal pueblos and had to leave and go live in another community. Some have had very serious problems, and have even been threatened that their entire family would be killed if they continued living where they were.

756. This has happened in various communities, and those who converted and became Protestants had to flee. A lot of them went to Ixmiquilpan and became concentrated in a community called Santiago. Many who decided not to return to their village are now living there. They are still flowing in to the barrio I am talking about, and it is becoming very highly populated.

757. According to what people remember, it was some foreign mestizos, early in 1944, who began to proselytize the people and get them to convert. 758. Since then many small communities have had problems of every sort, and the problems have not been eliminated to this day. This new religion has torn apart many pueblos and divided the people who live in them. 759. For example, the pueblos of El Olivo and El Espíritu have been having these difficulties for many years, and no one knows when it will end. Sometimes people just find pretexts to start the troubles again.

760. Sometimes the Protestants involve themselves in community border disputes, or in disputes over the borders between individuals' plots of land.

When those arguments erupt, men and women discuss the problem together and, if they see that the problem is getting serious, they call for a face to face confrontation between the parties in front of the local, or state, or federal authorities. One of the parties gets fed up and backs off, and then weeks or months pass before the trouble erupts again.

761. People from one faction or the other wind up being mixed up in the affair, even if they don't know much about it, or how it got started, because otherwise they would be accused of siding with someone's enemy. 762. The mestizos who got the parties to confront one another are nowhere to be found when people want to fight each other. Nowadays there are people living everywhere who have converted to the Protestant religion. In some villages everyone knows who they are, and in other places they go to their own church in secret. If a man's neighbors get suspicious, then two or three may follow him and find out where he goes. When they return from spying, they tell others what they have learned, and that is how people find out about someone's habits. 764. In communities where these divisions are present, they have not been able to progress, because everyone does what he feels like doing and people don't work collectively for what is needed.

765. Now we continue along the road that goes to Las Emes, the "Ms," and we go through a little pueblo known as Ojo de Agua. From there we go up the mountain to Puerto de Piedra[83] and down the other side. This is the road that goes to La Lagunita. At Puerto de Piedra, things begin to get green, and this is where people say the area called the "wet mountains" begin. 766. Behind the mountain called "Zuhuä" in Ñähñu, or La Muñeca, there is a forested area that runs north and south. Among the trees there are pitch pines, Mexican firs, evergreen oaks, other shrubs, and a kind of maguey called "i'ta." 767. It is colder in La Lagunita; it is different from the flat land of Orizabita where it is a bit more hot. The cold climate begins in La Lagunita and beyond, in Banxu for example, and beyond that in La Pechuga de Gallina. That is as far as the cool region goes; after that comes Bonanza and from there it becomes really hot again.

768. In La Lagunita they celebrate the fiesta of Santos Reyes[84] on January 6th. The images worshipped there are crosses that have been there from the beginning.[85] Sometimes they invite other villages to come in for the celebration. Among them is Defay, which is invited to bring the image of El Sr. del Buen Viaje, of Orizabita, to participate. 769. The fiesta lasts for three days. The mayordomos stay there for two or three days to receive the alms given and to give out relics to all who ask for one.

770. The custom of asking for an image from some other village to come and participate in a fiesta is a bit delicate, because after the fiesta is over the mayordomos from the other village have to go home and leave their pueblo's image in the church of the community that invited them. That is, they leave their icons in the charge of the mayordomos from the community that asked them to participate in the fiesta. People are sometimes not careful and the images get scratched or knocked over. They fall down, or get broken and then not only is the mayordomo blamed, but the entire community. 772. The people of the pueblo themselves accuse the mayordomo. 773. They all take part in reprimanding him, and they say things like: "How could such a thing have happened? What, were you drunk, or something? Can't you see? What are you, still a child that you don't know what you are doing? It seems like you just don't think about God." The people get very angry, women as well as men, and what happened really affects them deeply.

774. The mayordomo, or the mayordomos, can only listen to what they are being told, for to answer wrongly would only worsen matters and the people would only punish them more. 775. This is what happened in 1981. The mayordomo of La Lagunita knocked over the statue; it did not fall to the ground, but just fell over on the altar. Still, one of the arms broke off at the armpit, and one of the right ribs broke. 776. The mayordomo of La Lagunita was afraid that the people from Defay would do him harm for having broken their statue. So he decided to first tell the mayordomos of Defay. They decided that they should not be the only ones who knew, and they told their own judges, and when they analyzed the situation they decided to tell everyone in the community in order to avoid a lot of problems. 777. And so it was that the whole community was informed and they were asked if they wanted to receive the statue as it was, or if they preferred to have it reconstructed first.

778. Many of them were very angry that this thing had happened to their holy image. The people who were best informed about such things asked that the mayordomos send the statue out to be repaired. Others said that the mayordomos of La Lagunita and Defay should go themselves and look for someone in some city who knew how to repair religious statuary. 779. They found such a person right in Ixmiquilpan, and he charged them 1,500 pesos. The mayordomos of La Lagunita paid the sum. La Lagunita and Defay are both in the pueblo of Orizabita so they informed the authorities there about the problem so that they could intervene. What they did was to draw up an agreement, which was signed by all the mayordomos, the judges and witnesses. 781. When the statue was repaired, it was returned to its home. The people of La Lagunita

gathered for this occasion and went to Defay to return the statue, and to ask the authorities and all the people there for forgiveness for what had happened to their sacred image.

782. When the statue arrived in Defay, there were many people gathered there, including pilgrims from other places, waiting for a mass to be celebrated in honor of the statue. 783. That mass was just for the arrival of the statue at his home church, and then the people of La Lagunita organized another mass celebrating the reconstruction of the image.

784. The fiesta in La Lagunita is much like those in other villages we have seen. The people organize to assign someone responsibility for the mass, someone to provide the candles, someone to be in charge of the torito, and so on. Someone is also named to provide food to the string musicians. They do not hire professional bands there, because they cost a lot and there are not enough people there to collect the money needed. There is no castillo, for the same reason. 785. There are flutists and drummers, of course, who stay all day and all night playing songs. People coming with floral offerings from their houses to the church see those musicians there, as well as string musicians. That is the custom that has existed for a long time. 786. The people who come to this fiesta come from El Banxu, La Pechuga de Gallina, La Bonanza, La Palma, Ojo de Agua, and sometimes from Cantamayé. 787. Some of the festival goers are not there just for the celebration, but bring something to sell like pulque, various fruits, tamalitos dulces and beer. These are the things that are generally found at all fiestas.

788. Years ago the people used to fight a lot when they had their fiesta. Men would get drunk and take out knives or pistols. A man with quick hands would live and the other would die. There used to be at least two people shot dead around there the day after the fiesta. 789. Then the people would say that the fiesta had been really good, with lots of action. But if no one was killed, they said the fiesta had been sort of low-key and dispirited. Sometimes the killer was taken into custody, and other times he would flee. Then after a while he would return to live in his own house again. 790. If the dead person had living relatives, they could take revenge at any time, and kill the assassin. They would give the killer back his own medicine at another fiesta.

791. If the killer was taken into custody on the spot, then he had to carry the body himself, on foot, in a large ayate, all the way down the mountain. Two or three local constables accompanied him, pushing him, driving him like a mule, to get to Ixmiquilpan quickly so that he could testify to the authorities about how things had happened—how the fight got started, who threw the first blow, and so on. The killer was subjected to a thorough interrogation.

The fiesta had been really good, with lots of action

Religion 789

792. The constables simply accompanied the man into town, left him with the authorities, and returned home. When they got back, their neighbors asked them if the prisoner had escaped from them, and they answered: "We don't play around with anyone and let them beat us. We took him and left him at his new house." That is what the constables said who took a killer to jail. 793. New problems arose when relatives of the dead man and the killer started fighting with each other. The father or a brother of the victim might get angry and want to take vengeance. 794. These fights go on for years between families, and the quarrels might not stop until all the members of the family are dead.

795. The custom of lending things for fiesta obligations also exists here in La Lagunita. Sometimes people lend each other maize, or whole tortillas, or pulque, or fowl. Chickens are lent separately from female turkeys and from male turkeys, and when the woman goes to repay the loan she has to give back exactly what she got unless she has some prior agreement to repay in some other goods. The woman who lends fowl may request that the loan be paid off with some other product.

All the people gather at the mayordomo's house, including those who have made some kind of loan and those who have been invited, and other guests. They are all there eating what God has provided. 796. Many are there all day and night, chatting and asking each other how things are, both in their personal lives and with regard to the fiesta. They agree to come and visit one another at their homes when they have some free time. The people just don't seem to tire when they celebrate their fiesta in this pueblo. The assistants come and go, bringing beer and great jarros of pulque to whoever wants some.

797. The owner of the house bids goodbye to his guests the next day, but not before asking his helpers to heat up something to eat. From this custom comes the saying that "reheated food tastes best." These words mean that the meal that has been reheated the next day is more delicious than the meal taken straight off the fire.

798. The church in La Lagunita was built by the people there themselves. They chipped in their own labor and money to build it. The walls are made of stone covered with a mixture of limestone and sand. 799. The roof is made of lámina[86] and it is about 15 meters high to the top of the little tower. The entire outside is painted white. There is a cross on the point of the steeple, and the bells are hung just below the cross.

800. The cemetery is nearby, at the foot of a mountain, just above where the road passes towards Pechuga, going east. 801. In prior times, they used to hire a string band to play songs for a dead child when they went to bury it. When they finished the burial, the mourners went home with those who helped him dig the

grave, and with the musicians, and gave everyone something to eat. 802. When they finished eating, dancing would begin; we can say, then, that while they danced and drank pulque their feelings of grief for the death of a child were not very profound. They used to do the same thing when an adult died. 803. Sometimes the grieving person killed a whole head of beef in order to feed everyone who kept him company during the time of mourning. There were people crying, others eating, others drinking aguardiente, and still others drinking coffee. This is where one could see that the pain was not very profound.

804. The inhabitants of the mountains generally keep the body of a dead person in their house for two days, and bury the body on the third day. The reason for this is that the mourners have to get together the money needed for the burial, and they may not have it. Sometimes they have to put a piece of land up for sale. It may be cleared and arable land, or just a piece of the montaña, but whatever they have, they must sell it. Then they can buy clothing for the deceased and a coffin in which to bury the body. 805. If they don't have extra land, then they sell a few dozen maguey plants so that they will have the money to do the right thing for the deceased. It took a long time for the body to leave the house of the bereaved, because they had to buy various things before burying the body, though the deceased did not object because he was dead. 806. It took a long time for the body to leave the house because someone had to go to the market in Ixmiquilpan and buy the things needed. Then they had to find someone to sew the manta so that they could dress the body. They dressed the bodies of children, as well as adults, in white manta.[87]

807. After the cloth is tailored they find someone to dress the body. Not just anyone can do this. This would be bad, according to custom. It is believed that dead people can reach out and "grab" people and make others in the family die, as well. 808. The person who dresses the body ought to be a compadre or a comadre, or someone else who is not part of the immediate family of the deceased. On no occasion is the wife or son or daughter of a person allowed to dress the body. 809. It is said that if they do, then not many days will pass before they, too, are dead. This is what is meant by the act of "grabbing" by the dead and that is why no one dresses his or her own dead.

810. This is why one has to find someone who had been the deceased's comadre or compadre and ask them to come and dress the body.[88] Neither must the person who sewed the manta for the body have any kinship ties with the deceased. Everyone who has any connection with preparing a body must be from outside the family. 811. A child's body may be dressed by its godfather or godmother, but no one in the family can carry the child, or dig its grave. The bodies of both children and of adults are sprinkled with holy water, and some

kind of religous items, or relics are put in the coffin next to the body. According
to the belief, this helps to drive away the Devil.

812. Some people put a few coins in the coffin, and this is supposed to be the
alms that the dead take to heaven. Sometimes, small brooms or brushes are
made for the children to take with them, and these, too, are put in the coffin next
to the body. Children are always buried with their arms folded across their
chests. 813. When the procession gets to the cemetery, holy water is sprinkled
into the grave pit and the coffin containing the body is lowered. Just before the
grave is filled with earth, someone comes forward and sprinkles a handful of
dirt over the coffin. This is supposed to be an act of saying goodbye. 814. When
all this is done, then the grave is filled, with the earth and stones making noise as
they fall on the coffin. 815. Many people at funerals carry lighted candles, and
a woman carries an incense burner which releases smoke during the whole procedure. When the grave has been covered with earth, a few candles are placed
on one side to burn; the mourners carry the rest of the candles back to the home
of the deceased where they are left to burn out. 816. Nine days after a death, a
novena is said for adults.

817. No prayers are said for small children on the day of their burial, but
people have to be found to recite prayers when adults die. The belief is that
adults have committed more sins which have to be forgiven by reciting prayers.
818. The prayer sayers pray all night, and there are usually two or three of them.
They pray at the spot where the person died. The clothing that the deceased
wore when he was alive is put there. A cross that has been made just for this is
set out on the ground, and in the morning it is picked up. This is why this act of
praying is also called the "picking up of the cross." Some people also call it "the
final night." 819. At dawn, the cross is taken to the cemetery where the body
was buried. A cross is not left for a child that dies. 820. With the picking up of
the cross, the mourning that has afflicted the family is ended. The picking up of
the cross is done for both men and women.

821. Banxu and La Lagunita used to be one community. What happened was
that not too long ago, Banxu built its own school and separated. However,
everyone in Banxu still practices the Catholic religion. 822. The religious image
worshipped in this little community is in a house, and the priest celebrates mass
right there. They don't have a big fiesta in Banxu; a priest comes to celebrate
mass when someone requests one. People also congregate for a mass whenever
someone makes a floral offering. 823. The people in Banxu generally go to La
Lagunita and La Pechuga to enjoy the fiesta celebrated there every year. They
bring along some kind of loan to leave with one of their acquaintances. There

doesn't have to be a big fiesta in Banxu for these loans to be paid back. These things can be repaid whenever there is need.

824. These loans can be repaid, for example, when there is a baptism, or when someone makes a floral offering, or when a mass is said in honor of some image. The loans are repaid in the same form as they were made; that is the custom. Nobody cheats anyone with regard to the amount of repayment for a loan. When an animal is loaned, for example, people are careful to note its size and whether it is a goat, or a sheep, or a chicken. In order for there not to be any problems for either party, people agree on the size of an animal at the time it is loaned so that it can be repaid in kind. Some people weigh the animals, because goats and chickens can have fur or feathers, whichever the case may be, which can make them appear larger than they really are. Once they have been skinned or plucked, the meat could turn out not to be very much, after all.

825. When one person (either the lender or the borrower) tries to cheat another, the person being cheated doesn't say anything at the time. Later, however, it will become very difficult for a person who cheats to borrow anything.

826. Someone is always there to help out at the house of the mayordomos. People don't like to leave the mayordomo alone with his responsibility. When he least expects it, here comes someone with a bundle of firewood. 827. It might be a man or a woman, or even a child. That is the custom. No price is placed on the wood, because it is given as a kind of loan. The payment is the food that the wood gatherer eats, and that is all. 828. Or here comes someone carrying a large jug of water, or two tin vessels made from cans. When people come forward like this, to help out without being asked, it is because they respect the mayordomo. When this is not the case, then no one comes. But sometimes it is poverty that forces people to look for someplace where God can help them find something to eat.

829. Now we can continue along the road that goes through La Lagunita. The first thing one comes to is a dip in the road, and then a barranca[89] that carries water. Further on, the road becomes winding, and on both sides there are big trees like evergreen oaks, pines, and Mexican firs,[90] along with other shrubs, and it is very beautiful. The road is like this all the way to La Pechuga de Gallina, which is situated at the bottom of a small river basin, surrounded by mountains. 830. There are orchards here, with apples, peaches and avocados. The houses look different from those in La Lagunita, and better constructed in La Pechuga de Gallina. To the east and to the west there are tall mountains, at least 1200 meters high. 831. There are no longer any large trees on these mountains, just various shrubs.[91]

The church, which is of average size, is in the center of the community. It is encircled by walls made of mamposteria[92] and inside the compound is a graveyard where they bury their dead to this day. The images that they worship are crosses known as "The Crosses of La Pechuga de Gallina." They are about a meter tall. The people in this community have a lot of faith in those crosses. These crosses have been coming for many years to the Fiesta del Sexto Viernes in Orizabita. 832. The church in La Pechuga de Gallina is painted all white. The bell tower is not very high, and there are three bells hanging in it with a cross on the top. The walls of the church are not heavily adorned like those of churches that we will see further on.

833. In other communities, February is the month that people dress up in masks and dance. The people in La Pechuga de Gallina don't try to disguise themselves, however, even though that is the object of the fiesta. The people there prepare meals in various houses and feed people whom they invite. They don't hire bands or firecracker makers, or pyrotechnists. 834. They generally hire string musicians who accompany the priest when he gives the mass at noon. The same group plays again at night when the dance is held. They play huapangos and other pieces called "rancheras" and "corridos" all night long until the morning.[93] Flutists and drummers also take part in this fiesta, accompanying the procession. Different people carry around the images and the crosses. During the procession, some people who know how to do so pray out loud and others answer them.

835. Before the procession leaves the church the crosses are adorned with garlands of flowers made beforehand. The people in this place are real believers; most of them can be seen following the procession. First they finish up in the church and then they all go to where the dance is to be held. Anyone can do whatever they want there. 836. If a man has money, for example, he can drink liquor and beer. But if it gets to him, then quarrels start. Anyone who lasts all night has to watch his movements carefully. They also get tired from dancing so many huapangos. But all this is a pleasure because it only happens once a year, and that is why it happens like this.

837. From here one can go on to another little community called La Bonanza in Spanish. There used to be a lot of active gold mines in this place, and they say that the Spaniards worked here for many years in the exploitation of those mines. 838. A lot of the people there have white skin and some have blonde hair because the Spaniards lived there for many years and these are their descendants. There are still a lot of very old houses there where people say the first Spaniards lived. There is a building which was once the Presidencia Municipal, and there is still a small bell hung at the top of the two-story structure.

839. When the Revolution began in 1910, a man named Nicolás Flores invaded La Bonanza with his followers. At that time they were from what used to be the jurisdiction of Santa María, which was a part of Zimapán and included La Bonanza. They burned all the houses, and one can still see the old burned walls today. 840. What Nicolás Flores wanted was to change the location of the presidencia to Santa María.[94] In the end he succeeded, and that is where it is today. Many people who lived in La Bonanza died in the fire, but some managed to escape and they returned to reestablish themselves when hostilities ended after the Revolution. They say that the church there was built by the Spaniards. It is going to ruin because it was built so long ago and because it was built on a slope of a hill.

841. From here one can continue along the road to a small community called La Unión. There is no church here, just a house in which the local image that is worshipped is kept, along with other images of both saints and holy virgins. As always, the priest is called in to celebrate mass. 842. They don't have a big fiesta here every year. It is about four kilometers from La Bonanza. To the east of this community is the road that goes to the pueblo of El Taxai. There is no church here, either. The same thing happens as in La Unión; that is, there is a little house where the image is kept that is worshipped, and the priest is called in to say mass. He comes from the cathedral of San Nicolás in the municipio of Ixmiquilpan. 843. The people in this place are also very Catholic. One can see this because when a mass is celebrated a lot of people gather.

844. We continue along the same road, but now we have to go about 10 kilometers before coming to Santa María, the birthplace of Nicolás Flores. This is the presidencia, where the other communities in the municipio meet. 845. The town is situated in a small river basin, encircled by mountains. There is an arroyo, with a lot of water flowing, along the west side of the town. 846. The path we have traveled has all been on foot. The dirt motor road goes only as far as El Taxai. To reach Nicolás Flores quickly, one must folow the footpaths, or one can go along the edge of the barranca. The other road into Nicolás Flores comes in from Zimapán and one has to go a long way around, through Zimapán, to get there. The road is tortuous and dangerous if one does not drive carefully.

847. The municipio of Nicolás Flores has a very beautiful church. The inside walls are highly decorated. The steeple is high, and the bells hang there. The front is painted white. 848. The Virgin venerated here is called La Candelaria. The date of her fiesta is the February 2nd. This is the date also known as "The Blessing of the Candles," and maize and beans are also blessed on that day. It comes at the time when people there say that planting season is near. This might, indeed be the case, but only in the irrigated zone. In the nonirrigated zone

it will be another four months before the rains come. The fiesta lasts five days. 849. Pyrotechnists are hired to make castillos and toritos. A band is also hired and it remains there for three days. They have two processions, one each night. Firecrackers are set off and people carry lit candles, and there are lit candles on the altar of the Virgin. A lot of people come to this fiesta, not just from the municipio of Nicolás Flores, but from Zimapán, Taxquillo, Cardonal, and Ixmiquilpan. 850. They have organized a dance there for many years. Both men and women like to dance huapangos all night. When they start dancing they make a lot of noise on the patio where the dance is held. Those who are not accustomed to dancing huapangos all night just don't last.

851. Not far from here is another place called La Ferrería in Spanish and "rä xeni gä hai habu di 'moe rä bojä" in Ñähñu or "the place where metal is melted down." From Nicolás Flores, or Santa María, one walks about four kilometers. A lot of people gather here because they have a lot of faith in the image of the Virgin of Guadalupe which is carved into a vertical, flat rock. It looks like someone had simply put a painting there; the image is very clear, as if someone had recently done it. 852. No one knows how it appeared there. The part of the the rock on which it is found is very high and practically impossible for anyone to climb. 853. Every year, on December 12th, a lot of people come to the fiesta. There are no houses there, just the image of the Virgin.

854. The image is about 80 centimeters high, and is pure stone, without any painting or anything! All the people who make the pilgrimage there do so out of faith and on their own. No one invites them. Neither full bands, nor string bands are paid by anyone to play, but they come on their own anyway. This is *their* offering to the Virgin. The priest comes to celebrate the mass. About a thousand people come because they believe that the image is very miraculous and that she will give her blessing and treat them with compassion. 855. Cars can not come in. The only way to get there is on foot or on horseback. The people who live around there put out food for sale, and that is what there is to eat. Others bring their own itacate and heat it there. Some stay the night, and may even stay for two or three days before returning to their homes. 856. When they do return, they walk to the highway where the busses pass. People from El Santuario, San Antonio Sabanillas, El Saúz, and other communities in this area, go all the way home on foot, walking an entire day. Despite this hardship, the next year they return for the adoration of the Virgin.

857. Some people buy new clothes when they go to worship a holy image. Some buy calzones[95] made of manta, or a white manta shirt, or new huaraches, or a new machine turned sombrero for the men. Women get new huaraches with leather soles, or a new white manta skirt, or a hand-embroidered blouse, and a

new rebozo[96] and earrings. 858. As time passes, they remember the day that they wore these things for the first time, and these are good memories, for it is not every day that people get new clothes. The old ones have to wear out first, before new ones are bought. 859. There is no cemetery in La Ferrería because no one lives there. Everything is brought in. When people fight and someone is killed, the killer has to carry the body, on his back or on a horse, to where he came from for burial. But of course, first the killer has to testify to the authorities.

860. Now we turn and go back towards the east to see what communties there are, and what kind of religion they practice. There is a pueblo that is right on the main road that goes to Pachuca. It is about four kilometers from Actopan. It is right on the highway and is called El Arenal. It has a church that looks like it must have been built a long time ago. 861. Pilgrims have gone to that place from around the Mezquital Valley and from other parts of Mexico for many years. 862. The image worshipped there is believed to be very miraculous and to help people who believe in him. 863. In earlier times there were no busses, and pilgrims walked to the veneration. They brought their food along with them, enough to last for two or three days.

864. There are people around who remember those days and they tell about how there wasn't any potable water at that place. They had to drink from the pools of rainwater. People brought chickens and goats and prepared them right there at the fiesta. There are no hotels in this village. Where did visitors sleep? They say that they slept out on the patio of the church. Though they suffered this lack of comfort, they returned for the adoration every year. 865. The fiesta was celebrated on the fifth Friday of Pentecost, and the celebrants came by the hundreds. There was no room to move around in the church, there were so many people. Everyone wanted to worship the holy image at the same time. The fiesta lasts five days, and the main day is Friday. 866. The santito there gets a lot of money from the pilgrims who come to give it. Some people ask that they be cleansed with the money they have brought; that is, that they be forgiven for the sins they have committed. Others ask that they, or one of their relatives, be cured of some illness, or that they be forgiven for having blasphemed against God.

867. At that moment, when people ask for forgiveness, El Arenal gets a lot of money in donations. Who knows how they have invested it? But every year the church gets thousands of pesos. 868. Perhaps the mayordomos of the holy church know the truth about where the saint's money is invested. The Ñähñu know the saint by his Spanish name, El Santito de Maravillas.

869. The land in this region is very arid because it does not rain much and there is no irrigation. The flora consists of such things as pirúl trees, mesquite trees, needle tipped cacti, tunas de coyote,[97] various kinds of cardón cacti[98] and sangre de grado.[99] The fiesta is celebrated at the end of March or the beginning of April. Around that time, the spring winds blow, and the celebrants may be covered with dust as they enjoy the fiesta. 870. The stalls that sell things come from various places. There are even professional merchants who come from distant towns because they know that they can sell their wares here. That is precisely where the red colored jícaras are sold that people like so much for drinking pulque. Some of the merchants there come from Metepec, and they bring some really big and beautiful jugs that hold up to five liters. People really liked to buy those jugs, which the mayordomos used when giving out pulque at a fiesta. Acocotes also were sold at this fiesta. They were huge and held about four liters of aguamiel.[100]

871. Forty years ago these things were not expensive. In those days, the coins that circulated were 6 centavos, 12 centavos, 24 centavos, 50 centavos, 72 centavos, one peso and one real. Those were the most usual denominations in those days. The parishioners carried their things back and forth, on foot, just to seek the mercy of the Santito de Maravillas.

872. Two fiestas are celebrated in Arenal. One, Christmas Eve, is celebrated on December 24th, and that is when we are supposed to remember the birth of God. Though a lot of people come to this fiesta, they don't buy as much as in the other one.

873. From Arenal we go back to Actopan where a very big fiesta that lasts several days is celebrated in July. However, one cannot compare the number of people that come to Actopan with the number that comes to Arenal; a lot more come to Arenal. There is a cathedral in Actopan that is much like the one in Ixmiquilpan. The one in Actopan has murals painted on the inside walls, and they look very old. Some of those murals have begun to peel off, possibly because of the humidity, or because the lime which was used to even out the surface of the walls has been eaten away by saltpeter. 874. Those murals are very beautiful, and one may enjoy the many colors of the figures. 875. The paintings, or frescoes, are of bishops. Perhaps they were the highest authorities then and that is why they painted their portraits. One can see how they used to dress in black, and how their long robes dragged along the ground. They wore a long skirt around their waist, and it came down to their feet. One can see also that they shaved part of their heads, around the crown. They almost always walked around with their hands clasped and their eyes looking up.

876. Possibly they were looking at God or the Virgin. One sees there also a likeness of Christ on the cross in the midst of some trees; it looks like a forest. There are flowers painted on other parts of the walls and there are other priests with their black robes and their shaved heads. There are also depictions of virgins and angels. Some of the virgins look very sad, and there is some writing with them in Latin. I could not translate them into Ñähñu; who knows what those inscriptions mean? May God forgive whoever wrote those phrases without translating them into Ñähñu. 877. There are also paintings of priests on other parts of the walls. On the upper wall there is a painting of two priests; one looks pensive and the other is reading a book. Below them there are three more seated figures that look like virgins. They are wearing long dresses, topped off with large bonnets.

878. A little further down there are some rather surprising figures of creatures that have the body and head of a horse, with the hoofs of a goat. The two animals are holding up a banner between them, each with a corner in its mouth. One can tell that what they are holding up is very heavy because they are straining heavily, as noted by the fact that their teeth are bared. 879. Their hooves are open, as if from the force they are exerting. Nowadays, no such monstrous animal as those in the mural have been seen. Perhaps that is what the Devil's horses were like in ancient times. There is a heart, with spears through it, on the banner the animals are holding.

880. Below the painting just mentioned, there is another of a small house with decorated walls. In the middle is a seated priest, perhaps a bishop, heavily dressed, and wearing a tall hat whose crown comes to a point. In his right hand he is holding a long rod, perhaps the priestly staff. 881. The wall is made of polished stone. At the bottom of the painting there are some pretty flowers and also some angels that are whipping something. If we look up towards the ceiling, we see some more flowers painted in the middle, with braids going off towards the corners with a winged angel standing at each corner. The angels appear to be girls and they are holding the ropes that radiate out from the flowers in the center of the ceiling. 882. The angels appear to be holding very tightly onto the ropes so that the great bouquet of flowers won't come loose. They hold it steady so it won't fall.

883. The middle of the altar, where the priest officiates at mass, also is beautiful. There is a small box there to hold the santito. There are seven saints on the wall above the altar, with two below, and the altar in the middle. There are smaller pictures of saints on both sides of the main altar, as well as on the pulpit where the priest goes in the middle of the mass to "scold" the people.[101]

884. The saint venerated in Actopan is known as Nicolás de Tolentino. A musical band is always hired here, to play songs for the santito. The procession does not leave the church, but goes around right there inside it. 885. There are five bells hung in the tower, with the largest hung in the middle. Its sound is very deep, but it can be heard a long way off. That is how it sounds when it is rung on Sundays and fiestas to call the people to hear mass.

886. From here one walks about five kilometers east to the village of Caxuxi. The virgin worshippped here is La Virgen del Carmen, whose festival is celebrated July 16th. Here, again, only a few people follow this virgin. They celebrate a mass for her and they bring floral offerings to place on her altar. 887. From here we continue along the same road, walking about two kilometers to the village of Lagunilla. There is a large church here, but not much movement; that is, not many come to worship, perhaps because the santito there is not very miraculous.

888. From the east of Lagunilla, there is a road that goes to Santiago de Anaya, where the image of Santiago Apóstol, or Saint James the Apostle, is venerated. The name of the community is the same as that of its saint, whose celebration is on September 20th. 889. The land here is very dry and the people are therefore very poor. There are no cultivated crops; the arable land that does exist is dry. The land itself is good; there are lots of mesquite trees, and all kinds of cactus. The most common ones here have already been mentioned. Goats are the most important economic resource for the people.

890. One returns from here to Lagunilla in order to take the road going east, and not far from there is Patria Nueva, a dip in the road, with its church. The image they worship here is the Virgin of Guadalupe on December 12th. 891. A band is hired to play mañanitas for the Virgin on her holy day. The mass is said at noon, and at night the toritos and castillo are set off. Even though castillos are expensive, the people there have money because they have irrigated land. This community, too, built its own church. They built it a piece at a time, but they are just about finishing it now. 892. Despite the fact that the Virgin of Guadalupe is considered miraculous throughout Mexico, not many people gather at Patria Nueva. Possibly this is because this celebration goes on at so many places.

893. Not far from Patria Nueva is another pueblo named Yolotepec. There is a statue worshipped there, too, of San Juan de Bautista (St. John the Baptist). The procession is made on June 24th, the very day of the fiesta. It goes out far from the church and all the images from the church are taken along. 894. The band follows the procession and the people carry candles, flowers and incense. Other men move along with the procession on their own, setting off firecrack-

ers, and many people from the community follow the procession. This is the only fiesta they have all year.

Next we walk about a kilometer and come to a community called Okäzaa, whose name comes from Ñähñu, meaning "wood that is full of holes." 895. Two churches can be seen here, and they have separated from one another. The separation is because of religious differences. 896. One part of the community is Catholic and the other practices the Evangelical faith. The part that lives on the north side of the road is Evangelical, and the part on the south side is Catholic. Each side has built its own church, with its own money. 897. The steeple on the church on the south side was not built well. There was an earthquake and the tower fell down but the bells remained on top of the piece of wall that was left.

898. When that earthquake happened, many of the houses split apart, and others lost their roofs. The houses that collapsed did so because the walls were made of adobe. 899. They are still standing there, as they were after the quake, and they have not been rebuilt because most of the people in the pueblo are very poor. There is no irrigation there, so they have to work as day laborers in the irrigated zone of Yolotepec in the municipio of Actopan. Every day they got up early to get to work on time, and they return late, arriving home when it is already getting dark. 900. Even after working so hard for money to feed and clothe themselves, they still don't have enough left over to fix their houses. Nor do they get paid what they should; they are paid a meager wage. Men, women and children work as day laborers in the fields. The children start at ten years of age.

901. The irrigated lands attract a lot of people to work, especially from the immediate surrounding lands. The santito there is the Virgen de Guadalupe. She has her mass, and they pray to her and sing songs of glory. They do not have a procession. The poor people are on the south side of the highway. 902. Some of the people in Okäzaa have irrigated plots of land. The community is in a splendid location, with the canal that irrigates parts of Ixmiquilpan running right through it.

903. We leave this community now and follow the same road down a winding stretch known as Pastores until it comes to the village of Taxadó. 904. Everyone in this community is Protestant. The people have organized to build their church[102] themselves, where they congregate every Thursday evening, and on Sundays to pray and sometimes to sing. They do not have processions for their santitos, and they do not have images like the Catholic people do. Another thing they don't do is throw big meals for their friends and

acquaintances. 905. They don't make loans to one another precisely because they don't have those meals for a lot of people. Some say that people who practice this religion have money because they do not spend it on images. It is not certain that this is the case, however, because the people of Taxadó are in the same condition they were before and have no money to spend.

906. Not far from there, touching the border of this community, in fact, is El Tepé, a place where there is a hot springs. 907. There is a church there, too, where El Sr. de Chalma is worshipped. They do the same things in that church as they do in Yolotepec: they celebrate the mass, and they hold a procession. One can tell that there is a fiesta going on from the noise of the firecrackers, and there is always a band. A castillo and a torito are set off. They do not have a procession outside the church; there is no place to turn around, because the patio is so small. They hold the procession inside the church.

908. In the prestigious churches like El Arenal, the priest holds weddings and baptisms for small children. The local people often get others from outside the community to accompany their child at a baptism, and when the godparents go back to their own communities they are compadres with those who invited them. 909. But they do not do this in Tepé, and not many people go to the fiesta there, perhaps because the image they worship is not very miraculous.

910. We retrace our steps a little in order to discuss a pueblo that we skipped over on the same route. In order to visit Xochitlán, we have to leave the highway, going south a little way. The village is located in a lovely spot. The church is located on the slope of a hill. It is a large church and the people there worship the image of Saint Sebastian, whose fiesta is celebrated February 25th. 911. It is the only community located there in the mountains, and few people come to the fiesta. Consequently, they don't have a lot of money in charity collections. The people are very poor because they they have no work and they have no crops because the land is completely dry.

912. From Xochitlán we go back over the route we came and pass through Tepé again in order to get to Dios Padre. There is a hot springs here, too, where people like to bathe during the cold season. 913. They worship the statue of Saint Augustine here, whose fiesta is celebrated in June. This is the main fiesta in this pueblo, though they also celebrate the 24th of December here, as well as the last day of the year, December 31st, and February 2nd, the fiesta of the Virgen de Candelaria.[103] Though these holidays cross two different years, in that community all those fiestas are the responsibility of the same mayordomos. 914. The people finance the fiesta cooperatively. They buy all the things needed; the castillo and torito are set off, and a band is hired. 915. Food is prepared for the castillo makers and for the band, who stay there for three days.

Only two castillos are set off; one for the day of vespers and one for the main fiesta day. Firecrackers are set off all night, like they were accompanying a mass. People also offer flowers to the santito; they leave bunches of flowers on his altar. 916. The flowers on the altar are distributed as relics to the pilgrims. People who give charity are given a relic to take home as a sign that they have returned from the fiesta or from the mass and that they have left some money for the image there.

917. Three mayordomos are named for the three fiestas—that is, Christmas Eve, New Year's Eve, and the fiesta of the Virgen de Candelaria. They are named from among the residents of the village at a general meeting. These are considered the major fiestas of Dios Padre. When the three men know that they have been elected, they get together and have a meeting. 918. This is to name a padrino who can help with the approaching fiestas. When they get together, they consider who to name as padrino, and this distinction is not given to just anyone.

919. The invitation is given only to someone whom they respect a lot. Sometimes the person is from the same village, and other times they select someone from another community. Though it may be far off, if the person they want to appoint is someone whom they believe in, then they go to pay him a visit. 920. The three mayordomos agree to pay, in equal shares, for some fruit, breads, and liquor for the visit. They fill two large baskets of twelve cuartillos each with tortillas, and bring everything to the man whom they think will accept their invitation to be the padrino for baby Jesus, and for the festivals of the New Year and the Virgin of Candelaria. 921. Once the man accepts the invitation they all enter into a relationship of great respect. 922. But the person who accepts such an invitation must think about it very hard, because he knows from the beginning that he will spend a lot of money for such things as boughs of flowers for the altar at the mass, and for six dozen firecrackers that he has to buy.

923. The padrino also has to hire the string band to accompany the priest when he celebrates the mass on Christmas Eve, and during the lullaby for the baby Jesus at midnight. He has to supply candles, sparklers that are distributed among the people so they can light them for the baby Jesus, and more firecrackers for when the procession leaves the church, because it is the custom there to make a procession for the baby Jesus. When all this is finished in the church, the people go to the house of the mayordomo to continue the fiesta all night. 924. The distribution of peanuts, sweets, tejocotes and jícamas[104] takes place at the house of the mayordomo. Each person is given his or her part with respect, and as the person receives it, he or she thanks the giver. 925. Other helpers give out liquor, but only to adults, and principally to men. Very few women accept

liquor to drink. Men "ask permission" before drinking. If it is cold, then they like to drink more because they say that one does not feel the cold that way. Sometimes it gets very cold around Christmas.

926. There have been times when it snowed in the mountains at this time of year. When there is a strong snow, it reaches all the way down the mountainside and the landscape looks beautiful, and all white. The string musicians are also there at the mayordomo's house, playing continuously. This music is part of what the padrino pays for. 927. When everything the padrino has brought is distributed, the meal begins, and this is the responsibility of the mayordomo. Everyone eats, adults and children alike. 928. The other mayordomos, besides the one serving that night, are also there. Right now they are just there as invited guests, but their day will come and then they have to treat the other mayordomos as nicely as possible. A week after the Christmas celebration comes the fiesta of the New Year, and another mayordomo is appointed for this.

929. The New Year's festival begins on the last day of the old year and ends on the morning of January 1st. On the night of the 31st, the baby Jesus is taken out again in a procession. The mayordomo has to buy firecrackers and candles which are given out to the people accompanying the procession; the firecrackers are set off in front of the parade. The priest celebrates mass at midnight and then baptizes the baby Jesus. 930. The padrino and the madrina carry the baby Jesus in their arms. They have been invited by the mayordomo specifically for this task. This is when the padrinos and the mayordomo begin their relationship of friendship and respect as compadres. There is a more profound respect among compadres, and once they enter this relationship they greet each other in the village as compadres, and not just as ordinary neighbors. 931. From then on they greet each other by kissing each other's hand. Some people take off their hats first, and then take the hand of their compadre or comadre, make the sign of the cross with it, and kiss it. This is the other form of greeting among compadres.

932. When compadres are apart they do not say bad things about one another. From the moment they become compadres in church, they show respect for one another. It is said that when compadres speak ill of one another, the Devil takes them when they die. 933. The three mayordomos become compadres with the person who carries the baby Jesus when he is brought to be baptized. The padrino brings the baby Jesus to the house of the mayordomo. At the house, they prepare an altar for the baby, along with flowers and incense, and someone lights firecrackers along the way as the baby is brought to the house. The same is done here as was done on Christmas. The same foods are prepared. The distribution of things is the responsibility of the padrino. 934. The meal is the responsibility of the mayordomo. Finally, in the morning, hot coffee and

They greet each other as compadres
Religión 930

tamales are given out. This is a fiesta of great repasts. The baby Jesus goes back to the church the next time mass is said.

935. The News Year's celebration is over, and the days pass, and exactly a month later is the festival called "The Blessing of the Candles." This is the 2nd of February, which is also the fiesta of the Virgen de Candelaria in some places. 936. The last mayordomo is responsible for this celebration. The padrino and the madrina are the same ones as the previous two fiestas. Paying for the mass falls to the mayordomo, while the firecrackers and the music are the responsibility of the padrino. The mass is said in the morning and the procession is made at night. On this procession, the baby Jesus, the Virgen de Candelaria, Saint Joseph, and other images of the baby Jesus that have been blessed that day, are all taken around on the procession. Each one is carried by its own padrino, and each image has been blessed. Every year they bless these things, and baptize the images of the baby Jesus. The images of the baby Jesus are taken back to the padrinos' houses. At each house there is a banquet where they await the arrival of the compadres who are carrying the baby.

937. When the procession in the church is over, the various santitos are put back in their accustomed places, with the baby Jesus in his showcase. The padrino takes the incense burner and censes each of the santitos there, crossing himself in front of each one, and finishing with the baby Jesus that he carried to be baptized. 938. The madrina does the same, and after censing them she kisses them goodbye. The invitation they received to be padrinos comes to an end, and it may never happen again in their entire lives. 939. The mayordomos do the same as the padrinos did. All three of them are there, and the people who participated in the procession watch them. When they finish saying goodbye to the santitos the mayordomos and the padrinos kneel face to face on the ground in front of the altar. They keep the images to their side so they won't turn their backs on them. Then the mayordomos thank their compadres for having accepted the invitation. At this moment one can see the deep mutual respect involved, because they thank them with all their heart.

940. By now it is night, getting to be twelve o'clock or even later. Though they have said goodbye in the church, they don't want to separate from each other just yet, so they go to the house of the mayordomo to have supper. 941. The padrino pays for the liquor and for the musicians who play beautiful songs. The cargo of the padrinos is finished when this is over. 942. What is not over is the respect initiated. This will always hold them together and they will always greet each other when they meet.

943. The three new mayordomos in charge of the following year's festivities are also at the mayordomo's house. As each one's name is called out, people

applaud. Garlands of flowers have been prepared, and one by one they are put around the necks of the future mayordomos. 944. The garlands reach down to their waists. The old mayordomos have prepared a gift for the new ones, which they present in front of all those present. The gift is a cooked chicken in a basket, and it is delivered to each one. The following year, the new mayordomos will have to do the same for those who will replace them. As each thing is done with the flowers and the chickens and so on, the musicians play tunes called "dianas."

946. Now we go back a little, and leave the road we have been following. We head east to a village called Pueblo Nuevo, where there is also a church where people come to worship God. 947. The image there appears not to be very miraculous because the fiesta is not talked about much in other places. What they do there is like what they do at Tepé, and in fact Pueblo Nuevo borders on Tepé to its north. 948. We take the road we were following before and come to a small place called El Fitzi. Two groups practicing different religions live here. 949. One group practices Catholicism; the other is known by the phrase "los hermanitos," the Protestants. They live mixed together in the village, with people of one religion in one house next to a house of the other relgion. The Catholics were the original inhabitants of the village and some of the hermanitos lived there, too. But others are immigrants who were banished from their own small communities. They fled because they were chased out. When their neighbors found out what was going on they changed how they felt about these people. All of them fled their own villages and came to seek succor in Fitzi, because the foreigners who came as heads of the group and who protected them lived there.

950. Even though many of them can not read, they still converted to the new religion because people lied to them and told them that whoever accepted the new faith would make money. Others were told that they would no longer have to work very much. The leaders of the sect went out into the villages to talk to the people and they told them other such things. 951. In order to induce people to convert they gave them books, and brought them photographs of the saints they worshipped, and photos of the pastors' houses. 952. That is when a lot of the problems began in the villages, and even today those difficulties have not been forgotten in many places. Some people who converted to Protestantism abandoned their land and their houses when they were chased out of their villages. 953. In some cases things got rough and people who converted were killed. Those still alive have not forgotten this, or the fact that they were thrown out of their village. Others repented their actions and did what they had to in order to return to their homes because they realized that they had been deceived.

The kind of work that people knew how to do did not exist in the new villages, so they returned to work the lands they had abandoned.

954. At first, no one said anything to those who came back. But there were some who were fanatic Catholics and they were very angry. 955. Those who returned were made mayordomos the next year in order to see if they had really repented. Like it or not, the man had to obey his neighbors and in this way they forgave him what had happened.

In the barrio of El Fitzi where other Protestants lived, many more of them have come recently. They have built so many houses that there is no room for any more. 956. They have built most of the houses right around the church. They have all helped in the building of their church. But one can see that someone is helping them out financially, because they have built a very large church which can hold many people.

957. Not far from there is the Catholic church. That church was built many years ago, and the village cemetery used to be right there. The santito they worship there is the apostle Santiago whose festival is the 27th of October. The priest celebrates mass and the torito is lit. There is no procession because they don't have a lot of room for one. Even though most of the inhabitants of the community are Protestants, many of them participate in the Catholic fiesta anyway. 958. Merchants come and set up their stalls and stands. They sell various fruits and several kinds of beer. People come who sell tamales dulces, coffee, tamales, and toys for the children. 959. In comparison, merchants do not come to the Protestants' fiestas. The Protestants just have their gatherings in their churches and return to their homes.

The most important holiday for the Protestants is Christmas and, after that, the celebration of the New Year. At those times people gather in Fitzi from the little villges—men, women, and children all come. 960. The santito they worship is Jesus Christ. That is who they always talk about, along with the Virgin Mary. The Protestants consider them to be their saviors. This community borders on Ixmiquilpan.

961. Now we head back east and come to another small community by the name of Carrizal. The distance between Fitzi and this village is approximately one and a half kilometers. They have a traditional celebration every year in this community, and they worship the image of San Miguel Arcángel (Saint Michael the Archangel) on September 29th. The festival lasts just three days, as in other places we have seen.

962. The church is not very big; in fact, it is really a chapel, and they have built a little tower on top where they hung the bells. They have a procession here, accompanied by a band, which is hired beforehand. 963. Mayordomos are

named for providing food for the musicians. The Ñähñu name by which this community is best known is "Xithi," because there is an abundance of carrizo there, owing to the fact that the village is in the irrigated zone.

964. From Carrizal one walks about four kilometers before coming to the community of El Nith. This is another of the pueblos that have a lot of people. The church there is big. It has a high tower and the bells in it are large. The fiesta of Santiago Apóstol (Saint James the Apostle) is celebrated on July 25th. 965. They light a torito and a castillo in this community. They hire a band; sometimes the band from the same village plays, because they have their own band. 966. There are meals at various houses in the village, in order to provide food for the helpers and for the visitors who come from surrounding communities. Some of those visitors bring loans to the houses of their acquaintances who are functioning as mayordomos for this fiesta. Others come just to see the fiesta, but while they are there they visit their acquaintances, and people have to provide food for the visitors because this is the custom.

967. The pueblo of El Nith can really celebrate their fiesta in style because the people there have resources. Most of the people own irrigated plots of land, and they can get at least two harvests a year. Also, their animals, like goats and sheep, multiply quickly, so it doesn't cost them a lot to kill a few for a feast. 968. The people of El Nith still maintain the custom of setting up arches in the streets where the procession passes. They adorn the framework of the arches with cucharilla. It takes a lot of work to make those arches, but when they are done they really look beautiful. Of course, there are firecrackers—a lot of them—during the mass as well as during the procession. In order to do all this, the people of the village must cooperate financially.

969. Going towards the east, down the road one can see the village of Capula that borders on El Nith. There, too, the villagers celebrate their fiesta in a special way. The icon of Santa Teresa is there, and her fiesta is celebrated on October 15th. The same ceremonies as in El Nith are performed for this fiesta. It is the same every year. 970. There are flutists and drummers in this village. They accompany the people who make floral offerings, or who bring escamadas to the saint or virgin being worshipped. These things may be offerings on behalf of individuals or families that have decided to ask God to save them from their troubles. 971. If someone is sick, then persons in the family beg God to save them by offering flower garlands and escamadas. These things are of different colors, and they look pretty when they are arranged around the santito people are praying to.

Others also come and make their offerings. One should not think that only one person does this on that day. 972. When someone is sick and they make a promise to a saint if he will make them better, then, if the prayer has been effective, the sick person gets better after a few days. In such cases, their faith is reinforced and they believe even more, and they say that it must have been God punishing them by making them sick. When it's not a floral offering, it might be a mass that someone offers. In either case, it is to ask God for a cure if one is sick and dying.

973. In the community of Pozuelos, they celebrate their fiesta like they do in Capula. A torito and a castillo are lit, and a band is hired. 974. They hire string bands there that play huapangos for an all night dance. Young people and older adults alike, of both sexes, like to dance to this kind of music. When there is this kind of atmosphere, then the people of the village say there is real merriment and there is a real fiesta going on. Very old people don't like the fiestas because when they were young they didn't have dances at the fiestas for the santitos. During their day, when the ceremonies in the church were over, they went back to their homes.

The people in Pozuelos are poor, but they are strong believers and they do all they can to pay their share so they will have enough funds to buy what they want for the fiesta. When the day of the fiesta is drawing near the people start working hard to fulfill their cargos properly. 976. Some men work at stripping fiber from maguey leaves; others work at stripping lechugilla. The women weave ayates. Together they find ways to make things work out.

977. Now we go up a hill and over a mountain and return to the plain which takes us to San Andrés Deboxta. There we find the apostle Saint Andrew, the image worshipped by the people in that community. His fiesta is traditionally celebrated annually there on November 30th. 978. Almost all the activities that go on in Pozuelos are found in San Andrés Deboxtha. They, too, hire pyrotechnists and a band of musicians; flutists come with their drummers and there are floral offerings. Of course, there are banquets in the homes of the mayordomos. Some of them kill goats, others slaughter chickens, and some even slaughter a head of cattle in order to have enough food for all the visitors and helpers who get together on that day. 979. Some of the women help each other cook the mole de olla, and others cook a thicker meat-sauce dish called, simply, "mole." This is an exquisite dish, but it takes a lot of work to prepare it. About three women work to prepare the seasonings. The dish requires a lot of condiments. This meal is usually only prepared for people who have higher social standing.

980. After passing through San Andrés Deboxta, one continues along the road another 10 kilometers. The entire distance is flat, but the earth is pure dust, and one comes to a community called El Saúz. 981. This village celebrates a

fiesta called "nt'eni," or Carnaval. The date changes every year, but it is always in February. 982. In Ñähñu it is known as a "joke" or "funny entertainment" because the men dress up; they disguise themselves as little old people and put on various kinds of masks. They put on skirts, or other kinds of clothing. It is a tradition for them to dress up like this and to dance in the church. 983. When they finish in church they go the plaza, and they go around making jokes and dancing. Sometimes they joust with the other fiesta-goers and make them laugh. Some of them dress up as the Devil. They go around the plaza making jokes and laughing with the people. One man has killed a badger, pieced its skin together, and stuck grass on it so that it looks like a real animal. Another is an armadillo shell. They fix up the skin of any animal they find and carry it around the fiesta. They thrust it at the fiesta-goers to make them laugh, and this is why the fiesta is known as the "joke." 984. Each mask wearer disguises himself differently. Sometimes it is the face of a very old man, or of a young person, or of a little old lady. Those folks are real jokesters. The other men attending the fiesta love to taunt the mask wearers and play with them.

985. Not far from this pueblo is a mountain whose peak is about 1000 meters high[105] where people have set a cross right on the peak. 986. Some people go up the mountain when this fiesta is celebrated and lay flowers at the cross. Firecrackers are set off, and the cross is censed with incense. There is a belief that the mountain will "scold" everyone in the community if they do not remember it properly. The people who go to offer the flowers simply go up the mountain, hang the garlands on the cross, and go back down.

The people of the community sell pulque to get the money to celebrate the festival every year. This place has an abundance of maguey. It also has some goats and sheep, and those who sell those animals get money which they spend on the fiesta. 987. Those who have not raised any animals, migrate in search of work far away. They usually go to the cities where they get paid better wages. 988. They can't plant any crops in El Saúz because it doesn't rain there steadily. When the earth gets dry there are dust devils all over the plain.

989. From El Saúz we continue following the road that crosses the plain and comes to San Miguel Tlazintla. The mountains and forest are close by. The place is called "'Matha Nsamige" in Ñähñu, which means "the San Miguel plain," because the community is located on a big plain.[106] There is a large church with a high tower, more or less like the one in Capula, and there are medium-sized bells hanging in the tower.

990. The celebration of the traditional annual fiesta takes place on the 29th of September. A full band is hired, as well as string musicians. The large band works first inside the church and later on in the plaza. The string musicians, on

the other hand, only work at the dance. They play huapangos and another rythym called "corridos." This is the kind of partying that the people here do. They adorn the altar of Saint Michael beautifully in the church. 991. They construct arches made of cucharilla in the street that goes around the plaza and adorn them with other things. They arches are very pretty. At around nine in the evening, the mayordomos organize the procession for the santito. 992. The people there are strong believers in Catholicism. A lot of people turn out for the procession. They carry candles and candlesticks with them, which they light as they follow the procession.

993. One hears the roar of the firecrackers going off, and of the castillo which has been installed in its usual spot. It is set off at one or two in the morning. The band plays songs continuously with the procession and then later at the plaza so that all the people who have come for the fiesta can hear them. 994. There are always toritos at this fiesta. They always build them and light them when the procession is finished. It is lit before the castillo, and it looks very pretty with its different colors. The man carrying the torito on his back cries out, imitating the bellow of an ox. 995. The dance is over at dawn. If the sun is about to come up and they are still dancing, the people say that it was really a dance. But if it ends earlier, then the people are not satisfied. The beer sellers have a lot of customers when a lot of people come to the fiesta, and people come up from the Tolantongo River area to take part. 996. Those people from the river really like to dance huapangos; it is their favorite music. Men and women alike come up to take part in the fiesta.

997. Around this time of year is when it starts to get cold. Cold winds blow from the east. Sometimes they bring fine, mist-like rain with them. Even though it may be raining, though, the dancers don't stop. It seems to just make them enjoy it more. When they start feeling the cold, they drink some aguardiente to warm up.

998. Now we continue and come to another small community near Ixmiquilpan called Los Cerritos which belongs to the pueblo of Los Remedios. In other words, it is one of the barrios of Los Remedios. The highway that goes to the municipio of Cardonal passes close by Cerritos. 999. The community of Cerritos does not have a Catholic church. There is a church there, but it is Protestant. The people themselves built their church some time ago. There are thus two religious groups in Cerritos. One is Catholic and the other Protestant. 1000. The Catholics congregate in the Centro Ñähñu[107] to worship the Virgin. It may be far for them to come in, but they attend the ceremony. The Protestants have their church nearby at a place called El Banco. They hold their meetings every Thursday afternoon, and also on Saturdays. The Catholics of the com-

They construct arches of cucharilla and adorn them

Religión 991

munity do not worship with them. They take on cargos in the Centro whenever they are called on to do so. Sometimes they take the cargo for hiring the band, or they take the torito.

1001. Even though the people of El Banco are divided by religion, when it comes to faenas they work together on doing chores for the school, or for cleaning the canal if they have land irrigated by it. The past few years they have not fought much over religion. But the Protestants keep telling people to come to their church so they will convert. Some have accepted and have converted while others haven't. 1002. Those who become Protestants do not want to continue fulfilling cargo obligations. They say that it is the cargos that make them spend so much money, and that they do not have the money to spend.

First the father of the house converts, and then he gets his wife to convert, and then he brings along his children, if he has any. Of course, they bring them if the children are small, because children decide for themselves after they are grown whether or not to convert. So, sometimes children decide for themselves, and sometimes their father makes them convert, because the father believes that he is doing something beneficial for his child. The people of El Centro despise those of El Banco.

1003. Continuing along the same highway one can see various little chapels along the sides of the road. They were built a long time ago because, in those days, people had greater faith in God, and it seems that in those times every family wanted to have its own chapel. 1004. They did not build towers on those chapels; instead, the roofs were domed. Nor did they decorate the insides. The roof was nearly all made of stone. The stones were cut so that they fit together well, and then they were fortified with lime. These chapels can be found all over the Mezquital Valley. Most of them have been abandoned. Some have been been used to store forage,[108] and others have been refurbished as houses. It is the rare community in which the chapels are used for what they once were, as we will see in the following pages. 1005. I am mentioning them here because they can be seen along the road we are following, and we see them along the way in various places. The images that were in those chapels, and that people used to worship, have all been taken into real churches now. When they were transferred to a church they had to have a fiesta for each one, because you can't just move images without any ceremony.

1006. When they got to their new home, the images were greeted with a mass, and with firecrackers, and with tolling of the church bells. In other words, they were awaited with all the enthusiasm and joy of the people when this happened. 1007. Some of those santitos continued being worshipped; in other cases people decided to seek another, more miraculous patron. The santitos that have ceased to be worshipped have been placed there in a corner of the church. Once in a while, someone lights a candle for them.

1008. We continue along the same road now to the north and we come to another church in a community called Nequetejé. It is difficult to spot this pueblo because it is nestled among the cacti. The church is surrounded by a wall, and inside is the cemetery where the people still bury their dead to this day. 1009. This church is also quite large, about the size of the church in Pueblo Nuevo. The image they worship here is an icon of what is called Corpus Christi, the "body of Christ."[109] 1010. They celebrate the fiesta in Nequetejé on the 10th of May. They invite the images from El Espíritu for this festival. They invite the Virgin of Peace and Good, and the santito called Espíritu Santo, and other, less important images which they carry. El Espíritu borders to the north of Nequetejé, and the people come south for the occasion. The neighbors of Nequetejé come bearing the images from El Espíritu and they bring everything needed for the fiesta. They don't have to walk far, just three kilometers to get to the church in Nequetejé. 1011. The images weigh a lot, and so they have to change bearers from time to time. The Virgin of Peace and Good weighs the most because the wood of her case is heavy, and the front door of the case is made of heavy glass.

1012. The Virgin herself is just a print, painted on cloth. The people at the front of the group are those who went to Nequetejé to fetch the images—that is, the mayordomos who organize everything. 1013. A mayordomo is named for the bringing of the images and is accompanied by the mayordomos of the church, the judges from the village, and, of course, ciriales. 1014. The mayordomo finds helpers who are put in charge of making the flower garlands, so that when the group gets to the church in El Espíritu, the flowers can be offered to the santitos. One of the flower garlands has been reserved to drape over the Virgin. They take firecrackers with them, which they light along the way and as the offering is made. 1015. On the way back to Nequetejé they come upon the ermitas that have been set up. For this, too, someone has been named to await the images and welcome them. Some shade has been improvised where the images can be set down. Special cloth is delivered to the person in charge of the ermitas so that he can set things up right.

1016. What he has to do is offer the flowers when the santitos arrive. He has also purchased firecrackers in order to worship his visitors properly. Finishing here, the bearers continue carrying the images, followed by all the people. If one of them wants a break, then one of the people can take a bearer's place. When they get to the next ermita, they do the same things again. 1017. Meanwhile, the bells in the church at Nequetejé ring constantly. When the images arrive at the church, they are given another floral offering by the mayordomos of the church. That is the promise that has been made to the images. Before the visiting images enter the church, there is a procession. This is a sort of "bidding welcome" to the visiting santitos. 1018. They don't take out the image from the church of Nequetejé on the procession that evening. The next day, however, the day of the fiesta, the image is taken out and accompanied by all the other images. On this occasion, the local santito goes in front and the visitors follow behind.

1019. Suppose they have lined up as follows: at the front of the procession are the ciriales. Next comes the santito of Nequetejé; then the Virgin of Peace and Good; and then the image of Espíritu Santo; and finally the band. 1020. The flutists and drummers select an image they will follow, playing their tunes. They come to these ceremonies on their own; no one pays them for their services. It is rare that a mayordomo invites them to accompany the people carrying the images.

1021. They only celebrate the religious fiesta in Nequetejé, and do not hold a dance. Apparently, the people there don't like dances, and they are also very poor and can not afford to pay the cost of the music. The men all work as day laborers, and the women weave ayates. Others make charcoal, and still others extract maguey fiber. 1022. The place is situated in a totally arid area. The only things one can see there are large rocks, tepetates, and spiny cacti of different kinds on the hills. The people of the village have not prepared much land for planting because there is no point when it doesn't rain regularly and the campesinos would just waste their time.

1023. Everyone doesn't cooperate at the same time in celebrating the fiesta. Instead, some eight people are named to be responsible for hiring the band. These same people must pay the cost of feeding the musicians, and they divide this responsibility among themselves. One does breakfast, and then another provides the midday meal, and another the evening meal, until each has had a turn. 1024. Separate mayordomos are named for the torito and the castillo. Those who rest from their responsibilities take part in naming others during succeeding years, and so it goes until all the adults of citizen age in Nequetejé have served. They hold the meeting here, to name the following year's mayordomos, the day after the fiesta ends. They change judges, mayordomos of the church, and two kinds of constables—those who go around telling people about meetings, and those who apprehend escaped prisoners and people who have committed some act of violence. 1025. It is not necessary that any superior authorities be present at these changes. The members of the community organize everything because they know best what is needed in their pueblo. Occasionally, an observer is invited who can report to his superiors in Ixmiquilpan. 1026. The reports given by the mayordomos and the judges must be complete and clear *before* the change of authorities takes place. If anything is missing, then it has to be returned first before making the change to new authorities.

1027. The people there remember the souls of their departed babies and they ask that a mass be said in their honor. They buy firecrackers for them and a day is set aside for them. Another day is reserved for remembering the dead adults. People set up altars in their homes where the dead used to eat, and they prepare the foods that the dead ate when they were alive. They burn incense for them, and light candles. 1028. As was said before, because the people are so poor, they do not have money to celebrate all the festivals in the calendar. Consequently, they do not celebrate the posadas as they do in other communities where they have them for nine nights, culminating with Christmas Eve.

1029. Without leaving the route we are following, we go up over a small hill and come down the other side to a village named San Antonio Sabanillas. It is situated on a small plain at the foot of a mountain called Juxmä'ye. This is a big mountain. 1030. They have a very large church here; it is about the same size as the cathedral in San Nicolás Tolentino, and perhaps a little bigger. The saint worshipped here is San Antonio Abad. His fiesta is on the 11th of June. They hire a band to play mañanitas to the saint on the day of his fiesta. 1031. As is traditional, there is a castillo; in fact, there are two, one on the day of vespers, and one on the actual day of the fiesta of San Antonio. They also make a procession out of the church.

1032. They do just about the same kinds of things here to worship their saint as people do in other communities we have seen. They buy firecrackers, they burn incense, and they make floral offerings. The flowers are brought to the altar in large wooden bowls. The people who come to the fiesta go in and out of the church, leaving alms and asking God to give them health and let them live a few more years. 1033. People who leave alms for charity generally perform a "cleansing" motion first, at forehead level, and then make the sign of the cross. They request a relic, a religious rememberance, to take home with them, which is supposed to help push evil aside.

1034. These people are like everyone else. They think that what they believe is good and they are free to do so to the limits of their imagination. They use relics to treat[110] any part of their body that aches. They also use relics to calm hurricanes and other violent weather, like hail, that comes to the valley. Hail destroys the little tomato plants, and the squash, jitomate[111] and chile pepper plants that people grow to get money. Sometimes hail destroys the fruit of the plants. People think about God, and believe that he sends all these punishments, and that he is responsible for these bad things. 1035. That is why they make these celebrations, to ask God not to send such calamities. Other times it is exactly the opposite; they hold a celebration in order to ask God to send rain when months and even years have passed without it. 1036. People still believe that God is in heaven and that he has all those things that happen on earth in his hands. That is why the fiestas are not just simply merry-making; the fiestas have their own reason for being within the thinking of the people.

1037. In addition, people believe what the priest tells them, because when he reads those books during the mass he says that those are the same words spoken by God when he was on earth. Moreover, the priest uses those words when he blesses the relics that people take home, and so people believe in those relics. 1038. Sometimes people get carried away with religion and become fanatic about it. Then they can not save anything; they use up everything they own, like the goats they raise, with no profit or payback. 1039. There have been times when mayordomos have been obliged to sell off part of their land in order to complete some cargo. Those same people wouldn't think of selling off anything when one of their children needs money to continue school so he could help his father out later. This is really bad. It's not as if people don't think about the future. They *do* think about it; they think about it a lot. It's just that men want so much for their cargos to turn out well that they don't think about anything else.

1040. In this part of the valley no mayordomo likes to have anyone speak ill of him. No one wants to be talked of as a cheapskate. Nor does anyone want people to think they let visitors go hungry at their home during the time of their cargo. 1041. No one wants any of his guests to speak with contempt when they finish eating, or hear men tell their wives and children that they were not treated well and not given enough to eat. The mayordomo thinks hard about the possibility of this kind of talk being directed against him. To avoid this, he does everything he can to prepare for as many people who might want to visit him so he can offer them a meal with full respect. 1042. Now if a visitor was treated well, and despite this he speaks against the mayordomo, then people say: "God in heaven only knows what this man is doing." They know that the mayordomo did everything he could to perform his cargo.

1043. In the village of San Miguel Jugí some of the people are Catholics and the rest are Protestants. The Protestants have their church in the same pueblo; they built it themselves and they congregate there to worship. 1044. The Catholics celebrate the fiesta of the village patron on the 29th of September. They don't have a big fiesta there because there are only a few Catholics left and they don't have enough money to make the cost of all the things needed for the church.

Fiestas have their own reason for being
Religion 1036

1045. They name one mayordomo for the mass, and he has to supply the flowers needed for the altar of Saint Michael. He also buys the firecrackers and the incense because sometimes the priest needs it to fume things when he is asked to bless them. The priest also uses holy water. 1046. Holy water is not purchased. It is merely potable water blessed by the priest so he can use it in church. He gives it to people who want to take some home, and he gives out relics of the plants and flowers, too. 1047. Escamadas are also always there next to the image of the saint. As was said a moment ago, the people don't have much money, so they don't hire a band anymore. Just a few flutists and drummers come to the church during the celebration of the mass and during the procession.

1048. There used to be a musical group known as Los Zopilotes, or The Vultures, and when they they were alive they were hired to play at the fiesta there because there were not many of them, only four. The instruments they used to carry included a large drum and drumstick; the stick was like a mallet and was used to beat the drum. The other three carried wind instruments that were blown in order to make them sound.[112] 1049. The band members have died out; they are no longer seen playing anywhere. They used to charge 10 pesos in those days, and they were on the job for two days. They were given food and pulque. There was a large jug full of pulque right there where they stood and played.

1050. The other group in the community, the Protestants, gather together twice a week in their church to pray. For them, however, there are no candles, no flowers, and no incense. They don't buy any of these things; they just come together and pray. 1051. They know how to pray better because they meet more often and go over their prayers well. By comparison, a lot of the people who are Catholic don't know how to pray because they only go to church periodically, when there is a mass or a fiesta. 1052. That is why the Protestants sometimes say that the Catholics don't know how to pray. Each group criticizes the other for what it does and for what it doesn't do.

1053. There were very bad problems in this community also when some people started converting to the Protestant faith. They fought with the rest of the people because they separated themselves from the group in which they had lived. Before that they used to work together through religion and through faenas to help make the community better. That is why religion is dangerous; it causes divisions and breaks up village cooperation. 1054. The worst danger, however, is not really in the division itself; the worst is when people start to kill each other, and then it becomes very hard to patch things up again and return village life to normal. 1055. Some people wind up hating one another for their entire lives. Some prefer the extinction of their family rather than reconciliation with their neighbors.

1056. Those hermanitos who are smart and save their money change their style of dress. One can see that they dress pretty well, and they dress their children well. They build better houses than do some people who are Catholics. 1057. The reason that they progress economically is that they don't spend much money in the religion to which they have converted. They don't pay for hiring bands; they don't pay for masses; they don't have castillos and toritos blasting off. There are no floral offerings, no candles, no buying of incense. They don't buy flowers and they don't hold feasts in their houses and await a lot of visitors.

1058. They stop having all these kinds of expenditures. That is an advantage that they can attain but only if they are smart, as I mentioned a moment ago. If they allow their co-religionists to make off with their money, then they wind up in the same situation as when they practiced Catholicism, or even worse. 1059. I mention this because there are pastors among them who abuse the people and ask for money from their parishioners. As some of those people tell it, the pastors tell them that everyone has to give a certain amount of money for God to help them and save them. The amount differs from group to group.

1060. Other times, as some members of that religion recount, the pastor tells them that the money is for him to travel to other places in search of good things for the community. Still other times, according to what people say, he tells them the truth, that the money is for him to be able to eat, because he can not work for money, what with attending to all his responsibilities in the church and visiting his superiors. He goes to his superiors to get new perspectives on how to advise his flock. 1061. This is what people in that religion say, as do people who didn't like the religion and have left it. They have said goodbye to the Evangelical religion, asking God to help them to forget it and to never let them go back to it.

1062. Now, to continue, we move along the same road that goes through San Miguel Jugí, so that we don't have to return to the main highway that we were on before. It is a long way back and we would get tired. 1063. Instead of retracing our steps we shortcut over foot paths. We cross the first valley where there are some foot paths that we can travel on quite well. 1064. The only thing inconvenient about this is that it is a little tiring because of the steep descending and ascending slopes that we have to cover, and because there are a lot of rocks on the road. But this is not important compared to the fact that one arrives quickly at the destination. 1065. The pueblo we are heading for now is called Cardonal. The presidencia municipal is there; in other words, it is a cabecera municipal. Whenever there is a serious problem in one of the communities, they send for the president to come and remedy the situation. 1066. The pueblo is situated on a tepetate mesa. The only vegetation that grows there is mesquite trees, cardones, capulines de ratón, and nopales de tunas pintaderas.[113]

1067. They say that a long time ago the Spaniards used to live there and excavate in the mountains to extract gold. There are still some big old houses where they used to live. Those houses are very high and have thick walls. Perhaps that is why they have lasted so long. 1068. They also withstood the fires set during the Revolution started by Francisco I. Madero in 1910. 1069. In those days there were people everywhere taking part in the war, killing those who had stolen their land. All the rich people in those days were sought out and everything was taken from them. Many of them did not relinquish their property voluntarily, so the revolutionaries had to kill them. They took them out of their homes or from their hiding places and shot them, or they put a rope around their necks and hanged them from a tall tree until, as people tell it, their tongues hung out of their heads.

1070. All those stories are told by old people from what they actually saw. They lived through it and so they remember it well. They were children in those times. They didn't take down those who were hanged; they just left them there for others to see, and little by little they were eaten by animals. 1071. Perhaps the vultures and the coyotes ate them, because in those days there were many such animals in the open countryside. The fires that were set were the result of the anger people felt during the Revolution. While they were poor and had nothing to eat, those who had a lot of money lived handsomely in their homes and even kept basic foodstuffs from the poor. Things like maize and beans simply were not sold anywhere. The poor were dying of hunger and this was the basis of their anger against the rich. Though the poor begged the rich to sell them maize, the rich would not sell them anything. 1072. Many of the houses in Cardonal, some of which still exist today, were found to be full of maize, beans, clothing, cloth, and many other things that were being hoarded. And that is why one day the people banded together and set fire to the houses of the pueblo.

1073. A lot of people who used to live there were fair skinned. They were the descendants of the Spaniards who lived there first. In other words, the people who first excavated the mountains were white, with rouged cheeks and blond hair. They were tall, and some were excessively fat. They looked pot bellied and had broad backs and wide feet.

1074. Those who have heard something of the history say that the ancestors of the Spaniards we are talking about here built the church in Cardonal. That church is big, with a high tower where the bells are. The bells are just medium size. 1075. The Virgin worshipped in Cardonal is said to be miraculous and is called Purísima Concepción (the Virgin of the Immaculate Conception). Her fiesta is celebrated on December 18th. 1076. The Virgin gets a lot of invitations to take part in the festivals of other communities. Every year she is invited to the traditional fiesta in the pueblo of El Santuario where they celebrate the fifth Friday of Pentecost. She also goes to Orizabita for the celebration of the Sexto Viernes de Dolores, and to San Antonio Sabanillas. These are the three places she goes every year.

1077. The religious activities undertaken are the following: they say a mass (the priest lives right there), and they light toritos and castillos. They buy flowers and put them on the Virgin's altar. On the day of the fiesta, they have a procession accompanied by a band they hire. 1078. A meal is prepared for the musicians at the houses of the mayordomos, and for the pyrotechnists. It gets cold during the season of the fiesta; the village is up on a mesa, and the cold winds blow from the east. They bring "cold clouds" with them that sometimes carry fine rain, and not many people come when this weather sets in because they are put off by the cold. This is the only fiesta they celebrate all year; it is the one that they consider the most important.

1079. We continue along the same road that goes through Cardonal and proceed towards a small community located in the mountains. Boxed in by a group of mountains is the pueblo known as El Santuario. 1080. From what people say, this name was given to the community by the Spaniards when they lived there while excavating the mines. 1081. They used to melt down silver there, and they built a foundry in the village. Supposedly, in order to wash out impurities in the ore, they used to bring it to a small trench nearby where water flowed, and because of this the place was named Mäpe'te in Ñähñu, which means "washing place." This is the legend that people from that place tell. 1082. The image of Christ there is known in Spanish as El Sr. del Santuario or El Sr. de Mapeté; the latter name is how he is known by most people. He is one of the images that people of the Mezquital Valley have the most faith in. It is said that he is very miraculous and that he saves whoever worships him with all their heart and devotion. Those are the people whom he helps.

1083. As was mentioned a moment ago, his fiesta is on the fifth Friday of Pentecost; it is celebrated every year on a Friday. The church there is big, and the tower is high. The bells ring when the mass is said. 1084. One can admire the decorations that have been painted on the walls of the church, as well as some wooden figures that have been set up. These are decorated in a golden color and are shiny. 1085. The figures are of different things. Some are copies of the body of Christ, some are angels, others are of the baby Jesus. Some are whole bodies, some are just the torso, and others are just heads.

1086. The decoration behind the altar is the most beautiful. On both sides of the church, on the left and on the right, other images are hung, large and small, of saints and virgins. Some are prints painted on cloth, others are carvings of wood or stone, and some are plaster. The latter are really well done, and the body looks like that of a real man or a boy. The priest's pulpit, where he gets up in the middle of the mass and advises people on how they must live better with their fellow man, is also beautifully decorated. The part that is not beautiful is the floor, which has holes in it in various spots. There is no explanation for this, since a lot of money comes into that church from the alms that people leave. Perhaps they use the money for some other purpose to benefit the people and thus neglect the church.

1087. How is it possible to say this? Because a lot of money goes to that church. The people who live in the surrounding areas always say "I'm going on a pilgrimage to El Santuario to leave some money for charity there." 1088. A lot of people go there from other communities, to worship the image, not just from the Mezquital Valley. They stay at the fiesta two or three days. A lot of people from the mountains come down on foot from their pueblos. They bring burros, laden with the things they use in the fiesta.

1089. The fiesta lasts for eight days. Every year the date changes, and the month changes. Sometimes it is in March, and sometimes in April. 1090. When the fiesta is in March it is during the last week of the month. When it is in April, it is in the first week. The people who gather there from other places say that this is a great fiesta because it is organized well and a lot of people come. 1091. They set off two castillos, as well as toritos, "remolinos," and "vistas".[114] All the saints and virgins there are taken out on the procession. 1092. The people following the procession carry boughs of flowers and candles, and some men go along setting off the remolinos and vistas as the procession moves along. At the front of the procession there are two ciriales. Then comes the Christo de Mapeté, and then all the other images from the church.

1093. The statue of Christo de Mapeté is 1.7 meters high. It is made of plaster and has been decorated. 1094. People who attend the fiesta with a child invite another person to act as padrino for the child's first communion. First communion is supposed to be a reaffirmation of one's belief in God and that one follows the doctine that he left on earth. The padrino simply accompanies the child into church to hear the mass. He buys the child a crown of flowers for the occasion and he puts it on the child's head during the mass.

1095. Now the father of the child and the other man are compadres, and the child is the new godchild. The people believe a lot in this santito. They say that if a person is sick and he asks with all his soul to be cured, he gets better.

1096. Many people come to offer flowers and to leave alms. This is apart from what goes on during the fiesta; people come at any time during the year. People who give money are given a relic to take home, like a piece of an escamada that has been blessed. They also give out a piece of ribbon called a "medida".[115]

1097. The name medida comes from the fact that the ribbons are purchased in rolls of different colors. There is a ruler that measures 25 centimeters that the mayordomo of the church uses in order to measure the ribbon, piece by piece. That is why they call that piece of ribbon given as a relic a medida. 1098. The priest is asked to bless the ribbons after the mass. Anyone who gets one of these ribbons ties it around his neck like a necklace. They are of different colors, like red, yellow, violet, green, pink, blue, orange. Black and brown are not used. Those colors are only used when they perform the lifting of the cross of the dead.[116]

1099. When they have a big benediction in Santuario, that is, whenever they are going to use something for the first time in the church, they invite a lot of padrinos from different communities. They send written invitations through the judges and they in turn are charged with giving out the invitations. 1100. People come from various places in order to be a padrino during the mass while the priest blesses the thing that was purchased for the santito to wear, or whatever else may have been bought for use in the church. 1101. All the padrinos arrive on the day of the fiesta, bringing new white candles which they have decorated with a white ribbon or with a white flower. They light the candle when the mass starts, and put it out later when it is over. They don't take the candle home, however, but leave it for the church. 1102. Since padrinos come from different places, there are a lot of people gathered, and almost none of them fail to leave some money in alms. That is why it was said a moment ago that a lot of money comes to this church. The mayordomos surely know how much is collected.

1103. Another custom of the pilgrims is to leave some money for the other images they find in the church. The priest gives communion in the middle of the mass. He gives it to those who have confessed, and not to those who haven't confessed. 1104. He gives it to adults and children who have confessed. Communion consists of a little round thing, made of white powder, which is put in the mouth of the person who requests it. The priest also give the person something to drink, which is supposedly wine.

1105. The priest also baptizes babies. Some people know this as "breaking the horns." Why do they say this? It is said that when a baby remains unbaptized the Devil puts horns on it, and so it is necessary to baptize babies so that God will have them at his side.[117] The bell ringing goes on practically all day in the church. The firecrackers can be heard in other pueblos, too, and in this way it is known that there is a fiesta. 1106. The merchants who come to Santuario from far away sell different things in the plaza, and they are there all week. Sellers of sugar cane come, and sellers of sombreros and of huaraches. Of course, there are always people who sell food.

1107. From the pueblo of Santuario one goes straight, cutting through on the foot paths, to a village called Cerritos. They practice a different religion in this place. Everyone who lives there is a Protestant. They have their gatherings on Thursdays and Saturdays, and do not celebrate any fiesta of importance. The people have built the church there themselves. When they get together it is to pray and to sing psalms.

1108. Again we go back to the road and move on to another community, larger than the last, called El Decá. There, too, the Protestants are the majority.

1109. The same things happen in both Cerritos and Decá. They have their congregation on the same days. They also visit each other, as do the Catholics, but only to pray together, and they do not bring each other any loans. 1110. When a small community is made up of all Protestants, they all go around visiting their co-religionists, whether in a city or a pueblo. They practice the custom of mutual visits. For example, one community goes to visit another, and then another day the second community visits the first. 1111. At the festival of the New Year, there are still some Protestants who remember the customs they had when they were Catholics and they prepare a meal to share with their neighbors. They kill goats in order to cook mole de olla. That is the meal that they usually serve. 1112. They do not serve pulque or any kind of alcohol to drink. All they serve their guests to drink is water sweetened with sugar. The people there who are Protestants appear to be nice folks. They always greet people whenever they meet others on the road. They greet people by taking off their hats, or they offer their hand if they are close.

1113. Apparently, most of the people who believe in that religion are like that. When they speak to one another they call each other "brother," as, for example, "brother Juan" or "brother Pedro." 1114. The women, too, call each other "sister." There is no harm in this form of speech. There are some people among them, however, who anger easily and who sometimes hit other people. 1115. There are men in Decá who have converted to Protestantism and who are big pulque drinkers. They are deceiving the santito that they believe in. Some of them, have, however, changed their lifestyle by saving money and building a nice house. Others continue to be extractors of lechuguilla fiber, or rope makers, or weavers of burlap sacks. The women continue as ayate weavers. They still can not live any better despite their conversion.

1116. Some young people, men and women, migrate from their lands in search of work in the big cities because they do not want to work at the jobs that exist in their own communities. Many of the men who migrate become masons' assistants, or construction laborers. This is really hard labor. 1117. They start at seven in the morning and don't leave until seven at night. The next day, they start again at the same time. It is very tiring. It feels like one's bones are going to break from weariness, and it is even harder for those not used to it. 1118. The work consists of preparing the cement matrix, and collecting the wood frames so the mason can use them again. 1119. The Protestants do not respect the masons, or construction bosses, who work in the big cities because masons curse terribly. They curse even more when the assistant doesn't rush. 1120. A young man on the job has to work, like it or not, because he needs money. He would like to be somewhere else because of the cursing of the construction bosses, but he can't.

1121. It is rare to find masons who are nice people. They curse the mothers of the men who work for them, and they tell them that they are "hijos de la chingada."[118] They tell them that the Devil is going to carry them away; they have a rich vocabulary for this sort of thing. 1122. The only thing a peon can do is listen to it all and hold back, because if he responds then they just tell him even worse things. It's even worse when they are roofing a house and the assistants are carrying the cement up to the roof. They have a lot of men on the job then, up to 20 or 30, depending on the size of the house. 1123. They start at seven in the morning and are there until they finish in the evening before they can leave. It doesn't matter if it's eight or ten at night, they have to finish roofing the house they are working on.

In order to haul the cement mixture up a house under construction, they use a large, rectangular tin can. The overseer orders the other men to bring their shovels and fill the cans to the top. 1124. The peon then has to climb up four, five or six floors, sometimes more, carrying those cans filled with cement. The peon carries the can on one shoulder. The man appointed to drive the workers does not carry anything. He just orders everyone else to hurry up, shouting obscenities at them. He curses at the workers who can not work any faster. Even though they may be old men, he curses at them. 1125. The work itself is not so bad; what really hurts are the insults thrown at the men. Some people resent it so much that they find it better to go home and to continue being extractors of lechuguilla fiber.

1126. Young women also migrate to become servants in the houses of the mestizos, as nannies or as laundresses, and to clean and polish up the houses of their masters. This is how they start out. Later they are given jobs as cooks. 1127. They are also not paid the wages they should be paid. They are paid a miserable pittance every month. Sometimes they get used clothing from the mistress of the house as a kind of supplement to, or in place of, part of their salary. They are not permitted to return home regularly, and months may go by before they visit their families. 1128. The girls never, or almost never, save any money because they are paid so little. Moreover, the work is very hard. They are treated this way by the mestizos because those girls don't know how to speak up for their rights. They don't know the laws pertaining to work.

1129. Sometimes this is the result of religion. That is, for going to pray all the time, one never learns anything about other ideas that are more important. Perhaps religion also teaches something, but it is not what people really need in order to live like they should. Another problem that older people have is that they fight over religion and neglect to send their children to school. 1130. That is why pueblos where people have been fighting each other for a long time have not been able to come out of their state of ignorance. Religion is what impedes them. Among men and women alike, the work in the cities saps their strength. What they do is return to work in their natal village.

1131. Not far from Decá, behind a big mountain to the east, there is another community called San Clemente that belongs to the municipio of Cardonal. The community borders on Orizabita, in the municipio of Ixmiquilpan. There are two groups in San Clemente, also, and they each practice their own religion. 1132. One group is Catholic and the other is Protestant. They used to fight, in the beginning, when people started converting to Protestantism. The religion that people in the Mezquital Valley practiced first was Catholicism. The religion of "the little brothers" arrived later. 1133. When it started, it spread quickly, like drops of oil sprinkled on different villages. People followed the new religion because they believed that they would better their lives if they did, as they had been promised. But many years have gone by and a lot of people are still day laborers in other people's fields, and masons' assistants in building construction. May their souls be saved, at least, when they die.

1134. There is no Catholic church in San Clemente. The image they worship is in a private house. The Protestants, on the other hand, do have a church where they gather to pray. What happens is that the Protestants often get more help from the mestizos to build their churches than the Catholics get. 1135. The Catholics in San Clemente do not celebrate any large fiesta where a lot of people gather. The priest from Cardonal only rarely comes to say mass. The most that people do for the santito is to make floral offerings.

1136. Right next to San Clemente is another small village called El Nogal. This community belongs to Orizabita and only has seventeen full citizens.[119] All together, among the men, women, and children, there are 55 people there. There is no church of either of the two religions. The people of San Clemente tried to impose Protestantism on the people of El Nogal, but the people of El Nogal did not like that religion. Because of that, and because of other things that they did to them, the people of El Nogal abandoned Protestantism, became even stronger believers in Catholicism, and opted to follow their pueblo, which is Orizabita. 1137. El Nogal borders on another small community to the north called El Deza. It is one and a half hours between them, on foot. 1138. There is no church there, either. The saints and virgins that they worship are in a private house. The santitos are prints on cloth. They have a print of the Virgin of Guadalupe.[120] The priest does not get to this place to celebrate mass, so the people bring the print to where mass is said. That is why they attend fiestas and go to the masses. Though these people live far off, they do all they can to come to where a fiesta is being celebrated. Their faith makes them walk all the way in; they have a lot of faith in God.

1139. We start back. Although it is far, we must do so in order to get back on the road that we left in Nequetejé. We go north now, not far, about three kilometers, and there we find a community called El Espíritu. It is located in a very arid and rocky area. The vegetation there consists of mesquite trees, garambullo, capulín cimarrón, sangre de grado, and cardonales.[121] There is a lot of rocky tepetate. 1140. There is a church there that has been built almost entirely from tepetate, and is covered with lime. It has a high tower, about 25 meters, at the top of which is a cross.

1141. The tower is built of finely worked red rock. There are figures made of the rock up the sides of the tower, ending with drawings on the part called "nanxa," in Ñähñu.[122] The red rock decorations are stuck on the walls, and the walls themselves are made of tepetate covered with lime. 1142. Three bells hang in the belfry. One of them is large and it hangs in between the other two. On each side of the tower, to the east and to the west, hang the "tumbling bells."[123] To the north of the main bell hangs a small bell. This is the one that accompanies the large bell when it chimes for joy. The door of the church is simple, and inside it is the same, without any decorations. The altar, on which is the santito of the church, is also unadorned. The floor is made of inlaid brick, and that is where the people kneel to hear mass.

1143. The image of Espíritu Santo, or the Holy Spirit, is located there, as well as the Virgen de Paz y Bién. The Virgen de Paz y Bién is the same one that is in

Candelaria. Thus, they celebrate a mass for her here on February 2nd. They only hold a mass and do not have any further fiesta activities for her here. 1144. The fiesta for the image of Espíritu Santo is held on the last day of December. It is also the last day of the year, and the celebration continues on through the first of January and ends on the second. The fiesta is known as the Festival of the New Year. December 31st is the day of vespers of this fiesta. The fiesta lasts into the night, and goes on again during the next day, on the 1st, and then into the night again until it ends on the morning of the 2nd. The people there gather on the last night of the year in the church to hear mass. The priest says mass at midnight and then the people wait until the castillo and the torito are over before going home to sleep. One castillo and one torito are set off that night.

1145. That is the joy there, because it is New Year's and the fiesta of the pueblo at the same time. Early on the first people get up and go to church to greet the Sr. del Espíritu Santo.[124] They play mañanitas for this greeting. Some people are there early to help sing the mañanitas; they carry boughs of flowers so that when they finish singing they can go into the church and make an offering to the santito. 1146. The mayordomos are ringing the bells and others are setting off firecrackers. When the priest arrives to celebrate mass, the mayordomos go here and there, up and down, helping out. These are the mayordomos of the mass.

1147. The mayordomos providing meals to the musicians and pyrotechnists get ready at their houses. The fireworks makers are also busy, hurrying to finish building their devices and hanging the fireworks on time. The floral offerings come to the church. They are brought by people who come from surrounding small communities. Sometimes, people come from far away, bringing escamadas. 1148. It is believed that the Sr. del Espíritu Santo and the Virgen de Paz y Bién are very miraculous. That is why many people come to pay homage and to leave alms. Those who leave alms go away carrying a relic such as the ribbon called "medida." These are of different colors. Some people put them around their necks; others keep them to put up at home, or to give to whoever is watching their house. Each of the pilgrims leaves a different amount of money there for the santitos.

1149. On the day of the fiesta the Sr. del Espíritu Santo is placed on the main altar. He is encased in glass. The people come to the base of the altar to worship and pray. They kneel and then they cross themselves. The children are taught how to cross themselves by either the father or the mother. Everyone there greets the santito with great respect; many of them come to bid their greetings every year. 1150. At the special mass for the fiesta the priest does baptisms and weddings and hears confessions. For children who are having their first communion, padrinos and madrinas are sought to accompany the child to hear mass.

1151. The person who accepts the invitation to be padrino for a child's first communion has to provide the clothing for the child. They buy white clothes, a white candle, and a book that has the prayers written out. If the child is a girl, then the veil she uses to cover her head must be white. It is transparent, like an ayate. 1152. When people are invited to be padrinos for first communion, one must prepare a meal for them; one does not just ask people to do this without offering them anything. Also, when someone is padrino for a child's baptism, a meal is prepared for them. In either case, the child becomes known as the "ahijado" or "godchild." 1153. Chickens or goats are killed to make the stew or the barbacóa. Chickens are generally cooked in mole and sometimes roasted or baked. When they are baked they are basted with salsa before going into the oven. 1154. The meal served to the padrinos is customarily offered after the mass or baptism is over. In the meantime, the people of the community are busy in the plaza, setting up the arches on the street corners where the procession will pass that night. The musicians are also there, playing beautiful songs continuously.

1155. At night, around nine, the mayordomos get together to organize the procession for the major images of the church, along with all the other prints or statues. At this church there are no images from outside. They don't invite anyone else. Many people gather to accompany the procession. The procession takes an hour and a half to make the rounds of the arches that have been built and decorated with different colored paper. 1156. Small groups are commissioned to build the arches, and so every year they are decorated differently. Some are decorated entirely with paper. Others are woven with cucharilla. Those are the ones that look the nicest. The men carry the santito and the women carry the virgin in the procession. Whether they are married women or girls, they withstand the weight of the statue and make the entire round.

1157. The roar of the firecrackers is heard as the procession moves along. Most of the people who follow the procession carry a candle to light the way. This is the time when the musicians have the most work, because they play almost continuously. 1158. No one in the procession wears a sombrero; all the men have their heads bare. The carolers go along praying to the images, and it goes on like this is until they all complete the round and return to go back into the church. When the procession is over, the statues are placed on the ground, both the saint and the virgin, each in its own case.[125] Then the people gather round to worship them. They cross themselves and kiss the santito and the virgin. A few people return to leave some alms.

1159. When the people finish worshipping, the mayordomos return the images to their usual places. When the the procession is over and the glorification is complete, then everyone leaves the church and heads for the plaza, where they stay until the castillo and the torito are lit. 1160. The noise of the firecrackers can be heard in the surrounding communities, and there is much merriment at the fiesta. People from Cerroblanco and Chalmita, the barrios that make up the community of El Espíritu, attend this fiesta. El Olivo used to be a barrio of this pueblo, but it separated because they had problems over religion.

1161. The barrio of El Olivo went over to Protestantism, and fighting started. What the people of El Olivo did was to separate in order to avoid confrontation with their neighbors. There is a special custom between the people of those two communities. Even though they do not have good social relations, whenever someone from El Olivo dies, the people there go to El Espíritu to ask permission from the authorities to bury the body. 1162. The authorities in El Espíritu have never denied permission to bury someone from El Olivo. They have always acceded to the request. Sometimes it is a Protestant being buried and they don't deny permission.

1163. Thus one finds there, in the cemetery, Catholics and Protestants lying together. Hopefully, they won't fight in heaven, because they could meet again there and that would cause problems for God. Bells are not rung for Protestants when they die, but they are rung for Catholics. This goes for children as well as adults. Also, the bodies of Catholics are brought to the church, while those of the Protestants aren't. They go directly to the cemetery.

1164. The day after the fiesta the new mayordomos are named who will be in charge of the next year's celebration. The changeover ends around five in the afternoon. The mayordomos for the band, the torito, the castillo, and the masses for the santitos are appointed at this meeting. People who know that a long time has gone by since they were mayordomos are ready in case they are chosen by their neighbors.

1165.The fiesta has passed, but the debts remain. The outgoing mayordomos have encumbered the most debt because they have spent a lot of money preparing the meals that they have offered to their guests. But in reality, this is nothing and no one regrets spending it. On the contrary, they are satisfied because it is said that they have served God. 1166. They are in debt once again to their neighbors and to some folks from surrounding communities who have brought them some kind of loan in the form of a cuarto or half a cuarto of pulque, or maize, or a dozen or half a dozen cuartillos of tortillas. There are some people whose economic circumstances permit them to lend both pulque and tortillas. Other bring maize and pulque. These are the things that are mostly loaned.

1167. Some people have lent things because the mayordomos asked them for a loan, but others make loans on their own initiative. They just come with things to lend because that is the custom. In this case, one can't say that there is no obligation to repay the loan just because one has not asked for it in the first place. No; both respect and tradition demand that one not turn away any loans that come on a fiesta day. Some of the loans that the mayordomos get will be recalled and paid the following year. The people who get the new cargos remember the loans they have made. But if only a few days remain before a fiesta, and if a loan has not been called in, then the person who owes back a loan can lend to someone else, to another mayordomo. Then some other time he will be reminded of his own borrowing.

1168. Animals such as goats, chickens and sheep are loaned. Cattle are almost never loaned because they are big and it would be very difficult for someone to repay. Some people brought money to lend. This kind of loan is called "alms" though it is for the mayordomo and not for the santito. Some brought a peso, or two or three or five, and some people lent fifty centavos. This is called "giving alms." These are the debts that an outgoing mayordomo was left with.

1169. From Espíritu one takes the north fork of the road and goes along a winding road which goes to a little place called Deeto. This is the original name of the place, but the people there have changed it and now call it Chalmita. There is a chapel which contains the image of Sr. de Chalma whose festival is on the fifth Friday of Pentecost, just like the one in El Arenal that we saw earlier. 1170. The fiesta of the small statue lasts only two days. The santito is made of plaster and has a small cross on it. It is about 70 centimeters high, or three and a half hands. The statue is kept in a glass case made especially for him. The santito is considered very miraculous because he saves people's lives, so a lot of people gather for his fiesta. Of course, it can not compare with the numbers who gather at Arenal.

1171. They celebrate the fiesta every year. Sometimes they hire a band and have a torito. The people there chip in for these things, but there are only about 20 adult men. The whole population is around 150. The floral offerings come from other nearby communities. Other pilgrims come to leave some alms; they stay for the celebration of the mass, request their relic to take home, and leave. 1172. The flutist and drummer are there all day and night, playing. They accompany the procession; though it does not go far from the church, there is one. Most of the people who come are from El Espíritu because they are neighbors.

1173. The little community of Chalmita is located on top of a hill and the people of this village are very nice. They, too, prepare meals for the members of

the band and for the fireworks makers. 1174. They have the custom of giving
out those ribbons that people put around their necks, and that we already know
are called "medidas." To ensure that a lot of people come, they sometimes postpone the fiesta. They wait until the fiesta of Arenal is over so that the celebrants
can stop by Chalmita on their way home. And that is how come there are so
many people there; if not for this, the santito would be all alone. They, too, have
a changeover in this community to name the new mayordomos and the new
judges. They don't have their meeting the day after the fiesta, however; they get
together on another day.

1175. Now we go back to Espíritu if we like, or we can take a shortcut over a
footpath, to El Olivo. The path is passable, though it is a little rough, owing to a
lot of stones and cactus spines. 1176. One can go back to Espíritu if one wants
to, but it is a long way around. On the other hand, the advantage is that the way
back is a good motor road. Traveling north over that road, it goes through
Espíritu and on to Olivo and continues on. We arrive there in El Olivo. The community is situated on a large, rocky mesa. It is practically all white tepetate.
Even so, there is a lot of maguey here that the people have planted with much
effort. When the plants are mature, they cut open the hearts and scrape them to
make pulque. They take the pulque to the irrigated zone where they sell it. They
sell it wholesale rather than retail. They bring home the little money that they
get and buy things they need for the house.

1177. The people in this community used to practice the Catholic religion,
though they didn't have a church there. They would come to pray in Espíritu
where they would fulfill their cargos, when it was their turn, to feed the
pyrotechnists and musicians, and to pay for the masses. They went to the meetings there when the changeover took place; they enrolled their children in the
school; and they did their faenas there. They also got justice there when they
needed it. 1178. Sometimes, people from Olivo acted as judge or they worked
closely with those in Espíritu. But everything began to fall apart when the
Protestant religion came in. That's when the problems began. 1179. Some
people in El Olivo began to follow the new religion. This angered those in the
Centro (El Espíritu), and they tried to stop people from converting. They
appointed people mayordomos who might have had a cargo only a short time
earlier. Men who were given those obligations simply ignored them. Those of
El Olivo no longer liked being part of El Espíritu and they separated from the
main body of the village. 1180. But the problems didn't stop there. They continued because the people of Espíritu did not like the separation, since they were
left alone to fulfill the cargos every year.

1181. Those of Olivo continued to practice Protestantism, but not everyone. A few families remain Catholic even today. Most believe in and practice the religion of the Protestants but they have not forced those who did not want to convert to do so. They haven't been like that. Each one knows what he is doing. Those who did not want to go into the Protestant faith continued going to the fiestas. Sometimes they go to El Espíritu when they celebrate the fiesta there, and no one in El Olivo says anything to them about it. But they no longer participate in fulfilling cargo obligations. They have left that behind. Who knows when or if they will participate again.

1183. The people who practice the Protestant religion chipped in equally to build their own church. That is where they meet today to pray what they believe. No one bothers them. 1184. The children also follow the religion practiced by their fathers and mothers. Many of those who converted early on are no longer alive. The young people now gather all the time to continue praying. They don't spend a lot of money when they have a celebration because they don't kill goats or chickens to give out to people to eat, and they don't hire musicians or fireworks makers either. If they ever spend money it's on New Year's when they all get together and buy some things to eat.

1185. To say prayers, the Catholics have a person called a priest. The Protestants, on the other hand, have a pastor.[126] The pastor says the mass because he knows best what is in the book they have. The Protestants are each given a book in which, according to what they say, the word of God is written. Among Catholics it is rare to find anyone with one of the books of his religion. One must know, too, that the books of the two religions are not alike. 1186. When one asks a Protestant what it says in the book that they were given, they know it well. More than anything else, they try not to commit so many sins, not to get drunk, and to treat their fellow man with respect. That is why they call each other "little brother," and why Catholics who have heard this have nicknamed the Protestants the "little brothers." 1187. One almost never hears them cursing. Though others may curse at them, they never respond in the same manner to the person who is offending them. There must be some of them who curse, but they are surely few.

1188. They are careful not to get drunk. When they are invited to drink liquor or beer they say that they don't drink. They say "Excuse me, but I don't drink." 1189. There are some who have been observed drinking and getting drunk. Perhaps, as in all things, they just can't resist, and they can not just stand around watching while others drink. 1190. The women in this religion are perhaps more good to their word; they have not been seen drinking pulque or liquor. But it seems somehow contradictory for them not to drink pulque, as we will now see. Even though they don't drink pulque, they make it to sell to those who do, and in this way they cause harm to their fellow man. For all their actions to be good they would have to refrain from selling pulque. In this way, the good works they think about doing would be more complete.

1191. Since they don't have any fiestas on which to spend their money, they have built nice houses with tile walls, concrete roofs, and metal encased windows. They do, indeed, have better houses, but only for those who work as builders and masons, or as teachers. Those who work as day laborers in the fields continue to have houses made of organ pipe cactus and sometimes of ocotillo[127] with dry stones laid over the outside. Those are the materials they use to make the walls of their houses, and they roof them with maguey leaves. From this one can deduce that one can believe in whatever one likes, but it takes work to get what is needed in life. 1192. The problems that they have with people of El Espíritu have not stopped yet. There are still times when they want to fight each other, because there is always someone who tells lies and defames others, and that is when problems start. 1193. After some more years pass, possibly those who are coming along behind, the children, will forget all this.

When one of them learns well the contents of the Bible that he reads, he leaves the village, accompanied by someone else, in order to go around convincing others to convert to their religion. 1194. This behavior is what their neighbors don't like, and this is where the problems start. Sometimes, when a person decides to become a Protestant, the rest of the Catholic people in the village get together to throw out the convert and this is how they avoid problems.

1195. Some of the converts have told how they get baptized again when they first enter their new church. Then they are given a new name, different from the one they had originally. For example, if a person used to be Juan, then after he is baptized into the new religion they might call him José. They say that they do this for men and women alike. 1196. In communities where the people are convinced to convert to the Evangelical religion, they are encouraged to help in building a church. The help might be in the form of faenas, or it might be money to buy calidra[128] or something else they need. When they inaugurate the church they all come together and invite their co-religionists, perhaps to bless it, and everyone who comes prays. When they are finished, they all eat together. 1197. They always ask God for permission before they eat. They say that God lives in heaven and for this they pray over the food they are going to eat.

1198. When the meeting that was called is over, all the invited guests return to the villages they came from. The people in this religion never laugh during their fiestas; they stay serious. None of them get drunk during their ceremonies because they do not hand out pulque or liquor. They only give out water, and that is what the people drink who are eating together. 1199. They kill some animals and prepare them to eat. They kill goats, chickens and sheep to make barbacóa. They do not boil and then fry any of these animals. They throw out the blood of these animals and only cook the meat to eat. By contrast, the rest of the people who are Catholics, collect the blood of the animals mentioned, and then the women cook it with condiments and make it very good to eat. 1200. Some Protestants believe that it is not good to eat the blood of the animals because that is what their leaders have told them, and that is what their books say. And they say that they don't just throw out the blood that they don't consume; they bury it so that dogs won't eat it.

1201. The Protestants try to induce others to convert, telling them that there is not much time before God comes to save those who have behaved well—to save those who have done something for the collective good, those who have lived well with their fellow men, those who have always believed in God and who have not blasphemed. They say that those are the people whom God will take to his side. And those who have done evil will be abandoned by God to go to hell. Some people believe this and convert, and before anyone knows it, there they are, Protestants. It is not known exactly who is telling the truth. From what it looks like, they just try to get more people into the religion so that they will be more numerous.

1202. From El Olivo one may continue walking north along the road, going down a slope at a spot called La Monjera, and continuing along the bank of the barranca. Then one goes up to hit the road again that traverses the brow of the mountain and comes to the community of Defay where they worship the santito of Orizabita. 1203.The real name of the santito is Sr. del Buen Viaje. They say that this is the santito that was originally worshipped by the people of Orizabita, and that the one in the church at Orizabita is just a copy that the people asked for. There is no church in Defay, and so the the santito is kept in the house of someone called the "mandante."[129] This person is named unanimously and is changed each year. 1204. The new mandante takes the santito to his house, along with the new things he has purchased for him, like his robes. When the mayordomo finishes his term, he holds a meeting to name someone else to care for the statue.

1205. When a person turns over the statue and makes his report to the community, everthing must be exactly as he received it. The person responsible for the santito is always a man and never a woman. This is because it is a santito; if it were a virgin, then a woman would be named and a man would not be. This is because the people say that each should be with its own gender. 1206. The celebration of the santito is the same as that in Orizabita, the Fiesta del Sexto Viernes. They show up at Orizabita every year for the invitation to participate in the fiesta. Those from Defay fulfill cargos for the fiesta of Orizabita, as was related in previous pages. They gather there for the changeover every year.

1207. A mayordomo is named for the santito of Defay. He is charged with receiving the statue, with soliciting the priest to say mass, and with making the floral offering. The mayordomo provides food for the people who accompany the santito and who will be at the fiesta. 1208. There are many pilgrims who believe that the Sr. del Buen Viaje is very miraculous, and that he saves and has mercy on poor people. Flowers are offered to him. The image is about 50 centimeters tall. The figure is nailed to a small, wooden cross. 1209. As was said, it is believed that this santito saves people and so he is invited to spend two or three days, or up to a week, at people's houses.

1210. They say that when a person is sick and can not get better, they invite the santito of Buen Viaje to be in the house of the ill person. They make floral offerings to him right there, in the house. They do a cleansing of the ill person with a candle or with some gift. That is, money and a mass are promised to the santito. 1211. Sometimes, by coincidence, the person gets better, and then people believe even more strongly that the santito has saved the patient. When people hear about someone being cured after the Sr. del Buen Viaje was in their house, then they do the same thing and invite the santito to the house of some other sick person. To invite the image, one asks the mandante of the Sr. del Buen Viaje and he checks to see if it is available, or if it is due to go out to someone else. 1212. If the mandante says that the santito has somewhere else to go, then the person who is inviting the image puts off the day. But he will do what he thought of doing, no matter what, and as soon as the santito is available he visits the house of the person inviting him.

1213. To prepare for the arrival of the santito, flowers are purchased, along with firecrackers, incense, and good quality candles, made of pure wax. There are candles that are made of a mixture that does not look like pure wax. The people can spot the difference, because the good wax does not smoke a lot when the candle burns. The poor quality candles make a lot of black smoke and they burn out fast; that is, they melt easily. These are the differences the people have observed. 1214. Why do they choose the good candles? Because it is a special reception for the santito, the objective being the curing of a sick person, and so everything promised must be done, including the purchase of good candles. Sometimes, people who have bees will get someone who knows how to make candles and they invite the candlemaker to make the candles that are needed. When they are made at home, then one can be sure that candles contain pure wax. 1215. Incense also is hand picked; there is a white incense that people like to buy because of its nice aroma. A lot of care is taken so the reception for the santito will be as it should.

1216. Care is taken also in selecting the flowers so that none are damaged. Sometimes they tie up a bundle of flowers and have the sick person make the offering he has promised to the santito personally, given that he is still capable of sitting up, of course. They do a cleansing of the sick person with a candle that has been kept aside especially for this. 1217. They do the cleansing over the whole body of the sick person, and then they light the candle. Some miniature whips, known as "ejotes" or "string beans" have been hung on the cross of the Sr. del Buen Viaje up near his feet. 1218. The mandante takes the ejotes and makes the sign of the cross in front of the santito, asking the santito's permission first. Then he comes near to where the sick person is seated and he makes the sign of the cross with the ejotes in from of him, and then he brings the santito near so that the sick person can venerate the image. 1219. Once the sick person has kissed the image, the mandante performs a cleansing of the sick person's head, shoulders and back. When he finishes the cleansing, the mandante gives the sick person several lashes with the whip, he does another cleansing, and then he gives some more lashes. When this is all done, the mandante crosses himself, gives the sick person the image to kiss, and then puts the ejotes back at the feet of the santito.

1220. When the mandante gives the lashes to a child, it makes the child cry. The belief is that the whipping will chase out the laziness and lack of will that is inside the body of the sick person, as well as the sickness in the body. 1221. Children who are thought to be lazy get lashings with the ejotes the most. A father or mother takes a child with them to a fiesta, and if they are informed that the santito has ejotes, then they ask someone to give the child a cleansing.

1222. Goats are killed at the house of someone who invites the santito. The people who go to bring home the santito, and all who accompany them, are given food to eat when they return with the image. The group of people who go to fetch the santito carry flowers. The flowers are strung into garlands to offer to the santito, and strung like this they can be carried. 1223. The case in which the image is housed is about a meter high. It is covered on the outside with a red cloth that has had a cross embroidered on it. This is what someone from among those who have come to get the image must carry. One person goes in front of the santito, carrying a small bell which he rings as he goes along, and someone else sets off firecrackers along the way. Sometimes, this is where a flutist and a drummer might be hired. They go along, playing tunes; but when a flutist and drummer are not used, then a string band is hired.

1224. There is always someone who carries a vase of flowers that also accompanies the santito. A small candle is placed among the flowers in the vessel. Sometimes it is the same woman carrying the vase who also carries the incense brazier containing coals and incense. When they get to the house of the person giving the reception, the man or woman of the house, whoever comes out first, greets the santito. He takes the incense burner from the person who accompanied the image and censes the image, crossing himself first. Then someone else comes out and does the same. This is the kind of greeting that people customarily offer to a santito or virgin.

1225. After the image is received, then they enter the house. The helpers of the person who awaits the santito keep lighting firecrackers. After the days which were planned for the stay of the image have passed, they prepare to return the image to where it came from, in this case, Defay.

1226. The santito is brought to various villages, either to be in some fiesta or to be in some family's house. Sometimes he goes around to the little communities in the Ixmiquilpan area, communities like Panales, El Maye, El Mando, San Juanico, Los Remedios, El Espíritu. These are some of the communities he goes to on the south. To the north, he goes to La Lagunita, El Banxu, La Palma, El Cantamayé, El Nogal, El Gundó. Gundó is as far as he goes, and then he comes back. 1227. A clarification should be made that he is not invited only to the houses of sick persons. No; he is also called to where someone is thinking of building a new house. When the people of the valley build a new home, they do not want to simply set up house and start living in it. They invite the santito, worship him right there, and then they can inaugurate the house.

1228. There is also the belief that it is not good for people to live in a house that has not been blessed first, because the Devil could be living there and he could cause some evil to befall any member of the family. So, it is necessary to bless the house with the presence of the santito. Those who do not invite the santito might call in a priest who prays over a new house and sprinkles holy water all over the walls. Once the house is blessed, the people can live in it, and it is said that in this way the house will not cause fright. These are the beliefs that many people have, and this is why they bless houses.

1229. From this place one can go south and go back through El Olivo once again. Then one goes down, following the road that goes down the brow of the hill to a barranca known as Barranca Hedionda. This barranca starts at the foot of the mountains at Defay and is joined by various small ravines along the way. 1230. Crossing the barranca one comes again to the flat land along the same road that goes to Orizabita. From there, one follows the road east. This is a dirt road; walking about three and a half kilometers, one reaches the community of

San Andrés Orizabita. It has this name because this piece of land is a part of the pueblo of Orizabita; that is, it is one more of its barrios.

1231. We could have also come on the road that crosses El Olivo and continued along the road that goes to El Espíritu, and from there we could have headed west, also walking along the road, crossing a hill where there is a cross. Then we would have continued down the small, white hill, coming exactly to the church at San Andrés. 1232. The church there is small, more like what is usually called a chapel. That is where the santito is that people worship, and that is where the pilgrims come every year on the 30th of November to celebrate the fiesta. The image is believed to make miracles, and so it has a large following and many people venerate it.

The people of the village organize the fiesta every year. 1233. Each citizen brings a sum of money so that all the money is collected for the band and for the fireworks makers, who are charged with building the castillo and the torito which are set off on the day of the fiesta. They take the santito on a procession. The image is not very big; it is about 80 centimeters tall and they keep it in a metal showcase. As is the usual custom, the mass is celebrated at midday on the day of the fiesta; this is considered to be the principal mass. 1234. It is called the principal mass because it is celebrated on the actual day of the fiesta; everything the priest says in the mass is the same as on other occasions. Here, too, there is the custom that the mayordomos prepare food for the musicians. This is done by those who have been named to do so. Other mayordomos provide food for the fireworks makers.

1235. Food is also given to other visitors who come with loans for their neighbors, and for those who come with loans from other villages in the surrounding area, and for those who come just for the adoration of the santito. The people who come the most to the fiesta there are from El Espíritu, Los Remedios, El Espino, Cerritos, Nequetejé, Cerroblanco, San Juanico, and other communities in the Ixmiquilpan area like Mandó in the irrigated zone. Some people from San Andrés have a lot of friends in Mandó because they work there in the fields and doing other things, and they sell their pulque there, too. That's how friendships start up, and they invite the people to visit them for the fiesta or for other celebrations that they are thinking of making. 1236. The people from San Andrés will be the recipients of a corresponding invitation from the people of Mandó to come and participate in their fiesta.

The people from the irrigated zone sometimes make loans of maize or tortillas. When the loan is repaid, the lender of maize will ask for pulque in return, because there is not much maguey in the irrigated zone for the people to extract aguamiel and make pulque. 1237. A person from the irrigated zone who lends twelve cuartillos of tortillas will ask for a barrel of pulque in exchange. Each person makes the loan personally, coming to the house of the receiver. This is the respect that people are accustomed to showing one another. To make loans, one has to go on foot. Even if the distance is great, that is not important when it comes to paying off loans. As we saw in earlier pages, a person who owes on a loan does not want to be shamed or have people say that he doesn't know how to pay off his debts as he should. He goes along carrying what he must pay off. Pulque weighs more, while a large basket of tortillas weighs less.

1238. Immediately after incurring a debt, a person starts working to accumulate the repayment. In this case the situation is considered somewhat delicate, because it has to do with the worship of a saint or a virgin. People believe that when one doesn't pay what one should, then the santito whose fiesta is being celebrated might bring on some misfortune. One might get sick, or fall and break a leg, or be bitten by a spider or a snake. These are some of the misfortunes in which people believe. They believe this if it happens while one is going to pay off a loan. But if such misfortunes happen at other times, then they are not believed to be caused by some image. Men almost always carry maize and pulque when making loans, while women carry tortillas.

1240. They have a changeover of judges and mayordomos in San Andrés every year. Two men are appointed as judges and two as mayordomos. This is done so that they can help each other, though the community does not have much population. 1241. The annual report in the church is made on January 6th. The outgoing mayordomos have to report how much money was collected as alms, and what works they performed for betterment of the church. All the things that belong to the church will be received by the new mayordomos. The judges too, report on their activities.

1242. When the report is over, the church is closed and the outgoing mayordomos invite everyone who attended the meeting to come and eat with them. They have prepared a meal for this, but this is not obligatory. It is just a way of showing happiness. All the authorities sit together, including the incoming mayordomos, and they are the first to be served; then they signal for everyone to join them. 1243. When the meal is over, then the baskets are brought out. Each basket has a whole chicken and they are given out to the new judges and then to the new mayordomos. The outgoing judges are not given anything, just the meal they were served, because they were given their chicken the year before.

1244. For this occasion, too, many loans come to the mayordomo who has the cargo; that is, the outgoing mayordomos receive a lot of loans so that they can fulfill their cargos. It is not as if the mayordomos who are leaving their offices do not have enough to fulfill their cargos on their own; it's just a custom that has existed for many years. 1245. Sometimes a mayordomo goes out to visit his acquaintances and invites them for a meal, and asks them to help him out with a loan. He does this because a lot of people gather at the changeover reunion, and he wants to make sure that no one who comes is without food to eat.

1246. Those people who are asked to make loans don't turn the mayordomo down because they know they have to provide one another with mutual help. That way, when they are named to fulfill a cargo, they will have people to help them out. Everything is on loan and it is not as if it will not be paid back. Whatever it is, an animal, or pulque or maize or tortillas—in amounts of twelve or six cuartillos, as is the custom for these loans—it is all repaid. One can thus think of the reunions as places where people meet new acquaintances and where they invite each other to visit.

1247. Now we return to Ixmiquilpan, the place where we began to organize our tour for this narrative. From there we will take another road that goes west, so that you will be introduced to the communities we will see as we go about. 1248. The highway that was mentioned divides into a Y before reaching Portezuelo, just before a place called Barranca Honda. The road that goes to the right goes around and to the north, on through the city of Tasquillo, on to Zimapán and on to still other cities. The other road, to the left, goes directly west. It goes through various places on its way to Querétaro and continues to the State of Zacatecas; from there it goes on to other parts of the country.

1249. We will begin by talking about the community that borders directly on Ixmiquilpan and is known as Barrio de Jesús, and Barrio del Cortijo as well. These are the two names it has. The traditional fiesta is celebrated in this place on February 25th. The fiesta usually lasts three days: the vespers, the day of the fiesta, and the overnight watch until the third day. 1250. The residents from the pueblo also gather each year to name the mayordomos who will be in charge of giving food to the band and to the fireworks makers. They only contract for one night of music, and they light two castillos and four toritos. 1251. They light one castillo and two toritos on the night of vespers; then they light another castillo and two more toritos on the main day of the fiesta. They also light remolinos and vistas, and sometimes corredizos, as they are called in Spanish.[130]

1252. The santito that they worship there is Jesus Christ. The image is about the same size as the Christ of Espíritu, and he has been fixed to a cross. The church of the santito is beautiful inside. Pictures have been painted on the walls, and the cross has been painted gold. The santito is on the altar. Three priests officiate at the mass on the day of the fiesta, and this is known as the grand mass. 1253. The people there, too, invite their neighbors from other communities to come and have their things blessed by the santito before using things for the first time. The things that the padrinos bring for this ceremony are the same as those we saw when we discussed the Espíritu Santo. The statue is taken out on a procession around the main streets. They have the custom here, too, of building arches on every corner of the streets. 1254. In front of the procession go people carrying a bundle of lit cardona twigs, a plant similar to órgano. Three or four people carry these torches to light the way for the procession. When those branches are lit, they produce a big blaze. The pilgrims accompanying the santito in the procession carry boughs of different flowers that they have gathered. Others carry candles and candlesticks; they light the wicks. And so, little by little, the santito winds his way around the street.

1255. Those who know how, go along praying to the image. The musicians tag along behind, playing tunes. In the steeple, the bell ringers ring the bells, while the assistants to the fireworks makers set off firecrackers. 1256. In the plaza there are people selling many things to eat, such as coffee, tamales, tamalitos, and tacos with cabbage, lettuce, onion and garlic added. The people who come to this fiesta most are from El Maye, La Reforma, La Otra Banda (also known as Progreso), and Ixmiquilpan. Almost all church processions are held at night. It is rare that they hold them during the day.

1257. From the Barrio of Jesús, we walk just a little to the south and come to the boundary with the community of El Maye in the municipio of Ixmiquilpan. 1258. Before getting there we have to cross a river which rises in Tula de Allende. This is the river that irrigates portions of the land to which water can be pumped, that is, where there is not much slope. The water is not very clean because it is mixed with the sewage from Mexico City.[131] But for the moment we will leave the subject of irrigation and continue on the road that goes to El Maye. There is a bridge that crosses the river. In the center of the village we find a small church and in it is an image worshipped by many people in the Mezquital Valley, as well as others who come from far away. 1259. The image in the church is a cross made of wood that appears to be oak. It is about two meters high, and the arms extend about a brazada. It is simply a wooden cross and has no image of any santito on it.

1260. Those who believe in the Catholic religion say that the cross has saving power, and that is why many pilgrims come together on the day they celebrate the fiesta, the 3rd of May. They have the same celebration every year. 1261. People come to make floral offerings at this place. Though they come from far away, they do everything possible to make it. There is a musical band, and the pyrotechnists build two castillos, one to go off on the day of vespers, and the other for the day of the fiesta. 1262. There is not enough room in the church for all the people who want to worship the cross and to leave flowers or alms as offerings. Others bring escamadas as offerings to the cross.

1263. The mayordomos can hardly keep up with receiving all that is given. They deliver relics to the pilgrims who offer alms. Dancers are outside the church door. They come on their own, because for them this is a promise that they are fulfilling. 1264. The dancers' apparel is red. They have embroidered a lot of designs on it, and the clothing is quite lustrous. They have put on feather head dresses which look beautiful. They keep on dancing, like they were tireless. There are men and women in the group, and sometimes children accompany them, and they, too, dance. Meanwhile, the pilgrims come and go, worshipping the cross.

1265. They take the holy cross out on a procession at night, and it is accompanied by a lot of people. A lot of the faithful who have come from far away remain for the procession and stay all night. Then the next day they return to their places of origin. 1266. On October 20th the people of the village take the cross to the top of a mountain known as Dexits'o for another fiesta in its honor. That mountain is near El Maye. 1267. A lot of people gather for this occasion, too. The fiesta is known as La Subida de la Santa Cruz (The Rise of the Holy Cross). The people take the holy cross from the church and some of them volunteer to carry it. A band is hired to accompany the holy cross on this day. They trek up the path that has been cut, and come to the top of the mountain. It takes about two hours to get there.

1268. There is a chapel on the top of the mountain where they go so that the priest can celebrate mass and the people can participate. People with floral offerings also get to this spot. 1269. People only gather during the day for this occasion and not at night, though they return very late; they arrive in Ixmiquilpan practically when the sun is going down. 1270. The belief about bringing the cross to the top of the mountain is that the cross was found there.

1271. They say that some people who were shepherding came upon the cross and that it is very miraculous. That is why so many people have faith in it. For example, they say that if a person is sick and goes to that spot to leave some alms or a floral offering, then he will get better. 1272. Sometimes, a sick person gets better, by coincidence, and then others believe. A lot of people bring food to the mountain to sell. There is barbacóa, and there are sellers of pulque; they bring different kinds of food to sell there. 1273. These are the two celebrations that are done in El Maye, in which a lot of people come from many parts. Though the fiesta of the Holy Cross is celebrated in other communities, the people are faithful to this cross because they say that it is more miraculous.

1274. The day of the builders is celebrated on May 3rd. It is what they call
The Day of the Holy Cross. They worship the cross right where they work so
that God will not let anything bad befall them, like a wall falling on them when
they are climbing on it. They ask God to always provide them with work as
masons and to see to it that the money they get multiplies. 1275. All the masons
who are working cooperate economically. They purchase flowers and firecrackers together. The flowers are for decorating the walls of the project on which
they are working. Only *some* of the masons ask the priest to conduct a mass—
those who believe in the Catholic religion.

1276. On the fiesta dedicated to masons, or building trades masters, they do
not work, and this includes the Protestants. They all relax and order someone to
prepare a meal and they eat together. Sometimes they make barbacóa, either of
goat or of chicken. They buy pulque to drink. If the fiesta falls in mid-week, then
they go to work the following day. This fiesta is celebrated in the cities, too. One
can tell because firecrackers can be heard wherever there is construction going
on. They put up a cross at the top of a construction site.

1277. From El Maye we go to another community called La Otra Banda, also
called Progreso. It is on the other side of the Tula River, on the west bank. There
are two roads that go there and end up at the church. This community is not far;
it borders on Ixmiquilpan. 1278. One of the roads that goes to La Otra Banda
crosses over the Tula River via a bridge that was built around 1760. The other
road goes around by the main highway, passing through the cemetery of Cruz
Blanca, and coming precisely to the church.

1279. The church is large and tall. It is built of stone. It has a tower in which
there are medium size bells, including a fixed bell and others that are hanging.
Inside, the church is painted white with gold colored columns. The altar is
beautifully decorated, particularly where they have the little santito that is worshipped there. 1280. The santito there is called Santo Niño de Atocha. It is wearing a sombrero and it has a little cane in one hand. The cane has a little gourd on
the end of it. It is believed that this santito is very miraculous. Many people
gather for his fiesta.

1281. The date of the fiesta is the 28th of January, and the priest holds mass
at midday. The church fills with believers carrying candles and flowers, and
there are even more when the mass is for blessing something that is being presented to the Santo Niño because of the custom of inviting padrinos from other
communities. 1282. The people invited to be padrinos are from Panales, Ignacio
López Rayón, El Dexto, El Mandó, El Maye, and other small communities
around there. 1283. A band is hired to play at the vespers, and it stays there until
the third day; that is, until the morning after the main fiesta. Fireworks makers

are also hired to make the castillos and the torito, and the remolinos, vistas, busca pies, and corredizos. 1284. Two castillos and two toritos are lit at the vespers. These are lit after the procession has taken around the Santo Niño. Four castillos are lit on the night of the fiesta. These have been set up a good distance apart from one another so that a spark from one will not set off another when they are lit.

1285. Different groups chip in to make up the cost of the castillo. One castillo is set up by the children; that is, they chip in to buy it. Another is put up by the women, a third by field laborers, and the last one by those who have greater wealth. Thus, there are four groups in charge of getting the cost of the castillos together. 1286. When the castillos are lit, they start with the one donated by the children. Then after a little time has passed, next comes the one given by the women, and then the field laborers' castillo, and finally the rich people's. 1287. The castillos differ from each other in how long they burn, and the children's castillo is also smaller than the others. The other three are all the same size. The castillo of the children is between seven and eight meters tall.

Aside from this, the castillos differ in the number of bangs they make. For example, one castillo might go off three times, and this shows that the people paid little for it. By comparison, one that goes off four or five times shows that the cost was greater. When a castillo burns, it shoots off one set of fireworks and then it stops for a few moments and lights up again. At the end, the whole thing lights up and shoots off, and one can admire the many colors. The firecrackers that have been attached to the castillo thunder away, and the whole thing gives off a lot of smoke, and it looks like a fog rolled in.

1289. When the castillo finishes shooting off, then a lot of firecrackers are set off—special ones. They are called "cámaras" in Spanish and they explode very loudly and can be heard a long distance away. When they explode in the air, the earth shakes. There have been times when misfortunes have befallen the fireworks makers when they did not take sufficient precautions. When lit off, these giant firecrackers have sometimes wounded their hands, blowing fingers off. Some of the fireworks makers who come to the fiestas have only one hand. This particular kind of firecracker sometimes kills people.[132]

1290. When misfortunes like these happen at a fiesta, people say that the mayordomos are not carrying out their cargos with a full heart, and so God is angry and sends punishment. 1291. This class of bad happening is called "desgracia" that is, "misfortune" or "disgrace." Sometimes it is the mayordomo who suffers the disgrace, and other times it is the fireworks makers. When accidents happen to the castillo makers, people believe that they must have come to work without really wanting to.

1292. The Santo Niño de Atocha worshipped in La Otra Banda is thought to be quite miraculous and he shows kindness to sick people. Since he is very miraculous, a lot of pilgrims leave alms. A lot of them have made a promise to the santito, and this is also called "limosna" or "alms." Floral offerings come, along with candles and escamadas. The believers ask the Santo Niño to protect them and ask that nothing bad should happen in their families. 1294. The Santo Niño, too, is invited to visit private homes. Sometimes he shows up in the same house as the Sr. del Buen Viaje from Defay. This is the only large celebration that they have in the community of Progreso. All the other masses that they have are just to worship the image, and for people to baptize their babies, or for weddings of those men and women who want to unite their destinies. The cemetery is located to the west of the church. That is where they bury the people from the community. They also celebrate the Day of the Dead in this village. The people remember their departed relatives and await their coming. They go to the cemetery and bring candles to light and flowers to put on the graves where their relatives are buried.

1296. Not far from this spot, in the same community of Progreso, there is another church, known as La Capilla (The Chapel). There is a virgin there known as the Virgen de La Soledad. People have a lot of faith in her, and many worship her. The Virgin is in a showcase, and that is where she remains. 1297. People worship the Virgen de La Soledad because they say she makes miracles and cures the sick. Sometimes a sick person will undergo a cleansing over the entire body with a new candle. Then, the candle is brought to where the Virgin is and is lit. Other times, the cleansing is done with money, and the money is brought to her and left in her church, or, better, said, in the house where she lives.

1298. She is the other virgin that is invited around to the homes in the valley. Sometimes she is invited to come by herself, and other times the Sr. del Buen Viaje, who is in Defay, is invited to be at someone's house at the same time so that both santitos can be offered flowers and candles. La Soledad is invited to houses farther away. Those who carry her go on foot because they want her to forgive the sins of those who carry her and those who await her. 1299. People are always coming to where she lives, in Progreso, to leave her things they have promised. They offer flowers, or they leave money. The person who receives the money is in charge of taking care of the Virgin. How is the money spent? I have no knowledge of that. The other communities invite the Virgin when they celebrate their traditional fiestas.

1300. From this community one can go to another called El Mandó. It is not far from the one we just saw because it borders on Progreso. The church there is also large, and looks like the ones in Progreso and Los Remedios, too. 1301. The image that they worship in El Mandó is a print of the Virgin of Guadalupe, whose fiesta is on December 12th. A band is hired for this fiesta, as well as fireworks makers. They, too, select the day for the celebration of this fiesta, as do other communities we have seen. If the fiesta falls on a Monday, then they do not celebrate it on that day, but postpone it until Tuesday. People prefer fiestas to be on Thursdays because they believe this to be the best day of the week, the "good luck day."

1302. In this pueblo also, they take on padrinos when they are going to bless something that will be placed before the Virgin. It may be a cloth, something to cover her head, or it may be for some repair done to the church. Mayordomos are named each year. The mayordomos of the church and the judges serve for a year and are then replaced. The people take the Virgin out on a procession around the main streets. 1303. As the procession moves along, firecrackers are set off, and when the procession is over the castillo and torito are lit, with a slight wait between the two. The band plays almost continuously. 1304. The mayordomos usually kill chickens and goats. Some even slaughter a head of cattle to provide food for the band or for the fireworks makers, depending on who they are appointed to feed. They always do so with respect and a good heart.

1305. In the community of El Mandó there is not much maguey, and so there is no pulque either. But since the mayordomos need pulque to offer and to drink with their assistants, they go around to other pueblos and ask their acquaintances to lend them barrels of it. As for the tortillas, the woman of the house asks other women to do her the favor and make them for her. She brings them maize, of course, from which to make the tortillas, and they lend their labor. The rest of their neighbors might show up with loans, as well. These are made of their own volition, but even so, these loans must be repaid when the givers call in the debt. And when they call in the debt, the loans of pulque also have to be repaid, with something given in return for the quantities of the delicious nectar. This is the agreement the lender and borrower have made with one another.

1306. The places where the mayordomos here go to ask people for a loan of pulque are: El Espíritu, Orizabita, Boxhuada, El Saúz. Some of the people in those places have long established acquaintances; they know beforehand what the mayordomos are going to need, and they bring the pulque to them at their homes. Some lend a barrel, others lend two. When the loan is paid back, they give a dozen cuartillos of maize that has been picked clean of stones. A dozen cuartillos is the customary measure. They also lend chickens and goats. Pigs are never lent for a fiesta because the custom doesn't exist to eat pork on a religious festival.

1307. When a pig is killed, the fat is removed and is used as lard daily in the kitchen and in the celebration of the Day of the Dead. This is the celebration in which pigs are slaughtered in order to prepare tamales for the dead. 1308. The mayordomos in the irrigated zone prefer to get loans of goats that have been raised in the arid zone because they have discovered that the meat tastes better. The meat of goats raised in the irrigated zone smells of grass because they feed on green grass, while goats in the arid zone eat grass that is drier and more firm.

1309. The fiesta of the Virgin of Guadalupe is the only fiesta of the year in this pueblo. Of course, they celebrate masses when necessary, and they have floral offerings. The cemetery is not far from the church. Those who die are buried in back of the church along the base of the church walls. There must not be any room left because the burials are already rising out of the ground.

1310. If you told the people to change the location of their cemetery they would get angry. A person with the audacity to suggest they change their cemetery runs the risk of being physically attacked. There have been some serious problems in several places arising out of this issue of changing cemeteries. 1311. People believe that it is better to bury the dead close to God, and that is why they do so next to the chruch.

1312. The pueblo of Panales is one of those that borders on El Mandó to the west. From one community to the other is a walk of about seven or eight kilometers. 1313. The community of Panales is on a dry mesa of tepetate. Potable water for humans and animals reaches the community only with difficulty. It is very dry; the vegetation is characteristic of the arid zone, consisting of mesquite trees, cardones, garambullos, sangre de grado, capulines, and tunas de coyote. These are the plants that predominate. 1314. People there work as field laborers in the city of Ixmiquilpan or in other places like El Mandó, La Otra Banda, El Maye, La Reforma. These are the places close enough for the people to go and come home on a daily basis. Despite this hardship, the people there cooperate economically to get together the money to celebrate the traditional fiesta every year.

1315. This is where they celebrate the festival of Carnival every year in February. Some people dress up as women. They are really men, but they disguise themselves by putting on women's clothing. There are about ten of them.

They are all men; none are women. They put on women's blouses and stuff something in the front so they look like women. They dress up like this so that people will think that they are going around with women. 1316. Those who dress up like this are called "masqueraders." Those who dress as women put a rebozo around themselves. The masqueraders dressed as women have their hair in braids and they put on red necklaces and thus they look like they were young women. They make conversation with men and dance with them. One or two of them play a stringed instrument.

1317. Those masqueraders are very playful. They dance in the plaza. One of them is dressed all in red as if he were the Devil. The others chase after him, trying to grab hold of his tail, and they carry a switch with which to whip him. 1318. The Devil goes far off and then doubles back to where the rest of the masqueraders are dancing. Some of the masqueraders carry an armadillo. The shell of the animal is complete, as if it were alive. It has its ears, and its tail and its feet. 1319. The masquerader who is carrying it in his arms approaches some of the fiesta goers where they are dancing. He goes up to the people and forces one of them to take the armadillo and carry it on his shoulder or in his hands, saying: "here, take this because it is your little brother." When the masquerader says this, the people who are watching break into great laughter.

1320. The masqueraders may also carry an animal called a "cacomixtle." In this case, too, it is just the skin that has been stuffed with grass, so it looks like a real, live animal. Other times they carry an animal called a "mapache," or racoon, or sometimes a "tejón," or badger.[133] 1321. They catch these animals live, or they trap them when they go out hunting in the mountains. Then they skin them very carefully to remove the meat. They lay the skin out to dry in the sun. Then they sew the skin back up, stuffing the carcass with grass as they go, until it takes the shape of a live animal. Other masqueraders have stuffed a snake skin and they bring it to the fiesta where people are dancing.

1322. They like to see the fiesta goers dancing and jumping around. They go up and down, from one to the next, goading the fiesta goers and saying all kinds of things. Nothing they do or say makes them ashamed because they are wearing masks and they disguise their voices, as well. 1323. No one hires the masqueraders; no one pays them anything. They go around at the fiesta entirely on their own because what they do on this occasion serves as fulfillment of a vow they have made. One of the mayordomos might give them something to eat. This is not because the mayordomos are cheapskates. No, it is because it has been the custom for a long time that the masqueraders do not want to cause any inconvenience as far as meals are concerned.

1324. All the customary things go on in the church. There is a mass, and the firecrackers go off. When the mass begins, about four dozen firecrackers are lit, and as the mass moves along there are more bursts of three and five dozen. Right in the middle of the mass, two dozen are set off at the same time. The mass continues and the person who has been put in charge of the firecrackers sets off bursts of three and four dozen, and when the mass ends he lights another three dozen.

1325. Flowers are brought to the church by the pilgrims, some in boughs and some in large wooden bowls carried by those who will make the offering. Arches have been built in the street so that the procession can pass through in the evening with the images. A band is hired, along with fireworks makers. One castillo is lit on the day of vespers and one on the actual day of the fiesta, and there are toritos, too. 1326. The people in this place have the custom of decorating the arches with cucharilla which they bring from the mountains. The priest does baptisms and weddings and offers first communion. Not many people from other parts come to the fiesta of this place. Possibly the image is not very miraculous and that is why a lot of people don't gather. Nor does one hear much about this santito around the valley. It doesn't go out visiting other villages and no one invites it to their home. They celebrate just one fiesta a year in this village.

1327. The pueblo of Ignacio López Rayón borders on the north of Panales. There are a lot of Catholic people in López Rayón, too, and they celebrate a traditional fiesta here once a year. It is not a very big celebration. They chip in just enough to hold the mass and, in general, it is not known who are the mayordomos for the fiesta. They don't hire a band or fireworks makers. The fiesta lasts for only one day, and the mass offered by the priest is just about all there is. The church was built by the people of the village, and inside the church there are no adornments. 1328. The people here, too, are very poor because there are only arid plots of land. The vegetation consists of mesquites, tunas de coyote, and cardones. The community suffers from lack of potable water. 1329. They take the image that they worship out on a procession, but they don't go very far, just to the door of the church. Also, there are not many streets for them to go around in a procession.

1330. From here we must walk a little to the north, about three kilometers, and we come to a small village whose inhabitatants are hard workers. The people there are united, and they help each out in solving really difficult problems by offering one another labor on a person-to-person and family-to-family basis. They also cooperate fully in the faenas to build new rooms for the

Those masqueraders are very playful
Religion 1317

school and to build a road. 1331. The adults of the community, men and women, and sometimes children, seek work in the irrigated zone. Most of them work as day laborers on farms; they work with horses as teamsters or plowmen. They do this because there is no water in their own community to enable them to work their small parcels of land.

1332. Others, principally young men and young women, go to work in Mexico City and return home every weekend to visit their families. In this community, everyone works; no one is useless. The elderly, both men and women, go to the mountains to tend flocks. They are out there all day and they don't return until evening. When a serious problem arises, the people come together immediately to see how they can best solve it by diplomatic means, and do not respond violently. 1333. They have had a lot of problems regarding the borders of their lands. They border on the community of Portezuelo, a community that has wanted to invade the small land holdings of Dexto. Though they have argued for many years before the authorities, the people of Portezuelo have seen that they cannot take over by violence what is not theirs.

1334. Many times they have tried to provoke the people of Dexto to take them on. That is, the people of Portezuelos have tried to get those of Dexto into a brawl so that they would have an excuse to go to the authorities and make away with the land. But they have not been successful because the people of Dexto understand that this is not the road to follow. Though they seem meek, they really know how to respect their fellow man. And so, in a community like this, where there is unity, it is impossible to provoke them into doing something bad. 1335. In the community of Dexto, when they name a judge and he starts to carry out justice, the people respect him and obey him. It is not like in other communities where the people reject authority. When they call for a meeting at a certain hour, that's the time when the people show up.

1336. The changeover of authorities in this community follows the same plan as in the other communities we have seen. Every year they appoint new judges, but the mayordomos are appointed every three years. The santito that they worship in Dexto is called San Pedro. It is made of plaster and is not very tall, possibly reaching 80 centimeters. 1337. The church is small. It is one of those generally referred to as a chapel, but it has a small steeple, about 1.7 meters high. The people in this region are very devout Catholics. On the day of the vespers, the priest celebrates mass, and he celebrates mass again the next day, the day of the fiesta. This is where one can see that the majority of the people in the village turn out.

1338. The santito is taken out on a procession at night, though he doesn't go very far, just around the chapel. There is no band hired for this fiesta, just a group of string musicians who accompany the procession, playing songs. A torito is set off on the day of the fiesta. The person who carries it goes up and down, running all around. It is always an adult who does it. The fiesta goers laugh at his antics because he jumps and runs around and everywhere he goes there is fire sprinkling out of him and firecrackers attached to him are going off. 1339. The torito is set off when the procession is over. The carolers from the village accompany the procession. Everyone does what they have been assigned to do for the occasion, and they do it willingly. One of the mayordomos sets up a temporary hut on one side of the church where cooks prepare food for the people who attend the fiesta.

1340. The mayordomos here are not stingy. They are right there at the fiesta, preparing the food—not just one of them, but around four persons who chip in and get everything needed. They put in animals, like goats and chickens. Sometimes they are the richer folk, and if they don't have goats, then they slaughter a head of beef to make sure that everyone who comes has enough to eat. The women of the community help out in the kitchen. This is a form of loaned labor, because when it is their husbands' time to take on the cargo, they will invite the woman whom they are now helping to come to their house and return the favor.

1341. On the day of vespers, the mayordomos are found in the hut; they stay there all night and the next day, and then again the next night. They return home on the third day, the last of the fiesta. They serve everyone who enters the hut until they are full and satisfied, and they give their guests an itacate to take home. 1342. If a visitor does not finish his food, the mayordomos wrap it up so he can take it home, because if he leaves it behind, then the family who invited him feels badly, as if their food had been rejected for not being good enough.

1343. It is one thing to give someone food to eat right away. Later, they are given more chunks of meat and another pile of tortillas to take home. People who know the custom come prepared, bringing a sack to carry their itacate. It is customary to give women as well as men their itacate. The amount of food in the itacate depends on how much the mayordomo has to offer. 1344. No one is discriminated against; everyone is given his or her itacate. For this courtesy, everyone is treated alike. All day and all night the mayordomos serve food. This is why they have to kill so many animals, so that there will be enough for everyone. 1345. Getting up after the overnight in the hut, the mayordomos serve again. The food they have is rice and thin noodles[134] which have first been fried in lard. After frying, water is added, and spices, and it is left to boil. When it is cooked it can be served.

1346. After midday, on the day after the overnight, the changeover takes place. The mayordomos for the next year's fiestas have been named previously at another meeting, and so the people of the village know who they will be. 1347. The mayordomos who will turn over their posts, who are leaving, report to the new mayordomos on the amount of charity money they have collected. This is the moment when everyone gathers around to hear how much has been collected. At the same time, they also see all the things having to do with the santito, whether everything is in order or not. They have to make sure that what is delivered is the same as what the mayordomos received the previous year.

1348. After the money is turned over, the old mayordomos put the keys, to both the church and the house in which the alms are kept, in the hands of the new ones. As the changeover takes place, the bells ring and firecrackers go off. Everything that happens that day is done with proper respect and nothing is done in a disorderly manner. 1349. The outgoing mayordomos have prepared a large basket of twelve cuartillo capacity, filled with bottles of liquor, bread, chocolates, and fruit. The new mayordomos are called up to receive the baskets in the courtyard of the chapel. They are called up by the outgoing mayordomos. The baskets full of gifts are there, laid out on a large, new petate.

1350. The rest of the folks are there admiring what the mayordomos of the fiesta are doing. The participants in the ceremony, the outgoing and the incoming mayordomos, kneel on the petate, taking their leave, and offering their hand. This is done by all the men and their wives as well. When the ceremony of saying goodbye is over, the outgoing mayordomos present the baskets with the gifts to the incoming mayordomos to take home with them. 1351. When all this is done, the assistants of the outgoing mayordomos take out bottles of liquor that they have helped to buy, and pour first for those who are taking over and then for other adults, men and women, who are there at the time. They also give out various kinds of breads. Those who drink a lot of liquor get very drunk.

1352. Once the gifts have been given out, the new mayordomos take the box that contains the santito's clothes. They take it to the house of the first mayordomo. There are four mayordomos; one is named responsible and the others are his assistants. 1353. The people carrying the box, or trunk, go to the house of the principal mayordomo. They don't go alone; they have hired string musicians to accompany them as they all go to deliver the trunk. At the house more aguardiente and pulque is given out. Pulque is served to those who like pulque. Then the new mayordomo starts to serve the meal that has been prepared. By this time it is supper. Here is where the whole fiesta of Dexto comes to an end.

1354. Of course, there have been loans. Many people in this community like to make loans, and so there are many people at the house of a mayordomo. Though the people of Dexto are very kind folks, the santito does not go out to any other pueblo. As was said a moment ago, the people are very devout

Catholics. Those who have contemplated converting to Protestantism have been punished very harshly. 1355. The members of the community call a meeting and call in those who are becoming Protestants, and they question them to find out if what they have heard is true. But the converts never want to admit it. They protest, saying that the others are liars. From this moment, the others in the village spy on them to find out where they are going all the time.

1356. Once, there were some men, about four of them, who were going around with Protestants from the community of Fitzi. That is where the people who were following them found them. At the time they said nothing to them, but came back and told the pueblo authorities. A few days later there was a meeting of the village and the novice Protestants were asked why they were doing this, why they were deceiving their fellow villagers. 1357. A lot of men at the meeting got angry and scolded the Protestants very harshly. Though they were treated like this, still the people who were in the other religion did not want to leave their pueblo. On the contrary, they went every day to the church of the Protestants, though they were advised not to do so. Despite being counseled against it, they did not obey, and so the people got together once again one Sunday—the same neighbors who had reprimanded them before—and they sent three local constables to bring those men in by force, because the new Protestants did not want to come on their own.

1358. It was about six in the morning on that day, which was an unforgettable one for them. The man who was the most angry about being brought in, and who was the most vociferous about it, was tied to a tree and made to drink urine which had been put in a liquor bottle. They did this to this man because he had been a big pulque drinker before becoming a Protestant. There were days when he was totally drunk, and when he went to the church of the "little brothers" he started telling everyone that he didn't drink pulque any more, or aguardiente, either. 1359. That is why they made him drink urine. Whose urine was it? I could not know; those who gave it to him to drink surely know. The companions of the man were just whipped because they recanted and promised that they would not return to the Protestant religion.

1360. Those who promised to forget their association with the Protestants continued to live in the pueblo, but those who decided to change their religion had to abandon their house and land to go forever to live with their co-religionists in Fitzi. It has been some years now since they left and they have not been back to their natal land. They know that if they return they will be ridiculed, and that is where trouble starts. 1361. The people there know that the law sides with letting each person practice the religion that appears best to them. But the people in this community don't want anyone dividing them and they want everyone to practice one religion. They also want everyone who is of citizen age to fulfill cargo obligations of mayordomos. No one there sits and does nothing; they all work.

1362. The community of Dexto participates in the life of the city of Ixmiquilpan. The people from Dexto build and install an arch on the 7th of September, which is the date of the great procession that we talked about. It is the final day of the fiesta that begins in August and is known as The Cloistering of El Sr. de Jalpa. The authorities, in cooperation with the mayordomos of the village, let the people know when the date approaches, so that they can get together and figure out how much each must pay to buy the firecrackers and the flowers. 1363. All the men work together to build the arch, and then each brings a piece of it to Ixmiquilpan and set it up around five in the afternoon. They set up the arch every year, and it is like a vow from the community of Dexto being fulfilled. 1364. The community does not have a cemetery. When one of them dies, the body is taken to Ignacio López Rayón, since Dexto belongs politically to that pueblo and is a barrio of it and is part of its jurisdiction.

1365. In prior days, the people of Dexto used to gather in López Rayón for their changeover meetings to appoint the new judges and the mayordomos of the church. In other words, López Rayón lent its public services to Dexto. But as years passed, the people of Dexto thought that it would be better if they had their own school, for example, so that the children would not have so far to go. 1366. The school is, in fact, the only public service that has separated from López Rayón. The cemetery function has not separated, and the people from Dexto still go to López Rayón to bury their dead. When the people of López Rayón want to do something in the cemetery, they call on the people of Dexto to fall in and help out.

1367. The people of Dexto, of course, worship their dead on the appointed day. They buy their things in Ixmiquilpan, and the first things they buy are candles and incense. Some people buy those things two weeks before the celebration, so that when the day comes they won't have to be walking on the highway.

1368. From Dexto we can walk on the footpath that traverses the side of the mountain called Cerro Grande on the north. Then we descend and come to the Tula River again, part of which serves as a border between Dexto and the pueblo of San Juanico. 1369. There is no bridge on this part of the river for the people to cross. At least, there is no fixed bridge made of cement. There is a hanging bridge, but most of the people have to go through the water to cross the river. The hanging bridge is constructed of two steel cables that have been strung from one side to the other and lashed to the base of a sabino tree.[135] The top part, where people step, has been laid athwart with wood poles so that the cables are held together. The toughest poles are used, and in some spots there are planks. The wood is lashed to the parallel cables along their entire length and this is what is known as a "hanging bridge." Bridges made of cement are called simply "bridges."[136]

1370. There are also other roads that lead to San Juanico. One of these comes from San Nicolás and another leads off from a part of Los Remedios. The church of San Juanico is in the center of the village. It is a large church, with a tower and hanging bells. 1371. The traditional fiesta of the pueblo is celebrated on June 24th. Here, as in other communities, if the fiesta falls on a "good day," then it is celebrated on that day, but if not, then it is postponed. 1372. The image that is worshipped is known by the name San Juan. Many people from Xochitlán, Los Remedios and San Nicolás come to attend this festival. Some of those who come from Xochitlán bring ears of maize to sell because this is the season when the maize starts to mature. Maize plants yield ears in the irrigated zone. In the other areas the prickly pears start to ripen and these are the fruits that some merchants bring to sell. 1373. They bring the ears raw and boil them there at the fiesta, and the fiesta goers buy them to eat.

Let's go back and see what is done in the church. On the day of vespers the merchants come from various parts to set up their stalls with things to sell. A band is hired, along with fireworks makers. 1374. The band arrives for vespers. It remains the entire afternoon and evening at the door of the church playing songs. There are mayordomos who have been assigned to this, and they give the musicians food to eat when they finish playing. The mayordomos also pay the cost of hiring the band. 1375. Some mayordomos slaughter a beef in order to feed the musicians, while others kill chickens and goats. Other mayordomos are named separately to take care of the castillo and torito makers.

1376. Of the two groups of mayordomos, those in charge of the music pay the most because there are many musicians and only a few pyrotechnists. The musicians go to the church very early to play greetings for the santito. They are accompanied by others from San Juanico who carry strings of flowers. The musicians start playing mañanitas. The people who are with the band start to sing. Then, when they finish singing, the mayordomos open the church door and enter to light candles and worship the santito San Juan. 1377. The priest comes at midday to celebrate mass. Those who have come to hear mass are there since the morning. There are women, men and children. Older people believe more in religion. The priest performs baptisms, hears confession, and offers first communion.

1378. If the people or the mayordomos have agreed to make some kind of benediction, then written invitations are sent out to the padrinos who are asked to come to the place where the benediction will be made. In the evening, or more precisely, at night, the mayordomos organize to take the santito out on a procession. The procession does not go far; it just goes around the little streets there, and then goes back to the church. 1379. Here too, they have the custom of making floral offerings, and vows of escamadas. The castillo and the toritos are lit at the end of the procession. The day after the fiesta there is another mass. This is where one can see that those who have kept the vigil all night have a hard time keeping their eyes open. The band is there, playing continuously because they are just about to complete their contractual obligation and will soon leave. They finish around two in the afternoon. They are brought their pay and then the mayordomos leave and walk a short distance to their homes.

1380. On June 24th, which is the day of San Juan, some women cut off the tip of their braids. There is a belief that if a woman cuts the ends off her hair on that day, then her hair will multiply and grow back even longer. 1381. It is not just adult women who have their hair cut; it is also done to little girls four and five years old. Men do not customarily cut their hair on this date, just women. 1382. The part they cut is just the ends. They cut off about four fingers in length. For this they ask someone who is known to have good hands. People who have "good hands" are those who do not get angry easily, do not fight a lot, and do not look for trouble. This goes for men as well as women.

1383. Now one can cross the mountain that abuts the pueblo of San Juanico to the west and follow the footpaths. Although there are footpaths, the route is very rough because it is full of big rocks and thorny thistles. Still, it is the most direct route to Juchitlán. The community is located on a slope that faces west and is exposed to the sun. They celebrate a traditonal fiesta in this pueblo also. 1384. They worship La Santa Cruz (The Holy Cross) there on September 14th. They hire a band there, too, and take the image out on a procession. Many folks from Tasquillo attend the fiesta in Juchitlán because Tasquillo is not far. 1385. There is a castillo and a torito. The people of this place are very nice, and so they have a lot of acquaintances who come to their fiesta on that date. The members of the Juchitlán community lend each other maize, tortillas, and animals.

1386. The sellers of pulque come from La Lagunita, El Naxtey, La Palma, El Ojo de Agua, Orizabita, El Dexthi. They come to this place to sell their product. Sometimes, when they sell their pulque wholesale, in bulk, they just turn around and go back home. But when they sell it a little at a time, they go from house to house offering their pulque to those who like to drink it. Because of this, the people of Juchitlán know many people who live to the east of them. 1387. The mayordomos of the fiesta invite some sellers of pulque to visit them on the day that it is their turn to provide food. What the mayordomos really want, of course, is for the pulque sellers to bring them pulque as a loan. Then, when the man who lends the pulque needs the loan repaid, he will invite the person from Juchitlán to reciprocate the visit. In this case, it is not to pay back with pulque. The man from Juchitlán will repay the loan with maize, and he will bring it to the house of his friend.

1388. This is where those of Juchitlán get really tired, because there are no roads for them to travel, just winding and narrow paths. They have to cross deep valleys, and go over mountains and hills and precipitous slopes. But, according to them, none of this is any obstacle. The important thing is not to lose face with the friend with whom they have begun relations. When it is like this, and both are good to their word, then they have confidence in each other on other occasions. Otherwise, they abandon the relationship and know where not to go for a favor in the future.

It is necessary to note that we are now in the jurisdiction of the Municipio of Tasquillo. 1389. From here we return again and follow the road that begins in Ixmiquilpan. We head west and find another community known as Portezuelo. One turns off towards Portezuelo at a "Y" in the road at a place called Barranca Honda. The fork to the right goes through Tasquillo and on to Zimapán and beyond. 1390. This community is well known in the Mezquital Valley, as well as in other parts further away, because in the church in the center of the village there is an image which the people of Portezuelo worship. And not just them, but people who live far away from there, as well. 1391. Since long ago, it is believed that the santito there is the most miraculous and is the savior who intervenes to keep evil away from those who have faith in him. 1392. They say that the Santo Niño there is a likeness of Jesus Christ when he was a baby. The people there have given him the name El Niño de Portezuelo, and they celebrate two fiestas a year there.

1393. The first fiesta is on December 24th, the date dedicated especially to this celebration. The pilgrims begin to arrive about three days before the day of vespers, and they stay there for a week. Every day the church is filled with pilgrims. Whole families come. Some people come on foot, others on horseback, walking all day and at night, too. 1394. They come to leave what they have promised to the Santo Niño. Some of them carry boughs of flowers, others bring beautiful escamadas, and still others bring garlands of flowers in large wooden bowls to the Santo Niño as an offering. Some pilgrims have nothing to give the Santo Niño, while others come with animals which they leave there as they promised; they bring ewes, female goats, and chickens. 1395. Those from the pueblo tell how the Santo Niño has his own flock, made up of ewes and female goats, and that a shepherd whom he has appointed takes care of them.

1396. Inside the church the mayordomos practically don't stop taking in money as alms and giving out relics to the pilgrims. The amount varies. Some people give a peso, others five pesos, and there are some who give hundreds of pesos. The people push and shove each other in their desire to approach and worship the Santo Niño, and all the pilgrims can not fit inside the church. Many stand ouside the church, and others go around in the plaza while they wait for the crowd to diminish in the church so that they can get in and worship the Santo Niño. 1397. The little plaza is filled with people. It is hard to move around because there are so many people and stalls and people buying things.

1398. In front of the door to the church is a group of dancers who are dressed up especially for this occasion. The clothing they wear looks lovely. The entire suit is decorated. They wear a kind of cap on their head, and it is decorated with feathers of different colors. No one hires the dancers to appear; they just come on their own to fulfill their promise to God. The group is made up of women and children who are dancing. 1399. Sometimes only one group comes, and other times there are two or three and they take turns dancing in front of the door to the church. The dancers don't return home right away; they stay there during the entire fiesta.

1400. Those attending the fiesta come from far away, and plan on staying two or three days. They look for a spot in the plaza, spread their petate that they carry with them, and lay down to sleep. The Santo Niño is taken out on a procession. It is not heavy because it is a small statue; it barely reaches 40 centimeters in height, and it is in a small showcase. Many pilgrims accompany him on the procession. All, or nearly all, carry a candle. This is their promise to God. Some buy the candle, while others buy the wax and ask someone to make the candle for them. Or they buy the candle from someone who has his own bee hive so that they will get pure wax and not the mixed kind that has been melted down and formed into blocks. 1401. When the procession is over, the Santo Niño and the procession go back into the church. The people continue to worship the image, and those who have recently arrived deliver the money they are offering. The musicians continue to play songs, staying at the front of the church. The Santo Niño is put back in his usual place and then the torito is lit, and then the castillo.

1402. In the mountains, and out on the open fields, the great bonfires that people have built can be seen. This is another of the many customs that have existed for so long, and the people who practice the Catholic religion continue to practice this one. They say that when Jesus Christ was born on December

The entire suit is decorated
Religion 1398

24th, it was very cold and so some shepherds helped his mother light a fire to keep the baby warm. 1403. People still maintain this tradition, and on this occasion they remember the birth of God and they light bonfires so that the baby Jesus will not die of cold. The people of Portezuelo burn bundles of cardón branches.

1404. A week after the celebration of Christmas the people of the community celebrate another fiesta, New Year's. This fiesta is celebrated in much the same way as Christmas. A band is hired, along with fireworks makers. Since this fiesta is celebrated in many places, there are not so many pilgrims as at the previous one. In many communities they have a fiesta in which they bid goodbye to the old year, and welcome the new one. 1405. Many of those who attend this fiesta were not there on the day of the fiesta for the Santo Niño, so they show up the next day, New Year's Day, to worship the santito. Bonfires are also lit on this occasion in other communities and in Portezuelo. 1406. The largest number of bonfires is lit for New Year's. Anyone who did not light a big fire for Christmas lights one now.

1407. There is a saying about bonfires: "Anyone who does not light bonfires, when he dies and goes to another life, God punishes him by turning him into a dung beetle." 1408. A lot of people still believe in this saying, and this makes them set fire to any wood or garbage they can find, or even to stacks of bushes. It is sad when they set fire to plants like this, because the vegetation gets used up and this leaves the valley more desolate than it is already by being arid. Then, when rain falls and the land is denuded of plants, it erodes the land and all that's left are piles of rocks. These are the two fiestas celebrated in Portezuelo, practically together in one continuous festival. After these, no other fiesta is celebrated during the year.

1409. The Santo Niño of Portezuelo is said to be very miraculous and that is why so many pilgrims follow him, especially those of the Catholic faith. The people say that the santito saves and cures those who have faith, who take him into their conscience, who await him at their homes, who pay for a mass in his honor, and who bring him floral offerings. 1410. The santito of Portezuelo, the Virgin of Soledad, the santito of Buen Viaje of Defay, and the Virgin of Los Remedios are the ones that people invite the most to visit them in their homes. There are times when the Santo Niño of Portezuelo is invited to someone's home for two or three days and he winds up staying for a week. Sometimes they invite both the Santo Niño and the Virgin of Soledad, or they invite the santito of Orizabita, located in Defay, and the Virgin of Los Remedios.

1411. The people believe that misfortune comes to anyone who does not worship the Santo Niño and other images as they should be worshipped. If they invite the images to their homes and promise to receive them, and then if they don't follow through on their promise, something bad will happen to them. 1413. When these images and the virgin come to someone's house for a visit, a certain amount of money is always collected. Those who come to the house to worship the images leave alms. They are invited to come and see the images by those who have invited those santitos to their homes.

1414. Of the four images mentioned, the one that gets the most money is the Santo Niño of Portezuelo. What happens to the money? Probably those who know best are the mayordomos, because they are the ones into whose hands the money is put. 1415. When the Santo Niño is invited to another pueblo, such as Espíritu, for example, the people who come to fetch the image have to carry it back. They come on foot and they return on foot, carrying the santito. They are accompanied by a string band that plays songs along the way. Those who do the carrying rest a moment so they won't get too tired.

1416. Continuing, we will now look at another small community in the Municipio of Tasquillo. The community is called Rinconada. They celebrate a fiesta to honor the Santo Niño there, too, just as they do in Portezuelo. 1417. The fiesta begins on the last night of December and ends on the first day of the new year, which is the main day of the celebration. The last day of the fiesta is the overnight to the second of January, and by then it is fully into the new year. In a celebration of this nature, there is, of course, a mass, celebrated by a priest. 1418. In Rinconada the priest celebrates mass at midnight, and then again the next day, the day of the fiesta, at midday. A band is hired, along with fireworks makers. It doesn't cost a lot, because there are not many men of citizen age who can chip in the money.

1419. The church in Rinconada is not large; it is one of those that are called "chapels." Even so, people worship their santito as they ought to, with all their souls. Women and children come to the fiesta. At this time of year it is cold, and they still are there at the fiesta, because this is the only fiesta they have, and there is no other during the rest of the year. 1420. They make floral offerings here, also. People bring their alms and get souvenir relics to take home in return. Pulque sellers from La Lagunita, La Palma and other communities mentioned in connection with Juchitlán come to the fiesta. Some come to sell their pulque, and others have been asked to bring it as a loan. Since people know one another, there is no distrust; they accede to one another's requests.

1421. When a mayordomo invites one of his friends, he only has to do so once. One time is sufficient, and there is no need to repeat it. When a person repeats an invitation, this sets people thinking that he must be regretting having made the invitation to them in the first place. 1422. If it becomes known that someone really does regret having made an invitation, then most likely no one will go near the man's house. The people of the valley say "Regret is the friend of stinginess." Sometimes, people use these words when they are talking about loans made at some place where a meal is being given.

1423. We leave Rinconada for the moment and start along the road that passes close by there. We head over a small hill where there are mesquites, cardones, capulines de ratón. There are some rises in the terrain, and the whole way is very arid.

1424. From there we head for a place called Tasquillo. It is very nice looking because there is irrigation here. This is due to the fact that the Tula River, which goes through Ixmiquilpan, turns and crosses Tasquillo, too. The people of Tasquillo have managed to construct partitions along the ground that capture and hold the water from the river, and they irrigate their milpas with it. They don't just grow corn, either. They have planted orchards where they grow different kinds of fruit trees. 1425. Among the vegetation one can see there are many walnet trees, and they are really green. When the walnut trees produce a good crop, they are one of the economic resources of the people there. But sometimes the trees get frozen during the winter and they shrivel up, or they get hit by hail and the nuts get knocked off. When this happens, the owners lose the entire crop.

1426. The church is in the middle of the city where they keep the statue of San Bernardino whose fiesta is celebrated on the 20th of May. A band and fireworks makers are hired. 1427. One castillo is put up on the day of vespers, and another on the day of the fiesta. Two toritos are lit, as well. The priest who offers mass doesn't come from far off because he lives right there, and he is the same one who goes out among the villages in the jurisdiction of Tasquillo. 1428. The band is up on what is called a "quiosco," or gazebo, playing songs. They are called to the church when mass is said, and they accompany the procession when it leaves the church.

1429. Not many people come to offer flowers at the church in Tasquillo. The few who come are from Motó, Tetsú, Candelaria, Juchitlán, Rinconada and other small communities that make up the Municipio of Tasquillo. 1430. The santito there is not really well regarded; it is not mentioned much as being very miraculous, and a lot of people do not congregate there, like they do in Portezuelo.

1431. From here we continue along the road that goes through Tasquillo and heads east. Not far from there is s small hill where the community of Candelaria is located. 1432. There is a small, chapel-like church there, and that is where the

Virgin of Candelaria is also. She is worshipped by the people there and her fiesta is February 2nd every year. 1433. This fiesta of Candelaria is also called La Bendición de la Vela, or The Blessing of the Candle, and this is when they do the blessing of the maize seed as well. On the day of the fiesta, the priest celebrates mass around eleven in the morning. People arrive from early in the morning, men and women, bringing seed with them. They put ears of corn in a basket, along with beans, and calabaza seeds, and all manner of seeds that they are planning to plant that year.

1434. The baskets are decorated. They put flowers on top of the seed, and two or three candles are crossed on top of that. These are the ones that will be blessed, and that is why the fiesta is called the "blessing of the candle." 1435. The priest begins by celebrating mass. When the mass begins, the mayordomos set off firecrackers. The thundering noise is very loud, and the mountains nearby make an echo. 1436. Everyone who has brought corn seed sits or kneels in front, near to where the priest is officiating. When he finishes mass, he starts to pray over all the baskets of seeds that have been laid out on the floor, and he sprinkles holy water on them. This is the blessing that they give for seeds. When the benediction is over, all those who have brought baskets collect them, and they head back to their homes.

1437. Now that they have been blessed, the seeds are stripped from the ears of corn and mixed with the rest of the seed they will plant. Suppose they are going to plant twelve cuartillos of seed; they mix the blessed seed into the whole batch. They do this with all their seed; that is, they mix the blessed seed with the maize, beans and squash that has not been blessed. 1438. When one has seed blessed by a priest, it is no problem to mix the blessed seed with the unblessed. Not many days pass before the campesino people begin to plant. This is in the irrigated zone; the only thing they need is for the cold season to pass.

1439. Some campesinos begin to plant during the first days of March. If it doesn't freeze again after that, then they will be the first to reap a harvest in July. But if a freeze comes when the plants are small, or even when they are big, then they die. When this happens, the campesino must plant again. If the freeze did not totally finish off the plants, then only those that were really killed have to be replanted. Those that were just singed by the freeze can be left to continue their development. 1440. Before starting to plant, the campesino crosses himself, whether he is the owner of a field, or just someone who is working it for someone else. Everyone does the same thing. This is to ask God to help make the planting successful. The poor people who live where there is no irrigation also bring their seed in to be blessed. For them, this is just on a bet, because they do not know if it will continue to rain or not. If a good rain comes, they quickly secure a pair of plow animals, either horses or oxen, to work fast before the moisture in the earth dries up.

1441. The people in the arid zone plant maize, along with beans and squash between the rows. When it rains they want to plant everything because it it not always possible to get a harvest out of this arid earth. Others plant sage.[137] Everyone who plants a crop in the arid zone can lose everything easily if it doesn't continue to rain. 1442. A lot of people who plant gardens do it out of tradition because they are not really sure if they will get a harvest. That is why they always ask God to help them make the planting successful. It is important to note that the plots of land are not just planted on any day, but that the most appropriate day is chosen. Friday is the day least accepted by the people, and we have already seen the reason behind this. 1443. A good day is chosen; that is, a day when the moon is good for planting seed. There is nothing special about the sun, as there is about the moon. The field laborer and the campesino[138] pay attention to the phases of the moon, especially the new moon. They believe that it is not good to plant during this phase because, according to what they have observed, corn plants will grow tall and leafy, but the ears don't develop.

1444. Another belief the campesinos have is that if they plant while the moon is young, then the corn that does come up will not last long in the bin, but will get eaten up quickly by insects. Another belief is that if one plants when the moon is full, then the corn bears many ears and does not easily get eaten by insects in storage, but lasts until the next planting. 1445. This belief is not just for planting seeds, but for other activities, too, like the planting of maguey[139] or the cutting of a tree trunk for house supports. 1446. A lot of work in the milpas is done according to the moon so that there will be good planting of seeds or a tree. Also, workers do not forget to thank God, because people believe that God in heaven governs the sun, the wind and the rain.

1447. The Virgin of Candelaria is also believed to be very miraculous, and those who believe this the most are the field workers and campesinos. A fiesta is held for her in several communities, not only in the Mezquital Valley, but in other parts of Mexico, especially where there are people who practice the Catholic religion. 1448. The people spend a lot of money to celebrate the fiesta of the Virgin, as we have seen. A band is hired, along with castillo makers in order to venerate her, because it is believed that she is very miraculous and that she cures the sick.

1449. From Candelaria we move to another municipio called Alfajayucan. Therefore, we return from Candelaria along the same road we came in on, towards Portezuelo. Not far from there, after walking about a kilometer, we come to the community of "X<u>ug</u>i".[140] 1450. This village is in the municipio of Alfajayucan. It is situated on very arid land, mostly tepetate, and dust devils are whipped up whenever the wind blows there. 1451. The church there is small, but despite that it attracts many pilgrims. The image they worship there is called San Isidro Labrador. They say that the saint went around on earth and worked like any other man, but that he was a very good person who looked out for his fellow man, and therefore God in heaven took him to his side. That is, God made him a god also, and now he is an apostle or emissary.

1452. The fiesta is celebrated in Xugi on May 15th, as in other places where they worship this saint and hold the fiesta on the same date. 1453. In the entire Mezquital Valley, the largest celebration for this saint is in this community. The mayordomos are appointed to provide food for the musicians and the fireworks makers. 1454. Many pilgrims come to the fiesta. Some come to make floral offerings, while others come to leave alms. Others attend as spectators only, and don't enter the church. They celebrate mass here at midday. A lot of people come to hear mass, but because the church is so small, they don't all fit and many listen from outside. 1455. The mayordomos have put flowers in front of the altar where the image of San Isidro is located. The mayordomos' assistants have brought along the firecrackers to light. 1456. The priest gives the blessing during the mass to whoever asks for it; he also does baptisms, marries couples who have decide to join their futures, and offers first communion. Communion is only given to those who have been confessed. The celebration in Xugi has a very special character.

1457. It is said that San Isidro Labrador worked in the fields, and because of this the field laborers, campesinos, and plowmen have chosen this santito to be their protector. He is the saint of the campesinos and also of cattle. 1458. On this date, all cattle, large and small, are venerated. Flowers are tied in necklaces around their necks, and firecrackers are bought to light in their honor. But who knows whether the cattle are happy, like people are when they celebrate their birthdays.

1459. On this day, cowboys make a special point of giving their animals fodder and grasses and all the food that they usually eat. The plowmen show up in the plaza before the mass. They have brought in their animals, yoked together as if they were going to plant a field or plough up fallow land. 1460. They put a flower necklace on each of their oxen. At this time of year, orchids begin to bloom, and this is what they put on them and make into a necklace. A clarification: the pair comes yoked, but not dragging a plow. This is left in the cattle corral. 1461. Some pairs of oxen are brought into the cemetery, like they were going to hear mass. A teamster watches over them because otherwise they start fighting, pair against pair. About twenty pairs of oxen come to the mass and then they go out on the procession.

1462. Some pairs of oxen wait in the cemetery, while others remain outside, awaiting the procession. When the priest finishes celebrating mass, he comes out and goes over to where the oxen are. He prays over them, blesses them, and sprinkles holy water on them. When the priest finishes all this, the mayordomos organize themselves. They take the saint off the altar and put him on his pedestal so that they can carry him and go out on the procession. 1463. The priest finishes the mass and returns to Alfajayucan, while the residents of Xu̱gi go on with the procession. At the head of the parade is the saint San Isidro Labrador. Then there are the pilgrims who have come to the fiesta, and then the band, and finally the oxen. The cows or bulls move along behind, bellowing. The reader should not think that they are praying, because bulls don't know what it is to pray. They are bellowing because they want to fight with the others, since they don't know each other very well, and don't see one another often.

1465. They see each other once a year and get to know one another. The next year, when they come back together, they meet others, and not the same ones as the year before. Sometimes they get loose and overpower the ploughmen and then they start fighting with other bulls. Then, the fiesta goers who are following the procession must get out of the way. When this happens, the men quickly rope the animals and yoke them together again so that they will follow the procession. 1466. Bulls act more or less like dogs. When they meet up at a fiesta or some other place, then if they do not know one another beforehand, they start biting. Two of them may start up, and pretty soon there are seven or eight of them going at it, and you can't tell which is helping which to beat the others.

The procession in Xu̱gi lasts about three hours because it goes in a big circle after it leaves the church. Firecrackers are set off along the way, and it takes nearly the whole afternoon; they leave the church around two o'clock and return around five. 1467. Ermitas are set up along the way so that those carrying the santito can sit for a moment. They also set up arches through which San Isidro Labrador passes. The people of this village also make offerings of flowers and escamadas, which come in a steady flow.

1468. When the procession is over some of the plowmen drive their oxen homewards. Others look for some place to tie up their oxen and then they go to the plaza to drink pulque. They find many people at the plaza who have set up stalls with things to sell. There is no procession at night, only during the day. At night, people who go to the fiesta just for the castillo and the toritos. 1469. During the day, from eight in the morning until noon, firecrackers can be heard going off in various places. What is happening at those moments is that people are putting flower necklaces on their cattle. They ask God for their animals to be "good cattle"— that is to say, that they work hard in the fields, and that a bull not attack his master, or the plowman, or the children who come around where the animals are tied up.1470. When a bull turns bad one seeks a butcher to sell it to.

In the whole Mezquital Valley, the community of Xugi is the only one where they allow people to bring bulls to stand in front of the church. This does not happen in other places; they just make flower necklaces for the bulls on the appointed day in order to honor them. 1471. Others in the valley do not simply honor bulls by making them collars. The bulls' owners prepare a meal, not for the bulls, but for themselves. They make chicken in mole and they kill a goat. So, May 15th is a big celebration in the Mezquital Valley, because they honor cattle in various places. 1472. Nobody crosses himself in front of the cattle; they just make necklaces and put them on the cattle. As for what would be the kiss, perhaps people taste it when they eat the cattle.[141]

1473. We have only come as far as Xugi, and for now we leave this arid land where the countryside turns green only when it rains. Then, the few plants bloom, and when it is not green it looks like there were no life in this place. 1474. This area is really dry. The people only get water for daily use and for drinking through a great amount of effort. Because of this, they have built traps called "jagüeyes or "reservoirs"[142] that collect rain water when it runs off the mountains and the slopes.[143] They also dig wells and get their drinking water from them. 1475. In digging wells, also, the people believe that if one worships God and has faith in him, then water will be found, and otherwise there will be nothing. When water is found, once again God is worshipped. Flowers and relics that were brought from the church are brought to the well. From what people say, this is what helps find water and also what keeps it from disappearing one day from the well.

1476. Now we leave the western part of the valley where we have been, and go back to the road we took to Portezuelos. This is the same road that goes to Xugi. We take this road now towards the south. 1477. The first community we come to is Maguey Blanco, which belongs to the Municipio of Ixmiquilpan. The boundary with the Municipio of Chilcuautla is nearby. There is another county seat there where the people of the small villages go to seek justice in the event of a problem. 1478. Anyway, the community that borders on Chilcuautla is Maguey Blanco. The area is very dry. The people have planted maguey, and a few have planted prickly pear. These are part of their small holdings. When the maguey plants are mature, they open them and take the aguamiel. They take the pulque that they make and sell it in the market at Ixmiquilpan.

1479. Other men leave the community to be field laborers in the irrigated areas nearby. The women weave ayates. They bring the ayates to Ixmiquilpan, or to the market at Mixquiahuala to sell. The market in the latter town is held on Sundays. 1480. The village is located on a small, long plain that runs more or less north and south. There are mountains on the east and west. When the hot winds blow strong[144] they create dust devils because it is hard for them to get out of the plain. 1481. Despite the aridness and the poverty these winds create, the people organize and name mayordomos to celebrate their traditional religious fiesta every year. Mayordomos are named for providing food to the musicians and the fireworks makers; mayordomos are appointed to be in charge of the masses. Sometimes a separate mayordomo is named who is in charge of buying the flowers placed on the altar of the santito.

1482. The image worshipped here is in the church. The church is large and it has a high bell tower, much like the one in Los Remedios. The statue worshipped there is Sr. de Jalpa. The mass is celebrated in the morning, and in the afternoon the image is taken out on a procession, as in the other communities we have spoke about. There are always people who bring the santito flowers. 1483. There are many images in the church of different saints and virgins. But the one who is considered the patron of the community is worshipped with more fervor. The fiesta lasts for three days. The first day is the vespers; the second is the main day of the fiesta; and the third day is the "overnight." Not many people follow the image in this village. One does not hear about this image as being very miraculous or as helping people. And so, for the moment we leave this community and continue along the road going south.

1484. We don't have to walk very far because we soon come upon a community called "Xot'i."[145] This village is also located on arid land. In place of fertile land, there is only a kind of tepetate. Despite this, the people have worked hard and have planted maguey. These are part of their holdings, along with some animals (for those who raise them, of course). Many people make ayates, men and women alike. The men work more at spinning the fiber. Wherever they go, they wear a shock of ixtle across their chests so they can spin while walking along. 1485. Those people in Xot'i also organize and name mayordomos to celebrate their traditional religious fiesta on January 6th every year. There is a church that has been built on a small tepetate hill. The door faces west.

1486. The images worshipped there are called the Santos Reyes. There are three of them called Melchior, Gaspar, and Balthasar. Copies of them have been made for the people to worship. The priest celebrates the mass at midday. The pilgrims bring their candles and light them during the mass. 1487. They don't have the custom in this place of taking the images out on a procession. Rosaries are said for them in the church; those who pray are residents of the pueblo. 1488. Those mayordomos who have been assigned to it prepare the meal for the musicians, and the others prepare the food for the fireworks makers. They also rush about attending to their visitors. The visitors bring loans to those acting as mayordomos on this occasion. 1489. The loans consist of pulque from the men and tortillas made by the women. They help each other, sometimes in groups of three, to make the tortillas.

1490. From Xot'i we continue along the same road on which we have been walking. If we wanted to, we could choose between two roads. One of them is a footpath that is more direct, going straight up over the hill to the south. But we take the road over which we came and continue over the rise known as Cocineras; we go around a bend and come to a community called Mejay. 1491. This part of the valley, and all these places, are very dry. There is nothing but tepetate, and under that there is sand. The plant life on the surface consists mostly of cardones and mesquites, and even they don't grow very big because the ground is not fertile. 1492. The mountains are very close to the village. There are no large trees on these mountains. The most prevalent plant is the chicle de piojo which only grows about a meter tall. These are the plants that make the mountains look greenish yellow. 1493. There are very few plots of farmland, and those that do exist are not worked very much because it does not rain enough.

They celebrate the traditional religious fiesta every year in Mejay December 12th. This is the date on which the Virgin of Guadalupe is venerated. 1494. There is no large church there, like those in other places. The people of the village have built a small chapel themselves where they congregate. They keep the image of the Virgin of Guadalupe there, and the priest says mass in the chapel. Not everyone can fit into the chapel, and some stand outside to hear the mass.

1495. The support for hanging the bells is a separate construction. The two bells are hung between two forked posts. One of the bells is medium sized and the other is small. The fiesta is more or less like the ones in other villages we have passed through. They hire a band and fireworks makers to set up the castillo and the toritos. The priest celebrates two masses, one on the day of vespers, and the other on the actual day of the fiesta. At night they take the Virgin out on a procession. I forgot to say that the image is a print. 1496. The only mayordomos they name are for providing food for the musicians and the castillo makers. Flutists and drummers come to this fiesta to worship the Virgin.

1497. The music that the flutists play is generally Ñähñu. Sometimes they play tunes composed by mestizos. Of course, they choose songs that are not sexually suggestive because they respect the Virgin a lot.

1498. When they do the naming of the mayordomos, the people come together in a meeting. First they see if all the adult males have already fulfilled a cargo. Some people at the gathering might not be from the village. They could come from another community, and hold some land in the jurisdiction of Mejay. In that case, they, too, can be named to fulfill a cargo. This is the custom here, and in some other communities such as Los Remedios, El Mandó, and San Juanico. Those from other communities who live in this village are asked to participate like any other citizen and to offer their service in the faenas that everyone does.

1499. When a person from some other place does not work, then he is asked to contribute money, and if he refuses, then they appropriate his land. But those who know the custom don't refuse and also accept cargos. After everyone else in the community has done cargos, then the outsiders are named again. Whether or not they have had a harvest on their land, the outsiders have to accept their turn as mayordomos. If an outsider dies and leaves his land to his sons, then they, too, must continue the custom of obeying the authorities of the community in which their departed father had his land. And if the new owner of a piece of land dies and leaves it to some other person, then the next owner must accept cargo obligations, even though the previous owner had no kinship relation with the new owner.

1500. Let's leave Mejay now and walk along the road that goes south towards the city of Tula de Allende. We are not going to that city; we will walk only four kilometers until we come to the pueblo of Tlacotlapilco. There is another church there in which a fiesta takes place every August 15th. The image that the pilgrims worship there is Sr. de Jalpa, the same one worshipped in Ixmiquilpan. The two pueblos celebrate their fiestas on the same date. 1501. The church there is large. There is a tower in which there bells are hanging that are rung with joy when they hold any celebration. The Tula River goes right passed the pueblo. It is the same river that goes through Ixmiquilpan and Tasquillo.

1502. The people of Tlacotlapilco also customarily appoint mayordomos for the celebration of the fiesta every year. They are in charge of providing food for the members of the band and for the castillo makers. The santito is taken out at night on a procession. During the day the priest celebrates mass, baptizes infants, and gives communion and first communion. 1503. No other images come to this village to visit, and neither does the image there go elsewhere. The pilgrims who come are from the surrounding communities. The image is not known for being very miraculous. It's not like in other communities where pilgrims just keep coming and coming. Tlacotlapilco is not like that, but the people of this pueblo worship their santito very much.

1504. With this village we finish discussing traditional religion. As we have seen, the people in various communities loved, worshipped, venerated, and gave their whole being to the images, whether saints or virgins, or baby Jesuses. There were no baby virgins. They don't exist because they are not mentioned in the religion of the Mezquital Valley. 1505. Many of the saints and virgins that were worshipped were made of plaster, others were drawn on paper. Stone is almost never used to make images. Stone is used only when a cross is made. Sometimes the images are painted on cloth.

1506. Some images are kept in a showcase of some kind, to preserve them, or frames are built on which they are kept. Some are not covered at all, but are just kept out, uncovered. 1507. The deep veneration and belief that people have in God and the Virgin is due to the hope that they will be granted life, health, and well-being. The people hope that God will grant them good luck and will protect them when they have to travel far from where they live. The people also pray to the images to bring rain so that they can plant and reap the production of the earth and have food to feed themselves.

1508. Sometimes one realizes that one does not know if they will ever get what they ask for, and they reflect on whether or not it is worth continuing to spend their efforts and funds on celebrating the fiestas. Other times one realizes that religion just blocks thinking and this makes one reflect on things. 1509. This happens even more when one sees that the things the pilgrims bring to the church disappear. The alms that are collected every year, for example; the money is almost never actually seen, and one does not know where it is going. We have to remember that we have talked about communities where the pilgrims leave a lot of money and the churches continue the same as always, poor in their appearance. Instead of being refurbished, they simply deteriorate more, and this is when the people think about whether what they are doing is good or not.

1510. The people have taken note of the fact that some mayordomos are looters; that is, they like to get their hands on the money for the santitos or images. Sometimes they steal the money. They are not appointed to do this, but to take care of the church. A lot of the pilgrims make great efforts to save their money, even not eating, so that they will have alms to give when they get to church. What would be their disillusionment if they knew that they were delivering their money into the hands of some unscrupulous mayordomos! When it isn't the mayordomos who take the money, it is thieves who open the door to the church and take the little money that has been collected.

1511. Religion is a touchy matter when a pueblo does not practice it as it should. Sometimes it unites a community and other times it serves only to divide it and to cause confrontations. Those responsible for what happens are the representatives of the church because they do not give proper counsel to their parishioners. They should know how to advise their flocks properly.

1512. In the narrative that follows, we will see how the Ñähñu people of the Mezquital Valley continue to celebrate the religious fiestas, how they organize cooperation among the members of a village, and how much money they spend. We will call this section Contemporary Religion. Everthing we will discuss from here on takes place after 1951 and continues until the present. And so we begin as follows.

CONTEMPORARY RELIGION

1513. Many communities continue to celebrate the fiestas just as they have traditionally. Others have forgotten, or have tried to forget, some of the customs they practiced formerly. There are pueblos that have replaced all the ceremonies they had before, and have introduced new ones. Other communities find themselves divided because many of their residents practice the religion of the Protestants, while the rest continue practicing Catholicism. 1514. The rest of the communities never practiced either kind of religion but have today opted for one of the two that exist in the region. The Protestant and the Catholic religion are the only two that are known in the the valley, and so some communities used to be "atheist," at the local level. Some of those communities have selected the Catholic religion, while others follow the Protestants. One by one, they decide on the religion that they believe is better. That is why, in some of the small villages, there are people who are Catholics but there is no church.

1515. The people in those villages try to build a small church where they put an icon or statue of a santito or virgin, whichever they think will make miracles for them. Thus, when those who follow the Protestant religion see that a community has no church—in either religion—they go in and try to advise the people of the village to adopt the Protestant faith. They have helped the people of the villages build churches. The leaders of the Protestants go abroad and acquire the materials to help build those temples. They get things like calidra, cement and steel reinforcing rods.

1516. The people in the community who are engaged in this work hurry to finish because they really need the church. Also, they are interested in getting others to join their religion. 1517. Further on we will see some small pueblos where Protestant churches are being built. Some have already been finished, while others are just now under construction. Others still are just at the discussion stage. That is, the "little brothers" want to build a temple and those who practice the Catholic religion won't let them.

1518. We will begin by looking at small communities where they recently built their churches—either Catholic or Protestant churches. We will look at both the villages where the construction is finished and those in which the construction is underway. In some cases, the members of the village chip in to build the church, and in other cases they look for outsiders to help them. 1519. It is easier for Protestants to find outside help in securing materials for building a church. By contrast, outsiders do not come quickly to the aid of Catholics. From what has been seen, the higher echelon among the Protestants appear to be quite wealthy. They have greater economic resources. This is apparent from the fact that they finish building their temples very quickly once they start them. Among Catholics, however, they start to build a church and then stop for a while because they don't have enough calidra or other materials needed for the construction.

1520. The priests have taken notice of the fact that the Protestants help their people out a lot, and so they, too, have begun to seek ways to help their flocks—that is, the people who practice the Catholic religion. 1521. Local groups have audiences with the bishop to ask for a grant of materials. In order for such a group to get the help they need, they have to present a written request for aid to the bishop. In the document they say which community they are from, and they solicit support for completion of the church there.

1522. Some days go by and the bishop calls back the appointed group that visited him in order to deliver the materials they requested. When the church is finished they go back for another audience with the bishop to invite him. This time, though, they do not come to ask for help; they invite the bishop to come and bless the new church. 1523. On the day that the bishop comes to bless the church, they decorate it all over, inside and out. Different colored paper is stuck on the walls, and flowers are also brought. As has already been noted for many different occasions, at this ceremony many people are invited who act as padrinos during the mass. When the bishop comes to render the blessing personally, then a lot of people show up, and many of them come up to kiss his hand. This makes him very happy and he smiles through it all.

1524. We will soon see which communities have acquired their churches recently and which are still building them. We will organize things as we did earlier so that we can know everything, and not just ramble without a plan. We will begin in the Centro, or Ixmiquilpan, and move out towards the north where our final destination will be Cuesta Colorada which belongs to the pueblo of Orizabita. 1525. A short time ago, three years to be exact, the "little brothers" finished building a new church very near the one that was first built in the community of Fitzi. The new church was built to one side of the older one, just a few meters off the main highway.

1526. The believers gather there every evening to pray. The church holds approximately seventy persons, all seated. And here is where one can see that the Protestants are multiplying their numbers. The pastors practically never stop trying to get more people to come to this religion. 1527. They have actually been quite successful in enticing people, not only from Ixmiquilpan. Many people from other communities also attend church there. 1528. Some of them come to seek work. Others are already working. They meet Protestants on the job and interact with them. The Protestants tell them about their religion and that is where the conversion process starts. Before they know it, those co-workers are attending the church and praying, even though they never prayed once in their life in their home pueblo.

1529. Now we leave Ixmiquilpan and walk a long way in order to see what is going on in the small communities to the north. Until very recently, those communities did all they could to build their own churches.

1530. The first community we will see inaugurated its church only five years ago. It was blessed in 1979. The bishop came to give the benediction, accompanied by his assistants to help him. His assistants live in San Nicolás. A lot of people came from all over on the day that that church was blessed. More padrinos came than anyone. Men and women gathered in the new church.

1531. The new church was built on a small declivity. The walls were made of tabique[146] and the roof was made of concrete. A tower was built and four bells hang in it. The people there are very religious and so they were very happy when the construction was finished and the church was blessed. The bishop who came on that day lectured the people not to change their way of thinking and to abandon what they had started to do in following another religion.

Today, the residents of Defay celebrate their fiesta every year, chipping in among themselves to pay for the mass for the santito. 1532. The santito is the same one we saw in earlier pages, the Sr. del Buen Viaje de Orizabita. The people in this place do not hire a band because they are too poor to do so. The land on which the church is built is all tepetate and produces nothing. The people there migrate to Mexico City in search of work. This goes on among young people, both men and women. Recently, some of the children have been going to school, and so they now have greater possibilities for better paying jobs, and they no longer just work as construction laborers, as before. The fireworks makers whom they hire do not build castillos. They just set up remolinos and vistas, and these go off as the procession moves along.

1533. The images from Orizabita are invited to attend the fiesta in Defay. Those images go to the church of Defay on the day of vespers, and they are brought back a week later. To get them there, the people have to carry the images ten kilometers to Defay. This custom of inviting the images began just a short time ago, but no one knows when it will end. It seems like this kind of social relation is good because people get together, meet one another, and come to respect one another. 1534. The celebration of the fiesta began when the community of Defay got its church. Now, every year some people have to fulfill cargo obligations. The mayordomos who are appointed are responsible for the mass and for the fireworks that are lit. There are always people at the fiesta who make floral offerings, and the faithful always give some money and they ask God for his grace to help them live.

1535. At the house of the mayordomo in charge of the mass there is food that has been prepared for those who have helped bundle the flowers. There is a custom that the mayordomo responsible for the mass must make a floral offering, and that custom has not been forgotten yet. The mayordomo also gives food to those who come to his house with some kind of loan, such as pulque, tortillas, and cases of beer. These last are expensive, but people make the effort to get the money to make this particular loan. When it is the turn of the lender to fulfill some cargo obligation, the loan will be repaid in kind.

1536. Nowadays, young men are participating more in the fiestas celebrated in the villages. They organize among themselves and send out invitations to other young men, in other communities, to come and participate in some form of athletic event. They have basketball games, or long distance races, but the favorite is basketball. Today, there can hardly be a religious festival without the participation of athletes; they play basketball and soccer. The team that wins gets a gold colored trophy cup. 1537. They play on a cement court, made especially for basketball. Soccer, on the other hand, is played on a dirt field. The earth is loose and powdery, and when the game is over the players are covered with dust and almost unrecognizable.

1538. From Defay we can walk north, going up the mountain. It is a rough road, but we have to take it because it is the only way to get to another little community called El Manantial. Some drummers and flutists live there, and when there is a fiesta in Defay or other places, they attend and play those unique instruments. 1539. There is no church in this village. Every house has the icon of some santito in which each person places his or her faith. After a while, they will probably consider building their own church. Now they fulfill cargos in Defay or they come down on fiesta days and fulfill some personal vow. There are no Protestants in this place; the people there are very Catholic. If a member of the village converts, the others become very upset and chase him off his land.

1540. Next one goes up over the mountain and down the slope on the other side, a distance of ten kilometers, to a village called Agua Florida. The high sierra begins here with these villages and the panorama of the mountains is very beautiful.

1541. The community of Agua Florida recently built its church, but the Protestants were the first to build theirs. At first, everyone there believed in Catholicism. But, as was said before, the Protestants never tire, never stop trying to get people to follow them, and so it was that they convinced the first converts to become Protestants. When those people who liked the religion converted to it, that's when the problems started and the people became divided where they lived united before. 1542. They got angry with one another and then the Protestants were the first to build their church. They had to get help in acquiring the materials for the construction. If they themselves had tried to chip in on their own, they would not have been able to come up with the money for the materials, because these people are poor and there are no jobs.

1543. The rest of the people, who remained Catholic, later on sought help to build their own church. The church walls are made of tabicón,[147] and the roof is made of concrete, which is made from a mixture of sand, gravel, and cement to make it hard when it dries. They just inaugurated that church in 1982. It is still not known whether the members of the village will continue to celebrate the fiestas.

1544. It is important to note that the people of Agua Florida are very divided. There are people who can not stand the sight of one another because of the hatred between them. Sometimes, when they feel like it, they fight. Then, when one of them goes in to lodge a complaint with the authorities, the latter never provide justice. But if the person who makes the complaint gives a little money, then the judge responds favorably. The problem is more serious when the person lodging the complaint does not speak Spanish. Instead of hearing the complainant out, the judge does the opposite and starts to scold the man in a deprecatory manner. 1546. People who are troublemakers, who like to fight and goad their neighbors into quarrels, are not corrected in their ways. They just get worse and worse, mistreating their fellow men because mestizo justice protects them.

1547. This is what happened in one case in 1981. Some neighbors in this place got into a fight and tried to kill each other. One man died in the fracas, and the other was wounded with slashes, stabs and bullets. He had four bullets in him and almost died; it took a lot of effort to save him. They had to take him to the general hospital in Pachuca to save him. If they hadn't done that, perhaps he would have died. The man who died left a wife and children in poverty. 1548. The judge tried diligently to get the authorities to apprehend the killer and to make him at least help out the children who had been left orphans. But nothing ever happened. The agent in the Office of Public Administration just got angry and said that he knew nothing of the affair, and the whole thing came to nought. 1549. So, the divisions provoked by religion really penetrate deeply into the thinking of believers, who sometimes fight one another physically. Although the people of the community remain angry with one another, nothing has stopped events, and both groups have finished building their respective churches. One of the churches is on the east side of the community and one is on the west side.

1550. No one is sure if the villagers can fulfill their cargos every year, because there are so few people, and because they are always fighting with each other. Religion itself helps each group for the moment. The Catholics see that it is important that no more of their number convert to the Protestant religion. Each person probably protects his own religion.

1551. We will not walk far from where we are before we come to another village. We just cross a barranca and arrive at Gundó. This place recently decided to adopt its own santito. 1552. The image they worship is Jesus Christ, whose fiesta is December 24th. There is no church, just a kind of enclosure of branches where the santito is. Despite this, the priest comes to celebrate midnight mass. The "church" is very small; it holds about 20 people, and others stand outside. The priest does baptisms and gives communion.

1553. The people of Gundó live in mutual respect with the people of Orizabita, and that is why they bring down their santito every year for the fiesta of the Sixth Friday of Pentecost. When the fiesta is over, a week later the santito goes back to his home. The people of Agua Florida and Cuesta Colorada attend the fiesta in Gundó because these are the closest communities. 1554. There are no wind instruments at the fiesta in Gundó. There is a group that plays stringed instruments. They accompany the santito in the church. They do not have a procession because there is no place for a procession to go around; the land on which the community sits is very uneven. 1555. Those who bring flowers for the santito cense them with incense as they deliver the offering. El Gundó, Agua Florida, and El Manatial all bury their dead in the same cemetery. The sacred ground is located at a place known as La Capilla (The Chapel).

1556. From Gundó we go down the mountain and come to a barranca in which there is water flowing. It takes about an hour, walking, to reach the summit again. 1557. Just about at the summit is the community of Cuesta Colorada. There is no real church here, either, just a house in which the santito of the village is kept. The santito is about the same size as that of Gundó. The people of Cuesta Colorada celebrate their fiesta on a different date than that of Gundó. 1558. The priest goes there to celebrate mass. Until just a few years ago, he had to go on foot. Sometimes he came on a burro they lent him to ride. Burros are not as fast as horses.

1559. In the old days, the priest used to dress all in black; it was a pretty sight to see him mounted on a burro. His robes were black and the burro was grey, and as they moved through the trees the priest would be sweating as the sun shone on his forehead. Priests are nice people, perhaps because they have a lot of education. Possibly this is what makes them compassionate with the poor. 1560. Even today, the priests still go to celebrate mass wherever they are asked, though the village might be far from the central cathedral. They even go at night, if need be. Perhaps this is because they have taken notice of the fact that the Protestants are very active in converting the faithful. As they convert more people, they build more churches where people gather to pray, as is the case with the recent construction in Agua Florida, in Cerritos, in Orizabita and in other communities in the southern part of the municipio.

1561. From Cuesta Colorada we return. If we could fly, we could get back quickly, and this would be wonderful. But no; it is better that we walk back and in that way nothing will happen to us. We will not fall, and thus we will always be safe and well. 1562. We will head south now, and see what kind of religion they practice in those communities.

In the southern part of the area there is a community known as El Alberto. 1563. This little community is on the other side of the mountains near El Maye. The area where the community is located is very dry. There is no potable water nearby for use by the local population. 1564. The water that the people use is brought back from the river that crosses there; it is the same one we know as the Tula River. The people of this village have followed the Protestant religion. Everyone there reads the book in which they say the words of God are written. The book is also called the New Testament. This is the book that the Protestants always use to teach people when they try to get them to convert.

1565. Those who have been assigned to convert more people have been well rehearsed about what they have to say. Also, they don't select just anyone to tell people about their thinking. Rather, they seem to choose those who can deliver the message easily. For the moment, this has been just a brief tour through this place; from here we return from where we started in Ixmiquilpan. 1566. As we have done from the beginning, we have followed a plan so that everything would be written in order, and thus we now go towards the east. It doesn't matter if we have nothing to say about these parts, but at least we give a cursory look around and return to the Centro.

1567. From the Centro we head north on the left hand fork in the road, to see what is happening nowadays in the communities of San Antonio, San Nicolás, Los Remedios and Orizabita. All these communities continue to practice many of the customs that they practiced earlier. Recently, amusement park rides and other diversions have come in to the fiestas.

1568. Amusement park rides are always there nowadays at fiestas. The judges of a community organize ball games. These games are enjoyed by many aficionados. People like to watch these games. Mechanical rides, such as are found in amusement parks, are set up in the plaza of the community and they attract children as well as adults. One of the rides that come to the pueblos is the merry-go-round. The children mount the horses and they go round and round and up and down. Those who get on really like it and have to go around twice. But they have to pay, because it is not free.

1569. The other type of ride is the revolving swing. The people who make it go around, the owners of the ride, sometimes do the work manually and sometimes the machine has its own motor that makes it go around. 1570. There is also a ride called the "wheel of fortune." This is a large wheel made of metal, and it too, has its own motor that makes it revolve. People get on the wheel and go up in it very high. 1571. Fiesta goers who get on the wheel with a full stomach wind up vomiting out on the other fiesta goers who are standing below and watching those who are enjoying the ride. But in the end, that's what the "wheel of fortune" is.

1572. The owners of those rides have realized a profit and so now they come every year to set up at the fiestas. Another kind of diversion always seen now at the fiestas are called "títeres," or puppets. They are great scoffers. They mimic what people do and laugh at them. Children love to watch them, and so do grown ups. One must pay in order to watch them, as always, and every year the price goes up. 1573. The games and rides do not reach the far off communities that we have seen here. This is because the proprietors choose only those places where there is enough of a population to make a profit. In the distant villages, they only organize ball games. But this is also good, because the young people get together in this way and relate to one another, and the people who want to watch the games don't necessarily have to pay.

1574. Those mechanical rides come every year to Ixmiquilpan. Sometimes the people get so wrapped up with them that they forget to worship the santitos. A lot of people gather around those rides. The owners probably make a lot of money. 1575. The santito is practically not even venerated any more in the celebration of the municipal fiesta. The whole thing has become all business. Most of the people at the fair just go around looking at things in the plaza; meanwhile, there are few people at the big parish church. Everything started when the mechanical rides came in.

1576. At first, the basketball games were played in front of the presidential hall. That was in 1970. Then the games moved to an enclosed area where people could not watch for free, but had to pay to get in. 1577. In that year, the mestizos charged one peso for the "entrance fee" to see the basketball games. The fair was set up in the plaza and there was no charge to see it.

1578. Now the mestizos in the city of Ixmiquilpan have figured out that they get a lot of money by charging people. So they looked for a more protected part of the city—that is, easier to enclose. They built barricades around a large area where they put all the rides and games that come to the fair every year. They have left open just three gates. At each one there is one of their assistants who charge the adults as well as the children who want to get in to see the rides and games set up inside. They have to pay before they are allowed in. [148]

1579. Those who have money can go in and can see everything; but those who are poor are not allowed access. And just in case the poor want to get in by force, they have put police at the entrance. 1580. Those policemen carry carbines and small arms. They wear a pistol on their belt and rest their rifle on their shoulder. They also carry a billy club, about 70 centimeters long. When people don't want to move aside, the police beat them with it. 1581. The club is thick and full of sweat from being carried for so long in the hands. This is all the policeman holds on to; this is what he is paid for. 1582. When a policeman hits a person with that club, the person gets knocked out.

The fiesta in Ixmiquilpan has become nothing more than a market. 1583. For many Ñähñu, it is as if this fiesta had disappeared, when before they loved it with all their hearts. Before, they used to come together at the fiesta every year. That was where many of them worked together so that the fiesta for Sr. de Jalpa would be lively. 1584. The little children came to the fiesta, even though they didn't buy anything to eat. Even so, they had a good time just watching the entertainment and amusements that used to be there. None of that exists today. They just sit in their houses, and as has happened with everything else, they don't get to enjoy any fiestas anymore.

1585. When the police can't handle the crowds and make them pay, the organizers of the fiesta call in soldiers to help maintain order. The soldiers carry their carbines on their shoulders and, from what people say, those guns are the best there are. Who knows why the mestizos say that those guns are the best? It is understood that they are best for killing. 1586. They also carry small pouches on their belts that contain bullets. It is obvious that those pouches with bullets weigh a lot because one can see that they practically drag down the soldiers' pants. When the soldiers see that some people are fighting, they take their guns down from their shoulder and they go up to the antagonists to separate them.

1587. If the fighters don't obey and separate, then the soldiers hit them with the butts of their rifles. 1588. The authorities in other communities also call in soldiers when the fiestas are celebrated, to make sure that no one fights. But it is unnecessary to bring in soldiers; after all, this is not the first time that people have celebrated fiestas. 1589. A lot of people don't like the soldiers being brought in to the fiesta. Villagers say that it is better if people work out proper behavior in the community. This is certain, because when people come to a fiesta and see soldiers there, they just hurry to leave and return to their homes.

1590. The mestizos organize a lot of attractions in order to make money. They organize a bullfight on the 15th of August, the date of the fiesta. They bring in bullfighters who live far from Ixmiquilpan, for example. They come from Mexico City and they come to fight the fierce bulls. 1591. At first, when the bull comes out of the corral, he acts fierce and runs around, trying to get to the bullfighter and gore him. The bullfighter carries a red cloth[149] that he uses to goad the bull into attacking. 1592. The bullfighter waits until the bull is tired out. Then a mounted horseman comes,[150] carrying a lance on one end of which is a pointed metal tip. This is what he uses to stab at the back of the bull. Perhaps the animal feels the pain because he cries out. But he gets angrier and he charges at the bullfighter and charges the sides of the horse. They cover the horse's flanks with old mattresses so that the bull can not get his horns into the ribs. 1593. When the picada is over, then another man comes out with banderillas which he thrusts into the back of the bull where the animal has been stabbed. The banderillas are made entirely of wood, including the part where the man grasps them. But the point that goes into the bulls's back is made of metal.

1594. The man has to chase the bull to insert the banderillas, and the bull runs too, trying to attack the man. But when the bull isn't watching carefully, the man sticks in the banderillas and the bull bellows. Six banderillas in total are inserted, and then one can see that the bull has nothing left. 1595. When all this is finished, then the matador comes out, carrying a sword, and he confronts the bull again for a moment. He fools the bull into thinking he can attack, but the bull just follows the cape[151] and nothing happens to the man. 1596. When the matador gets the bull good and tired, he prepares to thrust the sword into the part where the picador stabbed the bull. Once the bull has died, a team of mules comes out, driven by a teamster who trusses up the feet of the dead bull in order to drag it out of the ring. It is possible that the animal is taken somewhere and butchered.

1597. The people who come to see the bullfight drink a lot of beer. Not everyone does, but the majority do and that is where a lot of money gets spent. 1598. One can hear people scream with pleasure at seeing the bulls killed. Once one is killed, they bring out another from where they are kept, and they do the same thing to it. They kill four, and sometimes six in an afternoon. 1599. Sometimes three matadors are hired. They charge a lot of money. The other communities in the area of Ixmiquilpan can not compete with those costs. 1600. In the case of those who extract fiber from maguey leaves, or workers of lechuguilla, there is never a time, and there never will be, when they will go to see a bullfight because they do not have enough money. A seat in the plaza de toros costs at least 400 pesos.[152]

1601. Another kind of amusement in which the mestizos make a lot of money are cockfights. They have also built a special big place for this where those who want to see the cockfights pay to get in. 1602. The cocks belong to different owners who bring them to fight and who bet a certain amount of money. The cockfights end around two in the morning because there are a lot of cocks that are put in to fight. The cockfight men don't just put up any old bird. There are special cocks that like to fight. 1603. The rest of the people who have come to watch bet among themselves. One person goes in favor of one cock while someone else favors another bird. They look for many ways to amuse themselves where the cockfights take place. They hire singers who know how to sing different songs. 1604. If it is not a man, then it is a girl who sings with a beautiful voice. They don't sing by themselves. They are accompanied by a mariachi group, who are all dressed in their outfits, and who carry the sombrero of a charro or horseman. 1605. Some of the instruments they carry are wind, and others are guitars, violins and guitarrones.[153] When they begin to play the artist sings, and the people react immediately and yell with joy.

1606. They tie a small blade on one of the feet of the cocks that are fighting. As they jump and kick, pretty soon one cock cuts the throat of the other and kills it. 1607. When one cock sees that it has killed the other, it stands on its enemy and crows. The entrance fee is also very expensive in this amusement.

1608. A few years ago, they started bringing together the handicrafts that are made in the Mezquital Valley, both those made by women as well as those made by men. Sometimes, the people who make these handicrafts are invited directly to come to the fair and to set up their own stalls to sell their goods. That is where they sell their wares to people who come from far away. Those people like to buy handicrafts like little baskets for holding tortillas, embroidered bags, embroidered blouses, and belts. 1609. The local people can sell things at the fair at a better price. But when they deliver their wares wholesale to those who sell at retail, then they get paid very little. The merchants pay the price they fix, and do not listen to what the worker says.

1610. This is how the fiesta is actually celebrated now in Ixmiquilpan. If the people have money, then they can come to the fiesta; and if they do not, then all they can do is to stay at home, as always happens to poor people. 1611. The merry-go-rounds, revolving swings, and other rides also come to Progreso, El Maye, San Antonio, and El Nith. This is because a lot of people go to those places and the owners of the rides can make a good profit. They don't have bullfights or cockfights because, as mentioned a moment ago, the salary of the bullfighters is very expensive.

1612. Basketball and soccer are the games that always take place. The other competition is bicycle races. 1613. They start out from the plaza in Ixmiquilpan and take the road to Huichapan. The round trip is 100 kilometers. The racer who has the greatest stamina and speed is the winner.

1614. There is another competitive event that also takes place, and that is foot races. Today, there are no fiestas where they don't invite young men who like to race. They run 10 kilometers and sometimes more. The young men take part in these races and those who are fat do not get very far because they tire quickly. The ones who hold up more are thin.

1615. We leave Ixmiquilpan once again and go back where we came from towards the east. There is a community in these parts that practices Protestant-ism, and which recently built its church. Everyone who lives there practices this religion. 1616. In this way, there is no division; everyone is united because they think alike. The pastor who goes abroad to other communities and who holds meetings with his fellow Protestants lives there. The pastor plays the role of the priest among them. When they gather to pray, he stands at the front. 1617. The pastor goes around to various parts of the valley. He gets to El Olivo, El Boye, and El Defay, because some of his co-religionists live there, too. The one family that lives there in Defay and practices that religion wants to build its own church. 1618. But their neighbors won't allow it because they are mostly believers in Catholicism. Also, the place where they wanted to build the church is practically next to the school.

The man who practices this religion gets into a lot of fights; he tries to convert others to his religion, and he holds forth against the majority of the community in trying to build his own church. 1619. This man used to live in Fitzi, the place where his fellow Protestants live, but he left there and came back to his homeland to provoke his neighbors in Defay. 1620. From all that one can tell, he needs what is called a "good massage"; otherwise, he will be the laughing stock of everyone. Some of his neighbors have chided him, but it has not penetrated and so he goes around stirring up trouble with anyone he finds. If this man goes on bothering people, the day will come when his neighbors get good and mad and give him a "massage" with their hands over his ears.

1621. Another small community that only five years ago began to celebrate a different kind of fiesta is San Andrés. The fiesta is celebrated in the last month of the year, in December. The people chip in to buy the things that are most needed in the church. They buy candles and sparklers. They don't celebrate the nine nights of posadas there. 1622. The people themselves choose which night they want to hold the fiesta. They look for a night when people can attend. The mayordomos rush about getting everything ready. They invite people to sing prayers who know how to sing the carols for the posadas.

1623. When they finish singing the carols and all the celebrating is over in the church, then everyone goes to a place that has been selected beforehand where the coffee and peanuts are given out. If a string band is hired, they begin to play their best songs, and some people start to dance. Those who were appointed to organize the fiesta give out tamales and coffee. 1624. The dances are done to music known as corridos and also huapangos. They start around eleven at night and finish at around three in the morning. The corrido is a dance where the man and the woman hold each other's hands, while in huapangos they are separated and cross back and forth in front of each other.

1625. While we are talking about dances, in most of the communities we have been discussing they have a fiesta and a dance as well nowadays. Some of those communities charge an entrance fee for the dances and others charge nothing at all. 1626. When they charge it is because they hire a band that supposedly plays really well, and those bands charge a lot of money. Despite this, the young men pay to get in and dance. Some of them don't go just to dance, but because they know that they will find a girlfriend there. Sometimes they just make love, and other times they get married. Some couples make an arrangement and just live together. But it is customary to let the father and mother know about relations between young people and for the boy to ask for the girl's hand and for the parents to decide if the couple will actually get married.

1627. During the last ten years, musical groups have been formed that play modern music. When a religious fiesta is going to be celebrated in a village and a dance is to be held, then these are the groups that are hired. One member of the group plays a large guitar that has a powerful sound because it is connected to electric power. 1628. They also bring along a set of drums that one of them beats a lot. The drummer practically never stops beating on all the drums, with his hands and his feet moving all the time. Those who dance seem to just move their bodies from side to side, and dance back to back. It looks like they were bothered by some kind of pain.

1629. When people started dancing to this kind of music, the traditional string bands were pushed aside. A lot of their sources of work were eliminated. Previously, they contracted to play at the dances, and the cost of their services was not that great. The modern groups, however, charge by the thousands of pesos. 1630. If they play for five hours, they charge 20,000 pesos. That is why the people who want to get in to the dances must pay 300-400 pesos. It is not always the same charge. The price depends on the quality of the music.

1631. Another occasion on which bands are hired is when people get married and have a dance. Of course, this is only possible for those who have the resources; the poor can not do this. 1632. Nowadays, when young men get married, they invite someone to be the padrino for the music. The padrino for the music has to hire the band and, above all, pay their wages. 1633. Another padrino is invited to pay for the mass and for the decoration of the church. Those are some of the new customs that have come in recently. Another happy fiesta where modern musical groups are hired happens in those homes where the 15th birthday of a girl is being celebrated.

1634. In this celebration, the girl who is becoming 15 years old goes to church to hear a mass dedicated to her. This is only among Catholics. The Protestants do not have this custom. The mass for the girl who has completed her 15th birthday is for her to give thanks to God for having let her reach this age, and for her to ask that she continue to live in good health. For this, too, a padrino and a madrina are invited to solicit the mass and to pay the expenses of decorating the church. 1635. This is all done during the evening, and at night the dance is held. On this occasion, all the relatives of the girl are invited to celebrate her fiesta.

1636. The girl's parents prepare a meal for all the invited guests who come to wish her well on her 15th birthday. Sometimes goats and chickens are killed. Other times, tamales and atole are made for the guests. 1637. Another padrino and madrina are invited to find out where there is a good baker and to order up a big cake. The cake weighs about six kilograms, depending on the size. The cake is decorated beautifully. It is given to the girl who is celebrating her fiesta, and she is in charge of giving a slice to each of the guests.

1638. The custom of inviting padrinos is in order to help the family that is celebrating the fiesta so that they do not spend a lot of money. This custom is a kind of "loan" because it gets paid back. The person who is now invited to be padrino for one thing or another will one day have his own celebration. Then he will invite the person for whom he did the favor previously. It can be said that no one loses anything because the loans just go in a chain.

1639. As was already said, the string musical groups have lost a lot of work. They are still hired when a family goes to visit an acquaintance who is celebrating his saint's day or birthday. 1640. The musicians play in salute to the person who is celebrating. Very early in the morning, the family that had decided to visit a friend goes there, accompanied by the musicians. They play mañanitas to wake up the person.

1641. This kind of visit is not so simple. The family that is celebrating on that day has bought a cake like the one mentioned above. It is wrapped in paper and given to the people when they finish singing the mañanitas. 1642. Some people who do this kind of thing tell the person that they are coming to fete him on his saint's day. But sometimes they just show up by surprise. The first thing the person in the house knows about it is when he wakes up to the mañanitas. The gift is not just cake, either, but consists of other things as well. Some people give out flowers and cake.

1643. The celebration does not end there; that is, it is not over with the delivery of the cake. The person who is being feted on his saint's day prepares food to share with all his visitors, and they drink pulque together if there is any. That is where friendships start, and when the person visiting has his own saint's day, then they do the same for him. 1644. Very few people hold dances for this day. Some people who go to give mañanitas to another also bring along firecrackers which they set off when they go to visit. Others string together little rolls called "billos" or "bolillos,"[154] interspersed with flowers.

1645. When they get to the house where the celebrant lives, at the moment when he comes out to receive his guests they put the cordón of rolls and flowers around his neck. Also, schoolteachers are feted on the 15th of May. 1646. For this occasion, also, a string band is hired to accompany the children to sing mañanitas to their teachers. This is a way of showing their gratitude to the teachers for giving them new knowledge.

1647. The heads of families and those who have not yet sent their children to school cooperate to put on a meal for the schoolteachers on this day. It is not ordained by any formal authority; they just do it on their own. 1648. The authorities have fittingly decreed May 15th as a day to honor teachers at all levels of education; the people have a lot of respect for the teachers. They say the teacher is like a second father who instructs children on how to live in the future.

1649. There is another day that many Ñähñu have made a custom of celebrating every year. This is January 6th, the day of the Holy Kings. One of them is called Melchior, another is known as Gaspar, and the third is named Balthasar.

1650. Bakers await this date eagerly; they make oval-shaped cake breads that have a hollowed out center and that are about a half meter across.[155] A little toy, or doll, is baked into the wide part of the oval. The doll is about three centimeters long. The person who buys the cake invites his friends over to eat it.

1651. When everyone is there, they sit down at a table with the cake in the middle. They start to cut the cake with a knife into slices that are handed out to all the guests. At first, no one knows who has been given the slice that contains the little figure. The cake is sliced in equal parts and no one knows which one has the figure in it. 1652. When it is eaten, then one of the people must find out. The agreement is that whoever finds the figure in his piece of cake has to prepare a meal for everyone on the 2nd of February, which is the day of the fiesta of the Virgen de Candelaria. The person who finds the little toy kills chickens and makes the meal to offer to his friends.

1653. A great many roscas de reyes are made on this day. The bakers decorate the cakes nicely in order to sell them. The cost of one of those cakes is not less than 400 pesos. Some fathers buy toys to give out to their youngest children on this date, also. 1654. They deceive the children, telling them that the gifts are brought by the Holy Kings; they tell them that the Kings come at night to leave the toys when no one will see them. 1655. Before they go to bed on the night of the 5th of January, the children take off their huaraches and put them just outside the door of the room in which they sleep. The next day, when they get up, they see a toy on their huaraches and they believe that the Holy Kings actually brought it.

1656. Children whose fathers are poor get nothing, even though they see other children getting gifts. When the child asks his father why he didn't get anything, the father does not know what to say. Some fathers tell the truth and say that they don't have any money to buy toys. They say that toys will come later, because the first priority is that the family has food to eat. 1657. The children hear that and they go to find old toys that someone has thrown in the garbage. They retrieve them to play with them. They also look for ways to make toys out of rocks and mud that they find around.

1658. Other communities have considered getting close to God; that is, practicing the Catholic religion. They have begun to build their own church, even though it is slow and based on faenas every Sunday. The churches are not very big; they are about the size of a normal house. It is just a place where the santito is kept that people worship in a village. 1659. The community of El Durazno is located in the jurisdiction of San Juanico and borders on Los Remedios to the east. The construction of the church there just began in 1983. The people asked for help from the bishop at Tula, and he provided calidra, cement and reinforcing steel rods. 1660. No one knows yet which saint or virgin they are going to venerate there. They will likely choose the image when they finish building the church. The people in this community are real workers; they will probably finish the construction soon. Of course, this depends on the necessary support and the presence of the materials.

1661. The community of El Dexthi has had its church for about ten years. The people who helped out there were some foreign women who were called "sisters." They are the ones that believe in God a lot.[156] 1662. Those young women spoke English. They helped build the church and also houses with walls of rubble-work masonry for poor people who used to live in shacks made of maguey leaves. They don't celebrate a fiesta every year in El Dexthí. They just hold a mass whenever somebody requests one.

1663. The road is very rough in this part of the country. There are a lot of hills, covered with lechuguilla plants, mesquites and other cacti. Even so, we have to walk, though it is slow going, up the hill. Pretty soon we come to a wide mesa. 1664. On this landing we find a humble and solitary village sitting on this rocky piece of ground. The village is called Cantamayé. There are very few inhabitants, and all of them are Catholics. There is no church here. When they want to hear mass or go to some fiesta, they come to Orizabita. They come by foot, a distance of 10 kilometers. 1665. They have icons of different saints in the houses of the people there, and these are what they worship, lighting a candle for them. 1666. They bring their images down to Orizabita when the fiesta is celebrated so that the priest can bless the icons, or even simply so that the icons can be at the mass. The people of the village fulfill cargo obligations in Orizabita.

1667. Behind the mountains that one sees from Cantamayé, there is a village called La Palma, about an hour and a half by foot, that also lies in the jurisdiction of Orizabita. There is a barranca at the bottom of the mountain there in which water flows that people consume. 1668. The people there are very nice. When someone comes to visit them with respect, they take them into their homes. They offer visitors food to eat when they can. Though the people in this place seem very poor, no one there dies of hunger.

1669. A long time ago the people of La Palma used to be mayordomos for the music and the fireworks makers in Orizabita. But as the years went by, they stopped taking cargos because they got poorer and poorer. In those days it used to rain a lot and their plantings were successful, and it was thus not difficult for them to take on cargos. 1670. But, according to what people say, there was a great drought, and their animals died from lack of fodder. From that time on, the people have never recovered economically, and they continue in the same poor state today. That is when they stopped accepting cargos.

1671. Although many years have passed, they have neither forgotten nor left the Catholic church, but continue to believe. Just because the piece of ground on which they live is poor is no reason to change ideas about religion. Not at all. 1672. The ground on which the little community is located is very rocky, a kind of white tepetate which has been eroded by rains over the years. Three years ago the villagers began to build a little church on their own initiative. They haven't been able to complete it because there is no road on which to haul in the sacks of calidra and all the other things needed. When they started the work they had to carry in everything they needed on their backs to the village. 1673. People who had burros used those animals to carry in the materials. The new road that is going in to the village has been built mostly by the efforts of the people of La Palma. They do the work in faenas. Every week they dig out the road, using metal bars, shovels and picks.

1674. The surrounding communities, seeing the work that is being done on the road, have started to help out with labor loans. At various times the following communities have helped out: La Lagunita, El Naxtey, Boxhuada, Orizabita, El Gundó, El Boye and El Taxto. From 300-350 faena workers gather for this effort. The authorities in each community are responsible for turning out their own people. Because this is collective work on the basis of loaned labor, every week the people go to another community.

1676. There are bureaucrats in an organization that is supposed to help the Ñähñu. The organization is headquartered in Ixmiquilpan and is known as the Patrimonio Indígena del Valle del Mezquital. When the director of the agency noticed that the work in La Plama was progressing so well, due entirely to the efforts of the people of the village, he finally agreed to offer some small support for the project. Before that, the people of La Palma went back and forth many times, asking for support, but only came away with hopes. 1677. When the people showed up in the office, they were told "yes," they would be given financial support. Then they would go back home and wait for the day to come on which help was promised to arrive. But nothing ever came. 1678. So they went back again and tried to get an interview with the mestizos, and they always got the same answer. They were told not to worry, because help was coming soon, perhaps tomorrow or the next day. But it was the same old story repeated over and over.

1679. No one knows yet which santito the people of La Plama are going to venerate. Very likely they will agree on a santito or virgin when they finish construction of their church. What we have to do is just wait a bit more until they finish building their church. 1680. For the moment, we will leave this village to continue working as they have become accustomed. They have not lost hope that the day will come when all the good things they have hoped for will come to them.

1681. It seems important to note that recently some pueblos have stopped buying firecrackers which they used to set off during mass, at floral offerings and during the procession. 1682. The reason that firecrackers are being avoided now is that there have been some very unfortunate accidents. In Ixmiquilpan in 1980 there was one of the worst mishaps in local memory. It happened one Monday in November, at the rememberance of dead babies and the departed faithful. 1683. There were some firecracker makers close to the market selling firecrackers to the people in the plaza to take home and light in honor of the dead. One of the plaza goers wanted to see just how good the firecrackers were. This is the custom; before someone pays, he asks the fireworks merchant to test them, to set one off or to let the buyer set one off. They light two or three and in this way they know whether the firecrackers are good or not. 1685. On this particular occasion, the person who wanted to try the firecracker was not careful as he lit one. Right next to that were all the other giant firecrackers that the seller had made and bundled together. There was also some powder and suddenly the whole pile of firecrackers started to blast off in big bundles, by the gross.

1686. That day was one of the worst disasters, a huge conflagration. People didn't know where to run and they began to scream, according to the information gathered. 1687. When the smoke cleared, only then could it be seen that there were pieces of feet and hands and heads everywhere. There are some large trees there that provide shade for the fireworks makers and the plaza goers; and pieces of human flesh were hanging from the branches of those trees. Many people died that day. 1688. The people of the Mezquital Valley were very sad at that time because a lot of Ñähñu died. None of the fireworks makers that were there are around any more; they all died. Those that were accompanied by their wives and their children—they all died. People have not forgotten that terrible misfortune and many years will have to pass before it is forgotten.

1689. Since then, people have thought that it is best to stay away from where firecrackers are sold in the market and no one will buy them. This was not the first time that an accident happened. Other terrible things have happened elsewhere and in other years. In some of these disasters people have been killed and in others they have been left crippled. 1690. These days there are few communities in which one hears the sound of firecrackers going off during a fiesta.

The other side of this is that a lot of people who made fireworks have lost their source of livelihood because hardly anyone buys the firecrackers they make anymore. But perhaps, slowly, they will conclude that what is being done to them is not so bad. Anyway, it is silent nowadays in communities where they are celebrating a religious fiesta and nobody in other villages knows it's going on because there is no noise from firecrackers.

1691. Now we are nearly finished talking about Ñähñu religion. The religion that the Spaniards started teaching hundreds of years ago; the religion that the Ñähñu learned; that religion has sometimes allowed the Ñähñu to live in peace with one another and at other times it has caused them to suffer. 1692. In what follows we will see which churches attract a large number of pilgrims, not just Ñähñu. We have to take note of the fact that many non-Ñähñu practice and believe in Catholicism and go to church, and that the church is also called the "house of God and the Virgin." 1693. We will see which churches have the largest number of followers because many Ñähñu go out from the valley to leave alms in those places, even though they may be a long distance away. In times past, it used to to take the Ñähñu people three days or even a week to make those pilgrimages. They weren't put off by weariness, but just had to push on to get to the image that they had thought of worshipping and to see the celebration of the fiesta.

1694. The churches where people used to go, and to which they continue to go are the following: Chalma, in the State of Mexico; the Basilica of Guadalupe, in Mexico City; El Arenal, in the State of Hidalgo; and the communities of El Maye, in the Municipio of Ixmiquilpan; Portezuelo, in the Municipio of Tasquillo; San Juan de los Lagos, in the State of Jalisco. This last is the furthest place to which pilgrims from the valley go.

1695. According to old people, the pilgrims used to go on foot. A few of them who thought about going to a place to worship would get together and it took them some days to make the trek. They took along their itacate for the trip. 1696. Sometimes they were gone for two weeks because they rested along the way and spent the nights on the road. Sometimes people would invite them to stay over at their houses and then the pilgrims would ask for permission to heat up their tortillas right there.

1697. The only thing they used to take to the Sr. de Chalma were candles that the pilgrims used to have made in a special way. The pilgrims practically just went to see the celebration and returned home. Nowadays a lot of people still go, but they don't go on foot. Now they travel on buses, paying for their passage. They don't take long and they return quickly. 1698. Another thing that pilgrims bring to the Sr. del Chalma are pastillas. They are made of sugar. When people arrived they used to go directly to the santito and leave the pastilla for him.

1699. People have a lot of faith in the santito at Chalma because it is said he is very miraculous, that he saves people and keeps them from misfortune, and that whoever places all his faith in the Sr. de Chalma will be protected by him. The traditional celebration for him is the fifth Friday of Pentacost. Many people attend. Those who have gone there attest that many people from many pueblos attend that fiesta.

1700. People have a lot of faith in the Virgin of Guadalupe also because it is believed that she is very miraculous. Not just the Ñähñu believe in her, but also the mestizos who come to her church by the thousands. The pilgrims who go there leave a lot of money and they collect many thousands of pesos in her church. 1701. Some of the pilgrims, including men, women and children, walk on their knees before entering the church. Many people from the provinces know her as the Virgen de la Villita, or the Virgin of the Roadbed. She acquired this name because the train passes close to her church. Many high class mestizos, and also many rich people, come to the celebration of her fiesta, to worship the Virgin. 1702. It is believed that she is very miraculous. They don't just celebrate one mass in the Basilica, but several, one after the other with the priests taking turns. The church is filled all day long with pilgrims.

1703. A lot of pilgrims also gather at the church at Arenal. We already know that this pueblo is in the jurisdiction of Actopan. The icon there is also known as the Santito de las Maravillas. We have discussed this image in earlier pages.

A lot of pilgrims gather in El Maye on the 3rd of May. 1704. They say that the holy cross that is worshipped here is very miraculous and that it protects sick people who have faith in it. Another place where a lot of pilgrims gather is Portezuelo on December 24th and also on New Year's Day, because that is when people worship the holy child who is venerated in that pueblo.

1705. It is at the religious festivals that merchants gather to sell various things. There are also sellers of pulque who come from various parts of the valley. There are people who sell ceramic tableware. They come from Alfajayucan and from Chapantongo. The people in Chapantongo specialize in making ceramics. This is their livelihood and they go abroad to sell their wares at markets and they set up stalls at fairs, as well. They don't just sell ceramic plates. They also sell pitchers, jugs and large earthenware jars, as well as earthenware comales.[157] They sell more comales at fiestas because the fiesta goers use them to heat up their itacate. 1706. Since long ago, and today as well, many people gather at the churches just mentioned because they have faith in the icons there and the pilgrims come to worship those images.

1707. There are some places where the mayordomos charge people to get in to worship the saints and virgins whom they have come to see. People who have suffered for a long time with some illness, for example, and who have not been able to get cured, may be charged admission. 1708. The sick person or his family members go to worship an image that they have been told is a miraculous saint or virgin. The sick person is directed to worship there in the hope that the saint will help cure the sickness. Sometimes, the mayordomos—fortunately, not all of them—charge for worshipping there.

1709. The mayordomos, as was said earlier, are appointed by the people to carry out their cargos with honesty and they are considered as aides to the priest. A believer who wants to leave some alms asks the mayordomo to cleanse him, and the mayordomo accepts, making the cleansing with the candles or money that the pilgrim is carrying as his vow. 1710. But then the person who is acting as mayordomo asks the pilgrim for 100 or 200 pesos. This only started recently. The people who are asked, like it or not, try to come up with the amount of money requested, because they are afraid that if they don't, then they might suffer some misfortune sent to them by the saint or the virgin. Those asking for the money say that it is for repairing the church. 1711. I think that it is not right for the mayordomo to ask for a sum of money. The best thing is for the believer to give the sum that he wants to give, and the amount that he can give, according to his resources. Otherwise, it is like the faith they have in the images is being sold to them.

1712. After that, the next thing that happens is that icons and statues of the saints and virgins are mass produced for sale in the markets. This is not only going on in the valley, but in other places as well. The statues are sometimes made of plaster, or the icons are painted on paper. The people who believe in the Catholic religion are badly deceived like this. 1713. Some things are being sold these days that hardly even look like santitos or virgins. Despite this, the people buy them. They pay 100 or 300 pesos, depending on the size of the image.

1714. The other place where a lot of people come together to worship is San Juan de los Lagos in the State of Jalisco. It is necessary to mention this place even though not all the pilgrims there are from the valley. Many Mexicans go there to leave something in fulfillment of a vow. 1715. It is a long ways off, but this is apparently no obstacle. People find ways to go there, even if it is not every year. It is heard that the Virgin of San Juan de los Lagos also helps people who are suffering from some malady. She protects people from those who would do them harm—that is, people who are having problems with their fellow men—and she cures the sick. 1716. The place is very far away. People don't go on foot, but travel in buses instead. The cost of the trip is more than 1000 pesos each way.

1717. Every year young men organize pilgrimage on bicycles. Sometimes the priest at the cathedral in Ixmiquilpan organizes them. From 300-400 young men show up and they race the whole way along the highway. It takes them six days to go there and return. 1718. What they do is like a vow made to venerate the virgin. It is not only the young men of Ixmiquilpan, but also those from Actopan, Progreso, Pachuca and other places who go along on the pilgrimage.

1719. Another place that they go by bicycle to worship is the Basilica of the Virgin of Guadalupe. More young men go there, as well as older men. Around 600 pilgrims get together for this trip because it is closer. It takes a day to go and a day to come back.[158] 1720. There are people in other villages and towns who also organize in groups to go to the church of the Virgin of Guadalupe in Mexico City. Those who go on foot take around four days to get there, depending on the distance from where they start their trip.

1721. As we have seen, much of the population in the Mezquital Valley is Catholic. Sometimes the religious beliefs have penetrated so profoundly that people can not understand any new ideas that have developed in modern times. 1722. For the moment we will end this narrative. I just want to say a few humble words that are part of my badly trained thinking, and they go like this.

Observe the World Carefully

By: a man of the desert

My Brother! You are not alone in the world. You have had people who are your true friends for hundreds of years. Surely you will ask "Who are they?"

Brother, I must tell you, then. They are the earth that you walk on; the air that you breathe; the sun that gives you light so that you may see and walk and work, and so that you might live happily in the world.

"Who else is my friend?" you ask. It is the desert that you are always walking across and the bitter pains that you have suffered for centuries. The birds who sing to you out in the countryside are your friends, as are the other animals that go about on the surface of the earth and beneath the ground, as well.

The stars are also your friends, and so is the moon, and the darkness, and the meteorites that come from outer space and light their own way as they go along. The barrancas that sometimes bring you water are your friends; the mountains

My brother! You are not alone in the world
A Man of the Desert

that are part of the earth where you live; and the water, which is the indispensable element for existence on earth.

Then who are your enemies? Dirt and filth from the lack of water you suffer is your enemy; sickness that strikes you and kills you; lies told to you by hypocrites; and the lack of purity in the minds of those who deceive you.

Those who tell you that they respect you but who only exploit you daily for your work are your enemies. When you are young they respect you but when you grow old and can't work for them any more, they say they don't know you.

They pay you whatever they want to pay and not what your efforts demand of them. Whenever you sell them anything, they do the same thing to you. Be careful not to make them angry when you ask them for something because they are violent when someone says anything to them that they don't like. What they pay you is not enough for you to feed your family. A salary of hunger is what they give you, and they are always poor-mouthing, saying that they have nothing to give.

They formed their habits during the time when they lived as great hacienda lords. They paid you very little for your little piece of land so that they could build their mansion. When they get through snatching away the land, you find yourself on the street without even knowing what happened. So you must distrust the words of the patrones, because they invade and capture the land, and they don't care at all if they destroy homes in the process.

When they seek political office, they call on you to gather and applaud them.[159] But they reject with disdain the support you give them, saying that your support is worthless. They just use you as a bridge to the things they want, and to keep you happy they give you something to eat and put their arms around your shoulders to show you how much they care.

When you go to speak to them you will see how false they are. It is useless for you to sit there with them, because there is neither aid nor justice. They look at you contemptuously, pretending they don't see you. Yes, they will notice you, but only after they have attended to the rich who come dressed in nice jackets. In the meantime, you just wait because they see you as filth.

If you say anything bad to them, they call in their police to beat you. You are witness to the fact that when many people have protested to them, they have called in their soldiers with rifles to shoot you. They have always cheated you and because you speak Ñähñu they don't want to listen to you.

Think about all this now and send your child to school, for that is where all the falsehoods will be wiped out. They say that you are weak, but they will see in the future that this is not true. Follow those who are your true friends and keep those who deceive you away from your thoughts. If you just keep wishing for the moon, I don't think it will come soon. Perhaps what you wish for will be found in the Infinite.

Notes to Volume IV — Religion

1. There is a movement now in Mexico, among several native groups, to use their own words to refer to themselves. Hence, Ñähñu refers throughout this text to the people called Otomí in previous texts by Salinas, and in the literature on native Mexican groups generally. "Otomí" is from a Nahuatl word adopted by the Spaniards and rejected now by bilingual education leaders like Salinas (see Introduction). Tarascan people now self-identify as Purépecha, and the Tarahumara refer to themselves as Ralámulis. Other changes are sure to follow.

All the bilingual educational material produced by the Dirección General de Educación Indígena, and the publications of the Instituto Nacional Indigenista now use the self-identifying words selected by various bilingual educators. Indian educators understand that use of these terms in the Mexican bureaucracy is symbolic and that it has not produced major changes in relationships between mestizo and Indian people. Nonetheless, the symbols are considered important among the Indian educators of my acquaintance, just as the terms "Black" and "Ms." have been important in the United States. Unlike the United States, though, the symbolic power of self-referent words is low in Mexico because it is not backed up by economic and voting power.

2. At various places in the text I have translated the word "mengu" as "native," or "Indian" or "inhabitant" or just as "people." The word in Ñähñu refers to people who are native to a particular place—an entire continent or a village.

3. This is a reference to the pointed questions being asked by Indian political activists who point out that their forebears built the fortunes of Mexico but that they have not gotten any of the wealth passed on to them.

4. The words "zidaada" and "zinänä" in Ñähñu are translated as "saint" and "holy virgin." They also refer to God (that is, to Christ) and to the Virgin Mary. In Spanish, the generic term is "imagen,", and there is no single translation for this term in English. Throughout the text, then, I have used the English word "image" or the Spanish word "santito" to refer to any form of "imágen"; that is, to a painted icon on paper or wood, or to stone or plaster stauary, or to holy crosses. Most of the images in the larger churches are statues.

5.Throughout rural Mexico, it is customary to carry the statues or icons (or sometimes holy crosses) in a procession around the church, and sometimes out into the village after mass is finished. These processions are accompanied by musicians and worshippers, and usually end with a fireworks display. These customs are still practiced widely in rural Mexico today, and are still quite current among the Ñähñu.

Readers may reasonably question, then, why Salinas says that the "traditional period" of Ñähñu religion ends in 1950, and why he writes in the "ethnographic present," with 1950 as the benchmark. The choice of that year as the end of the "traditonal period" of Ñähñu religion is not arbitrary. That was when members of the Summer Institute of Linguistics (SIL) began to arrive in force in the Mezquital (a few missionaries had been in the area since the 1930s), and it is also about the time when the Patrimonio Indígena del Valle del Mezquital (PIVM) was established in Ixmiquilpan. The SIL is composed of evangelical missionaries who translate the Bible into the various indigenous languages of the world, and who use the Bible as their instrument for getting people to convert. The PIVM is a major development agency of the Mexican government; its job is to improve all areas of life in the Mezquital, traditionally among the poorest regions of Mexico. Both of these institutions have had a profound impact on the way of life of the Ñähñu (see Introduction).

The SIL built a major residential research facilty in Ixmiquilpan, the Centro Lingüístico del Manuel Gamio. Members of the SIL came to the Center from all over the Americas. They brought their informants and stayed in residence at the Center for months at a time, working on their translations of the Bible into the indigenous languages of the New World. Their presence in the Mezquital was prominent for three decades. In the late 1970s, the Summer Institute of Linguistics was asked by the Mexican government to leave Mexico. They began vacating their headquarters in Mexico City in 1989, but their legacy in the Mezquital is the presence today of thousands of Ñähñu converts, along with an increasing number of Protestant churches that are in competition with the Catholic churches for the allegiance of the people.

Conservatively, the PIVM has spent several hundred million dollars over the past 35 years (I have not been able to get reliable figures regarding its budget), primarily on infrastructural projects. They have built schools, potable water systems, roads, and clinics. They have brought electricity to the remotest villages. And they have developed a massive irrigation project that brings the sewage water from Mexico City (altitude 2,300 meters) by gravity to the lower parts of the Mezquital (altitude 1,825 meters).

Over the years, there have been accusations that the authorities of the PIVM were corrupt and that they diverted funds for their own use. Ñähñu almost universally say that the mestizo authorities of the PIVM treat the Indians like dirt. Only one of the directors of the PIVM, the late Maurilio Muñoz, was a

Ñähñu. In fact, Muñoz was an anthropologist who went into public service. His memory is revered in the Mezquital by the Ñähñu. Virtually all positions of power in the PIVM are held by mestizos who are not from the local area. Some of them have told me that they considered their stay at the PIVM as a kind of way station — a post on the way towards something better in government service.

For all the probable corruption; for all the possible diversion of funds from projects; and for the all the lack of goodwill between the Ñähñu and the people who run the PIVM, one thing is very clear: since the PIVM came to the Mezquital, massive infrastructural changes have taken place. Until recently, when the agency began closing down many of its operations, it employed hundreds of people directly, and its building projects provided temporary jobs for thousands over the years. When both the SIL and the PIVM arrived around 1950, then, the Mezquital entered a new era.

6. The main church in Ixmiquilpan is a major cathedral. It was begun by Franciscans in 1542 and took more than 60 years to complete. The interior contains frescoes depicting scenes of Ñähñu life, made by Indian artists of the time. The frescoes were covered over in the 1700s, but were rediscovered in the 1950s and have since been partially restored. The cathedral is now a national historical monument.

7. The familiar term in Spanish is "promesa"—"promise," "vow" or "oath." People will often vow to make an offering of money or candles or flowers to a particular saint or image of Christ or to one of the holy virgins (Mary, Guadalupe, etc.) after recovering from an illness, or after completing a successful business deal. They will also do this in anticipation of recovery or success. That is, they will ask one of the "santitos" (male or female) to help them over some trouble or give them health and luck, or make the crops grow or bring rain, or make their children smart, or whatever. I have used the terms "promise" or "vow" or "oath" to refer to these activities throughout the text. I have also used the word "alms," and sometimes "charity" to refer to the money left in the church by people making these offerings in fulfillment of vows or just as part of their normal worshipping activities.

8. Note that in the Ñähñu text Salinas uses the present tense though he is referring to the past. I have retained his usage here, even though it is now very rare to see traditional flutists and drummers at religious ceremonies. This is one of the many changes that have occurred in the past few decades.

9. This plant is called "planta aérea" in Spanish. It is an epiphytic bromeliad.

10. The Ñähñu word "jäpi" is translated as "relíquia" in Spanish but is not easily rendered as "relic" in English. It refers instead to something left at the church as an offering to one of the images, and to a "remembrance" given to a supplicant after he or she has made an offering or returns from mass. I have used both "relic" and "remembrance" in the text.

11. These terms will become clear in the text. Suffice here to say only that the "castillos," or fireworks towers, continue to be part of local celebrations today, but that "toritos" (a man hopping around with fireworks exploding off his back) are becoming rare.

12. The words "mayordomo" and "cargo" are well known to all students of Mexican culture. For those not familiar with these terms, they will become quite clear in their usage in the text. Rather than use any euphemisms, I have retained throughout the text the use of the Spanish word mayordomo ("mep̱äte" in Ñähñu) and cargo ("m'ep̱ina"). For fuller treatment of the mayordomo and cargo systems in rural Mexico, see Cancian, 1965.

13. As with many other Indian languages of Mexico, Ñähñu does not distinguish between green and blue with a single lexeme. The Ñähñu word for "grue" (green-blue), as it is known by linguists, is "nk'ami."

14. The word "assistants" here may seem somewhat awkward. As will become clear in the text, whenever anyone (man or woman) takes on any cargo or similar obligation (like offering a communal meal), he or she involves a number of "helpers." Later on, of course, these assistants have call on the aid of the first party when they perform cargos of their own.

15. This is "xadi" in Ñähñu.

16. A brazada is the distance between the fingertips of outstretched arms. In practice, it is about one and a half meters.

17. These arches are no longer built in Ixmiquilpan. In some of the rural villages, a token arch is built outside the church during local fiestas for village patron saints.

18. It is still common practice in many parts of rural Mexico for prisoners in local jails to sweep the streets and help clean up after market day.

19. This is the Ministry of Public Administration, the national level ministry which is in charge of local criminal justice, and which names local judges in towns like Ixmiquilpan. Village level judges are an entirely different matter, discussed further on.

20. The corruption referred to here is both past and present; the "hundreds of pesos" of course, refers to a time when the peso was worth much more than it is today. For nearly two decades, until 1976, the peso was valued at 12.5 per U.S.

dollar. In August 1985 the peso was valued at around 350 per dollar; by January 1989, it was 2,400 per dollar.

21. Aguardiente sometimes refers to any form of bootleg whiskey. Usually, however, it refers to the clear, potent liquor made from sugar cane, and sold under many different brand names in Mexico and elsewhere in Latin America. The name means "water that bites," and with good reason. It is usually 40% alcohol, but may be higher in some cases.

22. Here again Salinas is referring to prices around 25 years ago or more. In 1962, when I first started working in Ixmiquilpan, tamalitos were three for a peso, as were chalupitas and other tortilla- and maize-based snacks sold by street vendors.

23. "Masa" is the dough from which tortillas are made.

24. "Milpa" is the word used throughout Mexico to refer to a small plot of agricultural land.

25. "Nixtamal" is the final dough from which tortillas are made. Lime is added to the masa to make nixtamal.

26. "Mole" is the famous Mexican stew of meat or fowl, made with a hot chocolate sauce containing chile and sesame. "Atole" is a gruel, generally made by boiling corn flour in either water or milk. "Pinole" is ground, toasted corn. It may be mixed with water and sugar (or cocoa or cinnamon) as a drink.

27. A "cuartillo" is a quarter of a peck. It is the standard measurement for selling grains. The corn merchants at the markets throughout Mexico use a metal container, with a handle, which is exactly a cuartillo. They scoop up the corn from the great heaps they lay out on a ground cloth, and pour it into sacks or carrying cloths brought along by the clients at the markets. As they scoop up the grain, they wipe their hand across the top to level out the measure, and if they cause an indentation below the lip of the container, they are likely to lose customers, or even to be reported to the police. Most merchants throw in a "puño" or "puño de la mano" of corn at the end of a sale just to make sure that the customer is satisfied with the measure. A "puño" is a quarter of a cuartillo; a "puño de la mano" is the amount in two cupped hands.

28. The tejocote is the *Crategeus mexicana,* a fruit resembling that of the blackthorn bush. While some species of tejocote grow in the U.S., consumption of the fruit is limited mostly to Mexico. It is a bittersweet fruit, with a strong odor, orange-yellow pulp, and several small seeds in the middle.

29. There is a great variety of chile peppers in Mexico, with an even greater variety of names. Chile de arbol refers to the familiar short red chili peppers. I have not been able to determine the botanical names for these chiles. Suffice to

say that anyone in the Ixmiquilpan market would sell you exactly the right product if you asked for these chiles by their local names.

30. "Loló" means "fat" in Ñähñu. The word is also used as a baby-talk expression for tortilla or for food, in general. It is one of the rare words in Ñähñu with the sound "L."

31. Nopal leaves are the fleshy pads of the prickly pear cactus plant (genus *Opuntia*), of which there are many varieties (see Volume III). "Quelites" is the generic term for edible greens. Quelites of many different kinds are gathered, sold and eaten among the poor. Wealthy people in the cities, however, can sometimes be heard extolling the virtues of quelites as a kind of chic "soul food." "Quintoniles" are greens of the family *Malvaceae,* taken from the spike or ear of the corn plant. (But see also note 28, Volume I.) "Verdolaga" is the common name for a range of greens, including *Portulaca oleracea* and other of the genus *Potulaca,* or purslanes. "Hediondilla" in central Mexico is *Cassia occidentalis, Chenopodium album* and other members of the chenopodiaceous, or goosefoot plants (including beets and spinach), and *Covillea tridentada,* a member of the zygophyllaceous, or bean caper family. "Chicharrón" is pork rind, fried in its own fat.

32. "Barbacóa," of course, means "barbecue." The word is originally West Indian; it was taken into Spanish, and thence to English. In Mexico, however, the word does not refer to the open pit barbecue, or backyard coal barbecue familiar to most Americans. Barbacóa is meat roasted in closed ground pits. In the southeastern parts of Mexico, the meat (which may be fowl or goat or pig or beef) is wrapped in banana leaves, giving it a distinctive flavor. In the northern and central parts of the country, the meat is wrapped in maguey leaves, and of course, this imparts a distinctive flavor as well. Salinas refers here, of course, to the distinctive barbacóa of the central region, which may, indeed, have been invented by the Ñähñu, since they are the people of Mexico most associated with use of the maguey plant for food, clothing, and shelter (see Volume III).

33. "Cántaros" are narrow-mouthed ceramic pitchers for holding water.

The word "guaje" is from Nahuatl and refers to the hard rinds of gourds. These are used as vessels, for drinking and for storing small items. Specifically, guajes are *Leucanea esculenta*. The elaborate decoration of gourds is a folk art, indigenous to Michoacán, and is much appreciated by the Ñähñu. In recent years, the techniques of engraving and painting gourds have been transferred to other items (small wooden boxes, large wooden chests, trays), which are sold in the tourist shops in Mexico City.

"Acocotes" (*Lageneria vulgaris*) are elongated gourds, pierced on both ends, and used to suck the "aguamiel," or sugary nectar, from the heart of the maguey plant. A person who extracts the aguamiel is called a "tlachiquero." He or she sucks up the aguamiel, covers the hole at the broad, mouth end of the gourd, transfers the narrow end to an "olla," or large ceramic jug, carried over the back with a tumpline across the forehead, releases the hole and drains the nectar into the jug.

These days, it is rare to see anyone with a ceramic olla anymore. Most people carry large plastic containers (also carried by tumpline), and continue to use the acocote as a natural straw to extract the aguamiel. I have asked many people why they use plastic containers for the aguamiel and the universal answer is that the containers don't break when you accidentally set your load down on a rock when resting. No substitute has been found necessary for the acocote, however, and there are no more efficient ways of distributing the weight of burdens on a human than with tumplines.

"Raspadores" are metal scrapers. Every time a tlachiquero takes aguamiel from a maguey, he or she scrapes out a layer of the pulp from the bowl in the center of the plant. This cleans insects and dirt out of the bowl, or heart, and stimulates the production of more aguamiel by the plant. (For a detailed description of the process of making pulque, see Volume III.)

"Jícaras" are drinking vessels, made from the fruit of the jícaro tree (*Crescentia cujete*). The fruits are large and have a thick, ligneous rind. They are cut in half, scooped out, and dried. Jícaras are traditionally used in Mexico as cups for drinking chocolate. Among the Ñähñu they are also used for drinking pulque. Decorating jícaras is a folk art form. Like guajes, they may be painted, engraved and lacquered. The "white" or "natural" jícaras referred to here are undecorated and, hence, less expensive.

34. "Ixtle" refers to all forms of hennequen, or fiber from various plants of the genus *Agave*. Traditionally, the Ñähñu used the fiber from the maguey, or century plant (so-called because it takes from 4-15 years to mature) and the lechuguilla plant. Both are agaves. Very few people extract maguey fiber anymore, although a large number still extract ixtle from the lechuguilla. The lechuguilla plant is much smaller than the various maguey plants, and many more leaves have to be mashed in order to extract a salable amount of fiber. However, many maguey plants are left to mature for both their aguamiel and for the pulque made from that nectar. The leaves of those magueys are spent and are useless for extracting fiber. Many varieties of maguey are not used for making pulque.

However, extraction of ixtle from maguey leaves is a very arduous process. By contrast, the lechuguilla, which grows wild and in abundance all over the valley, yields its fiber quite easily and children can be enlisted in the family enterprise of extracting it. The Ixmiquilpan market has an entire section devoted to ixtle and products, such as rope, made from the fiber. Today, however, most of the ixtle sold in the market is from other parts of Mexico, such as Yucatan, where hennequen production is mechanized. Ñähñu weavers of "ayates" (carrying cloths made from ixtle) used to extract their own fiber from local plants. Today many of them buy the ixtle in the Ixmiquilpan market and dedicate their time to backstrap weaving of the cloths for sale locally. Purchasing ixtle and making more ayates in the time available produces marginally more income than does devoting one's time to extraction of free fiber and production of fewer ayates, at much lower energy costs to the producer.

35. Molcajetes are small, bowl-shaped mortars, with three legs, usually made from volcanic rock. They are used for making salsa from ground chile peppers, and for triturating hard condiments such as cumin. The stone molcajetes are always sold with a pestle of the same material. Wooden pestles, obtained separately, are used with the ceramic molcajetes. The ceramic molcajetes also have three legs, and have a rough inner surface, made by scoring the clay in a criss-cross pattern before firing. They are used almost exclusively for making salsa.

36. To this day, posts, axe handles and other articles of wood are sold by men from villages around Gundó, high in the mountains about 35 kilometers by dirt road from Ixmiquilpan, and about 20 kilometers from Orizabita. The men travel to the Ixmiquilpan market every week and set up in front of the eighteenth-century bridge in the center of the market. The climate in the mountain villages (which are situated above 2,500 meters above sea level) is very different from that of the valley. It is much wetter, but the elevation also means that coniferous trees grow very slowly. The natural stands of pines have been slowly disappearing as men cut them down for fuel and for sale in the market.

37. As noted above, castillo and torito are explained further on in the narrative. The castillo is a fireworks tower. It can be very, very elaborate and may last for more than 20 minutes. During that time, the tower spews roman candles, spinners, cherry bombs, and a variety of multicolored fireworks. It may have several crossbars, also laden with fireworks displays. Itinerant fireworks makers used to go all over Mexico, from village to village, setting up castillos for the fiestas. The trade is apparently dying out, although the major fiestas continue to have castillos and even more modern fireworks displays.

38. The system of loans described in the next few paragraphs is still in existence today, though with different commodities changing hands. Instead of lending a goat, a man might lend another the cost of the music for a fiesta, for example. Today, fiestas are often private affairs, rather than just responses to

church and village obligations. The wedding of one's children; the graduation of a child from primary or secondary school; the completion of a family head's fiftieth birthday; all these may be the occasion for holding a private fiesta. These parties include the killing or purchase of animals, the making of barbacóa, the hiring of professional musicians, and the purchase of large quantities of pulque, beer, and brandy. The brand name of the brandy reflects the financial circumstances of the person giving the fiesta.

Male friends help one another by bringing cases of beer, or paying for extra time for the musicians (beyond the regular five hour contract paid for by the host), or by bringing bottles of expensive brandy. In any event, the loans made between pairs of men to help pay for one another's fiesta obligations creates a network of debt relations that is highly structured. I am convinced that the network of debts was, and continues to be, an important component of village, and intervillage social structure. It serves to distribute risk (since one need not expend all one's capital at once on a fiesta), and to lock families into relations that translate into marriages among junior members of the family, and into business relations as well.

A full study of the way in which fiesta debt relations are established, how they are maintained, and how they serve to structure aspects of village and intervillage relations would be very important for our understanding of modern rural Mexico.

39. As in many poor societies, there is a lot of emphasis placed on eating meat. Throughout the text it is stressed time and again how important it is for a host to provide sufficient meat, even if it means killing a head of cattle to fulfill one's obligations. Herds of goats are considered wealth precisely because they are bank accounts filled with meat. Currencies may fluctuate in value; land may or may not be arable, depending on the vagaries of the weather; but herds of animals like goats that can fend pretty much for themselves in the desert are prized because they are a source of meat protein.

When villages in the Ñähñu area get irrigation, the very first thing people talk about is raising alfalfa. They do this for two reasons. First, as Mexico's middle class has burgeoned in the cities, so too has the demand for beef. Cattle ranching is among the fastest growing of Mexico's industries, and there seems to be no keeping up with the demand. Alfalfa is in very high demand for cattle fodder. Second, raising alfalfa allows people to keep a few head of cattle of their own. If chickens and goats are prized as sources of meat, then cattle are an order of magnitude more desirable. As Harris (1985) shows, this reflects a worldwide trend.

Foster (1965) maintains that Mexican peasants are envious of one another's wealth and that the cargo-fiesta system is a wealth leveling mechanism. By saddling the wealthy members of a village with mayordomo obligations, they are forced to kill off their animals and are thus reduced in their riches.

This may be a proximate cause of the system, but I think the underlying issue is meat protein distribution. We have very poor data on the actual food intake of Mexican rural people (or any other rural people, for that matter). I suspect that the actual protein intake in rural villages that practiced the fiesta system in the past, with all its cargo obligations, was (and remains) far greater than is generally imagined. After allowing for death from dehydration due to diarrhea (the primary cause of infant death), residual infant mortality and lack of growth may be due more in rural Mexico to lack of access to meat protein than to lack of access by the population in general.

40. "Itacate" ("t'egi") refers to food carried along on a trip, or to work. I have seen the custom of sending people home with extra meat and tortillas practiced widely in the valley today.

41. Mole de olla is truly a delicious meal, and one can see why, in an environment of very scarce meat resources, it would be reserved for prominent people. When they can get it, however, Ñähñu prefer plain broiled beef (the famous "carne asada"). Mole de olla is a stew and thus serves many more people per kilogram of meat than plain beef does. Moreover, the preparation of mole de olla results in tenderizing of otherwise tough meat. Being able to afford good quality, tender, beef to eat plain, without chopping it into stews is a sign of real wealth anywhere in rural Mexico.

42. Dianas are military, or marching songs, with a strong drum beat.

43. This refers to the fifth Friday after Pentecost.

44. These are the "jueces auxiliares," or local authorities who represent municipal justice at the village level. They are elected every year at village meetings. They mediate disputes and decide when one is serious enough to warrant bringing the parties to Ixmiquilpan. Throughout the text I have referred to them simply as "judges."

45. This is the name of the santito from Orizabita.

46. In the Ñähñu original, Salinas says that they go to the place called the "sementeryo, nu Ñähñu nt'agi," or "the cemetery, which is called nt'agi in Ñähñu." "Sementeryo," of course, is from the Spanish "cementerio," and is used in Ñähñu as a loan word. Salinas is building a Ñähñu dictionary at this time and often takes pains to use original Ñähñu words in place of more commonly used borrowings from Spanish. In this case he felt it was important to point out the difference in the text.

47. "Morral" in Mexico refers to a woven bag, worn over the shoulder by men. In the Mezquital, there are distinctive designs that have become quite popular as tourist items, and that are now sold outside the valley. Traditionally, morrales were woven from ixtle and these bags are still sold in the market and are still worn by men in the countryside.

48. Monday is market day in Ixmiquilpan. The markets are held on different days in the various county seats. Markets are on Sunday in Actopan and Al-fajayucan, for example, and on Saturdays in Cardonal, and so on.

49. The cucharilla is described at length in Volume III. It grows high in the mountains where there is more moisture than in the valley, and it grows along very steep slopes. It is hard to find and is prized for its bright, white, shiny, spoonlike leaf stems. This plant is a member of the genus *Dasilyrion;* it is short (about one meter high) and is made up of many narrow leaves (one to three centimeters wide) that have sharp thorns along both long edges. The leaves grow out from a central heart and when they are peeled off the heart, the bright, white leaf stem is exposed. The leaves are cut short and woven into flower arrangements.

50. "Cleansing" is done by the mayordomos using coins given to them by supplicants. The mayordomo passes the coin over the head, shoulders and upper back of the worshipper. Then the coin is added to the collection for the santitos.

51. "Cleansing," or "purifying" is done with ejotes as well as with coins. Both boys and girls alike are subjected to this particular form of cleansing.

52. "Carrizo" refers to common reed grass here, including *Phragmites communis* and other gramineous plants. It also is used to refer to *Olyra latifolia,* a plant that looks like bamboo and grows along river banks.

53. I have used the generic word "fowl" here because Salinas uses it in the original. The word "oni" in Ñähñu refers to both chickens ("onjä") and turkeys ("däm'oni"), and in fact either or both of these fowl may be lent between women.

54. The posadas are folkloric celebrations that go on for nine days before Christmas. Although originally a purely religious act, posadas have become a major part of Christmas secular celebrations, and now even include popular dancing. The most common act during the time of the posadas is what we would call "Christmas caroling." Groups of people go around to houses, carrying candles, and singing carols. They may be joined by those in the house they stop at, and they may just start dancing as well. Although this custom is still carried on in small villages to some extent, in the larger towns the time of the posadas is considered a time of general merriment, including many forms of secular entertainment.

55. This is the religious enactment of the posada, which became a house-to-house enactment, and eventually a general, secular revelry as well.

56. Replicas of the baby Jesus are usually made of painted plaster. Some are naked, and some wear tunics, depending on the level of modesty in the village.

57. There is a statue of El Sr. del Buen Viaje in the village of Defay, in the mountains above Orizabita. Defay is a very small community (about 20 families), which is part of the political jurisdiction of Orizabita.

58. One of the auxiliary judges of Orizabita. The word "Centro" here refers to the obvious, visible village of Orizabita. I say "obvious" because a lot of the pueblo is not obvious to outsiders who visit the Ñähñu for the first time. I have had some students out in the Mezquital who have asked me, "Where are the villages?" Traditionally, the Ñähñu lived in dispersed, nonnucleated communities. The population density is still very low (less than 10 people per square mile in the most remote parts of the valley), reflecting the harsh environmental conditions. It simply takes a lot of territory per capita to pull food from the desert.

When the Spaniards first encountered the Ñähñu, they found the scattered population an administrative nuisance. They built churches at strategic places throughout the Mezquital Valley as centers, in the hopes of attracting people to live in nucleated settlements. There was some success in the strategy, but it was by no means completely successful. In the 1950s, with the coming to Ixmiquilpan of the PIVM (see Note 5 above, and the Introduction), population patterns began to change rather dramatically. What churches and seats of religious power could not accomplish, schools, potable water, electricity, roads, and clinics have begun to accomplish to a great extent. In 1962, when I first worked in Orizabita, there were about 400 persons in the main village. Today, there may be 900, despite a lot of migration to Mexico City.

The pueblo of Orizabita is composed of a number of "barrios" or "manzanas," including the many small villages from Boxhuada to La Lagunita and Gundó to the north, and others which are mentioned in the text. Each of these communities is attracting the dispersed people from the countryside with their own schools, electricity, and so on. But Orizabita itself remains the Centro, the main judicial and administrative center of the pueblo. That is why, in most instances I use the word "pueblo" for a Centro-type barrio, and "community" or "village" to refer to smaller populations. When someone in Orizabita (or in La Lagunita, for that matter) says "I'm going to the Centro," however, he means "I'm going to Ixmiquilpan." In Ñähñu there is no ambiguity; one says either "I am going to Orizabita" or "I am going to Ixmiquilpan" or "I'm going to the market," which is the same as saying that one is going to Ixmiquilpan. The refcrence to Centro in the present context is to Orizabita, since there are no *auxiliary* judges in Ixmiquilpan.

59. The technical term in English for a master fireworks maker is "pyrotechnist." I have used this term along with "fireworks maker" in the text. Like many skilled craftsmen, the fireworks masters in Mexico take on apprentices, often from their own extended families. They are itinerant artisans who were once institutions throughout rural Mexico. As Jesús notes towards the end of this volume, however, the profession of pyrotechnist is on the decline. There are still many people practicing the craft, however.

60. Actopan is a town about 35 kilometers south of Ixmiquilpan. Like Ixmiquilpan, it is the seat of a major cathedral and a weekly market. There are dozens of small Ñähñu villages in the municipio of Actopan, as there are in Chapantongo, Chilcuauhtla, Cardonal, Alfajayucan, Tasquillo, and other municipios in the Mezquital Valley. Each of these municipios is a Centro for some group of Ñähñu. The most important municipio, in terms of population of Ñähñu, is Ixmiquilpan. There is, of course, a great deal of interpersonal exchange, including debt relations and affinal ties, across municipio boundaries *within* the Mezquital, but less contact between the Ñähñu of the Mezquital and those of the other areas. There is very little contact, for example, between the Mezquital and the Sierra Ñähñu of the state of Hidalgo (who, despite the name "Sierra," live at much lower altitudes than the Mezquital Ñähñu).

61. The pirul is the American pepper tree (*Schinus molle*).

62. Here the word "carrizo" refers to a bamboolike plant, probably the *Olyra latifolia*, rather than to reed grass, as in earlier instances.

63. Many stories of tragedies are told about pyrotechnists. In fact, as Jesús relates later on, several people have been killed in Ixmiquilpan as a result of carelessness in handling fireworks. It is assumed that a fireworks maker will lose an eye or one or more fingers in the course of his career, and indeed, most of the pyrotechnists I have seen over the years bear the unfortunate marks of their trade.

64. As noted earlier, there are many places in the text where Jesús refers to people getting their "assistants" to help them do something: women making large batches of tortillas; men killing goats; mayordomos serving food at a fiesta; and so on. Such assistants are not on anyone's payroll. Nor are they necessarily socially inferior to the person whom they are helping. In one year a man may be an "assistant" to another who is mayordomo; the next year, the roles may be reversed. The same is true for women who call on one another for help in fulfilling their obligations or those of their husbands' cargos. But this is not to

say that there are no gradations of rank, prestige, and economic status in these villages. To be sure, there are some people who are much wealthier than others and who have established patron-client relationships with persons who are beneath them, socially and economically. More respected, high status members of the community, such as school teachers, former judges, and so on, have many men on whom they can call for assistance in killing goats, or repairing their homes, or notifying other village authorities of a meeting, and so on.

65. At a private fiesta for a birthday in March 1985, a group of three musicians charged 20,000 pesos for five hours. The exchange rate was then 220 to the dollar.

66. The last time that the man came to Orizabita was in 1981, according to Jesús.

67. This is an icon print on cloth, about 2.5 by 1.6 meters. It is glued to the back wall of a large, glass-fronted case.

68. This custom of notifying guests in writing is still practiced, to a limited extent, in some villages, according to Jesús.

69. This Ñähñu word is borrowed from Spanish "huella," or "footsteps."

70. A "topo" is one-fourth liter.

71. Palm Sunday.

72. These are baskets for holding tortillas.

73. Here Jesús uses the Ñähñu word "enxe" which translates as "children who are not culpable for their sins." This usually means unbaptized babies in the Catholic church, but the general usage among the Ñähñu of the Mezquital is that children 13 or 14 years of age and younger are in this category.

74. Note the use of the word "angelitos," or "little angels," referring to children who have died. In Ñähñu it is the diminutive of "enxe." The infant mortality rate has been very high in the Mezquital Valley, although in recent years it has been dropping. In 1962, I estimated that infant mortality in the Mezquital might have been as high as 60 per thousand in the first two years of life. This has been cut in the last two decades, perhaps by as much as a fourth, but this still places the infant mortality rate at four times that of the United States. There has been some decrease in fertility, but it has not matched the decline in infant mortality. Despite this, the Ñähñu population of the valley seems to have remained fairly stable, probably due to migration. Census figures show about 80,000 Ñähñu in the Mezquital region, down from 90,000 in 1960.

These estimates are based on what I consider to be highly unreliable counts. The census takers do not always trek out into the distant countryside to enumerate the population. Many census takers are poorly trained. Probably most important, people are registered as Indians only if they claim to speak an Indian language. It is not known how many Indians claim *not* to speak their native language when asked by census takers about the matter, but the number must be substantial. The simple fact is that there are no reliable or accurate estimates of the Indian populations of Mexico. Jesús guesses that the Mezquital Ñähñu may number as many as 150,000, and that there are between a third and a half a million Ñähñu among the seven dialect groups (see Introduction).

75. These are rhomboid shaped lumps of masa, or tortilla dough, stuffed with beans.

76 Chayote is the product of the chayotera, a cucurbitaceous vine, the *Sechium edule*. It is eaten as a vegetable and is known in English as mirliton.

77. Also called "pan de muertos," these are small bread cakes made of wheat flour and covered with sugar on top. They are eaten especially on the Day of the Dead.

78. These are flowers of the common marigold.

79. This is the typical folkloric music of the Veracruz region, popular all through the state of Hidalgo. The songs are usually couplets, and the troubadours of the region take pride in being able to make up verses on the spot. The verses are often slightly risque, with double entendres a hallmark. At dances, the music may be played without verses for a while, but good huapangueros will always single out people in the group and make up verses poking fun at them. The host may feed information about people at the fiesta to the huapangueros so that the singers can make up verses that hit home.

80. Here Jesús is referring to the adult males of the community who are entitled to participate in the village meeting. When he refers to "the people" he usually means adult, married males, unless the text makes it clear that women are included.

81. As will become clear, many communities in the Mezquital (and elsewhere in Mexico) have split over the issue of Evangelical Protestant conversions. Boxhuada, however, is an example of a split in recent times that was based on population and land pressure, and where religion was not a major factor. The people of Boxhuada (which was at one time a barrio of Orizabita) built their own school in the early 1960s, and since then they have become more and more independent of Orizabita. They remain mostly Catholics, and continue to participate in both the religious and secular affairs of Orizabita.

82. The expression for "Protestant" in Ñähñu is "rä zi ku," literally "the little brother." As Jesús explains, this phrase is used because the Protestants address each other as "brother." When he says in Ñähñu that "most of the people (in

Boxhuada) believe in God," he means that they are Catholics. It is quite common to refer to Protestants as not being Christians and as being persons who do not believe in God or in Jesus Christ.

83. "Puerto" is a mountain pass. The Mezquital region changes dramatically here, from desert to almost lush mountain greenery. On the other side of the Puerto de Piedra is the little community of La Lagunita, so named because it has a small pond right in the middle of it. Cattle come to water at the pond, and there is a running brook at the rear of the village. In recent years several enterprising people in the village have planted fruit trees, some of which are now bearing. Further up the mountain, in Gundó, there are some successful apple orchards that produce sufficient crop for people to earn a living. There is no irrigation in the mountain terrain at the top of the Mezquital, but there is plenty of moisture, both from streams and runoffs, as well as from rain and frequent fog. More information about the change in terrain is contained in Volume III. See also Mc-Carty, 1985 for a discussion of life in La Lagunita.

84. This is the feast of the Holy Kings, or Epiphany.

85. The exact dates of the crosses at La Lagunita are not known, but it is thought that they were first installed during the middle Colonial period, around the beginning of the seventeenth century.

86. This is the common name in Mexico for corrugated asbestos sheets. It is also used to refer to zinc laminated tin, a very popular roofing material. The new church in Lagunita has a metal lámina roof.

87. Manta is a kind of coarse, white, bleached cotton cloth, used for making ordinary (nonfestival) clothing.

88. Deceased men are dressed by one or more of their compadres, ideally, while deceased women are dressed by their comadre(s).

89. This is "jote" in Ñähñu. A barranca is a steep-sided gulch, or ravine that is usually dry, except after heavy rains. It is sometimes called an arroyo, both in Spanish and in the American Southwest. The particular barranca referred to here carries runoff water after rains in the mountains, but it maintains a flow all year.

90. The evergreen mountain oaks of the Mexican altiplano are members of the genus *Quercus*. The pines are known in English as "pitch pines" or, in some regions, as "fire starters." The Mexican pines of the Mesa Central are highly resinous; the most saturated branches are chopped up and sold in small batches as fire starter wood. The particular fir referred to here is the *Abies religiosa*, known as the "oyamel" in Mexico.

91. The reason that there are "no longer" any large trees on these mountains is simply that they have been cut down for fuel and for sale. When Jesús talks

about the "people from the mountains" who sell poles in the Ixmiquilpan market (see Volume III, and also earlier in this volume), he is referring to the people from this area, along with those from Gundó, Cuesta Colorada, etc.

92. "Mamposteria" ("jädo" in Ñähñu) refers to rubble masonry construction.

93. "Rancheras" and "corridos" are ballads, usually about romance or adventures. They are very popular on the radio, even today, and are the equivalent of country music in the United States. They are the standard fare in rural fiestas, although rock and roll is becoming more and more popular, even in relatively isolated provincial areas like the Mezquital. During the time that most of Jesús's narrative refers to, however, the rancheras and corridos were the only styles of music at local village fiestas and dances at people's homes.

94. The "Presidencia Municipal" is the equivalent of the county seat in the United States. The municipalities in Mexico are generally known by the name of the presidencia. So, there is the Municipio de Ixmiquilpan, the Municipio de Cardonal, and so on. The Municipio de Santa María is today called Nicolás Flores.

95. Traditionally, since middle Colonial times, at least, Indian men throughout Mexico wore these baggy pants made of bleached cotton cloth, or manta. Among some groups, the men still wear calzoncs, but the Ñähñu of the Mezquital no longer do so. Before 1950, however, the "ethnographic present" for Salinas's narrative, some Ñähñu are reported to have still worn manta.

96. The rebozo is the ubiquitous shawl worn by rural middle- and lower-class women in many areas of Mexico. It covers the shoulders and is used both to carry babies and to hold babies while nursing. Rebozos were traditionally made of cotton, wool, and silk, and are now also made of synthetic fabrics. They are often highly decorated with embroidery, and the finest of them are used exclusively for attending festivals and for visiting.

97. This is *O. kleineae* or possibly *O. imbricata*. It has long, thin, spine covered branches rather than the familiar pads of the prickly pear plant, and it produces a small tuna that is not consumed by humans, but is eaten by goats.

98. There are many species of cardón, or "thistle" cactus in the Mezquital. They have long, hard, white needles. The cardón blanco is the *O. tunicata*. It was used traditionally to make combs and devices for carding raw wool, called "*card*adores" in Spanish, hence its name. See Volumes II and III.

99. One of the euphorbiaceous or spurge family of plants, the "sangre de grado" is known as the croton plant in some parts of the United States and is used in the Mezquital as a disinfectant and pain killer for wounds. The juice from the fleshy buds on the stems of the plant is rubbed on cactus punctures, for

example. From my own experience, it appears to have an immediate soothing effect, and reduces swelling.

100. Recall that these are the long hollow gourds (*Lagenaria vulgaris*) used for sucking the aguamiel out of the maguey plants in the making of pulque.

101. On more than one occasion in this narrative Jesús refers to the sermon in the middle of the mass as a scolding.

102. In Ñähñu Jesús uses the word "nijä" to refer to churches of both the Protestant and the Catholic faiths. In Spanish he always refers to the churches of the Evangelicals as "templos."

103. The image of the Virgin of Candelaria is a cloth icon there.

104. Tejocotes are the fruit of the *Crategus mexicana*. Jícamas are a sweet, bulbous tuber, the *Pachyrhizus angulatus*.

105. Jesús is measuring the altitude from the village of El Saúz on the valley floor rather than from sea level. The peak he refers to is about 2600 meters above sea level.

106. Readers will undoubtedly note that the word "matha" is the same as that in the phrase "Rä 'Matha Rä Bothähi," or "The Mezquital Valley." Although the common name of the area refers to a "valley," in Ñähñu the name refers generally to a large open plain at the bottom of the valley.

107. Recall that the word "Centro" is used to refer to the main barrio of a pueblo or town. In this case, the reference is to the main cathedral in Los Remedios.

108. In particular, Jesús refers here to "zacate," or fodder composed of the leaves of corn plants.

109. This is a framed cloth print, about one and a half meters square.

110. Treatment here refers to rubbing the relic on parts of the body, or to using the relic as incense to fume parts of the body.

111. The jitomate is the familiar, large, round tomato, the *Lycopersicum esculentum*. The fruit known in the Mezquital as the "tomate" is either the small, round, green tomato (*Physalis coztomatl*), used in the making of chile sauce, or the European tomato (sometimes known as Italian or plum tomatoes), the *Solanum lycopersicum*.

112. The instruments used were the trumpet, trombone, and clarinet.

113. The "capulines de ratón" are one of the many shrubs called "capulines"; they are related to the rose or possibly the almond family. The "nopal de tunas pintaderas" may be *O. cantabrigiensis*. In any event, the pintadera is considered of low class and is mostly eaten by goats.

114. These are wheels, about a meter and a half in diameter that revolve and spew multicolored sparks and flames, sometimes forming figures. The wheels

are mounted on poles, about two meters long, and are held aloft by a man as they spin around. "Remolinos" are small wheels, about 50 centimeters in diameter that are mounted on short poles and shot aloft to a height of 30-40 meters. As they spin and rise, they leave a trail of multicolored lights. They are sometimes also call "omnis."

115. "T'eni" in Ñähñu, means "measure." The Spanish noun for "measure" is "medida."

116. A cross is left on the floor of a house where a person has died. It is usually placed where the person used to sleep. After nine days, the cross is picked up and placed on the deceased's grave.

117. This is a somewhat opaque reference to the extremely high infant mortality rate that prevails among the Ñähñu. Unbaptized babies cannot go to heaven, so there is some urgency in baptizing newborns. The problem is that it costs (and still costs) a great deal of money to have a formal baptism, including the expenses for the feast that one must give. Many Ñähñu wait until they have accumulated sufficient funds before holding a baptism; they may wait until they have two children to baptize at one time. There is some feeling among people whom I have talked to that people are waiting longer and longer to hold baptisms as costs escalate, and as infant mortality comes down among the more economically successful. The principal causes of death were measles and diarrhea. Infant vaccination has cut down drastically on the former, while education on rehydration techniques has begun to cut down the latter. The problem of infant death from diarrhea, however, remains acute.

118. This is the phrase made famous by Octavio Paz in his book on Mexican national character, *The Labyrinth of Solitude* (1962). The literal translation is "son of the woman who has been fucked, or violated." According to Paz, the reference is to Malintzín, La Malinche, the Aztec woman who gave herself to Cortez. From then on, by extension, all Mexican men are "hijos de la Malinche" or "hijos de la chingada."

119. "Full citizens" here refers to adult (i.e., married) men.

120. This is a framed paper print.

121. The garambullo is the *Myrtillocactus geometrizans*. It is a large cactus which bears nutritious, very small, red fruit. Cravioto says that they provide as much as 2.12 grams of protein per 100 grams, in addition to substantial amounts of vitamins A and C (1951: 150). The capulin cimarrón is a large boraginaceous plant, possibly *Erehtia tinifolia*, according to the *Diccionario de Mejicanismos*.

122. "Nanxa" is a borrowing from Spanish "naranja," meaning "orange." Church towers do not come to a perfect point, but have a ball, or "nanxa" at the top on which the cross is fixed. The ball may be decorated, as it is in El Espíritu.

123. These are called "acrobatic" bells because they do complete flips on their cross beams when they are rung.

124. This is a statue of Christ.

125. These cases are called "andas" in Spanish. They are several tiers high (like a layer cake) and mounted on twin poles for carrying by up to six bearers in a procession.

126. Priest is "makjä" and pastor is "ma'yo" in Ñähñu. In fact, the word "pastor" in Spanish and "ma'yo" in Ñähñu both mean "shepherd."

127. The ocotillo is a large, spiny bush, *Fouquieria splendens*, with dense, resinous wood used widely in central and northern Mexico to make corrals and other enclosures.

128. This refers to dry building material made of crushed lime. It is mixed with water (and sometimes other materials) to form a cement.

129. In Ñähñu this is "mändande," a loan from Spanish, meaning "commanding officer."

130. Corredizos are small canisters that run along the ground on a wire, spewing fireworks from behind. The wire is strung at a height of less than a meter, between two posts, set about 30 meters apart. Buscapiés are small fireworks that rush crazily about on the ground. In a crowd, people scurry and jump out of the way as the buscapiés ("chases feet" in Spanish) whiz by.

131. Sewage water from Mexico City has been used for the past several decades as irrigation and fertilizer for crops in the states surrounding the Federal District. The cost of building the canals has been very high, in both money and lives. Orizabita, Jesús's natal village, is too high up for the water from Mexico City to reach there by gravity, and the cost of pumps and further canal works has been judged too great for the relatively small area of flat, irrigable land that would result from major effort. The gravity-fed irrigation line is about five kilometers below Orizabita, towards Ixmiquilpan. Twenty years ago the entire stretch from Ixmiquilpan to Orizabita was desert. Today, the break in the landscape is startling.

132. These monster firecrackers are also known as "bombas." They are inserted into meter-length metal pipes that are six centimeters across. The pipes are set into the ground and the firecrackers are sent aloft, up to 70 meters, to explode in the air.

133. The cacomixtle is called "mixkle" in Ñähñu. This animal (*Bassaricus astutus*), is related to the racoon, but with a longer tail. The name in Ñähñu is a borrowing from the Nahuatl "tlacomiztli," or "half cougar," as is the name in

Spanish. The raccoon is "metri" in Ñähñu, and the badger is "tsathá." See Volume II.

134. These noodles are known as "fidéo" in Spanish.

135. This is the ubiquitous Mexican conifer of the altiplano, the Montezuma bald cypress (*Taxodium mucronatum*).

136. Hanging bridges are called "raani" in Ñähñu while fixed bridges are "sä'ye." They are considered two different kinds of things, rather than one being a kind of the other, as in English.

137. They plant various menthaceous herbs, most importantly *Salvia chian*. The plant is called "chía" in Mexican Spanish.

138. The distinction between the laborer and the campesino is that the latter has his own plots of land, or milpas. English-language dictionaries may refer to "milpas" as plots of land cleared by the slash-and-burn technique in the tropics. However, the word "milpa" is used throughout Mexico to refer to garden plots.

139. Magueys propagate by shoots. These are removed from the ground when they are about 60 centimeters high, dried out, and replanted. See Volume III.

140. This village has no Hispanicized name, like Gundó, or El Maye, or Defay, all of which are Ñähñu names that have been rendered into Spanish orthography.

141. This is a humorous reference to the kiss of the fingers after crossing oneself.

142. These are simply large, open ponds dug in the ground.

143. In Ñähñu, there are two separate words, one for "small mountains" ("yä kati") and one for rolling slopes ("yä zi tsanä nguani").

144. The word "panthi," or "hot winds" refers to the warm air currents of spring.

145. This village also has no Hispanicized name on local maps. It would be spelled Xoti, without the glottal, in Spanish.

146. These are red, rectangular tiles, made of mud.

147. These are the familiar grey cement blocks used for house construction. The blocks are thicker than tabiques and are made of cement and sand rather than mud.

148. In 1985 the entrance fee was 25 pesos, or about seven cents USC. In 1970, when entrance fees for the fair were introduced, the tariff was one peso, or eight cents USC.

149. The "capote" is the cape referred to here.

150. This is the "picador."

151. Now the reference is to the "muleta" cape.

152. This was the 1983 price; the July 1985 price (when the peso was 350 to the dollar) was 1,400 pesos for the sunny side of the arena, and 1,600 pesos for the shady side.

153. These are oversized stringed instruments, with one side rounded. They are held like guitars and maintain the bass for a mariachi band.

154. These are white flour rolls, baked with a golden crust all around.

155. These breads are called "roscas de reyes," or "kings' twists."

156. The reference here is to a group of nuns.

157. A comal is a large earthenware plate, about 60 centimeters in diameter, slightly rounded on the bottom. It is placed directly on the fire for cooking tortillas or for heating up food.

158. It is approximately 160 kilometers from Ixmiquilpan to the Basilica of the Virgin of Guadalupe in Mexico City. It is a very long day's bike ride.

159. It is common practice in Mexico for politicians to let the word out that they are going to appear at such and such a place, and for their paid aides to go around the rural areas getting a crowd together.

REFERENCES

Aguirre Beltrán, Gonzalo (1973) "Teoría y práctica de la educación indígena." Sep Setentas no. 64. Mexico City: Secretaría de Educación Pública.

Ammar, Hamed (1954) Growing Up in an Egyptian Village. Silwa, the Province of Aswan. London: Routledge and Keegan-Paul.

Arana de Swadesh, Evangelina (1979) "Native bilingual education in Mexico," in Sanchez Cámara and Felipe Ayala (eds.) Concepts for Communication and Development in Bilingual and Bicultural Communities. The Hague: Mouton.

Bartholomew, Doris A., and L. C. Schoenals (1983) Bilingual Dictionaries for Indigenous Languages. Mexico City: Summer Institute of Linguistics.

Benitez, Fernando (1972) Los Indios de México. Vol. 4. Mexico City: Biblioteca ERA.

Benson, Lyman (1982) The Cacti of the United States and Canada. Stanford, CA: Stanford University Press.

Bernard, H. Russell (1966) "Otomí tones: A reevaluation." Anthropological Linguistics 8.9 (December): 15-19.

Bernard, H. Russell (1974) "Otomí tones in discourse." International Journal of American Linguistics 40: 141-50.

Bernard, H. Russell (1975) "Otomí obscene humor." Journal of American Folklore 88: 383-392.

Bernard, H. Russell (1980) "Orthography for whom?" International Journal of American Linguistics 46: 133-136.

Bernard, H. Russell (1988) Research Methods in Cultural Anthropology. Newbury Park, CA: Sage.

Bernard, H. Russell, and M. J. Evans (1983) "New microcomputer techniques for anthropologists." Human Organization 42: 182-185.

Bernard, H. Russell, and J. Salinas (1976) Otomí Parables, Folktales and Jokes. Native American Texts Series. International Journal of American Linguistics 1(2). Chicago: University of Chicago Press.

Boege, E., H. Diaz-Polanco, A. Medina, and G. López y Rivas (1983) El Idigenismo y los indígenas. Cuicuilco 11. Revista de las Escuela Nacional de Antropología e Historia.

Bravo H., Elia (1937) Las cactaceas de México. Mexico City: Universidad Nacional Autónoma de México.

Burnaby, Barbara [ed.] (1985) Promoting Native Writing Systems in Canada. Toronto: Ontario Institute for Studies in Education.

Cancian, Frank (1965) Economics and Prestige in a Maya Community: The Religious Cargo System in Zinacantán. Stanford: Stanford University Press.

Cancian, Frank (1979) Change and Uncertainty in a Peasant Economy: The Maya Corn Farmers of Zinacantán. Stanford, CA: Stanford University Press.

Cannizzo, J. (1983) "George Hunt and the invention of Kwakiutl culture." Canadian Review of Sociology and Anthropology 20: 44-58.

Caso, Alfonso (1954) Métodos y resultados de la política indigenista en México. Mexico City: Instituto Nacional Indigenista.

Costello, David F. (1972) The Desert World. New York: Thomas Y. Crowell.

Cravioto, R. O., G. Massieu, J. Guzmán, and J. Calvo de la Torre (1951) "Composición de alimentos mexicanos." Ciencia 11: 129-155.

Crawford, Clifford (1981) Biology of Desert Invertebrates. New York: Springer-Verlag.

de la Fuente, Julio (1964) Educación, antropología y desarollo de la comunidad. Mexico City: Instituto Nacional Indigenista.

Dow, James (1974) Santos y supervivencias: Funciones de la religión en una comunidad Otomí, México. Mexico City: Instituto Nacional Indigenista y Secretaría de Educación Pública.

Dow, James (1975) The Otomí of the Northern Sierra de Puebla, Mexico: An Ethnographic Outline (Monograph Series, No. 12). Latin American Studies Center. East Lansing: Michigan State University.

Dow, James (1986) The Shaman's Touch: Otomí Indian Symbolic Healing. Salt Lake City: University of Utah Press.

Dundes, Alan, R. Leach, and K. Ozok (1972) "The strategy of Turkish boys' verbal dueling rhymes," in J. Gumperz and D. Hymes (eds.) Directions in Sociolinguistics. New York: Holt, Rinehart & Winston.

Dyk, Walter (1938) Son of Old Man Hat. New York: Harcourt Brace.

Dyk, Walter, and R. Dyk (1980) Left Handed: A Navaho Autobiography. New York: Columbia University Press.

El Guindi, Fadwa [with the collaboration of Abel Hernández Jiménez] (1986) The Myth of Ritual. A Native's Ethnography of Zapotec Life-Crisis Rituals. Tucson: University of Arizona Press.

Elias, Thomas (1980) The Complete Trees of North America. New York: Van Nostrand Reinhold.

Ergood, Bruce (1983) "Material improvement or social change: Thirty years of Mexico's Patrimonio Idígena del Valle del Mezquital." Paper presented at the meeting of the Latin American Studies Association.

Foster, George (1965) "Peasant society and the image of limited good." American Anthropologist 67: 293-315.

Gentry, Howard S. (1982) Agaves of Continental North America. Tucson: University of Arizona Press.

Goncalves de Lima, O. (1956) El maguey y el pulque en los codices mexicanos. Mexico City: Fondo de Cultura Econonómica.

Grimes, E. (1980) "Systematic analysis of meaning." Notes on Linguistics 13: 21-30 (Dallas: Summer Institute of Linguistics).

Guerrero Guerrero, Raúl (1983) Los otomies del Valle del Mezquital. Mexico City: Instituto Nacional de Antropología e Historia.

Guerrero Guerrero, Raúl (1985) El Pulque. Mexico City: Joaquín Mortiz.

Hale, Kenneth (1965) "On the use of informants in fieldwork." Canadian Journal of Linguistics 10: 108-119.

Hamel, R.E. and H. Muñoz Cruz (1986) "Desplazamiento y resistencia de la lengua otomí," in R. E. Hamel, Y. Lastra y Suárez, and H. Muñoz Cruz (eds.) Sociolingüística Latinamericana. Mexico City: Universidad Nacional Autónoma.

Harris, Marvin (1985) Good to Eat. New York: Simon &Schuster.

Heath, Shirley B. (1972) Telling Tongues. New York: Teachers College Press.

Horcasitas, F. and R. Pozas (1981) "Del monolingüísmo en lengua indígena y nacional," in Pensamiento antropológico e indigenista de Julio de la Fuente. Mexico City: Instituto Nacional Indigenista.

Jones, Delmos (1970) "Towards a native anthropology." Human Organization 29: 251-259.

Katzner, Kenneth (1986) The Languages of the World. New York: Funk & Wagnalls

Kenyatta, Jomo (1938) Facing Mt. Kenya. London: Secker & Warburg.

Kim, Choong Soon (1987) "Can an anthropologist go home again?" American Anthropologist 89.

Krupat, A. (1983) "Foreword," in P. Radin (ed.) Crashing Thunder: The Autobiography of a Winnebago Indian. Lincoln: University of Nebraska Press.

La Flesche, Francis (1963) The Middle Five: Indian Schoolboys of the Omaha Tribe. Madison: University of Wisconsin Press. (Original work published 1900)

Lame Deer, John and R. Erdoes (1972) Lame Deer, Seeker of Visions. New York: Simon & Schuster.

Larson, Peggy (1970) Deserts of America. Englewood Cliffs, NJ: Prentice-Hall.

Lurie, Nancy (1961) Mountain Wolf Woman, Sister of Crashing Thunder. The Autobiography of a Winnebago Woman. Ann Arbor: University of Michigan Press.

Manrique, Leonardo (1969) "The Otomí," pp. 331-348 (Vol. 8) in R. Wauchope (ed.) Handbook of Middle American Indians. Austin: University of Texas Press.

Martín del Campo, Rafael (1938)"El pulque en el México precortesiano." Anales del Instituto de Biología 60:5-23.

Martínez, Máximo (1936) Plantas Utiles de México. Mexico City: Edición Botas.

Mathews, John J. (1968) Wah'Kon-Tah: The Osage and the White Man's Road. Norman: University of Oklahoma Press. (Original work published 1932)

McCarty, Christopher (1985) "Development among the Otomí of the Mezquital Valley, Mexico: The case of Lagunita." MA thesis, University of Florida, Gainesville.

McMahon, James A. (1985) Deserts. New York: Knopf.

Messerschmidt, D.A., [ed.] (1981) Anthropologists at Home in North America: Methods and Issues in the Study of One's Own Society. New York: Cambridge University Press.

Miller, Alden, and Robert Stebbins (1964) The Lives of Desert Animals in the Joshua Tree National Monument. Berkeley: University of California Press.

Milne, Lorus, and Margery Milne (1980) The Audobon Society Field Guide to North American Insects. New York: Knopf.

Momaday, N. Scott (1969) The Way to Rainy Mountain. Albuquerque: University of New Mexico Press.

Murdock, G.P. (1971) Outline of Cultural Materials (4th ed., 5th printing, with modifications). New Haven: HRAF Press.

Nabokov, Peter (1967) Two Leggings: The Making of a Crow Warrior. New York: Crowell.

Nahmad Sittón, Salamón (1982) Indoamérica y educación: Etnocidio o etnodesarollo? pp. 21-44 in Arlene Scanlon and Lezama Morfín (eds.) Hacía un México pluricultural. Mexico City: Secretariá de Educación Pública.

Neihardt, John (1972) Black Elk Speaks. New York: Pocket Books. (Original work published 1932)

Nida, Eugene (1958) "Analysis of meaning and dictionary making." International Journal of American Linguistics 24: 279-292.

Nolasco Armas, Margarita (1966) "Los Otomíes del Mezquital," in A. Pompa y Pompa (ed.) Summa antropológica en homenaje a Roberto Weitlaner. Mexico City: Instituto Nacional Indigenista.

Ohnuki-Tierny, E. (1984) "Native anthropologists." American Ethnologist 11: 584-586.

Parsons, Jeffrey, and Mary Parsons (1985) "Otomí maguey utilization." Preliminary Report to the National Geographic Society. Museum of Anthropology, University of Michigan, Ann Arbor.

Paz, Octavio (1962) The Labyrinth of Solitude: Life and Thought in Mexico. (Lysander Kemp, trans.) New York: Grove Press.

Peterson, Roger T., and Edward Chalif (1973) A Field Guide to Mexican Birds. Boston: Houghton-Mifflin.

Radin, Paul (1913) "Personal reminiscences of a Winnebago Indian." Journal of American Folklore 26: 293-318.

Radin, Paul [ed.] (1983) Crashing Thunder: The Autobiography of a Winnebago Indian. Lincoln: University of Nebraska Press. (Original work published 1926)

Richter, Paul O. (1966) White Grubs and Their Allies. Corvallis: Oregon State University Press.

Rohner, Ronald (1966) "Franz Boas, Ethnographer of the Northwest Coast," in J. Helm (ed.) Pioneers of American Anthropology. Seattle: University of Washington Press.

Rohner, Ronald (1969) The Ethnography of Franz Boas. Chicago: University of Chicago Press.

Roth Seneff, A. and C. Monzón (1987) "Desplazamiento lingüístico y definición regional en México." Paper presented at the meeting of the Society for Applied Anthropology, Oaxaca, Mexico.

Salinas Pedraza, Jesús (1975) "On the clan of anthropologists" (H. R. Bernard, ed. and trans.), in The Human Way: Readings in Anthropology. New York: Macmillan.

Salinas Pedraza, Jesús, and H. R. Bernard (1978) Ro Hnychnu: The Otomí. Albuquerque: University of New Mexico Press.

Sands, K. (1980) "Preface," in R. Savala, Autobiography of a Yaqui Poet. Tucson: University of Arizona Press.

Santamaría, Francisco J. (1974) Diccionario de mexicanismos (2nd ed.). Mexico City: Editorial Porrua, S.A.

Savala, Refugio (1980) Autobiography of a Yaqui Poet. Tucson: University of Arizona Press.

Scanlon, Arlene, and Lezama Morfín, Jr. [eds.] (1982) Hacía un México pluricultural. Mexico City: Secretaría de Educación Pública.

Sexton, James (1981) Son of Tecún Umán. Tucson: University of Arizona Press.

Sexton, James (1985) Campesino: The Diary of a Guatemalan Indian. Tucson: University of Arizona Press.

Simmons, Leo W. [ed.] (1942) Sun Chief: The Autobiography of a Hopi Indian. New Haven, CT: Yale University Press.

Sinclair, D. (1948) "Tonemes of Mezquital Otomí." International Journal of American Linguistics 14: 91-98.

Smith, Hobart (1946) Handbook of Lizards. Ithaca, NY: Cornell University Press.

Spicer, Edward (1980) "Introduction," in R. Savala, Autobiography of a Yaqui Poet. Tucson: University of Arizona Press.

Uchendu, Victor (1965) The Igbo of Southeastern Nigeria. New York: Holt, Rinehart & Winston.

Villa Rojas, Alfonso (1971) "Antropología aplicada e indigenismo en América Latina." América Indígena 30: 26-40.

Voegelin, C. F., and F. M. Voegelin (1977) Classification and Index of the World's Languages. New York: Elsevier.

Werner, O. and G. M. Schoepfle (1987) Systematic Fieldwork (two vols.). Beverly Hills, CA: Sage.

INDEX

Index of Otomi (Ñähñu) Words in the Text

ABOUT THE AUTHORS

H. Russell Bernard is Professor and Chair of the Department of Anthropology at the University of Florida. He has served two terms as editor of *American Anthropologist*, the official journal of the American Anthropological Association, and previously served as editor of *Human Organization*, journal of the Society for Applied Anthropology. Professor Bernard's work has spanned the full range of cultural anthropological concerns, from traditional ethnography and linguistics to applied work and statistics. His fieldwork settings include Greece, Mexico, and the United States and cover such diverse subjects as sponge divers, scientists, bureaucrats,and prisoners. He has developed, with a native speaker, a writing system for the Otomi people of Mexico and, through it, experimented with native-generated ethnographies. He is cofounder of the Sunbelt Social Network Conference and is a leading figure in the study of social networks. Books he has edited or authored include *Technology and Social Change* (coedited with Pertti Pelto, two editions), *Introduction to Chicano Studies* (coedited with Livie Duran, two editions), *The Otomi* (coauthored with Jesús Salinas Pedraza), and *The Human Way: Readings in Anthropology*.

Jesus Salinas Pedraza is a bilingual school teacher in the national teacher corps of Mexico. He taught school in the Mezquital Valley for 14 years, until 1979. He spent the next nine years in Mexico City with the Directorate of Indian Education preparing curriculum materials for bilingual education. For the last year and a half he has worked in Oaxaca, in a project jointly sponsored by the Mexican Directorate of Indian Education, the Instituto Indigenista Interamericano, the Centro de Investigaciones y Estudios Superiores en Antropologia Social, and the University of Florida to establish a Latin American Center for Native Literature. He is training speakers of several Indian languages in the use of microcomputers for the production of books in those languages. Salinas and Bernard began working together in 1962.